AARON
COPLAND

Music in American Life

A list of books in the series appears at the end of this book.

AARON
COPLAND

The Life and Work of an

Uncommon Man

HOWARD POLLACK

University of Illinois Press
Urbana and Chicago

First Illinois paperback edition, 2000
© 1999 by Howard Pollack
This edition reprinted by arrangement with
Henry Holt and Company, LLC.

Manufactured in the United States of America
∞This book is printed on acid-free paper.

Library of Congress Cataloging-in-Publication Data
Pollack, Howard.
Aaron Copland: the life and work of an uncommon man /
Howard Pollack.
p.   cm. — (Music in American life)
Reprint: Originally published: New York : H. Holt, 1999.
Includes bibliographical references and indexes.
ISBN 0-252-06900-5 (pbk. : alk. paper) / 978-0-252-06900-0
1. Copland Aaron, 1900– 2. Composers—United States—Biography.
I. Title. II. Series.
ML410.C756 P6 2000
780'.92—dc21
[B]
99-057851

P 8 7 6 5 4

In memory of my grandparents
Anna and Julius Malamed

Contents

Contents

Introduction

For many years I took Copland for granted. Studying music at college, I may well have surmised his importance from Donald Jay Grout's *A History of Western Music* (the 1960 edition), which devoted more space to Copland than to any other American composer, and from Otto Deri's *Exploring Twentieth-Century Music*. Yet he remained a shadowy figure at some distance from the central concerns of myself, my classmates, and my teachers.[1]

During my graduate studies in musicology at Cornell University, my appreciation for Copland deepened. My teachers included William Austin, who would write the Copland entry for the *New Grove Dictionary*, and Robert Palmer, a Copland protégé. My colleague, the composer Christopher Rouse, also furthered my knowledge of Copland's music. And in 1979, I met Copland, who had agreed to let me, a graduate student, interview him about Walter Piston, my dissertation topic. Still, the significance and drama of Copland's accomplishment eluded me.

In the early 1990s, while investigating the friendship between Copland and the Mexican composer Carlos Chávez, I grew dissatisfied with the state of Copland scholarship. The two pioneering and helpful studies by Arthur Berger (1953) and Julia Smith (1955) obviously needed updating;

Neil Butterworth's handy monograph (1985) was limited in scope; and the two-volume Copland–Vivian Perlis publications (1984, 1989)—a magisterial compilation of autobiography, biography, oral history, and photographs—offered little in the way of critical commentary and left important areas of the composer's personal life unexplored. The time had come for a more candid discussion of Copland the man as well as for some new critical thinking about the music.[2]

Toward this end I made repeated visits to the Copland Collection housed in the Music Division of the Library of Congress, where Wilda Heiss and other staff members kindly made materials available to me even before the collection had been fully processed. The Music Division of the New York Public Library, the publishing firm of Boosey & Hawkes, and other institutions offered further help, as did Stephen Luttmann, Farhad Moshiri, and other resourceful librarians at the University of Houston.

I found letters, writings, sketches, drafts, and unknown pieces that shed new light on familiar and unfamiliar works alike; and I conducted interviews that helped me gain a better understanding of Copland and his world. I also came across widespread misconceptions about both the man and his music, in part the result of a lack of serious Copland research; as recently as 1994 the musicologist Larry Starr thought Copland "still widely underrated and insufficiently studied." Fortunately, this situation is rapidly changing, thanks to the scholarly interest generated by the opening of the Copland Collection.[3]

I decided not to write a straightforward chronological narrative, partly because many aspects of Copland's life cried out for more contextual study than they customarily have received. I further attempted to discuss the music without recourse to musical examples and with minimal technical jargon. Included at the end of this volume is a catalog of musical works that includes premieres and other information not necessarily found in the body of the text.

Many individuals aided me in various aspects of this project. A number of musicologists and theorists, including Elizabeth Bergman, Jessica Burr, Jennifer DeLapp, Terri Gailey Everett, Margaret Susan Key, Neil Lerner, Roberta Lindsay, Daniel Mathers, Mitchell Patton, and Marta Robertson, generously shared their ideas and findings with me.

I also received assistance from Samuel Adler, Edward Albee, Philip Alexander, Betty Auman, William Austin, Milton Babbitt, Walter Bailey, Stephen Banfield, John Bell, Arthur Berger, Rosamund Bernier, Nina Bernstein, Philip Blackburn, Alan Boehmer, Henry Brant, James Brown,

Introduction

Rudy Burckhardt, Carol Bushell, Ronald Caltabiano, Gena Dagel Caponi, Bridget Carr, Robert Citkowitz, Alfred Cochran, Christopher Cole, David Conte, Mervyn Cooke, Roque Cordero, John Corigliano, Robert Cornell, Camille Crittenden, Irving Dean, Henry Ellis Dickson, Helen Didriksen, Mike Doran, Stanley Drucker, Shelley Edelstein, Vivian Fine, Ray Fliegel, Lukas Foss, Ellis Freedman, Hershel Garfein, Jack Garfein, Philip Glass, Morris Golde, Sylvia Goldstein, Neil Gould, Judith R. Greenwald, Kim Hartquist, Richard Hennessy, Jeff Herman, Adolph Herseth, Timothy Hester, Michael Hicks, David Hogan, Mark Horowitz, Michael Horvit, Betty Izant, Edward Jablonski, David Jacobs, John Kennedy, Rick Kessler, Barbara Kolb, Karl Korte, Donald Koss, Kim Kowalke, Rheba Kraft, Rose Lange, Noël Lee, Luis Leguia, Keith Lencho, Jeffrey Lerner, Roger Levey, Erin Lynn, Robert Mann, Newton Mansfield, Burt Marcus, Ralph Marcus, Jean-Pierre Marty, Roberta Mittenthal, Paul Moor, Edgar Muenzer, Gayle Murchison, Thea Musgrave, J. Kevin O'Brien, Michael O'Connor, Carol Oja, Andrea Olmstead, Juan Orrego-Salas, Leo Panasevich, Donald Peck, Adele Pollack, Linda Pollack, Walter Pollack, Stuart Pope, Donald Plotts, David Price, Jennifer Rector, Ned Rorem, Laurence Rosenthal, Christopher Rouse, Amy Rule, Joel Sachs, Arnold Salop, Michael Samford, Nancy Schoenberger, Gunther Schuller, Harold Shapero, Jonathan Sheffer, Zoya Shukhatovich, Doris Sing, Leonard Slatkin, Michael Slayton, Leo Smit, Catharine Parsons Smith, Laura Snyder, Randy Snyder, John Solum, Stephen Sondheim, Florence H. Stevens, Michael Sumbera, Janis Susskind, David Tomatz, Jennifer Trent, Steven Tulin, Charles Turner, Laszlo Varga, David Walker, Michael Webster, Stefan Weisman, Samantha Whelan, David Ashley White, Ray White, Patrice Whiteside, Gottfried Wilfinger, John Williams, Hugh Wolff, Wes York, and Marilyn Ziffrin.

I am particularly indebted to David Diamond, Verna Fine, Alex Jeschke, Erik Johns, Kent Kennan, Vivian Perlis, Phillip Ramey, Wayne Shirley, and Darryl Wexler for their many thoughtful suggestions; and to the University of Houston for providing significant aid in the way of a one-semester sabbatical and travel and other grants.

AARON
COPLAND

1

A Copland Portrait

In maturity Copland stood just under six feet tall, a lanky figure weighing only about one hundred and fifty pounds. He had his mother's oblong face and craggy features, with sensitive pale blue-gray eyes that looked out from under heavy lids with a kind of bemused curiosity. When he was a young man, his spectacles, dark suits, and thinning brown hair made him look older than his years, whereas in old age his boyish grin gave him a remarkably youthful appearance. His countenance changed little over the years.

Interviewing Copland over the radio, the dance critic John Gruen pictured for his audience "this marvelous, strong, splendid Copland-esque face that we have all come to love and be familiar with." Minna Lederman, who for many years edited Copland's writings, concurred that artists and photographers found him "always the perfect subject, the face one could never forget—after Stravinsky's, THE face. A hawk, yet not predatory. Not what you would call good-looking—something much better, more striking." Others similarly described him paradoxically as "stunningly ugly," as "endearingly homely," as having a "wonderful ugly/beautiful Copland grin"—that toothy smile that even after one meeting the composer Robin Holloway found "unforgettable." More than one person thought of Ichabod Crane; and by coincidence he spent his later years in Washington Irving country up on the Hudson.[1]

Copland humorously deprecated his looks, finding in his gaunt physique, narrow face, prominent nose, and buckteeth a comic resemblance to a giraffe. He considered himself an "ugly duckling"; when his friends Irving and Verna Fine acquired a cubist painting of a clown, he told them, "I bet you bought it because it reminds you of me." Especially sensitive about his crooked teeth, he avoided smiling for the camera for years.[2]

He was likewise modest about his musical accomplishments. When honored or complimented, he reacted with almost disbelief, like a surprised, delighted child. He spoke about his work lightly, with a slight chuckle or sardonic inflection, and emphasized his good luck, never dwelling on any disappointment or sadness.

Copland's calm self-effacement struck many as extraordinary, especially in the context of the temperamental art world. "He is always perfectly relaxed," observed his lifelong friend Harold Clurman. Another friend, the Chilean composer Juan Orrego-Salas, wrote to him, "I admire greatly your serenity. You are a man and an artist at ease with yourself. I truly believe that it is exactly there from which the greatness of your contribution rises." "He exuded calm," agreed a painter friend, Richard Hennessy. When asked late in life what had "hurt him," Copland answered,

> I don't hurt easily and I don't bear grudges without working at it a little bit. So that nothing immediately jumps to mind, as to what hurt me. I'm very sensitive I think to the atmosphere in which we all live. At the time of Hitler, Hitler hurt me, if that's what you mean. I was considerably upset. You see, I think it uses up a lot of energy to get really angry. And I save my energy [laugh] for moments where I think it's really worth extending all that energy.[3]

Only occasionally did he show strong emotions of any kind. He was, in general, extremely discreet and low-keyed. In his hundreds of letters to friends, he rarely alluded to his own feelings, and when he did, he did so almost apologetically, as in a brief admission of depression to Leonard Bernstein on the occasion of his mother's death. "He masks his feelings," said Bernstein, "and there's a great deal going on inside him that doesn't come out, even with his best friends." He kept cool even at the time of his McCarthy hearing, prompting his friend Edwin Denby to write, "It is extraordinary even now I can't detect a sign in you that you have been through any trouble. I mean in the sense of wanting comforting. It is only by imagining how grueling it would be to me to be questioned by the police on suspicion, even if I were sure of my innocence, that I can imagine anything." David Diamond, Leonard Bernstein, and Phillip Ramey—three of his closest friends—all independently observed how strangely uncommunicative he appeared at the death of a beloved family member or friend. Diamond concluded, "There's never a scene with Aaron. He knows exactly what dignity means in the sense of how far you go emotionally."[4]

This temperament naturally paralleled his artistic taste, for example, his great affection for the composers Gabriel Fauré and Darius Milhaud and the essayist Michel de Montaigne. After Jean-Pierre Marty performed his Piano Sonata, Copland complimented this "brother spirit" on his "cold passion." In his journals, he wrote of hating "an emotion-drenched voice."[5]

In reminiscences by friends, the word *tact* in particular recurred, as in William Schuman's assertion that "Aaron was always tactful." Harold Clurman, recalling an episode in which Copland intervened during an argument between himself and Nadia Boulanger, observed,

> Aaron is one of the most balanced persons I know; the most tactful, knowing exactly what to say to each person. He wouldn't yield to anything that he didn't want to do. He wouldn't declare anything he didn't mean. But he is never aggressive in any way, and he always knows exactly the right thing to say in the right circumstances. It has helped him not just as a composer but as a man of the world. The United States could send him abroad with full confidence that he would represent it well because he has an extraordinary sense of justness. He had it when he was young and he has it still. Boulanger recognized this immediately.[6]

Such tact made Copland a moderator par excellence, and in the course of his life he chaired innumerable organizations, committees, juries, and panel discussions. In two concert readings of Stravinsky's *The Soldier's Tale*, he was the obvious choice to play the narrator, whether the Soldier and Devil were Roger Sessions and Virgil Thomson, as they were in one production, or Elliott Carter and John Cage, as they were in another. In his relationships with many younger composers and artists, his role even took on the earmarks of the psychotherapist. When on one occasion

Phillip Ramey said to him, "Aaron, you could have been a diplomat," he responded, "Or a psychiatrist."[7]

Although he was sometimes fidgety and skittish in his movements—he joked that he avoided Jell-O because the wobbly gelatin made him nervous—only a fear of heights noticeably disturbed Copland's equanimity. In 1932 the composer Vivian Fine accompanied Copland on a Ferris wheel only to find him, as the carriage reached the apex, terrified and clutching her for dear life. But it was precisely because he was so restrained that even the slightest confession or outburst took on a special intensity and a larger frame of reference. Verna Fine, for instance, never forgot her surprise when he responded to her request that he speak at her husband's funeral by saying, "I can't speak because I'm going to break down." And Minna Lederman felt ashamed of once provoking him to an "unbecoming display of anger" that "was so out of character." If he wished to communicate his disapproval or irritation, he usually did so with a glance that spoke volumes.[8]

Some close friends found Copland almost too reticent. Paul Bowles humorously reproached him for it in a 1933 letter: "You seldom write, you know, and when you do, you say nothing of importance. Sometimes I find an old letter of yours in a trunk, and upon reading it over, manage to imagine that it was written recently and is still valid." "Aaron, for once, tell me," pleaded Leonard Bernstein in reference to Copland's private life.[9]

Some even regarded his reserve suspiciously. In 1930, the writer Chard Powers Smith, who had met Copland at the MacDowell Colony, wrote to a mutual friend, "There is a strange hypocritically good-humoured aloofness about him which, unless he dislikes me, I must put down to a self-consciousness either of race, of humble origins, or perhaps of habits—all of which should be beneath Aaron." Virgil Thomson viewed Copland's reticence as a kind of Machiavellian career tool, while Ned Rorem saw it as a way of distancing people. A few rival composers and their wives simply thought him devious.[10]

But friends like Minna Lederman and Robert Cornell sensed in Copland's reserve nothing more nor less than a "mode of self-protection." "Copland had a way of being pleasant and affable and very noncommittal without being aloof," recalled Cornell. "There was a veneer of self-protection in the way he handled encounters with people that he was not intimate with. And he was very, very skilled at this." Another friend, Sylvia Goldstein, described him as "basically shy."[11]

Copland's reserve, at the very least, was something of an idiosyncratic family trait inherited from his mother and maternal grandmother. "If ever she was depressed or irritable, she managed to hide it well," said Copland about his mother. "I can only conclude that I must have inherited some of my own comparative evenness of temperament from my mother." Copland's older brothers, Ralph and Leon, were similarly inscrutable. "Leon usually keeps his emotions inside," wrote Leon's third wife to Copland, "while I let them out which is good for *me* at least."[12]

Moreover, Copland's reserve should not be thought of as being in the least unfriendly or imperious. On the contrary, he encouraged a fun-loving, high-spirited atmosphere, often punctuating remarks with a laugh or giggle. His own conversation sparkled with a delightfully wry humor, made all the more winsome by his somewhat arch speech; John J. O'Connor, reviewing a televised appearance in 1976, observed that beneath the mild-mannered gentility he could be "almost devilishly droll." With women friends especially he showed physical warmth, cradling Rosamund Bernier consolingly after a difficult divorce and squeezing Verna Fine's hand during a memorial concert for her husband. Friends and colleagues typically described him as "warm," "sweet," and "lovely." He became "Aaron" to thousands of mere acquaintances, thus setting the precedent for Bernstein's adoption of "Lenny."[13]

Indeed, he maintained an extraordinary number of friendships, devoting a good portion of nearly every day to the reading and writing of letters. Moreover, he relished companionship. "He never, never liked to be by himself," remembered David Walker, his secretary for many years. He enjoyed traveling and sharing rooms with friends, hosting small parties, and introducing people to one another. "Copland bores himself without crowds of people which I consider an immense weakness," complained Paul Bowles to a friend. "Aaron loves parties more than any man I know," Bernstein would say.[14]

Aside from his family, with whom he stayed in regular but rather distant touch all his life, his social world largely consisted of artists or intellectuals of one sort or another—or at least art lovers. This included intimate friends, casual acquaintances, lovers, even cooks and secretaries. Only a few other composers could boast so dazzling an array of artist friends and acquaintances, both in and out of music. The apartments of Montparnasse, lofts of the Upper West Side, brownstones in Greenwich Village, and rustic artist colonies outside New York and Mexico City formed his natural habitat.

His relationships with friends—especially the younger men with whom he formed the bulk of his close friendships—could be, in their own way, highly volatile. One finds a recurrent pattern of a year or two of intense intimacy, a year or so of drifting apart, and the settling of the friendship onto a stable but cooler footing. While this often transpired in the context of romantic or would-be romantic relationships, it characterized more purely professional friendships as well. At the same time, Copland prized loyalty and, often over the objections of well-wishers, remained at least cordial to people who annoyed, used, or even betrayed him, as Oscar Levant humbly discovered.[15]

Copland lived simply and unpretentiously. He dressed modestly, often wearing a simple dark suit, white shirt, and tie or, more casually, an open sport shirt and corduroy pants. When friends teased him about his clothes, he would protest, "But what's wrong with them? They're comfortable." "Can you imagine Aaron wearing a ring, a jeweled cufflink?" asked Leonard Bernstein. "It's unheard of! Or wearing some kind of natty leisure suit? Plain, plain, plain! It goes with *Appalachian Spring* and *Our Town*, which I think of as a self-portrait of Aaron. No conspicuous consumption." If he showed a greater interest in having stylish furnishings or nice wines in his later, more prosperous years, he did so usually to please younger friends.[16]

Some of these same friends were surprised and troubled to find that Copland, having become well-to-do, spent money so cautiously. But others contended that such habits derived from decades of poverty and from an instinctual sense of economy. "It was part of his plainness, it was part of thrift," explained Bernstein. "One of those Puritan virtues like being fair—you're thrifty." Clurman even related Copland's frugality to his tact: "He never spent more than was necessary on anything; but his economy was a sign not of parsimony but of an almost instinctive sense of measure." "I adore extravagance," Copland would tell his friend John Kennedy, "but I abhor waste."[17]

In fact, he was very generous. "When Aaron traveled all over the world as a conductor," remembered Verna Fine, "he always brought back gifts—a Yemenite necklace from Israel for me, books for Irving, and toys for our three daughters. We never saw the thrifty side of Aaron that everyone talks about." Even during his impoverished years, he supplied loans and cash gifts for friends in need. By the end of his life, he was supporting whole families. If he occasionally hurt a friend like Richard

Hennessy by lending him money cautiously, it might well have been because so many of his loans were never paid back, as Hennessy himself acknowledged. He showed special generosity to fellow composers. "Considering that I am a person who lacks no possible human failing," wrote Oscar Levant, "I have been constantly amazed by Copland's generosity."[18]

Copland was a diligent and constant worker, yet another facet of his rather spartan makeup. How else to explain the scores, the books, the mountain of letters, lectures, and speeches? Even when friends visited, the time would come, as Vivian Perlis relates, when he would send everybody back to work, with the command "au travail!"[19]

A night owl, he usually began his day around nine or ten in the morning with a small breakfast, during which he lingered over newspapers and magazines. After breakfast, he read his mail, wrote letters, made phone calls, and otherwise attended to business. Following a light lunch at about one, he might study a few scores at the piano, prepare a lecture or article, meet with musicians, or simply read; at least in later years, he also napped for an hour in mid- or late afternoon. Unless pressed by a deadline, he did his real composing only after dinner, from about eight in the evening to midnight or later. "Music is largely the product of the emotions," he explained to Arnold Dobrin, "and I can't get emotional early in the day." After a late-night snack, he might stay up still later reading. "This was not a man who wasted time," observed his friend the composer John Kennedy.[20]

Copland composed primarily at the piano, working directly on the instrument's music stand or on a nearby work table. Having grown up with the belief that a serious composer should be able to hear his music in his head and reproduce it directly onto paper, he felt somewhat defensive about this practice until he learned that Stravinsky did likewise. This did not mean, he reminded one interviewer, that he merely improvised at the piano:

Actually, it's more like using the piano as a large typewriter: the instant before you start to work, you know what it is you're going to "type." You're one instant ahead of yourself all the time . . . primarily it is a feat of the musical imagination. Otherwise why write certain notes down rather than other notes. No, music must be heard in your head; something must be guiding you toward the notes you put down.[21]

Copland usually sketched out a few musical ideas—perhaps a particular motive or harmony or bass line—before plunging into a composition per se. He once explained,

> Somehow, suddenly, a musical idea occurs to you; either a whole phrase, or three notes, or a series of chords, something that seems pregnant with possibilities for development. Once you have the kinds of ideas that fascinate you, you're no longer in a position to decide the nature of the animal. It's going to take its essence from the musical ideas that occur to you. . . . Some musical ideas are too short, they don't seem long enough to carry you through ten minutes of music, so you have to start searching about for other ideas; contrasting ones that seem to fit with the original ones.

In another such discussion he emphasized the fact that he worked not necessarily with a single idea, but with multiple ones: "You might collect a series of ideas without thinking about how they go or where they go, but then, one fine day, looking at them, you get the impression that Idea A and C and G go together in some curious way which you didn't realize before when you were thinking about them separately."[22]

When writing for orchestra, Copland first prepared a piano score of from two to four or more staves, orchestrating the music only after he had completed it thus. He argued for the advisability of this method, as opposed to scoring a work from the start: "Since balance and contrast of instrumental effect are prime factors in good orchestration, it follows that any decision as to timbre, too quickly arrived at, is itself a limitation, since it prevents freedom of action on other pages."[23]

Nor did he compose straight through from beginning to end. At the least, he used themes sketched out in advance, but he often composed whole sections out of their eventual order; especially well known is the fact that he put together the *Piano Variations* and the *Twelve Poems of Emily Dickinson* only after completing their separate parts. Such an approach characterized his working methods in general. William Schuman once related Copland's response when asked about the progress of his *Connotations* (1962):

> He said that he had completed writing the end of the movement. I said, "I did not realize that you had finished it." Aaron said, "No, I am not finished. I am just writing the ending." He was astonished

when I told him that I never wrote a piece out of sequence, that it was impossible for me. I start at the beginning and work my way toward the end. I never could stop and write an ending.

"I don't compose," he once said. "I assemble materials." This openness to collage—for all his emphasis on stylistic and motivic unity—prefigured postmodernist aesthetics while helping to explain his enthusiasm for such earlier composers as Mahler, Ives, and Nielsen.[24]

Often he used music that he had composed years earlier. As with all his written documents and personal effects, he fastidiously preserved sketches and manuscripts, which he recycled from time to time. For a climactic scene from his film score to *The Heiress*, for example, he resorted to a long-discarded variation from the *Piano Variations*; one can find numerous such economies in his work. Some knowing friends even complained to him about this tendency toward self-borrowing. While it seems that he reused only a relatively small percentage of his work and typically only music that he had discarded or suppressed for one reason or another, the materials at the Copland Collection are helping scholars like Daniel Mathers clarify this particular matter.[25]

If necessary, as in the case of his film scores, he could write quickly, but he usually worked slowly and deliberately. When looking over his music with friends, he would often point to a spot with undisguised pleasure and say, "That was the note that cost." One of his most frequent complaints about certain pieces was that they seemed "facile." You have to be more "*choisi*," he would lecture David Diamond. He personally found it beneficial to put his work aside for a few weeks from time to time: "The passage of time is then a big help in reaching a true and just estimation of what you've accomplished." The eleven-minute *Piano Variations* took about two years to complete.[26]

For all the care and thought he brought to the creative process, he considered composition as, fundamentally, an emotional experience, an act of "self-expression" and "self-discovery." He spoke of "musical instinct," of the "heat of inspiration," of music as "the product of the emotions." In his Norton lectures, he quoted Santayana, adding, "Yes, I like this idea that we respond to music from a primal and almost brutish level— dumbly, as it were, for on that level we are firmly grounded. . . . That is fundamentally the way we all hear music—gifted and ungifted alike— and all the analytical, historical, textual material on or about the music heard, interesting though it may be, cannot—and I venture to say should

not—alter that fundamental relationship." His characterization of a composer as "cerebral" or "intellectual" carried somewhat negative connotations. He identified rather with the image of Beethoven—attributed to
Schubert—as maintaining "superb coolness under the fire of creative
fantasy."[27]

Copland realized that not every work of his would be well received.
Noting that his family thought it "impractical" of him to write something
that would be hard for performers and audiences to grasp, he reflected,

> But I don't think one composes to be practical. That's *too* sensible.
> You have to be more adventuresome than that. But you do have to
> be truly convinced about the value of what you are doing, otherwise
> there are many reasons for not doing it—minimal financial gain, no
> favorable criticism in the papers the next morning. You really must
> be brave, but the bravery is derived from inner conviction.[28]

But although he neither condescended nor pandered to the average listener, he never lost sight of him or her either. Reviewing Roger Sessions's
Violin Concerto, he questioned the composer's seeming disregard for
"audience psychology," writing, "It is not a question of giving an audience what it wants, but of *not* giving it more than you can reasonably
expect it to be able to digest. It is difficult to set those limits." "The ideal
listener, it seems to me," he wrote on another occasion, "would combine
the preparation of the trained professional with the innocence of the intuitive amateur."[29]

Between composing, writing, and eventually conducting, Copland had
little time for much else. Although a skilled pianist, he rarely played the
piano simply for fun. As a young man, he went to countless concerts, but
after his return from Europe in 1924, he became much more selective
about what musical events he attended, generally restricting himself to
contemporary music and unusual repertory. When he traveled (as he did
extensively throughout his life), he kept busy, allowing himself little time
for sight-seeing or mere loafing. Rather, he concentrated on the tasks at
hand: composing, conducting, meeting local musicians, hearing new
scores. For all his sociability, he had little taste for small talk.[30]

Not really athletically inclined, in his younger days he nonetheless
became somewhat adept at tennis and enjoyed playing it. During his more
senior years, his physical activities were largely restricted to taking walks
in the woods or puttering about in his garden. He liked dogs and cats and

kept pets throughout much of his life, including in later years a Great Dane named Nadja (in honor of his teacher, Nadia Boulanger) and a cat called Helen.[31]

Copland's involvements with the other arts often centered on connections with one or another friend or collaborator. On his occasional visits to museums, he often headed straight for sculptures rather than paintings, an understandable attraction given the sculptural qualities of his music. His most valuable piece of art, a Picasso print of a bull and a horse, was a gift from Thornton Wilder. "Aaron was not visual," friends often claimed, though Robert Cornell noted that he had, in fact, a "definite aesthetic" and a "visual philosophy," namely, that art and decor should be "pure, simple, and have guts." Michael O'Connor, who served as Copland's cook for a while in the 1980s, thought him "very visual in a sense," recalling his strong reactions to table settings; once, after O'Connor had set out some red napkins, Copland exclaimed, with his characteristic lilt, "You could put this in a museum, *just* the way it is."[32]

For many years he enjoyed going to the theater and movies. He admired and, as he once admitted, almost resented drama's "naked" emotional power, as opposed to the less engulfing, more distilled musical experience: "Not infrequently I have been moved to tears in the theater; never at music." Leonard Bernstein confirmed that the only time he ever saw Copland weep was at a motion picture: "When at a Bette Davis movie that caused me to ooh and ah and marvel and groan 'No no no!' at the unbearable climax—I am always very vocal at Bette Davis movies—he turned to me, his cheeks awash with tears, and sobbed, 'Can't you shut up?' "[33]

After 1950 he attended plays and motion pictures with less regularity. Although he purchased a black-and-white television set sometime around 1960, he showed little interest in the medium, tuning in only for particular cultural events. Once, at home, he tried to lure his young friend Phillip Ramey away from the television set with the suggestion that they look over some scores together. After Ramey declined, explaining that he was watching an episode of *Star Trek*, Copland shook his head and left the room, saying, with a laugh, "What an ape you are!"[34]

His only real preoccupation outside of music was reading. "Composing and reading were most important to him," remembered his friend Gerald Sykes. In 1921 Copland wrote to his parents, "I am doing my usual amount of devouring of books." The following year he further told them, "I wonder if you ever realize what a large part the reading of books on all imaginable subjects plays in my existence. I read, not to learn anything, but from the pure love of it." All of his studios featured a corner with a comfortable chair, a table of current reading material, and a lamp so that he could alternately read and compose, his reading time usually tran-spiring before and after his major compositional work at night. He enjoyed memoirs, letters, biographies, poetry, novels, history, philosophy, aesthetics, psychology, and the natural sciences. "I read all the time," he stated in 1978. "I prefer what the French call belles lettres—essays and collections of articles about different subject matter."[35]

Some of Copland's friends found his personality—the reserved, charming man with the friendly giggle—embodied in his music. And yet his music had other qualities—sarcasm, sorrow, violence, and nostalgia—that did not seem to fit his public or private image. In a 1979 speech, Bernstein acknowledged that Copland's music "can have an extraordi-nary grandeur, an exquisite delicacy, a prophetic severity, a ferocious rage, a sharp bite, a prickly snap, a mystical suspension, a wounding stab, an agonized howl—none of which corresponds with the Aaron we loving friends know; it comes from some deep mysterious place he never reveals to us except in his music." Copland himself mused on the relation of art to one's inner life:

An artist can take his personal sadness or his fear or his anger or his joy and crystallize it, giving it a life of its own. Thus he is released from his emotion as others cannot be. The arts offer the opportunity to do something that cannot be done anywhere else. It is the only place one can express in public the feelings ordinarily regarded as private. It is the place where a man or woman can be completely honest, where we can say whatever is in our hearts or minds, where we never need to hide from ourselves or from others.[36]

In Copland's music, we find that fundamental tension between the outer and inner man made whole.

2

Background Matters

Copland and His Family

Aaron Copland was born in Brooklyn, New York, on 14 November 1900. His parents, Harris Morris Copland (c. 1860–1945) and Sarah Mittenthal Copland (c. 1860–1944), were both Jewish immigrants from Russia. Harris, a furrier's son, left his native Lithuanian town of Shavli (Šiauliai) in the mid-1870s in order to avoid military conscription and arrived in Brooklyn in 1877, via Glasgow and Manchester; along the way, he adopted a more Anglicized version of his original surname, Kaplan. For many years, Aaron assumed that an Ellis Island immigration official was responsible for the altered surname, but while in Scotland in the 1960s, he came to suspect that the change had occurred in Glasgow: the Scottish pronunciation of *Copland* ("Cupland," as in "Scutland"), he realized, resembled the Russian-Jewish pronunciation of *Kaplan*.[1]

Soon after Harris arrived in New York, he helped safeguard passage to America for the rest of his immediate family, including his brother Alfred and two sisters, Sadie and Becky, all of whom adopted the name Copland; his brother Abe, who chose the more conventional spelling, Copeland; and, lastly, his parents, Sussman and Frieda, and three younger sisters, Lillian, Rose, and Fanny, who kept the name Kaplan.

Sussman and Frieda were both around sixty years old when they arrived in the States, and they learned little English, preferring to speak and read in their native Yiddish. Aaron remembered these paternal grandparents as out of their element, as "very dépaysé in America. But they lived a good long life." From all these older relatives, he heard stories about the hardships of life in Russia that left an indelible impression. The majority of Coplands—however they spelled their names—became store owners of one kind or another.[2]

The composer's mother, Sarah Mittenthal, was a child of about six when she and her mother, Bertha ("Boshie"), arrived in America from Vishtinetz (Vistytis), a small town on the Russian-Lithuanian border near Kaliningrad, to join her father, Aaron, in Chillicothe, Illinois. In contrast to the Coplands, Aaron Mittenthal and his brother Ephraim were frontier peddlers rather than urban retailers, moving about small towns in the Midwest and Southwest. Sarah went to elementary school in Peoria and high school in Dallas; she thought of herself as a Texan. Most of the Mittenthals wound up in Dallas (one cousin, Herbert Marcus, cofounded Neiman-Marcus) or in New York, where the twenty-year-old Sarah moved with her parents in 1881. After her husband's death, Bertha settled in the Bronx with the youngest of her nine children, Nathan, a bachelor. Sarah eventually named her fifth child Aaron, in honor of her deceased father. This younger Aaron remembered his grandmother Bertha as "a nice little old lady, very sweet, never made any trouble for anybody as far as I know." He seemed especially intrigued by his bachelor uncle. The entire Mittenthal clan struck him as considerably more "American" than the Coplands.[3]

At first Harris went into business with a cousin, but at about the time of his marriage to Sarah in 1885, he opened his own business, H. M. Copland's, at 628 Washington Avenue in Brooklyn, a successful venture that in its heyday required about twelve employees. Aaron often described the store as a kind of neighborhood Macy's. Sarah assumed an active role in running the business, including keeping the accounts, doing much of the buying, and designing the displays. After leaving Washington Avenue in 1921 and selling the store in 1922, Harris managed real estate, including the Brooklyn apartment house to which he and Sarah had moved.[4]

Harris and Sarah had five children: Ralph (1888–1952), Leon (1890–1974), Laurine (1892–1972), Josephine (1894–1967), and Aaron. They lived comfortably if modestly amid the three floors of rooms above the family store. By the time Aaron was born, Harris and Sarah, in their forties and preoccupied with a demanding business, left him largely in the care of their daughters and of one or another maid; the 1900 census lists, as a servant in the household, a recent Russian immigrant, Fanny Kafkin, though Copland remembered only Tessie Tevyovitch from Hungary and especially Lillian ("Lils") Coombs from Barbados, whom he described as warm and gentle. "I had a sense of being on my own from an early age," he often said, considering himself lucky in this respect. At the same time, as "the sort of baby of the family," he was "fussed over." "I don't know whether that had a good effect or a bad effect, but anyhow it gave me the elements of being a performer." All five children were expected to help out in the store, unpacking and marking stock, dusting items, and manning the cash register.[5]

In his autobiography, which he dedicated to their memory, Copland sketchily portrayed Harris and Sarah as genial entrepreneurs, loyal Americans, staunch Democrats, and loving but busy parents. Success in business had made his father "justifiably proud," and photographs of Harris suggest a contented burgher, especially in his old age, when he acquired the kind of heftiness Aaron carefully warded off. Everyone referred to Harris as "the Boss." Harris's principal diversion was pinochle at the local Democratic Club, prompting Aaron's ironic remark upon hearing in 1922 that his parents were about to retire: "What does Pop intend to occupy himself with (since one can't play pinochle *all* day long)." He doubted that his parents would enjoy themselves traveling about Europe: "This applies particularly to Pop, whom I imagine, would have a better time in a decent Yiddisher hotel with plenty of pinochle than in the swellest dumps in Europe. . . . And yet, after all is said and done, I may be all wrong. You may enjoy some good Pilsner Beer in a good old German beer garden very much." Among friends he described his father as "bourgeois to the core."[6]

One particular outing with his father—a trip to the Lafayette Baths followed by an evening at Minsky's Burlesque—apparently had special importance for him, perhaps because it betokened some connection with his own taste for the risqué. In later years, he recommended to friends J. R. Ackerley's memoir, *My Father and Myself*, a book about how unaware a father and son can be in regard to each other's sexual and emotional lives.[7]

Aaron's decision to go into music came as "a blow" to his father. "Where did you get such a strange idea?" he asked. "Can you make a living at it?" Harris had no particular interest in music; but doubtful or not, he supported his son's musical education, and over the years took increasing pride in his career. In his last years, Harris suffered from dementia and became extremely difficult, "very mean" to the attendants Laurine had hired to take care of her ailing parents. After Sarah's death in 1944, the children placed Harris in a nursing home, where he died the following year.[8]

Copland admitted being "closer" to his "more sensitive" mother. "She was affectionate, and a very nice mother to have," he wrote. Sarah had some musical abilities; she sang and played the piano (at least in earlier years), and provided her children with music lessons. The proudest moment of her life, she told reporters in 1927, was watching her son perform his own Piano Concerto with the Boston Symphony. If he ever married, she announced in 1937, she expected to "share him in half."[9]

Nothing Copland ever said suggested the least unhappiness as a child, aside from contending with bullies and the occasional illness, including a bout of typhoid fever. He often told the story, however, of returning home from a Paderewski concert at age fifteen all fired up about the music, only to find his parents too involved with playing cards to pay him any mind. Feeling that his family would never appreciate his deeper aspirations, he went off in a sulk. Harris and Sarah never did, in fact, develop more than the vaguest understanding about Aaron and his world, including his homosexuality, a subject simply not discussed in family circles. "He's married to his music," explained his niece Felice Marlin when her young son once asked why Uncle Aaron was not married.[10]

Still, Copland remained close to his parents—more so than was commonly thought. During his three years in Paris, he wrote to them every week, letters that Harris proudly read aloud at his Monday night pinochle game. These warm letters, always addressed "Dear Ma & Pa," mostly detailed the price of food, rent, taxis, and concerts, gratifying their shared sense of economy. They also carefully deflected any unrealistic expectations that his parents might have about his financial or personal prospects.[11]

After he returned from Paris, Copland saw his parents regularly, Harris and Sarah often visiting him in Manhattan. He wrote to his parents when he traveled, telling them as of old about the cost of living here and there, but also about what the critics had to say of his work and about how his career was shaping up. He also sent them reviews of his music.

"Reviews bothered me only when they upset my parents," he would later recall.[12]

Of his four siblings, he retained weakest ties with Josephine, who married Louis Bergman in 1915 and, as far as he was concerned, essentially disappeared into suburban New Jersey. In contrast, he remained very close with Laurine (pronounced "La-rine," with a strong emphasis on the first syllable), or "La," as he called her. Laurine had studied voice and piano, learning enough to entertain the family with ragtime and popular songs and to accompany her brother Ralph at the violin. She helped teach Aaron to play the piano, to dance, and to drive a car. A strong, attractive, and vivacious woman (Aaron inevitably referred to her as "the lively one"), she married Charles Marcus, a successful clothier, in 1914, and, like her mother, assisted in the running of the family store. After the Second World War, the Marcuses moved from the Flatbush section of Brooklyn to Long Island; her children thought of her as "a woman ahead of her time," someone who drove cars and played golf at a time when few women did.[13]

Laurine was thoroughly devoted to Aaron. She not only promoted his early musical education but proved instrumental in persuading their parents to let him study in Paris. In later years, she became the principal intermediary between him and the rest of the family, she providing all the family gossip, he sending his love to "all the folks," or "the mob," or "the mispochat" (Yiddish for family), through her. She did whatever she could to lessen family burdens for him. Following their mother's heart attack in 1944, she wrote to him, then away in Hollywood, "They [the doctor and others] wanted me to telegraph you, but I was sure it was not that bad and hated to disturb and worry you if it were not necessary." Whenever he traveled, she carefully followed his itinerary, fretting about his comfort. "About sending things to Israel for me," he wrote to her in 1951, "thanks for the offer, but I don't think it would look right for me to 'have it easy' while the regular citizens have it tough." "Let them treat you like a Lord," she wrote to him in 1961.[14]

Laurine regularly attended concerts of his music in New York and Tanglewood and encouraged him to conduct: "I'm carrying out your plans for me by conducting the orchestra here tomorrow night," he wrote to her from Montevideo, near the beginning of his conducting career. But none of their correspondence suggests on her part anything more than a vague familiarity with his music. Her son Burt recalled with amusement how she would tell Aaron what was "wrong" with certain pieces, saying, " 'This is too wild, and this is too this, and da-da-da-da-da-da,' and Aaron would say, 'You're right, you're right, you're right,' and never change a thing."[15]

Aaron thought Ralph a "more serious" musician that Laurine, remembering especially their "fair rendition" of the Mendelssohn Violin Concerto. Although Ralph studied law, music remained "his greatest enjoyment," according to his wife, Dorothy. Like Laurine, he followed Aaron's career with keen interest and attended various concerts and lectures; a letter on the "considerably abridged" adaptation of El Salón México for the motion picture Fiesta revealed, for an immediate family member, an unparalleled knowledge of the music.[16]

Copland considered Ralph the intellectual of the family. "You're not the simplest person to write a letter to," he told Ralph in a letter from Paris in 1922. "I am capable of writing two sorts of epistle—one like I write home, having as its warm topic of interest what I had for supper last night and the other like I write to [his friend Aaron] Schaffer, for instance, telling of the marvels of the 'Group of Six.' " He chose the "happy medium" of describing his teachers, Nadia Boulanger and Ricardo Viñes, and informing Ralph about his progress with the French language. "Perhaps you could tell the folks about Boulanger and Viñes now, in less technical language," he suggested.[17]

It's possible that Ralph had hoped to pursue a career in music himself, but as the oldest boy, he felt he had little choice but to study law or medicine. He attended law school at Columbia University, became an attorney, and settled, like Laurine, in the Flatbush section of Brooklyn. For a while he represented Copland's legal interests. Then, on 24 March 1952, depressed and in financial straits, Ralph, at age sixty-three, jumped from the sixteenth story of his Manhattan office building just as Aaron and Laurine were having lunch to discuss his problems. "Ralph was such a mild-mannered individual that I could never have dreamed that he—of all people—would do such a thing!" exclaimed Copland, who was "shocked and shaken." He supported Ralph's widow for the rest of her life. She wrote him stacks of appreciative letters; "Your generosity helps me go on," said one.[18]

Copland thought his other brother, Leon, less intelligent than Ralph. For many years, the two went their own ways, Aaron helping Leon out financially from time to time. An unsuccessful businessman, Leon married Vivian Pinckney in 1917, Irene Cole in 1963 after Vivian's death, and

Mildred Roseback in 1966 after Irene's death. Leon and Mildred met at a retirement community in Croton-on-Hudson, where Leon had moved to be near Aaron's home in Cortlandt. During these later years, Leon and Mildred sometimes lunched with Copland; but like his other siblings, Leon scrupulously honored Aaron's need for quiet and privacy. "We do not see him often as he belongs to the world," explained Mildred to the positive-thinking Norman Vincent Peale, "but we were at his home for Thanksgiving. He joined us for Leon's birthday and he *always* keeps in touch, no matter what part of the world he has traveled to."[19]

For her part, Mildred thrived on the connection with Copland, to whom she wrote scores of letters. "Sometimes we ride in on your coattails," she confessed. Mildred regarded Leon's taciturn but sympathetic nature a Copland trait, writing, "No one but a woman who lives with him would know the *real sentimental* side of your brother. He can be real tough (*especially* on himself) and others too if they do not measure up—but they never know it as he understands human nature and goes along with everyone. He is a real lover of the world at heart." Above all, Mildred wanted Copland to know the deep veneration in which Leon held him.[20]

Copland also grew up with a large extended family of uncles, aunts, and cousins. One cousin, his exact contemporary Percy Uris, played a particularly important role in his career. The sons of Harris Copland's sister Sadie and Harris Uris, Percy and his brother Harold emerged in the course of the 1920s as leading New York builders. By 1970, their corporation, Uris Buildings, had accrued assets of $350 million. Architects criticized their policy of "the greatest amount of space for the lowest cost," but Percy Uris defended himself by stating, "To me a building is beautiful if it performs the function it was designed for."[21]

During the Depression, Uris occasionally made apartments and hotel rooms available to his struggling cousin Aaron. He further offered to support him financially for an entire year, an offer Aaron accepted, but not before writing a somewhat overpunctilious response, in which he remarked that it was "easier to accept help from a stranger" than from a relative, especially one who could "have no personal conviction about the value of the stuff I turn out, but must take it on hearsay. When a person has a real appreciation of the product I turn out, it is easier for me to accept the wherewithal for turning out that product." Rereading this letter years later, Copland was somewhat mortified by its ungrateful tone, but at the same time, he gave himself credit for its lofty idealism. During these later years, he declined a generous offer from Uris to compose a fanfare for the opening of a Hilton hotel in Manhattan.[22]

Throughout his life Copland maintained at least distant ties with a large number of other cousins, nephews, and nieces. Although most kept their distance, Laurine's daughter Felice Marlin basked in her uncle's glory and became, at least from the perspective of Copland's friends, an intrusive presence who discomfited him at public events in the years after 1960. Even so, Copland made a point of including Felice—Laurine's daughter, after all—on many a guest list.[23]

From financially supporting his widowed sister-in-law to welcoming his niece, Copland showed a strong sense of family duty. Yet he regretted not having a relative with whom he could more fully discuss his work. A lack of understanding even underscored, albeit in a humorous way, a 1922 letter to his parents in which he suggested the name Gina for a new baby in the family: "Lou [Bergman] will think it too stuck-up, Dorothy will think it too stagey, La will think it too old and so forth,—but Lils [Lillian Coombs, the maid] will agree with me!"[24]

Copland's Brooklyn

When Harris Copland arrived there in the 1870s, Brooklyn was its own city of more than one hundred thousand inhabitants, distinct not only from Manhattan but from such outlying towns in Kings County as Flatbush and Flatlands. By the time Aaron was born, Brooklyn's population had grown to over one million. It had annexed all of Kings County and had itself been incorporated into New York City, with a total population of about three and a half million. The only city in the world larger was London.

For his home and business, Harris staked out the corner of Washington Avenue and Dean Street in an area of Brooklyn then thought of as southern Bedford, but today considered part of Crown Heights. Although Copland described Washington Avenue as a "drab" and unlikely background for a composer, its drabness more or less resembled that of most American middle-class neighborhoods, neighborhoods whose "commonplace prosperity" Hawthorne had found inimical to art decades earlier.[25]

Turn-of-the-century Brooklyn actually enjoyed an enviable peak of economic prosperity and cultural vitality. Within walking distance of Copland's home lay the borough's greatest cultural institutions, all brand-new: the Brooklyn Museum (1897), the relocated Brooklyn Academy of

Music (1908), the Brooklyn Botanic Gardens (1910), and Grand Army Plaza, with its towering arch (1892) and its imposing Central Library. Copland heard his first concerts at the academy, survived his "first 'cultural' shock at the sight of a nude statue" at the museum, and discovered the latest books and musical scores at the library.[26]

Washington Avenue itself, writes Eric Salzman, "was often described as the most beautiful street in the United States." In close proximity were Prospect Park West, Eastern Parkway, and Bedford Avenue, fashionable boulevards where such Brooklyn luminaries as the department-store magnates Abraham Abraham and Frank W. Woolworth had their mansions. A few crowded tenements dotted the area as well. For the most part, however, turn-of-the-century Crown Heights, like the rest of Brooklyn, was solidly middle-class.[27]

At the beginning of the century, Brooklyn's population consisted largely of German and Irish immigrants and their children, with significant pockets of English, African-American, West Indian, Finnish, Italian, and other ethnic populations, and Jewish (mostly German-Jewish) inhabitants scattered throughout. In the year Copland was born, most residents on his block were either first- or second-generation Irish; others were of German, Welsh, Scottish, or Swedish descent. The Coplands at that time were one of the relatively few Jewish families in the neighborhood. Farther east, Crown Heights laid claim to the borough's largest West Indian community as well as to a historic African-American district that dated back to the early nineteenth century.

With the opening of the Williamsburg Bridge in 1903, Brooklyn suddenly became a popular destination for Italian and Eastern-European Jewish immigrants fleeing the crowded ghettos of Manhattan's Lower East Side. By 1920, such immigration, which helped double Brooklyn's population to over two million, dramatically changed the character of Crown Heights as well as the entire borough. Still, while Copland lived there, Crown Heights retained its essentially Irish character, whereas other areas of Brooklyn became predominantly Jewish. Copland's world thus differed somewhat from those two archetypal Brooklyn-Jewish neighborhoods of the early twentieth century: the slums of Williamsburg and Brownsville, from which many famous Jewish comedians emerged, and more suburban Flatbush, the birthplace of Arthur Miller and Bernard Malamud.[28]

Accordingly, Betty Smith's 1943 novel about her early life in Williamsburg, *A Tree Grows in Brooklyn,* presents at least as telling a literary portrayal of the Brooklyn of Copland's youth as do the tales of Jewish immigrant life by Henry Roth and Daniel Fuchs or the reminiscences of Miller and Malamud. The novel tells the story of one Francie Nolan from her birth in 1901 to her seventeenth birthday in 1918; and although the Nolans are Catholic, German-Irish, and poor, Francie's environment resembles that of the young Copland's in many particulars, including the uninspiring teaching in the public schools, the mean city streets, and the ethnic tensions among the Irish, German, Italian, and Jewish populations.[29]

Copland felt such tensions during his school years in Brooklyn—first at Public Schools 111 and 9 (1906–14) and then at Boys' High School (1914–18). On the way to school he had to walk through a "tough and slightly scary" neighborhood, as he told Vivian Perlis:

> I wasn't a toughie as a youngster. I must have run into kids who were much tougher than I was. You had to sort of be careful of what you said and did to stay out of trouble, that kind of thing. That was a kind of vague atmosphere around. Not all the kids. There were some proper kids from the brownstone houses who were all right. But there were some toughies from the Irish section, down on Dean Street and Vanderbilt Avenue.

He further told Irving Fine that when he attended Boys' High School, he "felt very different," though Fine reasonably supposed that this had more to do with his homosexuality than with his being Jewish; as *A Tree Grows in Brooklyn* documents, homosexual or at least effeminate boys were commonly taunted, as well as Jews. Even so, he made friends with boys of varying backgrounds, including Jewish, Italian, Irish, and African-American.[30]

Summers provided welcome alternatives to Brooklyn life: Camp Carey, a Jewish camp in the Poconos (1910–13), a YMHA camp (1914), a stay at a hotel in the Catskills (1915), berry picking in Marlboro, New York (1916–17), a few weeks at the Fairmont Hotel in Tannersville, New York (1916), jobs for a Wall Street brokerage firm (1917–18), and playing in dance bands in hotels in the Catskills (1919–20). Copland was not entirely in his element at camp: "I wasn't one of these manly young fellows who were completely adequate in that atmosphere," he remembered. "No, I was rather delicate by comparison with the other kids." He had, in particular, a fear of water, and although he joked about the camp counselor who threw him into the water, screaming, "Swim, you son of a gun, swim," it must have been a traumatic experience. Yet overall he enjoyed camp, where he made friends, learned to play tennis, and displayed his innate leadership qualities. "Those summer camps," he stated, "were very educational in that sense, of learning how to live with others in a tent, at close quarters. Not the family." Karen Mittleman notes the cultural importance that Jewish summer camps held for Copland's generation in general, writing, "In their heyday, camps were the vehicle for shaping what it meant to be an American and Jewish. That's something beyond nostalgia. It's about the meaning of a Jewish-American identity." For its part, the Fairmount Hotel offered contact with intellectuals who would prove supportive and influential.[31]

After leaving home at age twenty-one, Copland never returned to Brooklyn to live, nor did his speech reveal more than a faint trace of a Brooklyn accent. Buy he remained an exuberant, down-to-earth New Yorker. Moreover, he absorbed not only his Jewish background but something of the Irish-American milieu in which he grew up, as suggested by the quotation of "The Sidewalks of New York" in *Music for the Theatre* and *Statements*; as for his succession of maids from around the world, including Lillian Coombs from Barbados, one can only assume that they made their mark as well.

Copland and Religion

Harris and Sarah Copland both left Russia some years before the huge emigration of Russian Jews that followed the accession of Czar Alexander III in 1881. They consequently were more isolated from the Russian-Jewish culture of their youth than later immigrants, who packed into the ghettos of the Lower East Side and Brownsville. Furthermore, the Jews they met in America were likely to be of German origin, that is, Jews not necessarily immersed in Yiddish and other aspects of Eastern European Jewish culture.

The Coplands maintained a strong Jewish identity nonetheless. They apparently spoke some Yiddish at home (Aaron wrote to his parents in 1922 that the Yiddish he knew would make it easier for him to learn German) and they observed the major Jewish holidays, even to the point of owning a separate set of dishes for Passover. They were "more traditional than religious, but observant," explained Copland. When in later years, Laurine humored her children with a tree during the Christmas holidays, she would hide it when her parents visited.[32]

Harris and Sarah joined Congregation Baith Israel, Brooklyn's second-oldest synagogue, an Orthodox institution that over the years resisted numerous attempts at reform, including a short-lived introduction of pipe organ and mixed choir in 1904. In 1905, the congregation, located in Boerum Hill since 1862, hired Rabbi Israel Goldfarb and moved to Cobble Hill, about a forty-five-minute walk from the Copland home. In 1905, Harris became treasurer and chairman of the Talmud Torah (which offered instruction on various topics, including Jewish music); he served as president from 1907 to 1909, during which time he helped establish a sisterhood for women congregants. Ralph also was active in the synagogue, serving for a time as superintendent of the Sunday school.[33]

In his annual report to the congregation in 1908, Harris proposed that the synagogue reduce its mortgage and secure its future by selling pews to the members. In defense of establishing a sisterhood, he stated, "By meeting in a social way, and by arranging occasionally some concert, lecture, or any other feature, [the women members] would come to know each other more thoroughly; they would help this Congregation in its struggles and would add a good deal of importance and dignity to our Chevra, augmenting the feeling of friendship and increasing the spirit of fraternity and harmony." One can detect in this rare record of Harris's synagogal activities something of the source for Aaron's financial savvy and fraternal sensibilities.[34]

Aaron learned at least enough Hebrew to get through his bar mitzvah, in 1913. Rabbi Goldfarb composed the bar mitzvah speech, which Aaron read in synagogue, as well as the toast spoken the following day at a party at the family store. Both speeches took as their theme a boy's essential unworthiness and his consequent need to prove his worth before his parents, God, and mankind. Copland would later describe Goldfarb as "a composer of liturgical music and the possessor of a fine baritone voice," as well as "a sensitive human being and an effective leader of his congregation."[35]

Otherwise, his recollections of growing up Jewish typically involved music, especially the dance music at traditional Jewish weddings and the singing of Hebrew chant, both of which impressed him. "Not being precise as to the musical pitch," he said of the latter, "it seemed colorful and different." In adult life, he read with interest books on Jewish music by Lazare Saminsky and Peter Gradenwitz, and he closely followed the progress of David Diamond's Friday evening service, amazing that composer with his knowledge of the Jewish holiday services.[36]

Like many contemporaries, Copland regarded Judaism alternately in terms of religion, culture, and race; but he showed relatively little involvement in any aspect of his Jewish heritage. For some years, he partly seems to have associated Jewish life with the hardships of the ghettos of Eastern Europe, as reflected in his piano trio *Vitebsk*. A comment, made in Israel in 1951, about the local population looking "healthy and happy and very un-Jewish" underscored this association. He attended synagogue only for the occasional family bar mitzvah, wedding, or funeral, and, aside from the exclamation "Oy," he rarely used Yiddish expressions. In a 1974 letter, Phillip Ramey reminded him that he had spoken of having "resigned from the Jewish church." His will specified that his funeral service, if any, be "non-religious."[37]

Over the course of his career, he nonetheless wrote a handful of works with explicit ties to Judaism, including a setting of Aaron Schaffer's Zionist poem "My Heart Is in the East" (1918); a *Lament* for cello and piano (1919) after one of the traditional melodies for the Hebrew prayer "Adon Olom"; *Four Motets* for chorus (1921), based on Psalmodic fragments; the piano trio *Vitebsk* (1928), inspired by Ansky's famous play *The Dybbuk*, about social oppression and redemption in a Russian shtetl; the Jewish-Palestinian folk-song setting "We've Come" ("Banu") (1938); and a chorus based on the opening section of Genesis, *In the Beginning* (1947). In addition, he hoped to collaborate with Thornton Wilder on a theatrical work based on a Hasidic legend and with Clifford Odets on an oratorio adapted from the Noah story.[38]

Although, like many progressive Jewish artists and intellectuals of his time, he worried about the dangers of a theocratic state, "My Heart Is in the East" and "We've Come" suggested some early sympathy for Zionism. His first trip to Israel in 1951 thoroughly converted him to the cause; the country, he wrote to friends, would make Zionists out of both Hitler and the old guard American composer Daniel Gregory Mason. On his second trip to Israel, in 1968, he posed for the camera with a helmet and gun.[39]

At the same time, he had ties to Christianity, identifying with such profoundly Christian writers as Gerard Manley Hopkins and often spending Christmas Day at home with a special dinner with close friends. He used a Shaker tune in *Appalachian Spring*, set the sacred Christian songs "Simple Gifts," "At the River," and "Zion's Walls" in *Old American Songs*, and quoted "Amazing Grace" in *Emblems*. In general, his music seemed to evoke Protestant hymns as often as it did Jewish chant.

He also took an open-minded attitude toward Eastern religions, purchasing copies of Romain Rolland's *Prophets of the New India* and Ouspensky's *In Search of the Miraculous* for his friend Erik Johns, a Vedantist. In 1963 Johns brought the swami Nitya-Swarup Ananda to Copland's Cortlandt home, Rock Hill, to meet the composer, who seemed fascinated by him and "amused when told by him, 'You are living here like a yogi.'" Copland characteristically found connections among various religious traditions.[40]

Copland's relation to Judaism, consequently, contrasted with the more overt Jewishness of Leonard Bernstein, who would tease him by saying, "Aaron, you're not a real Jew." Samuel Lipman contended that the composer's 1941 "sanitized" autobiographical sketch "shrouded" his Jewish origins.[41]

But if Copland was discreet about his Jewish background, he never hid it either. Verna Fine remembers that at Harvard cocktail parties, at which sooner or later a local Boston Brahmin would query him about the missing "e" in his name, Copland would put on his thickest Brooklyn accent and say, "Well to tell ya the truth, when my family came over it shoulda been Kaplan. They just got it wrong at Ellis Island." Moreover, throughout his life, Copland spoke warmly of the Jewish traditions he had grown up with.[42]

While Copland had no real religious affiliations and showed no particular interest in theology (he even apologized to Carlos Chávez for setting Scripture), he had his own metaphysical worldview, feeling, according to David Diamond, that there was "a mystery behind the whole aspect of being with a capital B, as he used to call it." Arnold Dobrin similarly reported,

> Aaron Copland has not followed the religion of his parents. He is an agnostic but one who is deeply aware of the grandeur and mystery of the universe. When speaking of religion, Copland refers to the vastness of space and "the sense of oneself in the universe."
>
> "And isn't that religion," he asks, "... the connection with something larger than oneself?"

He occasionally referred to God—Robert Cornell, for instance, remembered his saying, in reference to his homosexuality, "God made me the way I am"—but he apparently rejected the idea of a personal deity who intervened in human affairs.[43]

Copland further took an interest in contemporary metaphysics, in particular the writings of Henri Bergson, William James, and George Santayana. However these writers may have influenced him—Diamond stressed the importance of Bergson's concept of the "élan vital" ("vital impulse") to Copland's own beliefs—he shared with them a certain religious ambiguity, a denial of old orthodoxies, with a sensitivity to the spiritual essence of the great religions, one directed toward creativity, goodness, optimism, and order, and one, moreover, reflected in the great art of the world. Copland may well have shared, too, the related sentiments of his close friend Harold Clurman, who declared, "Art is my religion only insofar as it serves my greater religion, which is the respect for life, the respect for creation, the respect for human beings and for the totality of existence, which some people might call God." Copland himself wrote, "I must believe in the ultimate good of the world and of life as I live it in order to create a work of art." Whatever the exact nature of his beliefs, friends widely described him as one of the most "spiritual" people they had ever known.[44]

3

Early Education and
First Works

Childhood and Adolescence

Copland took all the usual classes at school but quickly gravitated toward literature and music. Like many American boys of his time, he developed a special fondness for the novels of Horatio Alger (1832–1899), stories that typically feature an underprivileged teenaged boy whose innate nobility helps earn him a place in society; although these heroes confront a variety of villains, they fortunately find some older, benevolent male patron to provide a helping hand. Many leading figures associated with the political left read Alger as children—not only Copland and his friend Harold Clurman, but Theodore Dreiser, Jack London, Upton Sinclair, and Richard Wright.[1]

Something of Alger's sensibilities can be detected in a one-act "playlet" by Copland entitled *The Home Coming*, written when he was twelve years old. The play opens with attorney Charles J. Gordon in conversation with his secretary, Jenny Marlo, whose missing "sweetheart," Jim Corland, has gone off "in search of fortune" so that they can "live comfortably together." Upon Gordon's exit, Jenny's mother enters, accompanied by their villainous landlord, Dan Farley, demanding the rent. When Jenny spurns Farley's offer of marriage, he threatens to kiss her. In the nick of time, Jim, coincidentally on his way to Gordon's office to see about an inheritance, enters, saying, "What is the meaning of this, Jen? How do you happen to be running away from this brute in a well-to-do lawyer's office?" Gordon returns, orders the landlord out, and informs Jim of a "legacy of $10,000, providing you marry on April 2 three days from today." As with Alger, the good and upstanding find their rewards on earth.[2]

In writing *The Home Coming*, complete with its lecherous landlord, Copland took his cue not only from Alger but from the period's stock melodramas of stage and screen. For a dime, recalls Betty Smith in *A Tree Grows in Brooklyn*, one could sit in the gallery of a Williamsburg theater and watch any number of small companies perform such plays (though Smith's juvenile protagonist, more practical than Jenny Marlo, "couldn't understand why the heroine didn't marry the villain. It would solve the rent problem"). Copland no doubt attended such plays and films himself.[3]

The young Copland's imagination was fired by European melodramas as well as by American ones; he eagerly read the libretti that his sister Laurine brought home from the Metropolitan Opera. At age eleven he even devised his own opera scenario, *Zenetello*.[4]

The plot of *Zenetello* shows some familiarity with the popular Italian and French operas of the day. In Act I, Naomi (a peculiarly Jewish name for the work's Italian heroine) and Lorenzo, a "reformed gambler," celebrate their wedding in a small Italian town, Naomi ignoring the warnings of her friends, Louis and Louise (names equally curious for Italians). In Act II, set in Paris a few months later, the newlyweds' marital happiness is disrupted when Lorenzo goes off with a few cronies, leaving behind some empty wine bottles. In Act III, five years later, Naomi, now in rags and the mother of a four-year-old boy, prays before a church on a "lonely Paris street." Warnery, a stage manager, persuades her to leave the child on the church's doorstep and become an actress. The monks Dalmore and Amadeo discover the abandoned child and resolve to find him wealthy parents. Act IV takes place in an inn on the road from Paris to (Le) Havre fifteen years later (shades of *Manon*). Naomi, now a celebrated singer (apparently the "Zenetello" of the opera's title), enters an inn, where she espies Lorenzo playing cards (though he fails to recognize her). During a robbery attempt at the inn that night, Lorenzo shoots a young man, Maurice. Naomi cries out, realizing, thanks to a locket the young man is wearing, that Maurice is their son, whereupon "Lorenzo kills himself as Maurice dies in Naomi's hands."

Copland's youthful stab at Italian-French opera reveals, unwittingly as it were, some telltale American features. The treatment of Lorenzo's gambling and alcoholism has something of the temperance movement about it; Copland's idea of a French inn was probably the "corner saloon with its occasional neighborhood drunks" near his home. The armed robbery also strikes an American note, as does Naomi's sudden discovery by Warnery and her radically changed persona as "Zenetello." If this is verismo, it is the verismo of the American dime novel and Hollywood silent film.[5]

Copland composed about seven bars of music for *Zenatello* (now spelled with an "a") before giving up; he quickly realized that an entire opera would require more than the two harmonies at his disposal. This sketch still survives as his earliest extant music.

Copland had the "great luck," he would later state, to have been "born with a musical gift." He started studying music at age seven with Laurine, who taught him the rudiments of the piano. "From the start," he remembered, "I was always arguing with her about how I should play." After six months, Laurine, having taught him all she could on the family upright, suggested that he find a professional teacher. At first, Harris, feeling that he had already wasted so much money on music lessons with the other children, refused; but Aaron persisted, and some six years later, when Aaron was thirteen, Harris relented.[6]

Word of mouth led Copland to Leopold Wolfsohn, who had a studio in Brooklyn at 345 Clinton Avenue. Wolfsohn, with whom he studied from 1913 to 1917, assigned him the standard pedagogical fare: Hanon exercises, Chopin waltzes, Mozart and Beethoven sonatas. According to Copland, he was "a competent instructor, with a well-organized teaching method," but a *"routinier* kind of man: Chopin was the highlight of his life, and Stravinsky was a madman." Copland made his debut as a pianist performing Paderewski's Polonaise in B in a recital of Wolfsohn's students at John Wanamaker's. "Ironic," he noted to himself, "that I made my debut in a department store boxing my ears to take my mind off my 'nervousness.' "[7]

Meanwhile he had started, by age eight, to compose, or at least to improvise and make up tunes at the piano. By age twelve, as *Zenatello* reveals, he had begun to notate such melodies. About the time he started lessons with Wolfsohn, he attempted another opera, this time his own version of *Cavalleria Rusticana*; he got as far as an unaccompanied setting of the Metropolitan Opera libretto's translation of Turiddù's opening offstage serenade, which he entitled "Lola!" Copland's version, with its prominent augmented seconds, bears the obvious imprint of Russian-Jewish melody; the melismatic "Ah"s suggest some awareness of the Mascagni original as well, but only vaguely.[8]

In 1916, Copland produced the beginnings of a piano piece, *Valse Impromptu,* a Schubertian effort again hampered by a restricted harmonic vocabulary. In the same year he acquired a "mail-order harmony course" and essayed his most ambitious piece to date, a *Capriccio* for piano and violin. Derived largely from Italian opera and Russian-Jewish dance music, the piece also incorporated something from popular American styles. At about this time Copland composed some less finished things: a rudimentary *Theme and Variations* for piano, which is of interest because its main theme, in its compression, looks ahead to the *Piano Variations* (1930); and a song à la Victor Herbert about the "innocent days of childhood." He also planned an "imaginary oratorio" with sections entitled "With a Mighty Hand and an Outstretched Arm," "Song of Miriam," and "Burial of Moses."

In the spring of 1917, Copland completed a solo piano piece, *Moment Musicale—a Tone Poem,* inspired by a poem, "Fear," by his friend Aaron Schaffer. The music awkwardly pieces together little ideas derived from Beethoven, Liszt, and Tchaikovsky before veering off into some Jewish-sounding meanderings ostensibly meant to depict Schaffer's "vague mysterious figure" that arises from the fire, leaving the poet's mind "enwrapped in haze." Still unable to modulate, Copland realized that he needed formal instruction and, on the recommendation of Wolfsohn, began lessons with Rubin Goldmark in the fall of 1917, during his senior year at Boys' High.

Copland attended few professional concerts during his years with Wolfsohn, even with the Brooklyn Academy in his own backyard; his serious concertgoing began only after he started traveling into Manhattan for his lessons with Goldmark. One notable exception—and one of the defining moments of his life—was a concert he attended, presumably in 1915, of the Polish pianist-composer, Ignacy Paderewski. An electrifying musician with a magnificent range of colors and a compelling sense of line, Paderewski thrilled the young Copland, as well as millions of listeners all over the world. "Up to now," writes Arnold Dobrin, Copland's "future had not been clear to him—simply vague years ahead that were in some way connected with music. For the first time now he realized he wanted to *write* music." Others claim that Copland left the Paderewski recital wanting to become a pianist and that he decided to become a composer only after studying with Goldmark. It's fair to say that during his formative years, he entertained more or less concurrently the ideas of becoming a pianist, a composer, and even, at one point, a music critic.[9]

Rubin Goldmark

Copland studied theory and composition with Rubin Goldmark (1872–1936) for four years (fall 1917 to spring 1921), meeting privately with him in his Manhattan studio every Saturday morning. During these years, he also changed piano teachers, first to Victor Wittgenstein (1917–19), then to Clarence Adler (1919–21). Thus, after graduating from Boys' High School in 1918, he essentially charted out his own three-year program roughly comparable to a conservatory education. He later regretted never attending college, but the decision presumably fostered his growing individuality and daring. Throughout this entire period, he lived at home with his parents, who purchased a six-foot Steinway grand for him in 1919.[10]

One reason Copland studied privately in New York was that it allowed him to take advantage of the city's sophisticated musical life. He frequented concerts by Walter Damrosch and the New York Symphony Orchestra and took out a subscription to the Metropolitan Opera (his first opera, *Boris Godunov*, left him spellbound); he heard the Philadelphia Orchestra play Debussy's *Nocturnes* and the Chicago Opera perform *Pelléas et Mélisande* with Mary Garden; and he saw Prokofiev in concert and attended dance recitals of Isadora Duncan and the touring Ballets Russes. He also scoured the standard literature by playing four-hand piano arrangements of symphonic works with his organist friend John Kober. Meanwhile he made considerable progress as a composer under Goldmark's tutelage.[11]

A composer of some repute, Goldmark was one of New York's most eminent composition teachers; his other students included Nikolai Berezovsky, Vittorio Giannini, Alexei Haieff, and Frederick Jacobi (George Gershwin, who had little patience for this sort of pedagogy, lasted only three lessons in 1923). The grandson of a Hungarian cantor, nephew of the prominent Viennese composer Karl Goldmark, and son of an American businessman, Goldmark had studied with Johann Nepomuk Fuchs at the Vienna Conservatory and with Dvořák at the National Conservatory in New York. In discussing Goldmark's music, Copland thought it interesting to note "a certain need to identify his music with the

American scene if only in the titles of some of his orchestral works: *Hiawatha Overture, Negro Rhapsody, The Call of the Plains*, and his best-known composition, *Requiem,* suggested by Lincoln's Gettysburg Address."[12]

Copland remained grateful to Goldmark "for the kind of solid basic training that he gave me and which accounted, I think, for the high opinion in which he was held as one of the leading composition teachers of his day." In a 1956 tribute, he honored him as a "musical pioneer," a "genial and vivid" teacher who "made it clear to me from the outset that the career of composer was not to be lightly embarked upon, and that the composer's discipline was a severe and arduous one." He thought it "significant" that when Juilliard opened its doors in 1924, Goldmark headed the theory and composition department, an appointment he held until his death.[13]

At the same time, Copland noted that Goldmark had "little if any sympathy for the advanced musical idioms of the day." Upon finding a copy of Ives's *Concord Sonata* in Goldmark's studio and expressing some interest in the work, he received the following admonition: "You stay away from it. I don't want you to be contaminated by stuff like that." At a 1921 celebration dinner in Goldmark's honor, the usually deferential Copland had some fun by anonymously submitting a chorale tune purportedly harmonized "in the Goldmark manner" but that turned, after two conventional phrases, waywardly Debussyan. By this time, Goldmark knew better than to have to ask who the "culprit" was.[14]

Copland was not entirely fair to Goldmark, for the latter admired Strauss, Ravel, and Debussy, of whom, according to Bernard Wagenaar, Goldmark "stood in awe." "Contrary to a fairly general impression, he was not intolerant of the more advanced music of his contemporaries," wrote Frederick Jacobi. But at the same time, he rejected Schoenberg and Stravinsky as "ugly," and held up German Romantic music as best representing "universal" ideals. "Of course Bach, Beethoven, Brahms, and Wagner were Germans, to the everlasting honor and credit of their people," he stated during World War I, "but I had all my life singly regarded their works as Music, the universal property of Mankind." He regarded the classical sonata as representing "the top point of one's training" and the "key to all future composition."[15]

Try as he might, Goldmark could not impart this kind of reverence for the German Romantic tradition to Copland, whose tastes, even as a child, ran more to Chopin and Verdi. Now, as Copland explored the repertory in 1917 and 1918, he rarely reacted to any German music as favorably as he did to Grieg and Tchaikovsky, both "ravishing" in his estimation; or Mussorgsky and Scriabin, whom he deemed "exceptionally fine"; or Debussy, who deeply affected him. Although Goldmark might not have found this music objectionable, he apparently would have questioned the kind of centrality it held for Copland.[16]

Significantly, the formation of Copland's musical tastes coincided with the height of anti-German and pro-French sentiment in the United States occasioned by the First World War. Copland felt strongly about the conflict, composing a song, "After Antwerp" (1917), to words by the Belgian poet Émile Cammaerts ("Sing, Belgians, sing, / Although our wounds may burn . . ."); picking berries in Marlboro, New York, in the summers of 1916 and 1917 in order to help the war effort by substituting for drafted soldiers; and undergoing military training himself in 1917. Such activities may have helped weaken the prestige and relevance of German Romantic music for him. At the same time, in 1919, he composed *Schumanniana*, an arrangement for cello and piano of melodies from Schumann's *Papillons*, *Carnival*, and *Kreisleriana*—presumably for himself and his cellist friend Arne Vainio to play. And after arriving in Europe, he developed an enthusiasm for more recent German and Austrian composers, Mahler in particular.[17]

In any case, during his years with Goldmark, Copland's interests continued to outpace his teacher's. In 1919, as he continued his independent study of Debussy's songs and piano preludes, he performed and discussed Ravel's *Sonatine* in a Clarence Adler studio class. He sought out whatever new music he could, attending a recital by the city's enfant terrible Leo Ornstein and discovering a sonata by Cyril Scott. In 1920, he heard Ernest Bloch's Violin Sonata, and began acquiring that composer's work, including the Viola Suite. He also gravitated toward such late Scriabin as *Vers la Flamme* and the Tenth Sonata, music that for the moment surpassed even Debussy and Ravel in his estimation. All this represented a dramatic plunge into uncharted and, from Goldmark's perspective, rather dangerous waters.[18]

Before leaving Goldmark's studio, Copland obliged his teacher by delaying study in Paris for one year in order to complete a three-movement sonata for solo piano as a graduation piece. Completed in 1921, this sonata demonstrated a capable handling of Romantic technique and rhetoric, like the music of such established Americans as Arthur Foote, Amy Beach, or Goldmark himself. Still, the sonata, with its resemblances to Chopin, Tchaikovsky, and MacDowell, contained far less personality than those shorter, more original pieces, composed during these same years, that Copland never showed to Goldmark, for fear that their "modern harmonies and unconventional rhythms" might meet with his disapproval. Copland once again might have underestimated Goldmark; upon receiving, in 1922, a published copy of Copland's piano piece *The Cat and the Mouse* (1920), composed right under his nose, Goldmark declared the work "very good—clever, musicianly and not too extreme for my tastes."[19]

Early Friendships

While in high school, Copland made friends with Bob Gordon, Daniel Burns, Gus Feldman, Frank Carroll, and John Kober, all classmates at Boys' High; and with Aaron Schaffer and Martha ("Marty") Dreiblatt, both of whom he met in 1916 at the Fairmont Hotel, a "gathering place for well-known Jewish literary people."[20]

Born in Baltimore in 1894, Schaffer—his "first intellectual friend"— played a particularly important role in the young Copland's life. When the sixteen-year-old Copland first met him, Schaffer, a rabbi's son, was a twenty-two-year-old graduate student in literature on the Johns Hopkins University faculty at work on a book of poems, published later that year. In 1917, he completed his doctoral thesis on Georg Rudolf Weckherlin. He taught at Johns Hopkins for another two years, did some postdoctoral work in Paris, and then, in 1920, joined the faculty of the University of Texas, where he taught French language and literature until his death in 1957, publishing major studies on Parnassian poetry (1929, 1944).[21]

Schaffer shared Copland's passion for music and literature; when they met, his heroes included Mozart, Chopin, Keats, and Judah ha-Levi. He encouraged his young friend's loftiest ambitions, dissuading him from writing for the popular stage. A fervent Zionist, he suggested that they immigrate to Palestine together.[22]

He also offered Copland guidance in French literature, in 1918 recommending Romain Rolland's *Jean-Christophe*, which made "a deep impression" on him. Published in ten volumes between 1904 and 1912, *Jean-Christophe* brought Rolland (1866–1944) to the forefront of European intellectual life, earning him the Nobel Prize for Literature in 1915. This magnum opus traces the life of its eponymous composer-hero—a composite of Beethoven, Hugo Wolf, and other composers—from childhood in his native Germany through old age in his adopted France. A somewhat radical composer of the generation after Debussy, he tells his friend Olivier, "Your Debussy is the genius of good taste: Strauss is the genius of bad taste. Debussy is rather insipid. But Strauss is very unpleasant." Jean-Christophe aims rather to create a vigorous music closer to the reality of everyday life. The novel surely helped shape Copland's developing aesthetics, including the notion of a humanistic, progressive nationalism.[23]

In 1918, Copland set three of Schaffer's poems: "My Heart Is in the East" (composed in May), "Summer Vacation" (April to May), and "Night" (composed July to December). (Although he referred to these as *Three Songs*, he did not specify any particular order for them.) "My Heart Is in the East," though the least distinguished musically, is noteworthy for its quasi-Zionist text, in which the poet (Schaffer as, presumably, Judah ha-Levi) pines for Zion amid "the abundance of this Spanish land." The choice of this text—especially the references to Zion "oppressed" by "Edom" and "Arab's bond"—suggests some sympathy for Schaffer's Zionist aspirations; perhaps not coincidentally Copland composed the song against the background of Wilson's support for the Balfour Declaration (1917), which established the idea of a Jewish Palestine as a patriotic war goal. At the same time, the music seems more melancholy than militant, reflecting a more general yearning for home.[24]

Schaffer may have brought Copland closer to his Jewish roots; in the same month as "My Heart," he began a *Lament* for cello and piano (completed April 1919) based on a traditional Hebrew melody, one sung to the hymn "Adon Olom" on particularly sad occasions. The piece, marked "Mournfully, very slowly," at one point has a passage, "with longing," that features the same sighing appoggiaturas found in "My Heart." Copland started but never completed an arrangement of this *Lament* for violin, cello, and piano, thereby anticipating his only mature work for this combination of instruments, *Vitebsk* (1929), which also quotes a traditional Jewish theme.

Although conservative in his musical tastes, Schaffer sympathized with Copland's growing daring and understood that Scriabin and other moderns offered "endless vistas." A month after receiving Copland's settings of his three poems, Schaffer, speaking for his family, told the composer that his discords "have won their way into our hearts." While studying in France in 1919–20, he sent Copland excited reports about Paris's new-music scene ("I am sure you would be in your glory here"), thus becoming, in Copland's words, "the source of inspiration in my desire to go to Paris."[25]

After Copland left for Paris in 1921, he and Schaffer drifted apart. But they remained in touch, seeing each other when Copland traveled to Austin and when Schaffer and his wife, Dorothy, visited Tanglewood. "I need hardly tell you with how much interest we read and hear of your numerous and varied achievements in the world of music," he wrote to Copland in 1943. One Texas graduate remembered Schaffer as "big, bearish, and formidable."[26]

Copland also stayed in touch with Martha Dreiblatt, one of his few close women friends from his high-school years. Dreiblatt lived in New York, where she pursued various work related to the theater. In the 1970s, she even proposed a collaboration with Copland; and in 1984, after reading the first volume of his autobiography, she wrote to him, "You never told me most of those things you were doing; how enterprising and steadfast you were in starting to achieve your career."[27]

After graduating from Boys' High, Copland played in dance bands in Brooklyn and in the Catskills in order to earn some money. This not only brought him in further touch with the kind of popular music that he would eventually absorb into his music but made him such new friends as cellist Arne Vainio, violinist Sidney Roof, violinist Abraham ("Abe") Ginsburg, and pianist Minnie Ruttenberg. They seem to have been a congenial group of young musicians, interested in and supportive of Copland's more serious aspirations.

Of these friends, Copland spoke most about Vainio, whom he described as a young, handsome, intellectual Finn "who played clarinet and cello and liked to talk about books, politics, music, and poetry." The two met playing in a dance band at the Finnish Socialist Hall in Brooklyn, perhaps in late 1918, when Copland composed his *Poème* for cello and piano, possibly for himself and Vainio. Vainio, a socialist, exposed him to leftist political thought. "Coming as I did from a thoroughly bourgeois environment," Copland wrote, "I found Vainio and his contact with Finnish socialism fascinating."[28]

Although Copland also came to terms with his homosexuality before leaving Brooklyn for Paris, we do not know if any of these friends were also homosexual or if he had any sexual experiences during these years. The preserved correspondence with friends—namely, letters to and from Schaffer and Kober—sheds no light on this matter, giving the impression of young men with nothing on their minds but books and music.[29]

Copland's musical compositions suggest otherwise. First, most of the songs composed around this time take love as their subject, usually unrequited or otherwise painful, a cause for tears, sadness, sleepless nights, and so forth. It is hard to imagine Copland writing these songs without feeling some such emotion himself. In discussing his juvenilia, he even wrote,

> I found that I derived profound satisfaction from exteriorizing inner feelings—at times, surprisingly concrete ones—and giving them shape. The scale on which I worked at first was small—two or three page piano pieces or songs—but the intensity of feeling was real. It must have been the reality of this inner intensity I speak of which produced the conviction that I was capable of some day writing a longer, and perhaps, significant work.

Moreover, a number of these early pieces feature, as poetic mottos, quotations from romantic poems, one of which—by Wallace Stevens—even associates music with sexual desire. Although the second piece of the *Three Moods* for piano, "Wistful" (1920), has no motto, it opens with a musical phrase borrowed from the song "Melancholy" (1917, words by Jeffrey Farnol), a melody that accompanies the words "Alack and woe, that love is so akin to pain." Taken as a whole, Copland's early music gives the impression of someone thoroughly absorbed by romantic yearning. In addition, he dedicated his *Sonnet I* (1918) and *Sonnets II and III* (1919 and 1920) to G.F. (Gus Feldman) and A.V. (Arne Vainio), respectively. Given that sonnets are often addressed to a beloved one, Copland possibly felt in particular some romantic affection for Feldman and Vainio.[30]

Apprenticeship Works, 1917–21

It would be an error, perhaps, to regard all of the music Copland wrote before leaving for Paris as mere juvenilia. As a composer he made enormous strides between 1917 and 1921 and wrote some lovely and interesting things before ever meeting Nadia Boulanger. He benefited, in this regard, only indirectly from Goldmark, for aside from the Piano Sonata, he wrote this music—little piano and chamber pieces and songs—without any supervision.

The individuality of these early works, even the humble and crude efforts of 1917, is impressive. To be sure, by then he had learned a few lessons from Debussy; and by 1920, he had assimilated something from

Ravel, Scriabin, and Bloch as well, which put him in range of such older Americans as Carpenter and Griffes, whose music he also knew. Surveying this youthful music, Peter Dickinson emphasized just such debts and similarities. But Copland's music emerged, so to speak, from scratch, from the composer's integral being, without a hint of affectation. In its unassuming, forthright tone, this music even occasionally evoked popular music, notwithstanding its relative daring and sophistication.[31]

As if by instinct, Copland avoided the more common resources of tonal music—major and minor triads and authentic cadences—in favor of seventh chords, diminished chords, augmented triads, and, above all, the tritone. These early pieces also tend to begin and end ambiguously; even when the music concludes with a triad, the actual choice of harmony is often unexpected. Keys change rapidly, the pieces or songs rarely ending in the key with which they begin. The music further experiments with elided phrases and deceptive cadences. And yet, for all their spontaneity, these early works do not sound amorphous; on the contrary, they display a subtle sense of architecture.

It is hard to explain how Copland developed such unusual procedures, but they clearly involved his practice of "exteriorizing inner feelings." This includes many colorful directives; the twenty-seven-measure *Sonnet III* for piano features the markings "slightly agitated," "hazily," "naively," "fancifully," "ominously," and "brightly" (the last two in the same measure!). This anticipates the use, for example, of such unusual directives as "searing," "muttering," and "uncertain" in the *Piano Fantasy* (1957), which prompted Leo Smit's comment, "Aaron's instructions to the performer in the *Fantasy* are so personalized that it's as though he was standing behind you looking over your shoulder."[32]

Copland's musical output begins in earnest, thanks to the combined influences of Goldmark's harmony instruction and Debussy's music, with three songs composed in the fall of 1917: "After Antwerp" (words by Émile Cammaerts), "Spurned Love" (words by Thomas Bailey Aldrich), and "Melancholy," subtitled "a Song à la Debussy" (words by Jeffrey Farnol). His songs from 1918 to 1921 are even more commanding: *Three Songs* (1918; words by Aaron Schaffer); "Simone" (1919; words by Rémy de Gourmont); "Music I Heard" (1920; text by Conrad Aiken); "Old Poem" (1920; translated from the Chinese by Arthur Waley); and "Pastorale" (1921; translated from Kafiri by Edward Powys Mathers). Although the texts for "My Heart Is in the East," "Old Poem," and "Pastorale" reflect the time's vogue for Asian materials, Copland's settings seem unusually cautious about exploiting exotic mannerisms, yet another sign of his individuality.[33]

Some of these songs compare favorably with the best American art songs of the period. They are historically interesting as well; the dreamy nostalgia of "A Summer Vacation" and the vivid tone-painting of "Night," for example, look ahead to many later works. "Pastorale," on the other hand, is a unique achievement; it is his only contented love song, the dream toward which all the more troubled love songs yearn (though again, the song's final three extremely soft notes in the high register of the piano anticipate the radiant conclusion of *Appalachian Spring*).[34]

The instrumental works from this period are, in comparison, less finished but of some interest in their own right, least so, perhaps, the flashy *Waltz Caprice* for piano (1918), a crude amalgam of Liszt and Debussy, with some scattered augmented seconds suggestive of Jewish music. Still, the work is revealing. It strongly inclines, for instance, toward the octatonic scale, which plays a part in Copland's later development. Moreover, the piece's static tonal language—an amplification of his still cruder efforts of previous years—reveals that the harmonic immobility of his mature work had deep-seated roots. And, as with his earlier *Valse Impromptu* fragment, it documents an early fondness for the waltz.[35]

A more persuasive work, *Poème* for cello and piano, completed at the very end of 1918, shows Copland now thoroughly under the influence of Debussy; the title itself, of course, reveals a French bias. In this moody piece—marked, at times, "passionately," "despairingly," and "with longing"—Copland pits the cello's expressive, lyrical lines against shimmering figuration in the piano, including, near the end, an astonishing bitonal flourish: two arpeggiated major triads a half step away from each other, played "as softly as possible."

The instrumental works from 1919 and 1920 represent still greater advances. Four of these pieces—*Sonnets II* and *III* for piano (1919, 1920) and *Preludes I* and *II* for violin and piano (1919, 1921)—bear quotations from recent poems by Conrad Aiken, Carl Sandburg, Witter Bynner, and Wallace Stevens, respectively. In this sense, they fall into the Romantic traditions of the song without words and the tone poem—Liszt still casts a shadow, as the title *Sonnet* suggests—but they show far more subtlety than *Waltz Caprice*. The poems in question are, after all, modernist, helping to inspire the music's jagged movement and intense compression. The quotation from Wallace Stevens—three years before the publication of Stevens's *Harmonium*—in particular shows a literary sensibility in sync with the music's daring. In his maturity, Copland remained keenly interested in contemporary poetry, an interest that, one imagines, continued to color his music in one way or another.[36]

In March 1920 he completed *Humoristic Scherzo* (better known by its subtitle, *The Cat and the Mouse*), a solo piano piece based on yet another poem, this one, however, old and humorous: Jean de la Fontaine's "Le Vieux Chat et la Jeune Souris" ("The Old Cat and the Young Mouse"). Upon hearing him play this work in a recital in Fontainebleau on 21 September 1921, the publisher Jacques Durand bought it outright for five hundred francs. Published as *Scherzo Humoristique* (subtitled *Le Chat et la Souris*), this debut publication became Copland's first recognized work, one still widely known and played.[37]

The La Fontaine fable tells of a young mouse captured by an old cat; the mouse appeals to the cat with various arguments, but the cat, unmoved, eats him just the same. The fable concludes, "Youth deludes itself into believing that it can obtain everything; Old age is merciless." The opposition of youth and old age, of hope and disillusionment, apparently spoke forcibly to the young Copland.[38]

The Cat and the Mouse is as adventurous and personal as any of Copland's apprenticeship works; some of its harmonies, in fact, derive from or at least duplicate a fragment for piano entitled "The Sea Fairies" ("Tone Poem for Piano After Tennyson's Poem of the Same Name"). But the portrayal of a cat stalking a mouse—unpredictably coy and sinister—inspires a more objective and ironic tone. The nervous scampering up and down the piano suggests, further, some connection with machine music of a decidedly ominous variety, as if the threat of age and death were related to that of industrial life. This includes the climax—crashing, dissonant chords followed by a soft passage marked "funereal" that anticipates the many far more solemn dirges of Copland's later music. The work ends with a whimsical but deathly whimper, like the end of T. S. Eliot's *The Hollow Men* or Stravinsky's *Petrushka*, a figure also caught in a game of cat and mouse.

In addition, the music contains certain elements related to Copland's explicitly jazzy works to come; the final gesture, for instance, anticipates the end of a piano piece composed the following year, entitled "Jazzy." In this respect, the piece warrants comparison with Zez Confrey's *Kitten on the Keys* and John Alden Carpenter's *Krazy Kat* (both 1921), though in notable contrast, Copland's effort contains a distinctively black humor verging on the grotesque. Such darkness distinguishes it as well from

Villa-Lobos's astonishingly similar *Cat and Mouse (O Gato e o Rato)* for piano (1917)—a work Copland surely knew nothing about at the time.

During the same Parisian concert that launched *The Cat and the Mouse*, Copland also performed his *Three Moods* (as *Trois Esquisses*) for piano, composed over the period November 1920 to July 1921. The work's very conception presumably owed something to *Three Moods* for piano (1914) by Leo Ornstein; Copland presumably heard these pieces, with their daring tone clusters, played by the composer himself (who at Copland's invitation performed them at a 1930 Copland-Sessions Concert). Copland's *Three Moods* remained in manuscript until 1981, when he halfheartedly published it at the urging of Leo Smit, to whom he dedicated the score.[39]

The work's individual movements ("Embittered," "Wistful," and "Jazzy") correspond vaguely to Ornstein's three moods ("Anger," "Grief," and "Joy") and more decidedly to those three moods later identified by Paul Rosenfeld as Coplandesque: "Embittered" to the "austere," "Wistful" to the "nostalgic," and "Jazzy" to the "ironic." Copland's music contained a certain wistfulness practically from the start (indeed, "Wistful" derives from "Melancholy," as mentioned); in contrast, the explosive anger of "Embittered" and the high jinks of "Jazzy" strike a new note, notwithstanding anticipations of both in *The Cat and the Mouse*.[40]

Shortly before playing the work in Paris, Copland wrote to his parents that the last movement "is based on two jazz melodies and ought to make the old professors sit up and take notice." This finale opens with a tune akin to Irving Berlin's "Alexander's Ragtime Band" (1911) while its contrasting theme quoted Jerome Kern's "The Siren Song" (1917). Although completed in July, during his first month in Paris, Copland began the work in Brooklyn, thus contradicting the notions that *Music for the Theatre* (1925) represents his first work in a "jazz" idiom and that he became interested in jazz only after hearing it in the bars of Paris and Vienna, or in imitation of European composers, or in emulation of the success of Gershwin's *Rhapsody in Blue* (1924).[41]

Of greater interest is Copland's individual use of the idiom, for "Jazzy" incorporates many of the qualities found in his earlier, more obviously anguished music: dark, surprising harmonic turns; shrill, exposed dissonances; carefully placed formal asymmetries; and even a triple-forte, whole-tone cluster related to the climactic "death" chords in *The Cat and the Mouse*. Copland left for Paris with a self-awareness and a maturity that no trend or fashion would ever undermine.

4

Paris

Nadia Boulanger

Copland sailed to France in June 1921 in order to spend a year studying abroad, including a summer semester at a new conservatory for young American musicians established in Fontainebleau, outside of Paris. On the trip over he met the painter Marcel Duchamp, who suggested that he forget Fontainebleau and head straight to Paris. The instruction at Fontainebleau proved, in fact, routine. Copland's composition teacher, Paul Vidal, struck him as a French Rubin Goldmark: "He is a man with Mr. Goldmark's tastes, and was therefore quite satisfied with the stuff I showed him and played for him," he wrote to his parents. "However, he is not the sort of man I shall want to study with, when I get to Paris in the winter." The students, furthermore, were "not a very talented bunch, since most of the Jews were scared away." But the town of Fontainebleau had its charms and Copland was able to work on his French. Moreover, he made a few new friends (including future Cleveland music critic Herbert Elwell), took some conducting lessons, and, most important, met Nadia Boulanger, with whom he would study for three years in Paris.[1]

This turn of events came as a surprise. Copland had planned on spending only one year in France, not three. He'd assumed, too, that he would work with an established, elderly male composer, not a woman harmony teacher thirteen years his senior. He enjoyed recalling his momentous meeting of Boulanger, how one of the students at Fontainebleau, the harpist Djina Ostrowska, virtually had to drag him to attend one of her harmony classes. After sitting in on a few other classes and having some casual contact with her, he realized that he had found the teacher he was looking for.

On October 26, a few weeks after moving to Paris, he visited Boulanger's studio with some of his scores; he was not sure whether Boulanger—known primarily as an organist, theorist, and critic—would even teach advanced composition, especially to an American. She listened to him play "Jazzy" from his *Three Moods* and immediately accepted him as a student, charging four dollars and twenty cents a lesson (as compared to Goldmark's fee of six dollars). "One could tell his talent immediately," Boulanger later remarked. "The great gift is a demonstration of God." Copland may not have been Boulanger's very first American composition student, as he believed, but he was one of her first few.[2]

Some weeks after this interview, he began piano lessons with Ricardo Viñes, the famed Spanish-born interpreter of Debussy and Ravel. But he learned little from Viñes, who would, he remembered, simply "shake his head" and "say goodbye." By the spring, he left Viñes and devoted himself wholly to Boulanger's guidance.[3]

The daughter of a French singing professor and a Russian contralto, Nadia Boulanger (1887–1979) enjoyed a pedigreed Parisian education, studying organ with Vierne and composition with Gedalge, Fauré, and Widor. Outperforming most of her male colleagues at the Paris Conservatory, she held her own alongside such classmates as Ravel, Alfred Cortot, George Enescu, and Florent Schmitt. By 1910, she seemed poised on the brink of a great career as a performer, composer, or conductor, but in the face of indifferent reviews, male chauvinism, a keen sense of her own limitations, and the death of her younger sister Lili, she devoted herself primarily to teaching. However, she continued to perform as organist and conductor, becoming the first woman to conduct a number of major orchestras, including the London Royal Philharmonic, the New York Philharmonic, and the Philadelphia Orchestra. (Copland was amused by her response to a reporter who asked how it felt to be the first woman to conduct the London Philharmonic: "I have been a woman for more than fifty years and it no longer astonishes me.") As for teaching, she was indefatigable; with classes and lessons at the American Conservatory, the

École Normale, and later at the Paris Conservatory, and as many as forty private students at any one time, she routinely taught seven days a week for as long as eighteen hours a day.[4]

Copland shared his early impressions of Boulanger with his brother Ralph:

> She is a woman of 40, I should judge, and is without any doubt the exception which proves the rule that there can be no great female musicians. This intellectual Amazon is not only professor at the Conservatoire, is not only familiar with all music from Bach to Stravinski, but is prepared for anything worse in the way of dissonance that I may choose fit to hammer out. But don't make the mistake of imagining her some sort of she-male, of formidable appearance and baritone voice. That's just what she isn't! A more charming womanly woman never lived.

"Of medium height and pleasant features," he similarly wrote nearly forty years later, "she gave off, even as a young woman, a kind of objective warmth. She had none of the ascetic intensity of a Martha Graham nor the toughness of a Gertrude Stein. On the contrary, in those early days she possessed an almost old-fashioned womanliness—a womanliness that seemed quite unaware of its own charm."[5]

Copland followed Boulanger's prescribed regimen, composing choral works, a passacaglia for piano, and eventually a whole ballet score. All the while, he studied orchestration, score reading, and analysis with her as well. His orchestration assignments included arranging other composers' piano music (including Mussorgsky's *Pictures at an Exhibition*) for orchestra and composing little original pieces for specified instrumental combinations. He also was required to make his way through orchestral scores at the piano at sight as Boulanger brought attention to details of harmony, rhythm, counterpoint, and form.[6]

On Wednesday afternoons, "Mademoiselle" extended a family tradition by holding an informal class at her home. She or her students would play through an unfamiliar score, debating its merits and faults; this included, during Copland's years in Paris, Berg's recently premiered *Wozzeck*. In addition, they might sing early choral music or discuss a new novel. For refreshments, Boulanger served tea and cakes. The atmosphere was far from luxuriant; the apartment's temperature was often frigid, the cakes typically stale. But this did not prevent musical and literary luminaries from attending, thus providing Copland with the opportunity to meet or at least observe Stravinsky, Milhaud, Poulenc, Roussel, Ravel, Villa-Lobos, and even the ancient Saint-Saëns. "In my own mind," wrote Copland, "she was a continuing link in that long tradition of the French intellectual woman in whose salon philosophy was expounded and political history made."[7]

Boulanger introduced Copland to a wealth of music, complementing discoveries made on his own. This included Renaissance madrigals, Bach's cantatas and organ works, and a wide range of modern music. "I discovered Mahler through Mademoiselle," he recalled. "How she got on to him I don't know, but she had the score for *Das Lied von der Erde* in 1922, and we pored over it together—especially the orchestration." She also apparently discussed both Schoenberg and Bartók during these years, devoting one tea in 1923 to Schoenberg's brand-new twelve-tone method of composition. Even as late as her 1925 American tour, she encouraged Americans to "grapple with . . . the tremendous scope of Schoenberg" as well as "the will of a Stravinsky" and "the complexity of a Milhaud." Only late in 1925, for reasons still not entirely clear, did her esteem for Schoenberg and Bartók noticeably diminish.[8]

Boulanger instilled in Copland, as with so many others, a special regard for Monteverdi, Bach, Fauré, Ravel, and Stravinsky, while strongly encouraging his own interest in popular music and jazz. But she was hardly indiscriminate. Her review of a Koussevitzky concert during the 1923–24 season took to task Roussel, Prokofiev, and especially Satie, whose "vulgarity . . . never seemed clearer to me than in this performance." "Too many notes," she would say about Richard Strauss, though his genius, she wrote, prevailed over "all aesthetic arguments." She generally avoided talking about composers whom she disliked, one exception being Rachmaninov, of whom she made no secret of her contempt.[9]

In an eloquent tribute (1960), Copland discussed at some length those lessons learned from Boulanger that he found most memorable and helpful. He recalled how her interests both inside and outside of music, including her friendships with Paul Valéry and Paul Claudel, proved "an important stimulus to her American students: through these interests she whetted and broadened their cultural appetites." He still marveled at her total grasp of music, her encyclopedic knowledge of the repertory, and her ability to imbue a young American composer like himself with confidence. Moreover, he praised her sensitivity to the formal rightness of a piece of music, her attention, especially, to "la grande ligne," the long line, defined as "the sense of forward motion, of flow and continuity in the musical discourse; the feeling for inevitability, for the creating of an entire piece that could be thought of as a functioning entity." He attributed as French her emphasis on "clarity of conception and elegance in proportion," though he added, "It was her broadness of sympathy that made it possible for her to apply these general principles to the music of young men and women of so many different nationalities."[10]

Boulanger's efforts on behalf of his career also earned his gratitude. In 1922, she arranged for and supervised the publication of some of his smaller pieces, including a few that had been composed back in Brooklyn. She also touted him to such influential conductors as Walter Damrosch and Serge Koussevitzky. Minna Lederman named Boulanger the person who did most to establish Copland's reputation; Copland himself wrote to Boulanger in 1950,

> It's almost thirty years (hard to believe) since we met—and I shall count our meeting the most important of my musical life. What you did for me—at exactly the period I most needed it—is unforgettable. Whatever I have accomplished is intimately associated in my mind with those early years, and with what you have since been as inspiration and example. All my gratitude and thanks go to you, dear Nadia.[11]

At the same time, he recognized Boulanger's limitations. He could laugh with friends like the Fines at her pronouncement, in her reverent contralto voice, of a work as "truly deep"; or with Jean-Pierre Marty, her successor at Fontainebleau, at her self-appointed role as, in Marty's words, the "arbiter of moral righteousness." After her death, he even publicly acknowledged her "very inflexible side," the way, for instance, he found her on his return to France in 1949: "rather set in her ways" and "rigidly aloof from the current excitement about serialism." But he remained utterly loyal, refusing, for example, to endorse Ned Rorem's *The Paris Diary* because he felt that the book belittled her. He also defended her against charges of anti-Semitism, writing, "I feel certain that anti-Semitism was not part of Nadia Boulanger's personality." Such devotion helped him form a bond with such colleagues as Walter Piston even as it resulted in tensions with Virgil Thomson and many others.[12]

As for Boulanger, when pressed in 1957 to supply a list of her favorite students in preferential order, she listed Copland first, ahead of many other star pupils from around the world.[13]

Harold Clurman and Montparnasse

When Copland moved to Paris after his summer at Fontainebleau, he joined Harold Clurman (1901–1980), a distant relative (the brother-in-law of a cousin) whom he had only recently met in New York and with whom he had agreed to share rooms. (Clurman was interrupting his work at Columbia University in order to study drama and literature at the Sorbonne.) After three years as roommates, both returned to New York, where they left a profound mark on their respective fields, all the while remaining the closest of friends and decisively influencing each other's life and work; Elia Kazan in particular credited Copland as an important force in the shaping of Clurman's "thoughts and his values."[14]

Like Copland, Clurman came from a New York Russian-Jewish family, but their backgrounds were very dissimilar nonetheless. Clurman's father was no contented merchant proud of his adopted homeland but a cultured doctor and writer disgusted with American materialism and nostalgic for Mother Russia. Moreover, the freethinking Clurmans were as quarrelsome as the Coplands were even-tempered. And whereas Copland grew up in a staid Brooklyn neighborhood, Clurman spent his childhood on Manhattan's Lower East Side, a shabby ghetto, he later recalled, that held "a recognition of a deeper vein of spiritual fortitude, a fount of lyricism, a nobility of aspiration, an irrepressible idealism."[15]

In addition, Clurman was heterosexual, though he thoroughly accepted Copland's homosexuality. They were opposites temperamentally as well; whereas Copland was frugal and reserved, Clurman was a spendthrift and, in maturity, extremely garrulous. Against stereotype, Copland dressed in plain, loose-fitting suits, while Clurman became something of a dandy, famous in his later years for sporting a silver-headed cane, his Legion of Honor ribbon pinned on his stylish coats. Friends remarked on Copland's "masculine" qualities and Clurman's "strong 'feminine' characteristics."[16]

In one of his most remarkable letters to Copland (1932), Clurman himself spoke of the two as opposite types, Clurman as the "man who cares," Copland as the "completely disinterested person." "Without me," Clurman wrote, "you would lose some hope or rather care less about living and enjoy life less (for your type hasn't too much 'life'), without you, I would destroy myself and others and do no end of mischief in this vale of tears. . . . Life without me might be a little dull and uneventful, without *you*, it would be impossible!"[17]

During their first year together in Paris, they roomed in "a crummy apartment" (Clurman's description) at 207 Boulevard Raspail (now the Carlton Hotel) in the heart of Montparnasse, a short block from a busy cluster of popular cafés. In 1922 they moved to more expensive quarters at the home of a singing instructor on the Villa d'Alésia, a secluded street just south of Montparnasse; located on a curved, quaint block a few houses away from the artist Auguste Leroux, this was, recalled Clurman, "the most pleasant" of all their Parisian apartments. In 1923 they economized, taking rooms at 66 Boulevard Pasteur, an expansive roadway running along the western edge of Montparnasse with a view of the Eiffel Tower. Thus, Copland and Clurman lived in or near Montparnasse during their three years in Paris.[18]

The Montparnasse section of Paris sits on the city's Left Bank, just south and west of the Jardin du Luxembourg. Whereas the nearby medieval Latin Quarter had long been home to students and artists, Montparnasse was traditionally a working-class neighborhood, with more spacious streets and accommodations. In the years just prior to the First World War, Chagall, Modigliani, Picasso, and other artists moved there from Montmartre, a picturesque but more cramped artists' quarter across town. At the same time, the area began attracting Russian and other political refugees of every persuasion. By the 1920s, Montparnasse (or the "Quarter" as it was called) had become a neighborhood in which workers, professionals, artists, homosexuals, indigents, political radicals, prostitutes, and hustlers tolerantly mingled with one another.

When large numbers of American writers visited or expatriated to Paris in the years following World War I, they gravitated toward Montparnasse. They included Gertrude Stein (who had lived thereabouts since 1902), Ezra Pound, E. E. Cummings, Ernest Hemingway, Sherwood Anderson, Sinclair Lewis, and Archibald MacLeish. Copland was one of the first American composers to take up residence in Montparnasse, followed, within a few years, by George Antheil and such Boulanger students as Virgil Thomson and Walter Piston (even though Boulanger's studio at 36 Rue Ballu, now 3 Place Lili Boulanger, was a distance away, on the Right Bank, close to the Place Clichy). American artists, including Alexander Calder and Stuart Davis, turned up in Montparnasse in the course of the decade as well.[19]

According to Jerrold Seigel, the American artists in Montparnasse provided the nineteenth-century concept of "bohemia" with a last gasp:

These Yankee Parisians exemplified one of the most favorable conditions for the continued vitality in the twentieth century of something like the original Romantic Bohemia: expatriation. Americans in Paris were natural Bohemians: free of ties to the surrounding society and culture, ready to devote their lives to their own self-development, able to participate in the city's pleasures while acting out their independence from tradition and convention, and predisposed to a life of liberated fantasy by virtue of having left their everyday identities, with their attendant restrictions, on the other side of the Atlantic.

These Americans met one another at the local bistros, including the Dôme, the Rotonde, La Coupole, and Le Sélect in the center of Montparnasse and the Café des Deux-Magots a little further north. Copland knew them well. Although these bistros served food—onion soup, sandwiches, ham and boiled potatoes—Americans often went there simply to drink, socialize, hear music (the Rotonde offered jazz as early as 1923), and watch the world go by. "People are dressed funny," wrote Copland to his parents about one such café, "have long beards, crazy ties and so forth. (Leon would call them nuts, I call them artists.) However, it's very interesting to watch them and we have already begun getting in with the bunch, altho I haven't grown any beards—as yet." Copland recalled, in particular, watching Erik Satie take meals by himself: "He had a funny way of eating, he'd put his face down near the plate and scoop the food up—almost animal-like. I couldn't stop looking at him."[20]

Although the abstemious and reserved Copland hardly fitted the popular stereotype, he was and in many ways remained something of a bohemian. He challenged the accepted mores. He successfully avoided steady employment, at the cost of many years of poverty and financial insecurity. For much of his life he eschewed material possessions and comforts, living in the most austere conditions. He also frequently moved from apartment to apartment, settling down only in his fifties. His romantic relationships were unconventional; lovers came and went and befriended one another. He always enjoyed the daring, the provocative, the new.

In the tradition of such nineteenth-century artists as, say, Whitman or

Verlaine, Copland's bohemianism was, in short, paradoxical. A model of propriety, he vicariously enjoyed the rebelliousness of others. Even as he lectured Diamond and Bernstein on acceptable behavior, he relished hearing about their sexual escapades. "Aaron was the most circumspect person I've ever known," observed Ned Rorem, "considering how he encouraged others to let down their hair."[21]

Copland recognized such contradictory impulses in himself. In some diary entries from the late 1920s, he expressed the fear that his "normal self" might repress the "latent possibilities" inherent in his "true nature," further wondering whether such fears themselves were "bourgeois to the core." This sort of reflection showed the influence of two icons of young artists during these years, Paul Valéry and André Gide, both friends of Nadia Boulanger's.[22]

The distinguished poet, critic, and aesthetician Paul Valéry (1871–1945) provided Copland's generation with a living link to the artistic fervor and lofty ideals of Mallarmé and the Symbolist movement. In 1921, he had just begun to publish again after a long hiatus, and, wrote Malcolm Cowley on behalf of fellow Americans in Paris, "it was his deliberate, twenty-year-long refusal to write for publication, that impressed us even more than the high poems and the noble essays he had printed since consenting once more to become a writer like anybody else." In these essays, Valéry proposed that art should be problematic, cerebral, and personal rather than accessible, emotional, and didactic; the creative act was a means toward "the study of the self for its own sake." Man's ultimate goal, he argued, was a detached consciousness of oneself.[23]

Valéry's aesthethics influenced, among others, Eliot and Stravinsky, who modeled his Norton lectures, *Poetics of Music,* on Valéry's *Art of Poetry.* Although Copland's own Norton lectures, *Music and Imagination* (1952), cited Gide, Claudel, Maritain, Sartre, and not Valéry, some of his statements—such as "I must create in order to know myself"—had a distinctly Valéryesque ring. The omission of Valéry possibly betokened the kind of ambivalence expressed by Copland's friend Edmund Wilson, who, in *Axel's Castle* (1931), criticized the Symbolists' preoccupation "with introspection sometimes almost to the point of insanity." Certainly, in distinction both to Valéry and Stravinsky, Copland emphasized the importance of "communication."[24]

Copland had no such conflicted feelings about André Gide (1869–1951), very possibly his favorite writer. As early as 1923 he described himself as an "ardent 'disciple' " of Gide's. He owned more than thirty volumes of Gide, mostly in French, and over the years quoted him in various contexts. He often recommended the French writer to friends, and he presented Rosamund Bernier with an essay by Gide signed by the author.[25]

Gide originally associated himself with the Symbolists, dedicating *Narcissus* (1891) to Valéry. But a trip to North Africa in 1893, which included a homosexual encounter with an Arab boy, awakened him to the pleasures of travel, action, and sensation, and he returned to Paris critical of the Symbolists for their "lack of curiosity about life." In his ensuing novels, he retained the Symbolist predilection for elegant, intellectual forms, but cultivated as well a certain psychological realism that concerned itself with the struggle between the material and the spiritual, promiscuity and repression, irresponsibility and duty, and isolation and social consciousness. He scorned categorical answers to such conflicts, viewing doctrinaire solutions as crippling, whereas the struggle itself was a sign of health.[26]

Copland had a special liking for *The Immoralist* (1902), one of Gide's most celebrated achievements, in which the novel's puritanical hero, through a rejection of marital fidelity, private property, and academic respectability, attempts to discover his "authentic being." He also admired *Lafcadio's Adventures* (1914), which similarly explores the extremes of mindless conformity and meaningless impulse; its satirical portrait of the French bourgeoisie made it a favorite with the young rebels of the 1920s. In the early 1930s, Gide's sympathy for the Russian Revolution helped sustain his relevance to Copland and his friends.[27]

During their years together in Paris, Copland and Clurman spent most of their time in each other's company. The latter attended Boulanger's Wednesday teas and became extraordinarily knowledgeable about the new-music scene; Copland himself admired Clurman's ability to sense meanings underlying a composition. In reviews of the Swedish Ballet (1922) and the International Society for Contemporary Music (1923), Clurman knowingly placed new works by Ravel, Stravinsky, Milhaud, and Bartók in the context of their careers, and showed a preference for these composers over Debussy and Schoenberg, for whom he expressed only a cool respect.[28]

Meanwhile Copland took classes in French literature and history at the Sorbonne and attended plays with Clurman, including productions of Chekhov, Shaw, Molnár, Wilde, Strindberg, and Andreyev, directed by

Jacques Copeau, Georges Pitoëff, and Stanislavsky. Although "dazzled" by Stanislavsky and impressed with Copeau, Clurman quickly developed the idea that drama was lagging behind music, painting, and literature in terms of relevance and modernity, a conviction that provided the springboard for his later career.[29]

Both men also frequented Sylvia Beach's English bookstore, Shakespeare and Company, located just north of the Jardin du Luxembourg, as well as a French bookstore across the street run by Beach's lover, Adrienne Monnier. Copland especially remembered a reading from *Ulysses* in French at Monnier's; he soon thereafter purchased the book's first edition (published by Beach in 1922), which he read in two weeks. To Copland's delight, these two bookstores provided the opportunity to observe and sometimes meet such figures as Joyce, Gide, and Proust. "Harold and I felt that we were living in a very civilized atmosphere," he would later write.[30]

While in Paris, Copland discovered, in addition, such American poets as Cummings and Pound, both of whose poetry he would soon set to music. And he met Hemingway, who once took him aside at the Rotonde to point someone out, saying, "A great fellow, that. He's had the clap five times." Eventually he would compose music for a dramatization of the writer's Nick Adams stories.[31]

Copland and Clurman returned to the States with certain attitudes that characterized their generation of artists, for whom Paris in the 1920s played such a decisive part: a stoical, ironic, earthy outlook skeptical of old-fashioned sentiments and shibboleths; a love of novelty and originality; and a fascination with the French and a concomitant interest in their own national culture. "I thought a lot more about Brooklyn when I was in Paris than I ever did in Brooklyn," Copland stated. He later observed, "It's curious that one can sometimes see America more clearly from across the ocean than when living right inside it."[32]

Although these shared sentiments made Copland, among American composers, a particularly representative figure of the "lost generation," he was in many ways unlike such writers as Cummings, Dos Passos, Fitzgerald, and Hemingway. To some extent, his Jewish background set him apart, as did his homosexuality. Nor did he succumb to the kind of self-destructive tendencies so prevalent among his contemporaries. "At 21, in Paris, with Dada thumbing its nose at art," he wrote to Bernstein in 1938, "I had a spell of extreme disgust with all things human. What's the use—it can't last, and it didn't last. The next day comes, there are jobs to do, problems to solve, and one gets gradually inured to things."[33]

And though Copland admired the celebrated American expatriate writers—especially Hemingway—he had only a passing acquaintanceship with any of them. Aside from Clurman, he would find his main literary and artistic friends only after returning to New York.

5

Copland and the Music
of Europe

Copland had arrived in Europe at an exciting time. As borders once again opened and musicians traveled from country to country, the continent was witnessing an amazing profusion of new styles from all over: Prokofiev from Russia; Milhaud, Honegger, and Poulenc from France; Schoenberg, Berg, Webern, Krenek, and Wellesz from Austria; Hindemith and Weill from Germany; Casella and Malipiero from Italy; Hába from Czechoslovakia; Bartók from Hungary; and jazz and popular music from the Americas.

Copland familiarized himself with all this repertory and more. He was by his own admission "insatiable." He studied the latest scores; read the critics; went to concerts "almost every night," as he told his parents; attended the opera and the ballet, including the Ballets Russes and the Swedish Ballet; and traveled to London, Milan, Rome, Florence, Bruges, Brussels, Berlin, and Vienna, hearing music and meeting composers everywhere. All this activity climaxed with six evenings of concerts presented at the first meeting of the International Society of Contemporary Music (ISCM) in Salzburg in August 1923.[1]

At the same time, he delved further into earlier music, especially that of the preceding generation. He continued his study of Debussy, Scriabin,

Ravel, and Bloch; he attended stage works by Dukas, Schmitt, and Fauré in Paris, and concerts of Schreker and Mahler in Berlin; and he perused the music of Bruckner and Reger in Vienna. Under Boulanger's supervision, he also studied music from Bach's era and before.[2]

By the time he returned to New York, the breadth and depth of his knowledge of European music—especially in its more recent stages—rivaled that of any other American. He soon found himself in some demand as a writer and lecturer about the latest trends and regularly offered classes on the subject at the New School for Social Research.

Copland began his association with the New School in 1927, teaching a class entitled The Evolution of Modern Music and organizing with Edgard Varèse six concerts of modern music featuring string quartets by Stravinsky, Bartók, Milhaud, Hindemith, Wellesz, and Cowell, along with works by Schoenberg, Webern, and others. Copland taught at the New School until 1930, taking five years off before returning there in 1935, by which time the much-enlarged faculty included or would soon include Henry Cowell, Charles Seeger, Hanns Eisler, Marc Blitzstein, and Elie Siegmeister. Copland resumed lecturing on contemporary music, but in 1936 also began offering the more general courses What to Listen for in Music and Intelligent Music Listening. In 1938, he taught his final course for the New School, Symphonic Masterpieces, which hardly ventured beyond the late Romantic repertoire.

During these same years, he regularly published articles in the *New York Times*, *Modern Music*, the *New Republic*, *Musical Quarterly*, and other journals (Norton brought out a collection of these essays in 1960 as *Copland on Music*). He also published his New School lectures practically verbatim as two books: the classic music appreciation text *What to Listen for in Music* (1939, revised in 1957 and still in print) and *Our New Music* (1941, revised in 1968 as *The New Music: 1900–1960*). These writings—along with some other sources—help illumine his thoughts on a wide range of European composers.[3]

From Machaut to Debussy

Copland's coolness toward the so-called standard repertory was unusual even in the context of Boulanger students who were often favorably disposed toward the Classical masters and the more classical Romantics. In dramatic contrast to most music appreciation texts, *What to Listen For* derived over three-quarters of its examples from Renaissance, Baroque, and twentieth-century scores; the chapter on melody, for instance, quoted melodies by Palestrina, Bach, Schubert, Carlos Chávez, and Roy Harris. If this seems unusual by today's standards, how much more so in 1939, when much less was known about early music and when the twentieth century was less than forty years old.

In his relatively brief discussions of early music, Copland intimated a special fondness for the English madrigalists, Palestrina, Gesualdo, Monteverdi, and Bach. By the 1950s, he showed as well a keen interest in Machaut and other medieval composers, thanking musicologists for reviving this music "of an extraordinary sadness and loneliness, with textural bareness that reminds us at times of the work of some present-day composers." At the same time, he wondered whether the music's seeming naïveté "encouraged a polite approach to the problem of actual performance" that he found "hard to connect with the more rugged aspects of the Middle Ages."[4]

He rated Palestrina and Bach especially highly. He praised Palestrina's "purity and serenity," writing, "Everything about it conduces to the contemplative life: the sweetness of the modal harmonies, the stepwise motion of the melodic phrases, the consummate ease in the handling of vocal polyphony." He held Bach in even greater esteem: "Americans should love Bach," he once stated, "for he is the greatest, as we would say." The mature organ chorale preludes in particular offered, he thought, "an inexhaustible wealth of musical riches, which no music lover can afford to ignore" and "a magistral illustration of the welding of thought and emotion." In another context, he wrote,

> What strikes me most markedly about Bach's work is the marvelous rightness of it. It is the rightness not merely of a single individual but of a whole musical epoch. . . . Never since that time has music so successfully fused contrapuntal skill with harmonic logic. This amalgam of melodies and chords . . . provided Bach with the necessary framework for his massive edifice. Within that edifice is the summation of an entire period, with all the grandeur, nobility, and inner depth that one creative soul could bring to it. It is hopeless, I fear, to attempt to probe further into why his music creates the impression of spiritual wholeness, the sense of his communing with the deepest vision.[5]

Copland displayed more ambivalence toward Mozart: "I number myself among the more critical of Mozart admirers," he confessed in

1956, "for I distinguish in my mind between the merely workaday beautiful and the uniquely beautiful among his works. (I can even complain a bit, if properly encouraged, about the inordinate length of some of the operas.)" He consistently expressed a preference for the more unpredictable Haydn. And yet Mozart's "rightness" made Bach seem "weighted down with the world's cares, Palestrina otherworldly in his interests." In his estimation, an ideal music might combine Mozart's "spontaneity and refinement" with Palestrina's "purity" and Bach's "profundity."[6]

Copland wrote little about Beethoven, but he rated him with Palestrina and Bach as a composer of the "first rank." In one lecture, he emphasized the music's psychological depth, its dramatic instincts, and its dynamic forms with their "sense of inevitability." He was amazed that with his dry sonorities, unlovely melodies, and gruff, unflattering manner (so unlike the "urbane" Haydn) Beethoven "was 'sold' to the big musical public," an amazing development comparable, in his opinion, to the public acceptance of Bartók after 1945. What made Beethoven so compelling?

How can one not be compelled and not be moved by the moral fervor and conviction of such a man. His finest works are the enactment of a triumph—a triumph of affirmation in the face of the human condition. Beethoven is one of the great yea-sayers among creative artists; it is exhilarating to share his clear-eyed contemplation of the tragic sum of life. His music summons forth our better nature; in purely musical terms Beethoven seems to be exhorting us to be noble, be strong, be great in heart, yes, and be compassionate.[7]

In 1970 he further singled out Beethoven's forthrightness. "When Beethoven is being suave," he stated, "as he occasionally is, you know it. When he's being tough, and very emphatic in manner, you know that too. There's never any question in your mind as to the expressive connotations of the music." He acknowledged, however, that such generalizations fitted the Fifth Symphony better than the late quartets, which "imply a more cultivated listener perhaps, because there you may justifiably wonder about the exact emotion suggested by a particular section."[8]

Although he appreciated the fact that the Romantics introduced a heightened expressivity to music (he considered Beethoven more Classical than Romantic), he was generally critical of nineteenth-century music. He preferred the most romantic of the Romantics—Berlioz and Liszt—precisely for their theatricality and passion, for their ability to reflect the times in which they lived; he thought Chopin "too elegant, Mendelssohn too polite, and Schumann too sweetly honest to reflect the seamier side of their epoch." Moreover, he relished the forward-looking qualities of Berlioz and Liszt: Berlioz for capturing "the feeling of romanticism classically controlled," something Copland recognized as modern in its sensibility (though he once spoke about the difficulty of knowing where Berlioz's music "is going or what the artist's intention is"), and Liszt for his sonorous imagination, harmonic novelty, and formal daring. He always spoke of Liszt with special admiration; in the 1930s, he astonished Arthur Berger by recommending that he study the *Années de pèlerinage*. In contrast, he seemed merely respectful of the more "perfect" Brahms, though when asked about his favorite composers in 1978, he stated, "other than [Stravinsky] . . . my tastes are quite regular. The three B's—Bach, Beethoven and Brahms."[9]

Copland hardly ever discussed Wagner, rarely mentioning that he studied the operas as a young man. Leo Smit recalled that Copland admired the way Wagner sculpted his ideas, but Phillip Ramey remembered only that Copland would make a face every time Ramey mentioned him. Copland cared still less for Bruckner, preferring Reger when he discovered both in Vienna in the 1920s; Ramey recalled that Copland once walked out of a concert in which one of his own works was performed because he could not abide the Bruckner symphony on the program.[10]

Copland perhaps felt closer to Mussorgsky than to any other nineteenth-century composer; he did not even consider him a Romantic, but rather a "realist." "He wishes above all to be true to nature—true to his own nature and to the humanity about him," he writes in a telling passage. "[Mussorgsky] dramatized not himself or his own private emotions, but those of whatever subject he had in hand. This is what gives his music the impersonal aspect that eventually was to guide all music out of the Romantic impasse." Boulanger surely enhanced this appreciation, though it predated his Paris years and may have helped draw him to Boulanger in the first place.[11]

Among nineteenth-century composers, he also made a special exception for Verdi. "What a pleasure it is to read about this man!" he once exclaimed. "What a relief from the grandiloquence of Wagner, the neurotic imaginings of Tchaikovsky, the sickliness of Mussorgsky" (this last phrase later replaced with "the self-pity of Rachmaninoff"). Copland praised especially the late Verdi operas for their sense of forward movement, their dramatic effectiveness, and their economic handling of materials. In addition, Verdi's "beautifully varied" orchestrations were not conceived of "from page to page" but with "the overall flow in mind"; far removed from Wagner's "useless, cluttered" doublings and Mahler's "pretentious" and "blown-up" handling of similarly simple materials, Verdi sooner deserved comparison to Gershwin: "Like Gershwin, the faults are obvious, but they don't in the end influence the directness of appeal."[12]

Copland considered Debussy, Fauré, Mahler, Strauss, and most other turn-of-the-century composers not so much transitional figures toward modernism as, less sympathetically, "late Romantics." Even though "their technical means . . . contained elements that were capable of being disengaged and used for new ends," they remained loyal "to a tradition that had already fulfilled its promise." He acknowledged the preeminence of Debussy (he always made special claims for *Pelléas*, which he considered a milestone of twentieth-century music), but his mature opinion of the French composer generally tended to be severe: "Debussy was the hedonistic poet of a thoroughly bourgeois world. There is something cushioned and protected, something velvety-soft and overcomfortable about his music." As for Debussy's virtues—"harmonic originality" and his "refusal to construct his music along academic lines"—they turned out to be hardly different from Liszt's. Copland's ambivalence reflected the anti-Debussy tendencies of the 1920s, especially among composers like himself who had fallen under Debussy's sway in the 1910s.[13]

In contrast, he adored Fauré and Mahler, notwithstanding similar reservations. Harold Clurman recalled that the one time he ever heard Copland "emit a semiarticulate cry signifying 'Bravo!' " was at a recital of Fauré's songs. In 1924 he published "Gabriel Fauré, a Neglected Master," his only extensive survey of another composer's work. Although he conceded that Fauré's earliest music smacked too much of the salon, he seconded those critics who saw his mature work as comprising some of the finest music of its time, including the opera *Pénélope*, deemed by Copland "one of the best operas written since Wagner." Fauré's piano music offered the special advantage of being modest technically, which Copland commended as "an individual trait in a day of post-Scriabinic terrors!" The world, he concluded, needed Fauré's "calm, his naturalness, his restraint, his optimism." However, in subsequent writings, he observed the music's limited emotional range: "What Fauré lacked more than anything else to make him a composer of the very first rank was broadness of scope." Still, he always acknowledged Fauré's influence on his own work, pointing especially to "the rhythmical side of his music and the orchestral colors he was able to produce, which were new and different from the older ones."[14]

In the early 1920s Copland also acquired an attachment to Mahler, whose *Das Lied von der Erde* he stumbled upon not only in Boulanger's studio but during a lonely stay in Berlin in 1922. In 1925 he wrote a letter to the *New York Times* defending Mahler against the disparagements of local critics, arguing that the composer's contrapuntal approach to choral writing and to orchestration anticipated the latest trends. And among Koussevitzky's papers can be found this statement by Copland, penned around 1931: "Gustav Mahler in my estimation belongs on a par with the greatest masters of symphonic art. . . . Once Mahler's significance is grasped, the world will make light of his apparent weaknesses, his banalities, his longueurs. To make his art better known should be the desire of every artist." In later years, he took a more moderate tone, granting that Mahler could be "long-winded, trite, bombastic," and offering this bon mot: "The difference between listening to Beethoven and listening to Mahler is the difference between watching a great man walk down the street and watching a great actor act the part of a great man walking down the street. The two experiences can be equally impressive, though in different ways." Still, he consistently recommended to listeners *Das Lied von der Erde*, his favorite work by the composer, along with *Kindertotenlieder* and at least portions of the First, Fourth, Seventh, and Ninth Symphonies.[15]

For all their differences, Fauré and Mahler similarly attracted him because of their subtle and invigorated counterpoint. He could not find such redeeming virtues in Scriabin, whose inspired ideas never found "a suitable form"; or in Sibelius, likable in his "pastoral" moments, "least impressive in his gloomy, pseudophilosophical broodings of a typically 19th-century mentality"; or in Strauss, whose brilliant orchestral writing was "overrich." Studying *Elektra* in preparation for a 1927 performance, he told Roger Sessions that he had more sympathy for Mahler's "naive . . . banality" than for Strauss's "heartless banality," allowing only that "Strauss's harmonic sense is extremely acute and he never fails one at the most dramatic moments." In 1970 he turned down tickets to see *Die Frau ohne Schatten* at Covent Garden with a friend, saying that of all the composers whom he had disliked in his younger days, Richard Strauss was the worst.[16]

Copland admitted only five contemporaries of Debussy to the ranks of true modernism: Satie, Busoni, Ravel, Roussel, and Nielsen. He considered Satie and Busoni particularly important in their dissemination of the ideals of clarity, economy, and objectivity to the young composers of France and Germany, portraying Busoni as a kind of Trojan horse, bringing liberating "Latin ideals" to the living German composers Copland most admired: Hindemith and Weill. As for Ravel and Roussel, he similarly applauded their move away from the "comfortable bourgeois world of the prewar era" with its "nebulous Debussian aesthetic" toward greater precision and lucidity, in the process establishing a connection with the "purely French traditions of a Couperin or a Rameau." To this pantheon of early modernists, he later added Carl Nielsen, whose music he knew but did not fully appreciate until the 1950s; although he most admired Nielsen's "original" and "sympathetic" Clarinet Concerto, he also liked the Fifth Symphony and the more conventional Flute Concerto, which had "interesting 'corners,' mostly because one never quite knows what he will do next."[17]

From Schoenberg to Britten

In *Our New Music* (1941), Copland viewed the contemporary European music scene as largely dominated by Schoenberg, Stravinsky, and, to a lesser extent, Bartók, Hindemith, Prokofiev, and Milhaud. *The New Music* (1968) more or less confirmed this perspective, except for Webern, to whom he accorded much more attention than before.[18]

Copland had mixed feelings about Schoenberg. On the positive side, he appreciated his formal economy, his contrapuntal sophistication, his "aural imagination," and his "fiery creative spirit, burning at full intensity." But he frowned upon the tendency toward overcomplexity and angst. He also criticized not so much Schoenberg's "Germanness" per se so much as his "Old World spirit" and his "unbounded reverence for past German masters" which made "for a kind of expressivity that is difficult to empathize with, despite the indisputable sincerity and conviction that lies behind the music." Such an aesthetic, he argued in 1941, offered "very little for a naïve but expanding musical culture such as is characteristic today of the United States (or the Soviet Union)."[19]

Copland also thought Schoenberg extremely uneven, generally preferring the so-called freely atonal pieces of the period around 1910 to both earlier and later works. He always considered *Pierrot Lunaire*—which he initially heard at its 16 January 1922 Paris premiere under Milhaud and then again later that year in Berlin under Schoenberg—a major landmark, comparable to Stravinsky's *Rite of Spring*. In contrast, he pronounced the twelve-tone Wind Quintet, heard in 1926, an "outstanding failure. . . . Except for certain parts of the scherzo and the final rondo, there seemed nothing but principles and theories of composition leading to complete aridity." Similarly, after hearing Schoenberg's *Serenade* in 1949, he confided to Irving Fine, "I liked it—but I don't think I 'enjoyed' it—it's so strained and strident." In 1968, without much change in his basic position, he added *Moses und Aron* and the late string quartets to the small list of Schoenberg works he deemed "indubitable masterpieces."[20]

Even after Copland adapted Schoenberg's twelve-tone method for some works, he touted Boulanger as a healthier mentor for young Americans, stating, "I don't think you can take Schoenberg as a model of broadminded, easy acceptance of different ideas with a philosophical point of view." His colleagues who fell under the influence of Schoenberg and Webern reminded him, to his considerable dismay, of those American composers who, decades earlier, had worked in the shadow of Wagner, Brahms, and Strauss.[21]

From his years in Paris, when Stravinsky became his "hero," to the end of his life, Copland named the Russian as his favorite twentieth-century composer. He loved, above all, the early Russian ballets, especially their "jagged and uncouth rhythmic effects," "bold use of dissonance," and "hard, dry, crackling sonority," traits he believed had helped revitalize Western music. Moreover, Stravinsky's use of folk materials encouraged Copland "to try to find a way to a distinctively American music," especially since Slavic "rhythmic drive" seemed analogous to American "rhythmic ingenuity."[22]

Copland followed each new work of Stravinsky's with eager anticipation. Attending the premieres of the *Octet* and the Piano Concerto in Paris, he found both works puzzling, thinking the former something of a "joke" and the latter disappointingly "dry" and "sober." But by the late 1920s, he recognized the continuity of Stravinsky's work—from the "subjective realism" of *Petrushka*, to the "objective realism" of *The Rite* and *Les Noces*, to the pure "objectivity" of the *Symphonies of Wind Instruments* and the *Octet*. With the exception of *Oedipus Rex* and the *Symphony of Psalms*, with its "majestic choral writing," he never seemed quite as impressed with Stravinsky's subsequent works; indeed their "mannerisms" often struck him as "reactionary" and "somewhat cold-blooded." But he found the entire oeuvre wholly admirable and interesting, programming the *Ode* as a conductor and citing for special praise the Concerto for Two Pianos, *Jeu de Cartes,* and the *Symphony in C,* which he thought less "pretentious" than the *Symphony in Three Movements.* With Stravinsky's later twelve-tone music, wrote Copland, one may not be sure "of having gotten the message," but "one is convinced that a new kind of musical communication is being forged."[23]

For his part, Stravinsky singled out Copland and Walter Piston among American composers (1945): "They have good musical ideas. They also have the requisite techniques. They are fine orchestrators, too." He went on record as liking in particular the score to *The City,* the Clarinet Concerto, and the *Dickinson Songs,* whose "distinctly American and very lovely pastoral lyricism" he also found exemplified in Carl Ruggles's *Men and Angels* and Milton Babbitt's *The Widow's Lament in Springtime.* Yet Copland and Stravinsky maintained a rather cool friendship, one troubled by conflicts similar to those between Copland and other prominent émigrés. David Matthews points out, too, that while Stravinsky's impact on Copland was "considerable," the "epic" and "heroic" qualities of a work like Copland's Third Symphony suggest "the very antithesis of the Stravinskian ethic."[24]

Copland long appreciated Bartók's distinction. Given ten dollars by Boulanger in 1922 to buy music "that's new and seems interesting to you" while in Berlin, he returned with Wellesz's String Quartet along with Bartók's *Improvisations,* which he described as "an exquisite little work." "When he is at his best, as in the *Music for Strings, Percussion, and Celesta,*" wrote Copland years later, "Bartók takes his place in the front rank of contemporary musicians." But for all this high praise, he had reservations about music that he found, at times, "expressive in the tortured manner of Schoenberg" and "profoundly pessimistic in tone." At any rate, Bartók's prime significance for Copland was ultimately like Falla's: as a model for modernist use of folk materials.[25]

Copland knew the school of French composers known as *Les Six* (Auric, Durey, Honegger, Poulenc, Milhaud, and Tailleferre) quite well; they were the talk of the town during his student years. He attended many of their famous premieres—including Milhaud's *La Création du monde,* Honegger's *Pacific 231,* and the collaborative *Les Mariés de la Tour Eiffel*—and learned Poulenc's *Mouvements Perpétuels,* which Clurman remembered him repeatedly playing during their first year in Paris. In later years he remained charmed by Poulenc, but of *Les Six,* he considered only Honegger and Milhaud of major significance. And as far as Honegger was concerned, it was only his early music that retained Copland's interest, specifically, the Piano Concertino, with its refreshing wit; *King David,* with its dramatic choral writing; and *Pacific 231,* which he regarded as a quintessential example of twentieth-century program music.[26]

Copland seems to have loved the music of Milhaud more than that of any other contemporary, with the possible exception of Chávez. He was captivated by the alternations of violence and tenderness, the unpretentious yet stylish harmonies, the earthy and dashing polyrhythms, and the incorporation of French, Jewish, and American traits. Milhaud's use of simple, modal strands to create subtle textures in particular influenced Copland, who adapted such techniques to even leaner, more economical ends.[27]

Meanwhile, Milhaud, who immigrated to the United States in 1940, acquired a knowledge and appreciation of Copland unusual for a European of their generation. "Among American composers, Aaron Copland outclasses them all," he wrote to Poulenc in 1945. "His latest works, tender, limpid, earthy, are very appealing. But his earlier works are also very good. His ballets, *Billy the Kid* and *Rodeo,* his piano sonata, and his piano and violin sonata—all have the stamp of an authentic personality." In 1953 he further noted,

What strikes one immediately in Copland's work is the feeling for the soil of his own country: the wide plains with their soft colorings, where the cowboy sings his nostalgic songs in which, even when the violin throbs and leaps to keep up with the pounding dance rhythms, there is always a tremendous sadness, an underlying distress, which nevertheless does not prevent them from conveying the sense of sturdy strength and sun-drenched movement. His ballet Rodeo gives perfect expression to this truly national art. His recent symphony [the Third] . . . has more grandeur and a deeper lyricism, but the melancholy simplicity of its themes is a direct expression of his own delicate sadness and sensitive heart.[28]

In emphasizing Copland's high regard for Milhaud and other French composers (sometimes with the intention of painting him as a Francophile), commentators have generally overlooked his keen interest in contemporary German and Austrian music during the 1920s and early 1930s. In the course of these years, he familiarized himself with the music of Weill (whom he met on his first trip to Berlin in 1922), Wellesz, Hindemith, Krenek, and others, including Webern, whose "magical" *Five Pieces for Orchestra* he heard in Zurich in 1926. The following year, he returned to Germany, where he met Hanns Eisler, saw productions of Weill's *Mahagonny*, Hindemith's *Hin und Zurück*, and Toch's *The Princess and the Pea* (all more or less engaging, in his opinion, though less so than Milhaud's *The Abduction of Europa*), and attended the premiere of Berg's *Lyric Suite*. He spent the remainder of the summer in Königstein, where he adapted Schoenberg's twelve-tone method for a setting of E. E. Cummings. In 1929, he and Marc Blitzstein toured some German opera houses, catching productions of Weill's *Threepenny Opera* in Wiesbaden and Hindemith's *News of the Day* in Darmstadt. By this time, Copland, who initially had not cared very much for Berlin, considered the German capital the most exciting center for new music in Europe; only New York rivaled it, in his estimation. In 1931, he once again returned there, this time passing quickly through Paris; the highlights of that year included a performance of Webern's Symphony, Op. 21, at Oxford.[29]

While Copland apparently felt that the indebtedness of Webern (at least in his earlier works) and Berg to German Romanticism lessened their ultimate significance, he quickly recognized their importance, lecturing on both regularly at the New School in the late 1920s. *Our New Music* commended the "exquisite" Webern and cited Berg's operas, *Lyric Suite,* and Violin Concerto as "among the finest creations in the modern repertoire," an opinion only slightly downplayed in the 1968 revision ("finest" being replaced by "most appealing"). This same revision notably expanded coverage of Webern from one to eight paragraphs; this new material consisted mostly of testimonials by Stravinsky, Krenek, and Boulez, whose opinions apparently helped Copland revise his own. And yet he sensed beneath the music's exquisite exterior the "firm and rigorous spirit of an Austrian schoolmaster," an observation that, like similar remarks about Schoenberg, Bartók, and Sessions, had negative connotations. He remained, moreover, frankly critical of Webern's emotional limitations.[30]

As for Hindemith, Krenek, Toch, and Weill, he could find individual works "dull," "meaningless," "conventional," and "monotonous," but he sympathized with their desire to create theatrical works for a general public. The unaffected sophistication that he so admired in Milhaud attracted him in particular to the early Hindemith, above all, the original

Marienleben, which featured "a searching, wistful, hopeless quality such as can be found nowhere else in contemporary music."[31]

After the Nazis came to power, Copland had little to say about the German scene. Nor did some of the previously admired Germans retain their appeal after they arrived in the States; although his esteem for Toch deepened in the wake of that composer's film score to *Peter Ibbetson* and his Third Symphony, he thought Weill's Broadway pieces "slick" and Hindemith's American work pedantic. And while he socialized some with Weill and Lotte Lenya, Hindemith, Eisler, and others, he enjoyed only distantly cordial ties with most of the older European refugees, German and non-German alike. Among other things, he worried about their influence impeding the cause of a distinctive and relevant American art music; in 1935, he explicitly cautioned young composers against taking either Schoenberg or Stravinsky as a model.[32]

That the older expatriates, especially the Germans, often assumed a dismissive and resentful attitude toward his own music did not help matters. (Younger émigrés, like Ingolf Dahl and Alexei Haieff, not to mention youngsters like Lukas Foss and Samuel Adler, were, in contrast, very responsive to Copland—as was Eisler, who admired the Piano Sonata, the Violin Sonata, and the *Lincoln Portrait*.) William Austin's remarks about the leading refugees bear on the situation in general:

> Schoenberg, Bartók, and Stravinsky all heard some of Copland's music broadcast on the radio. Whether or not they attended live performances of his most ambitious works, they knew he was a favorite of Koussevitzky. They could glance at his scores: the English publishing company, Boosey & Hawkes, was promoting Copland alongside the young prodigy Britten, before it signed up Stravinsky. Probably these composers assumed that Copland's successes gave him more power than in fact he ever wielded. In any case, they envied him. They let it be known that they preferred something of Gershwin, recently dead at thirty-eight, or perhaps Benny Goodman, current "king of swing." (They were aware that the older pioneers like Ives and Varèse were less successful than Copland.) Toward the refugee heroes, Copland was gracious when he encountered them, as he always was toward Ives and Varèse.

"Pretty pictures, that's all," Hindemith once told Harold Shapero in reference to Copland, whose teaching methods at Tanglewood he considered symptomatic of an undeveloped country. And while Krenek and others rightly perceived Copland as well connected, they apparently exaggerated his ability to land them academic positions and promote their music.[33]

Such tensions climaxed with an embarrassing contretemps that occurred after Schoenberg had settled in Los Angeles. Although on arriving in the States he had listed Copland with some thirteen other American composers of "talent and originality," on 11 September 1949 he gave a bitter radio address in which he accused American conductors of suppressing his music and ideas, concluding, "Even Stalin cannot succeed and Aaron Copland even less." Virgil Thomson published the talk that same day in the *New York Herald Tribune*, offering only the faint rebuttal "Mr. Copland has never, to my knowledge, acted to prevent the dissemination of Schoenberg's work, little as he may approve of it."[34]

Copland had every reason to be outraged, considering that, as he reported in a letter to the *Herald Tribune*, he had, in fact, "disseminated it [Schoenberg's music] in lectures and in arranging concerts for more than twenty years and was instrumental in seeing to it that the Columbia Recording Company issued 'Pierrot Lunaire' under the auspices of the League of Composers." But as always, he remained cool; he assumed that the misunderstanding stemmed from his participation in the World Peace Conference in which Shostakovich had condemned Schoenberg—remarks that "may make some sense as the statement of a citizen of the Soviet Union; but it certainly makes no sense over here."[35]

But as Schoenberg explained to Thomson, he knew nothing about Shostakovich's remarks; rather, it had come to his attention that Copland had made "malicious remarks about my dwindling attractiveness to audiences" and, further, had advised students "to use 'simple intervals' and to study the masters." Copland finally wrote Schoenberg directly, denying that he had ever advised students to write in a specific way. "I have composed in both a complex and a simple style. Insofar as my compositions exemplify a certain aesthetic other composers may be able to extract useable principles from them, but that is their own affair." This letter placated Schoenberg, who wrote back that he "appreciated" Copland's music "without restriction." How was he to know that Copland meant no malice when he "uttered surprise about my large audience in Los Angeles, in contrast to New York"? Apparently mutual acquaintances had fanned the flames of Schoenberg's resentment.[36]

Since the 1930s Copland's attention had, in fact, shifted increasingly toward the Americas, England, and the Soviet Union, where Prokofiev and Shostakovich were the preeminent figures. He never found Prokofiev as "significant" as Stravinsky, but he admired his "fresh, clean-cut, articulate" style from the first. Prokofiev's return to his homeland "only made him lean more strongly on music of utter simplicity and directness." On the ninetieth anniversary of Prokofiev's birth, he stated, "We here in America hear his music every day. It never ceases to astonish us by the richness of its invention:—the never-ending welling up of fresh melodies, the charm or bite of the harmonies, the bounce and dash of the rhythms. To us, Prokofiev is a profound national composer who knew how to speak in a universal tongue."[37]

Copland and Prokofiev also shared a close ally in Koussevitzky and thereby came to know each other fairly well. In the early 1930s, Prokofiev warned Paul Bowles away from Copland and other Americans, writing, "Music is not headed in that direction." "When I showed Aaron the letter he loved it," recalled Bowles. "He laughed and laughed."[38]

In contrast, Copland met Shostakovich only in rather formal circumstances. This included a rare 1949 visit by Shostakovich to the States, for which Copland served as his principal liaison, and a visit by Copland to the Soviet Union in 1960, in which he and Lukas Foss spent an evening at home with "Shostie," his family, Dmitry Kabalevsky, and Tikhon Khrennikov. At this soiree, the gathered company listened politely as Copland played his Piano Sonata; then, as Foss and Kabalevsky read through a Haydn symphony arranged for four hands, Copland closely watched Shostakovich, later remarking, "He loves music with a kind of innocent joy I have rarely seen in a famous composer. Music must have been a great solace to him in the tough days." In 1954 Shostakovich named Copland, along with Britten, Menotti, and especially Gershwin, as among those few Western composers who interested him; and in 1969, he wrote to Copland, along with Britten and the Bulgarian composer Lyubomir Pipkov, on behalf of the imprisoned Greek composer Mikis Theodorakis.[39]

Copland followed Shostakovich's career with some ambivalence. In a 1946 lecture, for instance, he praised him as a composer with "a personal note all his own and enormous facility and brilliance," though "not a deep thinker, not strikingly original by comparison with Stravinsky, and sometimes unnecessarily trite." In public, he honored him as a "symbol of achievement in Soviet music," writing, "During the 30's and throughout the War years, Shostakovich showed how one could speak of serious matters in a musical language that had a marked profile and a wide appeal."

Privately, however, he spoke of Shostakovich as having "a simple philosophical mind that gains a certain strength from a rather naive approach," contrasting the "spiritual profundity" of Byrd, Palestrina, Purcell, Bach, Mozart, and Beethoven with his mere appearance of depth. And near the end of his life, he expressed a clear preference for Prokofiev over Shostakovich:

> Well, I think I'm closer to, I'm more interested in, the music of Prokofiev. By comparison Shostakovich seems more conventional; he uses ordinary forms. Melodically, Prokofiev seems to be livelier, fresher, more adventurous. Shostakovich's music is very good of its kind, but it's a kind that's basically conservative and familiar. Prokofiev took more chances.[40]

For many years, Copland criticized the English scene as "stuffy and conventional." He thought the music of Arthur Bliss and Constant Lambert lacking in personality and Vaughan Williams's work, "noble in inspiration, but dull." Neither version of *Our New Music* so much as cited Elgar, Holst, or Vaughan Williams, while its 1968 revision deleted the simple mention of Walton's name (though during these same years, Copland regularly conducted *Portsmouth Point*). Throughout the twenties and into the thirties, Copland presumably found the English as uncongenially genteel and bourgeois as he did the older generation of American composers (with the exception of Ives, Ruggles, and, to a lesser degree, Griffes). Significantly, the first modern English composers to excite him—Britten and Tippett—not only had themselves assimilated something recognizably American in their music (for the same could be said of Lambert, Walton, and others), but had affiliations with the political left.[41]

Copland probably developed closer personal ties with Benjamin Britten (1913–1976) than with any other European composer. They first met at a 1938 ISCM concert at which Copland's *El Salón México* and Britten's *Variations on a Theme of Frank Bridge* were both performed. Britten thought *El Salón* "really beautiful and exhilarating" and "the brightest piece in the festival," while Copland admired "the technical adroitness and instrumental wizardry" of the *Variations*. At the conclusion of the festival, Copland spent a weekend at Britten's home in Snape. "Perhaps the fact that we were both represented by the lighter side of our wares drew us together," recalled Copland.[42]

At Snape, Copland was struck by Britten's closeness to the East Anglian countryside, contrasting his own Manhattan loft with Britten's studio in the converted tower of an old mill. He sang through *The Second Hurricane* at the piano, a work Britten instantly liked; and Britten played his recently completed Piano Concerto for Copland, who offered tactful but candid criticisms. "If anything," remembered Copland, "my frankly expressed opinion helped to cement our growing friendship." Before Copland returned to America, Britten helped him secure a contract with Boosey & Hawkes, writing personally to the company's head, Ralph Hawkes, on his behalf: "I feel he's a winner somehow."[43]

Copland provided some incentive for Britten and his friend Peter Pears to come to the States shortly before the outbreak of the Second World War. "Nice person," wrote Britten to Copland about Pears in advance of their arrival, "and I know you'd approve." In the summer of 1939, Britten and Pears rented a place for the summer in Woodstock so as to be close to Copland and his lover, Victor Kraft. "I thought of him as the voice of England in the contemporary musical scene," wrote Copland, "and he, in turn, considered me the American spokesman. We had many of the same sympathies, musical and other kinds, and we knew we faced similar problems." These "sympathies" included their leftist politics and their homosexuality, while their "problems" concerned the challenge of economic survival and social relevance in the face of public hostility toward modernist art.[44]

Britten described their Woodstock routine as one of composing all day, bathing and sunning in the late afternoon, tennis in the early evening (Britten "always won," remembered Copland), dinner in a local restaurant, and then a return to his place or to Copland's or else a visit to a cinema in Kingston. Both enjoyed the other's company immensely. When war broke out in August, Copland helped set Britten's mind at rest about staying in the States. "I think you absolutely owe it to England to stay here," he wrote Britten. "Whatever anyone may think now, I'm sure the future will justify your looking upon your own case as a special one. After all anyone can shoot a gun—but how many can write music like you?"[45]

Britten spent the following two and a half years shuttling back and forth between Amityville, Long Island, and Brooklyn Heights, before sailing back home in March 1942. During this time, he and Copland saw each other with some regularity, including "an innocent but jolly night on the town" in Chicago in January 1940 on the occasion of the American premiere of Britten's Piano Concerto. Copland introduced Britten to Koussevitzky and successfully arranged a film contract for him with his Hollywood agent.[46]

Copland and Britten never became intimates, however. "There's something about Ben that prevents us from becoming friends," Copland would tell Leonard Bernstein. Even so, they retained fond memories of Snape and Woodstock and kept in touch. Britten always remembered Kraft in his letters, and in 1967 the four held a reunion in New York. Upon Britten's death, Copland immediately cabled Pears, who wrote back, "Ben died quiet, with my hand in his, ready to go after three years of growing discomfort."[47]

Both Britten and Pears loved Copland's music. As early as 1940, Britten referred to Copland as "by far the best American composer," an opinion seconded by Pears. As a duo, they especially regretted the dearth of songs in the Copland catalog, and in 1950 they commissioned Copland's first set of *Old American Songs* for the Aldeburgh Festival. In 1963, Britten cited Copland along with Stravinsky, Shostakovich, and Tippett as the composers he most admired. In stark contrast to most European composers, he showed the influence of Copland's music. He composed one of his first distinctive works, *Paul Bunyan* (1941), under the stimulus of *The Second Hurricane*; and reviewing Britten's *Serenade* (1943), Arthur Berger commented that the work "affords striking evidence that at least one composer abroad is as profoundly conscious of the Copland style as so many young men here are. This is unprecedented for an American composer, perhaps because no one of us has ever had so individual a manner—something specific, that is to say, to emulate." English critics Peter Evans and Wilfrid Mellers similarly found traces of Copland's "lonely prairie" style in Britten's music. Copland himself wrote, "Occasionally, I've even had the illusion of hearing an echo of one of the choruses of the opera [*The Second Hurricane*] ('What happened, Where are they?') in a fleeting moment of a Britten work."[48]

Copland voiced his astonishment at Britten's "breath-taking facility" as early as a 1947 review of *The Rape of Lucretia*: "He combines an absolutely solid technical equipment with a reckless freedom in handling the more complex compositional textures. The whole thing is carried off with an abandon and verve which is irresistible." In later years, he similarly praised Britten for his "extraordinary flair, a dashing sureness of technique, and an attractive manner" and for the "wonderful asset" of being able to plan out his work "in its entirety and in its every detail," something that would have made him "a city planner of genius." He also liked Britten's Englishness, which he identified as "a certain forthrightness, a sense of—a lyrical quality that was very British," an attribute that made him a model for young composers from other countries. "His main impact," Copland observed, "has been the fact that his music shows it's not necessary to be an innovator in order to compose fresh music."[49]

Copland had great admiration, as well, for Michael Tippett (1905–1998). From the time they first met in May 1949, the composer's "un-English warmth," his "unabashed" and boyish enthusiasm, reminded Copland more of Roy Harris than of the British composers he knew, including Britten, Lennox Berkeley, and Richard Rodney Bennett. He similarly detected an American quality in the music; upon first hearing the *Concerto for Double String Orchestra*, he even assumed it the work of an American. Later, he came to know a different side of Tippett—a "darker, more philosophic side"—but the "basic impression" of a "vibrancy and exuberance" related to "American-derived rhythm" remained. As with Britten, the respect was reciprocal; Copland conducted the aforementioned concerto and Tippett performed Copland's *Quiet City*.[50]

Copland consistently evaluated music according to such criteria as contrapuntal finesse, rhythmic vigor, stylistic unity, and formal cohesiveness, along with such general attributes as freshness, sophistication, directness, accessibility, individuality, and objectivity. Such virtues, in his opinion, characterized not only the best European music of the distant past but recent scores by Stravinsky, Bartók, Milhaud, Hindemith, Prokofiev, and others. Even so, he maintained a certain distance from Europe's great composers. He believed that Americans needed to go their own way, without subservience or undue reverence for Europe's heroic achievements; and he wanted a place for American art music in a world crowded with European exports.

6

From *Sonata*

Movement to *Grohg*

(1921–24)

Shorter Works from Paris

Soon after arriving in France, Copland composed the *Sonata Movement on a Theme by Paul Vidal* for string quartet (which was discovered by Vivian Perlis in the music library at Fontainebleau only as recently as 1995). He presumably wrote this unremarkable work in the summer of 1921 while studying with Vidal, for it was common in those years for students to base a composition on one of their teachers' melodies. Copland submitted the piece for a Prix de Paris in December, receiving an honorable mention.

While at Fontainebleau, Copland also composed two love songs for voice and piano as an exercise in setting the French language: "Une Chanson" to words by Victor Hugo (1802–1885) and "Reconnaissance" to words by Fernand Gregh (1873–1960), the Parisian poet from whose name Copland would derive the title of his ballet *Grohg*. Both are sumptuous songs in Copland's best Debussyan manner and, like similar works composed back in Brooklyn, hardly recognizable as the composer's.

The first composition that Copland wrote after moving to Paris and beginning lessons with Boulanger was a little piano piece, *Petit Portrait*. Completed on 3 November 1921, Copland intended the work as a "supplement" to his *Three Moods* and, more specifically, as a portrait of his

Brooklyn friend Abe Ginsburg, whom he described as "rather moody and unhappy with himself." Repeating the three pitches A-B-E in the melody or, more usually, in the bass, he even wrote the letters ABE under the first such statement. Although a mere trifle, *Petit Portrait*, with its bitonal harmonies and extended ostinato, is historically important because it documents Copland's quick assimilation of the world of *Les Six*.[1]

Copland went on to complete *Four Motets* for a cappella mixed chorus in the fall of 1921 and *Passacaglia* for piano in the winter of 1922; Boulanger expected her more advanced students to compose motets and a passacaglia as exercises in contrapuntal and formal discipline. Copland thought of these works as "student pieces," especially the *Four Motets*, which he did not publish until 1979, and then only with "mixed emotions." But they are more than mere pedagogical studies, and today both enjoy a place in the repertory.[2]

Based freely on biblical passages, the motets feature two prayers for mercy ("Help Us, O Lord" and "Have Mercy on Us, O My Lord") and two songs of praise ("Thou, O Jehovah, Abideth Forever" and "Sing Ye Praises to Our King"). At the least, they are serviceable works that show, according to Phillip Ramey, "a surprising sureness and a certain sophistication." The suave choral writing seems particularly remarkable considering Copland's utter inexperience as a choral composer. "Those motets sound in the voices in a stunning manner," enthused Boulanger, who performed them regularly with her classes for decades, holding them up as a standard of contemporary choral writing to hundreds of young musicians from around the globe.[3]

Although Julia Smith identified a distinct Greek mode for each of the motets, Copland claimed that he never gave much thought to the modes as such during his time with Boulanger; and, in fact, the music, eschewing pure modality, might more accurately be described as modal-chromatic. These pieces reflect, too, an affinity to, if not a conscious assimilation of, such varied sources as Stravinsky, Mussorgsky, Fauré, Honegger, and Milhaud, as well as the music of the Renaissance; they also suggest connections to Jewish chant and American hymnody. The two songs of praise in particular anticipate Copland's mature works: "Thou, O Jehovah" looks ahead to his declamatory fanfare style, "Sing Ye Praises" to his folk song settings. But the motets seem rather pallid and stiff for Copland, though effective and appealing in their own way.[4]

If Copland had understandable reservations about the *Four Motets*, he had few, if any, about the *Passacaglia*, which was published by the

Parisian firm of Maurice Senart soon after he completed it in 1922. He himself cited it as an example of cancrizans, or retrograde technique, in *What to Listen For*. Indeed, the piece is a veritable textbook of contrapuntal devices, not only retrograde but canon, invertible counterpoint, augmentation, diminution, and basso ostinato, all subtly and expertly handled.[5]

Neil Butterworth describes the *Passacaglia* as a kind of step beyond César Franck; and appropriately enough, Senart published the work with an art nouveau cover, complete with Copland's name set in a highly florid script. The music more precisely recalls Busoni and, as with the *Four Motets,* Honegger, whose *King David* Copland had heard the year before. His strong musical personality notwithstanding, during his early years with Boulanger Copland seems to have concentrated more on mastering his craft than on asserting his individuality.[6]

Copland's remark about the *Passacaglia*'s technical difficulties—"I am told that it is not an easy piece to play"—seems something of an understatement; the (first) triple-forte climax, in three staves, is virtually unplayable as written. One wonders whether this passage has in any way limited the piece's popularity, because it is otherwise quite rewarding and idiomatic. The passage in question, incidentally, works perfectly well at the organ, and given the dedication to Boulanger, one suspects that Copland may have had the organ in mind.[7]

In early 1922, Copland also composed the song "Alone," for voice and piano, to an Arabic text translated by Edward Powys Mathers. This moody, slightly exotic song looks back to his Brooklyn settings of Chinese and Kafiri verse, but it is more stylistically unified and formally coherent than those earlier efforts. It marks, too, the end of his involvement with Eastern sources.

In the course of his studies with Boulanger, Copland wrote a variety of other things, including a double canon on a theme by Bach, a chromatic fugue, sketches for a woodwind quartet (that either gave rise to or derived from the wordless motet that eventually became "Help Us, O Lord"), and a series of duets for piano and flute, clarinet, oboe, trumpet, French horn, and trombone. These duets, intended largely as exercises in orchestration, are stylistically diverse. The very French-sounding piece for flute and piano shares material with the *Passacaglia*; the duet for piano and trumpet is a transcription of "Jazzy" from *Three Moods*; while still others have themes that would make their way into the ballet *Grohg*.

Only one such exercise evolved into an acknowledged composition, namely, "As It Fell upon a Day," for soprano, flute, and clarinet. The song originated as an assignment by Boulanger for a piece for flute and clarinet; while working on this duo, Copland chanced upon the poem "Philomel" ("As It Fell upon a Day"), by Richard Barnefield (1574–1627) and, moved by its "simplicity and tenderness," had "the idea to add a voice part." He composed the piece during that remarkable summer of 1923 while encountering torrents of new music in Vienna and Salzburg; such experiences apparently made a mark, because "As It Fell" stands as a work of early maturity, "one of Copland's best pieces," in the opinion of Otto Luening.[8]

The Barnefield text deserves some of the credit for the song's success. In this lovely poem, all the world celebrates the "merry month of May" except for Philomel, transformed into a nightingale, whose doleful song, like the poet's grief, goes unheeded. The "simplicity and tenderness" Copland found in the poem helped nurture one of his most characteristic moods: a gently wistful and quietly ironic melancholy. The vocal line recalls Elizabethan song, but freshly so, in a somewhat neoclassical manner that anticipates Copland's use of folk song.

The song also shows considerable personality in its ingenious writing for the woodwind accompaniment, including a dramatic use of dynamics, an unusual sense of texture (including large spaces between high flute and low clarinet), and striking counterpoint, sometimes quite dissonant. In all these respects, the influence of Stravinsky for the first time strongly imposes itself. The work concludes with one of those magical Copland endings, at once ravishing and utterly simple: a quintal sonority comprised of two open fifths (clarinet on E-flat, voice on B-flat, and flute on F).

Copland must have been pleased. He not only included "As It Fell" in his catalog but attempted a second movement for the same forces, "Encouragement to a Lover," a setting of the song "Why So Pale and Wan Fond Lover?" by another seventeenth-century poet, John Suckling (1609–1642). He never completed this song, however.

Another work from 1923, the "Rondino" for string quartet, also went far in defining Copland's individuality. The piece originated as the second of a two-movement *Hommage à Fauré*, the first movement being a transcription of Fauré's Prelude, op. 103 no. 9. Copland eventually brought forth the "Rondino" as the concluding movement of his *Two Pieces* for string quartet (1928).

Copland created the main theme of the "Rondino" by loosely corre-
lating the twelve letters of Gabriel Fauré's name to twelve solfège sylla-
bles. Designing a theme out of a series of twelve notes reveals a certain
temperament that could lend itself to the twelve-tone method, which it did
in 1927 and intermittently after 1950. Here, he arranges his notes to
create something closer to the octatonic scale of alternating half and whole
steps than to a twelve-tone row per se. No doubt Copland's increasing
familiarity with Stravinsky's music furthered his long-standing inclination
toward this type of pitch collection. In any case, he used the octatonic
scale extensively in other works from this period, including *Grohg*.[9]

However, the principal novelty of the "Rondino" concerns rhythm. As
made clear from the unusual time signature and dotted lines drawn within
bar lines, the music divides into uneven groups of three and five eighth-
notes (3+5), with the five eighth-notes further subdivided into units of two
and three eighth-notes (3+2+3). Moreover, Copland pits such rhythmically irregular ideas against other syncopated patterns (or the same pattern displaced) that result in complex polyrhythmic textures. At one
point, in the slower middle section, he juxtaposes an ostinato derived
from the 3+5 main theme with an expressive theme divided, conversely,
into 5+3. The resultant clash, along with the unremitting ostinato, which
uses both pizzicato and *col legno* techniques, creates the kind of "colt-
like" or "rocking horse" effect that Paul Rosenfeld spoke of in his reviews
of the early Copland.[10]

Although some American composers, such as John Alden Carpenter
and Henry Gilbert, had already begun the process of exploring smaller,
asymmetrical units (something that, according to Roy Harris, distinguished the rhythmic sensibilities of Americans from Europeans), their
jazzy rhythms, in contrast to Copland's explosive 3+2+3, typically took
the more conventional form of 3+3+2. More decisively, Copland placed
his jazzy lines in elaborate polyrhythmic combinations, something Milhaud had done in *La Création du monde* (1923), and something that both
composers apparently owed to emerging jazz practices.[11]

At some point toward the end of his studies with Boulanger (possibly
in 1923 as part of a larger work meant to include the "Rondino"), Copland composed yet another single movement for string quartet, one whose
parts Vivian Perlis discovered among the composer's papers at the Library
of Congress in 1983. At this late date Copland permitted the work's publication and performance, entitling it simply *Movement* for string quartet.
The work, which the Alexander String Quartet premiered on 18 October

1984, has a slow-fast-slow form of a sort destined to become a Copland trademark, while its atmosphere resembles the ghoulish *Grohg*. Copland wisely salvaged the best passage, the concluding slow section, for the opening of the *Organ Symphony* (1924).[12]

Still other obscure pieces and sketches from his Paris years resurfaced in later compositions. Copland used a little material from his wordless "Jazz Song" for voice and piano, which he wrote, he guessed, in around 1924, in "Blues No. 2" for piano (1926); the song itself, in conventional popular song form, comes as close to a Tin Pan Alley number as one finds in the composer's oeuvre. And for a planned ballet, *Longchamps,* to a scenario by dancer Carina Ari—a ballet seemingly named after the Parisian racetrack Longchamp, or more likely the leather-goods store of the same name (considering that it was to feature a mannequin and a tourist)—Copland composed some music that would provide the basis of the Piano Concerto (1926). Whatever the exact date of these ballet sketches—whether before or after Ari left the Swedish Ballet in the spring of 1923—they help substantiate the independence of Copland's Piano Concerto from Gershwin's *Rhapsody in Blue* (1924). In general, much of the music Copland composed in Paris spilled over into the rest of the decade and beyond.

Grohg

Copland's major Parisian composition was a ballet score originally called *Le Nécromancien* and later retitled *Grohg.* As he remembered it, he based the title on a Danish author named Grog (the *h* added "to avoid an alcoholic connotation!"), whereas it surely derived from the Parisian poet Fernand Gregh, whose poem "Reconaissance" he had set at Fontainebleau. Copland undertook the ballet—his first orchestral score—without realistic expectations that it would be produced; rather, he intended it primarily as a study in orchestration and form. He began the ballet proper in Berlin in June 1922, finished the reduced piano score in Paris in June 1924, and completed the orchestration back in the States in November 1925.[13]

"My Ballet is progressing very slowly but surely," he wrote to Boulanger from Berlin in August 1922. "I still can't find a satisfactory story to go with it, but I continue to develop the separate dances." Then, one evening that fall, Copland and Clurman saw the German silent horror film *Nosferatu, a Symphony of Terror.* "By the time we reached home that night," he remembered, "I decided that this bizarre tale would be the basis for my ballet. Harold had never written a scenario, but he was eager to try."[14]

A masterpiece of German cinema, Friedrich Murnau's *Nosferatu* (1922), starring Max Schreck, was a free adaptation of Bram Stoker's 1897 *Dracula* (making *Grohg* a Dracula ballet once removed). Partly in response to copyright considerations, Murnau and his screenwriter, Henrik Galeen, revamped Stoker's original story, using many of the English novel's characters, images, and ideas in new contexts. Both tales, however, are fundamentally psychosexual dramas that draw upon images of sexual hysteria, sadomasochism, and confused gender identity.[15]

Nosferatu takes, as its particular premise, an explanation for the outbreak of bubonic plague in Bremen, Germany, in 1838. Knock, a real-estate agent in the vampire Nosferatu's power, persuades his clerk Waldemar Hutter to travel to Transylvania to close a real-estate deal with one Count Orlock (or as we know him, Nosferatu, from *nosferat*, a Romanian word for a kind of vampire). Leaving behind his devoted wife, Ellen, in the care of friends, Hutter travels to Transylvania. An up-to-date businessman, he laughs at the local peasantry's superstitious fear of Nosferatu. Soon after arriving at Nosferatu's castle, Hutter cuts his thumb at the dinner table and is understandably startled when his leering host sucks his bleeding finger. The next morning he finds marks on his neck that he assumes are insect bites. Only Ellen's love, which telepathically protects him, awakens the obtuse Hutter to the danger he is in.[16]

Hutter and Nosferatu both race back to Bremen. Accompanied by coffins filled with rats, Nosferatu spreads the plague wherever he goes, including, at last, Bremen. Hutter safely returns, but he and Ellen cannot resume the bourgeois idyll of bygone days. In the meantime, Knock, now totally deranged, escapes from a mental asylum and is pursued by a frenzied mob. Taking her cue from the *Book of the Vampires*, Ellen offers her blood to Nosferatu and keeps him at her bedside until sunrise. As the sun rises, Nosferatu disintegrates; Hutter mourns his wife's death, but Bremen is saved and Nosferatu's castle ruined.

Copland and Clurman adapted the film to suit their own purposes, making their protagonist a necromancer, a "sorcerer who loves the dead and vainly seeks affection among them. He can make them dance in so far as he does not touch them." In a French sketch of the ballet scenario, they further described Grohg as having a hooked nose and gigantic eyes, a figure "tragic in his ugliness, tragic—and pitiable." The one-act ballet takes place in the "large courtyard of Grohg's domain. The stage is empty, except for a high, thick, semi-circular wall at the back, from the top of which, at right and left stage, descend two flights of stone steps pointing towards the center." In a preliminary note to the score, Copland and Clurman emphasized that the work was not intended as a "macabre or realistic ballet" in the tradition of the Grand Guignol, but rather as a "fantastic" and "symbolic" work. The dead should not look dead, they warned, the coffins not look like coffins, and the lighting "should be unrealistic and varied."[17]

The ballet opens with a short introduction featuring a portentous three-note knocking motive (presaging later Copland works as different as *Appalachian Spring* and *Night Thoughts*). One by one, four groups of "servitors" drag out four coffins (three in the revised version) to music terrifying or jittery. Grohg enters and calls for the first dead, an adolescent (of indeterminate gender). Grohg looks "tenderly" at the adolescent, who, at his command, begins a lively dance, the servitors joining in from time to time. Grohg—his sad, yearning theme pitted against the youth's perky music—is moved by the adolescent and begins to dance himself, albeit "awkwardly." When the adolescent finally becomes aware of Grohg, he (or she) recoils in horror, at which point the "wounded" Grohg violently strikes him (or her) down.[18]

The servitors bring forth the second dead, an opium-eater, about whom Grohg "wearily" begins a slow, static dance. At a moment in the score marked "Visions of Jazz" and "misterioso," the opium-eater joins Grohg in the trancelike music; when the servitors join in a little later, the music momentarily becomes hectic. "Moved to pity," Grohg removes the spell and the servitors return the opium-eater to his coffin.

The third dead, a streetwalker, begins an "apache dance," a flirtatious waltz alternately pert and mock-sentimental. When she attempts to flee Grohg's advances, the angry necromancer strikes her, too. The fourth dead, a beautiful young girl, dances as if dreaming; eventually Grohg partakes in her slow, hypnotic waltz. After a passionate climax, he gently kisses her, the kiss represented by a solo viola melody containing quarter tones. The girl awakens and shudders with disgust as Grohg, in a frenzy, grips her.[19]

Then, in a lively dance full of polyrhythms and changing meters, the servitors and the four dead mock Grohg, mimicking his authority and violently striking him. After failed attempts to assert his power, Grohg picks up the streetwalker and flings her into the crowd. At this point, the stage darkens except for a light illuminating Grohg's head. The gloomy introductory music returns as Grohg slowly retires, "as if the action had happened only in his imagination." He disappears from view as the curtain falls.

Although Nosferatu, with his hooked nose and bulging eyes, clearly provided the physical model for Grohg, the relationship between the film and the ballet has eluded commentators. Peter Laki characterizes the ballet as "one of those productive misreadings where an artwork inspires another artist to create something original." Ronald Caltabiano and John Mugge further argue that Grohg seems less like Nosferatu than it does The Cabinet of Dr. Caligari and Petrushka, both of which also feature ominous authoritarian figures. But whereas the conflicts in Petrushka largely unfold among the puppets themselves, in Grohg the drama takes place between Grohg and his subjects. Nor is Grohg a heartless manipulator like Dr. Caligari or Petrushka's sorcerer; on the contrary, Copland's yearning music for the "tragic and pitiable" Grohg evokes sympathy for the hopelessly repressed necromancer, who can bring his beloved dead to life but cannot touch them, who exists in an endless cycle of sadomasochistic episodes.[20]

This brings us back, after all, to Nosferatu, a figure of desperate sexual—at times homosexual—yearning, as such observers as Jack Kerouac, Robin Wood, and Lotte H. Eisner have pointed out; indeed, since the late eighteenth century, homoeroticism had been such a prominent feature of vampire tales that by Murnau's time, the vampire-as-homosexual had become a literary commonplace. At the same time, Max Schreck's Nosferatu—a sly and exotic creature of legendary wealth—projected stereotypically Eastern and, more specifically, Jewish associations, making it necessary, in the wake of Nazi propaganda, for friends like Lotte Eisner to vigorously deny any anti-Semitic designs on Murnau's part. Whatever Murnau's intentions—and a fascination with and fear of Eastern Europe undeniably underlie the film, as they do the Stoker novel—it is little wonder that Copland, himself homosexual and Jewish, should find Nosferatu an intriguing figure. Like Murnau, however, Copland took an ironic if not necessarily campy view of his antihero; Grohg is the composer's Pierrot, his Petrushka, his Miraculous Mandarin—a hapless and lovelorn outsider.[21]

In its portrayal of a city in decay, Murnau's film also contains a social context largely absent from the Stoker novel. Bremen appears modern, writes Gregory Waller, "in the sense that its people are isolated, trapped, and afraid in an impersonal urban environment." Upon hearing news of the plague, for instance, all the citizens of Bremen anxiously close their windows and bolt their doors. The film further implies some criticism of capitalism and eugenics, offering hope rather in the form of peasant tradition and what Siegfried Kracauer calls "inner metamorphosis," symbolized by Ellen's sacrifice. Murnau thus establishes ties not only with Dostoyevsky, as Kracauer points out, but with Brecht and other Marxists.[22]

Grohg lacks this kind of clear social context, but the servitors can be seen as an enslaved group that finally rises up against a tyrannical master, or perhaps as a mob in pursuit of a sacrificial victim, like the settlers in *Billy the Kid*. The portrayals of the prostitute, with her apache dance, and the opium-eater, with his "visions of jazz," more specifically reflect Paris of the times (opium was popular with such French artists as Jean Cocteau). In its own way, *Grohg,* with its impotent hero cast in a decadent underworld, suggests a musical parallel to Hemingway's *The Sun Also Rises.*

Copland's score is an impressive one, especially for a student work; upon hearing those parts of it arranged as the *Dance Symphony* (1929), Stravinsky admitted it to be "a very precocious opus" for a composer in his early twenties. The music makes stylish use of the octatonic scale, polytonality, polyrhythms, ear-splitting sonorities, even microtones, a technique apparently inspired by the work of Alois Hába and perhaps Bloch. Concurrently, it features considerable stylistic range, with echoes of Mussorgsky, Satie, Ravel, Stravinsky, and, by Copland's own admission, Florent Schmitt's *The Tragedy of Salome*, as well as jazz and Jewish music. Given the ballet's connection with film, this eclecticism possibly owes something to the music heard in the more sophisticated motion-picture theaters of the time; a 1921 showing of *The Cabinet of Dr. Caligari* at the Capitol Theatre in New York included themes culled from Debussy, Strauss, Schoenberg, Stravinsky, and Prokofiev. At any rate, in this one work, Copland seems to have integrated the wide range of contemporary European musics he was eagerly seeking out; remarkably enough, it features as well a recognizable personality all its own.[23]

Although Peter Laki notes a fundamental kinship—though entirely coincidental—to Bartók's *Miraculous Mandarin*, *Grohg* also resembles a similarly gothic score by an American contemporary, namely, Roger Sessions's *Black Maskers* (1923), likewise inspired by an expressionist source. Both works—composed at the same time, though independently, an ocean apart—initiate a new phase of American music, epitomized by the concert series Copland and Sessions would later codirect. At the same time, *Black Maskers* is a texturally denser work, closer to Debussy, with a more intensely subjective tone and no obvious connection with popular music; such distinctions portend later differences that would ultimately drive these two composers apart.

Having no opportunity to launch *Grohg* as a ballet, Copland extracted portions of it for two independent orchestral works, the *Cortège Macabre* (1923) and the *Dance Symphony* (1929). He submitted the *Cortège*, an expanded treatment of the opening dirge, to Howard Hanson, who premiered it at the first of the American Composers Concerts in Rochester on 2 May 1925; Copland later withdrew it, but when Hanson asked to replay it at the very last Festival of American Music in 1971, he "agreed, thinking if Hanson liked it, there must be something good about it!"[24]

In the meanwhile, when it became clear that he would not be able to complete the *Symphonic Ode* in time to enter it in a 1929 competition sponsored by the RCA Victor Company, he arranged large chunks of the still mostly unknown *Grohg* as the three-movement *Dance Symphony*. The first movement conjoins the introduction and the adolescent's dance, skipping the servitors' dirge, which had since become *Cortège Macabre*; the middle movement consists of the young girl's dance up through the eerie kiss accompanied by quarter tones; and the finale comprises the concluding mocking dance, without the final coda. RCA Victor awarded Copland $5,000 for his effort (the other winners were Louis Gruenberg, Ernest Bloch, and Robert Russell Bennett); Leopold Stokowski and the Philadelphia Academy of Music premiered the piece, which Copland dedicated to Clurman, on 15 April 1931.[25]

In 1934 Copland resurrected the only two unused sections of *Grohg*—the dances of the opium-eater and the streetwalker—for a ballet for Ruth Page, *Hear Ye! Hear Ye!* He left the streetwalker's dance largely intact, whereas he used only the more excited portions of the opium-eater's dance for the ballet's climax. In the meantime, something like the opium-eater's slower music had turned up, years earlier, in the *Organ Symphony*.

Copland also prepared a revised *Grohg* (1932), shortening the work from about forty minutes to a half hour, principally by omitting the character of the young girl and her solo dance. But he was reluctant to bring the score forth as such, not only because by 1934 he had recycled the entire work, but because, as he commented in 1967, "fantastic and symbolic ballets" had gone out of fashion. Nonetheless, Oliver Knussen, who championed this revised score in the 1990s, judged it "stronger whole than any one of its temporary homes" and "arguably Copland's most remarkable orchestral achievement prior to the *Symphonic Ode*," a strong recommendation considering such intervening works as *Music for the Theatre* and the Piano Concerto.[26]

Knussen premiered the revised *Grohg* with the London Sinfonietta on 20 June 1992, two years after Copland's death, and recorded it with the Cleveland Orchestra in 1993. Critics uniformly declared the finally aired ballet an astonishing find, even those who had long known portions of it through the *Dance Symphony*. Knussen pointed out, meanwhile, that although the 1932 revision was superior for concert purposes to the 1925 original, the ballet itself still awaited a performance in either guise. Copland himself had maintained an interest in seeing *Grohg* staged, suggesting that the ballet might work especially well with a new scenario.[27]

7

Return and Rediscovery

Making a Living

Although while in Paris Copland had briefly considered the idea of becoming a music critic, by the time he returned to New York in June 1924 he had been decided for some time upon a career in composition. Such a decision took courage and determination. Even the most renowned European composers of serious music—except for authors of operatic hits like Puccini or Strauss—had difficulty surviving on commissions and royalties; how much more difficult would it be for a young and unknown American. Most of Copland's colleagues took paths of less resistance and became critics, private teachers, or college professors, but Copland was determined to live primarily from his music.

He had an additional problem in that he worked rather slowly, producing about one work a year (works so finished and polished, however, that they rarely needed later revision). On the other hand, he could write in a variety of styles and mediums. Moreover, he had no family to support and could live frugally; he required only a bed, a desk, a chair, a piano, and a place to store books, scores, and records. And finally, he could capably manage his financial affairs, something he attributed to early experiences in his father's store. "Artists have usually been thought to be nitwits in the handling of money," he would later write. "No one has ever accused me of that particular failing."[1]

At first, he attempted to make some money, as he had in the days before Paris, playing in a dance band. In the summer of 1924, he formed a piano trio with his violinist friend Abe Ginsburg and booked with a resort hotel in Milford, Pennsylvania, assuming that he would have enough free time to make progress on a commission from Serge Koussevitzky and the Boston Symphony Orchestra. But the job turned into a nightmare; when not rehearsing transcriptions of Italian opera arias under the hotel proprietor's supervision, he found himself at the piano in competition with noisy plumbers and carpenters. In desperation, he rented a dark and dirty movie house with a dilapidated piano for some afternoon hours, but he eventually realized that he could not get work done this way either. He retreated to his sister's house in Brooklyn, his career as a popular pianist over.[2]

Copland stayed in Brooklyn only long enough to complete the piano draft of the Boston Symphony work. "I had to leave Brooklyn a little precipitately," he explained to Koussevitzky's assistant, Nicolas Slonimsky, "because the neighbors threatened to descend in a body and maul me if I continued 'playing' such awful music—i.e., my Concerto." He moved into a studio in Manhattan in the fall of 1924 and sent out cards, hoping to augment his income as a private teacher of music theory and composition. This plan also failed to pan out; he received not a single inquiry.[3]

Fortunately, his colleague Marion Bauer introduced him to the director of the League of Composers, Claire Reis. Through her he met the music critic Paul Rosenfeld, who, after hearing him play some of his music, helped him obtain a cabin at the MacDowell Colony; Rosenfeld also introduced him to the patron Alma Morgenthau Wertheim, who gave him $1,000. Meanwhile, his old piano teacher Clarence Adler made his Lake Placid home available to Copland for a month. All this assistance helped get him through 1924–25. Subsequently, he received two $2,500 fellowships from the Guggenheim Foundation—enough for him to live on for the next two years. But in the fall of 1927, he once again had to face the "difficult problem of how to make a living."[4]

Again Rosenfeld came to the rescue, this time getting him a part-time appointment at the New School for Social Research, a position he would hold off and on over the next ten years, providing an important mainstay during this period. His $5,000 award from RCA Victor covered expenses for 1929, and a comparable subsidy from his cousin Percy maintained him through 1930. In the years that followed, he gave lecture-recitals, taught briefly for the Henry Street Settlement Music School, filled in for Walter Piston at Harvard (spring of 1935 and fall of 1944), joined the Tanglewood faculty (in 1940) and wrote books and articles, all sources of income that helped supplement what he earned by his music.[5]

Even so, he made very little right up through the Second World War, averaging a few thousand dollars a year. He gratefully accepted relatively small commissions, earning, for example, $250 for the ballet *Hear Ye! Hear Ye!* (1934) and only $100 for the children's opera *The Second Hurricane* (1937). Vernon Duke reports that in 1938 Copland "readily accepted" fifteen dollars for an orchestral fanfare. In that same year Copland almost missed the Boston premiere of *El Salón México*, because with only $6.93 in his checking account, he could not afford a hotel room. Occasionally he borrowed money or accepted gifts from friends and family. At no time, however, did his own financial difficulties dampen his efforts on behalf of other American composers or his willingness to help out artists even more destitute than himself.[6]

During these difficult Depression years, a circle of enlightened and well-to-do New Yorkers came to the aid of Copland and the cause of modern music in general. These patrons—mostly women—included Claire Reis, Minna Lederman, Alma Wertheim, Mary Senior Churchill, Mary Lescaze, Dorothy Norman, and Kirk and Constance Askew. Most lived in gracious town houses on Manhattan's Upper East Side, hosting lavish receptions that gave near-starving artists an opportunity to sample fine food and elegant surroundings. The Askews, art dealers, were especially known for bringing together brilliant musicians, dancers, artists, and architects. In Copland's case, the support of such patrons went much further than an occasional meal. As director of the League of Composers, Reis commissioned new scores; and as editor of the league's influential journal, *Modern Music,* Lederman solicited articles. Churchill bankrolled the Copland-Sessions Concerts; and Lescaze, Norman, and the Askews helped underwrite *The Second Hurricane.*[7]

Moreover, Wertheim funded the Cos Cob Press (founded 1929), a nonprofit organization operated by the Edwin Kalmus company that published the work of a number of mostly young and struggling American composers, offering them a hefty 50 percent royalty as opposed to the usual 10 percent. As cofounder and adviser (along with Emerson Whithorne and Louis Gruenberg), Copland naturally received special consideration, and between 1929 and 1934, Cos Cob brought out the bulk of his catalog to date. Although not of the highest graphic standards, these publications helped him earn some money and further his career.[8]

Although profoundly grateful for such support, Copland hoped to see America's serious composers stand on their own feet financially. This dream—along with his natural abilities—led him to accept leadership of the American Composers Alliance from its founding in 1939 to 1945. The alliance, which enjoyed broad support, was established in order, first, "to regularize and collect all fees pertaining to performance of their copyrighted music" and, second, "to stimulate interest in the performance of American music, thereby increasing the economic returns." Composers traditionally had been timid about such demands for fear that they might jeopardize performances of their music; but the sweeping pro-labor sentiments of the 1930s finally caught up with them. The two principal agencies for collecting such fees were ASCAP, which had long worked primarily on behalf of America's popular composers (including some well-favored concert composers), and its rival BMI, active in controlling radio rights. In 1944 BMI took over collecting duties for ACA; because Copland's publisher, Boosey & Hawkes, was affiliated with ASCAP, he had to resign from ACA soon after. But by then the goal of establishing a composer's right to collect performance fees had been firmly established.[9]

Copland's break into Hollywood in 1939 brought considerable financial relief. Usually easygoing about commissions, he proved, to the apparent discomfiture of his agent, Abe Meyer of MCA Artists, a tough negotiator with motion-picture producers. For each of his first two films, *Of Mice and Men* (1939) and *Our Town* (1940), he made around $5,000, a large amount for an essentially untried and unknown film composer. "I thought if I was to sell myself to the movies," he wrote to Bernstein, "I ought to sell myself good." With the success of these scores, he began asking for $10,000 or more a film, making him, along with Max Steiner and Erich Wolfgang Korngold, one of Hollywood's highest paid film composers. In 1948 the scores for *The Red Pony* and *The Heiress* each earned him, more or less, an impressive $15,000.[10]

Still, because he did not want to devote himself wholly to writing film music, he began considering other available offers, including a position at Brooklyn College in 1941, then one at Juilliard in 1945. Even in the early 1940s, the principal moneys derived from his music—the performance fees collected by ASCAP and the royalties earned from Boosey & Hawkes— still amounted to only a few thousand dollars a year. But he never accepted a permanent college position.[11]

Although economic security continued to elude Copland in the immediate postwar period, his fortunes improved dramatically as the decade wore on, thanks to the growing popularity of his more accessible work and a newly prosperous worldwide market for recordings of classical music. In a 1947 survey of music performed by leading American orchestras, Copland led the list among native composers—far behind Strauss and Ravel, but comparable to Bartók, just then coming into his own as well. By the early 1950s, he had become a household name, writers typically referring to him as, among American composers, "the most significant," "the greatest," and "the most potent." For the rest of the century, he maintained such prominence alongside, though more typically ahead of, Gershwin, Barber, and eventually Ives and Bernstein.[12]

Such distinction brought financial rewards. By the early 1950s, he was averaging about $25,000 a year, an upper-middle-class income that allowed him to purchase a home (in 1953 for $9,500), buy a Buick, shop at the better stores, retain legal counsel, and hire a secretary and a housekeeper. In the years that followed, his annual income grew steadily; in 1958, he grossed $63,000 for the year.[13]

Finally able to live comfortably off his music, an almost unimaginable accomplishment for a serious American composer, Copland might have been expected to devote himself entirely to composition, but he continued to teach, lecture, and write as vigorously as ever. In 1958 alone he lectured at ten midwestern universities, as well as in other parts of the States, Canada, England, Brussels, and France. Moreover, from the mid-1950s to the early 1980s, he embarked on a highly lucrative conducting career, earning as much as $2,000 or more for a single engagement. All this took Copland more decidedly from the middle to the upper class. He purchased his second home for $65,000 in 1960 and bought a Mercedes.[14]

Copland's good working relationship with Boosey & Hawkes helped. In 1938, he signed a contract for two works with the prestigious English publishing house, thanks to the success of El Salón México and the efforts of Benjamin Britten; later, he signed on permanently. This arrangement proved mutually beneficial. Under the effective directorships of Ralph Hawkes, David Adams, and Stuart Pope, and the eagle eye of Sylvia Goldstein, a lawyer who became vice president for business affairs, Boosey ably represented Copland's interests. For his part, Copland joined the ranks of Richard Strauss, Stravinsky, and Britten as one of the firm's biggest money-makers.[15]

In 1962, Copland and his lawyer, Abraham Friedman, arranged an unusual contract with Boosey that returned him his copyrights and also provided, for the remainder of his life, a significantly higher royalty than the usual 10 percent, one that would drop below normal upon his death; in the words of Stuart Pope, head of the firm's New York office from 1964 to 1984, Boosey "took a kind of mercenary attitude, gambling on Aaron's longevity." Copland, who lived another twenty-eight years, to the age of ninety, made out very well. In the 1970s, his annual income had climbed into the hundreds of thousands, topping half a million dollars by the mid-1980s. By the time he died, his securities were worth several million dollars, his copyrights valued at three or four million dollars more. He could have earned even more money had he been less discriminate about commercial use of his music.[16]

Copland used an accountant, but he kept his own meticulous records of his finances, saving checkbook stubs, receipts, royalty statements, tax returns, lists of business expenses, investments, and so on. These records reveal a scrupulous attentiveness to financial matters. At the same time, Stuart Pope and Sylvia Goldstein agree that although he painstakingly went over his quarterly reports, he did not seem nearly as concerned about money as did Stravinsky and other clients. "I always found out what Stravinsky got paid," Copland would say about his fees, "and then I would know what to ask."[17]

Moving About and a Place of One's Own

In October 1924, Copland established his first Manhattan residence, a small studio at 135 West Seventy-fourth Street on the Upper West Side, an area that would remain his principal home base for nearly three decades, until 1947.

If Greenwich Village was New York's Montmartre, the Upper West Side was its Montparnasse, a sprawling mélange of apartment buildings, brownstones, and shops populated by immigrants, artists, professionals, and workers. Musicians liked the proximity to the Metropolitan Opera on West Thirty-ninth, Town Hall on West Forty-third, and Carnegie Hall on West Fifty-seventh, as well as the theaters on Broadway, the jazz clubs in the West Fifties, and the midtown publishing houses. For some years home to New York's German-Jewish community, the area also was fast becoming associated with intellectuals and artists of Russian-Jewish descent, though by the time it had crystallized as the center of Jewish intellectual life in America, Copland had already left it.

Like all of his Manhattan apartments, his studio on West Seventy-fourth consisted of a single room with a bed, a desk, a piano, and a few plain furnishings; for many years, he never had a kitchen—nor did he ever learn how to cook. He lived on West Seventy-fourth from 1924 to 1926 and then moved to a larger studio on West Seventy-eighth for another three years (1926–29). After a lengthy trip to Europe, he spent five years moving about Manhattan: he stayed, courtesy of his cousin Percy Uris, at the Hotel Montclair on Lexington and Fiftieth Street in 1930; sublet Clurman's apartment at 52 West Fifty-eighth Street in 1931–32; lived at two West Fifty-fifth Street addresses (63 and 100) between 1932 and 1934; and then, in 1935, moved to downtown apartments loaned to him by his cousins—the first at the Hotel Lafayette on Ninth Street and University Place, the second at 1 University Place. Reading about these many addresses in Julia Smith's biography, Copland's friend and former student Alex North was reminded of the Depression, "when we purposely moved every year in order to gain a two months rental concession."[18]

In 1936 Copland took a room at the Hotel Empire at 115 West Sixty-third; two years later, in 1938, he rented, in addition, a loft down the street at 113 West Sixty-third, where he could work at night without disturbing neighbors. The loft was situated on the top floor of a building that rented out to such daytime organizations as the Flesh Leather Company, the Comités-Femeninos-Unidos, and Flavors by F. W. Kaye and Company. "The hallways and four flights are richly inscribed with epitaphs more ordinarily scribbled on subway lavatories," wrote Herbert Kubly after a visit. The loft itself consisted of one cavernous room from front to back, with a divan, a desk, a piano, and shelving for books and music. A small kitchen was situated at the far end, with a gas range, a refrigerator, and a folding table. David Diamond, a frequent guest, recalled the spartan decor, which included a drawing by Copland's lover, Victor Kraft, a Mexican rug pinned to the wall, photographs of the composers Carlos Chávez and Silvestre Revueltas, and a Miguel Covarrubias caricature of Frida Kahlo. Kraft often slept at the loft when in New York. The Empire, on the other hand, offered a measure of elegance, although Copland's room on the tenth floor (1040) contained simply a bed, a bureau, a desk, a studio piano, and a small bath with a stall shower.[19]

Copland typically ate, by necessity, at the most inexpensive places, sometimes lunching at the YMCA or a cafeteria. During his years at the Empire, he often had dinner at one of the "greasy spoons" on Sixty-third Street, or at the Brass Rail on Columbus Avenue; only on special occasions did he frequent the hotel's fine dining room. He rarely entertained guests at the Empire, but he occasionally threw parties in his loft, serving beer and pretzels, unless someone else cooked. "The loft went over in a big way," he recalled. "It was a novelty before the time when composers and artists sought out lofts to live and work in." Clurman was less impressed: "Why, my beloved friend of all time," he wrote Copland in 1943, "must every one of your permanent residences have a hangover of Washington Ave. in Brooklyn?" Copland kept the loft and his room at the Empire until 1947.[20]

By this time, life in New York had become increasingly difficult. The Sixty-third Street loft, never in a safe area in the first place, had been burglarized a couple of times. Postwar New York as a whole was becoming a tougher, grittier place to live. In addition, with growing fame came more interruptions. In 1947, Copland hid out in Verna Fine's mother's Boston apartment in order to complete *In the Beginning*. "I plan to use the BSO [Boston Symphony Orchestra] as an address," he wrote to Fine, "and to be mysterious about my real whereabouts. It's come to this! A nice simple guy like me." In the same year, he more or less left Manhattan for good. "It's easier to say 'sorry' when you're not around the corner," he explained about his move.[21]

In 1947 he rented a "rambling white Colonial" (nicknamed the Ding Dong House by its previous owners) at Sneden's Landing near Palisades, New York. A small town on the left bank of the Hudson, Sneden's Landing was popular with artists: Noël Coward, Orson Welles, John Dos Passos, and John Steinbeck had lived there at one time or another. Copland loved the Ding Dong House, which he described as an "enchanting house" with "an upstairs veranda, New Orleans style, with a truly sensational view up and down the river." After receiving a Fulbright to spend 1950 in Rome, however, he left the house in the hands of pianists Robert Fizdale and Arthur Gold, never again to reside there. Upon his return to the States in 1951, he taught at Tanglewood, then moved to Cambridge for his 1951–52 Norton professorship at Harvard, at the same time maintaining an apartment at 9 Charlton Street in Greenwich Village, his last in Manhattan.[22]

While at Harvard, Copland purchased his first home—Shady Lane Farm—in Ossining, New York, in Westchester County, where he lived from 1952 to 1961. A converted barn, Shady Lane contained two stories in one large open space, with big beams and floor-to-ceiling windows.

The first floor included Copland's studio, a large living area with a fireplace, a kitchen, a bath, and a bedroom. Upstairs were Copland's bedroom and a third bedroom.[23]

With its open design and huge windows, Shady Lane offered little privacy; and Copland readily admitted in 1953 that he had yet to find the "perfect home" that "has been always in my thoughts." In this "perfect home," he mused, the studio would command central importance: "It will be sound-proofed and air-conditioned and have a majestic, ebony piano in it, and a work table from which the eye can look out on a broad expanse of rolling hill." Recalling all the many apartments and studios that he had lived in over the years, he granted that each had added "its special zest to life. And at least I saw places. All that was lacking, really, was a pleasant place to come home to."[24]

In 1960 Kraft encouraged him to buy a similarly airy but more spacious home, Rock Hill, at 1538 Washington Street in Cortlandt, outside of Peekskill, farther north, but still within an hour's drive or train ride of Manhattan. A dark green clapboard house built on a granite promontory on two and a half acres of wooded land, Rock Hill featured a main level that contained Copland's studio (with picture windows and a terrace that led down to the woods), his bedroom, his bathroom, two guest bedrooms, a guest bathroom, a kitchen, and a dining room; a downstairs level that had yet another bedroom and bathroom, along with a file room; and a two-story cottage connected to the garage, which held, above, a living area, a deck, and a kitchenette and, below, a bedroom and bath. One observer described it as "a very spacious log cabin." Copland liked it especially for its full view of the Hudson River. "There was a sense of space that you don't have now," remembered Erik Johns. "When other houses came in he let the trees grow."[25]

Copland lived at Rock Hill for the rest of his life, furnishing even this large home modestly and sparsely. After visiting the house, one journalist wrote, "There is the black Mercedes in the driveway, but the rest of the place could be a Shaker ad for simple gifts and related homilies of the rustic spirit."[26]

Throughout his life, Copland enjoyed traveling, in large part because it abetted his creative process. He told William Schuman, on turning down a position at Juilliard, "My deepest inner concern seems to be a need to think of myself as free to move about when and where I please and to let my mind dwell solely on my own music if I happen to feel that way." He regularly left Manhattan during the summer, usually for rural retreats in

upstate New York, New England, and Mexico. "It wouldn't hurt anybody to spend a couple of months in Rio," he once counseled, "a
delightful experience, or an awful experience, but it would be an experience. You wouldn't be left cold by it."[27]

At the same time, he never liked being far away from New York for
long; his letters from abroad typically yearn for Manhattan and its
goings-on. He especially disliked having to spend months in Los Angeles
scoring films. "Frankly, I would starve to death, musically, if I stayed
here," he told a Los Angeles reporter in 1948. "In New York, there are
twenty or thirty musical events going on practically every evening. No, of
course, I don't go to all of them. As a matter of fact, I don't go to any.
But, like a man with a harem—it's nice to know they're there!"[28]

Paul Rosenfeld and the Stieglitz Circle

Copland was happy to win the patronage of Paul Rosenfeld (1890–
1946), a music critic whose writings had offered welcome guidance and
stimulation during his years with Goldmark. "I very well remember the
excitement of reading his first articles about the young Stravinsky and the
young Ernest Bloch," he remarked. "That must have been around 1919
or 1920." After leaving Brooklyn for Paris, he had the *Dial* mailed to him
so that he could continue to read Rosenfeld; by any standard, Rosenfeld
was a remarkable critic.[29]

Born into a well-to-do and cultivated German-Jewish family from the
Upper West Side, Rosenfeld attended Yale and Columbia University and
established himself as a freelance critic and novelist. After hearing Scriabin and Ornstein in the mid-1910s, he became a particularly eloquent and
important advocate for modern music; for an American to write with
insight and sympathy about Schoenberg and Stravinsky in the 1910s, or
Bartók and Satie in the early 1920s, was no small feat. As Copland wrote
in a 1946 memorial tribute, Rosenfeld went on to become "one of the
very first to affirm the talents" of Sessions, Harris, Chávez, and himself.
"He took chances when some years back he wrote enthusiastically about
the neglected Charles Ives or the 15-year-old Lukas Foss. He took chances
when he gave a preeminent place to the music of Leo Ornstein or Edgard
Varèse." Such writings earned him, in the estimation of Edmund Wilson,
a "prestige" like that of H. L. Mencken and Van Wyck Brooks.[30]

As a critic, Rosenfeld emphasized the notion that music embodies or
criticizes or in some other way reacts to the values of the society from
which it emanates. Wagner's music, he wrote, represents the nineteenth

century's "cry of pride in its possessions," whereas Mussorgsky's "grows from the flesh of the nameless, unnumbered multitudes of men condemned by life throughout its course to misery." The great artist is one who speaks honestly and meaningfully about the world around him. After witnessing a "neurotically stupid" New York audience hiss Stravinsky, an outraged Rosenfeld fired back: "He comes to tell them what is at work in the world to-day, what the tenure of his own existence is, what is happening or about to happen to them." The artist cannot escape or ignore the world; one either transfigures its "forces" or succumbs to them—as Mahler did, in Rosenfeld's estimation, to Austrian anti-Semitism and Gershwin to American materialism.[31]

Because Rosenfeld regarded the world as increasingly barbaric, mechanistic, and violent, he inclined toward music that spoke to him of such things. He thus cultivated a critical vocabulary that in many ways resembled Ives's (both men, perhaps significantly, had studied with Horatio Parker at Yale); he spoke favorably of music that was "virile," "barbaric," and "savage," in contrast to that deemed "sterile," "decadent," and "soft." This inclined him toward Ornstein, Stravinsky, Varèse, and Ives, and away from Strauss, Fauré, Rachmaninov, and John Alden Carpenter; thus, too, he rated Borodin superior to Tchaikovsky and Sibelius to Grieg.[32]

As Barbara Zuck points out, Rosenfeld naturally equated musical Americanism "with the expression and representation of American life as music," as opposed to those who viewed it more in terms of its relation to the musical vernacular. Thus Varèse, in his opinion, is more "American" than Gershwin. Indeed, popular or "entertainment" music can lead the composer astray; it "is something which temporarily removes people from contact with reality," as does jazz, which he considered "just another means of escape." In contrast, authentically American music—whether by MacDowell, Harris, or Chávez—evokes potent images of the American continent and its peoples. For Rosenfeld, Ives is profoundly American in spite of, not because of, his use of the American vernacular; like Mussorgsky, Bartók, and Falla, says Rosenfeld in one of his typically provocative passages, Ives criticizes "folk music and the folk itself."[33]

Although Rosenfeld warmly supported Copland from the start, the two never established a close friendship, partly because Rosenfeld was somewhat retiring in nature. In addition, there were real differences in sensibility, evident from a comparison of their prose: Rosenfeld's was ornate and passionate; Copland's, clear and ironic. And while they might agree, say, on the importance of Chávez and Harris, they did not see eye to eye when it came to a number of other composers. In 1932 Rosenfeld actually assailed the programming of a festival organized by Copland, one that featured a number of graduates of Nadia Boulanger's studio.[34]

He also expressed reservations about Copland's music, perhaps no more than his wont, but more than in the case of Varèse, Chávez, or Ives. From the beginning he complained of Copland's "meagerness" of expression and "narrowness" of range, identifying three principal moods: a wistful mood, related to the blues; an ironic one, related to jazz, and (by 1931) an "objective" and "austere" one heard as early as the finale to the *Organ Symphony* (1925). In 1939 he frankly stated, "Mr. Copland works a little too steadily in a few tints—grey, whitey-grey, and greyish-green, and this is one of the limitations of his art." Harris "comprehends a more human experience," he noted in another context; significantly, he resorted time and again to an array of animal metaphors in his discussions of Copland: the frisky colt, the shrill cock, the gurgling frog, the cackling cat, and the gangly daddy longlegs. Finally, Copland's architecture, admirable though it was overall, lacked "cohesion" and was excessively repetitive, even, at times, "arbitrarily mosaical" and "sluggish."[35]

The gulf between the two widened in the course of the 1930s as Copland became more involved with ballet, film, and music for schools. Rosenfeld tolerated *Statements* as a piece of left-wing propaganda, *El Salón México* as a caper à la Chabrier, and *The Second Hurricane* as a little charmer; but he rejected *An Outdoor Overture*, *Billy the Kid*, and *The City* as seeming "altogether innocent of artistic intentions." By the 1940s he privately contended that the composer of *Rodeo* and *Appalachian Spring* had simply sold out.[36]

Concurrently, Copland and Rosenfeld had a running debate as to whether or not "social idealism could inspire good music." Clurman similarly quarreled with Rosenfeld for having "overemphasized the significance of the individual genius in the development of culture, while my conviction made me stress the role of the formative collective group from which the individual artist emerges. . . . I decided then and there that Rosenfeld and I represented two different generations, and that his generation thenceforth had very little to offer mine."[37]

Even so, as Clurman acknowledged,

He suggested the core and principle of our universal problem: to make man act on his responsibility to man, so that he might be conjoined through love to work and create with his fellow man, rather than isolate himself to destroy through power. . . . This is certainly what the men of the thirties were after, and if Rosenfeld was not explicit about it, his work might still be said to contain the seeds of this knowledge. He was moreover a pioneer in arriving at such knowledge through an understanding of music, and in seeing the role that music might play in its dissemination.

Presumably, Copland's ideal of a healthy interaction between the artist and society owed something to Rosenfeld.[38]

Copland and Clurman had yet another debt to Rosenfeld: he brought them into his circle of friends, a group of mostly older intellectuals and artists associated with the photographer Alfred Stieglitz. At a soiree at Rosenfeld's in November 1924, Copland played some of his music before no less an assemblage than Stieglitz, his soon-to-be wife Georgia O'Keeffe, Van Wyck Brooks, Hart Crane, Alfred Kreymborg, Marianne Moore, Lewis Mumford, Herbert Seligmann, Paul and Rebecca Strand, Jean Toomer, Edmund Wilson, and a French visitor, Jean Vatal. Copland and Clurman quickly established themselves in this milieu.[39]

As a reader of the *Dial*, the *Nation*, and the *New Republic*, Copland had, as with Rosenfeld, some familiarity with Van Wyck Brooks, Waldo Frank, and others in the Stieglitz crowd even before meeting them personally. Copland's early enthusiasm for Whitman, acquired at about age eighteen, may have owed something to their collective criticism. In any case, the artists and critics associated with Stieglitz formed the principal aesthetic and intellectual background against which Copland's mature music emerged.[40]

Born in Hoboken, the son of prosperous German-Jewish immigrants, Alfred Stieglitz (1864–1946) studied photography in Germany and in 1905 opened, with Edward J. Steichen, the Photo-Secessionist 291 Gallery at 291 Fifth Avenue, a gallery that established itself as a famous meeting place as well as a select showcase for contemporary painting and photography. There Stieglitz's coterie could hear him pontificate in a "quasi-prophetic vein" on painting, photography, and the future of the arts in America. Clurman, who visited 291 once a week after his return from Paris, wrote, "He was committed to the artists, not simply as individual talents, but as representatives of something astir in the country, something bigger than the art world—life in America itself. There was a kind of religious exaltation in Stieglitz's speech. He was pleading for the recognition of a new spirit, a new awareness he associated with the coming of age of the American consciousness."[41]

Stieglitz's conviction that the American artist should reflect, in Paul Strand's words, "the ideas of American Democracy," informed not only his own work, but that of a whole generation of photographers (including Dorothea Lange, Paul Strand, Walker Evans, Edward Weston, and Ansel Adams) who heeded his advice and went off to photograph America. Their slogan, "Affirm America," denoted nothing chauvinistic; on the contrary, these photographers typically depicted the bleaker aspects of American life: huddled immigrants, shadowy pedestrians crushed by towering skyscrapers, harsh desert landscapes, impoverished farmers, urban decay, and so forth. However, underlying all this was the "affirmative" and optimistic belief that such images could move Americans toward fulfilling their unrealized potential as individuals and as citizens.[42]

Copland admired Stieglitz's work more than he liked the domineering photographer himself. Moreover, Copland and Clurman shared the same reservations about Stieglitz that they felt about Rosenfeld—he was too much the aesthete, in their estimation, too much the romantic individualist. His followers, argued Clurman, made 291 "a haven in a storm" when it should have been "an outpost." Then, too, most members of the Stieglitz circle "were country rather than city people, whose America lay outside New York." Stieglitz, for his part, probably liked Copland's music less than that of Ruggles, whom Copland first met at 291 in the late 1920s. (Georgia O'Keeffe frankly wrote Copland, on receipt of some recordings that he had sent her, "It has always annoyed me that your music does not speak to me.") Still, as Copland himself suggested, his efforts on behalf of American music owed much to the example of Stieglitz.[43]

As the premiere champion and practitioner of photography in America, Stieglitz also influenced Copland, both directly and indirectly; for some of Copland's closest friends, especially in his early years, were photographers affiliated with Stieglitz, including Paul Strand (1890–1996), Ralph Steiner (1899–1986), and Rudy Burckhardt (1914–99).

Copland met Strand and Steiner at about the same time that these two photographers met each other, around 1927. Strand and Steiner rallied around Stieglitz's ideals while modifying his aesthetic to accommodate a leaner look and a more ironic tone; they further collaborated on various film projects, including Pare Lorentz's classic documentary, *The Plow That Broke the Plains*. Both were politically left-wing; Strand spent six months in the Soviet Union in 1935, while Steiner was, according to Elia Kazan, "full of devout admiration for the working class."[44]

Copland and Strand became chummy, enjoying time together in Mexico in the 1930s. Upon receiving an "unbelievably beautiful book" of his photographs in 1974, Copland expressed his appreciation for Strand's work in unusually warm terms, especially to someone outside of music: "The overwhelming impression is one of the utter 'rightness' of each separate photograph—and the sense of unity, despite the wide variety of subject matter. . . . I suppose what touches me most is the sense of human warmth and sensibility each of your pages gives off,—whatever the subject matter may be."[45]

Copland became even closer friends with Steiner; in addition to being nearer in age, they shared an interest in music. Copland included three short art films by Steiner on a 1931 Copland-Sessions Concert (to music by Colin McPhee and Marc Blitzstein); Steiner, who had next to no experience making films at this point, "induced" Copland to help him edit one of them. "He claimed he knew nothing about film," recalled Steiner, "but I persuaded him that a composer should know about unity and progression, and that these had to be important to film editing. Not long ago I saw that film for the first time in almost forty years, and I thought that Aaron and I did not do too well in organization. I saw that Aaron, in choosing a career of composing rather than film editing, showed splendid judgment." Steiner subsequently collaborated with Copland on the documentary *The City* (1939).[46]

Copland met Rudolf ("Rudy") Burckhardt, another distinguished photographer, through Edwin Denby in 1935. Having recently arrived in New York from his native Switzerland in order to live with Denby, his lover at the time (they had met in Switzerland in 1934), Burckhardt quickly became friends with both Copland and his lover, Victor Kraft. Burckhardt, who found Copland "charming," helped guide Kraft's own burgeoning career in photography.[47]

In 1936, Burckhardt filmed a short silent comedy, *145 W. 21*, that featured Denby, Copland, and other friends. In the film, Denby and Paula Miller (Lee Strasberg's wife in real life) live in a loft at the eponymous address (Denby and Burckhardt lived there in actuality). Their loft is a mess because workmen—Copland (dressed in overalls and a cap) and the lyricist John Latouche—are repairing a skylight on the roof. As Denby and Miller attend a burlesque (with Virgil Thomson, Paul Bowles, and Victor Kraft in the audience), Copland and Latouche ransack their loft and, finding four dollars, merrily go out for a meal. Denby and Miller return home to find their loft turned upside down. Despair turns to joy when Denby recovers an overlooked twenty-dollar bill. Burckhardt showed the film, with music by Paul Bowles, as part of a fund-raiser for the Copland-Denby opera *The Second Hurricane*. Burckhardt's more serious and characteristic work of the period focused on the discrepancy of scale between city dwellers and skyscrapers.[48]

The work and ideals of this whole New York school of photographers left a mark on Copland. This is at least suggested by Rosenfeld's description of him as someone who worked essentially in whites and grays; by the phrases "photographic realism" and "virtually photographic," as applied to his music; or by *The Tender Land*, inspired by the photography of Walker Evans. Then, too, the preferred subject matter among these photographers—from cityscapes and industrial machinery in the 1920s, to Mexico and the far West in the early 1930s, to midwestern farmhouses, migrant workers, and New England churches during the Roosevelt years—paralleled trends in Copland's own development. More generally, the notion of art as an "affirmation" and an "effective communication" helped shape Copland's own aesthetics.[49]

Although Van Wyck Brooks (1886–1963) stood slightly apart from these photographers (he had little enthusiasm for modern artistic trends), the Stieglitz circle took a keen interest in both the man and his voluminous critical work, which focused on the historical role of the arts in America. His most influential book—*America's Coming-of-Age* (1915)—and his other writings set forth the thesis that American culture had failed to integrate a highbrow, imported culture and a lowbrow, native one. Consequently, America produced either "saints," like Emerson, or "millionaires," like Twain; only Whitman among America's poets and Jefferson among its political heroes offered a "usable past," that is, a centered tradition upon which a healthy culture could build. Brooks believed further that only a socialist America could overcome many of these ingrained conflicts. The novelty of Brooks's argument resided not only in recognizing the competing claims of high and low art but in demanding their unity and integration; Copland's allusion to Brooks in his Norton lectures showed a sensitivity to some of the argument's many implications.[50]

Brooks's later career had further ramifications on Copland's development, at least indirectly. In the wake of a 1927 nervous breakdown, Brooks underwent a rather startling about-face; Emerson and other nineteenth-century American writers, he now argued, were eminently "usable," after all. This reevaluation of Emerson (*The Life of Emerson*, 1932) concurred with Copland's championship of Ives at the 1932 and 1933 Yaddo Festivals; and Brooks's idealization of the New England small town (*The Flowering of New England*, 1936) coincided with Thornton Wilder's *Our Town* (1938) and the music Copland composed for its screen version (1940).[51]

Of all the writers associated with Stieglitz, however, Copland developed closest ties to Waldo Frank (1889–1967), his colleague at the New School in 1927. This was due to the fact that Frank, an amateur cellist, had an interest in the new-music scene and a great admiration for Copland's music. In one letter to Copland, he wrote, concerning the Piano Sonata (1941), "I was profoundly impressed and moved by its lucid, pure, potent beauty—the strong architectonic of the first movement, the brilliant intricate middle, and the deeply beautiful last movement." He hoped Copland would compose the incidental music for his play *Malva*, written for Katharine Cornell.[52]

Like Brooks, Frank assailed American culture as fragmented and impoverished, notably in his acclaimed book *Our America* (1919); and like Stieglitz and Rosenfeld (with whom he shared a German-Jewish background), he thought the artist could play a prophetic role and help make society whole. Like all three, he celebrated the achievement of Whitman, though in the political arena he was attracted more to Lincoln's visionary nationalism than, as with Brooks, Jefferson's utopian liberalism.

Frank struck a distinctive note in opining that an integrated America would require the kind of spiritual basis and collective identity that allegedly typified preindustrial times. He found himself drawn to tribal and peasant cultures, especially the campesinos of Spain and Latin America; the notion that the technological know-how of the United States and the spiritual depth of Latin America could merge to produce the ideal of "integral socialism" provided the central thesis of *America Hispana: A Portrait and a Prospect* (1931). We can readily observe connections not only to Copland's attraction to preindustrial societies, but to his belief that the fate of American and Latin American composers depended upon their mutual cooperation.[53]

In the 1930s, Frank's communist activities derived in part from the further hope—initially explored in *Dawn in Russia* (1932)—that the Soviet Union's presumed merger of industrialism with traditional art and folklore might give rise to "integral socialism." However, his attitude toward communism was always ambivalent; he worried that Marxist dogma was as likely to squelch as to promote spiritual growth. "Yet so long as I was convinced," he recalled in his memoirs, "in those early 1930s, that the Communists were the sole organized instrument for the transformation of the capitalist into a socialist society, I could not oppose them." He broke with the Communists after the Moscow trials of 1937, but remained wary of anticommunism as an ideology, and his last published book, *Cuba: Prophetic Island,* viewed Castro sympathetically. Frank's writings, well known to both Copland and Clurman, apparently influenced their own political views.[54]

Lewis Mumford (1895–1990) and Edmund Wilson (1895–1972), both also associated with Stieglitz, offered Copland further examples of socially engaged intellectuals. Taking off from Brooks and Frank, Mumford argued that for American culture to become whole and organic, modern technology would have to serve urban planning and ecological harmony rather than laissez-faire capitalism. Copland took a special interest in Edmund Wilson, whose concern about the artist's place in society, as expressed in his most celebrated book, *Axel's Castle* (1931), set the stage for Copland's work of the 1930s. In 1932, when Copland sublet Clurman's West Fifty-eighth Street apartment, he found himself living upstairs from Wilson; in later years, he regularly saw Wilson at Tanglewood, where the latter wryly compared the relationship between Koussevitzky and Copland to that between Lenin and Stalin.[55]

Of all the Stieglitz circle, however, Copland was perhaps closest to the petite, red-haired Mary Lescaze. He met her originally through her first husband, Ralph Steiner, whom she married in 1927. By September 1933, the Steiners were, as Mary wrote Copland, "manipulating the legal and mucky hocus-pocus necessary for a divorce," and later in the month she married the architect William Lescaze. A pioneer in his own right, the Swiss-born Lescaze helped establish the International Style in the States. His remarkable designs included his own residence at 211 East Forty-eighth Street (1933–34); he also undertook one of the first low-cost housing projects in America, the Williamsburg Houses in Brooklyn. In 1952 he helped design Copland's Ossining studio.[56]

Like Claire Reis, Mary Lescaze had the means to assist Copland; she helped him arrange concerts at the New School and raise funds for *The Second Hurricane.* Both she and William held his music in high esteem. After hearing *Appalachian Spring,* she wrote to Copland, "I meant to write you immediately because Bill and I both found it so pure and beautiful." Copland was very fond of Mary; from expressing thoughts about communism in the 1930s to voicing his concerns about the education of his godson Jeremy in the 1960s, he could speak his mind to her as with few other friends.[57]

One final association might be mentioned in the context of Stieglitz: Copland's friendship with the New York poet Lola Ridge (1871–1941). A romantic realist in the tradition of Whitman, the Irish-born Ridge earned a reputation in her time as a kind of New York Carl Sandburg. Her most famous volume of verse, *The Ghetto and Other Poems* (1918), took Manhattan's Jewish poor as its subject matter. A later volume, *Red Flag* (1927), celebrated the Russian Revolution.

Relations between Ridge and Copland attained some intensity in the years around 1930 as she became an ardent Copland enthusiast. Viewing him as representing—in contrast to Stravinsky, Schoenberg, Hindemith, and others—the "coming generation," she wrote to him in 1931, "I've heard enough of your music now to feel you belong definitely with the coming yea-sayers. You have experienced something of what the late dead that are yet alive have passed through, but you are already past it, with a perspective on it." This yea-saying, "this liberation," as Ridge also refers to it, had its debt to Stieglitz and his group of friends.[58]

8

The Usable Past

American Music Through Ruggles

Determined to create a distinctively American music, Copland took a cue from Van Wyck Brooks and sought a "usable past." The extent to which he seriously studied earlier American music is unclear—he already knew some of it, of course, growing up—but he suggested that the endeavor occupied him and some unnamed colleagues until the late 1920s, by which time "our search for musical ancestors had been abandoned or forgotten, partly, I suppose, because we became convinced that there were none—that we had none." As late as 1932 he proposed to his cohorts that they include older American composers at the Yaddo Festival, "as a sort of gesture," exclaiming, "I want roots for the Festival." But at the same time, when asked for specific suggestions, he demurred. "We did not have anybody, really," he reiterated in 1960, contrasting the American situation with that of the English, who had their madrigalists and Purcell. As with many compatriots, his Americanism, aside from the example of Whitman and some other literary figures, was shaped largely by popular culture and the texture and movement of everyday life.[1]

Copland never elaborated on this "search for musical ancestors," though in his Norton lectures he presented a bleak portrait of American

music before the twentieth century, especially in the years prior to the
Civil War. Regarding this earlier era, he spoke of "hardy primitives from
the Revolutionary War period, like William Billings," who wrote pieces
"a bit stiff in their contrapuntal joints," but whose "rough honesty . . .
keeps them alive for present-day listeners"; Louis Moreau Gottschalk,
who made historic use of Latin-American idioms, but who created only
the "exceptional piece" of "original quality," the others "too obviously
designed to dazzle the paying public"; and Stephen Foster, "our own
national hero," who possessed a "simplicity," "sincerity," and "naturalness" of a sort "that has inspired certain types of our own music in
the twentieth century," and yet who "was a song writer rather than a
composer."[2]

Copland felt only slightly closer to those late-nineteenth-century
American composers who had honed their craft in Europe and had
returned to the States "full of admiration for the treasures of European
musical art, with the self-appointed mission of expounding these glories
to their countrymen." They established "professional standards of workmanship" and communicated a "seriousness of purpose" to their students; but they had "little to offer us of a younger generation," in large
part because these composers—especially the leading members of the
Boston school, identified as John Knowles Paine, George Whitefield
Chadwick, Arthur Foote, and Horatio Parker—had an "over-reverence"
for European music. "They loved the masterworks of Europe's mature
culture not like creative personalities but like the schoolmasters that many
of them became."[3]

Copland made something of an exception for Chadwick, whose music
he found "smoothly written" and "varied in style" after he had an opportunity to examine it closely at Harvard in 1952. But he had greater respect
for the more original MacDowell, whose success in escaping "some of the
pitfalls of the New Englanders" he attributed in part to his early training
in Paris. Copland recalled that in 1925 it was MacDowell whom he and
his friends knew best among the older American composers, and that "his
central position as 'foremost composer of his generation' made him especially apt as a target." But over time he came to appreciate, especially in
the smaller pieces, MacDowell's "sensitive and individual poetic gift" and
his "special turn of harmony," features that gave his music the kind of
recognizable profile rarely encountered in American music of that time.[4]

Copland paid greater attention to those Americans still nearer in age,
those born in the 1870s and 1880s. He tended to group these composers

of the previous generation in one of five categories: conservatives (or "official" composers), sophisticates (or "decadents"), folklorists, jazz-related composers, and ultramoderns. The conservatives—like Daniel Gregory Mason, John Powell, and his old teacher Rubin Goldmark—held virtually no interest for him; he showed singular contempt for Mason, once referring to him as "an insufferable, self-righteous ass."[5]

By sophisticates, he principally meant Charles Martin Loeffler and Charles Griffes, both of whom he admired for their daring and polish; he featured Loeffler's Rhapsody no. 1 for oboe, viola, and piano at Yaddo in 1933, and in later years he conducted Griffes's *Poem* for flute and orchestra. But he deplored their detachment from "the grim realities of everyday life" that informed the writings of such literary contemporaries as Theodore Dreiser, Frank Norris, and Carl Sandburg.[6]

In contrast, he thought that the folklorists, including Arthur Farwell and Henry F. Gilbert, had more or less the right idea but lacked the requisite technique. Gilbert's interest in Negro and Creole music appealed to him more than Farwell's use of American Indian music ("We have Indian songs. But what do the songs of the Indians mean to me?" he asked in 1929), and he found Gilbert personally sympathetic when they met at the MacDowell Colony in the summer of 1927. But Gilbert had little influence on Copland, "for the truth is that we were after bigger game," not the "quotable hymn" but "a largeness of utterance wholly representative of the country that Whitman had envisaged."[7]

He seemed similarly removed from those older artists he associated with jazz, such as John Alden Carpenter, E. B. Hill, and Louis Gruenberg. One might have expected more affinity with this group, especially Carpenter, who, as William Austin points out, in particular anticipated his own work. Moreover, Carpenter twice invited Copland to lecture at the prestigious Chicago Arts Club and wrote him a glowing letter after attending a performance of *Billy the Kid*. But although Copland used recordings of Carpenter's music in the classroom and sent his own congratulatory note after the latter won the National Institute of Arts and Letters Gold Medal in 1947 ("As one of the 'runners-up,'" Copland wrote, "I particularly want you to know how pleased I am that the honor went to you—and how well merited I think it is"), he presumably found Carpenter too genteel for much enthusiasm. In any event, the friendship remained remote on both sides.[8]

At the same time, Copland seemed rather cool toward most of the so-called ultramoderns, largely regarding their work as providing only the raw materials for something more accomplished and accessible. He spoke highly, though, of Edgard Varèse's "astonishing percussive imaginings," especially *Arcana* (1927), vividly remembering its premiere by the Philadelphia Orchestra for decades. Moreover, as in the case of Webern, he expanded his treatment of Varèse in the revised *The New Music* (1968), writing, "In the '20s, his work seemed to us limited and somewhat sectarian, but as sometimes happens, it has now taken on a larger significance." During these later years, he led performances of *Ionization* and *Octandre*.[9]

However, of the older generation of American composers, only Charles Ives and Carl Ruggles—both also associated with the ultramoderns—won his real and continued support and advocacy. He initially discovered Ives via Henry Cowell's 1929 publication of the Fourth Symphony's second movement, music that struck him as unjustifiably complex, if not actually unplayable. But in the early thirties, some younger friends encouraged him to examine Ives's *114 Songs*, published privately in 1922. "When I did investigate, I was amazed," recalled Copland. "There we were in the twenties searching for a composer from the older generation with an 'American sound,' and here was Charles Ives composing this incredible music—totally unknown to us!" He subsequently programmed—and performed—seven of these songs with Hubert Linscott at Yaddo in 1932, six with Julius Huehn at a League of Composers concert in 1934, and two ("General William Booth Enters Heaven" and "Charlie Rutlage") with Mordecai Bauman at Town Hall in 1935. These successful airings contributed significantly to Ives's growing reputation.[10]

In addition, Copland published an article on Ives and his *114 Songs* (1932) that later became the basis of the chapter "The Ives Case" in *Our New Music*. Praising the songs for their amazing variety, their originality, and their authenticity and depth of emotion, he also criticized them as fragmentary, overcomplicated, inconsistent in style, and uneven in quality, "more successful as experiments than they are as finished artistic productions." A major problem, he opined, stemmed from Ives's "glorification" of the businessman-composer working in isolation and the resulting deprivation of an audience that "demands and rejects music, that acts as a stimulus and a brake."[11]

Ives appreciated the article, writing Copland a gracious note that took issue, however, with his alleged "glorification" of the businessman: "I was paying my respects to the average man (there is one) in the ordinary business of life, from the ashman down to the president—among whom, it seems to me there was more openmindedness and fair-fighting than among musicians—particularly of my age and generation." Copland remained convinced nonetheless that Ives had written important music in spite of his nonprofessional status, not because of it. He tried, in any case, to get Koussevitzky to play Ives; in 1945, he cited Ives as an American composer particularly deserving exposure abroad; and in 1946 he recommended *Lincoln, the Great Commoner* as "well worth a good struggle on the part of willing interpreters."[12]

Copland revisited the subject of Ives in his Norton lectures (1951–52). Comparing the "largess" of Ives's music to both the geographical immensity of the United States and the "inflated style" of American orators, he thought him analogous to Brazil's Villa-Lobos and starkly unlike Virgil Thomson and Douglas Moore, both of whom represented "another and different aspect of America." At its worst, the music was "amorphous, disheveled, haphazard—like the music of a man who is incapable of organizing his many different thoughts"; at its best was a work like *Central Park in the Dark*, whose various parts "exist independently on different planes." Whatever Ives's eventual significance, Copland discounted his influence on his own generation, "for our knowledge of his work was sketchy—so little of it had been played."[13]

Copland programmed Ives's music early in his conducting career: *The Unanswered Question* became one of the first pieces by another composer to enter his repertory, and in the 1960s he started conducting *Decoration Day* as well. He performed both pieces scores of times all around the globe; he considered them, along with the *Harvest Home Chorales* and the First Piano Sonata, "among the finest works ever created by an American artist." He also read Ives's writings and memos, excerpts of which he copied out into his own notebooks. And he penned the foreword to Vivian Perlis's oral history *Charles Ives Remembered* (1974), a warm if guarded tribute that praised the "richness of human experience" found in Ives's finest music and, more generally, his incredible "daring: no one before him had ever ventured so close to setting down on paper sheer musical chaos." He marveled most, however, at Ives's fortitude: "To write all that music and not hear it one would have to have the courage of a lion." At the Ives Centennial Festival-Conference (1974), he played the piano parts of the Ives songs he had introduced at Yaddo over forty years earlier.[14]

Copland championed Ives to the end. In 1980 he challenged Phillip Ramey's assertion that Ives's importance had been exaggerated in recent years: "Ives may not be everybody's cup of tea, but that's their problem. You're not going to get me to say anything bad about him. What an original character!" One of his great regrets was never meeting Ives; a sense of delicacy over the older composer's frail health kept Copland from calling on him at home.[15]

Ives arguably influenced Copland's late work and possibly some of his earlier music as well; "Charlie Rutlage," for example, which "stopped the show" at Yaddo, may have suggested ways in which a modernist style could accommodate evocations of the American West. But as in the case with Ruggles, Ives offered Copland more generally a model of integrity and courage—along with some cautionary lessons.

By the time Copland met Carl Ruggles through Stieglitz in the late twenties, he presumably had some acquaintance with Ruggles's music, given its high profile in New York's avant-garde community. In 1930 he visited Ruggles in his country home; in 1931 he arranged for *Portals* (1925) to be performed on an all-American concert conducted by Ernest Ansermet in Berlin; and in 1933 he programmed and arranged excerpts from *Men and Angels* at Yaddo. He greatly admired *Portals*—Ruggles's astringent grandiosity accorded with the tenor of some of his own work— and in the 1960s he added it, along with *Men and Mountains* (1924), to his conducting repertory. In 1964 he further made a private recording of his performance of *Portals* with the Boston Symphony for the composer, whom he described as "an interesting old codger—a real character in the American sense" who "wrote works that are surprisingly personal and passionate and very convincing." That he would champion an openly anti-Semitic curmudgeon who was basically interested only in his own music, speaks to Copland's utter commitment to the cause of American music. At the same time, he consistently observed Ruggles's limitations, criticizing in particular his tiny output and narrow emotional scope and taking issue with Virgil Thomson's attempt to "put Ives down to the advantage of Ruggles."[16]

If Copland came up shorthanded in his search for a "usable past," he considered the search itself something of a moral imperative and a professional obligation. "Composers nowadays seem to have no sense of history whatsoever," he complained in 1968, "and practically no interest in where they came from, or how they got here, or why we are where we are now. You can't imagine how distressing to me that is. It makes our younger men seem so primitive, like savages on an island who have no conception of how anything happened, and couldn't care less. It may have a healthy side to it, of course, but it seems to me somewhat poverty-stricken to have no curiosity at all as to your own historical background." On a more humorous note, he ironically identified with his previously scorned forebears. "Whenever I meet some 20-year-old composer nowadays who seems less than admiring," he stated in 1960, "I think 'Well, *we* were pretty tough on Edward MacDowell. I suppose it's *our* turn now!' "[17]

Jazz and Popular Music

Without a vital concert tradition to build on, Copland concluded that America's serious composers might well look to their folklore; and like Carpenter, Gershwin, and others, he considered jazz and popular music a kind of folklore and an especially appealing one. "If we haven't a folksong foundation, we must invent one," he argued in 1925. "I began by thinking—what is folksong after all? And I came to the conclusion that in my case it was the songs I heard when I was a child—rather commonplace jazz tunes and music of the 'Old Black Joe' variety. These, then, are my material, and I must accept them for what they are."[18]

During these early years, Copland obviously used the word *jazz* broadly, even more so than was typical in the 1920s, when it commonly described varieties of so-called real jazz (or "hot" jazz), arranged dance music (or "sweet" jazz), popular song, and ragtime and novelty piano pieces. For the young Copland, "jazz" formed a sort of continuum from the Stephen Foster melodies sung at school to the ragtime played at home to the improvisational jazz heard in clubs. Consequently, when he says that he and his Brooklyn friends listened to "the exciting, pulsating jazz rhythms" in one another's apartments, one cannot be sure what this means—especially considering that nothing now considered to be jazz had been recorded at this point in time—but it apparently included renditions of Irving Berlin and W. C. Handy.[19]

Copland initially considered all this music pedestrian. "You mustn't forget," he told Gilbert Seldes, "that I was born in Brooklyn, and that in Brooklyn we used to hear jazz around all the time—it was just an ordinary thing." Hearing jazz (or what passed for jazz) in a bar in Vienna in 1923 (apparently the Weinberg Bar, where the black Charleston-born Arthur Briggs had a long-standing engagement) gave him a new perspective; he was fascinated by how American this music sounded in such a foreign context: "When I heard jazz played in Vienna, it was like hearing it for the first time. It was then that I first began to realize the potentiality of jazz material for use in serious music." Copland remained intrigued; in

June 1924 he told a reporter that he had "nightly been haunting the Paris cafés where Jazz is played." In these cafés he might have heard real jazz musicians, including perhaps the clarinetist Sidney Bechet, who regularly performed in Paris during these years.[20]

With the full approval of Boulanger, he also began consciously abstracting jazz elements in his ballet, *Grohg* (1922–25). He had instinctively been leaning in that direction since 1920, but Europe's infatuation with American popular music no doubt encouraged such inclinations. Especially in these early years, he viewed such music as fodder for an art music that would surpass it in seriousness, sophistication, intensity, personality, and formal coherence. He considered figures like Kern and Berlin songwriters rather than composers and regarded their work as "limited." "You can only hear popular songs so many times before you want to hear another popular song," he would joke.[21]

Still, after his return to New York, he continued searching out jazz, venturing into some clubs in the West Fifties, where one could hear the likes of Bix Beiderbecke and Benny Carter, and up to Harlem's Cotton Club, where Duke Ellington and his band performed. In 1925 he took Koussevitzky to a few jazz clubs, reporting, "He listened carefully, then said, 'It's just like the gypsies; it's just like the gypsies.' And it is. Like the wild, impassioned, improvised music of the Russian gypsy."[22]

With *Music for the Theatre* (1925) and the Piano Concerto (1926), both composed, significantly, for Koussevitzky, Copland followed the path only tentatively explored in earlier works and made blatant, explicit, occasionally parodistic use of jazzy rhythms, colors, and moods. At the time, such works were called "symphonic jazz"; Copland employed the term himself, though he later referred to them more simply as his "jazz works." "Any piece based on jazz was assured of a mild *succès de scandale*," he recalled, and such proved the case with both *Music for the Theatre* and even more so the Piano Concerto. But for Copland the use of jazz meant more than mere notoriety; it signified a defiant badge of contemporary urban America.[23]

In discussions of symphonic jazz, Copland often used the adjectives *piquant* and *grotesque*. It is not clear exactly what he found piquant and grotesque, the use of jazz in concert music or early jazz itself, but he apparently meant both. The word *grotesque* betokened to him the wilder, "almost hysterical" side of jazz—as well as the ragtime-inspired music of Debussy and Stravinsky—while *piquant* he associated with the blues—as well as with Weill's *Threepenny Opera*. A 1929 statement further suggested a connection between the "grotesque" and the "excitement" of city life, and the "piquant" and the "sensuality" of sex.[24]

After the Piano Concerto, Copland more or less put the idea of symphonic jazz behind him. In one of his most controversial and oft-quoted remarks, he explained, in 1941, "With the Concerto I felt I had done all I could with the idiom, considering its limited emotional scope. True, it was an easy way to be American in musical terms, but all American music could not possibly be confined to two dominant jazz moods—the blues and the snappy number." He had criticized the "spirit" of jazz as early as 1927, in his article "Jazz Structure and Influence," written at a time when other composers—including Carpenter, Milhaud, and Krenek—similarly had begun to distance themselves from jazz. But many—including, recently, Martha Bayles—misconstrued Copland's 1941 remark to mean that he had written jazz off, whereas he essentially meant that he had renounced the parodistic mannerisms of symphonic jazz.[25]

In fact, "Jazz Structure" became the first of many statements that argued for and sought to explain jazz's crucial importance to the American composer. In this early essay he emphasized jazz's rhythm, whose growing complexities he traced from the ragtime hits of Irving Berlin to the fox-trot to newer techniques that could more definitely be described as polyrhythmic, including syncopation without any "evenly rhythmed bass," as in the Charleston, or conflicting metrical patterns, as in Zez Confrey's "Stumblin' " or Gershwin's "Fascinatin' Rhythm." He could not locate any comparable rhythmic phenomenon in the European repertory; even the polyrhythms of the English madrigalists did not contain the "peculiar excitement" derived from jazz's habit of "clashing two definitely and regularly marked rhythms." For Europeans, consequently, jazz represented an exotic novelty that they could take or leave; but "since jazz is not exotic here but indigenous, since it is the music an American has heard as a child, it will be traceable more and more frequently in his symphonies and concertos." Once "freed of its present connotations," Copland predicted, jazz will "stir" the American composer: "It may be the substance not only of his fox trots and Charlestons but of his lullabies and nocturnes. He may express through it not always gaiety but love, tragedy, remorse."[26]

"Jazz Structure" had its usefulness, including providing a theoretical foundation for Winthrop Sargeant's *Jazz: A History*. But as an analysis of real jazz, it left much wanting, as has long been pointed out; Copland, after all, primarily had in mind popular tunesmiths as opposed to improvising performers. It should be remembered, however, that this early article took as its subject not so much jazz per se as the influence of jazz on the concert composers of the time, and in that regard, the emphasis on Berlin and Gershwin made some sense. At any rate, he stood behind the article's basic tenets for many years.[27]

As large swing bands began to flourish in the 1930s, Copland took a renewed interest in jazz, perhaps spurred on in this respect by such younger friends as Paul Bowles, who as early as 1932 wrote to him, "I think Duke Ellington is really the best source for inspiration." Copland's 1936 course for the New School, What to Listen for in Music, cited Duke Ellington—his first public acknowledgment of a real jazz musician—and included some discussion of the jazz band under the subject of tone color. In a 1938 review, he praised recent recordings by Benny Goodman, Tommy Dorsey, Bunny Berrigan, Fats Waller, and especially Duke Ellington, "the master of them all. . . . Ellington is a composer, by which I mean, he comes nearer to knowing how to make a piece hang together than the others." His admiration for some of the commercially successful big bands did not hinder his appreciation, voiced in a 1939 review, for the more "untrammelled expressions of Negro folk art," as represented by the boogie-woogie of Meade Lux Lewis and Albert Ammons. "We mustn't make the mistake of 'Brahms or Wagner' over again," he warned his readers. "Duke Ellington may still be listened to." In the same review, he further recommended a recording of Congolese folk music: "They have a marvelous tang and savor, plus an intoxicating rhythmic intricacy that all the history books mention in relation to primitive music, but which we seldom have heard to so authentic a degree."[28]

These reviews and other writings from the period show a new respect for jazz: not only for its rhythms, but for the unusual sounds made with traditional instruments, the "supervirtuosity" of the individual jazz musician, and the idiom's "brazenly dissonant" harmonies. "A few more years of such harmonic liberties," he observed, "and Stravinsky's boldest flights in that field will sound quite tame to the man in the street."[29]

Throughout the 1930s, his own music continued to reflect jazz, at times quite explicitly, as in the ballet Hear Ye! Hear Ye! and the opera The Second Hurricane. By 1945, he even expected some near convergence of jazz and concert music, a development thought to represent "the levelling, the democratic trend, in contemporary music. The barriers are down, the classifications are disappearing." He himself contributed to this hope with his *Four Piano Blues* and his Clarinet Concerto for Benny Goodman (both 1948). But by the 1950s he had reversed himself, predicting that, despite the growing presence of jazz musicians with classical backgrounds and classical musicians with jazz backgrounds, jazz and concert music would remain distinct and separate. "The two fields will continue to borrow and perhaps eventually will overlap," he wrote in 1958. "But I don't feel that there ever will be one form."[30]

In his discussion of jazz in his Norton lectures (1951–52), Copland stressed, in contrast to his earlier writings, African-American culture, jazz's global connections, the art of improvisation, and the importance of the phonograph, which "makes it possible to preserve and thereby savor the fine flavor of what is necessarily a lucky chance result." Indeed, assertions by others to the contrary, he emphasized improvisation—as he had rhythm in the 1920s and timbre in the 1930s—as an aspect of jazz that offered considerable potential to serious composers, in that it stood opposed to the growing and questionable trend toward "absolute exactitude in the execution of the printed page." At the same time, he differentiated jazz from the chance compositions of John Cage, a distinction he maintained in later years.[31]

Although he admired jazz in all its phases, Copland particularly liked the "modern" or "cool" jazz of the 1950s. Again younger friends helped. Erik Johns, for instance, took him to a Dave Brubeck concert and played recordings of Lennie Tristano for him. But Copland also pursued such investigations on his own. In his Norton lectures, he discussed and played, in addition to Brubeck and Tristano, Oscar Pettiford and Bud Powell. Another friend, John Kennedy, recalled that Copland also liked the Modern Jazz Quartet. He may have felt especially close to these jazz musicians because their style and aesthetic came, in some ways, close to his own.[32]

Such interests climaxed around 1960, as suggested not only by scores like the *Piano Fantasy* and *Something Wild* but by written and spoken remarks, including two 1958 interviews with Don Gold and Gilbert Seldes. Discussing a wide range of jazz styles and figures—Dixieland, Louis Armstrong, Duke Ellington, Stan Kenton, Charles Mingus, Lennie Tristano, Teo Macero, Jimmy Giuffre, Shelly Manne, George Russell, Miles Davis, and Billy Taylor—he told Gold that he wished he could take a month off and listen to the latest jazz.[33]

In some of these publications, he expounded on what he felt to be the virtues and limitations of jazz. He praised its contrapuntal textures, its bold harmonies, and its lively spontaneity, singling out for special praise Ellington, Davis, and two of his favorites, Mingus and Tristano. If he ever regularly taught composition, he said he would introduce his students to the latest jazz, "for the freedom of invention present." At the same time, he criticized jazz's formal looseness and, while disavowing earlier remarks about jazz having only two primary moods, its expressive limitations: "Jazz does not do what serious music does either in its range of emotional expressivity nor in its depth of feeling, nor in its universality of language. It does have universality of appeal, which is not the same thing." And while he expressed a preference for jazz "free and untrammelled, as far removed from the regular commercial product as possible," he cautioned against jazz's becoming too sophisticated: "Erudition in jazz often has a phony sound."[34]

In 1968, Copland, citing Ornette Coleman and Jimmy Giuffre, appraised the changing relationship between jazz and concert music: "In recent times, the tables have turned insofar as jazz influence is concerned: jazz has been more influenced by serious music than the other way around." As for Gunther Schuller's "third-stream music," he thought such efforts hampered by the seemingly insuperable problem of getting classically trained musicians to improvise in a jazz style. On the other hand, the fusion of "serious and jazz idioms" in the work of Larry Austin and David Reck suggested that "the last word has not yet been said on the influence of jazz on serious composition, at least in America."[35]

Copland also took note of developments in American popular music, including in the 1960s, when rock—especially Simon and Garfunkel and the Beatles—caught the fancy of his younger friends. Copland, who had by this point long distinguished jazz from popular music, put rock into the latter category, even referring to it as "light" music; but he acknowledged its newness and its appeal. "The music is powerful," he stated in 1967. "I'm taken up with it too." The idiom, he argued, marked an advance for American popular music in terms of subtlety and complexity, which suggested that the rock generation was "more open to new musical experience than many of their elders." He worried, however, about the decibel levels at the discotheques he had visited; and as with jazz, he noted the music's limitations: "Marvelous as rock music may be, it's circumscribed by the kind of thing it's trying to do. There are other moods in life which are not able to be expressed in terms of rock." Moreover, he cautioned against such institutions as symphony orchestras engaging rock bands for financial reasons: "I can see the temptation. But it's dangerous. The minute you start matching the box office in terms of art you are going to get into trouble."[36]

Even in his eighties, Copland remained interested in jazz, thanking Barbara Kolb in 1982 for recordings of Chick Corea and Gary Burton. And he always acknowledged the "radical" and "unique" contribution jazz had made to concert music in America: "Even if you're not thinking about jazz rhythms, it just comes out that way." He also recognized that jazz's worldwide appeal helped nurture friendly feelings toward the United States. Yet he rejected the notion of jazz as the country's "major" contribution to the art of music and consistently pleaded that more be done on behalf of American concert music abroad.[37]

Copland's use of jazz in his own music initially won, at least among elite critics, a generally positive, sometimes even enthusiastic response. Listeners as different as Edmund Wilson, E. B. Hill, Paul Rosenfeld, Lawrence Gilman, Isaac Goldberg, and Henry Cowell commended the imagination, skill, and individuality with which he employed the idiom. The most extended such discussion, Goldberg's "Aaron Copland and His Jazz" (1927), further extolled his sincerity and ease:

A Brooklynite by birth, a New Yorker by residence, he grew up in the very midst of our musical capital during the period when our popular song was tearing through its race from rag-time to jazz. This was his folk music and his cradle song. He does not come to it from the background of a millennial culture; therefore, not even unconsciously does he condescend to it. He weaves it into his writing as naturally as one employs the rhythms and accents of one's childhood.

The negative reactions to Copland's jazz works—and they were many and sometimes violent—tended to take issue more with their modernist implications than with their jazziness per se.[38]

The critical consensus shifted in the early 1930s as writers like R. D. Darrell and Constant Lambert compared Copland's symphonic jazz unfavorably to real jazz. In the ensuing decades, many expert critics, including Hall Overton, Sidney Finkelstein, Wilfrid Mellers, David Ross Baskerville, and Hugo Cole, judged his use of jazz a mistake. Overton argued that he had failed to digest it the way Bartók had assimilated Hungarian folk music; Cole and many others felt that jazz itself defied assimilation into a concert idiom. Finkelstein and Mellers emphasized the superficiality of Copland's jazz works, their appropriation of the "hard-boiled surface" of jazz but not its "inner pathos"; Copland ironically came closer to the true spirit of jazz, argued Mellers, only after he had renounced such self-conscious appropriations. Baskerville similarly found Copland's jazz pieces from the 1920s "among his weakest works," writing, "He ended up sounding more American when he forgot all about jazz."[39]

Aside from the fact that Copland's jazz-inspired pieces from the 1920s continue, over seventy years later, to attract large numbers of listeners, a problem with such remarks resides in the idea that he subsequently "forgot all about jazz." On the contrary, his respect for jazz only deepened over the years; moreover, he made use of jazz throughout his career. Elliott Carter was one of those rare critics who observed the presence of jazz elements in his style quite generally. Copland himself often acknowledged the debt he and other American composers owed to jazz and popular music, writing, for instance, that "the rhythmic life in the scores of Roy Harris, William Schuman, Marc Blitzstein, and a host of other representative American composers is indubitably linked to Negroid sources of rhythm."[40]

The common notion that Copland left jazz behind in the 1920s seems, in short, simplistic. During the 1930s and beyond, he at times employed American and Latin folk tunes, but he adapted such tunes to a highly personal, jazz-related style, in a way not unlike the way jazz musicians themselves appropriated such materials. In still later years, he accommodated jazzy rhythms and gestures to Schoenberg's twelve-tone method; still later, to Ivesian multiplaned textures. But jazz remained central to his musical style and imagination.[41]

9

From the *Organ Symphony* to "Vocalise"

(1924–28)

Serge Koussevitzky

In the spring of 1923, upon hearing that Serge Koussevitzky would take over the Boston Symphony starting with the 1924–25 season, Boulanger took Copland to meet the esteemed maestro at his Paris apartment; she rightly assumed that Koussevitzky, an indefatigable champion of new music, would want to meet a talented young composer from his future homeland. Copland played his *Cortège Macabre* at the piano, with, to his dismay, a visiting Prokofiev looking over his shoulder. After he finished, despite a critical outburst from Prokofiev ("too much bassi osinanti"), Koussevitzky announced his intention of playing the work during his first year in Boston; realizing, too, that Boulanger was scheduled to make her American debut with Walter Damrosch and the New York Symphony Orchestra that same season, he further requested a new work by Copland for organ and orchestra for her to perform in Boston. Boulanger subsequently persuaded Damrosch to premiere this new work, thus securing for Copland two high-profile performances—a remarkable commission for someone who had never heard a note of his orchestral music. "It was very tempting," he remembered, "but *very* scary."[1]

Serge Koussevitzky (1874–1951) never performed the *Cortège*, but he played, as promised, the *Symphony for Organ and Orchestra* and went on to perform a number of other Copland works in the course of his long tenure with the Boston Symphony (1924–49)—a total of twelve works, culminating with the *Third Symphony*. A number of these pieces he himself commissioned and premiered. In addition, his recordings of *El Salón México*, *Lincoln Portrait*, and *Appalachian Spring* went far in furthering Copland's reputation. In short, he became the composer's most important advocate—at least before the emergence of Leonard Bernstein—and only Nadia Boulanger played, perhaps, a more decisive role in his professional life.

A virtuoso double bassist, a protégé of the conductor Arthur Nikisch, and a composer in his own right, Koussevitzky had a long track record promoting the work of young composers. Before leaving Moscow for Paris in 1920, he supported Scriabin, Stravinsky, Prokofiev, and other Russian composers, not only as a conductor but, thanks to the resources of his wife, Natalie, as a publisher and benefactor. Similarly, in Paris from 1920 to 1924, he championed Honegger and Milhaud. Now, with his Boston appointment, he nurtured an array of American composers, again not only as a conductor but, through the establishment of the Berkshire Music Center and the Koussevitzky Foundation, as educator and patron. Copland was only one of many to benefit from his largesse, but few if any profited more than he did.[2]

As for Koussevitzky's strengths as a conductor, Hugo Leichtentritt and others pointed to his brilliant and velvety sonorities, his rhythmic precision and vigor, his flexibility of tempo and line, his careful attention to detail, and his relaxed podium manner.[3]

In his own discussions of Koussevitzky, Copland used the same words time and again: "conviction," "enthusiasm," "excitement," "faith," "confidence," "vitality," "energy," "courage," and (as regards detractors) "unfazed," describing traits that enabled him to wear down the resistance of orchestral musicians, critics, and audiences to new music. "Dee next Beethoven vill from Colorado come!" Koussevitzky would exhort in his Russian accent. Other conductors, Copland observed, may have played more new music, but no one rivaled him in making the premiere of a new work seem so important—a perception attained through ample rehearsal time, consultations with the composer, and prominent placement of new works on programs, as well as through the exuberance of the conducting and the realistic expectation that the work might well enter his repertoire.

Premieres by other conductors seemed "perfunctory by comparison." "Just as every ten-year-old American boy dreams of being President some day," wrote Copland, "so every twenty-year-old American composer dreams of being played by Koussevitzky."[4]

Koussevitzky held Copland—or "Arosha," as he sometimes called him—in special regard. As early as 1929 he singled him out as outstanding among U.S. composers; ultimately he performed more of his music than that of any other American of Copland's generation. He also relied on Copland's good judgment, exploring the music of Roger Sessions, Roy Harris, William Schuman, David Diamond, Irving Fine, and others on his recommendation. When in 1940 Koussevitzky fulfilled a lifelong dream by founding the Berkshire Music Center for the training of young orchestral musicians and composers, as part of the summer Boston Symphony festival at Tanglewood, he appointed Copland assistant director.[5]

The importance of Koussevitzky to Copland's career is demonstrated by the fact that during those years when he performed twelve Copland works, even the country's most progressive conductors conducted only a few of his pieces. Frederick Stock performed far more Carpenter; Leopold Stokowski, more Cowell, Ives, and Riegger; Artur Rodzinski, more Barber; Dimitri Mitropoulos, more Schoenberg and Krenek. Despite Copland's residence in Manhattan, the New York Philharmonic gave surprisingly few performances of his music.[6]

At the same time, Copland apparently did little to ingratiate himself with other conductors, in part, perhaps, because he often found them in one way or another objectionable. He took a negative tone toward Damrosch; where he thought it courageous for Koussevitzky to program *Music for the Theatre* on the heels of the *Organ Symphony*, he dismissed the identical move on Damrosch's part as out of character, emphasizing, rather, that Damrosch had indiscreetly questioned a particular harmony of his in front of the entire orchestra. He criticized Pierre Monteux's uneven interpretations and Stokowski's alleged superficiality. "I can see he has no depth of feeling whatever and practically no sense of style," he said about Stokowski to Koussevitzky in an untypically severe critique that seems unabashedly pitched to the Koussevitzky-Stokowski rivalry. Copland even reproached his good friend Bernstein for unauthorized cuts and hasty rehearsals.[7]

The fact remains, too, that Koussevitzky could be a thrilling interpreter of Copland's music. Harry Ellis Dickson, the Boston Symphony violinist who played Copland's music under innumerable conductors, remembered Koussevitzky's Copland as the most exciting of his career. Koussevitzky's recorded performances of Copland offer weight to Dickson's claims, performances full of verve and warmth, and wonderfully attuned to the music's distinctively American sensibilities—remarkably so, considering the conductor's relatively late arrival in the States. In *El Salón México*, he encourages the players to go hilariously nasal in imitation of a mariachi band, revealing a bold sense of fun, and his *Appalachian Spring* remains one of the best on record, a lush reading marked by some fast tempos that practically swing. One can better understand Copland's regard for Serge Alexandrovitch, as he addressed the conductor, or "Koussey," as he referred to him, by comparing this latter recording with preserved radio broadcasts of the same work by Rodzinski and Monteux.[8]

For all its importance, one need not exaggerate this particular relationship. Discussing Koussevitzky's rendition of the Third Symphony, Copland wrote that although the conductor could "whip up a storm," his Russian "point of view" tended to make him "lean on" sections in a way unsuited to the music's "American simplicity." Others recalled that Koussevitzky had trouble coping with Copland's rhythmic demands, an assertion borne out by the recording of *El Salón*. For his part, Koussevitzky, whose tastes were relatively conservative, rarely retained a Copland work in his repertory—he was more likely to repeat a piece by Loeffler, Hill, Carpenter, Hanson, or Hadley. And although he championed Harris in the 1930s, he took little interest in other composers whom Copland held in high regard, such as Thomson, Chávez, Blitzstein, and Ives. In the course of his tenure, however, Koussevitzky performed over 150 American works with, in Copland's opinion, the right attitude. Both men knew that they were fighting the same fight.[9]

Copland also had warm and supportive associations with the two Madames Koussevitzky: Natalie, who died in 1942, and her niece Olga, Serge's secretary since 1929 and his wife after 1947. Natalie tried raising funds for Copland's causes, though "among the miserly Bostonians," as she wrote to him, this required "much eloquence" and sometimes brought "meagre results." Having a background in music publishing, she also helped advise him in matters regarding the Cos Cob Press. Olga and Copland similarly worked together closely, especially on the Koussevitzky Foundation, which she directed after Serge's death. In 1953, during Copland's troubles with McCarthy, she provided a four-page sworn affidavit on his worthiness to receive a passport; she reminded the authorities that her late husband—and Copland's principal champion—had twice been honored by the czar.[10]

The *Organ Symphony*

The 1924 *Symphony for Organ and Orchestra* (or *Organ Symphony* as it is commonly known)—the work with which Copland made his initial reputation—contains three movements: a short, reflective prelude; a jaunty scherzo, with a slower, bluesy trio section; and an imposing finale, moderate in tempo and varied in mood, and cast in a modified sonata form. Copland composed the first movement in France and the second two movements in the States, making it, quite literally, a transition between the more French-oriented *Grohg* and the more assertively American *Music for the Theatre*.

Copland originally intended a four-movement work that would open with what ultimately became the finale (which possibly explains the use of sonata form for this particular movement); but he eventually decided upon his unusual three-movement design (slow-fast-moderate, with each movement getting longer), defending the idea to Boulanger by citing Honegger's First Violin Sonata. If Copland actually took his cue in this regard from Honegger, then the French composer played a greater role in his development than one would have imagined; for such a format, or some derivative of it, became one of his most characteristic gestures.

The expressive qualities found in each movement also portend his later work. Although he criticized the piece early on as "too 'European' in derivation," he later recognized it as "closer to my natural expressive idiom than I had realized." The prelude, more wistful than sad, features that bittersweet, pastoral mood so characteristic of its composer. The scherzo reveals an equally familiar hallmark in its evocation of modern urban life—here propulsive, mechanical, jazzy, with an ironically robotized quotation of the French tune "Au Clair de la Lune," an homage, surely, to Boulanger, to whom the score is dedicated. And the finale, alternately dirgelike and urgent (the composer's prophetic voice already making itself heard), ends triumphantly, as his music often does.[11]

Neil Butterworth points out that all of the symphony's material derives from the prelude's opening four measures. In addition, Copland highlights a three-note motto (a B minor triad spelled D–B–F-sharp) not found per se in these opening bars but first stated obscurely by the solo organ halfway through the movement; the trumpet's first entrance, although pianissimo and muted, brings this motto, for the first time, to the fore. After further use in all three movements, Copland states the motto a final time, tutti and triple forte, near the work's very end. This growth—from obscurity to emblazoned climax—helps give the work its sweeping grandeur.[12]

Formally, the only problematic movement is the finale. Its sonata form—amply described by Copland as consisting of a first theme (incorporating the three-note motto) played by the violas; a second "more vigorous theme" introduced by the strings over a basso ostinato comprised of the three-note motto; a development section initiated by the solo organ followed soon after by a "vivacious" theme for solo violin; and a short recapitulation that juxtaposes the movement's "four main elements" (presumably the first theme, the "more vigorous" second theme, the basso ostinato, and the "vivacious" theme)—is not easy for even an experienced listener to grasp. In fact, the movement, in contrast to the neat hierarchy of the classical sonata form, feels more like a passacaglia, what with its opening unison theme, its contrapuntal exposition, its repetitive bass lines, its lack of clear thematic contrast, and, perhaps above all, its tonal stasis. Such an unusual, spontaneous design itself would prove characteristic; Copland used sonata form only occasionally, and then in idiosyncratic ways. As is often the case with Copland's more ambitious work, the listener might best focus on identifying the principal themes and noting their inventive developments and juxtapositions.[13]

Copland wrote that in this work, the "organ is treated as an integral part of the orchestra rather than as a solo instrument with orchestral accompaniment," the rationale, one imagines, for calling it a symphony as opposed to a concerto. Still, it is a concerto in every way but name; the soloist plays most of the time and even has some cadenzalike passages. In any case, the work's brilliant scoring announces the arrival of a master orchestrator. Here, the organ inspires complementary colors not necessarily found in his later work—for instance, the remarkable opening of the scherzo, as the little bits for flutes, clarinets, and oboes combine to create a breathy whirligig. In other respects, the work anticipates a century of American symphonic writing at its most characteristic, from the dry and sober (common assumptions to the contrary, Copland's oft-cited "sobriety" predates his Depression-era works) to the delicately sensuous, from the loud and brassy to the richly eloquent (as in the fugato for strings that opens the last movement, a coloring that anticipates Harris, Piston, Schuman, and others).

Stylistically, the work has debts to traditional Jewish music as well as to jazz; some of the prelude's melancholy lyricism evokes Jewish song, while the "vivacious" theme in the last movement suggests Jewish dance. At times these idioms seem to blend; when the jazzy rhythms break down into sprightly groups of 3+3+2, the music seems as close to the hora as to the Charleston. However, Copland draws upon such sources in a highly personal way, and though the work still seems eclectic compared to later scores, what comes to the fore is his own strong personality.

Overall the *Organ Symphony* seems less persuasive than some other Copland scores from the 1920s. Some of the music possibly goes on too long given the nature of the material, a criticism frequently leveled at Copland during these early years, but truer here than in other works. The last movement in particular sprawls. But such flaws are more than compensated for by the music's vitality, brilliance, and individuality. Still, the symphony became one of those works more talked about than played, without even a commercial recording until 1968, when Leonard Bernstein and the New York Philharmonic issued one with organist E. Power Biggs. Recently, Leonard Slatkin and the St. Louis Symphony Orchestra, with organist Simon Preston, also recorded the work, which remains something of a novelty.

In an attempt to make the work more practical, Copland transcribed the *Organ Symphony* for orchestra without organ, with added brass and saxophone to compensate for the missing solo part—first just the middle movement as *Scherzo*, introduced by Fritz Reiner in Philadelphia in 1927, and then the entire work as the First Symphony (1928), premiered by Ernest Ansermet in Berlin in 1931. He also transcribed the "Prelude" movement both for chamber orchestra and for piano trio. One naturally misses the contrast of the organ in all these versions, but they help clarify his intentions, making them a fascinating complement to the original. Moreover, the music appears less ghoulish without the organ, which, depending on one's taste, may or may not be an asset.

Copland recorded the First Symphony with the Orchestre National de France in his later years. This live performance lacked the polish of the Bernstein and Slatkin recordings of the *Organ Symphony*, but the interpretation was particularly incisive, with slower tempos that allowed for greater attention to detail. In Copland's hands, for instance, the prelude seemed less smoothly waltzlike than intensely songful. Copland also more clearly underscored the music's affinity with the objective modernism of Hindemith and Honegger, making its occasional moments of romantic effusion all the more effective, even heartrending.[15]

Music for the Theatre

In 1925, Claire Reis, on behalf of the League of Composers, requested from Copland a work for chamber orchestra for Koussevitzky and members of the Boston Symphony to be premiered in New York later that year—the very first work commissioned by the newly founded composers guild. Copland originally considered a setting of Rimbaud's *Une Saison en Enfer* (*A Season in Hell*) but decided, instead, on "a series of pieces to be called 'Incidental Music for an Imaginary Drama,'" later retitled *Music for the Theatre*. He composed most of the piece during the summer of 1925 at the MacDowell Colony, and he completed it in September at a summer camp in Lake Placid run by his former piano teacher Clarence Adler. Adler, who heard Copland working on the composition, left us this vivid reminiscence: "He bangs and hammers at the piano, at the same time singing in shrill, dissonant tones."[16]

Copland scored *Music for the Theatre* for a very small orchestra, as few as eighteen musicians, depending on the number of strings. He seems to have had in mind the kind of commercial pit bands that form the background to the work—as well as, perhaps, Milhaud's *La Création du monde*, which was similarly inspired by jazz. For the work's subtitle, *Suite in Five Parts,* he used the word *part* as opposed to the more traditional *movement*, thereby suggesting not only the relatively brief length of the individual sections but the striking emotional distance from part to part, which, like theatrical incidental music, almost presumes the kind of lapsed time that spoken dialogue or changes of scenery would bring.

Each of the five parts—entitled "Prologue," "Dance," "Interlude," "Burlesque," and "Epilogue"—forms an arch, as does the work as a whole. The first, second, and fourth movements are more specifically in ABA form, with a middle contrasting section. But throughout, Copland refashions his restatements to such an extent that these forms are less schematic than might appear thus described; indeed, the music's often slight but ever-present variants provide some of its more subtle delights.

"Prologue" begins with a jazzy trumpet fanfare (featuring unmeasured accelerations of a type also found in the *Organ Symphony*) that puts forth a crucial motive that leaps upward by a fifth, then by a sixth; this fanfare leads directly into a cadential figure of three descending whole steps that forms the work's other major motto. The score directs the first trumpet to play "sharp, fast, clear, nervous"; the unusual directive "nervous" stands out—it is one to which Copland will frequently return and which highlights a distinctive aspect not only of this often tremulous piece but of his art in general. The strings and winds develop the descending whole-step motive in a kind of blues chorale (anticipating many future hymnlike passages in Copland) that, by the end of the movement's A section, finally subdues the trumpet's opening fanfare. The movement's snazzy B section in essence restates the A material, but ingeniously masked beyond easy recognition. The return of A, drastically shortened, leaves a more full recapitulation of this material to the concluding "Epilogue."

As with the later "Burlesque" movement, "Dance" lovingly evokes the sassy vigor of America in the 1920s. The bold dissonances, knotty cross-rhythms, and dazzling colors allow Copland additional audacities of his own, in the process creating what such critics of the day as Warren Storey Smith called "super jazz." The B section, with its jazz mutes, its relentless vamps, and its directives for the instrumentalists to occasionally play "a little sharp" or "a little flat," further evokes jazz instrumental practices. Like popular musicians of the day, Copland also quotes an old tune, "The Sidewalks of New York" (1904), for ironic effect, recasting the song's waltzlike exuberance into an angular, mechanized 5/8. Besides reminding us that the work is, on one level, a portrait of New York, the fragmented tune puns the descending whole-step motive, raising the question of whether Copland had this tune in mind from the work's very inception.

The bluesy "Interlude" introduces for possibly the first time that lonely, night-in-the-city ambience so characteristic of the mature composer, including the sumptuous scoring for English horn, soft trumpet in its high register, and solo violin. In addition, whereas the work's other movements derive some of their bite from a kind of bitonal clashing of keys, "Interlude" effects its own mood through a kind of modal haziness one might call bimodality; the opening English horn melody cadences in one mode as the orchestra joins in another, like a traditional deceptive cadence, but here sounding quite fresh and made all the more captivating through the interlocking accompanying figures for piano and celesta. The music makes such a strong impression that one can barely recognize its origins in the Dance of the Opium-Eater from *Grohg* and the slow movement of the *Organ Symphony*.

Although European composers also wrote burlesques, Copland took his inspiration for "Burlesque" directly from America's burlesque houses, a distinctive theatrical milieu, even more earthy than vaudeville, that featured off-color comics and scantily clad women. Burlesque houses of various degrees of vulgarity had become especially popular in New York in the 1920s, especially in the Forty-second Street area, where they sat side by side with more "legitimate" theaters. While prudish New Yorkers viewed such entertainment with dismay, many young artists and intellectuals saw in burlesque, as in the equally controversial jazz, a vital American art form, comparable and yet different from the Parisian dance hall and the German cabaret. The burlesque houses of Forty-second Street, the hub of New York's gay ghetto in the 1920s, in particular attracted homosexuals, who appreciated their flouting of traditional sexual mores.[17]

Copland's music suggests burlesque's two most characteristic faces: the fast-talking, bawdy comics in section A and the sexually suggestive dancers in the contrasting middle section, which features a hilariously vulgar theme for trumpets (that rudely distorts the opening fanfare), marked "grotesco," against a plodding ostinato bass (derived from the descending whole-step motive). This surely was the passage that caused Roy Harris to jump up and shout, "It's whorehouse music! It's whorehouse music!" when Copland played some of the score for him. The climactic restatement of the "grotesco" theme at the movement's end even evokes the final moments (often the baring of breasts) of a burlesque striptease; if "Dance" is "super jazz," this is "super burlesque."[18]

Copland's admission that "Burlesque" was "partly inspired" by Fanny Brice provides further resonance to the movement. Born in 1891, the daughter of Jewish immigrants, the singer-comedian Brice, known for her "manic mimicry and exuberant buffoonery," was at her height in the early 1920s, a star attraction of American vaudeville and burlesque. Although she grew up in Newark, at an even further distance from New York's Jewish ghettos than did Copland, she cultivated Jewish mannerisms and dialect on stage, not only in her portrayals of Jewish immigrant characters ("Second Hand Rose") but in burlesques of such theatrical icons as Oscar Wilde's Salome ("Sadie Salome, Go Home!"), Theda Bara ("I'm Bad"), Pavlova ("Becky Is Back in the Ballet"), and Ethel Barrymore's Camille ("Yes, yes, Armand, I know—I know I have been a bad, bad voman—but awfully good company, nu?"). Most of these parodies satirized femmes fatales, drawing on the incongruity between the Hollywood vamp and the Jewish immigrant housewife. Copland probably had Brice as vamp in mind when writing "Burlesque," thus heightening the masquerade: the composer as Brice as Jewish immigrant as vamp.[19]

"Epilogue" freely recapitulates "Prologue," the music now more forlorn, like the atmosphere of an empty theater, with tender solos for clarinet, viola, bassoon, and solo violin. As with the gradual emergence of subsidiary material in the course of the *Organ Symphony*, a countermelody for solo cello from "Interlude" now returns, in altered form and put forth by a solo viola, as an important theme in its own right; played by the bassoon, it even has the last word. This somewhat pentatonic, hymnlike melody anticipates not only the later Copland but Roy Harris's Third Symphony; indeed, this music, encountered by Harris in 1925, may well have helped him toward his own distinctive style. The work's final two chords—the bassoon's isolated nonchordal tone surrounded by the orchestra's simple triads—shimmer exquisitely into silence.

What of the work's literary or dramatic connotations? Copland had been thinking about Rimbaud's psychodramatic poem *A Season in Hell*, whose disjointed form and emotional moodiness suggest a real, if unexpected, affinity to *Music for the Theatre*. And yet the move away from Rimbaud toward jazz and burlesque was momentous—a turn from European symbolism toward an American vernacular. And although he wrote that the work "was written with no specific play in mind," the American theater generally—its music, its plays, its actors—no doubt made its mark.[20]

Often in the company of Clurman, Copland attended Broadway plays and musicals with some regularity during these years. There were 228 shows in the 1924–25 season alone, including plays by O'Neill, Sidney Howard, John Howard Lawson, and Philip Barry; musicals by Gershwin, Rodgers, and Porter; and memorable performances by Fanny Brice and Laurette Taylor. In 1980 Clurman declared that season his all-time favorite, stating that although set against the decade's "exuberant optimism," its offerings taught Americans "to confront tragedy in the theatre and to give sober thought to our own life experience." Unlike later playwrights, opined Clurman, the writers of the 1920s in general benefited from the fact that they "still felt themselves at home in a society of more or less stable values, and if their plays reflect a growing distrust of these values, it was in their name that they protested."[21]

Among the 1924–25 productions, Clurman recalled, for his "own special delectation," Lawson's *Processional*, a "semi-Expressionist play about labor troubles and the Ku Klux Klan, which annoyed some and exhilarated others." Whether or not Copland shared Clurman's exhilaration, *Processional* contained features not unlike those of *Music for the Theatre*, including the use of vaudeville, jazz, ethnic humor, and American slang within a modernist context; both works shared, too, a satiric, jittery, almost apocalyptic atmosphere that Lawson explicitly associated with social conflict and nascent totalitarianism. (Copland and Clurman themselves felt "something like Nazism in the air" while in Munich in 1926.) Both Lawson and the play's scenic designer, Mordecai Gorelik, in later years became important contributors to Clurman's Group Theatre; significantly, Clurman requested that Copland write something along the lines of *Music for the Theatre* as incidental music for Lawson's *Pure in Heart* (1934).[22]

However, the subject of *Music for the Theatre* seems not so much the theater, or even the genre of incidental music, as New York itself, as the quotation of "The Sidewalks of New York" suggests. Or one might say that the work found inspiration in both New York and its theatrical life (which in the mid-1920s mirrored each other with unusual intensity). Copland took great delight in recalling how, when he and Clurman showed Boulanger the Times Square area in early 1925, she exclaimed, 'It is *extraordinaire*, but not very *raffinated*!" Although writers often use the term "Americana" to describe some later Copland scores, especially those inspired by rural landscape and folklore, the term as used in the 1920s denoted any characteristic depiction of the American scene. In this more authentic sense, *Music for the Theatre* is as much a work of Americana as anything Copland ever wrote.[23]

For all its American atmosphere, *Music for the Theatre* makes contact with European neoclassicism, not just in its elegant chamber orchestration but, more subtly, in gesture and design. The work as a whole seems to translate the Baroque suite in modern terms, one explanation for the use of the word *suite* in its subtitle. "Prologue," for instance, subtly recalls the Baroque French overture, while "Burlesque" descends from the "burlescas" and "vaudevilles" and "Epilogue" from the "envois" of the same period. Such neoclassical reverberations, largely overlooked, warn against facile pigeonholing of Copland.

Although many listeners initially heard *Music for the Theatre* as the raucous bellowings of an enfant terrible, it remains one of Copland's most accessible works. To be sure, it has its shocks, its subtleties, even considerable technical difficulties (Koussevitzky found the rhythms more challenging than those of the *Organ Symphony*), but its allusions to popular music and its formal tautness make it particularly approachable. This aspect of the piece discredits the common idea that Copland had a "severe" period followed by a "popular" one, but rather underscores the fact that works of greater and lesser accessibility alternated throughout his entire career.[24]

The verve, drama, and immediacy of *Music for the Theatre* attracted a wide range of dancers over the years. Most notably, the distinguished English choreographer Anthony Tudor choreographed it for the Ballet Theatre as *Time Table* (1941). Set on a station platform in a small American town at the end of World War I, the ballet depicted "casual goings-on," including, most poignantly, according to John Martin, "the farewell of a Marine sergeant and his sweetheart." When Tudor restaged the work for the New York City Ballet (1948), Martin could now see that the ballet anticipated Tudor's masterpiece, *Pillar of Fire* (1942), as well as Jerome Robbins's *Fancy Free* (1944). Other choreographers who used, in Martin's words, "the excellent Copland music," included Doris Humphrey, Peter Darrell, Jochen Ulrick, Eliot Feld, and Joel Schnee.[25]

Despite its long popularity with dancers, *Music for the Theatre* remained for many years something of a connoisseur's delight, with Leonard Bernstein and the New York Philharmonic holding sway with their performances and recording of the work. One aspect that helped recommend the piece to dance companies—its chamber orchestration—apparently stood in the way of wider exposure. In recent years, however, the work has enjoyed growing popularity, its discography now including, in addition to a second Bernstein performance released after his death, brilliant performances led by Dennis Russell Davies, Yoel Levi, Hugh Wolff, and Gerard Schwarz. While none of these recordings quite supersedes Bernstein's landmark recording, they all offer their own attractions, including a number of memorable solos; indeed, *Music for the Theatre* turns out to be something of an orchestral showpiece.[26]

These recordings raise the essential performance practice question—aside from how many strings to use—of how jazzily to play the work. Davies and Levi deliver particularly straightforward readings, thereby throwing the music's more modernist qualities into sharper relief. At the least, such renditions offer, as Larry Starr notes, "a stimulating alternative, a reminder of just how open to varying interpretations—and of how resistant to 'standardizing'—Copland's remarkably rich music can and should be." Copland, who thought that most musicians played his jazz works too squarely ("everything was supposed to be off the beat," he would say in reference to the Piano Concerto), probably would have preferred a more uninhibited and idiomatic approach, like Bernstein's or Wolff's.[27]

The Piano Concerto

In 1926, Copland composed the Concerto for Piano and Orchestra for himself to play with Koussevitzky and the Boston Symphony; he completed the work in November. By this time, the press had begun to link Copland's name with Gershwin's, and in later life, Copland entertained the idea (albeit doubtfully) that he was somewhat propelled toward writing this work by the success of Gershwin's *Rhapsody in Blue* (1924) and *Concerto in F* (1925). More decisive, he thought, was the fact that Koussevitzky had told him, "If you write a piano concerto, you can play it yourself," a "temptation" he thought "too great to pass up." He dedicated the score to his patron Alma Morgenthau Wertheim.[28]

The concerto contains two connected movements: a slow, preludial movement that leads into a larger fast one. The work evokes popular music—blues in the first movement, jazz in the second—but as in *Music for the Theatre*, Copland uses such styles metaphorically, in order, if not actually to portray New York, at least to impart a sense of life in a great American metropolis. Brassy, percussive, at times shrill and noisy, the work requires a big, unusual orchestra, including alto saxophone (doubling on soprano saxophone) and five players to handle the large percussion battery. Copland's intentions are clearly more symbolic than picturesque, though one particular passage in the second movement for the brasses in stretto vividly evokes, for this listener, city traffic (without the benefit of Gershwin's taxi horns). Meanwhile, the piano soloist functions alternately as reflective observer and high-spirited participant.

If the concerto takes its place alongside Gershwin, it also recalls more hard-edged evocations of city life, such as George Antheil's *Ballet mécanique* (1923), John Alden Carpenter's *Skyscrapers* (1924), and Edgard Varèse's pieces for chamber orchestra and percussion from the early 1920s. Copland was more indebted to their work, as he was to Gershwin's, than he was inclined to allow, for he was more aware of differences than of similarities; but at the very least such music helped prepare the ground in which his own work took root. This entire movement, in turn, stemmed above all from Stravinsky's *Rite of Spring*; and the Piano Concerto employs a full range of Stravinskyian techniques, including biting harmonies and complex polyrhythms that make the work challenging for players and an earful for listeners.[29]

Whatever its debts, the Piano Concerto has its own personality, with the familiar Copland moods—melancholy, playful, ironic—all on display. The first movement features three distinct ideas: an opening declamation, somewhat Jewish in profile, to the point of recalling traditional shofar calls; a sweeping, romantic theme heard shortly thereafter; and a more intimate, bluesy melody derived, said the composer, "from a traditional blues" used about the same time by Gershwin for the second of his *Three Preludes* (1926). The second movement similarly builds on two principal ideas: a hectic, bustling theme, announced by the piano in an opening cadenza that incorporates Charleston rhythms; and a more relaxed second theme, one parodistic to the point of goofiness.[30]

Copland integrates all these elements into a complex web, including a dramatic return of the romantic theme near the conclusion of the second movement and a climactic augmentation of the declamatory theme even closer to the end. Although the first movement roughly traces an arch and the second movement comprises a modified sonata form, the work unfolds, even more than in the *Organ Symphony*, a series of short passages that explore and juxtapose its main ideas in a kaleidoscope of colors. The work might even be compared to a mobile: separate but related ideas appear and reappear in various combinations. Copland does not so much develop these ideas as order and reorder, merge and transform them; beginnings are vague, endings uncertain, and climaxes unpredictably spaced. The conclusion intentionally leaves one hanging; Leonard Bernstein and Harold Shapero used to debate whether the piece ends in B or E. Such formal complexities pose challenges that complement and enhance the work's stylistic ones and that contribute to the sense of urban jumble.[31]

Despite its manifest kinship with Gershwin, the Piano Concerto, like most of Copland's music from the 1920s, never caught on with the large concert-going public. Of course, Copland was working in a more modernist idiom than Gershwin, enjoying, at age twenty-five, some moody introspection and barbaric yawping. Nor does the piano part, for all its difficulties, offer much in the way of virtuosic dazzle. One would as soon expect his contemporary settings of Ezra Pound or E. E. Cummings to enjoy the popularity of a Gershwin song.

In any case, for many years the only available recording of the concerto was that by Leonard Bernstein and the New York Philharmonic, with Copland himself at the piano, a wonderful and certainly historically important performance that may have scared off other interpreters. Copland plays the solo part with unmatched élan, and Bernstein communicates the music's big-city edge—which provided no small foundation for his own cityscapes—with inimitable gusto. Still, in later recordings, with Earl Wild and Noël Lee at the piano, Copland, now as conductor, turned in a more poignant first movement and a funnier last movement than Bernstein, who seemed somewhat ponderous in comparison; the recording with Wild and the Symphony of the Air may even be the most persuasive to date.[32]

Two more recent recordings of the work—one with pianist Lorin Hollander, conducted by Gerard Schwarz, the other with pianist Garrick Ohlsson, conducted by Michael Tilson Thomas—presented still other approaches. The latter made an especially strong case for the music's continued relevance and viability. It seemed that after seventy years the work was finally making its way into the repertory.[33]

Smaller Works from the Mid-1920s

In 1926, while working on the Piano Concerto, Copland composed *Two Pieces* for violin and piano ("Nocturne" and "Ukelele Serenade") and "Blues No. 1" and "Blues No. 2" for piano. *Two Pieces* he wrote for himself and violinist Samuel Dushkin to play in an all-American concert of (mostly) Boulanger students in Paris on 5 May 1926. (He dedicated "Nocturne" to Israel Citkowitz and "Ukelele Serenade" to Dushkin.) "Nocturne" gave rise, at least indirectly, to both the *Symphonic Ode* (1929) and the *Piano Variations* (1930), while Copland used both it and "Ukelele Serenade" in his incidental music to *Miracle at Verdun* (1931) and his ballet *Hear Ye! Hear Ye!* (1934). All this qualifies the common view of an early Copland jazz period that ended in 1927.[34]

The history of the two "Blues" is even more convoluted. Copland apparently intended them as the first and second movements of *Five Sentimental Melodies* (1926), an incomplete suite for piano itself based on the unpublished "Jazz Song" as well as sketches to the Piano Concerto. He published "Blues No. 1" as *Sentimental Melody: Slow Dance* (1929) and "Blues No. 2," with a dedication to John Kirkpatrick, as the last movement of *Four Piano Blues* (1949). Still another movement of the original 1926 suite—one subtitled "Hommage à Milhaud"—provided the basis for the "Dove Dance" from *Hear Ye! Hear Ye!* and the second of the *Four Piano Blues*. Such complex transmutations of material were not uncharacteristic of Copland.

Both *Two Pieces* and the two "Blues" explore, like the Piano Concerto itself, what Copland once characterized as jazz's two principal moods: "the slow blues and the snappy number." The slow movements are both moody, the forlorn "Nocturne" providing an early example of Copland's celebrated quiet-city style, the more ironic "Sentimental Blues" anticipating a century of American ballet music at its most characteristic. The lively and humorous fast movements—"Blues No. 2" and "Ukelele Serenade"—offer contrast. At the same time, both sets feature inner correspondences, and pianists might find it revealing to reconstruct the two "Blues" as a pair. All four pieces are rounded in form, with the longer violin-piano pieces more explicitly ternary. "Ukelele Serenade" gets its name, incidentally, from its middle section, which contains piano chords to be played "like a ukelele"; as an additional novelty, the violin part features quarter tones "meant to achieve a blues effect."[35]

All four pieces also explore bitonal textures, frequently pitting a melody in one key against harmonies in another or juxtaposing two simple triads. Such bitonality provides a distinctive context to the melodies, which derive mostly from octatonic and other modal scales, with the violin pieces featuring some melodic inflections related to Jewish music as well as to jazz. Copland recorded *Two Pieces* with violinists Jacques Gordon and Louis Kaufman, lovely recordings that came in at about eight minutes, making Robert Davidovici's recent rendition of the "Nocturne," for all its enveloping sound, rather protracted in comparison.

Meanwhile, in 1925, Copland set Edwin Arlington Robinson's "The House on the Hill" for unaccompanied four-voice women's choir and Ezra Pound's "An Immorality" for three-voice women's choir, soprano solo, and piano, extracting his texts from Robinson's *Children of the Night* (1897) and Pound's *Ripostes* (1912). In 1927, he composed "Song" (later retitled "Poet's Song") for voice and piano, a setting of an untitled E. E. Cummings poem from the collection *is 5*. Copland wrote the *Two Choruses* (as they became known) for the Women's University Glee Club of New York; even this early, he obviously concerned himself with practical needs. In contrast, he composed "Poet's Song" for more personal reasons, perhaps as a love song for Israel Citkowitz, for whose birthday he copied it out; the song went without a public performance until 1935.

Copland dedicated "The House on the Hill" to Thomas Whitney Surette, who helped get him his 1925–26 Guggenheim, and "An Immorality" to Gerald Reynolds, conductor of the University Glee Club.[36]

The use of texts by Robinson, Pound, and Cummings reveals Copland's continued receptivity to modernist American poetry. Such verse may well have abetted his development—teaching him something about the use of irony and colloquial speech, about the avoidance of worn, romantic rhetoric, about the bold acceptance of contemporary life, about concision and the "mot juste." At any rate, he continued to read contemporary American poetry avidly—including, in later years, Elizabeth Bishop and John Ashbery—and not for the reason of finding song texts (he wrote relatively few songs) but rather for nourishment and pleasure.

Two Choruses presents considerable contrast: "The House on the Hill" reflects on death and decay; "An Immorality" celebrates "love and idleness" (Copland adds his own sighing "Ah"s in the former and "Tra la la"s in the latter). Both pieces compensate for an almost unrelenting harmonic stasis with rhythmic and contrapuntal subtleties: "The House on the Hill" dispenses with bar lines, favoring instead an unmetrical flow of quarter notes; "An Immorality" pits the chorus's 4/4 against the pianist's jazzy 3/4. Both also make extensive use of canon and imitation, "An Immorality" featuring, like the Piano Concerto's opening movement, a climactic three-voice canon. As with the little instrumental pieces discussed above, the melodic materials recall Copland's Parisian exploration of the ecclesiastical modes ("The House on the Hill") and the octatonic scale ("An Immorality"). Julia Smith long ago observed their neoclassicisms, writing that "The House on the Hill" possessed the "archaic modal flavor" of a Renaissance motet, while "An Immorality" suggested "a 'hot' jazz madrigal." Copland clearly was sensitive to ways in which Robinson and Pound accommodated the American vernacular to European traditions.[37]

Copland wrote "Poet's Song" in August 1927 while in Königstein, Germany, a town under British occupation that he found depressing. His only completed composition from that year, this little song shows the direct influence of the second Viennese school, including Webern, whose *Five Pieces for Orchestra* had so impressed him the previous summer. He even admitted using Schoenberg's recently unveiled twelve-tone method of composition for this song, though he was rather inscrutable about the matter, later hedging specific questions about tone rows and such. At the very least, he used the method with complete freedom. Indeed, the song reveals Copland at his most idiosyncratic. A virtually atonal composition despite its rather bluesy harmonies, the voice puts forth its expressive melody "freely," as the piano repeats the same brooding sequence of harmonies, plausibly reflecting Cummings's "Doom," which "will smooth entirely our minds."[38]

However, "Poet's Song" represented no isolated phenomenon, but rather was part of a concerted effort by Copland—as with many composers during the late 1920s—to reconstitute a musical language stripped of all fussy complications. The song takes us to the brink of a new sensibility in Copland's music, one related to such popular slogans as "the new objectivity" (*"die neue Sachlichkeit"*). This trend embraced tendencies not always easily reconciled: some composers emphasized earlier European styles; others, militant opposition to an oppressive world order; still others, the desirability of finding a larger audience for new music. In any case, the nervous splendor of *Pierrot Lunaire* and *The Rite of Spring*, which had cast such a long shadow for over a decade, had simply, for the time being, exhausted itself.

This worldwide trend represented, to some extent, a shifting focus from Paris to Berlin, as the waning era of the Ballets Russes gave way to developments in the Weimar Republic, with its attention to social criticism. The composers spearheading these new developments—Hindemith, Krenek, and Weill—were all German and the trend seemed to crystallize in Germany in 1927, specifically at that year's Baden-Baden Festival. Copland had attended the festival and, tellingly, he composed "Poet's Song" shortly thereafter. Schoenberg and Stravinsky themselves contributed to this so-called new sobriety: Schoenberg with his twelve-tone method of composition, Stravinsky with his neoclassical works, including *Oedipus Rex* (1927), which Copland, poring over the score in Königstein, immediately recognized as one of the great masterpieces of his time. "My enthusiasm," he wrote to Roger Sessions about the piece, "begins to rival your own."[39]

Sessions himself may have veered Copland in this direction; their friendship was at its height. In *Our New Music*, Copland quoted at length a 1927 manifesto by Sessions that read, in part,

Younger men are dreaming of an entirely different kind of music—a music which derives its power from forms beautiful and significant by virtue of inherent musical weight rather than intensity of utterance; a music whose impersonality and self-sufficiency preclude the exotic; which takes its impulse from the realities of a passionate logic; which, in that authentic freshness of its moods, is the reverse of ironic and, in its very aloofness from the concrete preoccupations of life, strives rather to contribute form, design, a vision of order and harmony.

Copland could not embrace this agenda whole; his music remained intense, ironic, and very engaged with the "concrete preoccupations of life." But his responsiveness to such trends had no small impact on his continuing development.[40]

Two short works by Copland from 1928—the single-movement "Lento Molto" for string quartet composed in New York in the spring and the textless "Vocalise" for voice and piano composed in Santa Fe that summer—continued the momentum toward objectivity and restraint. He composed the latter for A. L. Hettich, a professor at the Paris Conservatoire and editor of ten volumes of vocalises. "Lento Molto" he paired with his "Rondino" (1923) as *Two Pieces* for string quartet (1928). He subsequently arranged *Two Pieces* for string orchestra (1928) and transcribed "Vocalise" for flute and piano (1972).

Copland created both "Lento Molto" and "Vocalise" out of the most commonplace materials: major and minor triads and plain diatonic scales. The juxtapositions of diatonic scales in particular suggested the influence of yet another landmark of the new sobriety, Bartók's Piano Sonata, which Copland had heard in Baden-Baden in 1927. In any case, the familiar Coplandesque voice of the famous ballets—pastoral, luminous, strong, and deeply calm—could be heard coming into greater focus in these works; significantly, both scores instructed the musicians to play, above all, tranquilly ("tranquillo") and simply ("semplice"). Boulanger appreciated this accomplishment at once; on receiving a copy of "Lento Molto," she wrote to him, "This piece for string quartet is a masterpiece—so moving, so deep, so simple."[41]

The simplicity of this music from 1928 reflected, in addition, Copland's personal desire for some serenity. While working on the "Lento Molto," he expressed the need for "quiet time," subsequently retreating to "the sleepy old Spanish town" of Santa Fe, where he wrote the "Vocalise." Copland chose Santa Fe, as opposed to the MacDowell Colony or rural France, primarily because he needed to perform his Piano Concerto at the Hollywood Bowl in July; but he welcomed the opportunity, writing Boulanger, "I suppose it is time for me to see America a little." Ever since they had met in 1925, Roy Harris had been strongly encouraging him to travel out West, teasing him "about not having been further west than Ithaca." Copland had Harris very much on his mind in 1928; he dedicated both the "Lento Molto" and *Vitebsk* (also completed in 1928) to him, later recalling that Harris's "enthusiasm for the opening phrase" of the "Lento Molto" gave him "the incentive to finish it." The plain triads of this phrase—wavering between major and minor—suggest a reciprocal influence between the two during these years.[42]

Consequently, the restraint of "Lento Molto" and "Vocalise" ultimately seems as related to Harris and the American West as to Sessions and German aesthetics; both pieces exemplify, as do the earlier jazz works, Copland's desire to create a distinctively American music balanced by an awareness of worldwide trends. Before leaving New York, he wrote Sessions that he was off to "see New Mexico and America!" and that he would "probably return a rampant affirmer." Behind such joking lay an optimism that might be tempered but not squelched by the new objectivity.[43]

10

From *Vitebsk* to the
Piano Variations

(1928–30)

Vitebsk

Upon returning to the East in September 1928, Copland completed a piano trio, *Vitebsk (Study on a Jewish Theme)*, at the MacDowell Colony. Commissioned by the League of Composers for violinist Alphonse Onnou, cellist Robert Maas, and pianist Walter Gieseking, this one-movement trio featured a Yiddish folk melody that Copland had heard in a 1925 production of S. Ansky's *The Dybbuk*. He titled the piece after the Belorussian town in which Ansky had grown up and first heard the tune.

Vitebsk was one of the many towns and villages (shtetls) located in the Pale of Settlement, a large area to which the many Jews straddling Russia's western border had been deported and confined. The prevailing conditions were appalling; in addition to widespread poverty and discrimination, the governing Russians condoned and often instigated violent pogroms by the local Christian populations. About half of the Pale's four million Jews fled the area in the late nineteenth century, fueling the large Jewish immigration to the United States during those years. "It was my intention," stated Copland with regard to *Vitebsk*, "to reflect the harshness and drama of Jewish life in White Russia."[1]

For this rumination on shtetl life, Copland could draw on stories he heard as a child from older relatives who hailed from that area. Perhaps he also found stimulation in the paintings of Marc Chagall, who, like Ansky, was born in Vitebsk; Copland himself referred to the trio's fast section as having a "Chagall-like grotesquerie." But *Vitebsk* took its principal inspiration from *The Dybbuk*, the play that provided its main theme.[2]

The Dybbuk is the only complete play by S. Ansky, the pseudonym of Shloyme Zanvl Rappoport (1863–1920), a Russian-Jewish collector and writer of Jewish folktales. Ansky completed *The Dybbuk* in 1914; he originally wrote it in Russian, then rewrote it in Yiddish at Stanislavsky's suggestion. In 1920, only weeks after Ansky's death, the play opened in Warsaw; and in 1921, under the direction of Stanislavsky's protégé Eugene Vakhtangov, a Hebrew version premiered in Moscow to great critical acclaim as performed by Habima, a Hebrew-Russian troupe that flourished in the early days of the Russian Revolution. *The Dybbuk* premiered in New York in Yiddish, but in 1925 a Habima member directed an English translation in the style of Vakhtangov for New York's Neighborhood Playhouse, the production Copland attended.[3]

Ansky based *The Dybbuk* on a folktale of the Hasidim, a mystical and pietist Jewish sect that arose in the early eighteenth century in response to the Talmudic strictures of Orthodox Judaism; Ansky himself came from a Hasidic family. The Hasidim resembled certain Christian sects that originated at about the same time, including the Shakers (another group who would inspire Copland); like the Shakers, the Hasidim sought spiritual ecstasy in music and dance. Hasidism eventually ossified into its own orthodoxies, but the movement left its mark on the Jewish enlightenment of the late eighteenth century as well as on the Jewish existentialism of Martin Buber.[4]

The Dybbuk takes place in a small Hasidic community in the Pale. Chanon, a poor scholar, and Leah are in love, but Leah's father, the wealthy merchant Reb (Mr.) Sender, wants a more prosperous son-in-law. In frustration, Chanon consults the occult practices of the Kabbala. On hearing that Sender has found a husband for Leah, he collapses and dies.

On her wedding day, Leah dances with the crippled and blind village women. She invites to the ceremony various persons who have died before their time, including Chanon, who takes possession of her in the form of a dybbuk ("attachment" in Hebrew), a migrant soul that, not able to fulfill itself in its lifetime, can attach itself to a living person. Although dybbuks, according to Hasidic lore, can be exorcised by religious rite, even the efforts of the wise and saintly Rabbi Azreilkeh fail. Prompted by a dream, Azreilkeh summons Sender to stand trial in a rabbinical court. At the trial, the ghost of Chanon's father reveals that, as young men, he and Sender had promised that their children would marry, but that Sender knowingly forsook his vow.

The court decides that, as punishment, Sender must give half of his fortune to the poor. Although Azreilkeh still cannot exorcize Chanon, the wedding ceremony goes forward. Chanon's soul finally leaves Leah of its own accord, but she freely dies so that her soul can merge with Chanon's. The cosmic scales have been set right at a terrible cost.

The world depicted by *The Dybbuk*, with its penurious merchant, its pathetic and impoverished townspeople, its inadequate rabbinical law, and, looming over everything else, the remembrance and threat of violence, teeters on the edge of madness and chaos. Only self-awareness through love offers redemption. The play's social implications—Ansky apparently had socialist affiliations—help explain its enormous popularity in Moscow and New York during the 1920s.

Recalling the Neighborhood Playhouse production many years later, Harold Clurman pointed out that Vakhtangov's direction had underscored the play's "social aspect" in ways that later productions had not. "The play was viewed as a kind of phantasmagoria of a past civilization, a world beautiful in its depth of feeling but condemned for its practical organization. All the props (furniture, etc.) stood askew, the characters' faces were strangely masklike as though they were phantoms of a bygone age, while the beggarly poor—crippled, hunchbacked, blind and stunted—danced at the wedding with hate-filled grotesquerie." Clurman cited this production as one of the most memorable of his life.[5]

The play's success owed something to its incidental music, which Joel Engel composed for the work's Warsaw premiere. A close associate of Ansky's, Engel had collaborated on the project from the beginning, and together the two chose the Hasidic song "Mipnei Mah" ("Wherefore, O Wherefore?") as the work's musical motto. The song, which both opens and closes the play, has a Yiddish text that translates as "Wherefore, O wherefore / Has the soul / Fallen from exalted heights / To profoundest depths? / Within itself, the fall / Contains the ascension." Its sad melody features a three-note motive that outlines a minor triad, not unlike the motto to Copland's *Organ Symphony*.[6]

Copland cast *Vitebsk*'s single movement in an ABA form, with slow outer sections and a fast middle section; all three sections are themselves ternary in design. The first A section puts forth a dramatic declamation, proceeds to the "Mipnei Mah" tune in a still slower tempo, and returns briefly to the declamatory music. The contrasting center section reworks this idea of surrounding the "Mipnei Mah" tune with declamations, except that the material is grotesquely distorted. The concluding A section, which functions as climax and epilogue, reverses the arch by stating the "Mipnei Mah" tune before and after the declamatory music. Although "Mipnei Mah" consequently permeates much of the work, Copland does not so much set the melody as use it as a springboard for a highly personal discourse, in the manner of some of the music of Bartók, whose Piano Sonata possibly influenced this work as well.

The declamatory music requires the violin and cello to play in quarter tones, here employed more extensively and systematically than in the jazz works, including use of a special notation. These declamations, with their microtones, iambic snaps, and falling intervals, evoke the shofar calls associated with the Jewish High Holidays and featured in *The Dybbuk*'s exorcism scene. If the work's slow music reflects the play's gloom, the fast section suggests Leah's dance with the blind and crippled villagers; the music even faintly resembles Engel's incidental music for this particular scene ("Bettlertänze"). In his recording of the work, Copland, at the piano, syncopates some of its rhythms in ways not indicated by the score, evoking a kind of hobble.[7]

Certain aspects of the score—the microtones, the syncopations, the alternating sadness and irony—strongly recall Copland's earlier jazz works, in particular "Prologue" from *Music for the Theatre*: both unfold slow-fast-slow forms, with opening sections that contain "sharp" and "nervous" declamations along with quiet, melancholy melodies, and fast contrasting sections that mask these materials practically beyond recognition. Such correspondences highlight the convergence of African-American and Jewish features in Copland's music during this period. Over the years, some critics argued that Copland's Jewish background predisposed him toward jazz in the first place; many more observed the fact that American Jews of Russian heritage in general played a conspicuous role in the creation and dissemination of jazz and jazz-related idioms. Various explanations proposed for this have included bona fide musical similarities between Eastern-European Jewish and

African-American folk musics, traditional black and Jewish roles in commercial entertainment, and shared experiences of persecution.[8]

The Jazz Singer (1927), a popular film based on Samson Raphaelson's melodrama about a Jewish vaudevillian who defies his stern cantor father, presumes just such interactions; as Robert L. Carringer observes, it mythologizes the idea that the Jew's jazz singing is "fundamentally an ancient religious impulse seeking expression in a modern, popular form," a duality symbolized by his blackface. Significantly, *The Jazz Singer* and *The Dybbuk* resemble each other in a number of respects; both concern young, rebellious Jews who reject a rigid father figure, an oppressive ghetto, and rabbinical puritanism in favor of a forbidden love and new identities. Ansky subtitled his play *Between Two Worlds*, while Raphaelson similarly described the "singer of jazz" as "lost between two worlds." Copland was not the only Jewish composer associated with jazz attracted to *The Dybbuk*; Gershwin considered adapting the play as an opera (1929) and Leonard Bernstein composed a *Dybbuk* ballet (1974).[9]

The Jazz Singer suggests that for American Jews, as for many others, jazz represented a generational break from the customs of the past—a break also manifested, in more specifically Eastern European terms, in *The Dybbuk*. In the 1920s, America's black and Jewish communities, for all their differences, both largely consisted of persons displaced from a ghettoized rural society—marked by lynchings and pogroms, spirituals and Hasidic dances—to great urban centers at once liberating and threatening. *Music for the Theatre* and *Vitebsk* drew upon both currents.[10]

At the same time, *Vitebsk*'s pared-down language exemplifies those new trends toward hardness, sobriety, and objectivity discussed in the context of Copland's smaller pieces from 1928; like them, it suggests in this sense the influence of Roy Harris, its dedicatee. One hears this new leanness in the work's juxtapositions of plain triads and scales—for example, the biting clash between a C-major and C-minor triad at the very opening, or the counterpointing of an E-major scale against a simple but dissonant accompaniment in the fast section. Critics have agreed—as the composer himself maintained—that the acerbic simplicity of *Vitebsk* anticipates the *Piano Variations* (1930) and, in general, his mature style. *Vitebsk* also captures a new mood, a tragic sense that goes beyond the bittersweet sadness of the earlier jazz pieces. This quality, although related here to the "harshness" of shtetl life, entered Copland's emotional vocabulary quite generally and resurfaced in subsequent scores, including his next two major works.[11]

Symphonic Ode and Piano Variations

The *Symphonic Ode* (1929) and *Piano Variations* (1930), two darkly personal works, reveal yet further stylistic development. Most striking, perhaps, are their stark textures that tend toward simple unisons and two-part writing, textures that seem all the more sinewy thanks to a prevalence of sharp dissonances—in particular, simultaneous-sounding minor seconds and their inversions. Fuller harmonies, like triads, appear only sparingly, for effect. Both scores contain tonal centers, but the highly dissonant writing so contradicts these centers that they are sometimes hard to perceive.

These two scores further contain particularly jagged melodies, with big leaps and crooked shapes, accompanied by staccati and accents; "marcato," "deliberamente," "incisivo," and (in the *Variations*) "strike each note sharply" become key directives. In contrast to Copland's earlier music, often enlivened by jazzy syncopations over a regular pulse, these works tend to unfurl a fairly steady flow of notes in the context of irregular meters (especially 5/4 and 7/4) or rapidly changing meters, making their connections with jazz more elusive. While such motoric elements arguably represent a certain simplification over his previous scores, the lack of a regular pulse actually creates a more complex rhythmic atmosphere. The avoidance of clear root movement and repetitive patterns only intensifies such rhythmic intricacies.

Copland matches these stylistic severities with formal ones; each work is based on a short motive that largely determines not only principal themes but accompanying voices as well. Both works relentlessly, exhaustively develop such ideas, procedures that might be described as "continuous variation" and that show, by Copland's own admission, the influence of Schoenberg's twelve-tone method. Such tactics provide more formal flexibility than seen previously in Copland's music and arguably greater emotional range as well.[12]

Copland worked on the *Symphonic Ode* from August 1927 to September 1929, carrying sketches with him all across the United States and Europe. The work satisfied a commission from Koussevitzky for a work in celebration of the fiftieth anniversary of the Boston Symphony. The piece was originally scheduled for a February 1930 premiere, but Koussevitzky felt, after looking over the score, that the orchestra could not manage its rhythms with the available rehearsal time. He invited a skeptical Copland to rehearse the work himself, but after one rehearsal, the composer agreed to rebar it using more regular meters, and the premiere was put off until 1932. "I can't hold it against the poor dear," Copland wrote to Marc Blitzstein; "he seemed as disappointed about not producing it as I was at not hearing it."[13]

After completing his revision, Copland came to the troubling realization that although his rebarred version would be easier for conductors and musicians to play, it looked distorted to the eye. This notational dilemma became one of the major preoccupations of his career. Although it was never fully resolved, he concluded that, for chamber and especially orchestral music, the more conventional the barring, the more performances were "likely to materialize." He occasionally offered some half-way solution by means of explanatory footnotes and dotted barlines.[14]

"The title *Symphonic Ode* is not meant to imply connection with a literary idea," wrote Copland. "It is not an ode *to* anything in particular, but rather a spirit that is to be found in the music itself." Nonetheless, he apparently had in mind the kind of heightened style associated with literary odes. He scored the work for a huge orchestra requiring eighteen brass players (including eight horns and two tubas) and an enormous percussion battery; at times the work erupts in massive torrents of sound. Moreover, its very rhetoric is exalted, even heroic.[15]

For such a big piece, the *Ode* uses a surprisingly small number of motives, all put forth at the start of the work, especially the five-note motto theme introduced by the violins in the work's eighth measure. These motives, themselves rather similar, constitute fragmented workings of a two-measure phrase from his "Nocturne" for violin and piano (1926), where it appears marked "nobilimente" (*sic*) and "grave." In its original context, the melody—which appears closest to its original form at the start of the *Ode*'s slow middle section—suggests connections to both the blues and Jewish cantorial; but here the music is more or less divested of such allusions.

Copland identified the work's form as ABCBD. The declamatory A music debuts, in mature fashion, that stern and grim expression sometimes referred to as the composer's prophetic voice. The jazzy B section is humorous in a hectic, edgy way. The introspective middle slow section—with its periodic tollings in the brass, yet another Copland trademark—offers relief. The designation of the last third of the piece as BD seems rather ambiguous; even before the end of C, elements from both A and B begin to encroach on the music, and as the tempo suddenly quickens, designating the return of B, one hears fragments of A, softly, in the brass.

By D, Copland presumably means the delightfully weird passage spot-lighting the timpani, Chinese block, and wood block; this short section, however, quickly moves on to a noble transformation of the B music, followed by a coda in which elements from both A and B are climactically stated at once, suggesting some reconciliation between the tragic and the affirmative. Because of such fluctuations, Arthur Berger viewed the Ode not as sectional but as a forerunner of the more explicit continuous variation form found in the *Piano Variations*. But one can readily hear the work's form as described by Copland, especially if one recognizes that D comprises both new material and a coda that recapitulates material from A and B, and that music associated with A lurks about the whole second half of the work.[16]

Copland often mentioned Mahler when talking about the *Ode*, by which he presumably had in mind not only the work's huge instrumentation but its grandeur and perhaps, too, its bell-like tollings. But in contrast to Mahler, the piece is terrifically sober and austere; if Mahler informs the work, so do Varèse and Ruggles. It can even, like the Piano Concerto, be read as a cityscape—Berger described it as "sad city music"—though the piece evokes a colder and harsher world, shorn of the glamour and giddiness that characterize the earlier score. In this more serious world, the heroic flourishes near the end—with "marcatissimo" timpani and snare drum—signal the kinds of nascent hopes that kindled America's political left in the 1930s.[17]

Despite earning the almost fervid affection of so sophisticated a musician as David Diamond, who considered it one of Copland's greatest masterpieces, the *Symphonic Ode* proved a monumental failure. Whereas other large, controversial works at least won champions and occasional performances, the *Ode* seemed headed, until very recently at least, for oblivion, a somewhat awkward misstep on the road to greater success. Even Koussevitzky, the work's dedicatee, who allegedly held the piece in "high regard," never performed it again after its premiere season.

In 1955, for the occasion of the Boston Symphony's seventy-fifth anniversary, Copland scaled back the work's instrumentation and filled out its textures in an attempt to make the piece more accessible, one of the very few substantial revisions of his career. Charles Munch introduced this revamped version in Boston and New York, where it still met with a mostly poor reception. "Even the most intelligent listeners such as Walter [Piston], Harold [Shapero], Arthur [Berger] felt that the ending did not come off," wrote Irving Fine to Copland. "Harold thought it ended in the wrong key. My own feeling is that this is unmistakably intentional but I am inclined to agree with Walter that it comes too late."[18]

Copland published the revised *Ode* (1957) and recorded it with the London Symphony Orchestra (1973), but the work remained ignored. No stranger to disappointments, he sounded a defiant note in his memoirs: "I have always regarded the *Symphonic Ode* as an important work. I tried hard for something there, and I feel that I succeeded in what I attempted." In the mid-1990s, both Gerard Schwarz and Michael Tilson Thomas recorded it, suggesting a more appreciative climate for this piece. Still, one wonders whether it will take still other performances to win over the large public, perhaps interpretations that combine Copland's sweep with Thomas's finesse.[19]

The neglect of the *Ode* seems, perhaps, especially surprising in view of the fact that the *Piano Variations*, a kind of pianistic companion piece completed the following year, quickly became one of Copland's most admired compositions. But admittedly the piano work is tauter in form, leaner in texture, and still more direct and personal in tone, free from the sort of portentousness that characterizes some of the *Ode*. The *Variations* sounds like a denuded version of the *Ode*; indeed, in its original guise as the first movement of an unfinished *Suite for Two Pianos* (1928), the *Variations'* famous four-note motto began life not as a bold theme in its own right but as the support for the same "Nocturne" fragment used in the *Ode*. When critics, consequently, refer to the *Variations* as stripped down, they are closer to the mark than they realize.[20]

Although its premiere in New York in 1931, with Copland at the piano, left its audience baffled, a reprise performance at Yaddo in 1932, also by the composer, established the piece, at least among an influential elite, as a major landmark, a distinction it has held ever since. "Within modern-music circles," wrote Arthur Berger, "this extraordinary piano work made a profound impression, and went a long way towards establishing him as a composer of great consequence." Wilfrid Mellers deemed it "a key-work in his career and in the history of American music," while H. Wiley Hitchcock reported that "for many" it marked "the summit" of Copland's achievement."[21]

The *Variations* consists of a short, compact theme, twenty variations, and a coda. The theme, which moves from minor to major and back to minor, features a pungent four-note motive (E–B-sharp–D-sharp–C-sharp) related to Copland's penchant for the octatonic scale (thus explaining noted resemblances to Stravinsky's *Octet*, and unremarked ones to Shostakovich's "D–S–C–H" signature motive) and his admiration for Bach, who uses an identical (though differently ordered) four-note motive in the fourth fugue from *The Well-Tempered Clavier*, Book 1. This four-note motive colors the entire piece, generating its own inimitable harmonic language, including juxtapostions of the motive that result in a series of piercing dissonances. The ingenuity with which Copland uses this theme won the admiration of musicians like Berger, who pointed out that "each chord or figure may be traced directly back to it. If only for this aspect, the work is a masterpiece of construction."[22]

While composing the *Variations*, Copland undertook a systematic and chronological study of music literature, in particular keyboard works and variation form; Berger, Smith, and others have detected likenesses—both in the work's material and in its formal design—to a number of composers. At the same time, critics agree that the form—which sweeps along through nine variations, climaxes in the tenth, dissipates in the eleventh, accelerates in the twelfth, starts deceptively slowly in the nineteenth, crests in the twentieth, and concludes grandly in the coda—is utterly original; Mellers goes so far as to state, "There has never been a work more decisive in its originality." This originality involves, to some extent, what is widely referred to as the work's "cumulative" effect, the fact that, as Smith puts it, "each variation is related to the following in the sense that it builds architecturally, solidly, one after the other."[23]

Berger thought the "exciting character" of the theme's "transmutations" even "more remarkable" than its form. While he and other critics discussed these "transmutations" in technical terms, Copland showed less reserve, marking certain of the variations "naively," "boldly," "warmly," and "threatening." Rosenfeld and Mellers, both of whom stressed the work's relation to industrial America, possibly overemphasized the more steely moments; for within its short frame, it explores a wide range of sounds and emotions. Significantly, at the time of its premiere, Copland felt that Walter Gieseking, a subtle colorist highly regarded for his Debussy, was the "only concert pianist" who could play the piece. Unfortunately, Gieseking missed the point; he turned down Copland's offer to premiere the work, citing its "crude dissonances" and "severity of style."[24]

Since then, many pianists, including Gilbert Kalish and Nina Tichman, have brilliantly exploited the music's color potential. So has Copland himself—not so much in his recording of the piece as in a transcription composed for the Louisville Symphony Orchestra, the *Orchestral Variations* (1957). This orchestral version contains interesting color contrasts within as well as between the individual variations; and although some of the music's motoric elements transfer less well for orchestra than, say, its more grandiose passages, the work as a whole not only strikingly illuminates the original piano version but constitutes an impressive work in its own right, one deserving to be better known.[25]

The *Piano Variations*—a defiant howl of a piece, rather Beethovenian in its balance of intellectual rigor and prophetic fervor—struck a responsive note among America's young composers of the 1930s, not only because of its technical command but because its predominantly stark and tragic tone spoke to a world made bleak by economic collapse and political despair. While such gloom recalled both *Vitebsk* and the *Ode*, here the tragedy moves beyond the crushing portraitures of shtetl and city life into some more personal terrain, its moments of innocence and humor only heightening the prevailing darkness. "To live on," Copland wrote Lola Ridge in reference to the work, "to develop means, as I see it, to enter always more and more deeply into the very essence of tragic reality."[26]

Such a breakthrough may have had something to do with the work's dedicatee, Gerald Sykes (1903–1984), a Canadian-born writer whom Copland had met through Paul Rosenfeld in 1925 and with whom he lived during the composition of the *Variations*. Even though Sykes was only three years younger than Copland, their relationship bore the earmarks of many to follow: the sympathetic composer supporting a troubled, talented younger man. Sykes befriended Harold Clurman as well, suggesting to Copland in 1928 that the three of them form some "gigantic combine." By 1929 this close-knit circle had expanded to include Marc Blitzstein and Eva Goldbeck as well.[27]

Copland's letters to Goldbeck suggest some romantic attachment on his part toward Sykes. In any case, their friendship peaked in early 1930, when Sykes left Brooklyn to spend some months with Copland in a rented house in Bedford, New York. By the end of the year, however, a certain coolness had set in, Sykes finding Copland "in a rather non-committal, dissatisfied state"; and by early 1931, they had begun to drift apart, Copland complaining that Sykes was in love only with his manuscripts, Sykes assuring Copland, "Surely you must know that you play a part in my life that no one can ever play." One senses the frustrations of a failed or unrequited romance. In any event, they remained fond of each other, staying in touch if only from a distance.[28]

After years as a freelance journalist and novelist, Sykes emerged in the 1960s as a prominent social critic in the tradition of Ortega y Gasset. *The Hidden Remnant* (1962) urged his time's educated elite (or "remnant") to study the work of Freud, Jung, Adler, and Fromm. His best-known work, *The Cool Millennium* (1967), viewed contemporary America as divided between the large masses ("Aztechs") and an enlightened minority represented by artists and scientists ("Toltechs"); whereas Stravinsky and Picasso had presented a Toltech challenge to modern materialism, he argued, the postwar avant-garde, co-opted by the Aztechs, had sold out.[29]

These writings represented a latter-day manifestation of the kind of Stieglitzian idealism that had helped bring Rosenfeld, Copland, Clurman, and Sykes together in the first place; *The Cool Millennium* warmly remembered Stieglitz as "one of the most outspoken leaders of a poor but still unterrified avant-garde." But Sykes's taste for the formidable, including his high regard for Varèse, as expressed in *The Perennial Avant-garde* (1971), seemed closer to Rosenfeld than to Copland and Clurman or, rather, fitted the *Piano Variations* more than some other Copland scores. One naturally wonders whether the *Variations* helped shape Sykes's aesthetics, whether Sykes's presence during the work's composition affected its uncompromising nature, or whether, as is most likely, such influences were reciprocal.[30]

The Reception of Early Copland

Copland's work quickly won the support of some adventurous musicians. Pianist John Kirkpatrick, for instance, who in later years was instrumental in bringing Ives's music before the public, wrote a laudatory article about Copland in 1928 and performed, in addition to the *Variations*, the Piano Concerto and the *Symphonic Ode* in his own two-piano arrangements—a labor of love. Fellow composers as different as Virgil Thomson and Roger Sessions similarly reacted strongly and immediately to his music; Thomson even wept upon hearing the *Organ Symphony*, later writing, "I thought that it was the voice of America in our generation. It spoke in the same way that Kerouac did thirty years later."[31]

In the course of the 1930s, Copland became a revered figure, especially for somewhat younger composers, and in particular those residing in the New York area, including Paul Bowles, Arthur Berger, Elliott Carter, David Diamond, and Leonard Bernstein. These composers held the music composed around 1930 in especially high regard; the *Piano Variations* in particular became a kind of rallying cry.[32]

By the 1930s, New York's avant-garde dance community had begun to take an interest in Copland as well. On 7 January 1930, Helen Tamiris (née Helen Becker) and her group premiered *Sentimental Dance*, the first known dance to Copland's music (ostensibly to the piano piece *Sentimental Melody: Slow Dance*); and on 3 February 1931, they launched *Olympus Americanus*, after the *Passacaglia*. At the time Tamiris was considered, along with Martha Graham, Doris Humphrey, and Agnes de Mille, as one of America's preeminent modern dancer–choreographers; all four regularly performed on the same stage throughout the 1930s, often accompanied by the pianist-composer Louis Horst, who had apparently introduced Copland's music to Tamiris and her distinguished rivals.[33]

Tamiris's work was highly uneven—neither Graham, Humphrey, nor de Mille thought much of it—and *Olympus Americanus*, which attempted to merge motifs from Broadway and ancient Greece (including a "priapic ritual"), had little success; at least one critic, in fact, found it distasteful. But the work helped introduce Copland to the dance community, anticipating his collaborations with Graham, Humphrey, and de Mille, all three of whom—remarkably enough—would create their best-known ballets to his music.[34]

On 6 December 1931, Tamiris, Humphrey, and de Mille had the opportunity to watch Graham, fresh from her triumph earlier that year with *Primitive Mysteries*, dance to Copland, this time the *Piano Variations*, in a work entitled *Dithyrambic*. A ten-minute solo evocation of the god Dionysus, *Dithyrambic*—a dance of "orgiastic abandon . . . concerned with rituals of worship," according to John Martin—met with roaring applause and bravos. Those relatively few who saw it remembered it as one of the most remarkable experiences of their lives; the strength and stamina displayed by Graham—in particular, the ease with which she repeatedly fell back and rose—stunned even those familiar with her dancing. "Its emotional impact is irresistible," wrote Martin in 1932. "At each reseeing one is impressed more deeply with the magnitude of this composition, not to speak of its masterly performance, and with the strange, hard beauty of the music, Aaron Copland's *Piano Variations*, to which it is danced. Louis Horst contributes substantially to its success by his playing of it." Years before *Appalachian Spring*, the careers of Graham and Copland became entwined; Graham boosted Copland's reputation among New York's artistic elite, while Copland provided the music for the dance that John Martin later would recognize as the "ancestor of so many of Miss Graham's later compositions."[35]

Copland did not achieve widespread popularity, however, until the U.S. premieres of *El Salón México* and *Billy the Kid* in 1938. On the contrary, the reviews of his early music typically represented it as ugly, uncouth, mocking, audacious. True, an occasional critic like Edward Cushing (not to mention Rosenfeld) found these very attributes appealing: "We like its brutal and Asiatic colors, its barbarism," Cushing wrote of *Cortège Macabre* in 1927. But most did not, including Warren Storey Smith, who (in a review entitled "Barbaric Music by Symphony") declared the *Organ Symphony* "ugly"; James Davies, who said of the *Dance Symphony*, "It never touches the hem of beauty's dress"; and Linton Martin, who declared the "sour harmonies" of the "empty and uninspired" scherzo (of the First Symphony) "as labored as they were unlovely." The Piano Concerto comprised a "concatenation of meaninglessly ugly sounds and distorted rhythms" (Smith), displayed "a shocking lack of taste" (Philip Hale), and was simply "a harrowing horror from beginning to end" (H. T. Parker); for still others, it evoked "a jazz dance hall next door to a poultry yard," a "barnyard and stable noises," and "a herd of elephants engaged in jungle rivalry of the Charleston and dances further south." As for the *Symphonic Ode*, Smith thought Copland's ambition "to make the orchestra sound, save in a very few passages, as harsh and strident as possible," while the usually sympathetic Lawrence Gilman envisioned its composer "lost in agonizing lucubration, praying Heaven to make him Hard and Stripped and Sharp-Edged and Astringent." One critic described *Hear Ye! Hear Ye!* (1934) as full of "wails and squeaks and other hysterical modernisms." As late as 1944, Norman Houk characterized *Lincoln Portrait* as "such as we have come to expect from the composer—angular, dissonant, and, as a setting for Lincoln's noble words, anachronistic." In the same year Robert Sabin wrote, in a review of *Appalachian Spring*, "One hates to use the word beautiful in response to anything, most of all the work of Aaron Copland, which only a few years ago was being described in far more sulphurous terms."[36]

Many of these critics felt that Copland was purposefully baiting his audience, and the phrase "thumbing his nose" frequently turned up in reviews. The Piano Concerto seemed particularly mocking. Frances Goldwater thought that the work made fun of its audience, while Pauline Schindler, more subtly, believed it to caricature "the life of our American cities—nervous, irrelevant, and pitched almost to a scream." Letters sent to H. T. Parker at the *Boston Evening Transcript* accused Copland of "poking fun at America." Philip Hale and E. B. Hill, in turn, had fun laughing at those proper Bostonians who thought Copland the "anti-Christ in music, or a musical bolshevik of dark and sinister deeds" and who believed his concerto "a unique example of musical depravity which should be suppressed, if necessary, by the District Attorney." And yet Hale and Hill themselves had fanned the flames: Hale by publicly chastising the concerto's arrogance and Hill (who privately dismissed *Music for the Theatre* as "close to rotten") by writing, "In his zeal to assert a kinship with the radical style, Mr. Copland may have overdone matters."[37]

These reviews often mentioned Arnold Schoenberg, a telling association because, by the mid-1920s, the Viennese composer had become, for some, a symbol of cultural anarchy and, for others, an anguished response to an insane world. Lawrence Gilman called the first movement of the *Organ Symphony* "a kind of Prospect Park Schoenberg." Another writer declared *Music for the Theatre* "a more cheerful Pierrot Lunaire, with atonality less evident, and irrepressible American fun healthily uninhibited." In his review of the Piano Concerto, Isaac Goldberg noted, "No such snickering has been heard in Symphony Hall since the playing of Schoenberg's *Five Pieces for Orchestra*." And Jerome Bohm thought that the *Piano Variations* made Schoenberg sound "as naive as Mozart."[38]

Other associations with the musical avant-garde were made. One review of the *Organ Symphony*, for instance, stated, "To the names of Cowell, Ruggles and Varèse (potential volcanoes, all three) must now be added that of a new and seething crater, Aaron Copland, of Brooklyn." Rosenfeld himself grouped Copland with Sessions, Ruggles, Chávez, Harris, Weiss, and Ruth Crawford in 1928 and with Chávez and Varèse in 1929 and 1931.[39]

Meanwhile, audience reactions to Copland's early music ranged from enthusiastic cheering to cordial applause to jeering sneers to catcalls and hisses—occasionally all at the same performance. Although the chamber and piano works were generally played before courteous if sometimes uneasy audiences, nearly all the orchestral works were greeted, at one pont or another, with hisses. The hissing began with Copland's first important premiere, that of the *Organ Symphony* in New York in 1925, prompting the beleaguered Walter Damrosch to announce, in the hopes of disarming his patrons, "Ladies and gentlemen, it seems evident that when the gifted young American who wrote this symphony can compose at the age of twenty-three, a work like this one"—here he paused for what some expected would be a proclamation of genius; then he concluded, with a smile—"it seems evident that in five years more he will be ready to commit murder." Friendly partisans in the audience, in turn, booed Damrosch's remark, and Lawrence Gilman fumed in the *New York Herald Tribune*, "The real murderers of music are the unimaginative standpatters among composers."[40]

The Piano Concerto came in for an especially rough time, with audiences hissing during as well as after performances. In Boston, the first-night audience added to the confusion by filing out during the performance. Playing the solo part in Mexico City, Copland wondered, sitting at the piano, "whether it was the correct thing to take a bow to hisses." But the performance at the Hollywood Bowl must have represented a low point; the musicians themselves hissed the work during rehearsal.[41]

Sometimes audience members responded simply by laughing. When *Music for the Theatre* was played before a Frankfurt audience in 1927, reported Henry Gilbert, "The people refused to take it very seriously. They were too busy laughing." Sometimes the laughter was highly incongruous, as at the premiere of *Vitebsk*. "For some reason," wrote Lehman Engel of this brooding work, "the nature of the piece and its strange name continued to strike the audience as funny!" In describing audience reactions to early Copland, critics often noted nervous laughter, using terms like "tittered" and "giggled" that recalled Copland's own giggling personality.[42]

Copland neither concealed nor dramatized the jeers and laughter that met his early work (though he generally tended to put a good face on things by emphasizing the more favorable parts of reviews). "I never left a concert hall or read a writeup and felt hurt because I wasn't being understood. I was, on the contrary, rather brazen about it, thinking, 'Those dumbbells, they'll see, just give them time.' " In fact, he enjoyed "bucking the tide and feeling part of the avant garde out there fighting new battles." Something of this attitude can be gleaned from an exchange between Copland and the future author of *Lexicon of Musical Invective*, Nicolas Slonimsky, who sent Copland from Boston the worst reviews of the Piano Concerto he could find, and to whom Copland responded by saying that the next time the concerto is played, "we must see if we can't get the police to raid the concert hall to give a little added interest to this 'horrible' experiment." And in a 1927 letter to the Koussevitzkys, he referred to his booed performance of the Piano Concerto at the Hollywood Bowl as a "succès de scandale," adding, "I have the impression of being a true pioneer." Even in later years he took a kind of pride in poor reviews. "The reviews were so bad," he wrote Bernstein after the 1950 premiere of the *Dickinson Songs*, "that I decided I must have written a better cycle than I had realized."[43]

Soon after the *Variations*, however, he determined to establish a better rapport with both critics and audiences. At the First Yaddo Festival (1932), he organized a conference entitled Critics and Composers, in the hopes of furthering better communication between these two largely antagonistic groups. Stung by the meager response from the critical community (only four critics showed up), he strongly castigated the press; one statement in particular made its way into the New York dailies: "Frankly, I consider newspaper criticism a menace, and we would be better off without it!" The remark, in fact, had been taken out of context and misquoted, but Copland nonetheless recanted in a letter to the *New York Times*, writing, "Far from being a 'menace' to the composer, he is an absolute necessity, if only because he serves as middle man between the public and the creative artist." At the same time, his own music began showing a more consistently accessible profile. For all its performing difficulties, the *Short Symphony* (1933) found a warm and enthusiastic reception at its 1934 premiere in Mexico City. The days of hissing were, for the time being, over.[44]

Copland observed two trends among composers in the 1930s: first, a continuing attempt to "simplify their musical language" and, second, a desire to "make contact" with as wide an audience as possible. Since 1927, he had been in the process of simplifying, or at least paring down, his musical language, though in such a manner as to sometimes have the effect, paradoxically, of estranging audiences and performers. By 1933, as he completed the *Short Symphony* and started work on *El Salón México*, he began to find ways to make his starkly personal language accessible to a surprisingly large number of people.[45]

11

Copland Among His Peers

Once Copland returned to the States from Paris, he immediately sought out other composers his own age. Not only did he enjoy having "pals" around, but he recognized the advantages of banding together. "When I was in my twenties," he recalled, "I had a consuming interest in what the other composers of my generation were producing. Even before I was acquainted with the names of Roy Harris, Roger Sessions, Walter Piston, and the two Thom(p)sons, I instinctively thought of myself as part of a 'school' of composers. Without the combined effort of a group of men it seemed hardly possible to give the United States a music of its own." In this he was inspired by the example of *Les Six*, a group of French contemporaries who had rallied together, in part to promote their own music.[1]

With an article for *Modern Music* entitled "1926: America's Young Men of Promise," Copland quickly established himself as an expert spokesperson for his generation of composers. He assumed this role largely by default, noting that although Europe enjoyed a tradition of established composers promoting young talent, America's composers were "left to shift for themselves."[2]

This 1926 survey of seventeen young American composers revealed an appreciation for good craftsmanship, individuality, originality, and accessibility wherever found. Still, the author more or less staked his ground, placing at one end "well-known" composers like Howard Hanson, who, he would later say, produced a "kind of palatable music," and, on the other end, "revolutionary" composers like Henry Cowell, deemed "essentially an inventor, not a composer." From the start, he showed a preference for those composers more toward the center, in this early outing intimating a special respect for Randall Thompson, Herbert Elwell, and George Antheil.

Copland's initial reactions to Hanson and Cowell did not bode well for future relations with either composer. His friendship with Hanson remained decidedly cool even though the latter conducted his music with some frequency. Copland simply had little interest in the "archconservative" Hanson, whose music he found dull and "uninspiring," as he told Roger Sessions in 1928. When, over fifty years later, Phillip Ramey referred to Hanson as "the American Sibelius," Copland tartly remarked, "You flatter him." Still, in 1975, on the occasion of an honorary doctorate from the Eastman School, Copland received from Hanson (who directed Eastman for many years) a warm letter that purportedly left him deeply moved.[3]

Similar tensions marked Copland's relationship with the African-American composer, William Grant Still. In 1936, while discerning "a certain natural musicality and charm" in Still's work, Copland decried its "marked leaning toward the sweetly saccharine that one should like to see eliminated." Such a remark was no harsher than Copland's wont—and less severe than criticism of his own music by some friends and foes alike—but Still and his future wife, the writer Verna Arvey, took it badly. Copland further upset the two the next year by referring to Still as an able orchestrator currently working in a style of American music "often based on the slushier side of jazz." The comment wounded and festered; Arvey bitterly recalled it as late as 1953. By this time, as Catherine Parsons Smith has documented, Still had privately and in 1950 even publicly implicated Copland in an antiblack communist conspiracy allegedly aimed at impeding the careers of conservative composers like himself. Such a charge represented a twist on the period's more typical innuendos of a Copland-led Jewish or homosexual cabal, but was no less preposterous for that.[4]

Copland's relations with Henry Cowell (1897–1965) were also fraught with difficulties. In the 1920s, they traveled in different circles: Cowell with the composers associated with Edgard Varèse's International Composers' Guild and with his own New Music Society, Copland with the League of Composers. Copland never revised his early opinion of Cowell as an "inventor" (though he conducted *Synchrony* in his later years), while from the start, Cowell contrasted the successful and French-influenced music of the Jewish-American Copland with the "more serious" but overlooked masterworks of those two "real" Americans, Ives and Ruggles. According to Frank R. Rossiter, Cowell even felt "a petty hostility toward Copland," one possibly exacerbated by racist leanings. After Cowell's death, his wife, Sidney, outspokenly denounced Copland as haughty and wily. Whether Cowell's hostility toward Copland was "petty," as Rossiter claimed, or justified, as Sidney Cowell imputed, one can only conclude that Cowell harbored resentments.[5]

Even so, Cowell—who, like Copland, resisted sectarianism—never repudiated Copland as did Dane Rudhyar and some others in his circle. Cowell wrote respectful, even admiring things about Copland's early music and published "As It Fell" in his *New Music Quarterly*, to which Copland subscribed. Though they never, according to Sidney, "clicked," they maintained a cordial professional correspondence and even socialized to an extent; Ruth Crawford recalled a party in 1930 in which the "elusive" Copland defended Stravinsky's *Oedipus Rex* to Cowell. The two discovered mutual interests as both became involved with the Composers' Collective and began to make occasional use of American folk music; Cowell, incarcerated in 1936 on morals charges involving homosexual activity, also appreciated Copland's efforts in helping to procure his parole in 1940.[6]

In addition, the two shared a dear friend in Colin McPhee (1901–1964), the adventurous composer and ethnomusicologist who incorporated aspects of Indonesian music into his own work after travels to Southeast Asia in the 1930s. Copland included McPhee's music at a 1931 Copland-Sessions Concert and recommended his *Tabuh-Tabuhan* for orchestra (1936) to Koussevitzky, writing, "I think you will find it full of exotic charm and new sonorities." And yet Copland apparently regarded McPhee's music as peripheral in importance; his writings rarely took any notice of it, and he seems to have disapproved of the composer's reliance on Balinese idioms. For his part, McPhee, while admiring the "vitality, exhilaration, and pungent orchestration" of Copland's jazz works, expressed doubts about his later efforts, including *Lincoln Portrait*, whose "eloquent simplicity," he wrote, "does not ring quite true to my ears." Their friendship survived such artistic differences, however, and in the 1950s, Copland helped the alcoholic, troubled McPhee obtain a Koussevitzky Foundation commission and came through with loans and cash gifts as well.[7]

Of all the Americans surveyed in 1926, Copland had particularly high hopes for his exact contemporary George Antheil (1900–1959). "One needn't be particularly astute," he ventured, "to realize that he possesses the greatest gifts of any young American now writing." Copland had met Antheil and his wife in Paris in 1923; in October of that year, he heard Antheil perform three of his piano sonatas at a tumultuous concert at the Champs Elysées Theater that helped promote him, at least among the French, as the foremost American composer of their generation.[8]

Copland was immediately impressed, calling Antheil "extremely talented" in a short article for *Modern Music* on the composer (1925), his first piece of published criticism. "When he plays his own compositions the effect is electrifying," he reported. Years later, when Oscar Levant asked him if he had ever been jealous of anyone, Copland replied, "When I first went to Paris I was jealous of Antheil's piano playing—it was so brilliant; he could demonstrate so well what he wanted to do." At the same time, he immediately criticized formal and stylistic weaknesses; and after attending the 1926 premiere of *Ballet mécanique*, he confided to Israel Citkowitz, "I am in all honesty bound to repeat my unshakeable conviction—the boy is a genius. Need I add that he has yet to write a work that shows it. If he keeps on exactly as he has started the sum total of all his genius will be exactly nothing."[9]

The following year, Copland played one of the pianos in a performance of *Ballet mécanique* in a disastrous all-Antheil concert in Carnegie Hall that signaled the composer's precipitous fall from stardom. Copland made sure New York gave Antheil a second chance by commissioning his Second String Quartet (1928) for a Copland-Sessions Concert. By this time, Antheil had moved on to a more neoclassical style, and the *Quartet*, observed Copland, "received a particularly poor press and was viewed as an apology for his earlier and scandalous *Ballet mécanique*." Undeterred, Copland asked him to perform some new piano music at Yaddo; Antheil responded with his Sonatina (1932), dedicated to Copland "in admiration of your work, and in appreciation of your friendship."[10]

During these same years, Antheil privately rebuked Copland for his 1925 article and dismissed him as the composer of passé "recluse" music who, as the promoter of other people's work, could not of necessity be a good composer himself. For his part, Copland concluded by 1936 that

Antheil had not fulfilled his promise; his dubious claim to fame remained *Ballet mécanique*, which Copland described as "a reductio ad absurdum of Stravinsky's emphasis on furious rhythms and pitiless dissonances." While disappointed with the outcome of his colleague's career, Copland respected Antheil's subsequent work in Hollywood, turning to him for advice about film scoring and citing Antheil's score to *Once in a Blue Moon* as one of Hollywood's best. Such deference was mutual. "I think of you, read through your new scores, and admire you," Antheil wrote Copland in 1946. "The *Appalachian Spring* is a fine piece, and I approve deeply of your present direction."[11]

When, in 1963, Copland reprinted "1926: America's Young Men of Promise," he noted its omission of George Gershwin (1898–1937), who, he wrote, "was famous in 1926, but was down in everyone's book as a composer of popular music with only two concert pieces to his credit." While this explanation appears credible, the absence of Gershwin from the survey's 1936 sequel (in which the author apologized for his earlier exclusion of Walter Piston and others), seems, in the light of *An American in Paris* and *Porgy and Bess*, less defensible (except, perhaps, that Gershwin needed no boosting on Copland's part). Even after Gershwin's death, Copland remained for a while somewhat remote on the subject.[12]

Copland's interest in Gershwin found little encouragement from their rare personal contacts. When they first met (through Nicolas Slonimsky in 1932, at the latest), they discovered they had, in Copland's words, "nothing to say to each other." On their few subsequent meetings, recalled Copland, "We weren't together very long before he was sitting at his piano and playing me his latest composition." Even Gershwin's devoted sidekick, Oscar Levant, would quip, "An evening with George Gershwin is a George Gershwin evening."[13]

What might have also hindered their friendship—besides disparities in circumstance and temperament—was the fact that critics typically paired and often compared them, especially in the 1920s, when both were widely associated with jazz. Carl Van Vechten and Lazare Saminsky stated a preference for Gershwin; Virgil Thomson, Edmund Wilson, Paul Rosenfeld, and Henry Cowell considered Copland the greater artist; still others, like Isaac Goldberg, Vernon Duke, and John Kirkpatrick, seemed to admire both in about equal measure. Whatever the range of opinion, Copland and Gershwin very likely felt the strain of finding themselves cast as rivals. One senses some envy on Copland's part in a 1932 letter to Koussevitzky from Mexico, in which he writes, "At last I have found a country where I am as famous as Gershwin!" And according to one source, Gershwin resented Copland's "ascendancy in serious music circles."[14]

One Gershwin biography, however, sensationalized this essentially distant relationship by portraying its subject as victimized by a "threatened" Copland, who "went out of his way to separate himself from a Tin Pan Alley–trained Jew." In fact, the two were cordial to and respectful of each other. Copland publicly expressed admiration for Gershwin's originality and individuality as early as 1927. In 1929 he performed one of Gershwin's *Three Preludes* in a lecture-recital of young American composers that also included pieces by Sessions, Harris, Chávez, and himself. Gershwin, meanwhile, seemed especially taken with *The Second Hurricane* and agreed to sponsor Copland for membership in ASCAP.[15]

Copland's appreciation for Gershwin deepened over time. In 1945 he named Gershwin as one of ten serious composers "most worthy to represent American culture to European nations." And in 1972, he said of Gershwin, "He became ambitious and justified his ambitions by writing the works which are still very much alive, like the *Rhapsody in Blue* and his Piano Concerto," works Copland often conducted, along with *An American in Paris*. "Copland liked things not necessarily for their perfection, but for their vitality," remarked John Kennedy. "Certainly Gershwin was an example of that." Still, Copland never accorded Gershwin the esteem he showed his most admired American contemporaries: Roger Sessions, Roy Harris, Virgil Thomson, and Walter Piston.[16]

Copland first singled out these four "exceptional" composers in a 1935 article, the same year arranging five one-man concerts of their—and his—music at the New School. *Our New Music* (1941) further discussed American music largely in terms of these four and himself (plus the younger Marc Blitzstein). Because these composers observed all this from the sidelines, they cannot really be compared to the Russian Five or *Les Six*, whose members actively banded together. Thomson, at least, gave the association his blessings, gaily referring to the group as Copland's "commando unit."[17]

Copland's 1936 sequel to his earlier survey clarified his special regard for these four in the context of the larger scene, while also acknowledging Randall Thompson, Bernard Rogers, and Quincy Porter as important in a somewhat lesser way, clearly more to his taste than Howard Hanson, Leo Sowerby, Henry Cowell, Douglas Moore, Robert Russell Bennett, or William Grant Still. Copland would later take a brighter view of Moore on the strength of his subsequent stage works, but 1936 found his views of his own generation of composers largely established.

Copland first met Sessions (at the latest) at Nadia Boulanger's in May 1926. Born, like Copland, on Washington Avenue in Brooklyn, Sessions (1896–1985) grew up in Northampton, Massachusetts; attended the Kent School, Harvard, and Yale; and studied with Ernest Bloch. Also like Copland, he came under the influence of Romain Rolland's *Jean-Christophe* as a teenager, but to somewhat different effect; he declared himself, in 1917, an "internationalist." After his years with Bloch, he consulted briefly with Boulanger, but he found France "fundamentally alien" and spent the years from 1925 to 1933 primarily in Florence, Rome, and Berlin.[18]

Copland and Sessions reacted immediately and strongly to each other's music. Reviewing the 1926 all-American concert that occasioned their first recorded meeting, Sessions declared Copland "artistically the most mature" of the composers on the program; like Thomson, he subsequently found the *Organ Symphony* "a revelation." Copland meanwhile wrote Sessions about his First Symphony (1927), "I've played it over and over again and it seems to me more lovely and more profound each time."[19]

Copland vigorously promoted Sessions, practically serving as his agent. He provided encouragement, recommended him for Guggenheim Fellowships (1926, 1927), raised money for him, brought him on board *Modern Music*, and introduced him to Koussevitzky, who in turn helped him win a Rome Prize. "It was Copland," writes Andrea Olmstead, "with his ambition and savvy, that helped Sessions's career more than any other single person was to do."[20]

Differences between Copland and Sessions quickly emerged, however. In the same 1926 letter that praised the *Organ Symphony*, Sessions gave Copland "hell" for "wasting precious energy" on young American composers for the sake of "anything so vague and dubious as the 'future of American music.' " He further reproved his assuming the role of the "New York composer" or "American composer" in works like *Music for the Theatre*. Such forthright criticism of Copland's attempts to foster a national school and create a recognizably American sound produced a cycle of debates, apologies, and reconciliations until, finally, the friendship collapsed in the mid-1930s.[21]

Sessions simply had little sympathy for Copland's immersion, whatever the mode, in the American scene. Pained by scandals in Washington, the case of Sacco and Vanzetti, and American anti-Semitism, he sought, rather, to escape it all. "I am really more conscious of the America that I really believe in, America as she may become in the future, that is, over here than I am at home," he wrote to Copland in 1928. Some months later he further confided, "You are the only person over here [in the States] with whom I feel quite myself." On his disillusioned return from Europe in 1933, he allied himself with such émigrés as Schoenberg and Krenek; after the war, he felt most himself with Luigi Dallapiccola.[22]

Despite his general disdain for most American composers and his determination to remain uninvolved with the music scene at home, Sessions lent his name and prestige to a concert series, the Copland-Sessions Concerts, which has become legendary for its promotion of new American music. Copland did nearly all the work; Sessions mostly just approved programs from Florence or Berlin. Deeply wary of the entire enterprise and frequently critical of the composers represented, Sessions—away in Europe—rarely attended the concerts himself; he had trouble simply getting his own Piano Sonata composed in time for a 1928 concert for which it had been advertised. When it came to the concert series, says Olmstead, he "posed more obstacles than he offered solutions."[23]

The Copland-Sessions Concerts sponsored two or three chamber music concerts annually over the four-year period 1928–31. The concerts were all held in New York, except for one in Paris's Salle Chopin (1929) and one in London's Aeolian Hall (1931). A program note to the first concert stated, "This series is not in any sense designed to compete with the work of existing organizations already so admirably engaged in presenting modern music. But we feel that the youngest American composers have been, till now, without a proper vehicle, an institution explicitly devoted to the interests of the developing artist."[24]

The reference to "existing organizations" alluded to New York's two rival modern music associations: the International Composers' Guild (1921–27), which had just evolved into the Pan-American Association of Composers (1928–34), and the League of Composers (founded 1923). All of these new-music societies were largely bankrolled by well-to-do women patrons: the guild by Gertrude Vanderbilt Whitney, the league by Alma Wertheim, and the Copland-Sessions Concerts by Mary Senior Churchill. These women, writes Carol Oja, "established a fragile but crucial network for the early performance and reception of the avant-garde in New York."[25]

The received wisdom holds that the guild, run by Edgard Varèse, favored the ultramoderns, whereas the league, directed by Claire Reis, tended toward more conservative American and European composers, especially those associated with Stravinsky. The clearest difference between the two groups actually concerned the guild's reluctance to repeat performances of new works; the two groups originally split up over just this matter. But this squabble barely disguised the central underlying conflict: the league's unwillingness to submit to Varèse's leadership. "Either you were a pal of the League of Composers or you were a pal of Varèse's," recalled Copland, summing up the matter neatly. "You couldn't be a pal of both."[26]

Although the guild and the league mounted programs much more similar than commonly thought, the latter, the more politically left-wing of the two groups, more clearly aspired to reach as large an audience as possible. Such differences sometimes masked a bias among a number of leading guild members against homosexuals and Jews. Whether or not the guild—as seems to have been the case—limited the participation of homosexuals and Jews, the league provided a more welcoming atmosphere in this respect. Indeed, Jews by and large founded the league and were so well represented therein that Virgil Thomson sourly referred to it as the "League of Jewish Composers."[27]

The Copland-Sessions Concerts carved their own niche, targeting American composers of various types between the ages of twenty-five and thirty-five, overlapping to some extent with both the guild and the league. It was evident from the start, however, that they would bypass such established figures as Hanson and Gershwin. As for the ultramoderns, Copland and Sessions included pieces by Crawford, Weiss, Rudhyar, and Cowell in 1928, but thereafter bypassed them, reasoning that, with the Pan-American Association, the ultramoderns had their own forum. But neither Copland nor Sessions had much sympathy for that whole group; this was one thing that they could agree on. Rather, the concerts favored mainstream modernists, including, as the years progressed, émigrés from Europe.

After the demise of the Copland-Sessions Concerts, Copland spearheaded and organized, with the financial support of Elizabeth Ames, two weekends of new music in the summers of 1932 and 1933 at Yaddo, New York, near Saratoga (the First and Second Yaddo Music Festivals). When Paul Rosenfeld and others took the First Festival to task for merely reflecting Copland's personal predilections (and, in particular, for shunning the ultramoderns), Copland privately explained to his confreres, "I prefer that we be called a clique rather than that we take in a man who would put unjustifiable pieces on the programs. I want to be broad, but if one includes everyone that seems to me being too broad." Years later he further explained that since neither scores nor parts of new music were generally available, he needed to rely on personal contacts. Nonetheless, he tried to make the Second Festival more inclusive and democratic by appointing a Central Music Committee and regional representatives, including Wallingford Riegger and Henry Cowell.[28]

Meanwhile, his long-standing dispute with Sessions over the idea of an American school continued. In a letter to Copland in the summer of 1932, Sessions wrote at length about how Copland's attempt to win over critics to the cause of American music at the First Yaddo Festival had been misguided. "I certainly hope that no music of mine will ever be played or praised simply because anyone feels it his duty to encourage American music," he remonstrated. They continued the debate for another year, Copland arguing that Sessions, having spent the better part of a decade abroad, did not fully appreciate the plight of the American composer, Sessions contending that Copland exaggerated the situation. Despite such disagreements, they remained friendly, and in the spring of 1934, Sessions generously accepted Copland's lover, Victor Kraft, as "a nonpaying pupil."[29]

By 1935, however, relations had become increasingly strained, and by 1936 the friendship essentially ended. Olmstead suggests that the 1936 divorce between Roger and Barbara Sessions may have estranged Copland as it did Nadia Boulanger. If so, the divorce precipitated the decline of a relationship long beset by deep artistic and temperamental differences. Among other things, Copland had begun to find Sessions's music "almost too difficult," while Sessions seems to have felt just the opposite about Copland's. Other factors no doubt played a part as well, including Sessions's possible resentment over Copland's growing success.[30]

Copland, however, remained admiring of Sessions's work, usually singling out for praise something from the 1920s or else the Violin Concerto (1935), which he once cited as unfairly neglected. In *Our New Music*, he described the composer as the consummate, painstaking craftsman of "tactile sensibility," limited melodic inventiveness, and textural complexity, creating, at his best, "music of ineffable pessimism—resigned, unprotesting, inexpressibly sad, and of a deeply human and nonromantic quality." In 1967, he reassessed a still complex but much more productive Sessions, whose "creative energies" had been released and stimulated by his "absorption" of the twelve-tone method. His work was still "not easily lovable"—privately, he admitted, too, that the complexity of some of the late scores baffled him—but it was music "of serious import and permanent value."[31]

For his part, Sessions's attitude toward his American contemporaries grew steadily more patronizing. Pressed for his opinions during the course of the 1930s, he would begrudgingly single out Copland, Harris, or Piston. In a 1938 letter to Elizabeth Sprague Coolidge, he expressed greatest respect for Piston: "Copland and Harris, I feel, both have more talent, but I have thus far been able to enjoy their music only in spots." In 1956, he granted that Copland defied pigeonholing; rather, he "summed up" a number of prominent trends in American music, remaining "a strong and well-defined personality, easily recognizable in the differing profiles his music has assumed." Privately, however, he complained that Copland's more popular scores compromised his integrity; and he would say to Milton Babbitt, somewhat equivocally, "Copland was more talented than he realized."[32]

Copland met Roy Harris (1898–1979) at the MacDowell Colony in the summer of 1925. Whereas Sessions struck him as more philosopher than composer, Harris, who grew up in Covina, California, seemed "like a farmer" with "a simple charm and a winning personality." He was also impressed with Harris's looks. "He was a very attractive young man," he would tell Phillip Ramey. "He looked like a movie star." Harris once claimed that Copland had made some sort of sexual overture in the 1920s. "Of course, I wasn't interested," he added.[33]

Copland was immediately affected not only by Harris's person but by his strong artistic individuality, which remained for him that composer's most appealing trait: "You can punch that personality full of holes," he wrote in 1940, ". . . but the fact will still remain that his is the most personal note in American music today." Significantly, Copland defined Harris's "personality" in terms of his Americanism—not the clichéd association of Harris with the "open prairies and woolly West," but with "the corner drugstore, the movie house, the public high school" of small-town America. This national ambience took other manifestations:

What Harris writes, as a rule, is music of real sweep and breadth, with power and emotional depth such as only a generously built country could produce. It is American in rhythm, especially in the fast parts, with a jerky, nervous quality that is peculiarly our own. It is crude and unabashed at times, with occasional blobs and yawps of sound that Whitman would have approved of. And always it is

169

music that addresses itself to a big public, sure sign of the composer of a big country.[34]

Copland vigorously championed Harris, including touting him to Koussevitzky as an "American Mussorgsky." In 1931, as his career began to take off, Harris wrote to Copland, with characteristic grandiloquence, "You were the very first one to believe in me when I had nothing but a sublime faith in myself, and so many times I have said to myself— sometime Aaron will be glad he picked me for 'a winning horse.' " At the same time, Copland recognized Harris's technical shortcomings and advised that he study with Boulanger, which Harris did from 1926 to 1929—not long enough, in the opinion of both Boulanger and Copland. For all Harris's progress made with Boulanger, Copland still regarded him deficient in technical matters, finding his "rudderless" forms especially problematic. Among Harris's output, Copland often singled out the Piano Sonata (1928) and the Concerto for Clarinet, Piano, and String Quartet (1929)—both composed under Boulanger's tutelage.[35]

Harris wrote these works, too, at a time when his friendship with Copland was at its height. Even so, he was beginning to try Copland's patience, as he wrote him a series of letters in the early 1930s at once warmly affectionate and teasingly provocative. One four-page letter (1930) haranguing him about the placement of his String Quartet on a Copland-Sessions Concert shows what Copland was willing to put up with for the sake of his profession. Copland changed the program as requested, but wrote to a friend the day after receiving Harris's letter, "His Quartet is his best piece so far and makes me wish I only knew him thru his music."[36]

In later years, Harris made no secret of his feeling that Copland had usurped his reputation as the country's "truly American" composer: "What diabolical plan have you up your sleeve now to scoop all my small public away from me—what there is left," wrote an at least candidly resentful Harris to Copland in 1942. In 1949, he composed *Kentucky Spring* for orchestra in a transparent attempt to rival *Appalachian Spring*. He remained convinced that he represented the real America, and would sardonically refer to the "New York City boys," by whom he primarily meant Copland. Copland responded in kind, referring to Harris, in a 1943 letter to William Schuman, as "the Patriarch Himself."[37]

Copland's friendship with Virgil Thomson (1896–1989) dated back to 1921–22, when the latter took a year off from Harvard to study with

Boulanger in Paris. This early bond was important. They met at a time and place—Paris in the early 1920s—when Satie and Jean Cocteau reigned as central figures. Although Copland neither identified that strongly with Satie nor ran with the Cocteau crowd, he was better prepared than most to appreciate Thomson's self-styled role as a Satie disciple. When many years later Phillip Ramey would complain to Copland that Thomson's music was "dumb, dumb, dumb," he would retort, "Yes, I know, but it's intentionally dumb. He's the American Satie."[38]

As early as 1926 Copland further appreciated not only Thomson's "melodic invention" and "fine feeling for prosody" but the fact that his wit and mock naïveté offered a refreshing contrast at concerts of modern music. He included Thomson's *Five Phrases from the Song of Solomon* on the very first Copland-Sessions Concert (1928) and his setting of Gertrude Stein's *Capital Capitals* at a subsequent one (1929); the latter especially was such a hit that Copland featured it again on their one concert in London (1931). In 1932 he further programmed Thomson's *Stabat Mater* at the First Yaddo Festival—another triumph—and then persuaded the League of Composers to perform it and Cos Cob to publish it, providing Thomson's first publication.[39]

The Copland-Thomson relationship was probably warmest in the early 1930s, when together, like older brothers, they fretted over the musical education of Paul Bowles; during these years, Thomson signed his letters to Copland "love, Virgil." Even then, however, they remained reserved with each other, this partly due to their different attitudes toward Nadia Boulanger, whom Thomson had come to scorn. But there were temperamental differences as well: Copland "never felt personally comfortable with Virgil," writes Anthony Tommasini, "what with his airs, his cigarette holder, and his effeminate mannerisms."[40]

Although Thomson appreciated all that Copland had done on his behalf—"I hope I can do something half as nice for you one day," he wrote Copland in 1932—one would not necessarily know it from his article "Aaron Copland," for *Modern Music* (1932). Whereas in 1925 he had praised Copland's *Organ Symphony* as "honest, personal music written by an American young man," this essay, written at Copland's personal request, found him in a different mood, emphasizing Copland's Jewishness. And while admiring Copland's "nobility of feeling" and "force and elegance," he criticized the music as comparatively ineffective and dull, falsely grandiose, eclectic, derivative, and lacking in "style" and "personal integrity."[41]

The notion—which appears strange to us today—that Copland lacked a distinctive style had been voiced earlier by the composer Theodore Chanler (1902–1961) in his article "Aaron Copland up to Now" (1930). "I've decided that your style is full of impurities," Chanler wrote to Copland shortly before the article came out, warning him that he was about to be "thickly buttered in spots." Although Chanler's "roast" turned out to be largely respectful, he criticized Copland's "poverty of harmonic resource" and noted, like Thomson, the absence of a "unifying integrity of style." A friend and fellow graduate of Boulanger's studio, Chanler immediately apologized to Copland about the article; Henry Cowell, who anthologized the article in 1933, even felt obliged to append some nice words at the end. But as with the Thomson essay, Copland took no offense. On the contrary, he kindly thanked Chanler for the constructive criticism, and he continued to program Chanler's music at Yaddo as he had for the Copland-Sessions Concerts. Their friendship similarly survived Chanler's severe review of *Our New Music*; Copland remained respectful of Chanler's sensitive songs and conducted his own *Nonet* at Chanler's memorial service.[42]

As for Thomson, he handed back the charge of eclecticism but not that of dullness; *Four Saints* (1928), he wrote, "made all other American musical stage pieces seem dull by comparison." Copland acknowledged that some colleagues were reluctant to take Thomson "seriously as a composer" but argued that the "idea" animating his work—"that the purpose of music is not to impress and overwhelm the listener but to entertain and charm him"—was a perfectly valid one. His own preference went to Thomson's vocal works and their "extraordinary felicity in the handling of the vocal text. His gift for allowing English to sound natural when sung is almost unique among American composers. We can all learn from him in this respect." He liked *The Mother of Us All* (1947) less than *Four Saints*, however, writing to Leonard Bernstein, "It's as if a new music idea hadn't occurred to him in ten years. The prosody, as per usual, is superb—but then it's easy to have good prosody if you have nothing else on your mind."[43]

Thomson and Copland criticized each other's prose as well. "Your book I read through twice and I still find it a bore," wrote Thomson about *What to Listen for in Music*. "Not that the book doesn't contain a hundred wise remarks about music. But it also contains a lot of stuff that I don't believe and that I am not at all convinced you believe." For his part, Copland found *The State of Music* amusing but disingenuous, especially the author's attacks on the "International Modern Music Ring," which, in a jab at Thomson's well-known remarks about a "Jewish conspiracy" and a "Jewish mafia" among American composers, Copland compared to "Father Coughlin's International Bankers": "This is just our old friend Virgil having a good time. For fifteen years now he has been repeating the same thing, as if we didn't know that this same style of Modern Music which he supposedly abhors, has served as the perfect foil for the simplicities of Thomson, Sauguet and Co."[44]

Whatever their differences, Thomson and Copland worked together closely and efficiently. In 1937 they helped organize the American Composers' Alliance and cofounded, along with Lehman Engel and Marc Blitzstein, the Arrow Press. Thomson often showed Copland his music and welcomed his comments, and Copland tried to get Thomson a contract with Boosey & Hawkes. "Aaron and I were sold on the same general idea," wrote Thomson, "that composers are not rival cheats at some show game on the street. We're all members of the same Fifth Avenue Merchants' Association, and our future and our present depend on being good colleagues."[45]

By the time Thomson permanently settled in New York in 1940, he and Copland had developed peacefully coexisting coteries. Ned Rorem, a Thomson acolyte who distinguished his "faction" as "Satie-French," as opposed to Copland's, which was "Stravinsky-French," exaggerated the situation, however, when he wrote, "Aaron had an entourage, so did Virgil; you belonged to one or the other, like Avignon and Rome, take it or leave it." In fact, both circles extensively overlapped, as in the case of William Flanagan. But a rivalry undeniably existed, at least on the part of Thomson, who felt that he deserved some of the fame won by Copland in his later years. "I'm jealous of Aaron," he once told David Diamond. "He's had too much success." When Diamond asked how he could envy a man who had worked so hard for so many American composers, he retorted, "We all did, baby, we all did."[46]

The uglier side of such resentment found expression in unpublished drafts of John Cage's book on Thomson, in which Cage unquestioningly assumed the truth of Thomson's accusation that Copland, as the "de facto head" of the League of Composers, had annihilated the International Composers Guild, "the Jewish question having been raised against the Copland organization in a city where it is suicide so to further one's interests." "For nearly one quarter of a century," wrote Cage, "composers promising serious competition to Copland's position of power in

New York either left town of their own accord or indirectly received honorable positions in distant places." Thomson wisely thought twice, however, about letting such slander go into print.[47]

In attempts to at least demystify Copland's reputation, Thomson also suggested ulterior motives for what seemed like simple generosity on the other man's part. Moreover, he took some of the credit for Copland's popular ballets and film scores, claiming that he had both anticipated and influenced these works. Indeed, aside from discussing him as a "career man," Thomson's treatment of Copland in his text *American Music* primarily concerned this very topic: *Four Saints,* he argued, inspired *The Second Hurricane*; *The Filling Station* encouraged *Billy the Kid*; and his work in general provided Copland with both a musical vocabulary for American atmosphere and a model for folk-song setting.[48]

Long before Thomson published such claims, some knowing listeners recognized his importance to Copland. As early as 1948, for instance, Bernstein told Harold Clurman that Thomson had inspired Copland to write "simple jolly music." In more recent years, Ned Rorem in particular argued along these lines: "Virgil's 'Americanness' predates Aaron's. Virgil's use of Protestant hymns and, as he calls them, 'darn fool ditties' dates from the twenties. Aaron's use came later, filtered through Thomson's. One may prefer Aaron's art to Virgil's, but give Virgil full credit: Aaron knew a good thing when he saw it." Rorem and others even implied that Thomson's prime significance might have been as a stimulus for Copland.[49]

This whole matter, however, awaits careful scrutiny. Thomson clearly had some influence on Copland, especially in the late 1930s, and perhaps most noticeably in *Billy the Kid* (1938), an important work, if not as pivotal as sometimes presumed. Some of the ballet's more daringly rough-hewn moments—as found, for example, in Billy's solo, the pas de deux, or even the very opening measures—seem to leap from the pages of any number of Thomson scores. *The Second Hurricane* (1937) at times also suggests Thomson's imprint, as do some other works, including parts of *Rodeo* (1942). But Copland absorbed a wide variety of sources (*Billy,* for instance, has one dance, "Billy's Demise," that strongly recalls Stravinsky's *Apollo*) and ultimately one needs to place his assimilation of Thomson in this more inclusive context.

Although Walter Piston (1894–1976) was the oldest of the "commando unit," Copland recognized his significance less immediately; he thought the *Three Pieces* for flute, clarinet, and bassoon, performed at the opening Copland-Sessions Concert, "little more than well written." In addition, as a Harvard professor, Piston was somewhat removed from the New York scene. However, two works from 1933—the *Concerto for Orchestra* and the First String Quartet, the latter performed at the Second Yaddo Festival—more clearly revealed his stature: "A work like the First String Quartet," observed Copland, "with its acidulous opening movement, the poetic mood painting of its second, and its breezy finale, sets a superb standard of taste and of expert string writing." The Second Yaddo Festival itself, which represented a "swing away from the experimentalism of the twenties," may well have contributed to this increased receptivity to Piston. In any event, Copland recommended the *Concerto* to Chávez in 1935, describing it as "very able, though influenced by Hindemith."[50]

Copland valued the sheer technical finesse of such music; it provided, he thought, the kind of foundation required for a "full-fledged school of composers in this country." In addition, the music played well with critics and musicians both at home and abroad. "A good many more pieces of just this caliber," said Copland of the *Concerto*, "are needed to give American music more definite standing in the community." Such virtues, he implied, more than compensated for the music's conventional forms and modest scope. Ultimately he may well have liked best the ballet suite from *The Incredible Flutist*, which he occasionally conducted in later years; he described its finale as "an all-around knock-out job by an American, and a college professor at that."[51]

Copland argued with Piston—as with Sessions—over the feasibility of an American school of music. Recalled Piston,

> Copland and I had a friendly war about American music. Aaron and I were very thick. We practically grew up together. He had hopes of producing an American music that was just as recognizable as French and German music. I told him that America had so many different nationalities that it would be nearly impossible. I felt the only definition of American music was that written by an American. He had to agree, but he felt there ought to be a vernacular.

William Austin further observes, "Copland in Paris was shocked to realize how separate were 'classical music' and American life. . . . Piston could understand Copland's shock and resolution; he could judge both as naive, while continuing to admire Copland's strong talent and growing skills. . . . In Boston, the [Piston] family lived in ways as American as

Copland's family in Brooklyn, so the 'separateness' that struck Copland and many others as a problem seemed to Piston an oversimplification and exaggeration."[52]

But Piston had an open-mindedness like Copland's, and such differences never led to any rift or animosity; indeed, Copland thought Piston "one of the most tactful, discreet, and warm human beings." Moreover, as Austin notes, Piston admired Copland's music. "The orchestration is superb," he wrote Copland after hearing *El Salón México* on the radio (introduced by the announcer, to his delight, as the work of one Aaron Piston). Piston's widely used *Orchestration* (1955) cited Copland's music far more than that of any other American composer.[53]

In addition, while both Sessions and Thomson very possibly would have liked to teach at Harvard, their alma mater, it was Copland whom Piston asked to take over his classes during the spring semesters of 1935 and 1944. Piston surely had a hand, too, in Harvard's commissioning *In the Beginning* (1947) and in bringing Copland to campus for the 1951–52 Norton lectures—the first American composer so asked. Nor did turf tensions develop as they did with Sessions, Thomson, and others; on the contrary, some Piston students, including Elliott Carter, Arthur Berger, Leonard Bernstein, Irving Fine, Harold Shapero, and Noël Lee, became particularly devoted to Copland. Finally, their music shared some real stylistic and aesthetic affinities, as critics occasionally noted, especially in the 1940s.[54]

After World War II, the "commando unit" more or less dissolved as a group. The great communal ventures—the Copland-Sessions Concerts, Yaddo, the New School concerts, the founding of Cos Cob, Arrow, and the American Composers' Alliance—were over. In 1946, the League of Composers ceased publishing their in-house organ, *Modern Music,* which had published so many reviews and articles about and by them. All five were now firmly established on the musical map. They had won their fight.

During all this time, Copland had largely formed the glue that kept them together. Although the other four more or less shared a real respect for one another, their relations, marked by personal resentments and artistic conflicts, were more professional than anything else. Only their admiration for Copland and his music enabled them to band together to the extent that they did.

In his later years, Copland himself grew distant from these old colleagues. They corresponded sporadically, seeing one another mostly at premieres and memorial concerts. If Copland always enjoyed Piston's company, he took less pleasure in socializing with the others. At the same time, in the 1970s Copland and Sessions had something of a nostalgic rapprochement after decades of coolness, and in 1986, at a rather advanced stage of senility, he asked that Thomson visit him, a very rare kind of request.[55]

In 1974, Copland offered a cautious but upbeat assessment of what he and his most admired colleagues had accomplished:

> I think that group has left a mark on American music. How important a mark, nobody knows. What it will seem like a hundred years from now, I don't know. But certainly it was necessary that such a thing should have happened. There had to be a group of composers who imposed themselves. I think in that sense, it was a success.

In a 1980 interview with Ramey, he offered especially frank appraisals of his old friends ("What's the point of being my age if you can't be candid?" asked the eighty-year-old composer). Sessions's importance lay in "his seriousness, solid culture and broad musical background and knowledge," as well as his influence on a sophisticated elite, but his music did not present "an especially striking stylistic profile" and had made "comparatively little dent." Harris's "great weakness was that he seldom was able to shape a piece so that it made sense from beginning to end and seemed logical and inevitable," though the Third Symphony remained "a terrific piece . . . in some ways . . . the most impressive symphony ever produced in America, this despite an unfortunately conventional ending." Thomson's work was "so plain and direct, so baby-simple, so to speak, in its harmony and rhythm, that it was startling." Piston he thought more academic than Sessions and "rather conventional, although not dull."[56]

As for his colleagues, they looked upon Copland's astonishing success with varying degrees of pride, disbelief, and jealousy. But as with veterans of some distant war who had gone their own ways, the memory of battle together proved an inviolable bond.

12

Copland and Younger American Composers

Upon returning home from Paris, the twenty-five-year-old Copland not only sought out contemporaries but began befriending and sponsoring younger composers. Such solicitude was remarkable for a composer himself so young and unestablished. In 1933 Roy Harris even expressed shock over his determination to "hand over the musical destiny of America" to the young. "Being an Amer-Irishman," Harris protested, "I cannot be counted on to have had my say before they nail the lid on."[1]

Over the years, Copland met and assisted hundreds of young composers. Some remained casual acquaintances; others became good friends, even lovers. It seemed as if nearly every American composer of his time enjoyed some beneficial contact with him. Bernard Heiden (b. 1910), for instance, recalled that in 1938, soon after arriving in the States from his native Germany, he met Copland in a library while copying parts for his First Symphony. "You shouldn't be copying parts," Copland told Heiden. "I'll arrange for the parts to be copied." And Copland promptly did so. This sort of helpful intervention—often behind the scenes—was not untypical.[2]

Aside from summers at Tanglewood and a few semesters at Harvard and the State University of New York (SUNY) at Buffalo, Copland had little institutional context for such involvements; his unflagging interest and remarkable acuity simply drew composers to him. Those composers who actually studied with him were small in number and did so for only brief periods; rather, Copland helped younger composers more informally, with intermittent advice and aid.

Copland's first protégé was Israel Citkowitz (1909–1974), whom he met in New York in early 1926. Citkowitz, then sixteen, had been born in Russia but had grown up in the States. He was Copland's type: young, talented, literary, politically aware, lithely built, and delicately featured, with a mass of curly hair—"very handsome," wrote Arthur Berger, "in a poetic way." (Alfred Stieglitz captured his smoldering good looks in a dashing portrait.) The two worked side by side during the winter of 1926, Copland dedicating his bluesy "Nocturne" (1926) to Citkowitz, who admired the "tenderness and longing and simplicity" of Copland's music.[3]

Like many later protégés, the often depressed Citkowitz looked to Copland for sympathy: "I know I will never be completely happy," he explained early in their relationship. "And you must not take what I say as coming from a despondent adolescent. . . . I am not satisfied with as much as is given for me to know and to do. The idea of time persecutes me like a mania and my fear of death is active enough now and as I grow older it will obsess me." Even as late as 1934, he was "in a catastrophic state" and enduring "a veritable *Saison en Enfer*." "You sound very forlorn," he wrote to Copland in 1930, "almost as if our roles had changed and it was up to me to console you."[4]

Copland not only comforted Citkowitz but offered practical guidance and support. He encouraged him to study with Boulanger (which Citkowitz did from 1927 to 1931) and helped raise the funds to make it possible for him to do so. When Citkowitz spoke in 1930 about the possibility of returning home, Copland advised "a room and piano of your own. You're used to different things now and I feel sure it will be difficult to live at home for any extended period of time. Have you thought of that?" He also suggested that Citkowitz take a personal inventory of his good and bad points—the kind of introspection long practiced by Copland himself. In addition, he programmed Citkowitz's music at Copland-Sessions Concerts and at Yaddo and arranged for Cos Cob to publish his Joyce settings (1930), two of which were dedicated to him. Such songs were enough to establish Citkowitz's reputation as a song composer's song composer, according to Ned Rorem, who noted the influence of Copland on his work.[5]

Copland fell for Citkowitz—no doubt early on—though such affection by all accounts went unrequited. In any event, they had their personal ups and downs. A turning point came when an "infatuated" Copland spent the summer of 1929 with Citkowitz in the small French town of Juziers. The experience must have been unpleasant; Citkowitz wrote soon after, "I think it's one of the most unfortunate things in my life that the first time we two lived together should have coincided with such miserable depression on my part. An invalid is an impossible person to live with, and spiritually sick as I was it must have been trying for you." The two subsequently drifted apart; both felt, for a while, neglected by the other. In 1931, Copland told Citkowitz, "We can't go on for two years, as we just have, with impunity." Further reconciliation took place in 1933. "As for forgiving you," wrote Copland, "es kommt garnicht in Frage—all your sins are forgiven in advance in my religion."[6]

By 1934, their friendship had reestablished itself; Citkowitz was approaching the end of his compositional career, a move that apparently brought him some peace of mind. During his subsequent years as a distinguished piano teacher and coach, he remained devoted to Copland, filling in for him at an all-Copland concert in 1943 and joining friends for a visit to Sneden's Landing in 1949.[7]

Copland met Marc Blitzstein (1905–1964), one of the younger colleagues he most admired, in the fall of 1927, just after the latter's one short year of study with Nadia Boulanger. Blitzstein immediately judged Copland a "nice, stimulating fellow" and a "good contact." They both spent the following summer at the MacDowell Colony, where they renewed their friendship and developed a shared liking for the lively critic-novelist Eva Goldbeck (1901–1935). In September 1929, the two toured Germany together for a week, engaging in a variety of pursuits, including homosexual escapades. "Aaron and I are sampling celestial beer," Blitzstein wrote Goldbeck from Darmstadt, adding, with a wink, "In other departments, the ground has been looked over, tested, but not yet plumbed." They discovered that they had opposite tastes in men: Copland liked young men ("too young," complained Blitzstein to Goldbeck), whereas Blitzstein preferred "rough trade" ("men who could only make him miserable," Paul Moor would write).[8]

After their week together, Blitzstein realized that the friendship had gone awry, as he explained to Goldbeck: "From time to time we exchanged bits of information ... and then tucked in somewhere, a danger signal, such as telling the other how one acts when deeply angry. . . . What took place, in sum, was an estrangement—one complicated by an intimate mutual knowledge." The phrase "intimate mutual knowledge" suggests sexual matters, but whether or not the two had any physical relations remains a matter of conjecture.[9]

Copland and Blitzstein remained friends, but not as close as the latter would have liked. "Aaron and I are rather worse off," he wrote Goldbeck in 1931. "He will not get close—I begin to believe something out of the past is responsible." By this time, Copland had become somewhat protective of Goldbeck, the relationship among all three taking on some of the earmarks of a love triangle, despite both men's homosexuality; one imagines that Copland looked askance at their marriage in 1933. After Goldbeck's death in 1935, Copland and Blitzstein continued to work closely together professionally, but it appears that socially each largely went his own way.

Throughout, Copland informally offered Blitzstein guidance. "Aaron has skated carefully around the rims of my music," Blitzstein told Goldbeck in 1931, "liking here, distrusting there." Copland early on expressed a preference for the ballet *Cain* (1930) and subsequently recommended Blitzstein to choreographer Ruth Page as a possible collaborator. He also publicly defended the ridiculed *Serenade* for string quartet (1932), with its one tempo indication, "largo," for all three movements, though privately he advised Blitzstein, "Always cajole a listener, never frighten him away." Copland later wrote, "In the very early part of his career he was something of a problem child. He seemed to have all the requisites for composing—talent, ability, technique—but somehow he had more difficulty than most composers in finding out exactly what he wanted to do. . . . Either a composition was too obviously derivative, or it tried too hard to be astonishing, or the style adopted was too rigidly abstract. It wasn't until Blitzstein began writing primarily for the stage that he really found himself."[10]

These later stage works, such as *The Cradle Will Rock* (1936) and *No for an Answer* (1940), offered, thought Copland, a unique and exciting blend of "social drama, musical revue, and opera," their character alternately "satirical, tender, bitter, or pessimistic." Copland especially praised Blitzstein's prosody as well as his ability to musically depict the "typical American tough guy" and to find "a voice for all those American regular fellows that seem so much at home everywhere except on the operatic stage." Alluding to the Marxist bias of these works (Blitzstein—like Goldbeck, a communist sympathizer since 1932—joined the party in 1938), he defended their "so-called propaganda angle," writing, "If Blitzstein, like many other artists in every field, was moved to expression by the plight of the less privileged in their struggle for a fuller life, that was entirely his right." The only problem posed in this regard was "a certain sectarianism" that limited the pieces' "circulation as works of art and therefore their effectiveness as propaganda." As for Blitzstein's *Regina* (1949), after Lillian Hellman's *The Little Foxes*, he noted some flaws, but nonetheless rated it one of the most significant American operas of the twentieth century. As a whole, Blitzstein's career provided an important reminder that "humanity's struggle for a fuller life" was as "valid" as "new techniques" in providing "a moving force in the history of music."[11]

Blitzstein in turn was a responsive listener to Copland's music. He heard "sorrow" in the *Symphonic Ode* and "pain" and "a stunning rebound from pain" in the *Piano Variations*. He recognized, better than most, the coherence of Copland's oeuvre, sagely observing, "No element ever appears abruptly in a work, or gets cut off in another." Like Virgil Thomson, however, he found some Copland scores somewhat dull and monotonous; similarly, as a lecturer, Copland was, in his minority opinion, "no felicitous phraser; he has little grace of speech, few quips; and sometimes one stops listening." *El Salón México* he dismissed as "up-to-the-minute travel-slumming music." But he remained deeply respectful of the man and his music and made him, along with Leonard Bernstein, coexecutor of his estate.[12]

The complex dynamics of Copland's friendship with Paul Bowles (b. 1910) followed closely along the lines of his relationship with Israel Citkowitz. Bowles was born in Queens, New York; his father, a dentist, he despised. While attending the University of Virginia in the late 1920s, he wrote music and poetry; on his frequent visits home, he explored the new-music scene, including the Copland-Sessions Concerts. In early 1930, he showed his music to Henry Cowell, who recommended that he see Copland, saying, "He likes glittering stuff." Bowles charmed Copland, who accepted him as a student and taught him daily (including figured-bass exercises and analyses of Mozart sonatas) until Bowles returned to Virginia in March. "Paul was not a student in the sense of being a beginner," Copland explained to Gena Dagel Caponi. "Working with Paul was more like showing things to a professional friend."[13]

Copland visited Bowles in Charlottesville later that spring, and Bowles stayed with Copland at Yaddo and in New York in the fall. Bowles came to "wholeheartedly" admire Copland, stating, "He seemed to me the ideal of what a composer should be because he knew exactly why he put down every note." On another occasion he acknowledged, "My whole musical and intellectual background was formed by him." For his part, Copland praised Bowles's "alert, quick mind," adding, "I can't imagine him ever being dull."[14]

When Copland first met him, the nineteen-year-old Bowles was, writes Christopher Sawyer-Lauçanno, "an exceedingly elegant and well-groomed young man with delicate features: a long, thin, perfectly shaped nose, small mouth with full lips, wavy blond hair always neatly coiffed, blue eyes bright and attentive." Bowles must have dazzled Copland, as he did Thomson, whom he met the following year. Indeed, by the time Copland arrived in Paris with Bowles in the summer of 1931, he had fallen "madly in love with this youngster of his," according to Eva Goldbeck, who disapproved: "Twenty, a budding composer, false good looks, and general falseness," she wrote to her ex-husband. "If Aaron has really fallen in love with him I am very sorry. . . . Israel [Citkowitz] is much preferable, with 'character' at least."[15]

As with Citkowitz, Copland's romantic feelings for Bowles apparently went unrequited, though Bowles was, says Sawyer-Lauçanno, "coy about the matter and did nothing to prevent suspicions of a homosexual affair." "Paul made like being queer," explains Thomson, "and he got money out of that and friendships. But he was really not interested in the physical side." Bowles unquestionably had sexual anxieties; for advice in such matters, he looked to Copland, who told him not to worry, writing, "When you really want to [make love], you will."[16]

In April 1931, Copland and Bowles met, by arrangement, in Paris, where Bowles proudly introduced him to his new friends Gertrude Stein and Alice B. Toklas, both of whom he had met through Thomson. Copland and Bowles subsequently left for Berlin, staying in separate quarters and lunching nearly daily at the Café des Westins with Stephen Spender and Christopher Isherwood. Bowles and Isherwood shared a friend in the real-life Sally Bowles (as in Isherwood's Berlin novels and their musical adaption, *Cabaret*), Jean Ross, whose offer of a "prairie oyster" cocktail, made with whiskey, raw eggs, and Worcestershire sauce, Copland turned down. Although Isherwood liked Copland at once, he only slowly warmed up to Bowles, whom he initially found aloof (he soon enough adopted his surname for the character of Sally Bowles, "because he liked the sound of it and also the looks of its owner").[17]

After returning to Paris in July, Copland and Bowles, at the suggestion of Stein, traveled to Tangier rather than to the Riviera, as planned; the two duly spent the rest of the summer and the early fall in Morocco.

Bowles fell in love with Morocco at once (he eventually made it his home, living there as of this writing), whereas Copland had mixed feelings. "It's terribly exotic of course and picturesque and all that," he wrote to Eva Goldbeck from Tangier, where he and Bowles had rented a spacious villa, "but it's also rather ominous and weighs on the mind." He found the lack of such modern amenities as hot water bothersome and the Arabs and their nighttime mountain drumming rather frightening, but most of all, he despaired over the lack of a competent piano tuner. "Of course, Aaron being Aaron," recalled Bowles, "he tried to make the best of it, but when we were in the souq [market], he would grumble that he'd seen it all on President Street in Brooklyn." As for Fez, which they visited at Bowles's urging, Copland thought the city "wonderfully regal," but was disgusted by the rats and flies. He quit Morocco in early October, leaving Bowles behind.[18]

For a few years thereafter, Copland continued to oversee Bowles's career, though typically from a distance. He had long tried to discipline the irrepressible Bowles; in *The Autobiography of Alice B. Toklas*, Stein writes, "Bowles told Gertrude Stein and it pleased her that Copeland [*sic*] said threateningly to him when as usual in the winter he was neither delightful nor sensible, if you do not work now when you are twenty when you are thirty, nobody will love you." Although Copland liked Bowles's music, he recognized certain technical failings and hoped that Bowles would study with Boulanger; but after two lessons in the fall of 1931, Bowles, with the backing of Thomson, gave her up. "It doesn't matter what pet ideas the teacher happens to have or what means are employed to drive them home," a disappointed Copland wrote Thomson, "the pupil should swallow it whole for a time and if he has any guts he'll throw them overboard soon enough."[19]

In the years 1931–35, while Bowles restlessly wandered the globe, Copland helped promote his music at home, as he had Citkowitz's, by including it on a Copland-Sessions Concert and at Yaddo. All the while Bowles wrote Copland letters, alternately self-pitying, pleading, confused, and flirtatious, including one from Monte Carlo in 1932 that read, in part, "No one is interested in me in the sense that there is no one in the world who manages to understand me as well as you do. So, if you see something worth saving, wouldn't you do something to save it?" "Did you tell me *to*, or *not* to sleep with someone different each night? I have forgotten," wrote Bowles in a more capricious mood. Copland continuously advised Bowles to move back to New York, though he remained respectful of his reluctance to do so: "These are difficult times for young composers, and I'm sure it's better to eat in Africa than starve in N.Y. So there's no reason for disapproving as you seem to suggest—only the natural desire to have you back soon where I can look at you."[20]

By the time Bowles returned to New York in 1935, he had grown, perhaps, closer to Thomson, but he resumed his friendship with Copland. Quickly establishing himself as a prominent composer of incidental stage music, he married Jane Auer in 1938 and for a few years belonged to the Communist Party (1938–40). In 1947, he immigrated to Morocco, where both he and his wife pursued successful writing careers, their life and fiction opening up, in Norman Mailer's words, "the world of Hip." Copland became a faithful reader of Bowles's books and was struck by how strangely dark his fiction was compared to his music, whose freshness and charm he had long admired. During these later years, he and Bowles stayed in distant contact. At a 1969 reunion, he introduced Bowles to Phillip Ramey, who felt snubbed; Copland assured him, "Don't be upset. Paul's always been something of a cold fish." When pressed by Ramey in later years to discuss Bowles, he would only say, "Oh, he was a bad boy."[21]

Given his involvement with the League of Composers, the Copland-Sessions Concerts, and Yaddo, Copland naturally met a large number of other young, aspiring composers in the late 1920s and early 1930s. Although always empathetic, he was, at the same time, frank in his criticisms. Turning down a work submitted by the twenty-four-year-old Ross Lee Finney (1906–1997), he explained, "As a whole, even to me, the work seemed to be under the shadow of the later Stravinsky to a disturbing degree." However, he encouraged Finney to submit other works, and a warm friendship ensued; in later years, he often stayed with the Finneys when visiting Ann Arbor. On the occasion of Finney's sixtieth birthday, he sent the following greetings: "I have met hundreds of composers in my time, but I have known none more generous in spirit, more devoted to his art, more continuously and effectively open to every new manifestation of our rugged musical times."[22]

In 1932 Copland helped oversee and facilitate the short-lived Young Composers' Group. Its members—all under the age of twenty-five—met at his apartment on West Fifty-eighth Street every two or three weeks in order to play and discuss new music, including their own. Elie Siegmeister (1909–91) essentially founded the group, which also included Irwin Heilner (1908–91), Israel Citkowitz (1909–74), Lehman Engel (1910–82),

Bernard Herrmann (1911–75), Arthur Berger (b. 1912), Henry Brant (b. 1913), Vivian Fine (b. 1913), and Jerome Moross (1913–93). All were Jewish and most had grown up in New York. Siegmeister and Citkowitz had studied with Boulanger; the rest, except for Fine and Berger, were enrolled at the Institute of Musical Arts (later Juilliard). Berger propagandized on their behalf, eventually writing an article about them for *Trend* magazine.[23]

Copland already knew a number of these composers, even the nineteen-year-old Henry Brant, whom he had met in 1929 through Clarence Adler. Copland immediately declared Brant a find, writing enthusiastic letters about him to both Citkowitz and Blitzstein. He even informally took Brant on as a student, urging him to study Mahler and Ravel in order to learn orchestration and dissuading him from pursuing his self-styled "oblique harmony," in which the music held one way sounded avant-garde and held another way sounded conventional. "Whatever it is," remarked Copland, "it's so sick. Sick like a sick cow." (In contrast, Cowell immediately began disseminating Brant's experiments around the world.) In 1932 Brant rightly predicted that the thirty-two-year-old Copland would soon be known as the "Dean of American Music," a tag that the Young Composers seem to have popularized.[24]

The Young Composers were a feisty and pugnacious group, contemptuous of the academy, the press, established composers, and even one another—especially Herrmann and Moross, whom Oscar Levant once described as "two remarkably unpleasant young men." After anything at all was played at one of their meetings, Herrmann would often exclaim, in his thickest Lower East Side accent, "It stinks!" "There was not a lot of brotherly and sisterly love," remembered Fine. The group more or less divided into two camps, the avant-garde Schoenbergians and the more neoclassical Stravinskyites, with Herrmann a "devout Schoenbergian" and Citkowitz the leading "oppositionist to the Schoenberg regime." And although the group veered strongly toward Marxist politics, here, too, dissension reigned, especially between those, like Siegmeister, already toeing the Stalinist line and those, like Citkowitz and Berger, heading toward a more independent, Trotskyite viewpoint. They found common ground, however, in their admiration for jazz, Copland, and Ives; indeed, the Younger Composers played a significant role in the unearthing and dissemination of Ives's music.[25]

Copland sympathized with their interests—at the urging of Herrmann and Moross, he reconsidered Ives—but he avoided taking part in their quarrels. "He sits with an air of serene impartiality that makes everyone else seem like a youthful barbarian," Citkowitz would later write. "Aaron listened, giggled, was interested, never interfered," remembered Lehman Engel. "It was thus," added Berger, "that Copland was a stabilizing influence for the jealousies and inevitably violent dissensions of budding young talents. At times the sessions of the Young Composers' Group became so stormy that even his powers of assuagement were taxed, and on one occasion a card inviting us to a meeting warned us succinctly, 'no polemics.' But when Copland was away, complete disunity was likely to set in among its ranks." Only once did Copland castigate a group member: when Herrmann took a flippant attitude toward his own music.[26]

Soon after a concert of the Young Composers in early 1933, the group disbanded, but not before a few others joined their ranks, including Oscar Levant (1906–72) and John ("Johnny") Green (1908–89). Both Levant and Green were already famous, Green for such hit songs as "Body and Soul" (1930), Levant less for his songs than for his performances of Gershwin at the piano, his character bits on stage and screen, and his eminently quotable wit. A high school dropout who had risen through the ranks of Broadway, Levant entertained serious ambitions after the fashion of his idol and friend George Gershwin; Copland encouraged him to complete a piano sonatina for the 1932 Yaddo Festival after hearing him play the work's first movement at an evening at the Gershwins'. Copland also introduced him into the group, though the other members made him feel like an interloper, Moross and Herrmann denouncing his participation at Yaddo as "a cheap Copland trick to leaven the festival with 'Broadway.' "[27]

For a brief period, Levant showed his serious compositions to Copland, who criticized one of his more pretentious attempts as "a cross between Scriabin and Berg." In contrast to Gershwin, who remained coolly ambivalent toward Levant's higher aspirations, Copland—like Schoenberg after him—clearly hoped to nurture his extraordinary and, alas, unfulfilled potential; Copland gave him, states a recent biography, "the faith in himself as a composer that George Gershwin was never able to give." "For dozens of American composers of my generation," Levant stated in 1940, "Copland has had a potent influence completely unknown to the public, in its sphere unmatched by that of any other native musician of the time."[28]

Copland programmed other group members at Yaddo; but privately he voiced his concerns about all their work, especially the lack of individuality. "None but Citkowitz has what I would call a personal style," he wrote to Brant in 1933, "and even his is far from being fully developed." In Brant's case, he worried about the influences of Stravinsky and Sessions and thought, further, that Brant simply wrote too much too fast. "I always felt, Henry," wrote Copland, "that your main problem is not musical, at all. It's a matter of deepening your experience and your contacts with peoples and things. Travel could aid that. So could friends. Think about it." Brant, however, decided against his advice to study with Boulanger and in 1935 began lessons instead with Antheil, who motivated him to compose more than ever. Copland watched with similar concern as Heilner and Fine joined Sessions's "crib." No one in the Young Composers' Group—or any member of what Copland called the "depression generation"—came off particularly well in his sequel (1936) to his survey of American composers (1926). "For they live," he explained, "in a moral climate that is none too good for the nurturing of new talent."[29]

By the late 1930s, Copland and the Young Composers had largely drifted apart. He remained closest to Engel and Berger. Heilner "abruptly" broke off their friendship around 1935; only in 1968 did he apologize, telling Copland, "At that time I said harsh things about you which for many years I've regretted since I realized that they weren't true." Brant assisted Copland in orchestrating *The City* and *From Sorcery to Science* in 1939, but then maintained only distant contact.[30]

During his stays in Hollywood in the late 1930s and onward, Copland had occasion to see Moross, Green, Levant, and Herrmann, all of whom had established themselves there at least intermittently. Moross and Green remained loyal and helpful, the former assisting in the orchestration of *Our Town* (1940), the latter, who described *Appalachian Spring* to Copland as "a big thrill in my life," arranging *El Salón México* for the film *Fiesta* (1947).[31]

In contrast, Copland had an unpleasant tiff with Levant. Upon visiting Hollywood in 1937, he toured the town with Levant, who arranged for four studio musicians to play his latest effort, a string quartet composed under Schoenberg's tutelage. Although Copland praised Levant's progress, he wondered whether the style was not "excessively chromatic." After angrily retorting that Copland's own *Piano Variations* was "completely lacking in harmonic style—and full of dissonant clichés as well," Levant told Schoenberg about the incident, "building, as I went, a complete case *contra* Copland. With elaborate embroideries I outlined a Copland who had practically demolished Schoenberg, with my work as a mere pretext." He later apologized to the "justifiably furious" Copland, who, to his amazement, subsequently recommended the quartet for a League of Composers broadcast. In 1949 an appreciative Levant recorded "The Open Prairie" from *Billy the Kid* as arranged for piano.[32]

As for the equally explosive Herrmann, he purportedly wrote a scathing letter to Copland accusing him of plagiarizing his film score, *The Devil and Daniel Webster* (1941), for *Lincoln Portrait* (1942); but both men retained a high regard for each other's film music. Copland remained closer to another film composer he admired, Alex North (1910–1991), who studied privately with him between 1936 and 1938 and who turned to him for guidance as late as 1957. "I think the American composer (plural) would give anything for that 'Feel' for jazz that you have," confessed North, whose own jazz-inflected film scores—such as *A Streetcar Named Desire* (1951)—showed traces of Copland's influence. After North praised the Third Symphony as "truly profound and moving," Copland wrote back, "If everybody listened with your ears life would be 'hunky dory' "; characteristically, he suggested that North "sit down" and write his own symphony.[33]

In 1938 Copland discovered Texarkana-born Conlon Nancarrow (1912–1997) through the publication of two of his works in Henry Cowell's *New Music*. "These short works show a remarkable surety in an unknown composer," declared Copland, "plus a degree of invention and imagination that immediately gives him a place among our talented younger men." Upon Nancarrow's arrival in New York in 1939 from Spain (where he had fought in the Abraham Lincoln Brigade), Copland met and befriended the young composer; the two stayed in casual touch after Nancarrow immigrated to Mexico in 1940. "He's really an original character," Copland wrote John Kennedy in 1953, "a rather rare phenomenon these days." As for the "fascinating" polyrhythms of his music for player piano, he added, "You have to hear it to believe it."[34]

By the mid-1940s, however, Copland considered William Schuman (1910–1992), Samuel Barber (1910–1981), and David Diamond (b. 1915) outstanding among American composers of the "depression generation."[35]

Copland first met Diamond in 1935, while the latter was studying with Sessions. Diamond subsequently became a close friend of both men—an uncommon feat made possible, in part, because he shared their reservations about each other's music; he preferred both the early Sessions and the early Copland to their later work. Diamond went so far as to offer this Sessions-like warning (rather bold for a twenty-three-year-old) to Copland in 1939: "By having sold out to the mongrel commercialists half-way already, the danger is going to be wider for you, and I beg you dear Aaron, don't sell out yet." Still, his friendship with Copland was far less fitful and turbulent than that with Sessions.[36]

Copland was immediately impressed with Diamond's work: "Not yet twenty-one," he wrote in his 1936 survey, "Diamond has a musical speech that is, of course, only in the process of formation. But already one can recognize an individual note in his last-movement rondos with their perky, nervous themes and quick, impulsive motion." Copland assumed his customary advisory role; he warned Diamond against facility and recommended that he study with Boulanger, which Diamond did in 1937; and while he did not disapprove of Diamond's membership in the Young Communist League, he dissuaded him from becoming a party cell member.[37]

Over the next ten years, Copland helped buoy up the often emotionally distraught Diamond: "I'm miserable . . . so long until I hear from you," Diamond wrote him in 1940. His personal life, described by Copland as "a mess," involved drunken sprees and romantic affairs with heterosexual men that usually turned out badly. In February 1947, after an inebriated Diamond picked a fight with some people at a concert at Carnegie Hall, Copland angrily sent him home in a cab and wrote him a long, tough letter telling him it was "imperative" that he seek medical treatment,

> first, for the drinking (if that is necessary) and second for the deeper reasons which set off the drinking and which obviously go far back in to your very psyche. . . . Everything else is unadulterated crap: the liquor that you "like the taste of," the arguments, the posturings, the abusiveness, the insults, the belligerencies, the later sophistries, self-justifications and letters of explanations—all of it is just meaningless and senseless crap. The whole goddam thing spells one word: i-l-l. The remedy for illness is medical attention. Think it over and remember who it is that writes this to you.

Diamond immediately sought psychoanalytic treatment with funds that Copland and Leonard Bernstein helped raise.[38]

During Diamond's years in Italy (1951–65), he and Copland saw less of each other, but they wrote often. Copland was also around to calm his nerves after Diamond was summoned to appear before the House Un-American Activities Committee. "What if I'm asked a question about Lenny [Bernstein]?" Diamond worried. "You say what you feel you have to say," advised Copland. Diamond remained solicitous in his relations with Copland and dedicated a number of works to him, including his Eighth Symphony.[39]

Copland also became an early advocate for William Schuman, bolstering his reputation with a 1938 review of a choral work, *Pioneers,* that read in part, "Schuman is, as far as I am concerned, the musical find of the year. There is nothing puny or miniature about this young man's talent." He similarly admired the Second Symphony—"What I like about it," he told a friend, "is that it seems to be music that comes from a real urge"—and he recommended the composer to Koussevitzky. A 1951 review of Schuman's Fourth String Quartet occasioned a fuller appreciation, one that once again emphasized the music's "urgency" but also mentioned its "uniformity of style," "masterful handling of instrumental color," "rhythmic ingenuity," "compactly shaped" forms, and "varied and well-balanced content." Copland was especially intrigued with this particular work's dark harmonies, which contrasted with the "basically optimistic—sometimes boyishly optimistic—tone of his earlier music." He sensed the possible influence of Roger Sessions.[40]

Unlike Diamond, Schuman was not in the least troubled by the "surface accessibility" of Copland's more popular scores. He wept over *Lincoln Portrait,* a work that immediately influenced his own *Prayer in Time of War* (1943). *Rodeo* and *Billy the Kid* he later described as having transformed "traditional American folk material into the most sophisticated art by discerning potentialities in simple music that could only be perceived by an artist of extraordinary imagination."[41]

Schuman never officially studied with Copland—his formal education came to an end after two years with Roy Harris (1936–38)—but in the late 1930s and early 1940s he regularly showed his manuscripts to Copland, whose critiques often led to revisions of one kind or another. Copland performed this kind of editorial service for many composers, the informality of the relationship not always referred to as a teacher-student one per se. Schuman, nevertheless, spoke unequivocally of Copland as a teacher:

As a teacher, Aaron was extraordinary. . . . Copland would look at your music and try to understand what *you* were after. He didn't want to turn you into another Aaron Copland. He would sit down at the piano, read through a score, and make comments. When he questioned something, it was in a manner that might make you want to question it yourself. Everything he said was helpful in making a younger composer realize the potential of a particular work. On the other hand, Aaron could be strongly critical. . . . Because of his agreeable disposition, Aaron is never thought of as being exacting, but this does him an injustice.[42]

In 1945, shortly after Schuman became president of Juilliard, one episode put a strain on their relationship. Having accepted Schuman's offer to join the Juilliard faculty in 1945, Copland, upon receiving a contract in early 1946, suggested instead a guest lectureship; Schuman was not only disappointed but hurt by what he perceived as a flippant rejection letter. They quickly made up, however, and during Schuman's long tenure at Juilliard the two worked harmoniously on many professional matters. In 1960, at an all-Copland festival sponsored by Juilliard, Schuman asked Copland, for the first time in his life, to narrate *Lincoln Portrait*; and in 1965 he praised him as "the father of us all." Meanwhile, in discussing American works of major significance, Copland often singled out the Schuman symphonies—especially the Third, Fifth, and Sixth—for their big sweep and striking rhythms, complaining only that the music, while "never dull," was not always "entirely fresh."[43]

It took Copland longer to appreciate Samuel Barber. In 1936, he coolly observed, "Barber writes in a somewhat outmoded fashion, making up in technical finish what he lacks in musical substance." Koussevitzky championed Barber without any special promotion on Copland's part. But by the 1940s, they had grown closer to each other's music: Barber to *El Salón México*, the Western ballets, and the Piano Sonata, Copland to Barber's more "sophisticated" later work, including the *Capricorn Concerto* (1944; a work that Charles Mills claimed showed the salutary influence of Copland's music), the Piano Sonata (1948), and his Agee setting, *Knoxville: Summer of 1915* (1947). Copland told Barber that he regretted not discovering the Agee text first, adding, to Phillip Ramey, "It's just as well it happened the way it did or we wouldn't have Sam's beautiful score."[44]

This mutual respect eventually encompassed their early works: the *Piano Variations* remained "a ripping piece," Barber told its composer in 1967; Barber's *Adagio for Strings* came "straight from the heart, to use old-fashioned terms," opined Copland in 1982. After Barber's death, Copland further remarked, "He chose to write in a fairly conventional romantic idiom, but if his music is unadventurous, it is always beautifully made, is often affecting and sometimes dashing. His work is expert, high-toned and serious. I admire that, even in some of his scores where I may find the sentiment not quite to my taste."[45]

Copland and Barber became personal friends as well, though in some ways they could not have been more unalike; Copland enjoyed the new-music scene as much as Barber avoided it. "Life here is heavenly," Barber wrote to Copland from Munich in 1960. "Don't see no musicians at all." He made an exception for Copland, however; they socialized with their respective lovers throughout the 1940s and 1950s, especially after Copland's 1952 move to Ossining, not far from Barber's Mount Kisco home. "Bless you, dear Aaron, have we become friends, perhaps? It would be nice," wrote Barber in 1953. Moreover, the two worked together professionally, for instance, in trying to establish more equitable policies at ASCAP. They also shared the belief—only occasionally articulated by Barber—that the American composer faced the problem of finding, in Barber's words, a "contemporary national style."[46]

And yet although Barber grew closer to Copland than to practically any other American composer outside his immediate circle, their relationship, if not wholly expedient, was not entirely easy either. Certainly Barber never developed the intimacy with Copland that he did with William Schuman, let alone Poulenc. And at least in later years, some friends of Barber's took a decidedly condescending attitude toward Copland's music; Gian Carlo Menotti told Barbara Heyman that Barber himself "rejected any serious comparison of his own works with Copland's." If Copland felt any resentment, it seems to be have been toward Menotti, especially in the light of that composer's many operatic hits and the luke-warm reception of his own *Tender Land*; but at the same time, he liked Menotti personally and admired his stagecraft.[47]

Copland's relationship with Leonard Bernstein (1918–1990)—the most legendary of all such friendships—had an element of the fateful. They met seated next to each other at an Anna Sokolow dance recital in New York in 1937 on Copland's birthday. (The poet Muriel Rukeyser introduced them.) On that same day in 1943, Bernstein skyrocketed to fame as a last-minute replacement for an ailing Bruno Walter. And both men died within a two-month period in late 1990. Without Bernstein, Copland probably would not have found so large a public for his music;

without Copland, Bernstein certainly would not have written the kind of music he did. Their careers were inextricably linked.[48]

When they met, Bernstein, eighteen years younger than Copland, was a junior at Harvard and already a "fanatic lover" of the Piano Variations, a work he knew from Copland's 1935 recording, recommended to him by Arthur Berger. He liked to say that he could "empty the room, guaranteed, in two minutes, by playing this wonderful piece"; one particularly violent performance, accompanied by the stomping of feet, caused a chandelier in the apartment below to crash to the floor. Bernstein had pictured its composer "as a sort of patriarch, Moses or Walt Whitman–like figure, with a beard" and was "blown away" when he realized that the charming, giggly, bespectacled man sitting next to him was the "patriarch" he had envisioned. That same evening, Bernstein, on a dare, played the Variations at an after-recital party at Copland's loft, leaving everyone "drop-jawed."[49]

Over the next few years, as he completed his last two years at Harvard (1937–39), studied conducting with Fritz Reiner at Curtis (1939–41), and then settled in New York, Bernstein frequently visited Copland, especially for help on his compositions; in sessions that were as close to formal composition lessons as Bernstein ever received, Copland scrutinized his choice and spacing of musical intervals, something he often did with composers. He also pointed out weak spots in Bernstein's orchestration and warned him away from self-conscious Jewish or American mannerisms, advising, "Sit down and write what comes into your head; if it's good it will be American." Above all, he encouraged him to develop a personal style; after Bernstein admitted that his new song cycle I Hate Music was "a little on the Copland side," Copland replied, "I want to hear about your writing a song that has no Copland, no Hindemith, no Strav., no Bloch, no Milhaud and no Bartók in it. Then I'll talk to you."[50]

In spite of all such advice, Bernstein continued to borrow heavily from Copland, as many have observed. In a conversation with Copland, Bernstein himself spoke of the "many aspects" of Copland's influence on his own music: "They come wafting through and when I become conscious of them I try to avoid them, naturally, especially if they're like quotes. There are some actual quotes I can point to. There is a bar in West Side Story that I always cringe at. It's perhaps the most beautiful bar in West Side Story, too, but I always cringe because I know it's Aaron." To which Copland wryly responded, "I had an idea how you might cringe less. Just send me some of the royalties that you collect!"[51]

Although none of Bernstein's recent biographers has asserted un-equivocally that Copland and Bernstein had a physical relationship, they all presume that they did, at least in the early days. Most concretely, Meryle Secrest interviewed someone who had discovered them in bed together in a Tanglewood boardinghouse around 1940. Copland's close friends Erik Johns and Paul Moor confirm that for a while the relation-ship had a sexual dimension. Their affair, such as it was, proved intermit-tent and lasted a few years at most, probably from around 1939 to 1942 or 1943. During this time, Bernstein would sometimes stay overnight with Copland, proposing, in 1939, that the two of them rent a cabin together. After six weeks together in Tanglewood, a lonely Bernstein wrote to Cop-land, "I've never felt about anyone before as I do about you, completely at ease, and always comforted with you. This is not a love letter, but I'm quite mad about you." Humphrey Burton detects a shift in the relation-ship around March 1942, citing an apologetic letter by Bernstein (including—shades of both Citkowitz and Bowles—the assurance "You must know that there can never be one closer to me than you are, and I hope will never cease to be") and a cool reply from Copland. And yet Copland wrote Bernstein from Hollywood in a quasi-romantic vein in September 1943, "You're one of the reasons I am coming home—and please don't forget it."[52]

In any case, the two remained extremely close throughout the 1940s, maintaining a lively correspondence, with Bernstein writing letters to "Dear Venerable Giggling Dean," or "Dear Judge-Nose," or "Aa," and Copland writing back to "Lensk" or "Lentschk" or simply "Lenny." To Bernstein's confessions of sexual escapades with both men and women, Copland responded alternately with fatherly scolding (as in this 1942 reply: "You sound so Newyorky, no sleep, mauled liver, psychiatrists, etc. Not at all the sound and confident fellow that should be seeking a job") and avuncular indulgence (as in this 1943 letter: "You write the most wonderful letters—just the kind I love to get: The 'I miss you, I adore you' kind, while sailors and marines flit through the background in a general atmosphere of moral decay"). "I miss you terribly," Bernstein wrote Copland in 1944. "I need your cynical ears for my latest tales of love and limbs."[53]

In later years, after Bernstein's continued rise to stardom and his 1951 marriage to Felicia Montealegre, the two men communicated less often. Copland never became a member of the Bernstein household as he did that of Irving Fine. The bond between them, however, remained strong.

"Mahler makes me think of you, hard," he told Copland in 1959, "and of our music, which I don't think I understand the direction of any more (or the purpose), and I long to talk to you and have you explain it to me, and reassure me that new music is just as exciting as it was when you showed me all about it 20 years ago." In 1967 he wrote Copland, "I suppose if there's one person on earth who is at the center of my life it's you."[54]

From the time Copland watched Bernstein supervise the music to a production of Aristophanes' *The Birds* in 1939, he vigorously promoted the younger man's conducting career, helping him find work and introducing him to Koussevitzky, Fritz Reiner, André Kostelanetz, and others. "I keep being properly impressed by all the offers, interests, contacts, personalities that flit through your life," Copland wrote Bernstein in 1943. "But don't forget *our* party line—you're heading for conducting in a big way—and everybody and everything that doesn't lead there is an excrescence on the body politic." Copland seemed cooler about Bernstein's compositional aspirations; when Bernstein excitedly wrote him that Reiner had decided both to program his *Jeremiah* Symphony and to let him conduct a program, Copland thought the latter development of greater moment. On meeting Chávez in 1945, Bernstein found out—with what emotion we can only guess—that, quite unlike his own situation, Copland continually urged Chávez to curtail his conducting so that he could compose more.[55]

Copland certainly never accorded Bernstein's music his highest endorsement. In 1949, he gave it, in fact, a very mixed review: "At its worst Bernstein's music is conductor's music—eclectic in style and facile in inspiration. But at its best it is music of vibrant rhythmic invention, of irresistible élan, often carrying with it a terrific dramatic punch. It is possible that some form of stage music will prove to be Bernstein's finest achievement." Remarks about the music are otherwise scarce. He liked *On the Town*—he described it to Irving Fine as "lively, fast, and lots of fun"—but the later works elicited little comment. When the subject of Bernstein came up with the composer David Conte in 1982, Copland cited him with Britten as "one of the most fabulously gifted musicians I've ever encountered"; but when questioned specifically about his music, he responded elliptically, "One has the impression that it isn't always entirely necessary."[56]

Bernstein meanwhile supported Copland in a variety of ways, arranging *El Salón México* for solo piano, writing a few bars of *Rodeo*, producing *The Second Hurricane*, giving the premiere of the two-piano *Danzón*

Cubano with the composer, and recording his favorite work of Copland's, the Piano Sonata. "Boston is all agog and all aware!" he wrote Copland about the production of *The Second Hurricane*. "What a team! You write 'em, kid, and I'll do 'em." After assuming the musical directorship of the New York Philharmonic Orchestra in 1958, he began recording Copland's music for Columbia Records, an undertaking that continued even after he resigned from the Philharmonic in 1969. These recordings represented only a portion of Copland's orchestral output, but they were expert performances neatly packaged and widely distributed, and they contributed significantly to Copland's reputation. Bernstein also commissioned Copland's last two major orchestral works: *Connotations* and *Inscape*. "Lenny helped Aaron more than the other way around," opined David Diamond.[57]

Moreover, Bernstein revered the music. "It's the best we've got, you know," he would say. He deeply identified with the bulk of it: "Aaron's music just always seemed so natural for me to play or conduct—as though I could have composed it myself, so to speak"; and Copland himself thought Bernstein the conductor who most "intuitively" understood his work. Appearing as a guest on one of Bernstein's Young People's Concerts, he joked, "Maestro Bernstein conducts the music as if he wrote it. But I just want to make one thing clear. He didn't write it, I did!"[58]

At the same time, Bernstein was not shy about criticizing and even revising certain scores. While arranging *El Salón México*, he changed one section because, as he explained to Copland, "there had to be some theatrical interest at that point (which is, I'm afraid, a bit dull—even in the orchestra). Don't take it too hard." He shocked Agnes de Mille with his youthful "impudence" toward Copland during *Rodeo* rehearsals. Copland himself thought it "pretty nervy" of Bernstein to make "a sizable cut" in the Third Symphony while on tour in 1948. A 1952 letter criticizing the Clarinet Concerto—for resemblances to Richard Strauss, for its "cute but arbitrary" cadenza, for its finale which "doesn't seem to work"—may have irked as well. Bernstein felt "rather close to the tonal way" in which Copland used the twelve-tone method in the Piano Quartet (1950); but he seemed rather distant toward such later twelve-tone works as the *Piano Fantasy* (1957), Copland's first piece that he felt he himself "couldn't have composed."[59]

Bernstein's growing identification with Mahler placed additional strain on their friendship, in part because Bernstein often programmed Copland's newer scores with Mahler, lavishing greater attention on the latter.

When Copland learned that he had cut rehearsal time for the premiere of *Canticle of Freedom* in favor of Mahler's *Resurrection Symphony*, he refused to attend the performance, a rare display of temperament that astounded David Diamond. Copland also felt that, because of Mahler, Bernstein had begun to play many things too slowly, as in his recording of *Inscape*. During a 1980 rehearsal of *Lincoln Portrait* with Bernstein conducting and Copland narrating, the latter could even be seen gesturing with "mild frustration" at Bernstein's tempos. In addition, like many old friends, Copland may well have disapproved of the way in which Bernstein's involvement with Mahler had begun to displace his earlier devotion to American music. In 1958 he even wrote to Bernstein with concern about the lack of American music on a round of guest-conductor appearances in Europe: "Maybe you could squeeze in ten minutes worth [of American music] in front of the Mahler [Second]—what do you think?"[60]

During these later years, Bernstein said some provocative things about Copland, publicly asserting, for instance, how sad it was that he had been abandoned by America's young composers. Typically, such remarks never seemed to offend Copland; on the contrary, he worried about Bernstein, telling David Diamond, "Lenny wants to die." As Copland succumbed to dementia in the 1980s, he greatly welcomed Bernstein's increasingly rare visits to Rock Hill; after telephoning in 1988, Bernstein received an appreciative note from Copland's secretary: "Aaron seemed to have a very good time, and even now, some two hours later, he remembered that you called. These days that is just about unheard of. . . . Thank you for making him happier than I've seen him in a very long time." Although Verna Fine urged him to visit Copland more often, Bernstein explained that it was "too painful" to see him so debilitated; he even warned Lukas Foss against doing so, saying that he would find the experience too unsettling.[61]

In his 1949 survey of young American composers, Copland discussed, in addition to Bernstein, another six composers of the "generation of the 1940's" identified as being "near the top of the heap": Robert Palmer, one of his "own particular enthusiasms"; the Russian-born Alexei Haieff, with his "alert musical mind that often gives off sparks of mordant humor"; Harold Shapero, the "most gifted" of the group, although inclined to "hide the brilliance of his own gifts behind the cloak of the great masters"; Lukas Foss, the German-born "Wunderkind" made "more human" through his contact with America; William Bergsma, "a sober and serious workman"; and John Cage, whose music, "fascinating as it is . . . has more originality of sound than of substance."[62]

At about the same time, he cited Haieff, Shapero, and Foss—along with Arthur Berger, John Lessard, and Irving Fine—as comprising an American "Stravinsky school." This idea of a Stravinsky school enjoyed wide circulation, quickly becoming a standard textbook item. Berger himself adapted it for his article "Stravinsky and the Younger American Composers" (1955), expanding Copland's list to include Ingolf Dahl, Charles Jones, Paul Des Marais, Leo Smit, and Louise Talma. In 1957 Fine similarly referred to Berger, Foss, Shapero, Smit, Talma, and himself as a group.[63]

In his article, Berger pondered the widespread devotion that the Stravinsky school felt toward Copland, offering his own explanations:

This may be because his own debt to the Stravinsky of such works as the Octet places him in the family and because, in or out of this family, his own stature on the American scene casts a sizeable shadow as inescapable to many Americans as Stravinsky's. Certain works of the 'forties by members of the Stravinsky school might have been very different were it not for Copland's contribution. Of these I might mention Shapero's Sonata for Piano Four Hands, Lukas Foss's *The Prairie* (a cantata), Irving Fine's *Music for Piano*, Louise Talma's Piano Sonata, and Leo Smit's earlier piano pieces and ballet music.

But the Stravinsky school, continued Berger, parted ways with Copland in their "internationalism" and their disinclination toward "developing the American characteristics that occupied Copland's attention." Indeed, they were generally wary of what Fine called Copland's "popularist tendencies."[64]

Copland developed close ties with many of these composers, particularly in the late 1940s and 1950s. He dedicated individual songs from his *Twelve Poems of Emily Dickinson* to Berger, Dahl, Haieff, Fine, Foss, and Shapero, and the first of his *Four Piano Blues* to Smit. Aside from Berger—whom he had known since the days of the Young Composers' Group and whom he "saw quite a lot of" while in Cambridge in 1935— he became especially friendly with Fine (1914–62), Shapero (b. 1920), Smit (b. 1920), and Foss (b. 1923).[65]

Copland had met Foss in 1937, when the fifteen-year-old looked him up at the Empire Hotel, his dirty laundry in tow; and Shapero in 1939, after receiving in the mail, via Nicolas Slonimsky, some music by the nineteen-year-old Harvard undergraduate. During the summers of 1940 and 1941 at Tanglewood, he got to know them both better; sometimes he had to mediate between these two outspoken students and their teacher, the formidable Hindemith. While at Harvard in 1944, he frequently socialized with Shapero and Foss, along with their close friend Irving Fine, then a young instructor on the Harvard faculty, and his wife, Verna (who called Shapero, Foss, and Fine "the three musketeers"). Copland regularly saw Fine and Foss at Tanglewood over the next two decades. Moreover, in 1960 he and Foss spent six weeks together in the Soviet Union, courtesy of the State Department. Meanwhile, in 1943, Copland met Smit, a pianist-composer who befriended Fine, Foss, and Shapero as well, and who championed their piano music.[66]

"It was love at first sight," Verna Fine remembered, describing the Copland-Fine friendship. "Aaron became like an older brother to Irving. They were both soft-spoken, and they loved to talk about music—I never remember them talking much about anything else." Fine and Copland regularly kept in touch by telephone or mail, Copland addressing his letters to "Oiv" or "Oiving" or, if writing to both Fines, to "Honeychiles" or "Babes in the Woods." He similarly became a beloved figure to the younger Shapero, Smit, and Foss—a nice change for Copland, who usually did the adoring. "I had fallen in love with America because of people like Aaron," remarked Foss.[67]

All four deeply admired Copland's music, but they held one or another work in special esteem: Fine, the *Dickinson Songs*; Shapero, the *Short Symphony*; Smit, the Piano Concerto; and Foss, *Billy the Kid*. They followed each new work with interest and sympathy. They also supported Copland in practical ways. Shapero coached Benny Goodman on the Clarinet Concerto, Smit played and recorded almost the entire oeuvre for solo piano, and Foss conducted a good deal of the orchestral music, once writing, "Yours is the only American music I have performed consistently over the years, and with genuine pleasure (with the possible exception of Ives' *Unanswered Question*, which I also love)." In addition, Foss proofed the orchestral score to *Billy the Kid* and arranged it for solo piano, Smit arranged *Danzón Cubano* for solo piano, and Fine arranged some of the *Old American Songs* for chorus. All four offered criticisms and opinions about the music as well, especially the irrepressible Shapero, who in 1942 wrote, with characteristic bluntness, "I liked the *Lincoln Portrait* a lot, but wondered if anybody else had pointed out to you one fast section which sounds a little confused." Copland made light of Shapero's critiques; in discussing his Third Symphony, he quipped, "Sonny was a severe critic—he listed only about thirty objections, so I figured it must be a marvel of a piece!"[68]

Copland provided these younger composers with the kind of informal guidance long his trademark. He supplied as well a sounding board for various personal problems. After the late 1940s, however, he rarely wrote about their music. As one exception, he penned in 1973 an extended liner note on Fine for a release of that composer's major orchestral work, a note prompted, in part, by Fine's early death in 1962. While praising Fine's "elegance" and "craftsmanship"—and raising the possibility of still greater things had the composer not died so young—he also alluded to "problems" concerning "matters of aesthetics, of eclecticism, of influence." One can read between the lines: for all their admirable qualities, Copland found Fine and his neoclassical colleagues too derivative, "a little too schoolish," as Foss himself put it. "Aaron didn't completely endorse that school," Foss recalled. "Aaron was not altogether wrong, because in a sense that classicism was something we had to overcome eventually." Indeed, Copland criticized Foss's Second Piano Concerto (1953) as too "classical" and approved of the direction taken with his *Time Cycle* (1960).[69]

Copland's personal closeness to Fine, Shapero, Foss, and Smit—along with Berger, Dahl, and Haieff—made it easy for some to overlook his criticisms of their music and to assume that his advocacy of American music was partisan. Copland certainly supported those composers he admired more than those he did not, and he occasionally favored friends with an extra boost. But no evidence suggests that he ever hampered or thwarted anyone's career; the principal distinction seems to have been simply the degree to which he assisted all composers. His essential criteria remained good craftsmanship and, above all, a fresh, individual personality. In the late 1940s, for instance, he championed Stefan Wolpe, publicly deploring the "isolation" of this "grimly serious" and "uncompromising" artist; in 1946 he declared Wolpe "the most unjustly neglected composer in America today." And in 1950, he pronounced Leon Kirchner, a student of Sessions's who belonged "to the Bartók-Berg axis of contemporary music," one of the most important composers to appear in some years.[70]

The career of Easley Blackwood represents a case in point. Although the young Blackwood wrote in an atonal, expressionistic style at some remove from his own leanings, Copland warmly supported the fifteen-year-old immediately upon hearing some of his music in 1948; indeed, he offered Blackwood the first "genuine encouragement" he had ever received. "No one else writes quite like you at your age," he told him. "You must groom yourself to be a composer." Although they subsequently enjoyed little personal contact, Copland sympathetically followed his career, helping him obtain a Fulbright (1954) and a Fromm Commission (1957).[71]

Nonetheless, in the course of the 1950s and 1960s, a number of younger composers—especially those working in complex serial idioms—perceived Copland as biased in favor of more conservative styles. Some even felt that he exerted "monopolistic control" of the new-music scene and prevented those composers not aligned with "the Copland empire" from obtaining performances, commissions, and grants.[72]

That many of these "serialists" were not aligned with Copland is perhaps something of an understatement. More than a few apparently regarded him as somewhat middlebrow, interpreting his more adventurous work as a sign of a conflicted personality, seeing his loyalty to Boulanger as suspect, and seemingly forgetting his efforts on behalf of Ives, Sessions, Schoenberg, Webern, and other heroes of the avant-garde. Such deprecation influenced critical and academic opinion—if not that of the large concert-going public. Once the postwar avant-garde successfully carved a niche for themselves, tensions eased; but resentments over perceived slights lingered.

Ironically, some of the more conservative composers of the postwar era felt betrayed, as with Stravinsky, by what they considered to be Copland's capitulation to the serialists. They pointed to Copland's twelve-tone works, though without necessarily knowing how occasional and personal his adoption of the twelve-tone method actually was. In any case, Copland clearly found himself in the midst of a highly polarized musical world.

Among composers of various aesthetic persuasions, the long familiar notion that Copland was prejudiced in favor of Jewish or homosexual composers gained ground as well. For instance, after rebuffing his sexual advances, Karl Korte—then his student at Tanglewood—felt that Copland's efforts on his behalf lessened; although the two remained cordial and supportive colleagues, Korte believed that he had paid a price for not being homosexual. Such perceptions, however, failed to square with

Copland's widespread patronage of younger composers of varied backgrounds. And although many of his friends were Jewish or homosexual or both, little suggests that personal ties and affection influenced the extent to which he helped advance careers.[73]

More to the point is the fact that, by the late 1950s, Copland, always a rather tough critic, viewed with some concern the profusion of technically proficient composers who, to his mind, did not necessarily have anything to say. The situation reminded him of the Kapellmeister tradition in Germany, which, he argued, was not an altogether bad thing, as it implied "a lot of people with training, and you can't have a musical country without such people." Still, this new generation did not "feel on the top of the wave. It is different from the feeling we had in the 1920s. We felt we had to fight the good fight—that there were reactionary forces against us. But nowadays there is a down-in-the-mouth feeling. No one is very much for or against." This proliferation of composers prevented him from surveying young Americans as he had in 1926, 1936, and 1949, but in an article entitled "1959: Postscript for the Generation of the Fifties," he gave it his best shot and named for special commendation Easley Blackwood, Kenneth Gaburo, Billy Jim Layton, Noël Lee, Robert Lombardo, Salvatore Martirano, Edward Miller, Seymour Shifrin, Gunther Schuller, Mordechai Sheinkman, and Yehudi Wyner.[74]

In this same article, Copland observed a worrisome development: by following the lead of the European avant-garde, this younger generation had, with the exception of Cage and his followers, failed to make their own mark. He thought this a "retrogression," writing, "The older generation fought hard to free American composition from the dominance of European models because that struggle was basic to the establishment of an American music." Nor had the example of Elliott Carter proved particularly helpful: "His theories concerning metrical modulation and structural logic have engaged the attention of our younger composers. Their own music, however, lacks similar directional drive. I detect in it no note of deep conviction."[75]

Thus, in 1959, Copland finally brought up the subject of Elliott Carter (b. 1908)—and as a dubious model for young Americans. This wariness resounded loudly. The two men had been friends since the mid-1930s. A prolific critic during these early years, Carter extensively wrote about Copland with insight and authority, valuing the entire oeuvre, from the most complex chamber work to the most popular ballet score. "Each new work of Copland," he wrote in 1939, "only goes further to prove that he is one of the most important, original, and inspiring figures in contemporary music either here or in Europe." Such interest continued at least through the *Piano Fantasy* (1957), a work that, like Stravinsky's *Agon*, represented an "emancipated musical discourse" comparable to Schoenberg's "emancipation of dissonance."[76]

Copland, in turn, offered guidance to Carter on his First Symphony (1942), and tried—unsuccessfully—to interest Koussevitzky in both it and Carter's ballet *Pocahontas* (1936). "I need not tell you about the quality of the piece [*Pocahontas*] as you can see that for yourself," wrote Copland to the conductor, comparing Carter's "workmanship" favorably to Piston's. Copland further helped Carter win a prize for his *Holiday Overture* (1944)—a work he himself conducted in later years—and recommended him for a 1948 Composers Forum concert. Yet he omitted Carter from his surveys of young American composers; perhaps he had matured too slowly to make it into the 1936 survey and was too old for inclusion in the 1948 one. In any event, Copland seemed surprised and upset by suggestions that he had not adequately supported Carter over the years, telling John Kennedy that "he thought he had been very even-handed with Elliott."[77]

Copland's evenhandedness, however, was hardly commensurate with the critical esteem that greeted Carter in the 1950s and beyond; if anything, Copland preferred Carter's more modest efforts from the 1940s. Kennedy remembered, for example, that Copland respected the First String Quartet (1951) more than he liked it. In 1961, privately musing on "the upsurge of interest in Elliott Carter's later music," Copland noted that it reflected "the passion of our times for methodology, for cool calculation in the creation of unusual relationships," but that the result was not "dull" because "he successfully dramatizes the elements he chooses to work with."[78]

Copland was even more equivocal about Carter's still later work. He admitted to Phillip Ramey having trouble making sense of the Piano Concerto (1966) and the Third String Quartet (1971). And when at about the same time Karl Korte asked him if he felt that Carter had gone "too far," he replied, "My boy, it's always possible to go too far." Such uncertainty made him hesitate about writing a tribute for a New York Philharmonic program book on the occasion of Carter's seventieth birthday. His eventual statement recognized Carter's originality but cautioned, as had his remarks about Sessions in years past, "It is clearly not music for everyone. It presupposes a listener with a sophisticated musical ear. One cannot hope to grasp it all on a single hearing." In interviews from the period, he similarly hedged, describing Carter in 1975 as "a brilliant mind, and a supremely intelligent musician."[79]

Carter, for his part, rarely mentioned Copland in his writings after 1960. He might reasonably have felt disappointed that his own work never won his friend's unqualified praise, but he surely understood that Copland's concerns were genuine. In any case, their mutual respect and affection endured till the very end, Carter remaining one of Copland's most loyal colleagues.[80]

Copland followed John Cage's career with similar ambivalence. In a 1960 lecture he called Cage's "playing around with silences a rather dangerous thing," adding, "On the occasions when I have listened to some of this music that makes an important use of silence I get the impression that if the silence is too long the mind begins to wander." This part-amused, part-skeptical response recalled his feelings toward Cowell, a comparison he drew himself: "There is something about him [Cage] that I connect with California, where he comes from. They try everything in California—and Cage is like that. . . . He derives from men like Varèse and Henry Cowell, people who themselves wrote in new ways."[81]

At the same time, he sympathized with Cage's inclinations—in an age of "total serialism"—toward spontaneity and improvisation. And he especially admired Cage for joining with like-minded composers in staking out and creating an audience—even if the audience consisted largely of avant-garde painters and poets; too few American composers, he thought, reached out in this way. Moreover, Copland and Cage liked each other personally, socializing together both at home and abroad. Copland once told David Diamond, "David, I want you to stop fighting with those boys. You be nice to John Cage!" For his part, Cage wrote Copland a kind letter about *Connotations* in 1974.[82]

Copland's interest in Cage and his circle extended to his personal support of the dancer Merce Cunningham—the original Revivalist in *Appalachian Spring*—and the composer Morton Feldman, who had booed the premiere of his *Piano Fantasy*. "At forty-two," wrote Feldman to Copland ten years after the event, requesting, like so many composers, a recommendation, "I not only find I have stopped booing—but also find I have stopped being booed! Having reached this enviable plateau, the only thing now needed seems to be money, for which I am applying to various foundations."[83]

Copland's association with Tanglewood's Berkshire Center brought him into contact with many other young composers; aside from suspended operations due to the war (1943–45) and two sabbaticals (1955 and 1962), he taught there every summer from 1940 through 1965. During most of his tenure, he worked side by side with distinguished Europeans: Hindemith (1940–42), Martinu and Lopatnikoff (1946), Honegger (1947), Milhaud (1948), Messiaen (1949), Ibert (1950), Dallapiccola (1951 and 1952), Chávez (1953), Toch (1954), Petrassi (1956), Berio (1960 and 1961), Fortner and Gerhard (1961), Lutoslawski (1962), and Xenakis (1963). For a few of these years, the center did without a European composer: in 1957 and 1958, he taught with Milton Babbitt; in 1959, with Leon Kirchner.[84]

From the perspective of Copland and his closest friends, the Koussevitzky years (1940–51) constituted Tanglewood's heyday. Neither Charles Munch nor Erich Leinsdorf—Koussevitzky's successors—were as devoted to new music. In 1963, after assuming the helm, Leinsdorf discontinued Tanglewood's long-standing tradition of conducting the work of all guest composers, citing the difficulties entailed by a composer like Xenakis. Allegedly disturbed by the increasing isolation and marginalization of the composition department, Copland scaled down his involvement with the center, spending his three last years on the faculty there in a part-time capacity and consenting to Leinsdorf's suggestion that Gunther Schuller take over the composition program.[85]

Harry Kraut reports that Copland's growing estrangement from Tanglewood predated Leinsdorf's arrival and primarily concerned his burgeoning career as a conductor and the unwillingness of the Boston Symphony to regularly perform under his baton. In any case, the new Schuller regime "embodied the new generation of composers whose philosophy, for better or worse, was to take the place of the school of thought represented by Aaron Copland and his followers," according to Tanglewood historian Herbert Kupferberg. "Henceforth, the center was to be more attuned to the avant-garde, the electronic, the experimental." Even so, Copland remained a revered figure at Tanglewood, with birthday celebrations staged there in his honor in 1975, 1980, and 1985.[86]

Copland usually had between five and eight students at Tanglewood each summer, including, over the years, Robert Palmer (1940), Gardner Read (1941), Robert Ward (1941), Blas Galindo (1941, 1942), Barbara Pentland (1941, 1942), José Pablo Moncayo (1942), Allen Sapp (1942), Jacob Avshalomov (1946), Alberto Ginastera (1946), Julián Orbón (1946), Ned Rorem (1946, 1947), William Flanagan (1947), Jacob Druckman

(1948), Charles Strouse (1948), Samuel Adler (1949), Martin Boykan (1949), John Kennedy (1953, 1954), Toshi Ichiyanagi (1953, 1954), Joel Mandelbaum (1957), Mario Davidovsky (1958), Thea Musgrave (1958), Karl Korte (1959, 1960), John Duffy (1960), Ezra Sims (1960), Michael Horvit (1961), and David Del Tredici (1963).

Druckman (1928–1996) was initially wary of studying with "a totally establishment person" but was soon won over by Copland's erudition and catholicity of taste. Copland's principal impact on him, however, "was more as an example, particularly in the kind of citizen that he is in the world of music—shouldering of responsibility and not being out for his own personal glory and gain. He feels as though the advancement of the art is his responsibility, and this is a wonderful influence on many of us." For his part, Copland declared himself "an admirer" of Druckman's music, the kind of endorsement that, modest though it might appear, had become quite rare in his later years; in 1979 he nominated him—as well as Bernstein and Barber—for a MacDowell Medal.[87]

In the 1970s, Copland also touted, alongside Druckman, another former student, the Argentinian-born Mario Davidovsky (b. 1934), an electronic composer who hoped to persuade Copland to write electronic music himself. Copland played a significant role in getting Davidovsky to combine electronic and traditional instruments, leading to pieces that largely established his reputation. Like Druckman, Davidovsky praised Copland's open-mindedness, as did Karl Korte, who remembered him as "extremely tolerant."[88]

In contrast, Ned Rorem (b. 1923) argued that Copland, "although in theory unbiased as to your style, was in fact disposed to praise music that most sounded like his own." Rorem was thinking uppermost of his own music, which, in his estimation, contained French-related textures like Copland's (indeed, partly modeled after Copland) but French-derived impressionist sonorities as well. "Our respective Frenchnesses were at opposite ends of the scale, and that, I think, put him off." Copland certainly disapproved of Rorem's facility, wondering if he wrote "too much." Although Rorem was disappointed that Copland never praised his music, he appreciated the composer's lifelong readiness to write him recommendations and meet with him socially; after Copland died, he eulogized him, saying, "With Aaron gone, whose upcoming works can we now look forward to with the throbbing joy of our youth? Where anymore is expertise combined with nostalgia, simplicity combined with power?"[89]

Having Copland accept you as a student or write a letter on your behalf was itself a mark of distinction. Samuel Adler (b. 1928) recalled that Copland admitted him to Tanglewood only at the urging of Irving Fine; he thought the young man's well-schooled music lacked freshness. At their first meeting, in 1949, Copland asked Adler what a plain C-major triad meant to him. "Well, it doesn't mean much," answered Adler. "And that's your problem, Sam," replied Copland, "you've got to love every note. You don't." In their lessons at Tanglewood, Copland criticized Adler's music at each turn, saying, "This note is wrong" and "That chord doesn't fit." By the summer's end, Adler at last produced music that Copland liked. "For the first time in your life," he remarked, "you have some judgment on your music. And if I did that, I was successful." He rejected Adler's request for a letter of recommendation nonetheless, saying, "When I feel I can write you a letter from the heart, then I'll write you a letter." Keeping abreast of Adler's career, eleven years later, in 1960, he finally offered to write a recommendation on the strength of the more recent work.[90]

Another Tanglewood student, William Flanagan (1923–1969), became a particularly ardent devotee; according to Ned Rorem, Copland was, along with Ravel, "the twentieth-century musician closest to his heart." "You know well that I have always been hopelessly addicted to your music," Flanagan once told Copland. "But addicted or not, I couldn't be convinced that there is a composer living who could move *me*, at any rate, as you do with the music of the mother's closing song [in *The Tender Land*]." He also defended *Connotations* against the widely circulated "Total Gloom descriptions" surrounding the work. In 1962 he described Copland as "the guy whose work has been the most important single influence on one's way of thinking about the profession he has chosen to occupy his life." Over the years, Copland regularly offered Flanagan advice and guidance; after Flanagan took his life in 1969, Copland eulogized him at a memorial concert.[91]

David Del Tredici (b. 1937), who also developed an intimate friendship with Copland, originally introduced himself by mail, via a tape of his own music; he subsequently received a scholarship to Tanglewood, apparently thanks to Copland, who never mentioned it. At Tanglewood, remembered Del Tredici, "Aaron showed me that it was OK to be making music and be gay. And he had a true interest in young composers. He wasn't the type to use sex as a tool of power—he never put the make on me." Copland also impressed on him the importance of restraint and subtlety: "Remember, David, it is the illusion of inevitability that we are all after, as though all those notes just fell from heaven."[92]

In later years, Del Tredici visited Rock Hill about once a month, often bringing some new piece along with him. "If I played a piece, he'd say something noncommittal at first, such as 'It's very nice.' Maybe an hour or so later, at dinner, he would turn to me, apropos of nothing, and say, 'I think the bass line is too regular, and the percussion should not always underline the main beat and would you pass the butter.' " Copland continued to abet Del Tredici's career from afar, without taking any credit for it. "Things would drop in my lap occasionally," Del Tredici recalled. "I'm sure he said a word. It was wonderful. He didn't make you pay for it in one way or another the way most other composers inadvertently do."[93]

Copland thought Del Tredici "that rare find among composers—a creator with a truly original gift. I know of no other composer of his generation, at least among those who write within the normal concert idiom, who composes music of greater freshness and daring, or with more personality." He himself performed Del Tredici's *Lobster Quadrille* with the London Symphony Orchestra in 1969, though he purportedly became more critical of the composer in the wake of *Final Alice* (1976), telling Phillip Ramey that he was "having too much fun" and needed to broaden his scope. Although not as close in later years, the two men remained good friends; as late as 1982 Del Tredici confided to Copland about his "suddenly drab and a bit lonely" life. And he always acknowledged Copland as his principal influence.[94]

Copland met the composer Phillip Ramey through Del Tredici in 1967. The two instantly hit it off; Ramey accompanied Copland to Europe in 1967 and 1969. He subsequently became perhaps Copland's closest friend during his final twenty years; he prodded him to compose, defended him in the press, unearthed and prepared unpublished manuscripts for publication, wrote liner and program notes on the music, and published a number of interviews with him. The two became confidants (contrary to speculation, they were never romantically involved); even so, Ramey felt that he never reached that "sad core that is perhaps responsible for the wonderful bittersweet lyricism heard from time to time in his music."[95]

Like so many of Copland's friends, Ramey was single, talented, literary, good looking, and interested in people and politics; but he had an especially irreverent wit, taunting everybody, including Copland. His acerbic humor—expressed in campy letters and devastating imitations of other composers—often delighted and sometimes exasperated Copland, who enjoyed, in either case, having him around.[96]

Ramey's disaffection with America in the sixties was higher pitched than the glum disillusion of Sessions in the twenties, the bemused detachment of Bowles in the thirties, or the quiet anxieties of Fine in the fifties. A critic of the Vietnam War, he railed at President Nixon as "that Swine in the White House" and Mayor Richard Daley as "Pig Daley," though he showed equal contempt for communist Eastern Europe and had little patience for SDS and other far-left radicals. "America is so VULGAR!" he complained to Copland in 1970. "These hideous super-markets, giant drug stores, hamburger stands, and fat, smug, self-righteous members of the so-called Silent Majority are EVERYwhere!!!" Copland took such outbursts in stride, telling Ramey with a laugh, "Calm down, you're foaming at the mouth."[97]

Throughout the century's second half, Copland remained an important model and influence for scores of composers with whom he had minimal contact—or none at all. For example, the successful opera composer Carlisle Floyd (b. 1926), who hardly knew Copland, wrote, on the occasion of Copland's death, "I have never ceased to be grateful to those composers—in particular, to Aaron Copland—for providing composers of my generation a legitimate, vital alternative to the musical language of Stravinsky, Schoenberg and Hindemith, distinguished as they unquestionably are. Also, I must confess that the Copland 'sound' is the only sound I ever have consciously appropriated in my own writing." Similarly, Stephen Sondheim (b. 1930), who met the composer only once, partly grounded his style—as *A Funny Thing Happened on the Way to the Forum* (1962) makes patent—in the work of Copland, along with Ravel, one of his favorite composers. "Copland's general harmonic language (when it was tonal)," wrote Sondheim in 1998, "colored my general musical thinking, just as it did almost every other subsequent American composer of tonal music." Because Floyd and Sondheim had only the merest acquaintance with Copland, their remarks about the pervasiveness of his influence carry a special resonance.[98]

For his part, Copland, in his eighties, discovered, to his delight, the musicals of Stephen Sondheim—at least *A Little Night Music* and *Sunday in the Park with George*, if not *Sweeney Todd*, whose subject matter he purportedly found inimical to the genre. That he was surrounded by young musical theater types during these years no doubt played a part in this regard. Betty Auman, who annually traveled up to Rock Hill in the late 1980s on behalf of the Library of Congress, recalled one visit during which Bernstein telephoned and, upon hearing Copland in the background merrily singing "A Weekend in the Country" from *A Little Night Music*, protested, "He never sings any of my songs!"[99]

Although Copland's personal involvements with composers tapered off in the years after Tanglewood, he continued to follow the new-music scene. In a 1975 article on recent trends, he declared Milton Babbitt (b. 1916) "an extraordinary fellow. In a way he's a man of the people, very broadminded, but when he sits down to write his own music, he turns out this music which you have to be very cultivated to appreciate and even then you might have a hard time. . . . I expect he knows what he's doing." This same essay noted the current interest in Charles Wuorinen (b. 1938), who "writes a very complex music which is not easy to latch on to, but he writes very easily," and George Crumb (b. 1929): "Well, he's obviously a very gifted fellow. His music has a colouristic appeal all the time that would seem to me to have the danger of wearing off once you get used to the colour. Obviously, though, he writes very inventive and attractive music of wide appeal. I should hear more of it."[100]

Copland also had some familiarity with the music of Steve Reich (b. 1936) and Philip Glass (b. 1937). He met Glass in 1960 at Aspen, at which time he made a "great impression" on the younger composer, who by virtue of his Juilliard education knew Copland's work well; in later years, Copland listened to recordings of Glass's music with such friends and associates as Ronald Caltabiano. Meanwhile Reich, a self-described "fan" of the *Piano Variations* since his college days, began sending Copland scores in the late 1970s. "Your comments back in 1978 about my *Music for 18 Musicians* were much appreciated," Reich wrote Copland in 1980, "and you may find the number of repeats in the *Octet* somewhat less than in earlier works of mine." Both Glass and Reich may well have owed something to Copland's work; Glass himself acknowledged some kinship to Copland (though less so than to Virgil Thomson), while Reich referred to his *Octet* as "perhaps a distant cousin of your wonderful Sextet." And whatever Copland thought of their work, he presumably would have admired their success in finding so large an audience at home and abroad.[101]

More to his taste, apparently, were John Corigliano (b. 1938) and

Barbara Kolb (b. 1939). Copland, who thought Corigliano "the real thing," especially admired his Clarinet Concerto, notwithstanding some concerns expressed to Ramey about the work's stylistic eclecticism. Corigliano for his part credited *Billy the Kid* with initially sparking his interest in classical music at age fifteen; in maturity he thought Copland, not Ives, "the great American composer."[102]

Barbara Kolb meanwhile became the last composer Copland assisted in a major way; as with Druckman and Del Tredici, he helped secure her a contract with Boosey & Hawkes. Given her involvement with Boulez and electronic instruments, she also proved one of the most far-out of his enthusiasms; but it was precisely her accommodation of new trends— wedded to a vibrant imagination, a freedom from academic restraints, and a rhythmic vigor, including some assimilation of more popular styles—that probably recommended itself so strongly to Copland.

Copland befriended Kolb at Tanglewood in 1968 after hearing a performance of her *Three Place Settings*. In the ensuing years, he periodically invited her up to Rock Hill and regularly included her, along with Del Tredici, on the guest lists of the many parties and receptions now regularly held in his honor. On one trip to New York, he made arrangements to take her out for dinner. "He was such a mensch, such a phenomenal human being," Kolb recalled, noting how Copland never condescended to young composers but treated them as equals. Kolb reciprocated with cards, gifts, and warm letters. "There will always be a future for American music," she wrote to him in 1980, "if enough personalities choose to follow in your footsteps."[103]

This friendship bears on the topic of Copland and women composers. In his critical writings, Copland rarely mentioned specific women composers, aside from passing references to, say, Germaine Tailleferre or Marion Bauer. He knew none whom he considered of the stature of many male composers past and present. He even titled his surveys of young American composers, "America's Young Men of Promise" and "America's Young Men—Ten Years Later," omitting mention of "men" only in his 1949 survey, though still not including any women.[104]

Copland occasionally mused on the seemingly limited achievements of women composers, stating in 1952, for example, "I have sometimes wondered whether this problem of the successful shaping of musical form was not connected in some way with the strange fact that musical history names no women in its roster of great composers. There have been great women musical interpreters, but thus far—I emphasize, thus far—no examples of women composers of the first rank." Puzzled by the fact that Nadia Boulanger forsook composition, he further asked, in a 1960 tribute to her, "Is it possible that there is a mysterious element in the nature of musical continuity that runs counter to the feminine mind? And yet there are more women composers than ever writing today, writing, moreover, music worth playing. The future may very well have a different tale to tell; for the present, however, no woman's name will be found on the list of world-famous composers." Recognizing that this was a "touchy subject," he would occasionally regret making such "dangerous" remarks, but he continued to speak his mind frankly, as in two 1978 interviews in which he stated, "Writing a forty-minute piece that makes sense is not a sympathetic task for the female mind," and "Music is too formal. The feminine mind doesn't like to concern itself with abstract things and that's what music is. But I think that's changing."[105]

Some interpreted these statements as revealing a hostility toward women composers. In his defense, Kolb argued that throughout much of his life there were relatively few women composers on the scene and fewer still of real distinction. Moreover, as can be seen, he spoke of "music worth playing." But however one reads his remarks, his inclusion of music by women composers in Copland-Sessions Concerts (including Ruth Seeger) and at Yaddo, his patronage of numerous women composers during his twenty-five years at Tanglewood, and the friendship and encouragement he extended to Kolb, as to, previously, the French Marcelle de Manziarly, the American Vivian Fine, the Brazilian Pia Sebastiani, the Canadian Barbara Pentland, and the Scottish Thea Musgrave, refute allegations of any prejudice against women composers.[106]

Nearly fifty years his junior, Christopher Rouse (b. 1949) was one of the youngest composers befriended by Copland. On 6 April 1962, the thirteen-year-old Rouse wrote his first letter to Copland, congratulating him on the twentieth anniversary of *Rodeo* and the premiere of *Connotations*, which he had heard broadcast on television and "unlike the rest of my family, enjoyed." Rouse continued to write Copland appreciative letters throughout his teenage years; he especially liked *Connotations* and *Music for a Great City* and bristled when William Flanagan treated the latter as something less than a work of major significance. "Of course, I like it (because I'm young)," he explained.[107]

As Rouse began to send Copland tapes and scores of his own music in the mail, the latter maintained a balance between candid criticism and thoughtful encouragement. In 1968 he counseled Rouse, now at Oberlin and feeling rather estranged from the current interest in Cage and Babbitt, with this advice:

> All I can tell you is this: that it is the strength of one's inner convic-tion as to the importance of what one does that justifies the doing of it. Naturally, it is also deeply satisfying to feel a part of one's own time, especially in a time such as ours, when music is in a state of flux. But nothing can be forced if one doesn't feel sympathetic, for that leads nowhere. At your age an open mind to new musical mani-festations would seem essential. In that sense your fellow-students are right—there is such a thing as being a stick-in-the-mud. But as for feeling old-fashioned stylistically,—if it is any consolation, don't forget that Brahms must have felt terribly old-hat by comparison with Wagner, and ditto for Fauré by comparison with Debussy and Ravel. Even Stravinsky, during the thirty-year period of his neo-classic manner, must have felt "backward" by comparison with Schoenberg and Webern. (He caught up, by the way!) But to come back to you: Don't get hung-up on what you are composing now, for it is certain to develop and change. The only thing you need be concerned about in that respect is to believe in it while you are doing it. Its eventual fate will be decided by others in any case.

Copland reserved full approval for a number of years, until 1971, when a new work convinced him of Rouse's "outstanding composition gift—and I am happy for you."[108]

One of the most intriguing exchanges between the two occurred at about this same time, when Rouse asserted that, to his mind, Copland's music possessed "an intrinsically violent nature . . . often disregarded in performance." After Copland wrote back suggesting that what he called "violence" could better be termed "a tragic sense of life," Rouse responded by arguing that, for him, "violence and tragedy are extremely closely related" and that "the most moving way of expressing despair or tragedy is through a huge, long cry, as in so much of Mahler, or in almost all of Varèse"; he heard such a cry—"virile, powerful, and a bit proud"— in Copland's work, especially at the end of *Connotations*. Rouse con-tinued to correspond with Copland throughout the 1970s and into the 1980s, though with less frequency; in 1977 he admitted a special liking for *Dance Panels*, admiring its "precision and restraint" as well as its "affecting sort of innocence."[109]

To the end, Copland was a sympathetic but frank critic. "After hearing four student works at Tanglewood in 1975, he commented, "I can't say there's anything in these works so striking that I'll remember them." About one work in particular, he said, "It seemed to me to be awfully spurty—it didn't seem to have any reason for proceeding the way it did. There were little globs of sound that didn't seem to be adding up. I'm being a little severe, but why not?" He was similarly "a little severe" with some students in Kansas in 1982, but as he told Ramey afterward, "They really should be doing better."[110]

Despite some declining prestige in his later years, Copland's reputation as the "Dean of American Music" remained uncontested. He himself did not like the epithet, which evoked the kind of dusty, academic world he had evaded his entire life. Surely the word *dean* hardly did his wide-ranging activities justice, for he offered the American composer much more than stewardship; he was an influence, a teacher, an editor, a guide, a patron, a benefactor, an advocate, a pen pal, a confidant, a psychiatrist, a friend. Virgil Thomson summarized this aspect of his life's work as follows:

As for his musical colleagues, young and old, Copland has befriended them all. For thirty-five years he has given concerts of their music, expounded it in books and lectures, organized publishing enterprises to make it available, produced it in Canada, the United States, Mexico, South America and Europe. He has founded a society that collects and distributes to them money in payment for performance rights. He has counseled the young, brought them up to maturity as artists, got them jobs, commissions and private subsidies, made enemies in their defense and taken the rap when their work has disappointed the backers. There is scarcely a composer in the hemisphere (and there are few even in Europe) who is not under the gratitude to Copland for valuable and specific services of a professional character.

Many younger composers may not have expressed or felt such gratitude. But Copland remained steadfast in his support of serious American music in all its diversity.[111]

13

South of the Border

Carlos Chávez

Copland's friendship with the Mexican composer Carlos Chávez, which lasted more than fifty years, was extraordinary: more enduring than with Sessions or Harris, more intimate than with Thomson or Piston, more coequal than with Blitzstein, Diamond, or any number of younger composer friends. Chávez, for his part, had no better friend than Copland, at least among composers. That they became the most venerated composers of their respective countries made the association all the more remarkable. In an essay on the subject, Robert Parker emphasized its wide-ranging aspects, pointing out that although both men were "first and foremost composers" they were also "pianists, conductors, teachers, entrepreneurs, writers, lecturers, administrators and statesmen for the arts."[1]

Raised in a suburb of Mexico City and later in Veracruz by his schoolteacher mother and five older siblings, Carlos Chávez (1899–1978) studied piano with Manuel Ponce and Pedro Luis Ogazón and harmony with Juan B. Fuentes. Unlike Copland, his formal education came to an early end in 1920 when he began publishing his own music. He never profited, consequently, from the kind of extended training Copland received with Boulanger, which perhaps explains why Chávez, for all his impressive technique, never quite acquired Copland's kind of technical mastery.[2]

In 1922–23, Chávez traveled with his new wife to Vienna, Berlin, and Paris, where Paul Dukas encouraged him "to concentrate on the rich popular music of Mexico as Manuel de Falla had done with Spanish music." On the way home, he spent the winter of 1923–24 in New York, where he so enjoyed the musical scene that he returned there for nearly two years (fall 1926–spring 1928) with the painter Rufino Tamayo, a friend of his. Chávez made a name for himself in New York, winning the support not only of Copland (whom he met in 1926) and Harold Clurman, but Paul Rosenfeld, Edgard Varèse, Henry Cowell, Roy Harris, and Colin McPhee, among others, thus bridging the gap between New York's two principal new-music factions—the International Composers' Guild and the League of Composers—better than practically anyone else.[3]

Whereas Chávez's earliest music reflected Ogazón's impressionism and Ponce's nationalism, in the mid-1920s he began to incorporate aspects of Stravinsky's rhythms, Varèse's "organized sound," and jazz. He occasionally subordinated all these influences to an interest in Aztec culture and indigenous Indian music that went back at least as far as his ballet *The New Fire* (1921), a work that grew directly out of the Mexican Revolution. Indeed, Chávez's life and work cannot be understood apart from the revolution, which had some bearing on Copland's artistic development as well.

The Mexican Revolution began as a popular revolt against the dictator Porfirio Díaz in 1910 and essentially ended, after ten years of domestic violence, with the assumption of the presidency by Álvaro Obregón in 1920; but in a broader sense, the revolution continued at least through 1940. The oligarchy that governed Mexico after 1920—institutionalized in 1929 as the PNR (Partido Nacional Revolucionario)—created a part-socialist, part-capitalist economy. Strongly antifascist, the government tolerated the Communist Party, which became especially influential in educational and artistic affairs; Mexico was one of only a few nations to support the Loyalists during the Spanish Civil War. At the same time, the country demonstrated its independence from both the United States and the Soviet Union by allowing the exiled Leon Trotsky to settle there in 1937.

The government's agenda included redistribution of land rights, restrictions on church authority, reform in education, freedom of the press, raised wages for workers, nationalization of some industries, and, when deemed necessary, expropriation of foreign-owned companies. Its anti-clericalism provoked the greatest controversy and resulted in violent conflicts not unlike those that led to civil war in Spain in 1936. The American public itself was occasionally alarmed by Mexico's anticlericalism; but the United States generally supported the government, a policy that climaxed with Roosevelt's rejection of "big stick" diplomacy in favor of the Good Neighbor policy in 1936 (the very year in which Copland completed *El Salón México*). By 1940 the revolution had gone far in transforming Mexico from a feudal agrarian society into a modern industrial one—though not nearly far enough, according to many contemporary historians on both the right and the left of the political spectrum.[4]

Taking its cue from the Soviet Union, Mexico began sponsoring art under the auspices of the Ministry of Education, headed by the visionary José Vasconcelos, described by Chávez as "a man of high caliber." Determined to create art for the impoverished masses, Vasconcelos commissioned the young Chávez to write his first ballet, *The New Fire,* and provided public walls for the murals of José Clemente Orozco, Diego Rivera, and David Alfaro Siqueiros. These murals quickly won the world's admiration, inspiring similar efforts in the United States and elsewhere. In his 1958 Norton lectures, Chávez said of the muralists, "In trying to be accessible to the people, as they called it (or, as we would prefer to say, to the average audience), they did not descend to a level of vulgarity. They maintained a classic dignity, at times truly superb, and whether or not they were accessible to the 'people,' it is good that their work was achieved and stands for posterity."[5]

In 1928 the government appointed Chávez director of both the country's leading orchestra, the Mexico Symphony Orchestra, and its principal conservatory, the National Conservatory of Music, a remarkable dual appointment for anyone, let alone an avant-garde musician under the age of thirty. These appointments intensified Chávez's determination to write music that would match the muralists in relevance, accessibility, and spontaneity; he set himself the goal of, in his own words, "writing simple, melodic music with a peculiar Mexican flavor that would have a certain dignity and nobility of style; music that would be within the reach of the great mass of people and would eventually take the place of commercial, vulgar music then in great vogue, meant to incite the low passions." Copland recognized a new accessibility in Chávez's Sonata for Four Horns (1929): "Well it certainly has your flavor," he wrote Chávez, "... but it is Carlos more humane and more cantabile. I also think it is easy for the public to listen to." In some new works, like the ballet *Horsepower* (*H.P.*) (1926–32, with sets by Rivera), Chávez began to use popular Latin-American folklore in addition to the more austere Indianist features that had dominated such earlier pieces as *The Four Suns* (1925).[6]

Chávez later interpreted this movement toward accessibility as a worldwide trend that also included Copland and Kurt Weill. Looking back on the 1930s in particular, he maintained that social and political concerns underscored such developments, though he acknowledged that the desire for money and fame may have constituted a factor as well; he contended that in any case, he and like-minded composers failed to establish a musical movement "comparable in magnitude or importance" to the muralists. At the very least, his biggest hit, *Sinfonía India* (1935), had enduring success.[7]

Chávez headed the National Conservatory until 1934 and remained with the symphony until 1949, when he appointed José Pablo Moncayo as his successor. For short periods he also directed the Ministry of Education's Department of Fine Arts (1933–34) and the National Institute of Fine Arts (1947–52). As a public servant in a politically volatile country, he had his vicissitudes with the government, but he remained a central figure in Mexico's cultural life, enjoying a power and prestige highly unusual for a modernist composer. He performed music by North and South American composers, taught and promoted colleagues like Moncayo, Silvestre Revueltas, and Blas Galindo, wrote books and articles, sponsored chamber music concerts, and published new scores. Although largely funded by public as opposed to private funds, these accomplishments strongly resembled Copland's multifaceted activities. "We had much in common," noted Copland. "His dedication to improving conditions for Mexican music was similar to my own efforts in American music."[8]

During the 1930s and beyond, Chávez—very much like Copland—needed to negotiate among various political and aesthetic points of view, including those promulgated by the Stalinists, the independent Communists, and the anticommunist left. Such disagreements resulted in personal tensions that sometimes exploded—as in a fist fight between Siqueiros and Tamayo in a Mexico City art gallery in 1954. Although Chávez wrote a number of works honoring and celebrating the Mexican Revolution—including the *Llamadas (sinfonía proletaria)* (1934)—his assimilation of modernist, Indian, and Spanish materials arguably recalled the stance of his old roommate Tamayo more than that of the militantly communist muralists. Chávez's departure from the conservatory in 1934 possibly had something to do with the far-left reforms ushered in during Lázaro Cárdenas's regime (1934–40). In the 1950s, Chávez and the pro-Soviet Rivera severed their friendship over a politically controversial mural; in a somewhat muddled account, Rivera bitterly portrayed Chávez as "having the typical Mexican sense of inferiority in matters artistic, and corresponding awe toward the culture of the Old World."[9]

The muralists as a group were aesthetically closer to Chávez's colleague and rival Silvestre Revueltas (1899–1940); like Siqueiros, Revueltas belonged to the Communist-dominated League of Revolutionary Writers and Artists and traveled to Republican Spain in 1937 to support the Loyalist cause. As Chávez's protégé, student, and assistant, Revueltas worked side by side with Chávez through 1934; but in the course of 1935 their friendship waned. For all their differences, the vibrant scores of Chávez and Revueltas comprised a distinctive movement, one that contrasted with the more restrained styles that dominated American and European musical trends in the 1930s. Their music arguably continued more directly along lines established in Paris in the early 1920s; and not surprisingly, a number of foreign artists, including Sergey Eisenstein, Paul Strand, and Copland, found Mexico in the 1930s comparably stimulating.[10]

In the years after their initial meeting, Copland and Chávez quickly set about championing each other. Copland programmed Chávez's *Three Sonatinas* (1924) and Third Piano Sonata (1928; dedicated to Copland) on no less than four Copland-Sessions Concerts, including one in which Copland performed the Piano Sonatina himself; and he included Chávez's *36* (1925) and *Unidad* (1930) at the First Yaddo Festival. Copland also persuaded CosCob to publish Chávez's Piano Sonatina and later helped get him a contract with Boosey & Hawkes. He further facilitated various commissions, performances, and guest teaching appointments, including those at Tanglewood (1953) and at the University of Buffalo (1958).[11]

Chávez, in turn, frequently conducted Copland's music in Mexico and around the world. During his many years with the Mexico Symphony Orchestra, he programmed one or another Copland work nearly every season, including world premieres of the *Short Symphony* (1934; dedicated to Chávez) and *El Salón México* (1937). He continued to conduct old and new Copland works for decades, including a performance of *Inscape* in 1970.[12]

Copland knew Chávez's work intimately; as early as 1928, he wrote an authoritative article on the composer. What impressed him above all was the music's modern and New World qualities, traits hardly distinguishable in his estimation: "His music is not a substitute for living but a manifestation of life. It exemplifies the complete overthrow of nineteenth-century German ideals which tyrannized over music for more than a hundred years. It propounds no problems, no metaphysics. . . . He is one of the few American musicians about whom we can say that he is more than a reflection of Europe." He thought Chávez's attempts at fashioning folk materials into "an art-form" at least as successful as the comparable achievements of Falla and Bartók; and while admitting that a work like the Third Sonata presented "formidable difficulties to even the sympathetic listener," with familiarity, the music revealed itself to be "packed with meaning."[13]

Copland remained most fond of some of the earlier scores, in particular, the "youthful and colorful" *Horsepower* (1926), the Third Sonata (1928), the *Sinfonía de Antígona* (1933), and the *Sinfonía India*. In some contrast, he took more and more of the later music to task: in letters to the composer he criticized the "ineffective" ending of the *Invención* for piano (1958; dedicated to Copland), the "sense of 'forcing' or strain" in portions of the Fifth and Sixth Symphonies (1953, 1961), and the stridency of *Clio* for orchestra (1969). At the same time, he found much else admirable and delightful, such as the scherzo of the Third Symphony. Even without the "specific national references," he wrote about Chávez's postwar music, "the *ambiente* remains pure Chávez."[14]

For his part, Chávez deeply esteemed Copland's music. At an all-Copland concert in September 1932, he spoke to his audience about Copland in much the same terms as Copland spoke about him, that is, as a composer of his time who had absorbed his distinctive culture. Drawing analogies to Mozart and Bach, he praised the *Piano Variations* as a work of "supreme intelligence, superior sensibility, and supreme culture." He liked even better the piece Copland would shortly thereafter dedicate to him, namely, the *Short Symphony*. After conducting the work's world premiere in 1934, he wrote to Copland, "The dialectic of this music, it is to say, its movement, the way each and every note comes out from the other as the only natural and logical possible one, is simply unprecedented in the whole history of music." In a 1946 symposium on neglected works, he mentioned only two, the *Short Symphony* and *The Rite of Spring*: "Their sense of movement is profound. A primitive and pagan but highly

221

co-ordinated strength runs through the Russian score. In the American piece the strength is agile, a bit playful and jazzy, but tender and fully disciplined." Ten years later, he still regarded the *Short Symphony* as "one of the most beautiful and original works written this Century."[15]

The strong attachment between Copland and Chávez involved a certain Pan-American resistance and solidarity in the face of European cultural domination. "European musicians are of the worst kind: conductors, pianists, violinists, singers and so on are mere 'prima donna' minded people—they are very important to themselves," wrote Chávez to Copland in 1931. "We must change the situation, Aaron. We must not accept to be in the hands of foreign conductors and interpreters whose mind and heart (if they happen to have any) is [*sic*] far away of [*sic*] the spirit and culture of this new world." "All you wrote about music in America awoke a responsive echo in my heart," answered Copland. "I am through with Europe Carlos, and I believe as you do, that our salvation must come from ourselves and that we must fight the foreign element in American music." "Together we will *clarify* the situation," Copland proclaimed in yet another letter from the time.[16]

They naturally found the differences between their music and that of European composers a source of mutual gratification. Discussing one of Chávez's works in 1933, Copland wrote, "The difference between our works and those of the Europeans was striking. Theirs were so smooth and refined—so very much within a particular tradition, and ours quite jagged and angular." In the following year, Chávez similarly wrote,

We had this summer a lot of Honegger, Hindemith, etc. etc. stuff here, and let me tell you that they are simply unbearable for me, they are artificial, full of literature, bad literature and worst possible taste, I cannot stand them any more, they should be shut up for ever, so much the better. And to think that it is that stuff what is taken for contemporary music? No it is not. And with such understanding about things I got the Little Symphony [*sic*]; and let me tell you what I thought: well, here is the real thing, here is our music, my music, the music of our time, of my taste, of my culture, here it is as a simple and natural fact of my own self, as everything belonging to oneself is simple and natural.

For such reasons, each composer's music held unparalleled importance for the other one; Copland continually encouraged Chávez, often saddled with administrative and conducting responsibilities, to compose: "I will never be really satisfied until I hear that you *are* composing again," he once wrote.[17]

The friendship between Copland and Chávez went beyond mutual support and shared ideals; they felt a deep spiritual and emotional bond. "You are something of my own self," Chávez told Copland in 1933, "you mean for me understanding, you are with me in the real center of thought and creation." And in 1951 he declared, "I always think of you no matter how long a time we do not hear from each other." Although a number of other friends—an astonishing number, in fact—similarly expressed themselves to Copland, none showed such sentiments for so long as Chávez. And one can hardly find among Copland's massive correspondence as effusive a declaration of friendship as this 1935 letter to Chávez: "I'm sure you must know how dear you are to me in every way—how close I feel to you mentally and spiritually and musically—and the idea that anything whatever should harm our friendship even temporarily is very painful to me. Even tho I may not write for long periods you are always in my thoughts—people are always asking me how you are—and I never feel really separated from you."[18]

Copland and Mexico

After trying for some time to persuade Copland to visit Mexico, Chávez finally lured him there in the fall of 1932 with various scheduled performances of his music. Copland borrowed his brother Leon's car and drove to Texas in August with Victor Kraft. Leaving the car in a garage in San Antonio, they took a train down to Mexico City, arriving there on September 2, just in time for an all-Copland concert at the National Conservatory, the first of its kind.[19]

Copland spent four months in Mexico. He rented an apartment in the heart of Mexico City and a small studio nearby so that he could continue work on *Statements* without disturbing his neighbors. Mexico City amazed him. He was particularly struck by its "great mixture of magnificence and of poverty" and its contrast of the new and the old, with "the poorer classes" going around barefooted on busy city streets lined with modern office buildings. "Mexico has turned out even grander than I expected," he wrote to Virgil Thomson, "and I expected pretty grand things. The best is the people—there's nothing remotely like them in Europe. They are really the 'people'—nothing in them is striving to be bourgeois. In their overalls and bare feet they are not only poetic but positively 'émouvant.' " And he wrote to Henry Brant, "I can't rave too much about the country itself—nor the populace, for that matter." Among other sites, the popular dance hall El Salón México especially intrigued him.[20]

Copland was also impressed with Chávez's clout—on his second day in Mexico, he met a cabinet minister—and his ability to arrange concerts accompanied by extensive press coverage. Some months after his return to the States, he wrote to Chávez,

> When I was in Mexico I was a little envious of the opportunity you had to serve your country in a musical way. Here in the U.S.A. we composers have no possibility of directing the musical affairs of the nation—on the contrary, since my return, I have the impression that more and more we are working in a vacuum. There seems to me less than ever a real rapport between the public and the composers and of course that is a very unhealthy state of affairs. So you can see that for me your work as Jefe de Belles Artes is a very important way of creating an audience, and being in contact with an audience. When one has done that, one can compose with real joy.

His experiences in Mexico clearly strengthened his growing resolve to communicate with a larger public.[21]

Copland remained in Mexico City for two months, acclimating himself to the food, working on his Spanish, and visiting nearby attractions, including the towns of Xochimilco, Chapultepec, and Cuernavaca. After attending a Hollywood film one evening, he wrote to his parents, with characteristic forbearance, "It was scheduled to begin at 9:30, but actually didn't get started until 11 P.M. It's a very Mexican habit to be always late, and nobody seems to mind."[22]

Under Chávez's guidance, he sought out as much indigenous music as he could, listening with special interest to mariachi bands. According to Arnold Dobrin, he began to question "the accepted idea of folk music as a rather static form that remained pure or simply disappeared," perhaps because he found himself in a milieu in which modernist and folk currents intertwined so closely. This notion of folk music as a vital art form had ramifications on his artistic development.[23]

Copland and Kraft spent most of their last two months in Mexico in the small town of Tlalpam. Then, after an excursion to Acapulco so that Kraft could swim in the Pacific, they left the country. From San Antonio,

Copland wrote to Chávez, "As soon as we crossed the border I regretted leaving Mexico with a sharp pang. It took me three years in France to get as close a feeling to the country as I was able to get in three months in Mexico." And from Savannah, he wrote to Mary Lescaze:

> Mexico was a rich time. Outwardly nothing happened and inwardly all was calm. Yet I'm left with the impression of having had an enriching experience. It comes, no doubt, from the nature of the country and the people. Europe now seems conventional to me by comparison. Mexico offers something fresh and pure and wholesome—a quality which is deeply unconventionalized. The source of it is the Indian background everywhere—even in the land-scape. And I must be something of an Indian myself or how else explain the sympathetic chord it awakens in me.

Traveling back through "our dear U.S.A."—with one-night stops in San Antonio, Houston, Galveston, New Orleans, Mobile, Montgomery, Atlanta, and Savannah—he thought "the non-existence of any cultural life worth mentioning . . . depressing even to a passer-by like myself. Perhaps it's only dormant and we need a new kind of pioneer down here to awaken the spiritual consciences of the people. I can easily see myself in the role." He hoped to find more "cultural life" in Charleston, Raleigh, Richmond ("Isn't that the country where the [Allen] Tate crowd functions?" he asked Lescaze), and Washington, D.C. But when he returned to New York, all he could talk about was Mexico.[24]

Copland spent subsequent working vacations in Mexico, especially in the 1930s and '40s. In 1936, he and Kraft revisited Mexico City, where they saw Chávez, Colin McPhee, and others before retiring for the summer to Tlaxcala, a small pre-Columbian town recommended by Chávez. "We live on the top of a hill opposite a 17th century church—one of the marvels of Mexico," he wrote to David Diamond on July 4. "It's all incredibly quiet and picturesque and hopelessly Mexican." During this same trip, he and Kraft traveled to the Yucatán and visited the ancient Mayan capital of Chichén Itzá. They returned to Tlaxcala the following year for a few months starting in August.

In 1941, Copland made Mexico the first stop of a government-sponsored tour of Latin America. Then in 1944, he and Kraft spent a few months in Tepoztlán. Years later, he recalled discovering Tepoztlán by way of a book by Robert Redfield, an anthropologist who had done work there in 1927; he apparently forgot that Rosamund Bernier's sister had suggested the town after he and Kraft decided against their original destination, Tenancingo; Tenancingo was "charming," he explained to Bernstein, but too much like Tlaxcala. The stay in Tepoztlán, a village without newspapers, radios, telegraphs, or electric lights, proved a remarkable experience. The one telephone in town did not work and a piano needed to be brought in from a neighboring village. He and Kraft resided—with a cook, maid, and gardener—in the village's "only livable" house: "If that sounds too snooty," he wrote Bernstein, "I'll amend it by saying that we boast the only bathroom in town." Twice a week, the residents held a public dance in the open market. "Instead of doing jarabes and huapangos," Copland informed Arthur Berger, "I was amazed to see them attempting a kind of Tepoztlán version of a fox trot. The nearest movie house is 15 miles away, but obviously it had its effect." Their cook, an elderly woman from the Yucatán, left Copland with a yen for Yucatán-style Mexican food.[25]

Copland revisited Mexico as a guest conductor in 1947, 1953, 1962, and 1972. On the 1947 trip, he took Elliott and Helen Carter to El Salón, where the men were frisked for firearms; and on the 1953 visit, he toured Oaxaca and Puebla with a young friend, John Kennedy, who remembered Copland loving Mexico for its color and vibrancy. "Mexico fascinating as ever," confirmed Copland to Irving Fine in 1953. He also spent the winter of 1959 in Chávez's Acapulco home; "I am simply enchanted with the set-up," he thankfully wrote Chávez. After Minna Lederman returned from a trip to Mexico in 1964, he told Chávez, "Minna talks about Mexico in terms that we used to use in the '30s. It is nice that she got such a kick out of her visit and that Mexico has not become so Americanized that it doesn't retain its old charm."[26]

From the time he first heard his music played by the Mexico Symphony Orchestra under Chávez's baton in 1932, Copland also felt a special affection for that particular ensemble. Rosamund Bernier observed him "in absolute delight" as he played his Piano Concerto with Chávez and the symphony in 1936. In spite of his dire finances at the time, he refused royalties for this particular performance, telling Chávez, "My feeling for you and for the success of the Sinfónica is much too close. To me it is not just like any other orchestra." He always spoke fondly and indulgently about the group. "In the old days (1932) they made a mess—but it was a pretty mess," he told Bernstein.[27]

Copland also kept up with Mexico's new-music scene to the point of becoming something of an expert on the subject. On his very first trip in 1932, he befriended Revueltas, whose Second String Quartet he had featured at Yaddo a few months earlier (probably on Chávez's recommendation). Kraft in particular admired Revueltas and his music, and a warm friendship ensued all around. When Paul Strand's film *Waves* opened in New York in 1937, with a score by Revueltas, Copland took advantage of the occasion by writing an article on the composer for the *New York Times*. Describing Revueltas as an "inspired" composer in the tradition of Schubert, whose works flowed from his pen as he sat absorbed at his desk, he praised the composer's colorful orchestral tone poems, which reminded him of "the bustling life of the typical Mexican fiesta" and Mexico's "highly spiced" cuisine.[28]

This article avoided the touchy issue—at least in Mexico—of Revueltas versus Chávez, other than to state that Revueltas "deserves to be equally well known" to American music lovers and to note that his greater closeness to the Mexican vernacular made him "more quickly appreciated" in his native country than Chávez. But a few years later, in 1941, Copland came down squarely on the side of Chávez. Although he realized that Revueltas's "untimely death" in 1940 only intensified many Mexicans' preference for him over Chávez, he contended that Revueltas "never was able to break away from a certain dilettantism that makes even his best compositions suffer from sketchy workmanship"; Chávez, he opined, remained "the more mature musician in every way." Still, there was no need to choose between them: "We can have both men and their music for exactly what each is worth to us." In 1944, after hearing Chávez perform Revueltas's *Windows*, he told Arthur Berger that he found the work "amusing" but not very sound structurally. "He was like a modern painter who throws marvellous daubs of color on canvas that practically takes your eye out, but it doesn't add up. Too bad—because he was a gifted guy."[29]

Copland met a number of other composers on his first trip to Mexico, including Luis Sandi, Chávez's colleague at the conservatory and two of Chávez's students, Daniel Ayala and Salvador Contreras. In time, he also befriended two other Chávez students, Blas Galindo and José Pablo Moncayo, both of whom studied with Copland at Tanglewood in the early 1940s. Assessing the work of Ayala, Contreras, Galindo, and Moncayo (known as the Group of Four or *Los Cuatro*) in his 1941 diary, Copland thought Galindo the most technically advanced and possibly "the most gifted" of the group, but claimed that none had so far "exceeded" the accomplishments of Chávez or Revueltas. In 1944, he expressed even greater reservations about still younger Mexican composers, those born in the 1910s; he attributed their failure to produce anything truly noteworthy to "the lack of an outstanding composition teacher" in Mexico. "Chávez and Revueltas went abroad and the young men stay home. Something ought to be done about it."[30]

Copland and the Rest of Latin America

Copland's adventures in Mexico whetted his appetite for other places in Latin America. In 1941, he accordingly took advantage of the opportunity to tour South America as a cultural attaché for Nelson Rockefeller's Committee of Inter-American Affairs. His four-month mission included lecturing on American music in person and on the radio, performing his own music, investigating local talent (especially with an eye for composers who would make good candidates for in-kind visits to the United States), and, in general, promoting cultural relations in the context of the nation's Pan-American wartime efforts.[31]

Before leaving for South America, Copland spent the spring of 1941 in Havana, partly in order to complete his Piano Sonata and his textbook on modern music, partly to ready his Spanish for the upcoming tour: "One works in the morning, beaches in the afternoon, and listens to Cuban music at night. Perfect program, No? Oh, yes, and I mustn't forget my Spanish lessons—excellent teacher, still not out of high-school," Copland slyly wrote Bernstein. Havana reminded him of Paris: "It's a crazily mixed-up city with skins of all colors, clothes of all varieties, and everybody jabbering away at top speed. It just doesn't make any sense to be writing about the works of one R. Sessions in this atmosphere."[32]

He left Cuba in August 1941 for Mexico City, Guatemala City, Cristobal, Bogotá, Quito, Lima, Santiago, Buenos Aires, Montevideo, and Rio de Janeiro before returning to Havana, writing home to friends and family about his impressions: Cristobal resembled "a kind of glorified whore house full of drunken navy men," Quito reminded him of "a very faded version of some provincial Mexican capital," and Rio he thought "all it's cracked up to be." He also recorded his musical experiences in a diary and published an account of his findings, "The Composers of South America," the following year. "I examined the work of about sixty-five composers," he reported, "and didn't find a Bach or Beethoven among them. But I did find an increasing body of music, many well-trained composers, a few real personalities, and great promise for the future. Enough to make apparent the value for both North and South America of closer, more permanent musical ties, beyond any question of political expediency."[33]

Although he sensed the strong influence of the "modern French school" thoughout the continent, Copland discovered that conditions varied greatly from country to country. He thought Argentina's composers the most cosmopolitan and expert; Brazil's composers, in contrast, he found provincial and old-fashioned. He noted that Chile's composers were better organized than elsewhere in Latin America, but he criticized their music as overly nostalgic, excessively complex, and dangerously inbred. Unlike Mexico's composers, Peru's, he thought, had failed to assimilate their Indian heritage effectively. Similarly, although Cuba possessed a folklore as splendid as Brazil's, their composers had neglected to make comparable use of it.

Copland acknowledged Villa-Lobos's preeminence in South America, although neither the man nor his music were as much to his taste as some lesser-known composers. "As I see it, the Villa-Lobos music has one outstanding quality—its abundance," he remarked rather caustically. Although he admired the music's vigor and originality, he faulted its lack of formal coherence and stylistic unity. These virtues and limitations made Villa-Lobos, he would later write, "the pride and despair of his Latin-American colleagues." The United States, he further argued, had its own Villa-Lobos in Ives; both composers shared "the main drawback of an overabundant imagination: the inability to translate the many images that crowd their minds into scores of a single and unified vision." Such profusion stemmed, he suggested, from the sheer size of their respective countries.[34]

Whereas he had known Villa-Lobos's music since his student days in Paris, most of the South American music he encountered was new to him. As his most exciting discovery, he named Brazil's Camargo Guarnieri, whose "healthy emotional expression" and "warmth and imagination" were "touched by a sensibility that is profoundly Brazilian." Among Argentinian composers, he singled out the neoclassicist José María Castro, the serialist Juan Carlos Paz (no "caterwauling" in Paz's use of the method, he observed), and the nation's "white hope," Alberto Ginastera. He acknowledged Domingo Santa Cruz as Chile's foremost composer, though he admired, too, the sensitive music of Humberto Allende, the Indian-based scores of Carlos Isamitt, and the potential of the young Juan Orrego-Salas. Uruguay boasted an impressive figure in the eighteen-year-old Hector Tosar, whose "vivid imagination, dash, and *élan*" reminded him of Shostakovich. In Colombia and Peru, the only composers "worth serious consideration" were, respectively, the Paris-trained Guillermo Uribe Holguín and the Belgian-born Andrés Sas. Copland also addressed the situation in Cuba; he noted the recent deaths of Amadeo Roldán and Alejandro Caturla, the respectable neoclassicism of José Ardévol, and the popular scores of Gilberto Valdés, who had the potential to become the Gershwin of Cuba with "more training and greater discipline."[35]

In the fall of 1947, Copland took another four-month tour of South America, this time as cultural ambassador for the State Department. Because his itinerary included only Argentina, Brazil, and Uruguay, he had time to explore some of Brazil's provincial centers. Other than Pia Sebastiani of Brazil and Sergio de Castro of Argentina, however, he met very few young composers who impressed him. Indeed, he was dismayed to find a group of young Brazilian "dullards" writing "singularly humorless" music under the tutelage of the German serialist Hans Joachim Koellreutter. At the same time, he favorably observed that the ubiquitous French influence had subsided since his last visit. In an article for the *New York Times*, he recommended—as he had in 1941—José María Castro, Luis Gianneo, Ginastera, and Guarnieri as composers "worth anybody's time."[36]

In neither 1941 nor 1947 did he neglect folk music. "I have tried to hear as much native music as possible in each country," he wrote in his 1941 diary. On that earlier trip, he was particularly struck by an Indo-Peruvian ensemble who "produced a fascinating music on home-made harps, violins, flutes, rattles and ram's-horns," and by the Afro-Brazilian samba, an "overpowering" music whose "melodic line is savage and more guttural than any I have heard anywhere." On his return to Brazil in 1947, he complained that, due to the baleful influence of Broadway, the samba in Rio had become commercialized; he duly set off for northern coastal towns specifically to hear the real thing. In Bahia, he discovered with interest an instrument called the "berimbau," while further up the coast, in Recife, he was especially intrigued by a dance, the "frevo," and the music that accompanied it: "The brass were particularly amusing in the way they interjected upward thrusting phrases and sudden isolated chords. The precision and energy displayed were remarkable." Copland's interest in South American folk music seemed to peak around this time; he devoted most of his 1947 article to the samba and the *frevo*, privately bemoaning the lack of a comparable vitality in the work of South America's serious composers. He returned to the States with twenty recordings of samba.[37]

Copland's 1952 Norton lectures confirmed an awareness and appreciation for a variety of Latin-American folk and popular musics: for the Cuban "guajira," which "could be listened to for hours on end"; for the "deeply nostalgic" flute music of the Peruvian Indians, music "of an indescribable sadness"; for the Colombian "bambuco" and its "exhilarating rhythm"; and for the popular "danzon" of Cuba and the urban tango of Argentina. "I myself am far from being expert in this area," he admitted, "but I do retain vivid impressions of an unbelievably rich and comparatively little known territory of folk expression in Latin America."[38]

Copland returned to South America in 1954 and 1957 for two lavish festivals of contemporary Latin-American music held in Caracas. He reviewed the first festival, which featured forty orchestral works performed over a two-and-a-half-week period, for the *New York Times*. "It came as no surprise," he reported, "that Villa-Lobos and Chávez confirmed their reputation as the two leaders of Latin-American composition." He further named as "finds" the Venezuelan Antonio Esteves, along with one of the festival's three prizewinners, the Spanish-born Cuban Julián Orbón. He also offered a few "gripes," including the fact that Guarnieri and Orrego-Salas were "conspicuous by their absence." And in strong contrast to his remarks from the 1940s, he complained about the overemphasis on "folk-inspired" music and the neglect of experimental and twelve-tone scores. For the shorter 1957 festival, he sat on the jury that awarded prizes to Galindo and Guarnieri as well as to Panama's Roque Cordero and Peru's Enrique Iturriagi.[39]

Over the years Copland befriended a number of Latin-American composers, from such established figures as Villa-Lobos, Santa Cruz, and Guarnieri to the young composers he helped bring to Tanglewood, including Cordero, Esteves, Ginastera, Orbón, Orrego-Salas, and Tosar, as well as Cuba's Harold Gramatges and Puerto Rico's Hector Campos Parsi. His vigorous support resembled his efforts on behalf of his countrymen: sympathetic yet exacting reviews; sponsored concerts of their music; recommendations for scholarships, fellowships, and commissions; and personal guidance and advice.

And as at home, he became a revered figure in Latin America. "All your letters, pictures, programs, your old pocket watch—the camera—all this I keep as souvenirs of the happiest days of my life," rhapsodized Villa-Lobos in 1947. Fleeing the Castro regime in 1960, Orbón sent birthday greetings to Copland that read in part, "We know that you are celebrating your birthday and you are receiving the homages of admiration and gratitude for [sic] everybody that love [sic] music and human greatness." "Thank you for what you think, for what you say, and for what you do," wrote Orrego-Salas in 1981. "It is my privilege to be considered among your friends," stated Cordero in 1987.[40]

His music exerted a strong influence on a number of Latin-American composers as well, including Ginastera, eventually described by Copland as "the foremost creative figure in the musical life of South America." In the years following their 1941 meeting, Ginastera eagerly obtained everything Copland published, praising his work as "very interesting and original." After buying a recording of the Clarinet Concerto and the Piano Quartet in 1953, he told Copland,

> In these as in some of your previous works, like *Lincoln Portrait*, *Appalachian [Spring]* and [the] Third Symphony, we can see a composer who masters completely his technical means and an artist who has attained his true personality. I think I told you this before, but I cannot help thinking of it when I listen to some of your new works: your music is not only the expression of a strong personality, but it represents the deep and real sense of your country. This is what I would like to do myself. To be not a voice but the condensed voices of a whole country.[41]

This ability to express, in Roque Cordero's words, "the soul of his country" influenced a wide range of Latin-American composers, not only Ginastera and Cordero, but Tosar, Esteves, Orbón, and other important figures. At the same time, Copland never presumed any nationalist agenda for his Latin-American students, to the relief of Chile's Orrego-Salas, for whom Copland's directness and simplicity and his reflective attention to detail—his admonition, for instance, to "save timbres"—made a "deep impact." Copland's Latin-American students and friends agreed that the importance of finding one's own musical personality represented his guiding principle as a mentor and champion.[42]

Copland loomed so large south of the border not only because of his concern and support ("a deep interest, not just a Good Neighbor policy," says Orrego-Salas) or because his kind of enlightened nationalism often hit a responsive chord, but because his music itself made profound contact with Latin America. He assimilated not only the sounds and rhythms of Latin America—beginning with Mexico in the 1930s and continuing with South America and the Caribbean in the 1940s—but something of its landscapes, its customs, and its peoples.[43]

14

Personal Affairs

Copland and Sexuality

When he met Copland in the summer of 1921, Harold Clurman thought him mature beyond his years and was amazed to discover that he had even psychoanalyzed himself. In later years, he wrote, "The secret or source of his wisdom can be traced to his utter acceptance of himself at an early age. He made peace with himself and so could be at peace with the whole world." In highly guarded language, he implied that Copland overcame the "suffering" and "guilt" related to his homosexuality and accepted it as "inevitable," thus becoming a "source of great strength" to others. "You had your 'big crisis' in 1920," Clurman once reminded Copland, suggesting a precise year for when this might have transpired.[1]

Copland's early acceptance and understanding of his homosexuality was shaped in part by literature, including the poetry of Walt Whitman and, later, the novels of André Gide. He also discovered with particular interest Gide's defense of homosexuality, *Corydon* (commercially available in 1924), a work that argued not only on behalf of what Gide called the "natural pederast" but of the societal advantages of homosexual mentoring of young men. According to David Diamond, the book made a deep impression.[2]

Even before Paris, Copland read the work of Freud and Havelock Ellis, whose landmark studies in sexuality, including Ellis's classic *Sexual Inversion*, published in 1897 in collaboration with John Addington Symonds, he discovered in the Brooklyn Public Library. Ellis's explanation for homosexuality—that people are born bisexual and that a congenital "predisposition" leads one either toward heterosexuality or homosexuality—possibly influenced Copland's belief that homosexuality was a natural and inherited phenomenon. Whatever its limitations from a contemporary point of view, Ellis's work—with its panoramic appreciation of "homosexuals" from Plato and Michelangelo to Verlaine and Whitman, its association of homosexuality with "artistic aptitude," its highly skeptical view of "cures," and its plea for a reform of England's penal codes—must have made for enlightening and supportive reading in the 1910s. Copland also perused the writings of another pioneering sexologist, Richard von Krafft-Ebing, most likely in the 1920s, when the vogue for Krafft-Ebing was at its height.[3]

Despite their old-fashioned use of the word *invert* (implying a male preference for a passive role), Freud, Ellis, and Krafft-Ebing more inclusively defined "homosexuality" as simply the desire for the same sex, thus reconceptualizing the very notion of sexual identity. They also asserted that the homosexual subculture of their time comprised three basic types, recognized as such by homosexuals themselves: effeminate homosexuals ("fairies"), more conventionally masculine homosexuals ("queers"), and essentially heterosexual men who engaged in homosexual sex ("trade"). Like most educated, middle-class homosexuals, Copland apparently identified with the second group; he himself used the word *queer* when casually referring to homosexuals, and he seems to have been somewhat put off by effeminacy.[4]

Nor did he seek out sailors and other "trade" as did a number of his friends. Rather, he was attracted to bright young musicians and artists. Most of his lovers were in their late teens or early twenties when he took up with them. Over the years, the gap in age between Copland and his boyfriends naturally widened; by the 1950s, he was sometimes more than thirty years older than they. Such romantic proclivities consequently left him somewhat vulnerable, and he occasionally wondered if he was being used for his prestige, his connections, or, eventually, his money. He also had to face the probability that his young lovers would eventually leave him, something he accepted graciously, typically conducting his affairs with a light, playful touch. (To the surprise of some of his boyfriends, it was Copland who often maneuvered the end of a relationship.) And while a breakup could have its sadness and difficulties, in almost every instance he remained on good terms with his former lovers, who over the years provided a primary source of companionship.[5]

According to Erik Johns, these relationships involved "the classic Greek thing with an older man adoring and mentoring a younger guy." Copland believed that, in love relationships, every man was either a father or a son. "He had been the baby," observed Johns, "and he'd had all of that. He wanted to dote." A number of the young men he became involved with had problems—including sexual identity confusion, alcoholism, and clinical depression—beyond those typically found among adolescents; even in his professional relations with composers, he often guided and supported troubled young men. A similar impulse animated his love life; indeed, the line was often a thin one.[6]

Erik Johns and John Kennedy—two of his more significant partners—found Copland sexually candid and uninhibited. Kennedy recalled how, in bed, Copland might read Goncourt or Gide in the original French, translating into English out loud; or tell risqué stories and naughty jokes, taking "shy pleasure in knowing he said things he shouldn't have." Johns and Kennedy further agreed that Copland was a gentle, sensitive lover. "It was very tender," said Kennedy. "He was a very loving, sweet man."[7]

Copland avoided discussing his own sexual mores. He himself was not promiscuous. Most of his affairs lasted at least a few months; some lasted years. At the same time, he occasionally had casual sex. In 1929, he spent a night, reported Marc Blitzstein to Eva Goldbeck, in Frankfurt with an "ingenuous-faced child" named Willy ("Ask Aaron about Willy," goaded Blitzstein, "to secure that desired characteristic look of mingled horror, annoyance and calm—all mock"). Another friend provided him with a list of "angel-type" boys prior to his 1960 trip to Japan, which led to "a nice time." But Copland believed in emotionally meaningful and committed relationships. He himself favored monogamy, though given the fact that he rarely lived full-time with his young lovers, he took it for granted that they would not necessarily be faithful to him. "Copland was old and wise enough to know that's what kids did," stated Johns. He made it clear, however, that he preferred not to know about such infidelities.[8]

Copland was discreet about his love life. Even after the 1969 Stonewall rebellion he showed no inclination to "come out." When urged to do so by Leonard Bernstein he responded, "I think I'll leave that to you, boy." For some of the very public events of his later years, he felt obligated to have a woman escort. And when asked about his private life by reporters, he cagily referred to himself as a "bachelor," as in this 1974 interview: "I'm a bachelor, in the tradition of Beethoven and Brahms, and I have no theory as to why."[9]

Even among friends, Copland avoided foul language and showed a rather genteel concern for such talk, especially in the presence of women. When conversation with "les boys" turned bawdy, he would often feign a kind of shock, his hand to his chest, what Erik Johns picturesquely describes as "clutching his pearls." For Copland, crude language—whether among heterosexuals or homosexuals—signified a loss of control, according to Harold Shapero, who duly watched what he said in front of him. "Copland had a very elegant sensibility, a delicacy, what Americans would call, 'class,' " he explained. Once, in a star-studded game of charades in which Judy Holliday, acting out *Die Kunst der Fuge*, pointed to her genitals, the avalanche of vulgarities she elicited from Leonard Bernstein and others, recalled Paul Moor, nearly "blew Copland out of the room," leaving him "literally gasping at each successive epithet, until he could gasp no more."[10]

Copland tolerated the campiness of younger friends like Diamond and Bernstein; he himself had fun acting out the parts (including the young girl and the prostitute) of *Grohg* with Harold Clurman or performing high kicks for the camera with Victor Kraft and Leonard Bernstein. But if he felt friends getting out of hand, he would plead, "Boys, stop that!" Nor did he feel comfortable with the assertive homosexuality of the 1950s associated with Paul Goodman, Ned Rorem, Frank O'Hara, and John Ashbery, much as he admired them as artists, according to Robert Cornell, who took O'Hara and their friend Joe LeSueur up to Rock Hill one weekend.[11]

In the 1970s and 1980s, when the still younger gay men who cared for him and his home became, to his mind, too raunchy, he might request, in a humorously reproachful way, that they tone things down. He tolerated their watching pornographic films on his video player but took little interest in the films himself, finding them, guessed Michael O'Connor, one of the staff, too crude and mechanical for his taste. If he saw an attractive man in a bathing suit on television, he might say, at most, "Well, he has sort of a dashing figure!" O'Connor found such remarks charmingly old-fashioned and was likewise amused when Copland absconded with one of his gay-interest magazines, such as *Christopher Street,* to read in the privacy of his bedroom.[12]

For all this, Copland lived a relatively open homosexual life, especially for someone of his generation. His sexuality was widely accepted in the musical and artistic circles in which he largely traveled; moreover, his friends—straight and gay alike—often socialized with his lovers. He never tried to "pass," nor did he ever seriously entertain the idea of a marriage of convenience, a commonplace among homosexuals of his time, including some of his closest friends. At a formal reception in Austin, Texas, in the early 1970s, when someone asked if he might photograph Copland with the beautiful blond wife of a fellow composer, he said, "Go ahead! It might help my reputation," a quip that not only revealed his sense of humor about such things but underscored the real difficulties posed by his lifestyle. And his two-volume autobiography, while not explicit about his romantic life, is more candid than generally recognized, as in, for example, his description of setting up house with Erik Johns. Indeed, he became one of the earliest homosexual composers of prominence to cohabitate with his romantic partners.[13]

All this required far more courage and self-assurance than suggested by glib references to Copland as "closeted," let alone presumptions that he was in any degree "tortured." On the contrary, he impressed friends as extraordinarily relaxed about his sexuality. "In private he was very open about being a gay man," recalled David Del Tredici. "He'd joke about it. It was perfectly natural." "Copland accepted himself," said John Kennedy, "no boasts, apologies, guilt."[14]

Victor Kraft

Copland's early sexual life is shrouded in obscurity, though as mentioned earlier, he seems to have had some romantic friendships while still in Brooklyn. On his various travels to Europe in the 1920s, he had some sexual experiences, according to the recollections of friends and an occasional bit of documentation, including a letter to David Diamond in Paris stating, "Sorry you don't find much sex-appeal in the native product. They make up for lack of attractiveness in savoire faire. You'll see." Upon settling in New York, he frequented bars known for their homosexual clientele, sometimes bringing heterosexual friends like Harold Clurman or Roy Harris along. During these early New York years, he developed crushes on Israel Citkowitz, Paul Bowles, and Edwin Denby, among others; it seems that at least in Bowles's case, the relationship may have had a physical component. Then, in 1932, he fell in love with Victor

Kraft, with whom he would have the most important romantic relationship of his life.[15]

Copland had just met the sixteen-year-old Kraft, barely out of high school, when he wrote to Carlos Chávez, shortly before leaving for Mexico in 1932, "I am bringing with me a young violinist who is a pupil, companion, secretary and friend. His name is Victor Kraftsov. I'm sure you will like him." "Kraftsov" was born Victor Hugo Etler on 8 August 1915 in Oneonta, New York, the son of Samuel and Bella Etler. His father had been born in New York City; his mother had emigrated from Alexandrovsk, Russia. The Etlers eventually returned to New York City, where Victor attended Public School 19 and De Witt Clinton High School. A violin prodigy, he gave concerts as a child and studied at Juilliard while in high school. After graduating from high school, he adopted his mother's maiden name, Kraftsov, later shortened to Kraft. The young Kraft set his sights on becoming a professional violinist or composer, thus explaining Copland's statement about his being a student.[16]

On their first trip to Mexico, Copland and Kraft spent some time—a veritable honeymoon—in Acapulco, where someone, perhaps even Paul Strand, took pictures of them in their bathing suits. In one photograph, Copland and Kraft gently hold each other, a rare document of their affection. Some of the photographs of Kraft by himself—taken, presumably, by Copland—are highly erotic, with Kraft in various suggestive poses, some in the nude.[17]

Over the next ten years and beyond, Copland and Kraft lived and traveled together as much as their busy schedules allowed; at the very least, they stayed in constant touch. At five feet, eleven inches and 165 pounds, the quietly intelligent Kraft matured into a strikingly handsome man, with wavy dark-brown hair, piercing blue-gray eyes, a statuesque physique, and a deep, mellifluous voice. He sat for the photographers Cecil Beaton and Carl Van Vechten at their invitation.

At first Kraft pursued music, including composition lessons with Roger Sessions, but he became increasingly interested in photography, partly in response to Copland's encouragement (Copland bought him his first camera) and partly due to his friendships with Paul Strand and Rudy Burckhardt. During the latter half of 1936, he studied photography at the Santuario de Ocotlán in Tlaxcala, following which he spent five months (December 1936–April 1937) covering the Spanish Civil War (in such

Nationalist strongholds as Seville and Toledo) as a photojournalist for Louis Aragon's *Ce Soir*.[18]

On his return to the States, Kraft continued working as a freelance photographer for a number of newspapers, magazines, and studios, including the *New York Times* and *Look* magazine. During the Second World War, he assisted and studied with the photographer Margaret Bourke-White, and managed a concert tour for Prince George Chavchavadze. From 1945 to 1947, he was on staff at *Harper's Bazaar*, a job he hated and from which he was eventually discharged.[19]

During these same years Kraft intermittently served Copland as a salaried secretary and chauffeur, with Copland's loft and residences providing his home base. Together they traveled to Bemidji, Hollywood, Mexico, and Cuba; Kraft further arranged the various moves to Bernardsville, Ridgefield, Sneden's Landing, and, eventually, Ossining and Cortlandt. At the same time, Copland supported Kraft's own career, cheering his accomplishments and offering advice; he apparently felt that photography was a more congenial pursuit for him than music. One photo historian, David Jacobs, contends that Kraft was a somewhat distinguished though ultimately second-rate photographer.[20]

Copland's closest friends also befriended Kraft, who was, in Verna Fine's words, "around a lot"; personal letters to Copland during this period—and for many years later—typically concluded with "regards" or "love" to Victor. Those who knew Kraft in his younger days remembered him fondly; even the often severe David Diamond softened at the thought of Kraft: "Oh, he was a sweetie-pie."[21]

Rosamund Bernier and Verna Fine especially liked him, partly because he so obviously shared their devotion to Copland but also because Kraft (who, as it turned out, was more heterosexual than homosexual) was something of a lady's man. "I was very fond of Victor Kraft in the early years," recalled Bernier. "He was terribly handsome, but so unsure of himself. . . . Victor was intuitive, affectionate, always taking up lost causes. He was like a character out of a Russian novel." "He was moody but charming and handsome and helpful," agreed Fine, "always working on Aaron's car and taking delightful pictures."[22]

One of Kraft's lost causes was communism. Paul Bowles referred to him as a Communist in a 1934 letter to Copland, and Kraft himself complained to Bowles about Communists defecting to Franklin Roosevelt in the 1936 presidential election. Kraft subsequently drifted toward Catholicism, then Quakerism. He went through a number of other phases in still later years, including some immersion in the philosophy of Buckminster Fuller.[23]

As for Kraft's moodiness, that was noticeable from the start. "Victor weeping still?" Bowles asked Copland in 1935. A 1937 letter from Kraft to Copland—one of the few such letters that survives—gives a fuller account of Kraft's state of mind during these years. Addressed to "Darling Heart," the missive continued,

> I hate myself. The whole world of people are—almost all—so foully dishonest and deceitful, really—deep within them. And I am most insidiously dishonest of them all—and can only watch helplessly and—hopelessly. What is there to write, it would be too much. Everything I think—is untrue and false and double. Better not write. Only Aaron is the single bright pure star.

In 1942 Copland wrote Leonard Bernstein, "Even V smiled benignly the entire time."[24]

By the early 1940s, the romance between Copland and Kraft had begun to unravel, with Copland, Kraft, and Bernstein embroiled in a muddled affair. In 1943, Bernstein wrote Copland, out in Hollywood, that he had "betrayed" him by prodding Kraft to join him there: "He'd be so much happier there than torturing himself here (and getting drunk, and forgetting the simplest obligations and duties). And especially *you* would be much happier? So why not? We've played squash together somewhat, and I know him better, and thus decided on this betrayal. As for my feelings, I can be awful controlled sometimes. I'm a good disciple, no, my love?" "I think it's great that V is finally going west," Bernstein exclaimed in a later letter. "He needs it, you need, I need it, and the best, of course, is that he made a decision at all."[25]

The romance, however, collapsed in the mid-1940s, possibly in 1944. Referring to the immediate postwar period, Ned Rorem observed that Copland's "rapport with Victor Kraft was ambiguous, and, in any case, pretty much deromanticized by the time I knew them both." Indeed, Copland sounded a bit fed up in a 1946 letter to Kraft urging him to go into psychoanalysis. By that time, both he and Kraft were having affairs with other people.[26]

Among other difficulties, Kraft was more sexually attracted to women than to men; such conflicts underscored the special rapport he felt with the photographer Rudy Burckhardt, who had been Edwin Denby's lover before marrying. "He wished he could be gay," Burckhardt stated, "but he wasn't quite. That's what we had in common, too."[27]

Even as Kraft began to date women in the 1940s—sometimes bringing them to the homes he and Copland still shared—the two remained emotionally attached; at the same time, Copland's relationships with other men may have forced him to attempt to make a life for himself. One marriage Kraft planned fell through in 1947. Then, in 1951, he married Pearl Kazin, a writer and the sister of the literary critic Alfred Kazin. "Everyone thought Victor's news was a great surprise," recalled Copland in his memoirs, "but I had realized long before his marriage that it was important for him to go it alone, or better still, with a woman to help him." At the time of his marriage, Kraft had been doing freelance work in Brazil; after their wedding, he and Pearl returned to Brazil, but within a few months—even before Copland's wedding gift of a Morris Minor automobile could reach them—they had separated, Pearl returning to the States, Victor remaining in Brazil.[28]

After a short stint in Guatemala, Kraft returned to the States with a Brazilian girlfriend. They settled in Brooklyn and later moved to Yonkers. Throughout the 1950s he stayed in close touch with Copland, often visiting and taking care of Shady Lane Farm. His sporadic appearances dismayed David Walker, Copland's mild-mannered secretary since 1952. "He sort of took over Aaron. He tended to father Aaron, to advise Aaron, don't do this, and don't wear that, and don't buy this."[29]

In 1960, Kraft married Rheba Robinson, a nurse and fellow dog enthusiast whom he met at a dog show. After moving to Croton-on-Hudson, he found Copland a house in nearby Cortlandt, where the composer obligingly moved in 1961, despite Walker and others' concern about the upkeep of such a large property. In the same year, the Krafts had a child, brain-damaged at birth, whom they named Jeremy Aaron. Jeremy's birth apparently pushed Kraft over the edge; refusing to accept the fact that his son was mentally handicapped, he exhaustively pursued various medical treatments and educational regimes. In 1968, he left his wife and kidnapped seven-year-old Jeremy from boarding school. Over the next eight years, he and Jeremy traveled around the world, to such places as England, Gibraltar, and Tangier, periodically returning to the servant's quarters at Copland's home. Kraft, who had a history of heart problems, died of a heart attack on 2 July 1976 while vacationing in Maine. Jeremy subsequently was returned to live with his mother.[30]

In the final decades of his life, Kraft grew progressively wilder. He let his hair and beard become long and disheveled, and he would parade about Rock Hill in the nude. In the 1960s, he became something of a hippie, smoking marijuana, dropping LSD, and donning headbands and granny glasses. Obsessed with the Beatles and the mass media, he wrote half-crazed notes on these subjects. At one point, he attempted to talk Copland into moving with him into a windmill in England. After Victor and Jeremy spent some time with Paul Bowles in Tangier in 1973, Bowles informed Copland that "most of the times, although not all of them, V. seemed to be in a state of desperate emotional turmoil." On another occasion, Bowles tersely observed, "They're both on the path of destruction."[31]

Copland rarely discussed Kraft's deterioration with friends other than to mutter, "Sad" now and then. Privately, however, he jotted down some of his thoughts. One such reflection read in part: "I had hoped that as a result of being forced to face himself—his true self—VK would be destroyed and eventually resurrected as a non-evil being—I knew him as a man with a thoroughly diseased soul. A gangrened limb must be severed if the body is to live. I feel that similar radical measures, in the sense of involving certain risk of total survival, is [sic] called for in the case of a psychotic masquerading among trusting souls."[32]

Kraft had always been something of an annoyance to Copland, from his habit of playing jazz on the radio to his emotional instability. On one of their trips to Mexico, he even threatened Copland with a wrench. But over the years his presence became ever more taxing and disruptive. "From the time I was there," recalled Walker, "I don't think that Aaron was very happy to have Victor appear. I don't think Aaron looked forward to that, because of the violence; but it obviously increased and increased." Kraft picked fights not only with Copland but with his staff and with his younger boyfriends; the only time Erik Johns ever saw Copland become enraged was in response to Kraft antagonizing someone. In the 1960s, Kraft badgered Copland about not being as famous as the Beatles. He had wild tantrums. Once he picked up the dinner table and threw it. Another time, after Copland fearfully locked himself in his bathroom, Kraft broke down the door. By the late 1960s, young, hyperactive Jeremy was often on hand as well, opening drawers, slamming cabinets, and throwing pots and pans around the kitchen. Many of Copland's friends reasonably contended that, whatever other problems he had in producing music in his later years, having Victor and Jeremy around could not have helped. Phillip Ramey remembered times when Copland would be trying to compose and Kraft would come screaming into his studio.[33]

Friends wondered why Copland put up with all this. When an exasperated Ramey once advised him to "get rid" of Kraft, he responded, "How can I do that? He's been my friend for so many years and he's in trouble. He's crazy, you know." Copland told Walker that he wanted to sever ties with Kraft and that he had gone to a psychiatrist to help him do so. But he put up with Kraft to the end.[34]

Marc Blitzstein and Leonard Bernstein believed that Copland felt such enormous responsibility and loyalty toward Kraft because he had in some sense corrupted him, distracting him from his natural inclinations toward both music and women. Richard Hennessy suggested further that for all the difficulties, Copland held on to the relationship because Kraft eased the loneliness of his later years. Robert Cornell similarly thought that Kraft's persona as the manly and explosive adventurer "played into what Copland craved."[35]

Kraft's death elicited ambiguous condolences from Copland's friends. "He was a beautiful young man," wrote Diamond. "I could never understand what happened to Vic." When Ramey told Copland that he was better off without him, he responded, "I think you're right. Best of all, I think Victor's better off now." Hennessy was similarly relieved: "Victor at rest, at last," he wrote to Copland. "What a consoling and reassuring image that is."[36]

As Jeremy's godfather, Copland continued to finance the boy's schooling as he had always done. After Jeremy left school in 1978, he helped him invest in a dog kennel and, later, become an automobile mechanic. He left $25,000 to Rheba Kraft in his will with the request that this gift "be used for the support and maintenance of my godson, Jeremy Aaron Kraft." It was a larger amount than he left to anyone aside from his secretary, David Walker.[37]

After Copland's death, his estate reportedly retrieved the voluminous Kraft-Copland correspondence from the Copland Collection, to the dismay of Betty Auman and others at the Library of Congress. Whether or not these letters survive remains unknown. In 1986 Vivian Perlis, in consultation with David Walker and Ronald Caltabiano, had written

Copland's attorney, Ellis Freedman, urging him not to destroy these letters; although Perlis, Walker, and Caltabiano agreed that the "silliness" of some of them might prove embarrassing to one or another party, Copland had instructed Walker that he wanted this correspondence preserved, saying, "There might be some things of importance or interest contained in the letters." Perlis never received a response. Whatever the fate of the Copland-Kraft correspondence, its disappearance deprives posterity of a deeper understanding of Copland's life. For as the few letters that slipped by reveal, throughout much of his adult life, Copland confided more in Kraft than in perhaps anyone else.[38]

Other Amorous Friendships

In the course of the 1940s, Copland commenced a series of affairs with Alvin Ross (1920–1975), Paul Moor (b. 1924), and Erik Johns (b. 1927). Like Kraft, all three were in their teens or early twenties when he first met them.

Born in Vineland, New Jersey, Ross studied painting at Temple University in Philadelphia, where in the late 1930s he entered a circle that included Leonard Bernstein and Ned Rorem. He loved music; Morris Golde recalled his special fondness for Beethoven's *Grosse Fuge* and Berg's *Lyric Suite*. After moving to New York, he taught art at the New School, the Pratt Institute, and the New York School of Interior Design until his death at age fifty-five. Rorem remembered early "Balthusian portraits" of "pubescent females," but in maturity, Ross painted mostly still lifes; reviewing a memorial exhibition in 1975, Hilton Kramer respectfully noted, "His paintings are small, quiet, affectionate and utterly faithful to the objects they embrace with a grateful precision."[39]

Copland met Ross through Bernstein and the two conducted a highly discreet romantic affair in the early 1940s; but as was typical for Copland, the romance soon evolved into a platonic, lifelong friendship. Rorem remembered Ross as "gentle to a fault, winsome, wry, smart" with a "velvety voice" and "hooded eyes." Robert Cornell similarly described him as "soft-spoken, thoughtful, with lovely manners, very intelligent." According to Arthur Weinstein, "Everyone loved Alvin Ross."[40]

A graduate of the University of Texas, Paul Moor, a skilled pianist, first met Copland upon his arrival in New York in 1943 via a letter of introduction from Copland's old friend Aaron Schaffer. Moor and Copland became reacquainted in 1945 while the latter was collaborating with Moor's lover at the time, playwright Lynn Riggs.[41]

Moor and Copland started seeing each other during the summer of 1946 and then more regularly beginning in late 1947. "I think you are much cuter, but God knows Ricardo Montalban is prettier," Moor wrote to Copland after seeing the film *Fiesta* (1947), which featured a version of *El Sálon México*. Moor recognized that the affair meant much more to him than to Copland and admired the way he "managed the relationship, especially its denouement, in the sense of supervising and guiding."[42]

Moor left for Paris in 1949, settled in Munich in 1951, and then in Berlin in 1956, where he established himself as a musician, writer, and photographer. He remained in touch with Copland, visiting him in the States nearly every year. When Copland and Vivian Perlis began collaborating on an autobiography, he hoped that they would "exercise candor and honesty about personal details," but Copland explained to Moor that he intended the book to be a "musical" biography. Moor's own candid discussions of Copland appeared in the *Advocate* and the *Harvard Gay and Lesbian Review* after the composer's death. In the former he wrote, "Aaron's beak-nosed, buck-toothed, somehow thoroughly endearing homeliness, his Jewish origins, his lifelong exclusive homosexuality—those factors combined into a background tailor-made to engender a seething mass of neuroses, exacerbated by social complications which came, inevitably, with fame. Yet by some miracle, Aaron remained about as free of neurosis as anyone I've ever known." In 1997 he remembered Copland as "one of the dearest, kindest, most thoughtful and fundamentally good human beings I've ever known."[43]

Copland's involvement with Erik Johns was more involved than his rather casual affairs with Ross and Moor. Johns was born Horace Eugene Johnston in Los Angeles. His father, a carpenter's foreman, worked on Hollywood studio sets; his mother was a schoolteacher. Although raised in a Christian home, he early on acquired a lifelong interest in Eastern religion and, in particular, the Vedanta Society, through which he encountered Christopher Isherwood and Aldous Huxley.[44]

Copland first met the young, handsome modern dancer (whom Diamond described as having a "wonderful, fresh beauty") at a 1946 New Year's Eve party at Alvin Ross's. Having studied modern dance in Los Angeles (during which time he adopted Erik Johns as his stage name), Johns was spending a brief six months in New York and was thrilled to meet the composer of Martha Graham's *Appalachian Spring*, which he had seen in California earlier in the year. The two subsequently began an affair. After Johns returned to California, where he continued his dance studies with Lester Horton and became a member of the Horton Dance Theater Company, he kept up a correspondence with Copland, saucily writing in March 1947, "I'm keeping my legs crossed that you will do the movie [*The Red Pony*] and come to Hollywood." Copland agreed to score the picture, at least partially in order to be near Johns, to whom he later dedicated the Suite from the score. Their affair duly resumed some months later when Copland returned to Hollywood to work on William Wyler's *The Heiress*.[45]

After completing the film in late 1948, Copland returned East with Johns, who moved into the house in Sneden's Landing and began classes with Graham. Johns assisted Copland in a variety of secretarial chores, while maintaining a professional association with a touring dance company directed by Graham dancer Miriam Pandor. In the spring and summer of 1949, they traveled to England, where they visited Benjamin Britten, Wilfrid Mellers, and William Walton, and to France, where they lunched with Boulanger, called on Alice B. Toklas in the apartment she had shared with Gertrude Stein, and heard Olivier Messiaen play the great organ in the Church of the Madeleine in the company of John Cage and Merce Cunningham. Alvin Ross joined them in Paris, and when Copland left for Tanglewood, Ross and Johns rented a pension on the Riviera.[46]

In 1950, Copland and Johns returned to Europe accompanied by Louisa Pierce, Johns's dance colleague from his Lester Horton days. After some time in Paris, the three left for Rome, where Copland had a residency at the American Academy. When he returned to the States in order to give the Norton lectures at Harvard (1951–52), Copland found a pied-à-terre for Johns and himself in Greenwich Village, during which time Johns continued his dancing and painting as well as his secretarial work. From the beginning of their relationship, Johns saw other men, but he remained Copland's lover as late as 1952, in the course of which they parted. No serious rift occurred; rather, career choices and demands precluded a continued intimate relationship.[47]

Johns reflected the kinds of shifting trends that characterized the postwar period: his interests in Eastern religion, Messiaen, Ravi Shankar, and modern jazz, as well as his boredom with all the old talk about "formalism vs. the proletariat," bespoke a new point of view, a greater concern for self-realization rather than political action as a means of bringing about social justice. Years later he recalled an argument in which he defended T. S. Eliot's *The Cocktail Party* to Harold Clurman: "The spiritual search was something that that generation [Copland's and Clurman's] had not dealt with in that way, and that was all coming in at that time, those ideas."[48]

Johns had some influence on Copland's work. An admirer of his instrumental music, he encouraged Copland to accept the commission for the Piano Quartet. Moreover, he wrote the libretto to Copland's opera *The Tender Land*, for which he adopted a second pseudonym, Horace Everett (Horace was his own first name, Everett his father's middle name). In later years, as he pursued other careers, Johns continued to write librettos, including ones for composers Jack Gottlieb and John Schlenck. Throughout, he remained one of Copland's most devoted friends; as someone who lived nearby, he was well positioned to assist him in his final years.[49]

In the spring of 1953, about a year after he and Johns parted, Copland met John ("Jack") Brodbin Kennedy (b. 1931), an aspiring composer in his junior year at Bard College, through his composition teacher, Paul Nordoff. Copland subsequently arranged a scholarship at Tanglewood for him that summer, during which time they began an affair. After Tanglewood, the two took a vacation in Mexico, reminiscent of similar trips Copland had taken with Kraft and Johns. In Oaxaca, Kennedy terrified him by brandishing a knife in bed, which brought back fearful memories of Kraft's violent episodes. "I was rather mischievous, playful, something of a bad boy," admits Kennedy.

The two remained lovers as Kennedy completed his work at Bard (1953–54), studied privately with Copland (1954–55), and attended Mannes and Princeton, each for a year (1955–57). (Copland once told Kennedy that he considered him, Bowles, and Citkowitz his only real students.) Kennedy typically saw Copland just on weekends, though they traveled extensively throughout Europe in 1955.

According to Kennedy, he and Copland enjoyed a "complete relationship." Each listened to the other's music, offering suggestions and encouragement. "I helped him stay young, and he helped me mature," Kennedy said. During much of their time together, Copland was at work on the *Piano Fantasy*. "He slugged those notes out," remembered Kennedy. "It was electrifying." Kennedy also assisted Copland on the orchestrations for *The Tender Land* and the television score *Nick Adams*.

Although Erik Johns thought him a "nice kid," Kennedy's behavior scandalized many of Copland's friends, who witnessed firsthand how he chortled over the bad reviews of *The Tender Land*. "I respected Aaron," explained Verna Fine, "I adored him, and I didn't like these young whipper-snappers treating him like that." After he and Kennedy spent the summer together in 1955, Copland himself sounded an exhausted note to Victor Kraft: "There was rarely a dull moment, and sometimes patience was severely tried." But when Diamond denounced Kennedy as an opportunist, Copland responded, "He's young, he's fresh, he's a lot of fun."[50]

In 1957, Kennedy fell in love with someone else and he and Copland sadly but amicably parted as lovers. For a while, they remained close friends, even maintaining sexual relations; Copland conducted Kennedy's *Lyric Ode* for orchestra on his 1960 tour of Asia. Later that same year, Kennedy argued with a cook in Copland's employ and threatened never to return to his home unless he fired the cook or made her apologize. After Copland refused, Kennedy wrote an angry letter, to which Copland responded:

> I thought that by now we had achieved a firm relationship which like the preacher says would be "better or worse till death do us part." Now you tell me I am selfish, ununderstanding, cowardly, indecisive, and guilty of humiliating conduct towards you in this matter. Naturally, I'm sorry you feel that way, but you could hardly expect me to agree with you. If I did, I could hardly bear to live with myself. One thing I am sure you are wrong about. Humiliating anyone is entirely foreign to my nature. I am quite ready to apologize, but what I definitely do not like is your air of putting me on trial for an unforgiveable crime that shocks your principles.

"I felt that I should have been backed up," explained Kennedy, who later recognized a similar pattern in Sylvia Plath's demands upon Ted Hughes. "I wanted to be loved, cared for, and respected unconditionally." Kennedy and Copland hardly spoke again after this incident, especially after a drunken phone call from Kennedy to Copland in 1966. Kennedy felt the failure of the relationship deeply: "You can lose for winning and you don't think of the consequences," he said.[51]

In 1958, a year after the breakup with Kennedy, Copland and Robert Cornell (b. 1931) began what Cornell calls "a prolonged semi-affair," one that lasted until 1965, when Cornell married. A graduate, like Copland, of Public School 9 and Boys' High, and a longtime admirer of Copland's music, Cornell was excited to meet the composer at an Alvin Ross party in 1953. They became better acquainted through Kennedy, Cornell's friend at Bard College. The relationship between Copland and Cornell, who during this period worked as Lincoln Kirstein's secretary and later for the New York City Ballet, had a sexual component, but was more companionable than anything else.[52]

Copland had other romantic attachments in his later years, sometimes with young men who had serious problems. One was the painter Richard Schiff (1932–1968), a 1953 graduate from Cooper Union whom Copland met around 1958 through David Walker. "He drank a lot, he was very unhappy," remembered Walker. "He went to Aaron a lot for guidance and help and perhaps money. He depended upon Aaron as a friend and Aaron worried about him." Boyish and blond, Schiff had a sarcastic wit that antagonized some of Copland's friends, though one, John Kenworthy-Browne, remembered him as "intelligent and very sympathetic." Few were surprised when at one point he landed in the Paine-Whitney Psychiatric Clinic. On 8 February 1968, only a few days after one of his ritual walks with Copland in the woods, Schiff was found dead in his East Village apartment from an overdose of pills and alcohol. The incident left Copland deeply shaken.[53]

Such involvements led Copland's friend Richard Hennessy to reflect:

Aaron was very patient. He would never hang up the telephone. I don't think he could help these people. He was a great listener. People knew that they weren't going to be judged harshly because they would never hear him say harsh things about anyone. So you'd be apt to open yourself up to someone like that. Also, one of the curses of fame is that you're viewed as a strong person with answers. The people who get through to you are the desperate ones with a secret project of tearing you down or getting something out of you.[54]

In at least one instance, however, Copland proved helpful. James Montgomery was a depressed young man when he and Copland had some brief attachment in the spring of 1963. "I sometimes think that my problems are so unbearable that I don't even have the desire to continue living," the tall, handsome pianist wrote Copland. Although Copland quickly ended the affair, he thought it might be helpful for Montgomery to move in with Robert Cornell. Cornell was somewhat discomfited, but the move helped Montgomery: "You should paint your name on your mailbox: Aaron Copland, M.D.," he wrote appreciatively.[55]

During the 1960s, Copland found welcome traveling companions in John Kenworthy-Browne and Donald Plotts. Born in 1931 in Hertfordshire and educated at Oxford, Kenworthy-Browne met Copland through a mutual friend in London in 1958, after a Festival Hall performance of Monteverdi's *Vespers*, which Copland attended with Richard Schiff. The two quickly became friends, and from 1958 to 1980, Copland often visited Kenworthy-Browne on his near-annual trips to England; the two usually met in London, and occasionally they traveled together—to Paris, to Dublin. They also saw each other during Kenworthy-Browne's trips to New York.

An art historian with a specialty in neoclassical sculpture, Kenworthy-Browne worked for the National Trust from 1959 to 1965; for Christie's from 1965 to 1969; and then as a freelance art historian and tour guide after 1970. He had little feeling for contemporary music, but he and Copland shared an interest in early music and English literature. He introduced Copland to Harold Nicolson, a meeting that not surprisingly fell flat, considering that Nicolson, as Kenworthy-Browne recalled, "apparently detested music" and "did not always care for Americans." At Cambridge they were more warmly received by E. M. Forster, whom Copland had met before and whose conversation, he warned Kenworthy-Browne, "would be utterly unmemorable, which was quite true."

Kenworthy-Browne described the relationship between himself and Copland as follows:

As one who had led a sheltered life, I was fascinated to know someone from a quite different world and who functioned efficiently; who had established himself and had always known clearly his own direction; someone so well organized and in control of his life; and I must say that it was a relief to be with him, the first person I had ever known who was not always worried about money. I admired his professionalism; and still there remained subjects which I could impart to him. I enjoyed his dry sense of humor and his tolerance. . . . He was certainly affectionate towards me and always kind and generous, but the affection rather lessened before 1970.[56]

Meanwhile, Copland met Plotts in 1961, again through Alvin Ross. An artist born in Brooklyn in 1937 and educated at Pratt, Plotts came up to Rock Hill on weekends and occasionally traveled with the composer,

251

whom he described as "wonderfully supportive." Like many friends, he found it painful to see Copland succumb to dementia and stopped visiting him after 1985.[57]

After 1967, Copland obtained some of the companionship and assistance that lovers had long provided from Phillip Ramey, who came up on weekends and accompanied him on trips just as so many former boyfriends had done. Still, he reportedly continued to have little affairs into his seventies.

Copland's involvements with young men mitigated against the kind of long-term, stable relationship that some friends believed he would have liked to have had. But even his closest friends could not say for sure whether Copland was content or not in his romantic life. He usually appeared remarkably cheerful and upbeat, but at the same time, some divined an inner loneliness. At the least, Copland's amorous friendships enriched and gladdened the lives of all involved.

Women Friends

Copland came of age in a period in which the modernist rebellion against Romantic sentimentality often took on, at the least, misogynistic overtones, even among women themselves. One detects a mild strain of this in, say, Copland's recollection of "all those nice ladies" who attended Friday afternoon Boston Symphony concerts in the 1920s.[58]

Moreover, Copland had relatively few close women friends and fewer still that could be considered confidantes. Ned Rorem remembered his joking that "he had trouble telling one woman from another." And Arthur Berger sensed that he was somewhat uncomfortable with women, associating this with his homosexuality or, rather, the mores of the day that generally inhibited candid openness between the sexes.[59]

However, such assertions—even if true—should not be interpreted as signifying any hostility toward women on Copland's part. He revered Boulanger, whose "old-fashioned womanliness" delighted him, and he abetted the careers of a number of women composers. He worked side by side with many women—patrons, musicians, dancers, businesswomen— with deeply mutual affection. Indeed, women often found his unique charm particularly appealing.[60]

He also enjoyed—more than the remarks of Rorem or Berger would suggest—some warm friendships with women, from Martha Dreiblatt in the 1910s to Vivian Perlis in the 1980s. We have mentioned, in the context of the Stieglitz circle, his relationships with Lola Ridge and especially Mary Lescaze, a lifelong friend. Another friend at least indirectly associated with Stieglitz was Claire Raphael Reis (1888–1978), the director of the League of Composers from 1923 to 1948.

Reis combined an indefatigable fortitude—somewhat indebted to her early years growing up in a Texas border town—with a sophisticated musical education acquired largely in New York and Berlin. Inspired by the progressive spirit of the times, including friendly contacts with Waldo Frank and Paul Rosenfeld, the young, well-to-do Reis dedicated herself to promoting classical music among New York's poorer denizens through educational programs and free concerts; such activities led to a more specific dedication to new American music. Whereas older reformers like Jane Addams and Lillian Wald "labored for the rights of children, new immigrants, and the poor," writes Carol Oja, "Reis took on another of society's underdogs, the composer." Following a brief involvement with the International Composers' Guild, she helped found the League of Composers in 1923. As the league's director, she tirelessly organized and promoted concerts of new music; issued commissions to scores of composers; facilitated contacts between composers and major arts organizations; and fought for the rights of composers—a volunteer service run from the top floor of her Manhattan home. In 1947 she also published an encyclopedic guide entitled *Composers in America*. Even after her retirement from the league in 1948, she continued to generously serve many composers and arts institutions.[61]

Copland was one of the first composers to benefit from her support. In 1924, she arranged under league auspices his first public performance in New York, which led in turn to helpful contacts with Paul Rosenfeld, Alma Wertheim, and others; and in 1925, she awarded him the league's first commission. He remained deeply grateful. When he received the Pulitzer Prize in 1945, he responded to Reis's congratulatory note by writing, "After all, you are an intimate part of my career, so you get the credit too!" He also appreciated all she had accomplished for American music quite generally, efforts close to his heart. He praised her loyalty at a memorial service on 21 April 1978 and shortly thereafter published an obituary for her in *Musical Quarterly*, the kinds of tributes he made only rarely in the course of his life.[62]

Copland felt more than gratitude for Reis, however. He retained throughout his life his first impression of her as "a rather small, lively, extremely pretty woman—very feminine, with a high degree of energy that visibly singled her out from any surrounding crowd." He enjoyed her formal sit-down dinners as well as her more informal parties, recalling some in the late 1920s "which ended with young people and even some middle-aged enthusiasts dancing till the early hours of the morning." For her part, Reis admired Copland's modesty and liked his company. "I always enjoy you on the podium or making a speech," she wrote him in 1966, "but I also like to gossip with you!"[63]

Copland's relationship with another of the league's major players, Minna Lederman, similarly evolved from a purely professional association to an enduring friendship. Lederman joined the league in its early days as a publicist and helped launch its journal, *Modern Music*. As the journal's sole editor for its entire tenure (1924–46)—though assisted behind the scenes by journalist Joel Lifflander—she oversaw the now legendary publication, editing it for most of its existence out of a spare room in her parents' apartment. "She developed the journal's distinctive literary style," writes R. Allen Lott, "and was responsible for bringing into its pages the writings of such rising young composers as Blitzstein, Bowles, Cage, Carter, Copland, Sessions, and Thomson, thereby nurturing an entire generation of composer-critics." Even so accomplished a stylist as Virgil Thomson publicly acknowledged an "enormous" debt to her. Lederman gave Copland his first writing assignment in 1925 and published as many articles by him as he was willing to write.[64]

Both Reis and Lederman regularly turned to Copland for guidance, especially after he joined the league's executive committee in 1932. "His influence and his judgment about works for performance, as well as his advice about the magazine, were invaluable," recalled Reis, "and his aesthetic opinions have always been sincere, never political." Copland even succeeded Reis as director of the league for two years upon her retirement. Lederman similarly relied on his wide knowledge of musicians and writers; he brought Sessions and many others to her attention. In a single communication from 1944, he suggested as possible contributors for various assignments a wide variety of names, including Salvador Moreno, José Ardévol, Juan Orrego-Salas, Carleton Sprague Smith, Everett Helm, Nino Rota, Francis Poulenc, Marc Blitzstein, Benjamin Britten, Irving Fine, Vincent Persichetti, and Samuel Barber.[65]

For all this, Copland's sway over Reis and Lederman was exaggerated in some of the more paranoid quarters of the musical community. Both women were strong and independent. They promoted and supported composers that he himself felt no great enthusiasm for. Reis consistently resisted his attempts to rename the league; Lederman showed no reluctance in publishing negative critiques of his music. Although Ned Rorem claimed that Reis, Lederman, and Alma Wertheim were "each touchingly, because hopelessly, in love with Aaron Copland," Lederman saw herself in relation to him quite differently, namely, as "a kind of sister, sometimes a younger, hectoring, teasing, pleading one, at others older, advising, giving counsel from the outside."[66]

Furthermore, Copland often found himself uncomfortably positioned between Reis and Lederman, whose conflicts, by the mid-1940s, had reached the breaking point as financial exigencies made the future of *Modern Music* more and more tenuous. Even long after both women left the league—Lederman in 1946 after the journal folded, Reis in 1948 after the death of her husband—they continued to air their grievances to Copland.[67]

Steering clear of their feud, Copland maintained as close a friendship with Lederman—or "Mink" as he called her—as with Reis. "He was such jolly good fun to be with," remembered Lederman. "No gloom-doom near him if he could help it, high spirits were his special ambience." The two socialized at one or the other's home in the country and spoke often by phone. "There was an easy sense between them that only comes with years and years of close contact," recalled Carol Oja, who, occasionally accompanying Lederman to Rock Hill, would observe the two "snuggle into a corner and chat away intensely." Copland also liked Lederman's gentlemanly painter-husband, Mel Daniel, whom she married in 1934.[68]

As a young man, Copland also enjoyed a friendship with the writer Eva Goldbeck, whom he met in 1928 at the MacDowell Colony. They established a warm rapport independent of the one they shared with composer Marc Blitzstein, eventually Goldbeck's husband. "I seem to have an inalienable and humorous affection for you," wrote Goldbeck to Copland, whom she regarded, along with Stravinsky, as the only modern composer with "sweep." "I thank the lord for your inalienable and humorous affection," replied Copland. They clearly liked each other enormously—Goldbeck apologized for constantly baring her soul to Copland—and had she not died of anorexia so young (in 1936 at the age of thirty-four) the relationship surely would have flourished in the years ahead.[69]

Copland had a similarly deep fondness for Rosemund Bernier. He first met her, as Peggy Rosenbaum, in 1936 in Mexico City, where she was on vacation from Sarah Lawrence with her fiancé, Lew Riley. Knowing Chávez through her father's connections with the Philadelphia Orchestra, Bernier attended a rehearsal of the Copland Piano Concerto (with the composer at the piano) and joined Copland and others for dinner after the performance. "I fell in love with him on the spot and never changed," Bernier recalled. In turn, she charmed and delighted him. She subsequently sought him out in the small town of Tlaxcala, where he played and sang parts of The Second Hurricane for her; because she especially liked "Gyp's Song," in honor of her 1937 marriage to Riley, he presented her with an arrangement of the song for harp and guitar, the newlyweds' respective instruments. Both very busy, she and Copland subsequently saw each other only occasionally—in New York, Mexico City, Havana, Bogotá, Paris. In the early 1940s, she spent a memorable weekend as his guest at a rented home in Tanglewood, later remarking, "I think he was quite pleased to have a feminine presence there. He seemed terribly proud to have me around, and he showed me off, introducing me to everyone." Copland often referred to her as "the only girl I could have married" and "my girl."[70]

Many of the traits that drew Copland to Reis, Lederman, Goldbeck, and Bernier also attracted him to Verna Fine: vitality, wit, intelligence, unpretentious sophistication, a passion for the arts, and a streak of non-comformity, including close friendships with homosexual men. Copland met her through her husband, Irving Fine, while both men were teaching at Harvard in early 1944. For nearly twenty years thereafter, Copland and the Fines spent most summers together at Tanglewood (sometimes under the same roof); Copland became "Uncle Aaron" to the Fines' three daughters, making the Fines something of a surrogate family for him. Verna was absolutely devoted to Copland, preparing meals, typing letters, even, on one occasion, making her mother's apartment in Boston available to him. "Oh, you don't know how lucky you are," she once told his sister Laurine. "How I would love Aaron for my brother!" After Irving's death in 1962, she remained closely in touch with Copland, especially after she divorced her second husband and settled in New York. In these later years, the two often attended parties and formal receptions together. Because they made such a good team, she would lightheartedly propose that they marry, mainly for tax purposes. Copland graciously declined.[71]

15

Copland and the
American Theater

Clurman and the Group Theatre

The Group Theatre (1931–41) provided the kind of background to Copland's music of the 1930s that the Stieglitz gallery had in the 1920s. Indeed, the Group could be seen as an outgrowth of Stieglitz's work and ideals. Its principal founder, Harold Clurman, regularly visited Stieglitz's gallery in the 1920s, and many of the Group's most ardent supporters—Copland, Waldo Frank, Paul Strand, Ralph Steiner, and William Lescaze—enjoyed some association with Stieglitz. At the same time, the Group represented the generation of Clurman and Copland come into its own, including the discovery and launching of an important new voice: playwright Clifford Odets.

In 1928 Clurman began holding weekly Friday-night sessions with fellow actors and directors who shared his dissatisfaction with the state of the American theater; some of his rantings brought a concerned Copland literally to tears. In 1931 Clurman, Lee Strasberg, and Cheryl Crawford cofounded the Group Theatre with the objective of presenting socially relevant American plays at popular prices. Strasberg trained and directed the actors; Crawford supervised the day-to-day administration; and Clurman served as spokeman, literary adviser, and, eventually, director. "There we were," quipped Crawford, "two Old Testament prophets and a Wasp shiksa."[1]

The Group touched a responsive chord in the theatrical community, catching the interest of, among others, Stella Adler (1902–1994), the daughter of Clurman's boyhood idol, the Yiddish actor Jacob Adler. Lovers since 1930, Clurman and Stella Adler married in 1943 and divorced in 1960. Near the start of their affair, Clurman drifted apart somewhat from Copland, who told Israel Citkowitz that his old friend was having "moments of real megalomania." Part of the problem may have involved Adler, widely resented by Clurman's friends—"This woman did not care what she did to this man," Odets would write—though Copland got along with her better than most.[2]

The Group eventually attracted a number of other distinguished actors—including Stella's brother Luther, Morris Carnovsky, Frances Farmer, John Garfield, Elia Kazan, Robert Lewis, Karl Malden, Sanford Meisner, Clifford Odets (who began his career as an actor), and Franchot Tone—as well as playwrights Maxwell Anderson, Sidney Kingsley, John Howard Lawson, and William Saroyan. Averaging at any one time about thirty members, the company spent summers in rural Connecticut or upstate New York, rehearsing the plays that they would bring to Broadway in the fall.

Strasberg's now legendary training and direction for the Group drew upon the work of Stanislavsky, whose methods he had studied under the Russian director's American disciples, Richard Boleslavsky and Maria Ouspenskaya. This included realistic and naturalistic ensemble work and rehearsals that involved improvisation and the use of "affective memory" (popularly known as the "Method"), a technique consisting, in Kazan's words, "of recalling the circumstances, physical and personal, surrounding an intensely emotional experience in the actor's past." To this Stanislavskyan framework, Strasberg added the theatricality of another Russian director, Eugene Vakhtangov, forging a distinctive style in the process.[3]

From the start, Copland involved himself with Group activities; his studio at Steinway Hall became one of their early meeting places. According to Clurman, the very creation of the Group had been inspired by Copland's efforts on behalf of American music. Copland counseled the Group on musical matters, located benefactors, composed incidental music, and, within his very limited means, offered donations. Like only a few other artists outside of theater, he became a Group associate. He regularly attended rehearsals and performances—he spent much of the summer of 1933 with the company—and became pals with Kazan, Lewis, Meisner, and especially Odets. "Aaron was around the Group Theatre a lot," recalled Clurman, "since he was my friend, and also the conception of the Group interested him."[4]

Copland was also curious about what Group members thought of his music, and Clurman obliged by reporting, for instance, that Stella Adler sensed that *Music for Radio* "had a whole philosophy, something about acceptance of the revolution and the difficulties attendant upon it," and that Frances Farmer, after listening to a recording of *Music for the Theatre*, "was struck by a melancholy or sad note in all of it." Kazan recalled Copland's "beautiful score" to *Quiet City* in his memoirs and acknowledged its composer as one of those "geniuses" whose "joyous intensity in work" he found inspirational.[5]

When the Group began operations in 1931, the founders had no agenda other than that of presenting topical theater for the average American. But by the summer of 1932, they had become considerably more political; discussions about "the masses" and "revolution" began to supplant previous talk about "the American man" and "life value." In May of that year, Clurman wrote Copland about his readings of Marx, Engels, Lenin, and Trotsky, though he warned that "a proletarian revolution (in the communist sense) in America to-day—even if it were possible—would be a most terrible catastrophe—more terrible surely than our sufficiently rotten capitalism." Under the pseudonym Harold Edgar, he published theater reviews in the *Daily Worker*; and in 1934 and 1935 he traveled to the Soviet Union. "The revolution is here," he enthused to Copland in 1934, "or, at least, we are on the verge of it."[6]

By the mid-1930s, some of the Group's plays explicitly concerned such issues as labor unrest, low wages, unemployment, fascism, and socialized medicine. Although none of the Group's three founders ever joined the Communist Party, Kazan belonged from late 1933 to early 1935, as did Odets for most of 1935. A seven-man communist cell even formed within the Group, taking orders directly from the American Communist Party. Although Kazan, Odets, and others soon lost patience with this sort of outside interference, the Group—party and nonparty members alike—remained strongly Marxist in orientation. This included broad support for communist candidates, an interest in Marxist writings, and a belief in the imminence of revolution and a new world order.[7]

The appeal of communism drew upon, in Odets's words, the "enormous prestige" of the Soviet Union and the Moscow Art Theater, one so great, in fact, that some Group members called their communal residence on West Fifty-seventh Street "Groupstroi" ("Group [Communist] System"). Clurman's experiences in the Soviet Union only enhanced the Group's Russophilia. "On my return from the Soviet Union [in 1935], where I had been so impressed by the sanity of the people I met, I was almost equally depressed in New York by a feeling that I was living in a mad world. Wherever I went it seemed to me I observed an inner chaos." In contrast, he considered the Soviet Union, as he wrote Copland, "a dream come true, an ideal created, a plan worked out and being."[8]

The Group's loyalty to the Soviet Union by and large survived the Moscow Trials (1938) and the Nazi-Soviet Pact (1939). Even after hostilities broke out, Group members more or less adhered to the party line that America should neither intervene in a conflict fought by Europe's "imperialist" powers nor involve itself in Asia on behalf of tin, rubber, or other capitalist interests. But as 1940 wore on, they increasingly agonized about the matter, Clurman finally supporting intervention after the fall of Paris, Odets waffling until the German invasion of Russia.[9]

For all their attachment to the Soviet Union, Group members thought their ideals profoundly American—more so than that of flag-waving chauvinists. Exclaimed Odets in 1935, "We are lovers of the honest words of great Americans—Jefferson, Walt Whitman, and Abraham Lincoln! We are Revolutionists!" Clurman argued that the turn leftward among intellectuals in the 1930s had more of a nationalist underpinning than was even appreciated at the time, when the American Communist Party adopted the slogan "Communism Is Twentieth-Century Americanism." The term "left movement," argued Clurman, was itself a "misnomer," as this phenomenon descended not so much from "the sources that produced the muckraking work of the Upton Sinclair and Lincoln Steffens era" as from "the humanistic traditions of the Emerson, Thoreau, Walt Whitman epoch." As for the attraction to Lenin, Trotsky, and Stalin, he cited a "definitive" explanation by Van Wyck Brooks, which read in part:

It is of no importance what the Russian leaders were: they became John Browns and Garrisons for our young people who had no Browns and Garrisons to contemplate at home. They seemed to be reliving the lives of our patriot fathers; they seemed to be translating into action the words of our Declaration of Independence. They were founding a great new civilization, just as our own forebears did, that answered the needs of the world they lived in. . . . We were producing advertising geniuses and President Harding. We Americans are the most romantic of peoples. More than any others, we need heroes; and we cannot make heroes of people who only make money. Not for long, not for a dozen years; and Russia was the world's romance for fifteen years because the search for social justice is the romance of our time.

"What they believed in, long ago," Kazan would write, "was not a fact, it was not substantial; it was a dream and no way less worthy because of that."[10]

The Group made theatrical history, enjoying a number of critical successes and even a few financial ones, most notably Clifford Odets's *Golden Boy* (1937). But behind the scenes, the atmosphere was tense, due only in part to incessant money problems. Strasberg's emphasis on affective memory made some of the actors anxious, as it led, they argued, to an overidentification with their characters. In 1934 Stella Adler studied privately with Stanislavsky in Paris and, to the relief of many in the company, reported back that Strasberg had overemphasized the importance of affective memory. The company subsequently dissolved into a Strasberg camp and an Adler camp, thus laying the foundation for the country's two principal schools of acting. On top of this, the company's Actor's Committee, moved by the radical spirit of the times, criticized all three directors as tyrannical, prompting the resignations of Strasberg and Crawford.[11]

With the collapse of the Group seeming imminent, Clurman, Kazan, Garfield, and other Group members joined Odets in Hollywood in early 1937 for financial and emotional relief. Dissatisfied in Hollywood, the Group reassembled in New York in the summer of 1937 and survived a few more seasons, until a rift between Odets and Clurman weakened the company beyond repair. The Group finally disbanded in 1941.

After the war, Clurman consolidated his reputation as one of New York's most accomplished directors and theater critics. His most acclaimed postwar directorial work was Carson McCullers's *The Member of the Wedding* (1949), which broke new ground in its treatment of race relations in America. (He was thrilled to hear from Copland that Stravinsky thought *The Member of the Wedding* comparable to the best of Russian theater.) His biggest hit was William Inge's *Bus Stop* (1954). No new American playwright, however (with the possible exception of Inge), excited him as had Hellman and Odets in the thirties, Wilder and Saroyan in the early forties, and Miller and Williams in the late forties; rather, he championed Jean Anouilh and Jean Giraudoux, whose plays he helped introduce to America. And on a European trip in 1956, he wrote Copland that the theater in East Berlin was "the best in many ways since what I saw in Moscow in 1935."[12]

In his voluminous critical writings, Clurman wrote with particular insight about Copland's music, often making two principal points. First, he argued that "the two Coplands—the popular and the reputedly esoteric—are the same man" and that the success of the popular scores should not impair the coherence and grandeur of his total achievement. Second, Copland's work, he opined, contained both an affirmative acceptance of and a resigned withdrawal from the world; in his review of Arthur Berger's book, for instance, he wrote that Copland represented the "well-tempered composer," defined as an artist "whose creation synthesizes the tensions between the loneliness, isolation, and desire for withdrawal a sensitive person must feel in our stony and increasingly joyless society with the equally strong impulse to affirm and assert with humor and an irrepressible vivacity the age-old aspirations of humankind."[13]

Clurman pursued this dialectic in his review of the Third Symphony. Over the years, Copland's "impulse to affirm" the world changed as the world itself changed: from the "embrace of the high-stepping twenties" (Music for the Theatre), to "a gay acquiescence and even affirmation of the dervish ferocity of the world's mechanics" (the Piano Concerto), to a "view of the world ... somewhat more severe, even austere" (the Ode), to "hope in the future" (the Variations), to "dreams of peace and quiet ... in terms of the halcyon days of the past, the relatively untroubled times of a pre-industrial America" (Appalachian Spring), to a readiness "to face the future with simple manfulness" (the Third Symphony). At the same time, one heard throughout the voice of a somewhat detached and lonely individual. These contrasts were found not in alternation but at once, giving, for example, Copland's use of jazz, for all its forthrightness, "qualities of affectionate irony, sharpness, and acidity that bespoke a slight apartness, a margin of reserve." "His own self," concluded Clurman, "is a fortress that remains pure and strong without turning away from or escaping above the fate of the outer world."[14]

Clurman and Copland remained the closest of friends until the former's death in 1980. Jack Garfein observed that while most people thought of Clurman as just a blustery "errand boy," Copland defended and protected him, discerning in him a sensitivity that often eluded others. In 1979 Copland served as the chairman of a "backstage bash" on the occasion of the naming of the Harold Clurman Theater in New York. During these later years, Clurman would visit Copland at Rock Hill more often than most friends. On one occasion, shortly before Clurman's death, David Walker was moved at the sight of these two old friends, sitting outside after dinner, gazing at the mountains in absolute silence; Copland was probably the only person who could have had such a calming effect on Clurman.[15]

Although guessing that Clurman died with a "secret ache" in his heart "from not having created the permanent theatre he'd spoken of so often and so eloquently," Elia Kazan thought his legacy vibrant and positive:

> Harold made me feel that artists are above all other humans, not only in our society but in all of history. I'm not impressed with any other elite, not of money, power, or fame, I got that from Harold. . . . He had the culture to know that if you attempt difficult tasks you're bound to fail as often as not, and that it was no disgrace to fail. Defeat was temporary, never a defeat of the essence.

Copland would have agreed. "Whatever else is true," he told Odets in 1951, "he's a *stimulus.*"[16]

Clifford Odets and Other Playwrights and Poets

Like Copland and Clurman, Clifford Odets (1905–1963) was the son of Eastern European Jewish immigrants. Born in Philadelphia, he grew up in the Bronx; after dropping out of high school, he took a series of odd jobs as actor and writer, joining the Group in 1933. He quickly established himself as an in-house playwright for the company, which within six years premiered seven of his plays, including *Waiting for Lefty* (produced in 1935), *Awake and Sing!* (1935), *Golden Boy* (1937), and *Rocket to the Moon* (1938). He also wrote for the Group the never-produced *The Silent Partner* (1936), for which Copland was to compose the incidental music.[17]

These plays, by and large, depict people—mostly New Yorkers—trapped by financial and social circumstances and looking for ways out. "The indictment of life in America was always his subject," notes William Gibson. "His central theme," says Clurman, "was the difficulty of attaining maturity in a world where money as a token of success and status plays so dominant a role." For all the overriding unhappiness of their characters, these plays feature an exuberant, streetwise humor and moments of wistful hopefulness. Odets himself acknowledged the influence, above all, of Chekhov and O'Casey.[18]

By the late 1930s, Odets had established himself as one of the foremost playwrights of his time. Critics and audiences especially liked his explosive language—a vulgar New Yorkese raised to a poetic level. As an example, Clurman cited the line "I'm so nervous, look, I weighed myself twice in the subway," commenting, "It is the speech of New York; half-educated Jews, Italians, Irish, transformed into something new-minted, individual, and unique. Above all it makes for crackling theater dialogue—ask the actors!"[19]

Copland and Odets met in 1933 through the Group and quickly became friends. On his first trip to Hollywood in early 1936, Odets gave up his New York apartment to Copland, who had been kicked out of his own apartment for playing "too much modern music." Through Copland, Odets befriended Victor Kraft, whose ambivalent sexuality he related to; Odets, who lived a heterosexual life, including two years of marriage (1937–39) to the actress Luise Rainer, expressed his conflicted feelings about his homosexual leanings, it might be argued, through the unsavory homosexual characters in some of his plays.[20]

In 1941, following two flops on Broadway, Odets relocated to Hollywood, where he worked for the rest of his life as a director and screenwriter. One project, *The Flowering Peach* (1954), an allegory based on the biblical story of Noah, originated as a dramatic cantata for Copland. Although some of these endeavors were highly remunerative, his later work brought him little of the kind of self-satisfaction or critical esteem he'd achieved in the 1930s. Comparing the fates of Odets and Clurman, Kazan observed that Odets "couldn't resist the money, the flattery, the apparent safety and security in the movie community. And he lost himself. Harold Clurman, one of the men I've most admired, was lucky: The people who ran the big studios did not want him, and he had to come east again; that saved him, for he seemed lost in southern California."[21]

Odets's later difficulties were compounded by a forced appearance before the House Un-American Activities Committee in the spring of 1952, in which he and Kazan agreed to name names. "The sad fact is," writes Kazan, "that what was possible for me hurt Clifford mortally. He was never the same after he testified. He gave away his identity when he did that; he was no longer the hero-rebel, the fearless prophet of a new world. It choked off the voice he'd had." Critics generally agree that his best plays are the Jewish-family dramas written for the Group and that his conflicts about being typecast as a Jewish-American playwright and his subsequent desire to purge his language of "Yiddishkeit" may have played a part in his undoing as an artist.[22]

During his Hollywood years, he and Copland maintained a warm and lively correspondence, Odets typically signing his letters "love, Clifford." "Adios to you, dear Aaron," he signed off in 1951. "You always have a friend in me who will do anything for you that is in his power or help." "You're a writer of warm and affectionate notes," answered Copland, "and I love you for it!" In one letter, Odets detected simply from Copland's handwriting "rather strong signs of strain, nervousness and considerable depression"; in another, evidence that he was "tired, irritable, depressed and nervous to a high degree." Odets's protective solicitude—he urged that Copland rest, that he see a doctor ("after all we have only one Aaron Copland")—reminds one less of Copland's friends than of his sister Laurine.[23]

Odets was passionate about music. He loved Mozart, Schubert, and especially Beethoven, in whom he saw, in earlier years at least, a prefiguration of communism. He became good friends not only with Copland but with Hanns Eisler, with whom he collaborated on a number of projects. He amassed a large record collection of old and new works; on one evening in 1940, he played recordings of Prokofiev, Milhaud, Ibert, and Shostakovich for some friends. In the 1950s, he presented Copland with all kinds of recordings, including (in 1956) works by Schoenberg and Stravinsky, along with Machaut's *La Messe de Nostre Dame,* which they both liked.[24]

Odets especially admired Copland's music, and in 1939, flush from the success of *Golden Boy,* he agreed to commission the Piano Sonata (1941), which was dedicated to him, for $500. After hearing a 1943 performance of the work, he wrote Copland, "It has real nobility and so it impressed many varied persons." And he felt "proud" of Copland upon attending a performance of *Lincoln Portrait* (1942). "You make me believe in art in America," he wrote to his friend in 1945. "You are a living proof of the becoming of art in our country; you encourage me by the very fact of your being." In the early 1950s, he attempted to interest Copland in writing another piano sonata or a string quartet in exchange for a Klee that he owned.[25]

Odets may have prized the Third Symphony more than any other work by Copland. After acquiring the Antal Dorati recording in 1953, he wrote a long letter about the piece to Copland, who thought it "one of the nicest I've ever received about my music." This letter read in part:

> Your Third Symphony is one of the most moving experiences I have had in years. Having played the recording about seven times, there was no time when I was not moved, excited and stirred generally beyond and above myself. Peace, a little peace, it was wonderful! . . .
>
> As for the music itself, dear Aaron, it is as lofty a nature as we in America have yet expressed. Of this there is not the slightest doubt—the loftiest our country has yet expressed in music. . . .
>
> You are a lesson and an inspiration for me in a time when I don't know if I have the strength to move upward but am trying. You can understand, of course, that I am thanking you.

For his part, Copland regularly attended rehearsals and performances of Odets's plays, admiring his willingness to tackle American themes and characters. He particularly liked *Awake and Sing!* The two periodically considered various collaborations, including the ill-fated *Silent Partner*, an adaptation of *Rocket to the Moon* as an opera, and the Noah idea that eventually became *The Flowering Peach*. Throughout the fifties, Odets regularly invited Copland to compose the music for this play or that film, while in 1956 Copland asked for possible suggestions for a one-act libretto. Answered Odets,

> Yes indeed!! Many ideas, but if you gave me some idea of what theme, what subject, what personages, what background, what milieu would stir and stimulate you—then I'd think more sharply. The range is wide: from an incident in Mozart's life up to anything in the U.S.A., 19th or 20th century. Civil War? Walt Whitman waiting to die? The dreams of a boy, the altercations of a cab driver—a father and son locked in a death grip, the love between men and women, death, birth—WHAT?

In response, Copland proposed a concert work for orchestra and a few voices, relating a story outline suggested to him by a young composer "in which a soprano and baritone converse on a bench in a hospital waiting room. The baritone is waiting for news of the birth of his baby and the soprano awaiting the news of the death of her husband." But nothing came of this either, to the deep disappointment of friends like David Diamond: "It's still my feeling that had Clifford come through with that opera libretto that they talked about doing—what an opera with Aaron's dramatic sense it could have been!" Such mutual friends thought Copland and Odets fundamentally complementary. "As Odets is my playwright," stated Clurman, "Copland is my composer."[26]

Through the Group, his film work, and related contacts, Copland met other esteemed American playwrights with whom he considered collaborating on a work of musical theater, including Thornton Wilder (1897–1975), William Inge (1913–1973), Arthur Miller (b. 1915), and Edward Albee (b. 1928).

Copland met Wilder in 1939 soon after signing a contract to write the music for the film version of *Our Town* (1940); they liked each other immediately. They also held each other's work in high regard, Wilder's appreciation of Copland extending to so late a work as *Inscape*: "You're at the top of your power," he wrote Copland. "The orchestration is of the richest and all so clearly signed by you. There are two Copland 'sounds'—the bleak one (and that's fine, too) and the plangent one."[27]

In the immediate postwar period, Copland considered adapting a number of Wilder works for the stage: the novella *The Bridge of San Luis Rey* (1927), the comic novel *Heaven's My Destination* (1935; a kind of *Candide* set in the American Midwest), and *Our Town* (1938). In 1948 he also proposed a collaboration based on *The Legends of the Chasidim*. The prospect of an operatic adaptation of *Our Town* especially intrigued him, particularly in 1950 after the general manager of the Metropolitan Opera, Rudolf Bing, expressed interest in the idea. But Wilder, although receptive to the notion of working with Copland, found this particular proposition unattractive: "I'm convinced I write a-musical plays; that my texts 'swear at' music; that they're after totally different effects; that they delight in the homeliest aspects of our daily life; that in them ever the life of the emotions is expressed 'contra musicam.' " Bing disagreed, suggesting that someone else adapt the play, but Copland "could not imagine an *Our Town* without Thornton Wilder." He apparently had his own doubts about the idea, remarking to Paul Moor, "But how can you write an entire opera in *andante*?"[28]

In 1955 William Inge, another friend, proposed a "musical" based on "a most appealing and melodramatic story about a girl from Boston who became an adored entertainer in the great saloon in Dodge [City, Kansas] when it was known as the 'wicked'st little city in the world,' back in the frontier days." Inge's scenario, which involved such legendary figures as Bat Masterson, Wyatt Earp, and Eddie Foy, drew somewhat on his hit *Bus Stop* (1955), while anticipating Douglas Moore's opera *The Ballad of Baby Doe* (1956). "All in all, it's something I can't resist," Inge wrote to Copland. "But I'd like to see it done with some authenticity." Copland turned the proposal down, explaining that he was not a "musical comedy composer." However, for a while he harbored some interest in adapting *Bus Stop* as an opera.[29]

At Clurman's urging, Copland also considered an opera based on Arthur Miller's *The Crucible* (1953), an allegorical treatment of the anti-communist hysteria associated with the McCarthy era. Although a number of composers immediately recognized its potential for operatic treatment, Miller offered it first to Copland: "I want you to do the opera," he wrote the composer, "and I will do anything I can to make that possible." But Miller did not have the time to adapt the play himself, and, as with *Our Town*, that may have been a major deterrent. After Copland decided against the idea, Miller gave his permission to Robert Ward to compose an opera (1961) based on the work.[30]

Copland met the young Edward Albee in the late 1950s through William Flanagan, the playwright's lover since 1949. Impressed with the *Zoo Story* (1958), Copland supported Albee, as he had so many young artists. For his part, Albee felt a kinship with Copland's music, writing to the composer in 1959, "Several of the Dickinson songs, and whole areas of *The Tender Land* affect me profoundly, convince me that you are the first man in I-don't-know how long—since Mahler, really, I guess—who can do full justice to feelings about loss and time: Areas that I feel a need to say something about, too."[31]

Albee proposed collaborating on a monologue about a dying woman looking back on her life: "What emerges is a cry for unattainable compassion." (Decades later he developed a similar theme in his Pulitzer Prize–winning drama *Three Tall Women*.) Copland countered with a suggestion similar to the one made to Odets: a small opera or dramatic cantata about two people in a hospital waiting room. He hoped to use a Paul Fromm commission to complete such a work by the fall of 1960, but once again the proposal fell through.[32]

The poets Archibald MacLeish (1892–1982), Elizabeth Bishop (1911–1979), and Robert Lowell (1917–1977) also proposed collaborations. MacLeish, who knew Copland from Paris (where his wife, Ada, had premiered "As It Fell upon a Day"), periodically suggested one idea or another. Bishop, declaring herself "an admirer of your music for a very long time," sent Copland her latest book of poems in 1956 and offered to write other poems or even a libretto for him. Robert Lowell similarly sent him his verse-play adaptation of Melville's *Benito Cereno* (1964), a study in the ambiguities of the American character; the third part of the poet's *Old Glory*, the play was originally intended as an opera libretto. It is intriguing to imagine what any of these collaborations might have yielded, but none materialized. As it turned out, for his two operas—*The Second Hurricane* and *The Tender Land*—Copland worked with writer-dancers.[33]

16

An Engaged Citizen

Copland took a great interest in civic and world events. He began each day poring over newspapers and public-affairs journals. Such preoccupations sometimes became all-consuming. In August 1938, as the world careened toward war, he thought it "nice" that Bernstein could "finish pieces in these troublous times," writing, "I haven't been able to do much more than read newspapers." Similarly, after the Kennedy assassination, he found himself "obsessed by public events," gobbling up "endless newspapers." To the very end of his life, he read newspapers and watched TV news with considerable intensity, sometimes reacting aloud to one thing or other.[1]

At the end of his Norton lectures, Copland hinted at the connection between such concerns and his music: "The artist should feel himself affirmed and buoyed up by his community. In other words, art and the life of art must mean something, in the deepest sense, to the everyday citizen. When that happens, America will have achieved a maturity to which every sincere artist will have contributed." He was even more explicit about such matters in a hearing before a Senate subcommittee (1953):

COPLAND: Musicians make music out of feelings aroused out of public events.

SENATOR KARL E. MUNDT: I can't follow this line of argument. I don't see how that line of reasoning makes sense with a hatchet man like [Communist Party member Harry] Bridges.

COPLAND: A musician, when he writes his notes, makes his music out of emotions and you can't create music unless you are moved by events. If I sponsored a Committee in relation to Bridges, I may have been misled, not through Communist leanings. If I had them, there was something about his situation that moved me.[2]

Copland inherited his interest in public life in part from his father, who briefly served as president of their local synagogue and who was active in the local Democratic Party. However, like many of his generation, Aaron must have looked askance at the corrupt Tammany politics that characterized the New York Democratic Party of his father's time, politics that often appealed to Irish, Italian, and Jewish immigrants (like his parents) but that widely alienated their American-born children. Indeed, he satirically quoted "The Sidewalks of New York," a song associated with Tammany, in both *Music for the Theatre* and the "Jingo" movement of *Statements*.[3]

Copland never joined any political party. He described himself as "sympathetic toward the American-Liberal principles," saying, "If one likes people, is sympathetic to them and concerned about their welfare in general, one's personal leaning is in the direction of the democratic or liberal viewpoint." Although he avoided getting much more specific than this, one can postulate some of his guiding political ideals, including freedom of speech and thought, civil rights for all men and women, and social and economic justice for the common man. This last in particular overlapped with more purely professional concerns; the fight he waged on behalf of the American composer reflected, in its own way, the larger economic struggles of the working poor.[4]

One friend further recalled that he "believed in socialism in the best possible sense." Such sympathies presumably dated back at least as far as 1919 and his friendship with Arne Vainio, who introduced him to the socialist newspaper the *Call*, and the political thinking of Eugene V. Debs, the head of the American Socialist Party. Around this same time, Copland defended the Russian Revolution to his father, who protested, "America has the only real idea when it comes to government."[5]

Copland also developed, early on, a deep admiration for the work of Frank Norris (1870–1902), Theodore Dreiser (1871–1945), and Upton Sinclair (1878–1968), all socialists whose novels passionately excoriated capitalism's physical and emotional toll on the average man. Copland recommended Sinclair's *The Brass Check* (1919) to his father in 1921 and Dreiser's *The Financier* (1912) to Clurman in 1934. As late as the 1950s, he considered composing operas based on Norris's *McTeague* (1899) and Dreiser's *An American Tragedy* (1925).[6]

Copland's socialist inclinations found support and guidance through his lifelong subscriptions to the *New Republic* and the *Nation*, as well as through those friendships in the Stieglitz circle made upon his return from Paris in 1924. The ideals that helped shape the Stieglitz circle—the emphasis on communal interaction; the interest in the ordinary man's experience in America, including its uglier side; and the call for an elite to help awaken and fulfill America's democratic potential—certainly accorded with socialist and communist tendencies. Many of Stieglitz's associates, including Waldo Frank, Paul Strand, and Edmund Wilson, voted communist in the 1930s.

Copland's music from the 1920s already suggested some such connections; Clurman discerned an affinity between *Music for the Theatre* (1925), for instance, and the work of communist playwright John Howard Lawson. The very use of jazz in concert music—indeed, practically any modernist music—often implied, to the general public, some identity with communism. In its portrayal of the "harshness" of shtetl life, *Vitebsk* (1929) further denoted a sympathy for the Russian Revolution.[7]

With the onset of the Depression and the rise of Nazism, however, the climate grew more militant, and Copland and most of his friends became bona fide Communists or so-called fellow travelers (a distinction sometimes so vague as to be moot), especially in the years 1932–38. The same happened with people Copland admired from afar, like Theodore Dreiser, Romain Rolland, and André Gide. Even the more conservative of Copland's friends and acquaintances during these years were largely left-of-center liberals.

According to his own testimony and those of his friends, Copland never joined the Communist Party. In fact, few of Copland's friends became party members, partly because membership entailed the risk of harassment or worse, partly because the ukases of the American Communist Party on artistic matters—represented, say, by the *New Masses* (established 1927) and its editor, Mike Gold, or by the popular John Reed Clubs (founded 1929)—often offended Copland and his colleagues. Primarily on account of the latter reason, most of those friends who joined the party—like Odets, Bowles, and Elia Kazan—lasted only a year or two as members. Some others, like Israel Citkowitz and Arthur Berger, drifted toward Trotskyite splinter groups that eventually coalesced around the newly formed *Partisan Review* (1937), specifically in response to the party's Stalinist aesthetics, which they decried as philistine.[8]

Still, whatever Copland and his friends thought of the party, they subscribed to many aspects of communist ideology; Kazan, for instance, recalls that even after quitting the party in some disgust in 1935, he continued to back the party line for a number of years. They identified with the "masses" and the "proletariat" and spoke confidently of the coming "revolution" and collapse of "bourgeois capitalism." They read Lenin and Marx, wrote for the *Daily Worker* and the *New Masses*, marched in May Day parades, traveled to the Soviet Union, voted for communist candidates, and defended the Stalinist line in foreign policy matters, at least until 1938—though sometimes right through the 1940s.[9]

This turn toward radical politics among Copland's friends can be traced most emphatically to 1932—a year in which one-third of the American work force found itself unemployed. In the course of that pivotal year, Waldo Frank visited the Soviet Union and published a sympathetic account of the revolution, *Dawn of Russia*. With the assistance of Edmund Wilson and Lewis Mumford, he also helped draft a manifesto recognizing the "fundamental identity of our interests with the workers and farmers of the nation" and advocating "a new order . . . in which economic rivalry and private profit are barred." In the fall Frank and Wilson both endorsed the Communist Party's presidential candidate, William Z. Foster; while acknowledging the party's shortcomings, Wilson even allowed the possibility of a nonviolent communist revolution by parliamentary means "if the politically vanquished bourgeoisie allowed themselves to be expropriated quietly." In the meanwhile, Clurman wrote about his Marxist readings to Copland, who attended to what all these friends had to say about such matters.[10]

Musicians felt the changing tide as well. The Young Composers' Group (founded 1932), over which Copland presided, leaned heavily in the direction of Marx. In that same year, Henry Cowell and Charles Seeger helped establish the Composers' Collective, an affiliate of the Pierre Degeyter

Club (named for the composer of the "Internationale"), itself an arm of the Workers' Music League (founded 1931), the principal musical organization associated with the American Communist Party. Whereas the league and the Degeyter Club oversaw wide-ranging activities, the collective comprised a small number of composers dedicated to the creation of proletarian music, in particular, the mass song. At its height in 1934–35, it had somewhere between sixteen and thirty-four members, including Cowell, Seeger, Marc Blitzstein, Henry Leland Clarke, Alex North, Wallingford Riegger, Earl Robinson, and Elie Siegmeister, some of whom adopted pseudonyms.[11]

The collective—later described by Seeger as "a bunch of crazy idealists"—puzzled over the question of finding a musical style appropriate to Marxist revolution. Rejecting folk music as reactionary and jazz as bourgeois, they welcomed Shostakovich as one possible model but embraced even more strongly Hanns Eisler, who regularly attended their meetings when in New York and who wrote, in Blitzstein's words, "stubborn, hard" music of "oppression and courageous resistance." They failed, however, to reach a consensus, as revealed by the wide stylistic range of their contributions to two songbooks published by the Workers' Music League: *Workers' Song Book No. 1* (1934) and *No. 2* (1935).[12]

One of the earliest indications of Copland's own involvement in radical politics is a 13 September 1933 letter from Mary Lescaze that referred to his "communism orgy" and his "emerging from it with an idea which applies to it but which lies in your own field, your Workers' Chorus." Perhaps he had attended a John Reed Club meeting.[13]

At any event, by early 1934, his association with communist-related activities had taken wing. On March 16 he participated in an all-Copland concert at the Degeyter Club that featured a wide range of chamber music and John Kirkpatrick's two-piano arrangement of the Piano Concerto (with Kirkpatrick taking the second piano part). Reviewing the concert for the *Daily Worker*, Charles Seeger reported that in a prerecital talk, Copland had proclaimed the need for the contemporary composer to identify "with the great masses of the proletariat," though he'd warned his audience "against viewing his compositions from a revolutionary angle, for, as he said with charming naivete, he had not, at the time of their composition, any ideas of that sort in his head." In view of such caveats, Seeger—who considered Copland "the best" of America's younger composers—nervously awaited "the avalanche to fall." But the only disturbance came from noise in the corridors, prompting him to write, "How about some show there, comrades, of revolutionary discipline, not to speak of courtesy and musical taste?"

Seeger discerned in this recital Copland's "progress from ivory tower to within hailing distance of the proletariat," writing,

> From the "genteel seclusion" of the earlier works (a Passacaglia and two pieces for violin and piano), through an intermediate stage of almost religious rage or, better, rage at religion (the trio, Vitebsk), and of a flirtation with Broadway (a jazz concerto for piano), he emerged by 1930 as the composer of one of the most undeniably revolutionary pieces of music ever produced here—the piano Variations. That he was not "conscious" of this at the time he wrote the work is merely to say that in 1930 he had progressed further in musical than in language development.

Following the concert, in a discussion of what this music had to do with the proletariat, a structural steelworker announced "that it seemed to him to be in keeping not only with the daily job but with the trip to and from it—even with the lunch hour," to which Copland admitted that he "felt that his music must be able to stand up against modern life," a remark that captured Seeger's fancy:

> For one of the finest definitions of revolutionary musical content yet made, we hail Aaron Copland "Up against!" And with vigor, too—that is the essence of the Piano Variations. There [sic] chief shortcomings seem to be that they are almost too much "against"— against pretty nearly everything. So some day, Aaron, write us something "for." You know what for![14]

At about this same time, in early 1934, the New Masses announced a contest for a setting of a poem by Alfred Hayes, "Into the Streets May First," sending out copies of the text to the Composers' Collective and other "accomplished" composers. The winning song was to be performed at the Second Annual American Workers' Music Olympiad on April 29 and published in the journal's May 1 issue. Copland, Seeger, Siegmeister, Riegger, and others submitted entries to a jury comprised of Degeyter Club members and some of the party's rank and file. Copland's song won. "He wrote a beautiful song," remembered Seeger. "It really was a splendid thing. It was magnificent. We all agreed."[15]

Copland always played down this two-page song for unison voice and piano, "my communist song," as he referred to it in a letter to Carlos Chávez. He never included it in his catalog; and during the McCarthy era, he publicly disowned it as "the silliest thing I did," adding that he wrote it simply "to prove to myself that I could write a better mass song than the next fellow." But at the very least, the song revealed his own solution to the problem that so baffled the collective, that is, how to create music that would be both revolutionary—or at least fresh and modern—in style and yet appropriate to mass taste and abilities. Copland resolved this dilemma by using stepwise melodic motion, marchlike rhythms, and triadic harmonies, while including some jazzy syncopations and pungent modal and chromatic shifts. In a 1 May 1934 article for the *New Masses*, Ashley Pettis, explaining the reasons behind the jury's unanimous decision in his favor, wrote, "Copland has chosen a musical style of time-honored tradition, but he has imbued it with fresh vitality and meaning. . . . Some of the intervals may be somewhat difficult upon a first hearing or singing, but we believe the ear will very readily accustom itself to their sound." This stylistic solution foreshadowed some of Copland's later work, such as *Fanfare for the Common Man*.[16]

Some weeks after the Pettis article, Copland published his own review of the Workers' Music League's *Workers' Song Book* for the *New Masses*. ("Into the Streets" would appear in the *Workers' Song Book No. 2*, published in 1935.) "Every participant in revolutionary activity knows from his own experience that a good mass song is a powerful weapon in the class struggle," he proclaimed. "It creates solidarity and inspires action." He attributed the popularity of Siegmeister's "The Scottsboro Boys Shall Not Die" to its text rather than its "rather flat-footed and unimaginative" setting; the composer was better represented, in his estimation, by some of his other contributions, including "Onward to Battle," based on "an old form of English folk music." Copland further criticized the songs of Lan Adomian as somewhat ungrateful, and those of Jacob Schaefer as "unnecessarily conventional in spirit." In contrast, he found Seeger's songs fresh and well crafted. "Those of us who wish to see music play its part in the workers' struggle for a new world order," he concluded, "owe a vote of thanks to the Composers' Collective for making an auspicious start in the right direction."[17]

On May 11, Copland joined Seeger, Siegmeister, and Roy Harris in a symposium entitled The Problems of the Composer in Modern Society, sponsored by the Degeyter Club. But his radicalism found its consummation a short time later while spending the summer with Kraft at his cousin's cabin in Lavinia, Minnesota, near Bemidji. In town, Kraft discovered a "little wizened woman" selling the *Daily Worker* on a street corner, who subsequently put them in touch with communist farmers in the area. After attending an all-day election-campaign meeting of the local Communist Party unit, Kraft complained about Copland's reticence before the local leaders; but at a subsequent communist picnic, he made up for it by giving his first political speech. Copland wrote to Israel Citkowitz,

> If they were a strange sight to me, I was no less of a one to them. It was the first time that many of them had seen an "intellectual." I was being gradually drawn, you see, into the political struggle with the peasantry! I wish you could have seen them—the true Third Estate, the very material that makes revolution. What struck me particularly was the fact that there is no "type-communist" among them, such as we see on 14th St. They look like any other of the farmers around here, all of them individuals, clearly etched in my mind. And desperately poor.

Clurman hailed the news when he heard it, writing, "Some people go east to the U.S.S.R. to become 'radicalized' but you went west to the U.S.A."[18]

When Minnesota's communist gubernatorial candidate, S. K. Davis, came to Bemidji for a stump speech in a public park, the farmers prevailed upon Copland to speak again. Copland told Citkowitz,

> It's one thing to think revolution, or talk about it to one's friends, but to preach it from the streets—OUT LOUD—Well, I made my speech (Victor says it was a good one) and I'll probably never be the same! Now, when we go to town, there are friendly nods from sympathizers, and farmers come up and talk as one red to another. One feels very much at home and not at all like a mere summer boarder. I'll be sorry to leave here with the thought of probably never seeing them again.

Such sentiments recall his feelings toward the people of Mexico after his first visit there.[19]

The events in Minnesota intimate the strong influence of Kraft during these years; in fact, in a letter to Copland dated December 1934, Paul

Bowles referred to Kraft as a Communist in such a way as to suggest that he and Copland were not. But as close to his vest as Copland may have played his cards—and as cautious as he remained about doctrinaire ideology—the summer of 1934 found him no mere fellow traveler, but rather an active, vocal "red."[20]

On his return to New York, Copland resumed some affiliation with the Composers' Collective. As early as June 1934, Siegmeister claimed that he had joined their ranks; Hanns Eisler explicitly referred to him as a member; and yet in later years Siegmeister and Seeger gave conflicting accounts of whether or not he ever officially joined. On record is the fact that on 11 April 1935 he attended a collective meeting for five minutes. At the least, the collective agreed on the desirability of his support and welcomed him to their sessions; and he, for his part, took an interest in their activities.[21]

Although joining the collective posed potential dangers to one's career ("It was dangerous to belong to the Collective," remembered Henry Leland Clarke), that in itself would not explain Copland's ambiguous position vis-à-vis the group. After all, he boldly used his own name in various party publications. More to the point, perhaps, is the fact that however much he may have shared some of their ideals, he was not much impressed with their music. In a spring 1935 article, he seemed singularly skeptical of the new so-called proletarian composer, writing, "the young composer who allies himself with the proletarian movement must do so not with the feeling that he has found an easy solution, but with a full realization of what such a step means, if his work is to be of permanent value to the workers and their cause." The following year, in discussing Siegmeister, Heilner, Jerome Moross, and Norman Cazden, he further stated, "It cannot be said that their works show the salutary influence of a collectivist ideal." As early as 1934, he wrote to Citkowitz that he regretted the idea that Siegmeister should be a "symbol of Communism" to Sessions—"whereupon all is lost there and then!"[22]

Concurrently, one doubts that Copland approved of the argumentative polemics that the collective went in for. Perhaps this explains his quick departure from the April 1935 meeting. In any case, his coolness toward the group reflected the same temperament that distanced him from the circle that sprang up around Varèse in the 1920s: a profound dislike of sectarianism. For their part, Siegmeister, Heilner, and doubtless others in the collective apparently regarded Copland's tastes and attachments as somewhat suspect.[23]

Nonetheless, the collective seems to have had some influence on Copland's aesthetics, including his developing interest in American folk music. In the course of 1935, the relation of folk and art music became a central preoccupation; Copland must have heard many discussions on the subject. The collective—in step with the American Communist Party—initially spurned folk music for a number of reasons, including its rural roots removed from the urban proletariat, its susceptibility to bourgeois corruption, and its association with fascism. However, in 1935 the party began reevaluating the matter in the light of the Kremlin's new emphasis on folk music, prompted not only by Stalin's personal liking for such music but by a new Popular Front policy that aimed to integrate the Communist Party into the larger fabric of American life. From 1935 to 1945, under the leadership of Earl Browder, the party adopted the slogan "Communism Is Twentieth Century Americanism," and recast itself as ultranational, appropriating political heroes like Jefferson and Lincoln, folk legends like Paul Bunyan and Jesse James, and American folk songs to the point that in some circles, writes Siegmeister, "anyone who was involved with folk music in those days was automatically considered a Communist."[24]

The collective slowly began to accommodate this new viewpoint. Earl Robinson contributed "Death House Blues" to the Workers' Music League's *Songs of the People* (1935), a tentative step toward the group's adoption of American folk song. By the end of 1935, Seeger had left the collective in order to embark on a celebrated career as a scholar of American folk music, while others started investigating such publications as Carl Sandburg's *American Songbag* (1927) and George Pullen Jackson's *White Spirituals in the Southern Uplands* (1933). But as a whole, the collective proved resistant to the party's growing insistence on accessible folk styles, inciting criticisms by Mike Gold in the *Daily Worker* in early 1936 and precipitating the collapse of the whole enterprise. (While most of the collective, like Siegmeister, eventually came around to the cause of folk music, Blitzstein remained true to its original, more Eisler-like orientation.)[25]

Copland probably regarded the growing interest in American folk music as a positive development; he much preferred Siegmeister's arrangements of folk songs to his more original work. And while he would not have identified with Gold's heavy-handed posturings, he might well have sympathized with his criticism of the collective's insularity and sectarianism, its attachment to Schoenberg, and its tendency toward complexity.

If folk songs could help the collective produce music of greater vigor and personality, he would hardly have objected. As for his own development, although he had long found popular and folk music a valuable resource, the Popular Front's emphasis on Anglo-American folklore undoubtedly fostered a growing familiarity with and receptivity toward that particular repertoire.[26]

Meanwhile, Copland's association with the far left continued unabated. He recommended communism's "classics" to friends (he himself acquired Lenin's *Imperialism* and *The State and Revolution*), sought out "full-length revolutionary plays for 8 characters" for possible musical treatment, and told Chávez that he felt he had nothing of importance to communicate "to those middle class people who up to now have been our audiences." In 1936 he donated free composition lessons to the winner of a competition sponsored by the Downtown Music School, the principal educational institution of the Workers' Music League. (The winner, Earl Robinson, emerged, following his work with Copland, as the American Communist Party's composer laureate with such pieces as the 1936 "Abe Lincoln" and the 1938 *Ballad for Americans*.) In 1936, he marched in a May Day parade and performed two recently composed piano pieces for children, *Sunday Afternoon Music* and *The Young Pioneers*, at a May 17 Festival sponsored by the American Music League (the renamed Workers' Music League).[27]

In 1936 he supported the communist presidential ticket, aligning himself with the Committee of Professional Groups for Browder and Ford and signing a statement that praised them for doing "battle against reaction and fascism." On this issue, he joined ranks with his friend Waldo Frank, who remembered Browder as "a dry, pleasant, reliable, transplanted Yankee, the sort that teaches in the Methodist Sunday school and helps out with the church finances." Although we do not know whether Copland actually voted for Browder in the 1936 election, it seems likely that he did.[28]

A youthful defender of the Russian Revolution, Copland remained strongly pro-Soviet; from 1934 to 1937, he repeatedly made plans to visit the Soviet Union, though such a trip never materialized. For his information about Russia he relied largely on the first-hand reports of such friends as Edmund Wilson, Waldo Frank, and Harold Clurman, who, unaware of the grim and brutal realities of Soviet life, similarly saw the Soviet Union as fundamentally a bulwark against Nazi aggression and as proof of the advantages of a socialist economy. Copland no doubt shared their idealistic view of the Russian Revolution (as did, during these years, Americans of many different political convictions). Even so, his attitude toward the Soviet Union remained one more of hopeful tolerance than infatuated enthusiasm; he typically assumed a cautiously relativistic position toward the country, arguing that what was right for the Soviets might not necessarily make sense in the States.[29]

Moreover, in the wake of Shostakovich's highly publicized reprimand by the Soviet authorities in 1936, Copland's remarks about Soviet policy began to acquire an ironic edge. Still, he apparently supported Russia even after the Nazi-Soviet Pact, at a time when only the most hardcore sympathizers among his friends—like Odets, Bowles, Blitzstein, and Kazan—advocated American nonintervention. "I'm not sure what the CP line is this month," wrote Bowles to Copland in 1940, "but it's probably the right one. As far as I can see, whatever line helps the Red Army helps the world. Any complication of that viewpoint seems unnecessarily cautious." In line with the American Communist Party, Odets and others reversed themselves after the Nazi invasion of the Soviet Union in June 1941. Blitzstein even became a rather impassioned soldier, criticizing Tippett's pacifism to Copland in 1943 as "defeatist."[30]

In 1943 and 1944, as the political objectives of the United States and the Soviet Union became practically indistinguishable, Copland's pro-Soviet sentiments hardly stood out from the prevailing atmosphere at home. In 1943, Stalin himself ordered the dissolution of the Comintern—the international communist agency established to promote world revolution—and in 1944, the American Communist Party renamed itself the Communist Political Association, offering no challenge to Roosevelt's renomination. "Uncle Joe" Stalin became the kind of hero to millions of Americans that he had long been to a small left-wing minority. But when the Soviet Union asserted its claims on Eastern Europe at the Yalta Conference (1945), American anti-Soviet sentiment revived and the American Communist Party regrouped.

According to government investigators, during the years from 1935 to 1949, Copland sponsored or supported over twenty left-wing causes and "front" organizations in addition to the ones already mentioned. When confronted with these allegations in the 1950s, he questioned the veracity of many of them, acknowledging only a close involvement with the National Council of American-Soviet Friendship.[31]

An outgrowth of the earlier Friends of Soviet Russia, formed in 1921, the National Council reorganized in 1941 under the leadership of the writer Corliss Lamont with the objective of promoting better cooperation and understanding between the United States and the Soviet Union. In 1946, the council outlined its four principal aims as fostering peace within the framework of the United Nations, encouraging cultural exchange, presenting factual information about the Soviet Union, and countering misrepresentations of the Soviet Union in the media. "Our Council is a non-political organization," stated Lamont in response to Senate investigations, "and welcomes to its ranks all Americans who favor cooperation with Soviet Russia, regardless of their political, religious, professional or other affiliations."[32]

At least as early as 1944, Copland served as vice chairman of the council's music committee, which along with the theater and literature committees hosted the First Conference on American-Soviet Cultural Cooperation on 18 November 1945. Copland chaired the music panel discussion, which featured talks by Siegmeister and Blitzstein. The music committee reconvened in 1946 as the American-Soviet Music Society, with Serge Koussevitzky as chairman; Copland, Bernstein, and Siegmeister as vice-chairmen; and a large, distinguished national advisory board. The society's goals included exchanging artists as well as promoting American music in the Soviet Union and "lesser-known" Soviet composers in the States. A 27 May 1946 concert sponsored by the society featured new works by Shostakovich and Vissarion Shebalin along with pieces by Paul Bowles and Ned Rorem.[33]

The fall and winter of 1946–47 constituted the society's heyday, notwithstanding some turmoil caused by the purported harassment of two Soviet singers by the Justice Department that led to a canceled tour in the fall of 1946. The society arranged panel discussions (one featured Henry Cowell and Alex North relating their experiences in the Soviet Union); exchanged folk and classical musicians; sponsored concerts, ballets, and operas; commissioned new works by American and Soviet composers; and, in December 1946, published their one and only copy of the *American-Soviet Music Review*. But Cold War pressures took their toll; Koussevitzky resigned in early 1947, and by the end of year, the entire society folded. Writes Eric Gordon, "The energy to push on with a task so obviously doomed and so clearly damaging to the careers of anyone associated with it simply vanished."[34]

Copland maintained a sympathetic posture toward the Soviet Union nonetheless. When in 1948 the Kremlin accused Prokofiev, Shostakovich, Khachaturian, and other Soviet composers of "formalism," Copland, while ridiculing the idea that bureaucrats could tell anyone how to compose, took the debate seriously: "They [Prokofiev, et al.] were rebuked for failing to realize that their musical audience had expanded enormously in the last several years (you have only to pass a record or radio shop to see that), and that composers can no longer continue to write only for a few initiates." In the same year he supported the Progressive Party's pro-Soviet presidential candidate, Henry Wallace. An enthusiastic New Dealer who had proclaimed the "Century of the Common Man" during his years in the Roosevelt administration, Wallace opposed the Democratic candidate, Harry Truman, by running on an anti–Cold War, anti–Marshall Plan, pro-labor, and pro–civil liberties platform. In the process, he won the endorsement, among others, of the American Communist Party.[35]

The 25–27 March 1949 Cultural and Scientific Conference for World Peace provided a last hurrah for the old left. A weekend of dinners, speeches, and panel discussions at the Waldorf-Astoria in New York, the conference brought together prominent figures to discuss "the effects of the cold war on the arts, sciences and professions, and the contributions that each craft and profession can make to the realization of world peace." The participants included Copland, Odets, Lillian Hellman, Arthur Miller, and Henry Wallace, but no figure commanded greater curiosity than the Soviet representative, Dmitry Shostakovich. Miller later explained his own participation in the conference as follows: "The sharp postwar turn against the Soviets and in favor of a Germany unpurged of Nazis not only seemed ignoble but threatened another war that might indeed destroy Russia but bring down our own democracy as well."[36]

The conference elicited enormous controversy. In the course of the weekend, thousands picketed outside the Waldorf, including nuns, disabled veterans, and Americans of Jewish and Slovakian descent. A newly formed group named Americans for Intellectual Freedom concurrently held a rival meeting nearby. At the conference's Friday-night dinner, Norman Cousins, editor of the *Saturday Review*, attacked the conference sponsors to boos and hisses, only to be assailed in turn by Lillian Hellman. In the panel discussions the following day, speakers faced angry accusations by anti-Stalinist participants. On Saturday night, both Odets and Shostakovich gave highly inflammatory speeches, the former assaulting capitalist greed, the latter accusing the United States of warmongering and defending Communist Party attacks on Stravinsky, Prokofiev, Hindemith, and others, including himself.[37]

In the context of this maelstrom, Copland's speech, "The Effect of the

Cold War on the Artist in the U.S.," given at a fine arts panel on Sunday morning, must have seemed like the voice of reason. He told his audience that he came "as a democratic American artist, with no political affiliations of any kind," concerned about how American policies will affect artists and the future prospects for peace: "I am here this morning, because I wish to protest an attitude that has turned the very word 'Peace' into a dirty word." Comparing the tension between communism and capitalism to other seemingly irreconcilable conflicts largely resolved, he urged his fellow citizens to work toward a peaceful resolution to this one. He emphasized the deleterious effects of the Cold War on artists:

> Lately I've been thinking that the cold war is almost worse for art than the real thing—for it permeates the atmosphere with fear and anxiety. An artist can function at his best only in a vital and healthy environment for the simple reason that the very act of creation is an affirmative gesture. An artist fighting in a war for a cause he holds just has something affirmative he can believe in. That artist, if he can stay alive, can create art. But throw him into a mood of suspicion, ill-will and dread that typifies the cold war attitude and he'll create nothing.

Imputing primary blame of the Cold War to the United States, he argued that such hostility in turn prompted the Soviet Union to officially adopt "a disapproving attitude toward much contemporary art, and especially in the field of music." He concluded his speech by quoting Franklin Roosevelt: "We have learned the simple truth, as Emerson said, that the 'only way to have a friend is to be one.' "[38]

The conference proved a great embarrassment for Copland. Just his participation made him look like a Stalinist apologist. On top of that, the Daily Worker, after devoting several columns to Shostakovich's speech, briefly reported Copland's concern about American policies possibly leading to a third world war, taking the remark out of context and ignoring his critical remarks about the Soviet Union. "I am very glad I went to that conference," he later told a Senate subcommittee, "because it gave me first-hand knowledge in what ways the Communists were able to use such movements for their own ends."[39]

For a while, he nonetheless remained affiliated with the National Council of American-Soviet Friendship, which invited him to a dinner in honor of Soviet Foreign Minister Andrey Y. Vyshinsky in the fall of

1949. Then, in June 1950, he withdrew from that organization. Copland began severing ties with other leftist organizations in the early 1950s. On 3 February 1954, he resigned from the Workers' Music Association, one of the last such groups he belonged to. In his Norton lectures (1951–52) he assumed a more critical tone toward the Soviet Union, arguing that the loss of freedom there had deprived the artist of one of his most important rights, "the immemorial right of the artist to be wrong."[40]

As McCarthyism gripped American life, Copland refrained from public actions of a political nature. He believed—correctly, as it turned out—that the FBI was keeping track of him and he feared—without grounds, it seems—that his phone was being tapped. He avoided discussing his leftist involvements in his autobiography, simply telling Vivian Perlis, "It seemed the thing to do at the time." While in Budapest in 1969, his companion, Phillip Ramey, made him nervous by threatening to participate in an anti-American march sponsored by local communist youth. "I'm here as a cultural ambassador," explained Copland, "and we have to watch what we say."[41]

Although he felt that he had been manipulated by the far left, Copland remained politically liberal, supporting Adlai Stevenson in 1952 and 1956 and John F. Kennedy in 1960. He was impressed with the Kennedy White House, especially the youthful vigor of the president ("No evil in the face, but plenty of ambition, no doubt," he remarked in his diary after meeting him), the stylish grace of his wife, and their support of the arts. In Munich on the day of Kennedy's assassination, a shocked Copland attended a memorial service at that city's Amerika Haus in order to mourn with fellow countrymen.[42]

By the 1960s, his position had taken on the kind of ambiguities associated with other survivors of the old left. He rejected anticommunism as an ideology; when he and Khachaturian met for an informal discussion in 1969, they were in remarkable agreement on many essential points, despite the volatile tensions between their respective governments. Copland also opposed the war in Vietnam, strongly supported civil rights, and kept up with such writers as Herbert Marcuse, Kurt Vonnegut, and H. Rap Brown. But he is said to have criticized the new left as somewhat nihilistic. He consequently found himself at odds especially with his younger friends. When he received a telegram from Nixon congratulating him on his seventieth birthday, two such friends rolled marijuana in it and suggested they smoke it; Copland grabbed the telegram, saying, "It's from the President of the United States. That goes into my scrapbook."[43]

Such conflicts came to a head when the Nixon administration asked him if they could play some of his music at the 1973 inaugural concert. In "a quandary" because he "did not admire Mr. Nixon," Copland decided to "allow the performances but not attend," a compromise that still did not sit well with some in the musical community. In contrast, he gladly conducted his music at the 1977 inaugural concert for President Carter, whose wife's "quiet charm" touched him.[44]

During these later years, Copland kept abreast of current events, hoping, in 1976, for government leadership of the caliber of Thomas Jefferson, "the greatest American of all time." He enjoyed cordial ties with Senator Jacob Javits—an avid Copland enthusiast—and Mayor Ed Koch, who in 1978 invited him to New York City's mayoral residence, Gracie Mansion, after hearing that he had never been there. "But you were born in Brooklyn and are one of our great composers," Koch exclaimed. "I am *shocked!*"[45]

Copland stayed particularly concerned about the role of the artist in society. Regarding the widespread dependence of composers on academic positions, he acknowledged that a university career was a suitable occupation for some, but fretted about an entire nation of composers so employed. Among other concerns, he noted a falling off of interest in writing for orchestra and a growing academicism among composers. "I don't think it is healthy for the whole composing community to move within university walls. The protected feeling and the small field of reference are a little worrying." Anything that isolated the composer from the large public and from fellow artists disturbed him. "Everybody gets encouragement from a small circle," he told Edward Cone in 1967. "I realize that encouragement is important, and there are plenty of examples of composers who began with a small circle of admirers; but one can overdo it. The tendency to lean back and depend upon that small-circle encouragement is, I fear, a lessening rather than an enlarging of one's capacities."[46]

As early as 1952, he went on record as a vigorous advocate for government support of the arts. Pointing to such subsidies in Europe and in Latin America, he dismissed fears of government control, writing, "Bureaucratic control of the artist in a totalitarian regime is a frightening thing; but in a democracy it should be possible to envisage a liberal encouragement of the arts through allocation of government funds without any permanently dire results." Among other benefits, he said, "Our people will show more concern for their artists as soon as the government shows more concern for the welfare of art in America." This included, crucially, support for America's composers. In 1955, he again brushed aside fears of "socialism" and "thought control," citing the dependence of earlier composers on court patronage. "It doesn't seem to have hampered Beethoven too much," he noted, adding, "Besides, it might be a good thing if the government were able to exert enough control to get more works by American composers on the average program." "The government should subsidize the arts," he reiterated in 1978. "It made a good beginning with WPA. This would increase worldwide respect for the United States. Government subsidy would not mean government control of music. The government wouldn't even know what sort of music it wants." He especially endorsed programs that would bring artists together, both at home and abroad; he even proposed that each state establish its own MacDowell Colony.[47]

He also continued to champion composers' rights. In 1975, he defended, before a subcommittee of the House Judiciary Committee, copyright legislation that would require the jukebox industry to more equitably compensate composers, arguing that the monies collected by ASCAP and other agencies benefited not only America's popular composers but, indirectly, its serious composers as well. And as late as 1986, he wrote to Senator Howard Metzenbaum protesting his opposition of a bill that would impose royalty fees on blank recording tapes. Although many typically thought of Copland's social and political concerns as limited to the 1930s, he remained a deeply engaged citizen from the beginning of his career to the very end.[48]

17

From the *Short Symphony*
to *A Prairie Journal*
(1933–37)

The Short Symphony

Copland composed the *Short Symphony* from 1931 to 1933. Both Koussevitzky and Stokowski hoped to introduce it, but its rhythmic intricacies demanded more rehearsal time than either had at his disposal. And unlike the *Ode*, the *Symphony* could not simply be rebarred; the difficulties were built in. In 1934, after ten rehearsals, Chávez (to whom Copland dedicated the work) and the Mexico Symphony Orchestra gave a shaky world premiere. As late as 1955, Copland needed the same number of rehearsals with the Südwestfunk Orchestra in Baden-Baden. In the meantime, in 1944, Stokowski finally presided over an American premiere.[1]

Critics often group the *Short Symphony* with the *Ode* and the *Piano Variations*, but while all three are sinewy, athletic works, the *Short Symphony* is as sprightly and charming as the earlier two works are tragic and defiant—the "antithesis of the *Ode*," as Copland explained to Eva Goldbeck. Cast in three connected movements (fast-slow-fast), the work begins with a first movement that is dancelike; its second movement is gently melancholic, with a pastoral middle section; and its third movement is vivacious. The sharp dissonances—which often unfold in the context of a major as opposed to a minor mode—are more comic or poignant than severe; the rhythmic jolts, more rollicking than violent. At one point Copland considered entitling the work *The Bounding Line* in reference to the first movement's "bounce." The piece's reputation as an austere and thorny work did not fool Gerald Sykes, who wrote to Copland, in reference to an arrangement of it by the composer, "Your wonderful sweetness of nature came across best for me in the *Sextet*," or Joseph Kerman, who described the same arrangement as "always interesting, never over-written, terse, bracing, neat, unpretentious, anxious to be liked and instantly likeable, musical to the bone."[2]

The *Short Symphony* can even be described as neoclassical, especially the taut first movement, which bubbles forward with the polished elegance of a Baroque concerto grosso. Indeed, Copland had at one point considered entitling the piece *Divertimento* or *Partita*; he presumably had this aspect of the work in mind when he wrote to Virgil Thomson that after his ten rehearsals with the Südwestfunk Orchestra, it sounded like *Eine Kleine Nachtmusik*. Surely relevant, too, is the fact that he was studying Mozart's string quartets and quintets in 1931; perhaps it is no mere coincidence that the last movement uses a well-worn motive made famous by the finale to the *Jupiter* Symphony. "I was determined to write as perfected a piece as I possibly could," Copland once said about the work.[3]

At the same time, the music's neoclassicism is thoroughly individual, even idiosyncratic. The instrumentation calls for singular forces somewhere between chamber and full orchestra: full winds (including a rarely used bass oboe, the heckelphone, doubling on English horn), four horns, two trumpets, piano, and strings—no trombones, tuba, or percussion. The music clearly represents a personal take on the neoclassical trends of the time.

Part of the work's distinctiveness derives, too, from its American qualities; Michael Steinberg argues that it represents a "remarkable synthesis of the learned and the vernacular," thus offering "a singularly 'complete' representation of its inventor." In addition to the already familiar gestures derived from jazz and Jewish sources, one discerns, in anticipation of *El Salón México*, some assimilation of Mexican music, especially in the finale. While composing the piece, Copland himself told Eva Goldbeck and Marc Blitzstein, "The Third movement . . . begins to sound rather Mexican to me." Significantly, some of the music, especially in the first movement, also looks ahead in unprecedented ways to his famous Western idiom.[4]

The finale further quotes a fragment of a Werner Heymann song featured in a German film operetta that Copland had seen while in Berlin, Erik Charrell's 1931 *Der Kongress Tanzt* (*Congress Dances*). Set against the political intrigues of Metternich's Vienna, this sophisticated comedy imagines an affair between Czar Alexander I and a Viennese glovemaker (played by the delightful Lilian Harvey) during the Congress of Vienna. Copland quotes the second phrase of the operetta's most famous number, sung by an enraptured Harvey as she drives through town in the czar's carriage on her way to his villa, the local Viennese townspeople and farmers cheering her on: *"Das gibt's nur einmal / Das kommt nicht wieder"* ("It happens only once / It will never happen again"). This particular fragment—highly disguised as such—provides the *Short Symphony*'s finale with climactic arrival points. Arthur Berger, who initially brought this quotation to public attention, wrote, "He was not trying to make any specific reference; he was merely fascinated by the notes." Still, the film's celebration of the bittersweet joys of young love seems somehow related to the work's vitality and humor.[5]

The forms of the individual movements are hard to grasp. Identifying the work's tonal structure—one is hesitant, with Copland, to speak in terms of a "plan" or "scheme"—Daniel Mathers has ventured schematic interpretations for each movement. Most recognizable, as such, is the ABA slow movement, described in like manner by the composer himself. In the outer movements, the listener most likely will hear not so much some sectional form as principal motives expanded, fragmented, developed, and restated in imaginative ways, procedures that apparently pertain to the work's special understanding of eighteenth-century music.[6]

In 1937, Copland arranged the neglected *Short Symphony* as the *Sextet* for clarinet, string quartet, and piano (first performed in 1939). Originally, both works ended somewhat abruptly with a harmony of an open fifth, but some years later, possibly at the suggestion of Leonard Bernstein, Copland revised the symphony so as to repeat this same concluding chord an additional two times, as found in the work's publication (1955). All performances of the symphony since have used this extended ending, while only some of the *Sextet* have done so.[7]

Like the *Piano Variations*, the *Short Symphony / Sextet* became a favored piece among elite listeners. Even Joseph Kerman, who found the *Sextet*'s "uneventful" forms and emotional reserve somewhat blithe as compared to string quartets by Carter and Sessions, thought it "the very best of Copland's early work." But in neither format did the music make significant inroads into the repertory. "One would think that most of the terrors of both versions would have worn off by now for players as well as listeners," mused Copland in the 1980s. "One learns to have patience." In the interest of securing more performances, he sanctioned an arrangement of the *Short Symphony* by Dennis Russell Davies for a more conventional chamber orchestra consisting of one flute, two oboes, one clarinet, two bassoons, two horns, one trumpet, piano, and reduced strings (1979). "Aaron seemed very pleased with the results," recalled Davies, "confessing to me that only in the third movement could he hear differences from the original."[8]

Whatever the work's fate, the interested listener at least has access to a number of fine recordings of the music in all its different guises. Most notably, Copland recorded the *Short Symphony* with the London Symphony Orchestra and, as pianist, the *Sextet* with clarinetist Harold Wright and the Juilliard Quartet. Leonard Slatkin and the St. Louis Symphony also issued an estimable rendition of the *Short Symphony*, one that neatly complemented Copland's earlier effort. In the meantime, the Orpheus Chamber Orchestra made a particularly compelling case for the Davies arrangement.[9]

Hear Ye! Hear Ye!

Copland wrote his second ballet, *Hear Ye! Hear Ye!*, for the Chicagoan choreographer Ruth Page in the fall of 1934. He had less than three months to compose, orchestrate, and revise the almost forty-minute work—and for a mere $250 (not including royalties). But he was eager to collaborate on a dramatic work and hoped to write something that might appeal to a larger audience than the seemingly prescribed one for the *Piano Variations* and the *Short Symphony*.[10]

Although a largely forgotten figure today, Page (1899–1991) was a well-known choreographer and dancer of the time, especially in Chicago. Having imbibed the traditions of St. Petersburg's Imperial Ballet and Paris's Ballets Russes through Pavlova and Adolf Bolm, Page, at age nineteen, was catapulted to fame in the title role of Bolm's ballet *The Birthday of the Infanta* (music by John Alden Carpenter). In the years between the two world wars, she served as première danseuse and eventually director of a number of small, adventurous, and short-lived Chicago dance troupes: the Ballet Intime and the Allied Arts (with Bolm) in the 1920s and the Ruth Page Ballets and the Page-Stone Ballet (with Bentley Stone) in the 1930s. Whether choreographed by Bolm or herself, most of these ballets featured music by contemporary composers and costumes and set designs by the gifted Russian artist Nicholas Remisoff.[11]

Page's choreography won a certain amount of prestige or at least notoriety for its assimilation of popular American dance. Inspired by the Carpenter-Bolm ballets, she incorporated vaudeville and musical comedy gestures and movement into her work. Discussing her best-known work, *Frankie and Johnny* (1938), choreographed with Bentley Stone to a commissioned score by Jerome Moross, Marcia Siegel described it as "equal parts pop art and dance theatre," as "raw, raunchy, and proud of it," as "good fun, if not precisely good form." At the same time, Page commanded a thorough knowledge of classical dance, and her Chicago studio, wrote Agnes de Mille, became "the focal point for all ballet training in the Midwest."[12]

Copland presumably met Page through Carpenter, who invited him to lecture at the Chicago Arts Club in 1930. When Page proposed a joint venture in 1934—a reasonable collaboration, given his nearness to Chicago that summer—he very likely played for her the never-performed *Grohg*, which he had recently revised and still hoped to see staged. But Page wanted something more in the spirit of his jazz works and devised a scenario about a murder in a nightclub in contemporary Chicago.

The action takes place in a court of law, complete with judge, prosecuting and defense attorneys, and six masked jury members. (Page described the prosecutor as "over-dramatic" and the defense attorney as an "ultra chic, well-dressed type, with cane, gloves and spats.") The plot pivots about the murder of the male member of a cabaret dancing team (danced by Page and Stone). The witnesses to the murder—a "Mae West type" cabaret hostess and her maid, a pair of newlyweds, and a black waiter—provide three conflicting accounts of the murder. The hostess testifies that the female dancer shot her partner, the newlyweds claim that a jealous chorus girl killed him, and the waiter swears that a maniac did it. The lawyers argue after each account, the bored jury finding everyone accused guilty. At the trial's end, the two lawyers shake hands and leave arm in arm. The judge and jury stand and then sit as three hammer strokes announce the next case. Writes Page, "And in that courtroom, hearts, though broken, are beating, beating as the hammer strikes calling the next case. Hear Ye! Hear Ye!"[13]

Like the Gershwin musical *Of Thee I Sing!* (1931), *Hear Ye! Hear Ye!* drew upon contemporary disenchantment with the American court system; Copland did his part by distorting a phrase of "The Star-Spangled

Banner" at both the beginning and ending of the ballet. But Page leavened the work's serious theme with the kind of tango, blues, and apache numbers close to her heart. By combining a roaring twenties ambience with a thirties concern for social justice, the ballet struck a strong transitional note.[14]

Page structured the ballet so that the sections for each of the three witnesses—the bulk of the work—contained two parts each: the first part consists of a dance for chorus girls that reflects that particular witness's point of view; the second features a flashback of that witness's account of the murder, including a gunshot heard at the climax. Since the three witnesses project their own personalities onto the dance team, these bifurcated episodes ultimately function as portraits of the individual witnesses—of the sensual hostess, the tender newlyweds, and the manic waiter. This elaborate design gave Page and Stone, who danced in all three flashbacks, an opportunity to refigure themselves according to each witness's perspective.

In creating this scenario, Page presumably took *Grohg* into account, for it can hardly be coincidence that their structures parallel each other so closely or that the three witnesses resemble in type characters from the earlier ballet: the Mae West hostess recalls the streetwalker; the newlyweds, the young girl; and the black waiter, the opium-eater. Copland even used some of the music for the streetwalker and the opium-eater for, respectively, the hostess's and waiter's account of the murder. In addition, he recycled some other scores from the 1920s: "An Immorality" for the opening overture, "Ukelele Serenade" for the first chorus-girl number, and the "Hommage à Milhaud" from the unfinished *Five Sentimental Melodies* for the second chorus-girl number, the "Dove Dance." The need both to write the work quickly and to establish a nightclub atmosphere no doubt encouraged such cannibalizing.

After the overture, the curtain rises as three hammer strokes announce that court is in session, followed by the discordant "Star-Spangled Banner." Three brief scenes successively portray the prosecuting attorney (including a specific accusatory motive consisting of accented triads for the brass), the more ingratiating defense attorney, and the two in argument. This entire section is more mimetic than balletic per se, as one might expect in a dance for opposing lawyers. Page choreographed "exaggerated, aggressive movement" for the prosecutor, while for the defense attorney she used "small, satirical movements, suggesting clever, rather smart-alecky answers to the pointed fingers, fists, and lunges of his opponent."[15]

All of the witnesses enter to similar music, including a brass recitative on a single pitch meant to represent the question "Do you swear to tell the truth?" and so on, and a falling third to describe the witness's "I do." Subtle variations in the witnesses' entrance music underscore their different personalities.

After the hostess takes her oath, the music explodes with "Ukelele Serenade," danced by twelve chorus girls. "They do a very sexy dance," instructed Page, "skirts pulled up high and legs, legs, legs much in evidence." For the hostess's subsequent account of the murder, Page requested "an extremely seductive Tango or habanera (jazzed) ending in a kind of apache dance," and Copland obliged with a suave tango (a rarity in his oeuvre) followed by the streetwalker's apache dance from *Grohg*. At the end of the scene, the accusatory motive sounds and the lawyers bicker.

For the entrance of the newlyweds, Copland quotes Mendelssohn's "Wedding March," sweetly reharmonized with chromatic triads. The chorus girls execute the "Dove Dance," a gentle, fluttering number, languidly orchestrated, that is the picture of innocence; Copland furnished this music in response to Page's request for "a minuet with a pigeon in one hand." At Page's suggestion of "a gavotte (or something very dignified, pure and beautiful)" for the newlyweds' romantic remembrance of the murder, Copland composed a kind of jazz siciliana, tinged with a bluesy, haunting melancholy. Once again, the accusation motive resounds and the lawyers argue.

For the chorus number associated with the black waiter, Page specified "twelve negro girls instead of white girls" doing "cartwheels" and "real jungle jazz." Copland responded with a violently jazzy dance that resembles his snazzy urban landscapes. The waiter's flashback opens with a contrasting blues section, moves on directly to a depiction of the maniac by way of *Grohg*'s opium-eater music, and climaxes with a return to the frenzied "jungle jazz." The ballet concludes with a return of the music for the court, including "The Star-Spangled Banner" and the judge's hammer strokes, signaling the next case. At the very end, a loud two-note cadential figure associated with the prosecution suggests, perhaps, that it is the American legal system which has been found guilty.

Hear Ye! Hear Ye! received a successful production, handsomely designed by Remisoff with tabloid headlines flashed on a large overhead screen during the overture and, for the ballet proper, a backdrop of tilting skyscrapers evoking a contemporary world out of kilter; the masks for the jury, wrote Page, "resembled Aaron Copland's extraordinary face." The work remained in Page's repertory for several seasons, winning favorable, if not extraordinary, reviews at both its premieres, in Chicago (1934) and New York (1936). A suite from the ballet was prepared and performed in 1937, but Copland subsequently withdrew both ballet and suite. "The music was really incidental to the dance," he explained, "and I have discovered that some music is more incidental than others!" Page's choreography, meanwhile, was lost, she herself hardly remembering the dance in 1969, writing, "I doubt now if it was a very good ballet."[16]

Now that the score is once again available and has been recorded in its entirety, one imagines that it will take its place as one of the real if minor pleasures of Copland's art. The *New York Times* critic Bernard Holland greeted a rare 1996 performance as "a delight" and "a happy half-hour." A suite that would include such highlights as the "Ukelele Serenade," the tango, the "Dove Dance," the siciliana, the blues, and the "jungle jazz" would probably make an even stronger case for the work. At the least, the ballet, as we can now see, is not the simple burlesque it was long taken for, but rather a work of strength and sophistication (notwithstanding the coarse parody of "The Star-Spangled Banner"). Nor can the ballet be regarded simply as a throwback to the composer's jazz period, despite its incorporation of earlier works. Rather, it makes some surprising movement toward the more commercial appeal of Gershwin, especially in the tango and blues numbers. But Copland never quite followed up along these lines, perhaps because they were geared to the strengths and limitations of Ruth Page from the start, perhaps because he discovered other strategies with which to reach the larger public. It was only the tenderness of the "Dove Dance" that he wound up salvaging. Otherwise, *Hear Ye! Hear Ye!* represents the road not taken.[17]

Statements

Like the *Ode*, *Statements* is a kind of companion piece to the *Piano Variations*; in fact, one of its six short movements quotes the *Variations*, where it fits seamlessly into the larger musical fabric. Begun as early as the summer of 1932 and composed intermittently between 1933 and 1935, the work satisfied a League of Composers commission for a piece for the Minneapolis Symphony and conductor Eugene Ormandy, who premiered, however, only the last two movements in 1936. Dimitri Mitropoulos and the New York Philharmonic finally presented the entire work in 1942 to enthusiastic reviews by Virgil Thomson and Donald Fuller; to Copland's delight Thomson wrote, "The whole group [of movements] is a manly bouquet, fresh and sweet and sincere and frank and straightforward." But again like the *Ode, Statements* remained largely neglected, even though Copland himself championed and recorded the work in later years. Its obscurity, however, helped make it a favorite of such enthusiasts as David Diamond and Leonard Bernstein, and over the years, it served Copland's friends as a means with which to disarm those who claimed that the composer held no surprises for them.[18]

The fact that *Statements* contains six short movements with vague titles cannot have furthered its cause. The scanty literature on the work has not helped either. By and large, its connection with the political left, for instance, has gone unremarked, despite the suggestiveness of the individual movement titles: "Militant," "Cryptic," "Dogmatic," "Subjective," "Jingo," and "Prophetic." In fact, while commonly thought of as the last gasp of the composer's so-called abstract period, *Statements* seems, on the contrary, very much the work of a man who in the summer of 1934 gave public speeches on behalf of communist farmers. Significantly, the earliest reference to the piece appears in a 1932 letter from Copland to Marc Blitzstein and Eva Goldbeck—already communist sympathizers—jokingly addressed, "Dear Dubrovniks." Not that one can pin a particular program on the work; but whereas in his earlier work he often seemed the ironic observer, in this work, more decidedly than even the *Ode,* he takes his stand as a public orator. This new rhetoric goes to the heart of the work's unusual title. At the same time, the music's taut expressivity and epigrammatic form bespeak a composer who in the late twenties and early thirties showed special sensitivity to Webern.[19]

The opening movement, "Militant," features loud, declamatory melodies, sometimes in unison, sometimes in acerbic two-part counterpoint, from time to time punctuated by noble chords in the brass. David Diamond asserts that "Militant" sought to capture the atmosphere of the Group Theatre and other left-wing associations, and the music, indeed, suggests a leftist speech or rally of the day. Significantly, in discussing the Group's production of Odets's *Waiting for Lefty* (also 1935), Clurman recalled, "We weren't putting on just shows. We were putting on exciting statements!" As in all of these little movements, "Militant" offers some internal contrast from the prevailing mood, here provided by way of a very brief interlude marked by quieter, "espressivo" melodies.[20]

Scored essentially for flute and brass, "Cryptic" is one of Copland's most unusual efforts; the title itself is suggestive, as are the dirgelike, dotted rhythms and the directive "dolce, misterioso" ("sweet, mysterious"). This movement serves as an obvious foil to the powerful rhythms, firm cadences, and blustery sounds of the following movement, "Dogmatic" (which quotes the *Piano Variations* in its middle section). Nothing about "Dogmatic" suggests ironic or satirical intentions on Copland's part; perhaps he was thinking of Marxist dogma. The juxtaposition of the questioning "Cryptic" and the assertive "Dogmatic" itself strikes one as dialectical.

The fourth movement, "Subjective," is virtually a note-for-note transcription of the first section of *Elegies* for violin and viola (1933), a short work withdrawn by its composer after its April 1933 premiere and November 1933 revision. Scored here simply for the violins, violas, and cellos, "Subjective" fills out the pervasive two-voiced texture of the original *Elegies* by adding a complex web of octave doublings and by taking full advantage of divisi scoring and double-stops. From the result, one would hardly guess that Copland adhered so closely to the violin-viola original.

The word *elegy* helps amplify the more vague title "Subjective." This is sad music, but calmly so, as implied by the directive "calmo." As movements two and three are opposites, so are movements four and five: the humorous "Jingo" follows. The opening three-note motive of "Jingo" apparently derives from the spot in *Elegies* where "Subjective" leaves off, underscoring their linkage. This movement's satiric depiction of chauvinism, including quotations of "The Sidewalks of New York," turns dark as the music evokes armed conflict and the horror of war. Then the more lighthearted music returns, and the movement concludes with a fade-out, as if such foolishness goes on and on. All in all, this movement in particular points to the possible influence of Shostakovich.

The last movement, "Prophetic," acts as a bookend to the opening "Militant," holding up the two inner pairs of movements. Like the other movements, this remarkable finale itself contrasts two opposing ideas: a stern, declamatory one in minor and a warm, lyrical one in its parallel major. The slightly faster lyrical music, associated largely with the solo trumpet, puts forth that distinctively diatonic language (sometimes referred to as "pandiatonic") associated with middle-period Copland and one of his most recognizable trademarks: a melodic and harmonic revitalization of the major scale. Here, used in its mature guise for perhaps the first time, the music poignantly suggests the prophet's utopian vision. The movement ends ambiguously and evocatively as the declamatory music gently reasserts itself in the flute and the glockenspiel, followed by a single triple-piano stroke of the tam-tam.

El Salón México

"It seems a long long time since anyone has written an *España* or a *Bolero*—the kind of brilliant piece that everyone loves," Copland wrote in Baden-Baden in 1927. On his first, memorable trip to Mexico in 1932, he began work on just such a piece using Mexican tunes, *El Salón México* for orchestra, which he completed in 1936. Perhaps Copland reasoned that much as Chabrier and Ravel worked with Spanish idioms, it seemed natural for American composers to make use of the music south of their border.[21]

El Salón México also followed in the footsteps of Milhaud's *La Création du monde*, one of Copland's favorite pieces. For as the Milhaud work found inspiration in a Harlem nightclub, this piece depicts a famous dance hall in Mexico City called El Salón México; to avoid confusion, Copland even subtitled the work "Popular Type Dance Hall in Mexico City."

Copland first learned about El Salón from Anita Brenner's guidebook to Mexico, which described it as a "Harlem type night-club for the peepul, grand Cuban orchestra, Salón México. Three halls: one for people dressed in your way, one for people dressed in overalls but shod, and one for the barefoot." Copland was startled to be frisked at the door and was amused by the sign on the wall: "Please don't throw lighted cigarette butts on the floor so the ladies don't burn their feet." Mesmerized by the sounds of the music, the young men in their fresh white shirts, and the women in their bright, colorful dresses, Copland closed the place—presumably with Kraft—at five in the morning.[22]

El Salón also made a deep impression on the Russian film director Sergey Eisenstein, who had visited there the previous year, 1931, before returning to the Soviet Union. He remembered it, however, as nightmarishly garish, like a trip through the "circles of hell," recalling the poor boys unable to afford the entrance fees shuffling at the entryway, the young girls with their cheap jewelry, the dancers with their love bites, and "the beat of the orchestra's screaming rhythm." Whereas Copland simply mentioned the overalled workers taking a few hours' snooze before returning to work, Eisenstein added that they slept there because they had nowhere else to go. Visiting El Salón in 1941, Ned Rorem commented that "it lacked sex"; but Eisenstein had observed photographs of naked women and dancing of "tormenting sensuality."[23]

Copland aimed not merely to depict this particular dance hall but to express his feelings about the entire country and its people—feelings far removed from Eisenstein's impressions of torment and hopelessness. "In some inexplicable way," he explained, "while milling about in those crowded halls, one felt a really live contact with the Mexican 'peuple'— the electric sense one gets sometimes in far-off places, of suddenly knowing the essence of a people—their humanity, their separate shyness, their dignity and unique charm. I remember quite well that it was at just such a moment that I conceived the idea of composing a piece about Mexico and naming it *El Salón México*."[24]

In writing the work, he availed himself of two recent collections of Mexican folk tunes, one edited by Rubén Campos (1928), the other by Frances Toor (1931). In his autobiography, he recalled using four tunes: "El Palo Verde" and "La Jesusita" from the Toor anthology and "El Mosco" and "El Malacate" from the Campos collection. But he adapted at least five other tunes: three more from Toor ("Camino Real de Colima," "Corrido de Rivera," and "Corrido de Lucio") and two more from the Campos ("El Mosquito" and "El Curripiti"). Most of these tunes, as transcribed by Campos and Toor, use meters of 6/8 or 3/4, sometimes in alteration, as in the traditional huapango. Only the ditty "La Jesusita" is in a simple duple meter.[25]

Gerald Abraham observes that while the work's principal melodic material derives from these Mexican tunes, "the operative word is 'derived.' " Copland freely deleted and changed pitches. He also varied rhythms, often prolonging or shortening a note or adding or omitting a rest. As a result, the tunes' downbeats appear, from the perspective of the Campos and Toor songbooks, in unusual places; a particularly striking example is the setting of "El Mosco," originally transcribed in 6/8, here revamped into 4/4. Copland thus frees the tunes from their metrical strait-jackets, so to speak, providing them with a delightful lilt and sway.[26]

For the refrain of "El Palo Verde," which appears three times (the last two times featuring a pounding bass drum), he did something slightly different; he used the original alternations of 6/8 and 3/4 but marked "ritard" above the 3/4 measures. At these 3/4 measures, Copland and most other conductors (including Bernstein and the Mexican Eduardo Mata) add an eighth-note rest to each of the two eighth-note rests already there, which results, essentially, in a 4/4 measure. Why not write these measures in 4/4 to begin with? Apparently, Copland wanted a special feeling of suspension, a 3/4 bar happening in the space of a 4/4 measure, perhaps his own response to Eisenstein's observation that "in the midst of the most sharp motion, a couple suddenly, for several beats, freezes completely motionless, facing one another, and stands as if rooted, until they again continue the tormenting sensuality, or the quick tempo of rhythmic body movements."[27]

Some of Copland's rhythmic ingenuity stems from the actual practices of Mexican folk musicians, whom he observed not only in El Salón but elsewhere in the country. Other aspects of the work similarly reflect folk practices: the wayward melodies in the bass, the harmonizations in parallel thirds and sixths, the clarinet cadenzas and the glissando strings, the slips in pitch, the responsorial volleys in the orchestra. The net effect is one of tremendous verisimilitude, so that the tunes seem much more true to themselves than in their songbook versions. Copland did not have Bartók's ethnomusicological expertise, but he had a similar ability to use modern techniques in order to get to the heart of a folk melody.

Aside from presenting "El Mosco" in its entirety near the work's beginning, Copland fragments these tunes, often separating verse and refrain, isolating single phrases, extending motives, even juxtaposing melodies, all the while developing a continuous logical argument. Throughout, however, some quoted phrase or other can be heard in a rather expository fashion; by thus stitching together the tunes, the music eschews the kind of development found in *Vitebsk* (which is based on a single melody). Copland thought such treatment—perhaps inspired by the kinds of collage and patchwork practiced by folk artisans—appropriate to the plain and nonmodulatory nature of the material. In any case, this approach— far too architecturally subtle to be characterized as a mere medley or potpourri—proved momentous for Copland, for it would inform such later works as *Billy the Kid* and *Rodeo*, especially their opening scenes. Along with the use of a folk tune as the basis for a set of variations (as in *The Second Hurricane* and *Appalachian Spring*), collage became the principal modus operandi for Copland's employment of folk music in a symphonic context.[28]

On a larger level, *El Salón* falls into four sections, comprising a slow-fast-slow-fast design. However, the actual relation of these parts to the whole is ambiguous, so much so that writers have variously interpreted the work as being in binary or ternary form; one might, in addition, hear the work as having (after a brief introduction) a slow prelude, a fast exposition, a slow interlude, and a fast return; that is, as a ternary form with an extended prelude. But Copland's collagelike structure largely undercuts all such schematic interpretations.[29]

The work opens with a lively statement of the verse to "El Palo Verde" in the strings and winds. The largely slow section that follows presents the chorus of "La Jesusita" in the trumpet, the tune "El Mosco" in the bassoon and bass clarinet, the refrain of "El Palo Verde" in the strings, and an only slightly altered version of the beautiful "El Mosquito." As the music suddenly picks up, Copland states fragments of "El Palo Verde" and "Camino Real de Colima," including the refrain of "El Palo Verde," climactically stated by the brass and percussion. The ensuing slower section includes a fragment from "Camino Real" for solo clarinet; an amalgamation of the waltz tunes "Corrido de Rivera" and "Corrido de Lucio" for winds; the verse of "La Jesusita" for solo clarinet and violins; a single phrase from "El Curripiti" for E-flat clarinet and guiro; the refrain of "La Jesusita" for muted violins; and a return of the waltz tunes. As the music once again quickens, we hear "Camino Real" in the clarinet, "El Malacate" in the E-flat clarinet, a third, even more climactic return of the refrain of "El Palo Verde," and a dramatic coda that rounds out the whole.

Copland scored *El Salón México* for full orchestra but made optional provisions for performance by a smaller group, arranging, if need be, for the omission of some of the woodwinds and the third trumpet. On the other hand, the unusual percussion battery, which includes timpani, snare drum, cymbals, bass drum, tambour de Provence, Chinese temple blocks, wood block, guiro, xylophone, and piano, is indispensable. Although not as exotic as Chávez's *Sinfonía India* (1934–35), which Copland would have known while orchestrating *El Salón*, the percussion writing creates a similarly vibrant atmosphere.

Copland made no great claims for *El Salón*, arguing that to write a work about the "deeper" aspects of Mexico—such as the Mexico of the ancient Mayans or "the Mexico of today, with its heartening message of land and a fuller life for the impoverished peon"—one "would have to be something more than a mere tourist." He was relieved that Chávez and his orchestra, who gave the world premiere in 1937, liked the piece as much as they did. But in describing the work as an "exotic travel souvenir,"

301

Julia Smith and others may have taken the composer too much at his word. Perhaps one can find in it something of ancient Mexico—especially that passage featuring the tambour de Provence that seems to jump out of the pages of Chávez's *Sinfonía India*—or detect some connections with revolutionary Mexico in the music's driving, streamlined vigor and the heroic sweep of its final pages. For Copland, after all, Mexico represented a hopeful alternative to modern life, not simply a quaint and picturesque getaway. Some interpreters of the work—for instance Leonard Bernstein, who transcribed *El Salón* for solo piano and who refuted suggestions that this was "light" music—seemed particularly sensitive to this political subtext.[30]

El Salón enormously widened Copland's popularity, winning worldwide performances and garnering raves in the press. It also helped secure his friendship with Benjamin Britten and a contract with Boosey & Hawkes. Koussevitzky and the Boston Symphony recorded it for Victor in 1939 (the first commercial recording of a Copland orchestral work), and Toscanini, who rarely performed American music, gave spectacular broadcast performances of it with the NBC Symphony in 1942. Doris Humphrey choreographed it as a showpiece for José Limon in 1943; the music remained a favorite with choreographers, including in later years Maurice Béjart (*Chapeaux*, 1957) and Eliot Feld (*La Vida*, 1978).

The music—or rather a facsimile thereof—even made its way into a 1947 MGM musical, *Fiesta*, produced by Jack Cummings and directed by Richard Thorpe, with a score by Copland's old friend Johnny Green and choreography by Eugene Loring, the creator of *Billy the Kid*. *Fiesta* is about a young Mexican composer, Mario Morales (Ricardo Montalban in the film that made him a Hollywood star), whose mother (Mary Astor) and twin sister, Maria (Esther Williams), support his musical aspirations but whose overbearing father, a famed retired matador (Fortunio Bonanova), pressures him into bullfighting. Mario runs away with an itinerant mariachi band, whereupon Maria (disguised as her brother) takes his place in the bullring in order to preserve the family honor and lure him back home. At a critical moment, Mario hears his orchestral composition, *Fantasia Mexicana*, premiered over the radio; the performance helps clarify his destiny and leads to a reconciliation with his family.

For the work of the imaginary Mario Morales, Green may well have considered using a real Mexican composition; but little about this film, aside from the on-location scenery, lent itself to any authenticity whatsoever. The jazzy appeal of *El Salón México* seemed closer to the mark; even so, Green dramatically watered down the score by compressing it into five minutes, eliminating some of its complexities, and retouching the orchestration, actually turning it into something of a piano concertino as the inspired Morales plays along with the broadcast in a dusty honky-tonk, adding Lisztian arpeggios and Gershwinesque trills along the way. Copland, who rarely consented to this kind of commercial exploitation, apparently could not resist MGM's tantalizing offer of an easy $15,000. Nonetheless, even the score so bastardized provided this vacuous film with its most compelling moments. Moreover, it helped win Green his first Academy Award and make *El Salón* that much more popular.[31]

Notwithstanding the great success of *El Salón México*, Arthur Berger, Hugo Cole, and others may well have exaggerated its seminal importance; its popularity allowed critics to minimize its ties to earlier works based on popular and folk materials, like *Music for the Theatre* and *Vitebsk*. What seemed most new, as Elliott Carter pointed out in 1939, was its "jubilance," something related not only to Copland's discovery of Mexico and his growing hopes for society but presumably to his blossoming relationship with Victor Kraft, to whom he dedicated the work.[32]

The Second Hurricane and Other Music for the Young

Moved by the spirit of the times, Copland started to write music—out of the blue, as it were—for children and adolescents. In 1935 he composed the two-part chorus "What Do We Plant?" for the Girls' Glee Club at the Henry Street Settlement Music School, where he was then teaching; that year he also wrote two short piano pieces, *The Young Pioneers* and *Sunday Afternoon Music*, for a collection of children's piano pieces edited by Lazare Saminsky and Isadore Freed and published by Carl Fischer. And in 1937 he collaborated with Edwin Denby on the children's opera *The Second Hurricane*, again for the Henry Street Settlement.

Speaking of his interest in composing music for young people, Copland explained rather matter-of-factly, "After all, they grow up and become our audiences." But the desire to reach the young—literally millions of whom, devastated by the Depression, lived in poverty, out of school, without jobs—had a strong social impetus. Like many other serious composers of the day, Copland felt the challenge of writing music that would uplift young people and prepare them for the complexities of modern life and art. On another level, such music represented a fighting response to the fascist youth music popular abroad.[33]

"What Do We Plant?" sets a rather homespun poem by the obscure poet Henry Abbey (1842–1911) that asks, "What do we do when we plant the tree?" Answers the poet: a tree provides the mast of a ship, the beams of a house, the staff of the nation's flag, and, finally, "the shade from hot sun free." This choice of text evokes the popularity of the Civilian Conservation Corps, one of the most effective New Deal stratagems for the problem of unemployed youth. Between 1933 and 1942, the government sent over three million young men to national forests and parks, where they installed telephone lines, built roads, and, above all, planted trees—over a billion of them; the government fed and clothed these "soil soldiers," paid them a salary, taught them to read and write, and, in general, provided this "army of pioneers" with much-needed self-esteem. The corps excluded women, however, and perhaps Copland chose this text for the Girls' Glee Club as a means of allowing girls a share in the excitement of the forestry program.[34]

Stylistically, "What Do We Plant?" continues along the lines of "Into the Streets May First," to the point that their opening gestures are virtually identical. But the melodies of this later chorus are less jagged, the harmonies less chromatic, and the rhythms more relaxed; the whole mood, while still somewhat militant (the work's opening directive reads "lively, with force"), is less strident, aptly capturing the period's more hopeful side.

The decade's idealism is also captured by the two children's piano pieces, in particular by *The Young Pioneers*, whose title itself alludes to the international communist youth organization along the lines of the Boy and Girl Scouts. Moreover, its music resembles "Into the Streets" and "What Do We Plant?," similarly beginning with four repeated notes. Yet Copland achieves another variation on this general style, something more playful and childlike in its swaying 7/8 rhythms and its carefree secondal harmonies.

Sunday Afternoon Music, a marvel in its own right, features a pastoral melody in the right hand juxtaposed against a dissonant pedal in the bass, as if to suggest an idealized dream pitted against reality. This sensitive piece sounds like Debussy recast in a harder, more forlorn light (as does "Queenie's Song" from *The Second Hurricane*). Neither of the two piano pieces in the least condescends to children; for all their modesty, they offer fine representations of their composer. Copland himself premiered them on 24 February 1936.

As early as 1931 Copland confessed to Marc Blitzstein "a terrible yen to write an opera," but it was not until a 1936 commission from Grace

Spofford, the director of the Henry Street Settlement, and Lehman Engel, the conductor of the settlement's children's choruses, that he had a real reason for doing so. The resultant work, *The Second Hurricane,* followed along the lines of Kurt Weill and Bertolt Brecht, whose "Lehrstück" ("learning piece") *Der Jasager (He Who Says Yes)* had recently been performed at Henry Street under Engel's direction. For his own didactic school opera—or "play opera for high school children," as he called it—Copland asked his friend Edwin Denby to write the libretto.[35]

Denby had only recently returned to the United States from an extended stay in Europe. Born in 1903 in China, where his father served as American consul, he attended Harvard and the University of Vienna. After studying modern dance in Vienna in the early 1920s, he moved to Darmstadt, where he joined a dance company and composed poems, dance scenarios, and opera libretti. With the rise of Hitler, he pursued his dancing career in Switzerland; after returning to the States in 1936 with his lover, the Swiss-born photographer Rudy Burckhardt, he continued writing poetry and libretti, though he made his greatest mark as a dance critic. As with Copland, he became a much beloved mentor to many younger, often homosexual artists in New York, including the poets Frank O'Hara and John Ashbery.[36]

Copland met the twenty-six-year-old Denby in Germany in 1929, at which time, according to Marc Blitzstein, he "fell for him like a load of bricks." Upon Denby's arrival in New York, the two developed a close friendship, in part because their younger lovers had so much in common, including photography. After *The Second Hurricane,* Copland and Denby gave some thought to another collaboration, but nothing materialized. They remained friends until Denby's suicide at age eighty in 1983, Copland often lending a sympathetic and confidential ear to Denby's troubles with the chronic depression that had plagued him for his entire life.[37]

Copland naturally thought of Denby for the Henry Street commission. He respected Denby's libretti as well as his aesthetics, as subsequently propounded in Denby's article "A Good Libretto" (1936). Denby's artistic and personal closeness to Brecht and Weill further made him a logical choice for the American "Lehrstück" Copland had in mind.[38]

The Second Hurricane upholds the revolutionary ideals of liberty, equality, and fraternity by way of the following parable. Somewhere in a town in the southern Midwest (later specified as Missouri), the students at a local high school, eager for glory, volunteer to help Mr. MacLenahan, an airplane pilot, deliver food and supplies to stricken flood victims of a hurricane. (Denby later confessed his error in thinking that hurricanes traveled far inland, a peculiarity of the plot that apparently eluded his other collaborators as well.) The high school's principal, Mr. Lester, selects six students, aged fourteen to seventeen, for this dangerous mission: Butch, the class president (tenor); the brawny Fat (bass) and his brother Gyp (baritone); the radio operator Lowrie (tenor); and Gwen (contralto) and Queenie (soprano), who have nursing skills. The six leave with great expectations, but engine trouble forces MacLenahan to make an emergency landing in deserted country. He leaves the six students and the supplies on high ground (which he calls Two Willow Hill) and resumes his risky flight. The stranded students find an eight-year-old black boy, Jefferson Brown (boy soprano), separated from his parents. The students begin to squabble and eventually depart in different directions, leaving Fat alone on the hill.

At this point, a second hurricane strikes. One by one, to their mutual relief, the students and Jeff make their way back to the hill. They realize that they should have cooperated and brought up the supplies to still higher ground, for now night is falling, the floodwaters are rising, and they have only a rubber boat they cannot inflate and a single flashlight. As they wait, cold and tired on the hill, they cheer one another up, eventually singing together the American folk song "The Capture of Burgoyne." Finally, a rescue plane saves them. Although they later get their chance to work for the flood relief, they cherish most the lessons learned on Two Willow Hill: "We got an idea of what life could be like / With ev'rybody pulling together, / If each wasn't trying to get ahead of all the rest. . . . A happy, easy feeling, / Like freedom, like freedom, like real freedom."

The work's musical numbers alternate with spoken dialogue; Denby thought of his approach specifically in the tradition of Lorenzo Da Ponte and Brecht. In addition to dialogue, three choruses—two (a young adult and a children's choir) to represent the pupils, the third representing their parents—relate and comment on the action, to the point that the work has often been referred to as an oratorio. The choral narration helps establish the work's detached and objective tone.[39]

In writing an opera for and about teenagers, Copland naturally simplified his style, drastically curtailing some of the harmonic and rhythmic difficulties long his trademark. "I wished to be simple to the point of ordinariness," he remembered. Still, the work's simplicity should not be thought of as simplistic; on the contrary, subtle details of counterpoint, harmony, and color make it a delight for the listener of any age attuned to such things. Moreover, for all its leanness, the work contains a nobility and grandeur, even a grandiosity, as at the end of the first act. Copland admitted that he intended the work to be "more ambitious" than mere "Gebrauchsmusik" ("music for use"); as early as the 1932 Yaddo Festival, he dismissed fears that American music for amateur ensembles might result in a "contaminated" style like German "Gebrauchsmusik," stating, "I think that's only because the Germans write music too facilely. It wouldn't be so easy for us, and that would make the music better."[40]

The opera's opening unison motto, F-sharp–B–D–A–F-sharp–D–G, epitomizes the work's noble simplicity; at the end, it accompanies the words "All feeling free and equal." Some aspects of the music's style recall Weill, including at times a certain leanness, while the work's dramatic modulations and contrapuntal choral writing point back to older traditions, like Fauré. When Copland first heard the work put together, he even thought of the finale to Beethoven's Ninth, telling Denby, "By that I meant that it had a surprisingly big sound, and a highly dramatic one. Also, the end has something of the same 'Freude, Freude' feeling, tho in completely different terms." Denby thought an analogy to Handel even more apt.[41]

At the same time, *The Second Hurricane* has its own very American personality, vividly capturing the vernacular rhythms of everyday speech, as in the parents' chorus "What's Happened, Where Are They?," with its taunting exchanges of "Did!" and "Didn't!" Reflecting the libretto's setting—city kids in the country—the music makes contact with both urban and rural America. "Gyp's Song" epitomizes this inclusiveness; it opens with a simple duet for winds that suggests the vastness of the American landscape (looking ahead to the opening of *Billy the Kid*) and then continues with the jazzy meditation "I wish I had a car and just could drive away." The introduction sounds somewhat like Thomson, the song proper somewhat like Blitzstein. Copland's ability to evoke both composers within the confines of his own unified style helps explain his special achievement.[42]

"Gyp's Song" is the first of the opera's four solo numbers. At the top of the second act, after an eerie orchestral introduction, Fat sings about his fears ("Fat's Song") in a song whose nervous repeated notes in the accompaniment shed light on this particular Copland earmark. Later in the act, Jeff sings a short upbeat song ("Jeff's Song") about his newly discovered courage; this leads directly into the opera's best-known number, a luminous solo for Queenie ("Queenie's Song"). Denby meant the song to express "the joy of being united, which I think is the root of society," and suggested music "floating in contentment that isn't rationally crystallized," like "our kitten's purring." To Copland's concern that the lyric was weak, Denby agreed, but argued, "Anything obvious would be Social-Democratic, 'Marx is in his heaven, and dew is on the Brotherhood of Man' wish-wash." Denby's obliqueness led later observers, like Wilfrid Mellers, to overlook a key phrase like "You dream along the sky with others, too" and to think of "Queenie's Song" as one of "adolescent love," as opposed to an exhilarated expression of comradeship.[43]

The setting of the American Revolutionary song "The Capture of Burgoyne" (1777) that follows "Queenie's Song" comprises the opera's climax. Copland discovered this song about the defeat and capture of the English General Burgoyne by the "gallant" American revolutionary army in S. Foster Damon's publication of Old American Songs (1936); he made some slight changes in music and text (including changing "sweet praise to high Heaven" to "sweet praises to Freedom"), but more or less set the melody as transcribed, with interesting changes of harmony and color throughout each of its four stanzas. This marks the first use of Anglo-American folk song in Copland's work; the climactic placement and the variation treatment look ahead in particular to the use of "Simple Gifts" in Appalachian Spring and "Zion's Walls" in The Tender Land.[44]

The incorporation of "The Capture of Burgoyne" serves multiple purposes. Most obviously, it allows the six principals to sing together in their newfound solidarity; in addition, it places their experience in a militant, patriotic context, suggesting a revitalization of the ideals of the Founding Fathers, as does the appropriation of Jefferson's name for the black farm boy. This nationalist context heightens the opera's relation to the Popular Front.

Copland accepted Denby's recommendation that the young Orson Welles direct the opera's first performance. Entering into the Brechtian spirit of the piece, Welles arranged the two choruses on bleachers on either side of the stage and the orchestra on a platform at the back, the conductor all the way at the rear of the stage looking out at the audience. The action took place, center stage, without any realistic scenery and lit by boxed-in overhead lights. The Henry Street Settlement and a local high school provided the choruses; the Professional Children's School in New York cast the leads; and although they can be played by children as well, the adult parts were assumed by adults—all amateurs, with the exception of Welles's friend Joseph Cotten, who played Mr. MacLenahan (at ten dollars a performance). The twenty-piece orchestra contained freelance professionals and Henry Street teachers. Mary Lescaze found wealthy donors to help raise the $2,250 needed for three performances.[45]

A fashionable audience of artists and patrons turned out for opening night on 21 April 1937. Critics mostly received the work, widely covered in the press, as an attractive contribution to the high school repertory. Composers appreciated the work, however, in ways that the casual observer would hardly have suspected. Virgil Thomson, for instance, wrote,

> The music is vigorous and noble. The libretto is fresh and is permeated with a great sweetness. Linguistically it is the finest English libretto in some years. It has the same racy purity about common speech that I called (a little unfairly) fausse naiveté in speaking of Cocteau and that is the very special quality of Bert Brecht's German librettos. Unfortunately the show peters out before the end, the plot falling to pieces at the very moment when our anxiety is greatest about the fate of the characters.

William Schuman spoke admiringly of its "wide gamut of feeling"; calling it Copland's "most lyrical work," Paul Bowles thought it contained, too, "some of his most nervously exciting passages." Blitzstein was more cautious in his praise—*The Second Hurricane* rivaled his own *The Cradle Will Rock* (1937) among a similar audience—but he deemed it "often effective"; aspects of the work (most notably its choral commentary) arguably influenced his *Regina* as well as some stage works by Leonard Bernstein, who supervised *Hurricane*'s Boston premiere in 1942 and who, "nearly weeping with nostalgia," whiled away a sleepless evening in 1967 singing one of its choruses.

The work made friends among the English as well. "I love *The Second Hurricane*," Benjamin Britten told Copland in 1939; he immediately set out to write a children's opera of his own, *Paul Bunyan* (1941). Wilfrid Mellers also found much to admire about the piece in 1964: "Though this insistence on everyone being Free and Equal may make us world-weary Europeans squirm a bit, we have to admit that the moral naiveté is, in a sense, the opera's strength. Only an American could have created this music-drama in which young people deal with an essential human issue of our time, without any hint of religious sanction, and in the American language—which generates also an American musical vernacular."[47]

Others were less forgiving. As he told Copland, Thornton Wilder, while admiring the composer's "faultless ear for spoken rhythms," found the "awful" libretto to contain "all the worst features of the Sunday School, the Boy Scout Movement and those radio serials where Fred aged twelve helps the F.B.I. clean up a nest of counterfeiters. It sounds to me as tho Mr. Denby had not talked to a young person for thirty years." Ethan Mordden similarly thought this "witless" work to reflect "the condescending faux naïf of the leftist Popular Front of the 1930s." When Bernstein produced the opera for television in 1960 and recorded an abridged version of it for Columbia Records, he substituted his own narration for nearly all of the spoken dialogue. Neither Denby nor Copland objected; on the contrary, Denby was critical of his own libretto, writing Copland in 1939, "It is too quiet, and doesn't have enough dramatic drive to get applause. That is my fault. I see I gave the kids too many scenes all alike, sort of wandering about with nothing to do."[48]

Other problems prevented the opera from acquiring the kind of widespread success Copland had hoped for. For one thing, the typical high school could not really cope with its demands, especially in supplying singers and instrumentalists for its solo and orchestral parts. Also problematic is the somewhat stereotyped portrayal of a black child in the character of Jeff. In his 1960 production, Bernstein simply deracinated the character, purging the dialogue of its dialect. However this matter may be resolved, it should be remembered that Denby and Copland had noble and even, for the time, daring intentions in making racial equality and harmony a subtext of the work.

Prairie Journal (Music for Radio)

In 1936 the Music Division of the Columbia Broadcasting System, headed by Davidson Taylor, boldly commissioned, for national broadcast, orchestral music from six relatively young composers: Copland, Louis Gruenberg, Howard Hanson, Roy Harris, Walter Piston, and William Grant Still. (Margaret Susan Key recently revealed that Copland was not among the original six, that CBS offered him the commission only after Gershwin turned it down.) Copland was happy to accept. The commission paid $500, a rather generous fee for a relatively short work. Moreover, nearly one hundred million people listened to radio daily. "Radio," recalled Copland, "was an exciting new medium—the very idea of reaching so many people with a single performance!"[49]

He worked on this commission alternately with *The Second Hurricane* and, thanks to a two-week extension, managed to complete the score in time for a 25 July 1937 broadcast. He originally called the work *Radio Serenade*, but shortly before the premiere CBS announced that the work "had a program, or scenario, that not even its composer . . . ventured to interpret," and that for the time being he would simply call it *Music for Radio*. He and CBS further invited listeners to propose a title. Soon after the premiere, Copland selected as the work's subtitle *Saga of the Prairie*, from over a thousand suggestions. For many years, he referred to the work as *Music for Radio: Saga of the Prairie*; in 1968 he retitled it *Prairie Journal* and dedicated it to Taylor.[50]

Copland approached this radio commission not simply as an orchestral work that would be broadcast over the airwaves but as a new genre, as suggested by his working titles *Radio Serenade* and *Music for Radio*. This was most apparent in the work's scoring, with its prominent parts for vibraphone, celesta, muted trumpet, muted trombone, tenor saxophone, and solo strings, a unique coloring among Copland's work, and one that reflected popular radio practices. He further requested that some of the solos be played "subtone (at the mike)." In addition, the piece made some contact with the kinds of music typically heard on the radio at that time: swing bands, folk song, and incidental music for serials, dramas, and news reports. It absorbed the world of radio much as *Music for the Theatre* captured the spirit of Broadway. One could almost hear the crackle of static.

Even the work's form—a programmatic seven-section design with a narrative feel—seemed responsive to its radio context. The first section, A, develops a nervous motive in unison (one of Copland's most arresting openings), against which a lyrical melody for the violins—the apparent main theme—emerges. The second section, B, which he labeled "march" in his sketches, features slower, dotted rhythms. The third section, C, contains a leisurely melody for solo clarinet marked "simply, in the manner of a folk song." The "snappy" fourth section, D, alternates jazzy music with a tuneful melody for piccolo and violins. The work subsequently recapitulates B, A, and (as a coda) C to form the slightly askew arch ABCDBAC.[51]

Although CBS implied that he had a program in mind, Copland never elaborated. He went as far as selecting *Saga of the Prairie* as the winning subtitle and *Prairie Travel, Journey of the Early Pioneers*, and *American Pioneer* as runners-up. (Listeners submitted titles as varied as *The Inca's Prayer to the Sun, Journey of the British Patrol Across Arabia*, and, from one disapproving sort, *Bull Shit*, though for most people who wrote in, the music carried associations of machinery and city life.) According to Ruth Leonhardt, who came up with the winning title, "The music seemed typically American and it reminded me of the intense courage—the struggles and final triumphs—of the early settlers, the real pioneers." The term *pioneers*, also found in two of the runner-up titles, obviously struck a responsive chord with Copland, recalling his own *Young Pioneers* (1935) and the word's leftist associations. As for the "prairie" connection, Copland wrote, "I had used a cowboy tune . . . so the western titles seemed most appropriate." And though he never really liked Leonhardt's title, as he explained to Eugene Ormandy in 1958, "for the simple reason that it sounds too corny and it wasn't my idea in the first place," he kept the word *prairie* for his eventual title, *Prairie Journal.*[52]

Copland did not mention that the work used a cowboy tune until near the end of his life, though in her pioneering study, Julia Smith, pointing to the clarinet solo, mentioned a "folklike theme presented in the manner of a cowboy song." Even with access to all of Copland's sketches and papers, researchers have not been able to identify the tune, and it is quite possible that he confused his own intentions with Smith's observation. The notion that he used a cowboy tune certainly contradicts Oscar Levant's recollection—much closer to the time—that Copland was surprised that for many listeners "the piece had distinctly Western overtones." In any case, the connection between the work and the American West remains vague, to say the least.[53]

What Wayne Shirley and others have discovered is that Copland derived the work's "march" section from an unfinished choral piece from late 1936 to early 1937 based on Langston Hughes's poem "Ballad of Ozie Powell," originally published in the April 1936 edition of *American Spectator*. The poem was a tribute to Ozie Powell, one of the so-called Scottsboro Boys, nine young black men who, traveling by train, were apprehended en route to Memphis in 1931 in the small town of Scottsboro, Alabama, on a trumped-up charge of rape. Convicted and in most cases condemned to death, the Scottsboro Boys became a cause célèbre in the early 1930s, as appeal after appeal kept them alive. The American Communist Party, who considered the case as symbolic of class oppression in the South, did much of the important groundwork on behalf of the accused men, in the process attracting to their fold such black artists as Hughes and Richard Wright. Copland's own leftist involvements surely deepened his awareness of the case. When he sketched out his "Ballade of Ozzie [sic] Powell," the matter had still not been resolved and all nine men remained incarcerated.[54]

One wonders how much *Prairie Journal*'s unspoken "program" had to do with the Scottsboro case. Wayne Shirley tellingly points to the trainlike music in the work's opening section; this reading gains further credence when one considers that a later radio piece by Copland, *John Henry*, depicts a locomotive, and that whenever Copland discussed twentieth-century program music, he immediately cited Honegger's *Pacific 231*. In any case, it seems significant that *Prairie Journal*, widely considered the first of the composer's Western works, should have in its background, if not in its very genesis, a choral work about racial injustice in the rural South.[55]

In the years following *Prairie Journal*, Copland continued to speak optimistically about the future of radio. "The new radio and phonograph audience . . . is a challenge to every contemporary composer," he stated in 1940. "I visualize a music which is profound in content, simple in expression and understandable to all." About the same time, he said of this new "mass" audience, "It is not without its political implications also, for it takes its source partly from that same need to reaffirm the democratic ideal that already fills our literature and our stage. It is not a time for poignantly subjective lieder, but a time for large mass choral singing. It is the composer who must embody new communal ideals in a new communal music." In the early 1940s, at the height of such enthusiasm, he served as a commentator for a series of broadcast concerts and composed two more works for radio, *John Henry* (1940) and *Letter from Home* (1944).[56]

Prairie Journal ultimately enjoyed even less success than *The Second Hurricane*. It attracted neither the cognoscenti nor the wide public, though it was aimed specifically at the latter. Copland himself never recorded it, nor did he regret its obscurity, as he did that of the *Symphonic Ode* and *Statements*. But a brilliant recording by Leonard Slatkin and the St. Louis Symphony Orchestra (1994) revealed that the music had considerable life in it yet. At the least, *Prairie Journal* proved an important milestone; in writing for radio, Copland forged a style that in the years ahead could be adapted to ballet and film.[57]

18

From *Billy the Kid* to *John Henry*

(1938–40)

Billy the Kid

In 1933, in the midst of the Depression, Lincoln Kirstein (1907–1996), a twenty-six-year-old poet and editor, cofounded the American Ballet with his former Harvard classmate Edward M. M. Warburg. This was an extraordinarily bold venture for such a time and for such young men, but Kirstein and Warburg were bright, ambitious, and armed with social connections and personal wealth. As the pièce de résistance, Kirstein lured George Balanchine from Paris to supervise the company and its ballet school. Even after Balanchine briefly decamped for Broadway and Hollywood, the American Ballet survived not only as a training ground but, from 1935 to 1938, as an in-house company for the Metropolitan Opera and, from 1936 to 1941, as Ballet Caravan, a small touring company that featured American talent. Kirstein and Balanchine reassembled in 1946 as the Ballet Society and then in 1948 as the New York City Ballet.[1]

Kirstein was a mass of paradoxes: an intellectual of volatile moodiness, an openly bisexual married man, a Jew who converted to Roman Catholicism, a Russophile who advocated American independence in the arts, a self-proclaimed foe of modern dance who championed Martha Graham and Paul Taylor. Having fallen under Balanchine's spell in 1932, he began proselytizing on the choreographer's behalf in writings that advanced the idea of ballet as an evolving "public spectacle," one that could be traced from the courts of Italy, France, and Russia to the Ballets Russes to Balanchine. He hailed Diaghilev's innovations—the presentation of three ballets from twenty to thirty minutes long, the depiction of exotic or ancient locales from a contemporary point of view, and the integration of dance, music, drama, and art—but complained that the celebrated impresario had stressed the musical and the decorative at the expense of the choreographic. Conversely, he criticized "modern dance," as represented by Isadora Duncan and others, for overemphasizing the choreographic. Moreover, he considered the modern dancer's rejection of traditional "materia choreographica" in favor of highly personal vocabularies a grave limitation. Indeed, it was not ballet that was decadent and elitist, he argued, addressing a commonly cited Marxist concern, but modern dance, with its cult of the individual and its rejection of the popular arts. He pointed out that much as it had used mazurkas and waltzes in the past, ballet—and not modern dance—could now accommodate tap and jazz dancing. The time had come to fine-tune the Diaghilev experiment and restore choreography and dancing to their proper place; and Balanchine was the right person for the job.[2]

Kirstein further prophesied a distinctively American ballet that would adopt native settings and gestures. He already recognized just such distinctive movement in the dancing of Fred Astaire, Eleanor Powell, Ray Bolger, and other film stars. "Instead of setting a stereotype of remoteness, spectral grandeur, and visionary brilliance [as in Russian ballet]," he wrote, "the Americans are volatile, intimate, frank, and they have an added theatrical flavor of close proximity to their public." American choreographers only needed to adapt the "strong technique and intense charm" of Astaire and others and use it "in other than a fragmentary, incidental, or merely diverting way." Kirstein insisted on American citizenship for all the dancers and instructors affiliated with the American Ballet.[3]

With the short-lived Ballet Caravan, Kirstein more fully realized such ideals than at any other time in the course of his long career. Acting as a self-styled Diaghilev, he brought together young American choreographers (in particular, Lew Christensen, Eugene Loring, and Erick Hawkins), artists, and composers, and commissioned a string of one-act ballets on

American themes, including Elliott Carter's *Pocahontas* (1936), David Diamond's *Tom* (1936, not produced), Paul Bowles's *Yankee Clipper* (1937), Virgil Thomson's *Filling Station* (1937), and, climactically, Copland's *Billy the Kid* (1938). Kirstein wanted a Copland ballet from the start, but the composer had just completed one for Ruth Page in 1934 and had other commitments besides; according to Thomson, he also wanted to see some other Caravan ballets before writing his own.[4]

At one point Kirstein devised a two-act ballet, *Memorial Day* (subtitled *Dances for Democracy in Crisis*), that was to have a score by Copland for brass band, Hammond organ, and percussion (as well as optional flutes or fifes) and choreography by Christensen, Hawkins, and Loring. Set in the years between 1858 and 1865, the ballet was to depict a New England picnic, an abolitionist raid, a ball in Virginia, the Civil War, and a Memorial Day celebration; but the project never went beyond the preliminary stages.[5]

At about the same time Kirstein had the inspired idea for Copland and choreographer Eugene Loring to collaborate on a ballet based on the legend of Billy the Kid (born Henry McCarty, 1855?–1881). Early in 1938 he brusquely thrust a copy of Walter Noble Burns's *The Saga of Billy the Kid* (1925) at Loring with the command, "Here! See if you can make a ballet out of it."[6]

Born LeRoy Kerpestein in West Allis, Wisconsin (near Milwaukee), the twenty-six-year-old Loring (1911–1982) had at the time only a few years' professional dancing experience. A homosexual actor-dancer of Dutch and German heritage, he had moved to New York City in 1934 on a scholarship to study dance and choreography at the American Ballet, where he worked with Michel Fokine. In 1936 he joined the newly founded Caravan, for which, the following year, he choreographed Bowles's *Yankee Clipper*. After a falling out with Kirstein and a Broadway debut as an actor in William Saroyan's *The Beautiful People* (1941), Loring moved to Los Angeles, where he acted in *National Velvet* and *Torch Song*, choreographed such lavish film musicals as *Funny Face* and *Silk Stockings*, founded his own American School of Dance, and eventually chaired the dance department at the University of California at Irvine. He continued to create dances for universities and professional companies, but none attained the success of *Billy*, which remained his best-known achievement. A vibrant and innovative choreographer, he brought a dramatic intensity to his ballets that required a deep identification between dancer and role (not unlike the kinds of methodologies associated with the Group Theatre and such colleagues as Agnes de Mille and Martha Graham).[7]

Walter Noble Burns's best-seller *The Saga of Billy the Kid*—a mix of lore, fantasy, and historical research—was the time's premier source about the legendary desperado. As related by Burns, Billy, a gambler and cattle rustler said to have killed a man for each of his twenty-one years, began his infamous career at age twelve by shooting someone who had insulted his widowed mother. At age eighteen, his leadership of one faction of the Lincoln County War (1878), a bloody feud in southern New Mexico, brought him national notoriety. Awarded amnesty, he continued a life of crime and violence, stealing livestock and killing those who stood in his way. In the hopes of establishing law and order in New Mexico, the local settlers elected Billy's friend Pat Garrett sheriff. After an arrest and a death sentence, a manacled Billy made a remarkable escape, killing two deputy sheriffs in the process. Garrett eventually tracked him down, stumbling across him in the dark of his hideout and shooting him on the spot.[8]

Burns portrays Billy ambiguously: as a cold-blooded killer, to be sure, but also as a loyal friend, a gallant ladies' man, and a courageous daredevil. He helps Billy's case by projecting his victims in a bad light, painting a rogue's gallery of cheating gamblers, villainous henchmen, and sadistic lawmen. He also presents Billy's faction in the Lincoln County War, which in fact pitted two entrenched powers against each other, as the good guys. He quite generally depicts Billy as a friend of the people—especially among the local Mexicans—against a background of corrupt government and moneyed interests, making the occasional comparison to the likes of Robin Hood (the hero of a hugely successful Hollywood film also produced in 1938). Billy even assumes a Christlike aura as his friend Garrett betrays him amid demands for his death by angry settlers; but as if to make amends for glorifying such a common outlaw, Burns concludes by elevating Garrett to an equally heroic stature as the man who, with a single bullet, brought stability and peace to the West.

Robert Utley points out that Burns's popular *Saga* appealed to readers as a coming-of-age story twice told: as a study in the development from adolescence to manhood and from frontier wilderness to industrial society. Indeed, Billy emerges as a barely disguised symbol for America; his frontier lawlessness must be crushed by a changing world. Unlike previous books about Billy, Burns struck an interwar note of nostalgia for a lost innocence and a bygone America.[9]

Loring liked the Burns book, but he had misgivings about turning it into a ballet. For one thing, he had never been west of the Mississippi. More important, he could not imagine a cowboy ballet without guns and horses, though guns would restrict a dancer's movements, and horses, of course, were out of the question. But then, he remembered playing cowboys and Indians as a boy:

> I thought if you did it like a child playing make-believe that you had guns and horses and cards and all that—that would be a feasible way to do it. But I wasn't sure that adult audiences would take to that. So, it just happened that there were previews of a certain Wilder play named *Our Town* playing in New York City at that time. So, I went to see it and sure enough, there they were doing exactly that; they pretended they had everything and had no props really. And that gave me the courage to go ahead with it.

As with the Wilder play, which also remembers a younger America, the absence of props ultimately served the ballet's sense of a lost world.[10]

Loring's scenario called for four principals: Billy; Garrett; Billy's mother, who also takes the role of his Sweetheart; and a character, Alias, created to represent all of Billy's victims. The ballet opens and closes with a slow processional of "pioneers, men, women, Mexicans and Indians" pushing across the open prairie. "What takes place between the introduction and the coda," states the scenario, "is merely a single episode typical of many on the long westward push to the Pacific."[11]

The story proper begins on a street in a frontier town, with sauntering cowboys and dancing Mexicans. A fight breaks out between two drunken men, one of whom is Alias (as cowhand). In the ensuing melee, Alias accidentally shoots Billy's mother. After the twelve-year-old Billy kills Alias "in cold fury," Garrett protects him from the angry mob. Billy dances a solo that depicts his troubled growth to manhood. At the finish of his dance, he meets and kills Alias (as land agent).

Playing cards under a starry night, Garrett accuses Billy of cheating and walks away from him in disgust. A posse, led by Alias (as lawman), tracks down Billy and his gang. A shoot-out ensues and Billy's side loses. After Garrett arrests Billy, the settlers rejoice with a bacchanal among the fallen dead. A jailed and shackled Billy kills Alias (as jailer) and escapes.

Alias (as Indian guide) pretends to lead Billy to a safe hideout. In the desert, Billy rests with his (imaginary) Mexican Sweetheart. Alias leads Garrett to Billy's hideout. Billy lights a match and Garrett kills him.

The local Mexican women mourn his death. The frontier processional resumes.

Much of the ballet's action, mood, and form reflects Burns's *Saga*, including the frontier processional that frames the dance. Among other details, the grotesque celebration following the shoot-out—which surely symbolizes the Lincoln County War—apparently derives from Burns's own such description. But Loring further mythologizes the story. He makes Billy that much more sympathetic by having his mother not merely insulted but killed; this not only provides more solid justification for the murder of Alias but establishes a psychological motivation and context for his later crimes, further intensified by the explicit identification of Billy's mother with his Sweetheart. (In his pas de deux with the ethereal Sweetheart, Billy never so much as looks at her, which emphasizes her essential role as the remembered mother.) The ballet also turns Garrett into an ambivalent father figure; Marcia Siegel speaks of Loring's Garrett as symbolizing "the lost father who can't ever really think badly of his son but who also represents authority and morality, the community Billy has renounced." In such ways, Loring gave Burns's social parable a new psychological twist.[12]

Loring underscored this in a narrative written for a telecast of the ballet for CBS's *Omnibus* series (1953). Billy's mother and Pat Garrett now clearly represent repressive parental forces: Billy's mother disapproves of the young hussies in town and Garrett, too, is "strait-laced." Billy, for his part, sounds like a troubled juvenile delinquent, at one point saying, "But who is to say who is wrong? I've seen a lot of terrible things done around here and nobody did anything about it. All the time I was growin' up, I've seen 'em. And now, I'm the guy who is wrong. Maybe I am, but I gotta figure it out for myself." Although this narration ostensibly attempted to update the story in the light of a new postwar climate, Loring had tapped into the notion of Billy as misunderstood juvenile from the start.[13]

After persuading Loring to tackle the legend of Billy the Kid, Kirstein then had to talk him into working with Copland; Loring had not liked the score to *Hear Ye! Hear Ye!* Meanwhile, Copland had his own reservations about a cowboy ballet and needed some encouragement from Kirstein, who assured him (mistakenly) that the real-life Billy the Kid had been born in Brooklyn like himself.[14]

Copland was, in fact, particularly well equipped for the project, as Kirstein knew. He already had composed some music—notably *El Salón*

México and *Prairie Journal*—that evoked Mexico and the American West; he had portrayed life at the violent fringes of American society in *Hear Ye! Hear Ye!*; and he had created poignant musical portraitures of young people in *The Second Hurricane*. Copland, however, was hardly being coy; the fact that the ballet was set in the late nineteenth century constituted a new challenge to an artist whose work had been so largely occupied with the present.[15]

To help provide period flavor, Copland wound up using six cowboy folk tunes: "Great Grandad," "Whoopee Ti Yi Yo, Git Along Little Dogies," "The Old Chisholm Trail," "Old Paint," "The Dying Cowboy" ("Oh! bury me not on the lone prairie!"), and "Trouble for the Range Cook" ("Come wrangle yer bronco"). Neither Kirstein nor Loring insisted that he use such material, though the former offered some encouragement by supplying him with some published arrangements of cowboy songs, including, it seems, *Songs of the Open Range*, edited by Ina Sires; *The Lonesome Cowboy: Songs of the Plains and Hills,* edited by John White and George Shackley; and assorted sheet music edited by John Lomax and Oscar J. Fox. Copland consulted all these sources, relying mostly on *The Lonesome Cowboy*; but he significantly reshaped the tunes to suit his own purposes.[16]

In a note issued shortly before the ballet's premiere, Copland wrote,

I have never been particularly impressed with the musical beauties of the cowboy song as such. The words are usually delightful and the manner of singing needs no praise from me. But neither the words nor the delivery are of much use in a purely orchestral ballet score, so I was left with the tunes themselves, which I repeat, are often less than exciting. As far as I was concerned, this ballet could be written without benefit of the poverty-stricken tunes Billy himself must have known.

Nevertheless, in order to humor Mr. Kirstein, who said he didn't really care whether I used cowboy material or not, I decided to take his two little collections with me when I left for Paris in the summer of 1938. It was there that I began working on the scenario as it had been outlined for me. Perhaps there is something different about a cowboy song in Paris. But whatever the reason may have been, it wasn't very long before I found myself hopelessly involved in expanding, contracting, rearranging and superimposing cowboy tunes on the rue de Rennes in Paris.[17]

Loring provided Copland with a scenario that included a detailed breakdown of timings. He also offered more specific guidelines, suggesting a march for the opening processional, possibly in the form of a fugue; a jarabe for the opening frontier scene; and a "macabre polka" for the bacchanal. When Copland returned from Paris, he played various "musical ideas" for Loring and together they worked on shaping and arranging the whole. "We didn't always agree," remembered Loring, "but the wonderful thing about Aaron was he doesn't have the kind of ego that gets in the way. If you convince him that certain thematic material belongs somewhere else . . . he was agreeable to that." After the ballet went into rehearsal, Copland further helped by expanding and shortening material as needed.[18]

The fact that Copland cast the ballet's opening and closing processional, "The Open Prairie," for the most part in a meter of three startled Loring. "I'd always thought of a march in four or six," the choreographer explained, "and that surprised me. Whereupon he reminded me that 'My Country 'Tis of Thee' is in three." Copland makes subtle use of the triple meter, however. After the woodwinds put forth their unforgettable open harmonies, evocative not only of the prairie but, a bit later, of birdsong, the basses enter with a syncopated, two-note motive. This plodding bass, moving dramatically from pianissimo to a triple-forte climax, vividly suggests the laborious trudging of the settlers. In addition, this marching bass throws the modally ambiguous prairie music into a dark minor modality, another effective stroke. As Marcia Siegel notes, this opening processional, used again at the end of the ballet as a coda, "has the effect of transforming Billy's story . . . into a kind of parenthetical incident in the panorama of American history" just as specified by Loring, whose scenario clearly brought forth from Copland a high level of inspiration.[19]

The "Street in a Frontier Town" that follows moves headlong from nonchalant innocence to bloody violence as Billy kills his first victim. The scene divides into five sections: a humorous part that uses "Great Grandad" and "Whoopee Ti Yi Yo," the latter in particular meant to suggest ambling cowboys; a more raucous section that features "The Old Chisholm Trail"; a brief return to the humorous music; the sudden appearance of a Mexican jarabe (music appropriately distinct from Copland's portrayal of a contemporary Mexican dance hall, *El Salón México*); and, as a climax, a setting of "Old Paint," which slowly evolves from pastoral innocence to mechanistic violence, the ominous ostinato underneath neatly recalling the plodding pioneers. Here, as in other parts of the ballet, Copland's flair for evoking both bucolic calm and urban anxiety allows him to explore precisely those conflicts between frontier and industrial America implied by the Burns-Loring story. As a whole, "Street in a Frontier Town" quickly established itself as a quintessential musical portrayal of the Old West; and in the decades ahead, many composers ransacked its trove of ideas and techniques for their own Westerns.

The rest of Billy's story unfolds in short vignettes, some musically continuous, some separated by pauses, but none conclusive enough to prompt applause. A gentle though sometimes ominous development of "Old Paint" serves as a transition, after which Copland presents Billy's solo-variation, declamatory music for the brass suggestive of a harsh and primitive frontier world (including a brief and telling anticipation of *Fanfare for the Common Man*); its chromatic lines and harmonic dissonances point specifically to the troubled Billy, while a short violent tag depicts the killing of Alias. In the starlit campfire scene, "Card Game at Night" (also known as "Prairie Night"), Copland draws upon the stereotype of the lone cowboy to the point of using the song "The Dying Cowboy." Adhering closely to the version of the tune as found in *The Lonesome Cowboy*—including the use of a 12/8 meter—he reconfigures the melody using duplets for greater flexibility; the haunting setting, at once neo-baroque in its stratification of parts and impressionistic in its evocation of a quiet and desolate though somewhat expectant landscape, is entirely his own.

Copland turns a motive from the "Card Game at Night" on its head by using it as the principal motive for the "Gun Battle" that follows. This hair-raising depiction of a shoot-out alternates a violent motive for timpani, bass drum, piano, harp, and lower strings with a nervous rat-a-tat-tat figure for trumpet and snare drum. The ensuing "Celebration After Billy's Capture" acknowledges Loring's proposed "macabre polka," Copland neatly transforming the trudging bass of the opening processional into a dissonant oompah bass. After this dance, whose crude bitonality satirizes the vulgarity of the pioneers, comes the understated jail scene, in which Copland, by way of wandering figures in the woodwinds and a circling ostinato figure in the bass, creates the "placid tension" requested by Loring.

Some dramatic music with tremolos follows, depicting Alias (as Indian guide) leading Billy to his doom. The ballet relaxes into a waltz-adagio, "Waltz," for Billy and his Mexican Sweetheart, based on the tune "Trouble for the Range Cook." Although clearly cognizant of the classical pas de deux, Copland gives this "Waltz" an ironic edge by using a comical ditty as its principal theme, by scoring its solos for bassoon and trombone, and by reconfiguring the original harmonic progressions in a way that reminded Arthur Berger of Picasso's cubist paintings. The music from the previous scene returns as Alias leads Garrett to Billy. For the mourning of Billy, "Billy's Demise," Copland writes a kind of apotheosis for strings, harp, and winds that functions as an epilogue to Billy's story proper. The ballet concludes with a stirring return to the opening march for America's inexorable movement onward.[20]

Loring devised some remarkable choreography for the ballet, including some strikingly novel staging for the corps in the westward-ho march, the gunfight, and the dance macabre. As Siegel emphasizes, he innovatively incorporated such film techniques as flashback, flash-forward, slow motion, and, in general, a cinematic sense of space and narrative. He also employed such abstract gestures as the use of flat hands to portray various objects. This amalgam of pantomime and symbolic movement came in for criticism by Edwin Denby and others; according to Siegel, it confuses especially first-time viewers. Having the Sweetheart, alone of all the characters, dance on toe also proved controversial; Loring apparently intended by this means to underscore her role as an idealized dream figure. Whatever its limitations, Loring's choreography profoundly influenced the development of American ballet.[21]

The Ballet Caravan first performed *Billy* in Chicago in a two-piano version on 16 October 1938, with Loring, Lew Christensen, and Marie-Jeanne in the parts of Billy, Garrett, and the Sweetheart, and costumes by Jared French. The ballet premiered in New York, this time with orchestra, on 24 May 1939. The work was an immediate critical and popular success. On the day after the New York opening, a line four blocks long formed outside the Martin Beck Theatre for tickets. *Time* magazine noted the event with a highly favorable review. "I cannot remember another work of mine that was so unanimously well received," remembered Copland. At the very least, viewers were struck by the novelty of the ballet's conception and subject matter. Shortly before disbanding, the Ballet Caravan revived this, its greatest success, for a final time in 1941.[22]

The [American] Ballet Theatre subsequently inherited *Billy*, Michael Kidd starring in some of its earlier productions. After leaving for California, Loring supervised the work for the company as best he could, making various changes over the years. Although he had danced the part of the young Billy himself (as a boyish and short character actor—he played a jockey in *National Velvet*—he could do so effectively), he some-times cast a child dancer in the role, depending on such considerations as the venue (as in his *Omnibus* [1953] and *Dance in America* [1976] televi-sion productions) or the height of the dancer playing the grown Billy. Most other revisions concerned such matters as blocking, lighting, and whether to use or mime a prop.[23]

Informed viewers who knew the original *Billy*, like Kirstein and Edwin Denby, criticized these later productions. Loring himself took many per-formances to task, mostly for one-dimensional interpretations that failed to communicate the characters' "emotional intent." In contrast, he thought performances by the Oakland Ballet in the late 1970s outstanding in this regard. After attending a 1980 American Ballet Theatre perfor-mance in which the characters wore *Rodeo* costumes, he forced the com-pany to drop the work from their repertory, a conflict still unresolved until 1999, some seventeen years after his death. In the meantime, Loring's artistic executor, Patrice Whiteside, oversaw numerous universi-ty and professional productions, including those by the Joffrey Ballet, the Hartford Ballet, Dance Theatre of Harlem, the Louisville Ballet, Ballet West, and Danza Maggio (of Florence, Italy)—all of which have helped to establish *Billy* as the first ballet by an American choreographer to attain repertory status.[24]

In 1939 Copland extracted a twenty-minute suite from his thirty-minute ballet score. This suite comprises "The Open Prairie," "Street in a Frontier Town," "Card Game at Night," "Gun Battle," "Celebration After Billy's Capture," "Billy's Demise," and the concluding "Open Prairie." Aside from a few small cuts, these movements appear as they do in the ballet. Although the suite has been much more widely performed and recorded than the complete ballet, the latter has its own appeal, notably, the inclusion of the score's romantic highlight, the "Waltz."

Some ardent admirers of Copland's more difficult music adored *Billy*, including William Schuman and Leonard Bernstein, who adapted aspects of it for Hollywood (*On the Waterfront*) and Broadway (*West Side Story*). The ballet became, furthermore, a critical influence on the work of Lukas Foss, who arranged portions of it for solo piano. But friends like Paul Rosenfeld and David Diamond had their doubts, and higher opinion looked askance at the very idea of a cowboy ballet.[25]

Certainly *Billy* never received the critical attention it deserved. This made the score, in the opinion of Larry Starr, "an exemplary Copland work for investigation ... precisely because its 'popularity' may cause even admirers of the score to overlook its enormous subtlety of compositional technique. In fact, not only is this ballet score as sterling an illustration of Copland's basic methods as either the *Piano Variations* or *Music for the Theatre*; it also reveals these methods at a stage of greater maturity and refinement." Starr cites especially "Card Game at Night" as a brilliant example of the composer's famed technique of spinning out melodies "through repetition and accretion."[26]

The general public, meanwhile, seemed endlessly bemused by the fact that this archetypical depiction of the legendary American West should be the work of a Jewish composer from New York. To give the circumstance added piquancy, some erroneously asserted that Copland had composed the score without ever having been to the West. Less intrigued by his depictions of, say, a Mexican nightclub or a New England town, reporters repeatedly asked how, given his background, he had managed so successfully to evoke the Old West. To this Copland would say that he had traveled there, that his mother was reared in Texas and sang folk songs popular to that region, and that he grew up surrounded by books and silent films about the West. "Every American has a feeling of what the West is like—you absorb it," he explained to *Newsweek* in 1976. "It was just a feat of the imagination." He also related this achievement to "Jewish adaptability" and "the melting pot aspect of American life."[27]

An Outdoor Overture, Lark, and "We've Come"

Both in its original form for orchestra and as arranged for band, *An Outdoor Overture* is one of Copland's most popular pieces, a staple especially of the high school and college repertory, as intended. Copland interrupted work on *Billy the Kid* to write the piece in the fall of 1938 on a commission from the New York High School of Music and Art. Alexander Richter, head of the school's music department, suggested to him "a single movement between five and ten minutes in length and optimistic in tone, that would appeal to the adolescent youth of this country." Copland duly wrote a work that met these specifications—with hardly a hint of darkness to shadow its radiant optimism—and, after Richter described the music as having "an open-air quality," titled it *An Outdoor Overture*.[28]

For all its subsequent popularity—or perhaps because of it—*An Outdoor Overture*, like *Billy*, has eluded close critical attention. It took so thoughtful a musician as Elliott Carter, who reviewed its 16 December 1938 premiere, to appreciate its distinctive qualities:

Its opening is as lofty and beautiful as any passage that has been written by a contemporary. It is Copland in his "prophetic" vein, a vein which runs through all his work. . . . The rest of the overture with its changes of pace, like the *Music for Radio*, develops very naturally with lots of charm and variety. Each new work of Copland only goes further to prove that he is one of the most important, original and inspiring figures in contemporary music either here or in Europe. But it is useless to expect the critics to hail him so, for they do not bother to hear or study his works.

Leonard Bernstein championed the piece in a more professional setting. "A lot of people thought it was kid stuff and refused to play it," he remarked in 1945.[29]

As with *The Second Hurricane*, a critical appreciation of *An Outdoor Overture* rests in part on the understanding that Copland wrote it for young people, however advanced in technical abilities. It has a fresh, direct vigor unusual even by his own standards. "Youth and freedom and tireless energy are the subject matter of the Overture," observes Cecil Smith. One can imagine its composer recalling his own adolescence in New York, when classical music seemed so remote from the life around him. There is nothing remote about this piece. It expresses a joyous today and a confident tomorrow. Perhaps only someone like Copland, who related so easily and sympathetically to young people on their own terms, could write a work like this in the first place.[30]

The *Overture* has five principal elements: an introductory fanfare (Carter's "prophetic" music) stated by strings, winds, and cymbals; a theme for solo trumpet that has something of the flavor of *Prairie Journal* and *Billy*; a faster repeated-note theme, stated initially by the violins (later developed into a subsidiary, "marcato" theme); a slower, more leisurely theme for the flute (and assuming even greater leisure when stretched out by the violins); and a resolute march put forth by the violins. Copland derived the fanfare and the solo trumpet theme from a brief fanfare for small orchestra, *Signature*, completed in February 1928 for Vernon Duke's short-lived High-Low Concerts—a fanfare that seems aware of its role not only as a concert opener but as a kind of arbiter between the kinds of concert works and jazz programmed by Duke. (Duke wanted something "similar to a radio theme-song.") The first minute or so of *An Outdoor Overture* puts forth *Signature* rescored but essentially intact (Duke reports nearly falling out of his seat the first time he heard *Outdoor*

Overture); the creation of a nine-minute work from this theme music resembles Copland's subsequent use of *Fanfare for the Common Man* for the finale of his Third Symphony.[31]

An Outdoor Overture forms a kind of binary sonata, with an exposition—comprised of an introduction (fanfare), first theme (trumpet tune), transition (repeated-note music), second theme (flute melody), and closing theme (march)—that leads directly into a recapitulation. The recapitulation doubles as a development, including, remarkably enough, the juxtaposition of the flute melody with the march. This unusual binary form, in which the second half comprises both development and recapitulation, represents a characteristic response to sonata form on Copland's part; the last movement of the Violin Sonata has a similar design. The relative directness of the form fits the music's festive, straightforward tone. Both form and content help explain the choice of the word *overture* for the title, the only such in Copland's catalog.

Since 1960, Louis Lane, Maurice Abravanel, Arthur Fiedler, Gerard Schwarz, and many others, including Copland, have recorded *An Outdoor Overture*. These recordings reveal how subtly challenging the work is, how easy it is for professional conductors and orchestras to sound as if they were usurping from young people what does not belong to them. For this listener, only Copland manages a thoroughly persuasive rendering, partly by avoiding the pitfall of playing the work too fast or too solemnly. Even at age seventy, when he recorded the work with the London Symphony Orchestra, he was able to communicate the ingratiating youthfulness that characterized both his person and his music.

Lark, a gem of a piece for baritone and mixed chorus a cappella also composed in 1938, enjoyed only a fraction of the success of *An Outdoor Overture*. Copland himself had little to say about this setting of a poem by Genevieve Taggard other than that its dedicatee, Alma Wertheim, commissioned it for a chorus to which she belonged, the Dessoff Choir. He could not recall why the premiere waited until a performance with the Collegiate Chorale under Robert Shaw at the Museum of Modern Art in New York on 13 April 1943.

Described by one critic as "a socialist who connected feminism to class and race struggle and who envisioned revolutionary, not just legislative, redefinitions of the economic system, cultural values, and sex roles," Genevieve Taggard (1894–1948) was a prominent "proletarian poet" on the New York scene in the 1930s and 1940s; Sessions, Harris, Schuman, and Henry Leland Clarke set her verse as well as Copland. The author of a groundbreaking biography of Emily Dickinson (1930), Taggard may have also helped introduce Copland to that poet's life and work.[32]

Taggard published "The Lark" in *Calling Western Union* (1936), a collection containing "her most vehement social protest," according to Jennifer Rector. Taggard herself described these poems as translating "the strong anti-fascist convictions of our times into living realities, with emphasis on the struggles of labor, the sufferings of the city and country poor, and the part of the humane middle class person in the intelligent movement against reaction." "The Lark" is one of the collection's less overtly political poems, however; its imagery of a bird arising "from the great dark" to announce "the great day-rise" only alludes to Taggard's hope that America might "achieve economic democracy and by this means lay a foundation for a great culture."[33]

Copland furnishes Taggard's invocation with an incantatory quality— sometimes sweetly prayerful, sometimes almost fervently celebratory. Among other devices, he refashions the timeworn device of contrasting minor and major modes in order to help distinguish images of dark and light. The expert choral writing shows the influence of both the polyphonic English madrigalists and the antiphonal Gabrielis. The style more precisely recalls Copland's own *Four Motets* (1921), thus underscoring a spiritual urge that runs like a distinct thread through his output. And yet *Lark* has the optimism and vigor of its time; and the rise and fall of its opening line is enough like the opening of *An Outdoor Overture* and other fanfares of the period to neatly mirror the fusion of metaphysical and social concerns that inform Taggard's work.

Copland's Jewish-Palestinian folk-song setting "We've Come" ("Banu") (1938), is even more obscure than *Lark*; neither Copland nor any of his biographers even mention it. One of thirty Jewish-Palestinian folk-song settings commissioned by the Nigun Press and published in Hebrew with English translations, "We've Come" by its very essence implied a sympathy for the Zionist movement. For many years prior, the leftist intelligentsia had tended to consider Zionism a reactionary movement, but with the emergence of the national-friendly Popular Front in 1935, even the American Communist Party adopted, in a volte-face, a pro-Zionist policy. This helps explain the participation of Copland and other left-wing composers in this project, entitled *Folk Songs of the New Palestine* and edited by Hans Nathan.[34]

Darius Milhaud, Stefan Wolpe, Ernst Toch, Kurt Weill, and Arthur

Honegger were among the series' distinguished contributors. Their settings differed considerably in style, as might be expected. Copland's features crashing chords and acerbic dissonances. The "Banu" tune, a hora, itself contains vigorous syncopations and direct triadic motion; the words celebrate the release of yesterday's "poor and needy" from "distress."

Quiet City and Other Music for Theater and Radio

Like such colleagues as Marc Blitzstein and Paul Bowles, Copland wrote incidental music for some Broadway productions in the 1930s: an English version of Austrian playwright Hans Chlumberg's *Miracle at Verdun*, directed by Herbert Bierman (1931); Orson Welles's compilation of Shakespeare, *The Five Kings* (1939); and Irwin Shaw's *Quiet City*, directed by Elia Kazan (also 1939). *Miracle at Verdun* was a Theatre Guild production; *The Five Kings* was a joint undertaking by the Guild and Welles and John Houseman's Mercury Theatre; and *Quiet City* came out of the Group Theatre.

Copland wrote *Quiet City* partly in order to help out his cash-strapped friends in the Group; *Miracle at Verdun* and *The Five Kings*, on the other hand, were well enough funded to be able to tempt him with higher-than-average fees (in the case of *The Five Kings*, $1,000 plus royalties). Considering his difficult financial circumstances at the time, it might seem curious that he wrote as little incidental music as he did; he certainly could have worked on any number of plays. But given the ephemeral nature of most incidental scores, he chose not to expend his time and energy too much in this way.[35]

There were other reasons besides altruistic or financial ones to suggest his participation in these productions. All three opened to considerable public and critical interest. They also were experimental in construction, including the use of cinematic techniques. And they all had leftist political implications, *Miracle* and *Quiet City* explicitly so. These similarities do not seem coincidental; Copland naturally would have been attracted to working with accomplished and innovative artists on socially relevant projects.

The sardonic *Miracle at Verdun* (1930), completed shortly before the death of Chlumberg (1897–1930), traces the repercussions of an international brigade of dead soldiers who rise from their graves at Verdun and return home. An irritant to their wives who have remarried, to the workers who have taken their jobs, and to the powerful captains of finance and government, the resurrected veterans eventually are ordered back to their graves. The Theatre Guild production opened 16 March 1931 and closed after forty-nine performances. Although the sets by Lee Simonson and a star turn by Claude Rains earned good notices, the show essentially received bad press, Dorothy Parker declaring it "pompous, pretentious, pseudo-artistic, and stuffy." Copland's music for small orchestra included a grim funeral march for the arising dead that anticipates *Statements*, as well as quotations of Gregorian chant, the "Marseillaise," and "Morgenrot" (a German soldier's song); for the more satiric moments, he recycled some of his music from the twenties, including "An Immorality" and "Ukelele Serenade."[36]

The Five Kings, Orson Welles's ill-fated compilation of Shakespeare histories, had even less success than *Miracle at Verdun*. Welles (1915–1985), who by this time had achieved considerable fame for his radio dramatizations, intended this five-hour marathon as the first part of a two-evening "sweep of the English history plays." Copland's incidental music for voices and chamber ensemble (including a Hammond organ) drew on English and French folk songs, traditional sacred music, and Dufay and Lully in order to provide (not necessarily historically correct) period flavor. During tryouts in Boston, Washington, and Philadelphia in early 1939, the production ran into numerous problems, including a climbing debt and malfunctioning equipment; in addition, reviewers criticized the play as overlong and Burgess Meredith, who played Prince Hal to Welles's Falstaff, as miscast. The play closed before its scheduled New York premiere.[37]

Irwin Shaw's *Quiet City* deserves special attention, since Copland's music for it survived the occasion (as the play itself did not) to become one of his most beloved pieces. Known today as a best-selling novelist, Shaw (1913–1984) was a young aspiring playwright in the 1930s; he first came to public attention with a somber antiwar play, *Bury the Dead* (1936), inspired, coincidentally, by *Miracle at Verdun*. In 1939 the Group Theatre had some mild success with his fable *The Gentle People*; regarding him as a possible successor to Odets, they had high hopes for the more ambitious *Quiet City*, which opened later that year under Elia Kazan's direction. Whatever the play's weaknesses, including its problematic mix of fantasy and realism, the Group failed to give it the production it deserved, and the show closed after only a few performances.[38]

Quiet City is about a half-Jewish, middle-aged businessman, Gabriel

Mellon, who has rejected his liberal Jewish background and his youthful dream of becoming a poet, Anglicized his name, married a wealthy socialite, and assumed the presidency of a large department store. His beloved brother and alter ego, the nervous, frustrated, and unconventional David Mellinkoff, awakens his social conscience and artistic aspirations with his trumpet playing. It is Gabe—not David, as recalled by Copland in his memoirs—who imagines "the night thoughts of many different people in a great city," along with, at key moments, his brother's trumpet playing. This music represents the fear and restlessness—alternately associated with sexual repression, material deprivation, and anti-Semitic violence—felt by David and the other characters. But it also signals a militant hopefulness; though Gabe turns against his better self at the end, as the curtain falls we hear "the trumpet, wonderfully clear, wonderfully promising, wonderfully triumphant."[39]

Shaw's play obviously struck a responsive chord in Copland, for it evoked some of his most personal and poignant music. Whether or not the thirty-nine-year-old composer actually identified with Gabe Mellon's struggles, he provided such tensions with a depth and nobility that the play only hinted at. One thinks at the very least of the kind of compassion he consistently showed friends beset by similar conflicts.

In 1940 Copland fashioned *Quiet City*, originally scored for two clarinets (doubling on bass clarinet and saxophone), trumpet, and piano, into a short suite about ten minutes in length for English horn, trumpet, and string orchestra. This suite, which roughly corresponds to the work's prologue, can be read as a kind of minidrama. The slow, soft opening for strings and English horn, an urban pastoral, evokes the quiet city at night, with Copland's oft-cited telescoped harmonies, along with bass pizzicati, suggesting underlying tensions. The trumpet enters with a repeated-note recitative influenced by Jewish chant; marked "nervous, mysterious," this represents David's music, which in the play reminds Gabe of his spurned Jewish roots and prompts him to examine his life. The music proceeds to a songful, expressive melody suggestive of Gabe's nostalgia for his youthful aspirations. Then follows another lyrical section, this one, however, in a minor mode and accompanied by a restless dotted-note figure in the strings, music associated in the play with Gabe's painful relationship with his father, Israel.

A brief and strong duet for strings clears the air, introducing a dirge that moves optimistically from a mixolydian to a major mode and, finally, to a stunning recapitulation of the nostalgia theme, now full of hope. The music winds down to the opening city music and, once again, like a reminder in the night, we hear David's nervous call. Whether one considers the final pitch an unresolved dominant or a more restful tonic, the work ends on a hesitant note; like Shaw's play, the music raises more questions than it answers.

The almost total inaccessibility of Shaw's play has made it difficult for listeners and critics to assess the music's relation to it. But since its premiere by the Saidenberg Little Symphony on 28 January 1941, audiences have needed no theatrical context—except perhaps for its atmospheric title—to make it one of Copland's most popular scores. A recent Schwann Catalog lists fourteen different performances; four of these are by English ensembles, supporting Copland's contention that the piece "for some reason is particularly admired by the British." Copland's own recording seems less outstanding than many of its competitors, partly because of the solo playing; there is also something to be said for pushing through the work, as Gerard Schwarz and the New York Chamber Symphony do in their dramatic rendition, which comes in at under nine minutes. Attempting to account for the music's popularity, Copland modestly remarked, "Since it is mostly quiet, it fills a niche in concert programs." But obviously its appeal goes much deeper than that. Like Ives's *The Unanswered Question* and Barber's *Adagio for Strings*, it holds a central place among America's most introspective musical ruminations.[40]

Jerome Robbins, who had wanted to choreograph *Quiet City* for decades, finally did so for the New York City Ballet in 1986 as a tribute to Joseph Duell, a promising young dancer and choreographer who had committed suicide. The audience and critics found the ballet very touching, though Jack Anderson predicted that, as a memorial piece, it was not likely to find a permanent place in the company's repertory.[41]

In the meantime, Copland reworked some of the unused portions of *Quiet City* for other scores. The slow waltz that underscored the shared remembrances of Gabe and Johnny Piper, his old friend now homeless and unemployed, turned up in the cemetery scene for *Our Town*. He similarly expanded the edgy music depicting the Cop's attempts to disperse Gabe's discontented workers for the "Fear in the Night" sequence from *Applachian Spring*. This appropriation of music from the very urban and Jewish *Quiet City* for two landmarks of rural Americana throws an unexpected perspective on them.

In 1939, Copland composed music for a puppet show, *From Sorcery to*

Science, for the New York World's Fair. The show featured twelve-foot-high puppets designed by Remo Bufano, the esteemed Italian-born puppeteer whose work had long attracted both sophisticated and general audiences. Bufano earlier had designed puppets for League of Composers productions of Falla's *El Retablo de Maese Pedro* and Stravinsky's *Oedipus Rex,* which helps account for this collaboration with Copland, an active and prominent league member from its very inception. In addition, the commission paid Copland $850, a handsome fee for a piece that took him less than a week to write and, with the assistance of Henry Brant, orchestrate.[42]

One of a number of corporate-sponsored puppet shows featured at the World's Fair, *From Sorcery to Science* commemorated the history of pharmacy from ancient China to modern times in short vignettes described by Copland as including "a Chinese medicine man, an old witch with a head seven feet long and an eye that lit up and popped, a hawk-faced medieval alchemist, an African witch doctor, two modern scientists, a modern druggist, and a modern beautiful girl." The narration, recorded by the popular radio commentator Lowell Thomas, portrayed pharmaceutical history as rather pitiful but took an upbeat look at the contemporary American scene, presented in two parts: first, "two modern scientists" in their "modern laboratory" concocting pills and potions; then, the "modern druggist" selling his merchandise to the "modern beautiful girl."[43]

In his ten-minute score—for a large orchestra containing two pianos and an exotic percussion battery (including temple blocks, claves, sleigh bells, and sandpaper)—Copland employed pentatonic melodies for the Chinese medicine shop, accented tritones and chromatic burblings for the witch, modal harmonies and mysterious dissonances for the alchemist, congalike syncopations for the "voodoo" witch doctor, noble triads for the laboratory researchers, and a spirited, tuneful march for the modern druggist. And yet he cast such hackneyed associations in a new light. The witch doctor episode, a wonderfully festive interlude reminiscent of Chávez, stands out as particularly fetching; Copland would not again essay so unrestrained an outburst for brass and percussion until *Dance Panels* (1959). Also noteworthy is the radically diatonic final march.

From Sorcery played several times a day in the Hall of Pharmacy's Medicine Chest theater, designed by Donald Deskey to resemble a glass bathroom medicine cabinet. Puppeteers operated the enormous figures from high above the stage. Reviewing the show in *Puppetry,* puppeteers

Frank Worth and Paul McPharlin thought the production compromised by its commercial context (including displays by Gillette, Bromo-Seltzer, Listerine, and other sponsors) but admired the "technical excellence" on display; moreover, Worth, a visiting Englishman, found Copland's music "stirring" and the Bufano puppets "truly American in size."[44]

Copland considered recycling some of the score, in particular the concluding march as a work for band. He eventually gave up that idea, but not before sketching some new music that subsequently served as the opening of *Rodeo*. In 1941 the manuscript to *From Sorcery* was lost in the same theft that cost Copland two completed movements of the Piano Sonata, thus thwarting any other plans to reuse the music. Eventually, however, a detailed sketch score turned up at the New York Public Library and orchestral parts at the Library of Congress, allowing Wayne Shirley to reconstruct and edit a full score in 1996. The music relies perhaps too much on the accompanying puppetry and narration to make it an entirely satisfying concert work, though conductor Jonathan Sheffer made just such use of the piece for a 2 February 1998 tribute to the 1939 World's Fair.[45]

In the context of these occasional pieces, one might mention, too, Copland's *John Henry* (1940), commissioned for fifty dollars by Alan Lomax and CBS for a radio program geared for children, *American School of the Air: Folk-Music of America*. Part of a series of orchestral arrangements of folk songs (other contributors included Henry Brant, Ruth Crawford Seeger, Ross Lee Finney, Roy Harris, Jerome Moross, and William Grant Still), *John Henry* featured the eponymous folk song as found in Lomax's own *American Folk Songs and Ballads*. "Knowing my audience was to be a young one," explained Copland, "and that young people like their music exciting and not too long, I kept *John Henry* down to less than four minutes and called it 'a descriptive fantasy.' " In fact, the commission apparently specified this length so that the music could fit on one side of a 78 rpm disc.[46]

A familiar subject of lore and song, John Henry, a black steel driver, became the most legendary figure to emerge from America's herculean laying of railroad track from coast to coast in the second half of the nineteenth century. In the version transcribed by Lomax, he dies of exhaustion after successfully competing against a steam-powered drill; like that of Billy the Kid, the legend of John Henry touches complex feelings associated with the industrialization of the American frontier. The tune's limited number of pitches (only four in the Lomax transcription), its syncopations, and its interjections of "uh-huh and "oh, yeah" bespeak its African-American origins; Lomax and others consider it a "blues ballad." At the same time, its driving rhythms suggest the influence of the sounds of trains. By the turn of the twentieth century, the song had become popular in many guises, both vocal and instrumental. As sung by Josh White in the 1930s and as dramatized by Roark Bradford in a production starring Paul Robeson (1940), "John Henry" became especially associated with the Popular Front.[47]

Copland's *John Henry* states the tune six times, although with some melodic variation, as one might find in an actual folk-song performance. (Only the third and fifth statements match Lomax's transcription.) The composer ingeniously shapes these six strophes into a little tone poem—or "descriptive fantasy," as he calls it—that depicts a train trip à la Honegger's *Pacific 231*, a work he very much admired. Copland even appropriates some of Honegger's strategies in his own portrayal of the released throttle, the crunch of wheels, the acceleration to full speed, and the braking halt. All the while, he establishes a distinctively American ambience, thanks in part to the picturesque scoring, which includes anvil, sandpaper blocks, and train whistle. The final statement of the melody functions as a somewhat uneasy coda, complete with hard dissonance, suggesting, like the conclusion of *Billy the Kid*, the human tragedy involved in America's expansion westward. In 1952 Copland reorchestrated a slightly shortened *John Henry* for full orchestra.

19

Music for the Movies and
for Keyboard
(1939–41)

Music for the Movies

In 1937 Copland set his sights on Hollywood. The motion-picture industry had recently begun producing some sophisticated film scores by formally trained composers, notably (as far as Copland was concerned) Ernst Toch's *Peter Ibbetson* (1935), Erich Wolfgang Korngold's *Anthony Adverse* (1936), Werner Janssen's *The General Died at Dawn* (1936), and George Antheil's *The Plainsman* (1937). "Hollywood has in several instances called on outstanding American composers to provide music for its output," reported the *New York Times* in late 1936. "The trend toward inviting men of serious purpose has been developing steadily." Copland read with interest about such developments—including rumors that Paramount was negotiating with Shostakovich and had engaged Schoenberg and Stravinsky—in Antheil's "On the Hollywood Front" column for *Modern Music*. Hollywood, which had seemed so remote to serious composers, suddenly beckoned with the promise of high visibility (motion pictures drew over eighty million people each week), rising artistic standards, and substantial financial rewards.[1]

Moreover, some of Copland's theater friends—including Odets, Clurman, and Kazan—were already out in Hollywood working for the major studios. Upon arriving in Hollywood in 1937, Clurman immediately met with music department executives Alfred Newman (at Twentieth Century Pictures) and Boris Morros and Nat Finston (both at Paramount) on Copland's behalf; Morros and Finston, he afterward wrote Copland, were "political hockers—and the atmosphere they give off is not fragrant. (But I'm afraid that is 95% of Hollywood.)" On Clurman's advice, Copland, en route from New York to Mexico, spent June 1937 in Hollywood in order to follow up possible leads. While there, he socialized with old friends and acquaintances, chanced into James Cagney and Harpo Marx at the Brown Derby, and interviewed with Morros—the executive most associated with Hollywood's current flirtation with concert composers—at Paramount.[2]

Copland had high hopes—"It is just a matter of finding a feature film that needs my kind of music," he confidently told Chávez before leaving New York—but nothing panned out; the studios were reluctant to hire a composer without film experience. "Hollywood is not nearly as composer-conscious as Antheil's articles would make one think," Copland wrote Victor Kraft. On the contrary, he found the level of musical taste low if not corrupt, with cowed composers producing banal scores for unsophisticated producers and directors. Moreover, working conditions were far from ideal; not only did composers have to work at a very fast pace, but the studios edited and dubbed their scores as they saw fit, without much regard for the composer's intentions. Antheil himself reported in late 1937, "Hollywood, after a grand splurge with new composers and new ideas, has settled back into its old grind of producing easy and sure-fire scores. . . . Meanwhile many excellent composers have come out to Hollywood and returned East again. Scarcely any of them have gotten jobs. . . . In other words Hollywood music is, at the present writing, a closed corporation."[3]

Undeterred, Copland persevered in his ambition to score a feature film. Not only could he use the money, but he hoped through film to enlarge both his audience and his capacities. The challenge of this new medium also attracted him, as composing for radio had and television would. The need for a film credit became, in any case, a factor in his decision to score the documentary *The City* (1939).

Sponsored by the Carnegie Corporation at a cost of $50,000, this forty-five-minute documentary was a high-profile, high-tone affair. Based on an idea by Pare Lorentz, it featured direction and cinematography by filmmaker-photographers Ralph Steiner and Willard Van Dyke, a scenario by Henwar Rodakiewicz, commentary by city planner Lewis Mumford narrated by Morris Carnovsky, and music by Copland—all accomplished, serious artists and thinkers. Both Steiner and Van Dyke had had a hand in the Pare Lorentz documentaries scored by Virgil Thomson: *The Plow That Broke the Plains* (1936) and *The River* (1937). Now they were collaborating on their own. *The City* premiered with considerable fanfare on 26 May 1939 at the New York World's Fair, where it played daily for the fair's duration. It quickly established itself as a classic of its kind, probably the most celebrated of all of Van Dyke's distinguished documentaries.[4]

The City embodies some of the ideals and attitudes characteristic of that New York intelligentsia of which Copland was the dominant musical figure. Propagandizing a progressive, humanistic, and essentially socialist approach to city planning, the film portrays, in visually striking and unusually realistic cinematic terms, four different types of American society: an old New England village, an industrial factory town and its slums, a metropolitan center, and a "new city" of the sort built by the Resettlement Administration in the late 1930s (the so-called Greenbelt towns). The New England village is idealized, with children frolicking, women at the loom, men at their farming tasks; one can hardly imagine a more pointed rendering of the period's slogan "Communism Is Twentieth Century Americanism" than its images of New England farmers with scythes and blacksmiths with hammers. The second section portrays the mighty furnaces and factories of an industrial coal town along with the squalid shacks, undernourished children, and environmental mayhem in their shadows. "Who built this place?" the narrator asks. "What put us here? And how do we get out again? We're asking, just asking."

The third episode depicts a day in the life of a large American city; frenetic, congested, violent, and grotesque, this section concludes with a satirical look at a herd of motorists fleeing the city for some elusive relaxation. The concluding sequence delineates a "better kind of city," one imagined to be between one and two hundred thousand people, with modest, semiattached homes close to parks, schools, factories, shops, theaters, medical clinics, and highways that take one to public swimming pools, golf courses, and skating rinks. The prevailing architectural style is Bauhaus; the medical treatments, preventative; the streets, clean. No church steeple dominates the townscape as with the New England village, but the film makes the point that the "new city" represents a translation of old village life into modern industrial terms. "This is no suburb where

The Copland family, 1899. Top row (from left): Aaron's uncle Abe Copeland, his uncle and aunt Harris and Sadie (Copland) Uris, and his uncle Alfred Copland; center row (from left): his aunt and uncle Becky (Copland) and Hyman Abrams, his grandmother Frieda Kaplan, his brother Leon, his father (Harris), his mother (Sarah), and his brother Ralph; bottom row (from left): his cousin Elsie Abrams, and his sisters Laurine and Josephine.

Copland as a boy, 1906.

Rubin Goldmark in his studio. The
inscription, dated 3 June 1921, reads,
"To my very good pupil, Aaron Copland,
with best wishes, Rubin Goldmark."

Nadia Boulanger at home, 1922.

At Nadia Boulanger's home, 1925
(from left): Virgil Thomson, Walter
Piston, Herbert Elwell, and Copland.

Harold Clurman, c. 1933.

Copland, 1933 (photograph © Ralph Steiner, Ralph Steiner Estate).

Copland, 1935
(photograph by Carl Van Vechten.
Reproduced by permission of the Van
Vechten Estate, Bruce Kellner, Trustee).

Victor Kraft, 1935
(photograph by Carl Van Vechten.
Reproduced by permission of the Van
Vechten Estate, Bruce Kellner, Trustee).

Copland in Mexico, c. 1936.

Of Mice and Men (1939), directed by Lewis Milestone (clockwise from left): Candy (Roman Bohnen), Carlson (Granville Bates), Whit (Noah Beery, Jr.), Slim (Charles Bickford), and George (Burgess Meredith), in the bunkhouse.

At Virgil Thomson's apartment at the Chelsea Hotel, New York, 1950 (from left): Samuel Barber, Thomson, Copland, Gian Carlo Menotti, and William Schuman (photograph by John Stewart).

Ballet Theater, c. 1941, rehearsing *Billy the Kid* (1938).

Agnes de Mille as the
Cowgirl in *Rodeo* (1942).

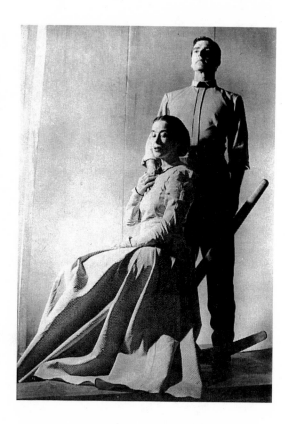

Martha Graham (as the Bride) and Erick Hawkins (as the Husbandman) in the 30 October 1944 premiere performance of *Appalachian Spring* (photograph by Arnold Eagle).

First page of Copland's condensed score to the as yet untitled *Appalachian Spring* (1943–44) (Copyright © 1945, 1958 by the Aaron Copland Fund for Music, Inc. Copyright Renewed. Reprinted by permission of Boosey & Hawkes, Inc., Sole Licensee.)

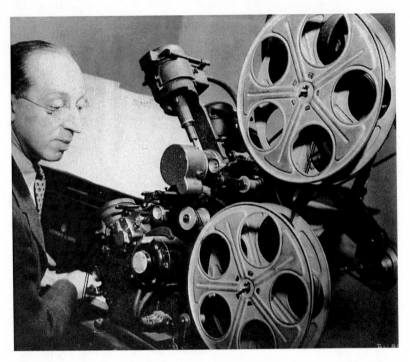

Copland, 1948, working on the film score for *The Heiress*.

The Red Pony (1949), directed by Lewis Milestone: Tom (Peter Miles) shows his new pony, Gabilan, to his schoolmates.

The Heiress (1949), directed by William Wyler: Montgomery Clift (as Morris Townsend) and Olivia de Havilland (as Catherine Sloper) exchange glances.

At Copland's home at Sneden's Landing, New York, 1949 (from left): Leon Kirchner, Copland, Gerhard Samuel, Israel Citkowitz, Donald Fuller, David Diamond, Arthur Berger, Elliott Carter, and Jerome Moross.

Serge Koussevitzky, c. 1950
(photograph by Victor Kraft,
courtesy Rheba Kraft).

Erik Johns, 1951
(photograph by Victor Kraft,
courtesy Rheba Kraft).

Copland composing, 1951 (photograph by Victor Kraft, courtesy Rheba Kraft).

Jerome Robbins's ballet *The Pied Piper* (1951), performed by the New York City Ballet.

Original production of *The Tender Land* by the New York City Opera at City Center, New York, 1954: "Dangerous thing, imagination can be," Mr. Splinters (Michael Pollock) tells Ma Moss (Jean Handzlik) (photograph by Gus Manos).

In Cannes, 1955 (from left): Gian Carlo Menotti, Thomas Schippers, Francis Poulenc, Copland, and John Brodbin Kennedy. Poulenc's inscription, dated August 1955, reads, " 'Avec génies réunis!!!' Avec toute mon amitié, cher Copland."

At the Second Latin American Contemporary Festival, Caracas, Venezuela, 1957 (from left): Domingo Santa Cruz, Alberto Ginastera, Copland, Carlos Chávez, and Juan Batista Plaza.

William Warfield, baritone, the Detroit Symphony Orchestra, and Copland, 1961, performing *Old American Songs* (photograph by Lare Wardrop, courtesy Detroit Symphony Orchestra).

Adlai Stevenson, narrator, the Lewisohn Stadium Symphony Orchestra, and Copland, New York City, 12 July 1964, rehearsing *Lincoln Portrait* (photograph by Marc and Evelyne Bernheim).

At Symphony Hall, Boston, November 1959 (from left): music critic Boris Yarustovsky, composer Dmitry Shostakovich, composer Dmitry Kabalevsky, conductor Charles Munch, composer Tikhon Khrennikov, composer Konstantin Dankevish, Copland, and composer Fikret Amirov.

Alexander Calder,
La grande Vitesse (1969).

"LA GRANDE VITESSE"

Benny Goodman, clarinet, the Los Angeles Philharmonic, and Copland, Los Angeles, 1976, rehearsing the Clarinet Concerto (photograph by David Weiss, courtesy David Weiss).

Copland and Leonard
Bernstein, c. 1980
(photograph by Walter
H. Scott, courtesy
Walter H. Scott).

Phillip Ramey, Copland, and Bennett Lerner, New York, 1985
(photograph by Susanne Faulkner, courtesy Lincoln Center).

the lucky people play at living in the country," intones the narrator. "This kind of city spells cooperation."

Although the film's strong utopian strain fit the tenor of the 1939 World's Fair and its theme, "The World of Tomorrow," some sensitive viewers like Edward Weston, who loved the film, including the music, had ambiguous feelings about the "new city." "Perhaps the artist can only want Utopia for others," he wrote to Van Dyke (who explained that he and Steiner wanted a shorter ending, but that the city planners they had collaborated with "said that that part was what they had made the picture for, that we had had our fun with the first part, and they were going to do the ending as they wanted it"). In any case, the filmmakers had noble motives. They believed that many Americans would welcome an opportunity to live in the "new city" or some place like it, and developments proved them right—although they imagined something more integrated and communal than the suburban sprawl of the postwar period. At the least, the principles espoused by the film—decent housing, good medical care, and a healthy environment for all citizens—remained central tenets of the political left.[5]

Copland, who spoke well of the film's "human intimacy," composed music for nearly all of its forty-five minutes, thus producing a score of about the same length as most of his later feature films. The music effectively matches the film's changing moods and locales: pastoral and quietly dignified for the New England village, harsh and desolate for the industrial wasteland and its slums, busy and frenetic for the bustling downtown, ironically jaunty for the Sunday getaway, and joyfully idyllic for the "new city." The Sunday outing music is a close if more sardonic cousin to the finale of *From Sorcery to Science*, while the "new city" music derives from the innocent "Dove Dance" from *Hear Ye! Hear Ye!* More distinctive and memorable is the haunting melody that accompanies the poor children of the mill town and the inner city.[6]

Copland obviously regarded his music for the New England village and the Sunday outing as of special intrinsic interest, for he excerpted these as "New England Countryside" and "Sunday Traffic" for his suite *Music for Movies* (1942). However, the score in its entirety contained many ingenious subtleties and picturesque touches, and rightly won wide critical acclaim, including a review in the *New Yorker* that praised not only its "bitter," "clangy," and "jocular" moments but its "pensive quality" and "optimism." The music earned as well the deep thanks of Van Dyke himself.[7]

The City opened up the doors to Hollywood. After viewing it at the home of a friend, producer-director Lewis Milestone resolved to hire Copland for his film adaptation of John Steinbeck's *Of Mice and Men* (1939), co-produced with Hal Roach of United Artists. Copland accepted Milestone's $5,000 offer—but only after rereading the Steinbeck novella. He flew out to Hollywood in October 1939 to quickly view and score the movie.[8]

Copland would compose three of his five Hollywood film scores for Lewis Milestone (1895–1980). Born in Odessa (as Milstein) and raised in Kishinev, Milestone immigrated to the States in 1913, moved to Hollywood in 1919, and emerged as a leading film director in the late 1920s. Although he directed comedies and musicals, he was especially admired for his gritty, often violently realistic dramas and war movies. Unusually sensitive about the use of sound in his films (his cousin was the violinist Nathan Milstein), in *The General Died at Dawn* (1936, screenplay by Odets), Milestone featured a pioneering Werner Janssen score that helped introduce Hollywood to more contemporary musical styles. Whether or not his strong revulsion toward McCarthyism diminished his artistic abilities in later years, as is widely believed, critics agree that *Of Mice and Men*, along with the earlier *All Quiet on the Western Front* (1930), represent his greatest achievements. Copland thought him "a classy and intelligent director."[9]

After screening *Of Mice and Men*, Copland immediately realized how fortunate he was to be making his Hollywood debut with this film. Milestone had skillfully adapted John Steinbeck's poignant 1937 novella, which already had had considerable success on Broadway as adapted by Steinbeck himself. The superb cast included Burgess Meredith as George, Lon Chaney, Jr., as Lennie, Betty Field as Mae, and Roman Bohnen as Candy. "They were directed with rare insight into the characterizations," recalled Copland. "Here was an American theme, by a great American writer, demanding appropriate music." Both the movie and its musical score would be nominated by the Motion Picture Academy as one of the best of 1939, a banner year for Hollywood.[10]

Moreover, Copland's working conditions were better than for most film composers. Roach and Milestone respected his integrity and abilities and avoided interfering with his work, a precious rarity then as now. They also gave him six weeks to compose the score, longer than the usual three or four. In addition, they refrained from cutting any of the music; Milestone actually added four seconds of film (when the barley wagons return at dinnertime) at Copland's request. After he completed the score, experienced studio musicians recorded it under Irving Talbot's expert direction. The only real disappointment for Copland was having to watch helplessly as the sound editor dubbed the score, adjusting the volume as he saw fit, sometimes to the point of oblivion. "I made some mild objections," remembered Copland, "but I was asked, 'Haven't you heard of the union?'"[11]

Unlike most film composers, Copland insisted on supervising the orchestration himself, arguing that Hollywood's orchestrators tended to make every film sound alike. Since he did not have the time to prepare a full orchestral score, he wrote out his condensed sketch in as many as four staves, indicating the scoring in shorthand to Talbot and other assistants. These indications could be as specific as the precise scoring of a single four-note chord for flute, clarinet, oboe, two trumpets, and trombone. He also provided extensive dynamic, slur, and attack markings, including such special techniques as "sul ponticello" and "slap tongue." When once challenged about his use of staff orchestrators for his Hollywood films, Copland retorted, "Look at this and answer me the following: If I dictate a letter and it is typed for me, who actually wrote the letter, me or my secretary?"[12]

The film *Of Mice and Men* tells the story of George Milton and his dim-witted but powerful companion Lennie Small, migrant ranch hands who have been friends since childhood and who dream of owning a ranch of their own. Forced to leave town because of one of Lennie's misadventures, they find work on a ranch run by the despotic Jackson, his weak and vicious son Curley, and Curley's neglected and shrewish wife, Mae (a household strikingly reminiscent of Shostakovich's *Lady Macbeth of Mtsensk*). George and Lennie befriend the other ranch hands, including Slim and the aging Candy, who has lost a hand to a thresher and who, in the course of the story, reluctantly lets another ranch hand, Carlson, shoot his mangy old dog. When Curley picks on Lennie, George encourages his impassive friend to fight back; Lennie breaks Curley's hand, but the threat of further humiliation prevents Curley from firing George and Lennie. Angry and frustrated, Curley orders Mae off the ranch; on leaving, she flirts with Lennie, who panics and strangles her. In order to prevent a lynching, George tracks Lennie down and shoots him himself.

Copland composed about ten musical cues spread out over the course of the movie. Most of these episodes contain two or three minutes of music, heard at intervals of about five minutes or more, though a few of these cues are more extended. Such restrained use of music for a big dramatic film like this departed somewhat from the time's norm. "Personally, I like to make use of music's power sparingly, saving it for absolutely essential points," Copland once stated. "A composer knows how to play with silences, knows that to take music out can at times be more effective than any use of it might be." The shooting of Candy's dog offers just such an example. Even when Carlson impatiently asks, "What do you say, Candy?" and Candy looks pathetically from ranch hand to ranch hand for a full twelve seconds, Copland refrains from adding music; only after Slim says, "Candy, you better let him go" does the poignant music steal in. In another example, this one from *Our Town* (1940), Copland waits until George and Emily have haltingly confessed their love at the soda fountain before sweeping in with Emily's love music.[13]

In another deviation from standard practice, Copland only slightly adjusted his already established style, one that contrasted with the lushly post-Romantic film scores of the day. "To some in Hollywood," he recalled, "my music was strange, lean, and dissonant; to others it spoke with a new incisiveness and clarity." The music's strong American flavor posited yet another distinguishing feature. Only certain sections of the score, however, could be described as folklike; rather, Copland focused on the drama's more contemporary aspects, seeing it as a stark Depression tale set in contemporary California, complete with trains and threshing machines. The few dubbed moments of so-called source music—the hobo's mouth harp in the opening credits, a bit of solo guitar, a little jazz blaring from Mae's radio, some music heard at the saloon, and an unaccompanied fragment of a hymn—only highlight the distance between Copland's score proper and more popular styles.[14]

Copland decided in advance that he would not use the leitmotiv method in which each character has his or her own theme. Nonetheless, he used certain key ideas to help shape and enhance the drama. Principally, these include a romantic melody associated with the dream ranch (first heard in the woods as George and Lennie turn in for the night), an earthy motive associated with Candy and the ranch hands (first heard when Candy takes George and Lennie to the bunkhouse), satiric music for the bosses (first heard at the threshing scene), and a death theme (first heard at Mae's death and later at Lennie's). Copland effectively interweaves and develops this material; in the dinner scene with the Jacksons, for example, he distorts a motive from the dream music to suggest a perverse connection between the aspirations of, on the one hand, George and Lennie and, on the other, Mae, who dreams of Hollywood and its glamour, a connection made explicit later in the story as Mae and Lennie alternately vent their hopes to each other. By such means Copland intensified the political subtext of Steinbeck's drama.[15]

Although he similarly chose not to underline all the action in an obvious way—the kind of "mickey-mousing" he objected to in the scores of Max Steiner and others—he showed rare attentiveness to nuances in the film narrative. Whereas most Hollywood composers of the time composed their scores largely from a time-breakdown cue sheet, he used a Moviola, a device that allowed a precise coordination of image and music. Taking full advantage of the instrument, he deftly phrased the drama in ways rarely encountered in a film score (even today, when videotape players have facilitated such synchronization). His subtle approach involved only slightly inflecting the score so as neither to engulf the film (as often happens, say, with Korngold) nor to disrupt the music's continuity (as occurs in most film scores, making it problematic to excerpt such music for concert purposes). For example, the walk to the bunkhouse inconspicuously darkens at the mention of the boss; the threshing sequence subtly brightens as Mae flirtatiously approaches George and Lennie; and the ranch music turns slightly chromatic when the ranch hands look ominously at Candy's dog. At the same time, Copland eschewed—for the time being—any use of the mechanically precise click track; he provided cues exclusively in seconds and in words.[16]

A few cues warrant special attention. In the killing of Candy's dog, Copland juxtaposes a dirge with high repeated notes, thereby vividly denoting the scene's poignance along with its tension. Dinner with the Jacksons is a masterfully shaped comic vignette. And the fight between Curley and Lennie contains, along with some other modernist features, a dissonant chord accompanied by a trill, held for close to twenty seconds as Lennie crushes Curley's hand. One doubts that Hollywood had ever heard anything like it before.

Copland's music earned him not only two Academy Award nominations (for best score and original score) but good notices by Paul Bowles and others in the pages of *Modern Music* and elsewhere. Virgil Thomson thought that, along with *Billy*, *Of Mice and Men* established "the most distinguished populist music style yet created in America." Some friends feared that Copland would now make Hollywood his home, but he had no intention of even primarily devoting himself to motion pictures. He had scored the film partly to see if he could rise to the challenge, partly to reach Hollywood's global audience, and partly to make enough money to sustain other projects and ambitions. Over the next ten years, even as he worked on another four Hollywood films, Manhattan remained his home base.[17]

He quickly returned to Hollywood in the spring of 1940, however, in order to score the screen adaptation of Thornton Wilder's *Our Town*, produced by Sol Lesser (also through United Artists) and directed by Sam Wood. He had seen and admired the play during its successful Broadway run in 1938. Further, he felt the allure of working on a movie so unlike *Of Mice and Men*; it offered, he wrote, "the perfect vehicle for putting to the test opinions I had voiced in the press—that film music should follow the organic structure of a story, and that the music must be appropriate to the nature of that story."[18]

Set in the small New England town of Grover's Corners at the turn of the century, *Our Town* attempts to show, in Wilder's words, "the life of a village against the life of the stars." The play opens in 1901 with a day in the life of two next-door households: Dr. and Mrs. Gibbs and their children, George and Rebecca; and Editor and Mrs. Webb and their children, Emily and Wally. George and Emily (played in the film by William Holden and Martha Scott), both in high school and still a bit callow, are falling in love with each other. The action proceeds to the marriage of George and Emily (1904) and a reminiscence of their courtship. The story jumps again, to 1913. Emily dies and is buried in the local cemetery, where she joins Mrs. Gibbs; her brother, Wally; and others since deceased. Emily's spirit goes back in time in order to observe her former life, but finding the routines of family life unbearably poignant, she rejoins the dead (or as devised by Lesser and sanctioned by Wilder for the film version, she awakens from a hallucination during childbirth).[19]

Given Copland's reputation as a modernist composer, Lesser was hesitant about hiring him; but when he expressed his reservations to Wilder, the playwright countered, "the non-sentimental tartness they [modernist composers] inject would be on the safer side." Still, Copland remained Wilder's third choice, after Thomson and Antheil, unless Lesser could "think of someone who might be simpler still." After he finally was hired, Copland met with Wilder in New Haven, the latter proposing appropriate hymn tunes for his consideration. "As usual," explained Wilder to Lesser, "I was shy of expressing much suggestion—believing always that such distinguished artists must have the rope to do things their own way. However, before we got through we had agreed on many things. He's a very likeable fella." Copland surely assured Wilder that, from his frequent stays at the MacDowell Colony, he well knew Peterborough, New Hampshire, the town upon which Grover's Corners was modeled.[20]

Wilder's trust was well rewarded. Whereas most Hollywood composers would have sentimentalized the film, Copland—assisted by his friend Jerome Moross, who helped prepare the orchestrations—created a masterpiece of understatement. Primarily writing slow, soft, consonant music for a reduced orchestra of strings, harp, and woodwinds, he avoided not only the full orchestral sound of the typical Hollywood film of the day but the bold contrasts found in many other of his own works. The smaller forces and high percentage of slow music allowed him and Moross to complete the score in a fast four weeks. "The usual impeccable Copland taste and high musical integrity are of course everpresent," observed Paul Bowles in a review, "although the music turns out to be practically unnoticeable."[21]

Within its prescribed limitations, however, the score contains considerable variety. As in *Of Mice and Men*, Copland juggles distinctive themes throughout, including those associated with the main title, Grover's Corners, the children, Emily in love, Cemetery Hill, and Emily's dream. And although simple triads and quintal harmonies characterize the entire score, Copland distinguishes these principal ideas through contrasting modal inflections. The C-major title music, for instance, features luminous triads with flats, capturing the play's "life of the stars" aspect; the Grover's Corners music, embroidering the familiar plagal or "Amen" cadence, contains a raised fourth, as in the lydian mode; the music for the children and Emily's beautiful love theme are more thoroughly diatonic; the Cemetery Hill cue mixes major and minor modes, while Emily's funeral march is more clearly in minor; and during Emily's anguished dream ("Oh, mama, just look at me one minute") augmented triads come to the fore, making a strong impact in the context of the score's harmonic restraint.[22]

In addition, Copland dramatically develops certain of these themes, especially Emily's love theme, heard first as she examines herself in the mirror. (For this initial statement, he strikingly suggests her ardor by alternating measures of 4/4 time with quadruplets in 3/4 time.) Later, as she leans out of her window at night, the theme reappears, languidly augmented and accompanied by harps; by this means, we realize that she is thinking about George—a timeworn technique, to be sure, but handled here with a touching delicacy. Copland uses this love theme on a number of later occasions as well, all of which have their own distinct stamp.

As with *Of Mice and Men*, Copland composed source music—hymns for the church choir and wedding music for the organist—but avoided using any folk tunes for the score proper. However, he discreetly wove into the music's larger fabric the final phrase of that nineteenth-century chestnut "Home, Sweet Home" (music by Henry Bishop, lyrics by John Howard Payne). The phrase—amazingly divested of its traditional bathos—first appears, appropriately enough, at the screenplay's mention of "Mrs. Gibbs coming down to get breakfast." It remains somewhat associated with Mrs. Gibbs, appearing, ethereally transformed, when she speaks in the cemetery scene. This allusion suits the dramatic material, which Harold Clurman once called "as unpretentious as, but even more effective than, *Home Sweet Home*." It also helps point up the play's universality; Copland grew up literally blocks away from Prospect Park's statue of Payne.[23]

The opening title of *Our Town* betokened Copland's growing stature in Hollywood; no longer relegated to the bottom of a long list of end credits, as in *Of Mice and Men*, his name received top billing, right after Wilder's. And again, the Motion Picture Academy nominated him for two Oscars. Written off by the studios barely two years earlier, Copland had spent a mere three months in Hollywood and walked away with four Academy Award nominations. Such acclaim not only consolidated his clout among film people but helped promote his name before the general public.[24]

Copland immediately arranged *Our Town* as a ten-minute, single-movement suite for orchestra (1940; revised in 1944 for the Boston Pops and Leonard Bernstein, to whom the work is dedicated), comparing the piece to Grieg's *Peer Gynt* and other concert works derived from incidental scores. The suite comprises the music for Grover's Corners, Cemetery Hill, the opening title, and a brief reprise of the Grover's Corners music. In 1944 he also arranged a short three-movement suite for piano: the first movement contains the Grover's Corners music, the second movement features Emily's love music (at the point when she scolds George on their way home from school), and the final movement contains music for Cemetery Hill and, near the end, the opening title. The presence of Emily's love music makes the piano suite the more inclusive of the two suites, though neither contains the lighthearted music for the children or the moving passage for the anguished Emily (which Copland arranged as *Episode* for organ). Both orchestra and piano suites—the latter championed by Leo Smit and Andor Foldes—enjoyed considerable success, eventually giving rise to a well-received ballet by Philip Jerry.[25]

Copland had less luck with the more ambitious five-movement suite for small orchestra *Music for Movies* (1942), derived from his three film scores to date: "New England Countryside" from *The City*, "Barley Wagons" from *Of Mice and Men*, "Sunday Traffic" from *The City*, "Grover's Corners" from *Our Town*, and "Threshing Machines" from *Of Mice and Men* (this last movement concluding with the film's opening title). "It struck me that a suite might successfully mirror in musical terms the wide range of American scenes in the three films for which I had written music," explained Copland. But he may have miscalculated in hoping to shape music from three diverse film scores into a satisfactory whole. Copland dedicated the score to Darius Milhaud, whose own film music encouraged and inspired him.[26]

While Alfred Cochran and others have begun studying Copland's early film scores, the question of their effect on the American motion-picture industry awaits investigation. Most musicians, such as André Previn, thought sooner of the influence of Copland's Western ballets, especially on the Hollywood Western. Film composer David Raksin—unlike Previn, someone on the scene in the late 1930s—likewise acknowledged Copland's importance to the Western, but singled out *Of Mice and Men* in this regard: "Not only was the score wonderful," he once told Copland, "you began something with that from which none of us have ever escaped: you created a definite style having to do with the Western film. Before that they used to think they were doing all right if they played 'Bury Me Not on the Lone Prairie.' And then all of a sudden we were face to face with this absolutely clear and pure and wonderful style." Whatever the particular source, *Of Mice and Men* or some other work, Copland clearly had a major impact on the Western, at least as represented by Jerome Moross's *The Big Country* and Elmer Bernstein's *The Magnificent Seven*.[27]

But Copland's early film scores offered Hollywood composers a model for authentic depictions of the American scene in general—city and country, past and present. Even more important, they established higher, more sophisticated standards. Hugo Friedhofer quickly profited from his example, notably in the film score to *The Best Years of Our Lives* (1946), which earned him an Oscar. "His influence helped me weed out the run-of-the-mill schmaltz," recalled Friedhofer, "and aim to do more straightforward and simple, even folklike scoring." At the very least, Copland's scores were ahead of their time and helped pave the way for such film composers as Bernard Herrmann, Alex North, Leonard Rosenman, and Leonard Bernstein.[28]

Copland on Film Music

After *Of Mice and Men* and *Our Town*, Copland began writing about the art of film music for *Modern Music*, the *New York Times*, and other publications; he also lectured on the subject, leaving behind notes that amplify these essays.[29]

Copland found the very nature of movie music somewhat contradictory. On the one hand, a good film score, he opined, did not draw attention to itself but rather had to be "secondary in importance to the story being told on the screen"; otherwise, one chanced losing the "narrative illusion." On the other hand, music played a pivotal role in most motion pictures. "To anyone who does not believe that the addition of music heightens the emotional impact and dramatic interest of a motion picture I suggest a visit to a studio projection room when a film is being shown before its score has been dubbed in," he wrote. "One reel of flat silences and interminable pauses is usually enough."

Should the viewer, then, consciously listen to a film's score or not? Viewers like himself, he admitted, could not help but listen, even at the risk of an "inferior score" ruining a good picture. But he thought this to be a matter of individual temperament, making the comparison to the female viewer who observes the costumes to which her husband is indifferent. In any case, he believed that film music deserved greater attention, especially considering that "a large part of music heard by the American public is heard in the film theatre. Unconsciously, the cultural level of music is certain to be raised if better music is written for films." To that end, he suggested that producers improve their musical standards, that filmmakers publicize composers of the better motion pictures "as an additional attraction to the merits of the film," and that music critics cover important film premieres.

Like Virgil Thomson, Copland felt that the principal purpose of film music was to supply "a sort of human warmth to the black-and-white, two-dimensional figures on the screen, giving them a communicable sympathy that they otherwise would not have, bridging the gap between the screen and the audience." But he specified five additional functions: establishing an appropriate atmosphere of time and place, signifying the thoughts of the characters, providing "neutral background filler," building continuity, and heightening and molding the drama. He thought background filler in particular difficult to write, given the fact that composers inclined toward self-expression. (How he himself faced this challenge can be observed in the scene for Mae and Slim in *Of Mice and Men*, for which he wrote a simple sicilianalike melody for woodwinds against a single-note pedal in the horn; for all its invisibility, he shaped even this thoroughly unassuming music, which intensifies as Mae confesses her unhappiness, into a neatly formed whole.)

Copland criticized the typical Hollywood motion-picture score of the day with unusual acerbity, raising three main objections to standard practice. First, most composers—such as Victor Young in his score for *Golden Boy* (1939)—tended to use a post-Romantic idiom for every motion picture, independent of the film's particular qualities. Second, composers abused the leitmotiv, a practice "reduced to its final absurdity" in Alfred Newman's score for *Drums Along the Mohawk* (1939): "One theme announced the Indians, another the hero. In the inevitable chase, every time the scene switched from Indians to hero the themes did too, sometimes so fast that the music seemed to hop back and forth before any part of it had time to breathe." Third, composers mimicked film action in ways more suited to a cartoon than to a serious drama. "Max Steiner has a special weakness for this device," he noted. "In *Of Human Bondage* (1934) he had the unfortunate idea of making his music limp whenever the club-footed hero walked across the scene, with a very obvious and it seemed to me vulgarizing effect."

Copland tempered such criticism, however, with healthy respect, writing, "While it is easy enough to poke fun at the movie music they turn out as so much yardage, it would at the same time be foolish not to profit by their great experience in writing for the films." This included Newman's use of a string orchestra for emotional scenes and Steiner's ability to exploit "atmosphere music almost without melodic content of any kind."

Copland distinguished these "composers created by the film industry" from those such as Werner Janssen, Erich Korngold, and Ernst Toch, who'd arrived in Hollywood "from the big world outside." This latter group posed another kind of problem in their attempts to accommodate sometimes overly complex concert styles to the requirements of the film medium. Still, Copland preferred their work to that of Steiner and

349

Newman. He especially liked Toch's *Peter Ibbetson*, writing, "On the strength of this job, Toch should be today one of the best-known film composers. But unfortunately there aren't enough people in Hollywood who can tell a good score when they hear one."

In the later 1940s, he welcomed the emergence of Miklós Rózsa and Bernard Herrmann, praising the latter's imaginative instrumentation, including his use of celestas for the sleigh ride in *The Magnificent Ambersons* and orchestra without strings for *Anna and the King of Siam*. "The other composers in Hollywood watch what Herrmann does," stated Copland, "and with reason, for he is one of the few men who have been able to introduce a few new ideas in the Hollywood musical scene." Similarly, Rózsa obtained unusually "macabre, unearthly" effects in films like *Spellbound* through the use of an "echo-chamber" (and, Copland might have added in his lectures, the theremin), though Copland preferred the opening of *The Killers*, "stark and dramatic, in an idiom which takes full advantage of modern musical resources" (music, incidentally, which eventually evolved into the theme music for the television show *Dragnet*).[30]

Copland rarely wrote about film music after 1950, but as a regular and alert moviegoer, he naturally kept up with the latest developments. In 1956 he singled out the work of Herrmann, Alex North, Leonard Rosenman, and Gail Kubik. All four verified his belief that Hollywood's best composers had classical training and aspired to write concert music and opera as well as music for the movies. One wonders, conversely, whether he had any special sympathy for concert composers who wrote film music; certainly, some of the composers he most admired—including Milhaud, Thomson, Blitzstein, Prokofiev, and Takemitsu—did so.[31]

Copland had other suggestions for reform. He thought producers should bring in the composer before the director completed his work, possibly so as to facilitate collaborations of the Eisenstein-Prokofiev variety, but at least in order to give the composer more time to do his job. He called for a new species of sound mixer who would be "half musician and half engineer," and for the standardization of sound levels in motion-picture theaters. Above all, composers needed good films. "At a practical estimate," he wrote in 1940, "90 percent of the films produced in Hollywood are getting just about the kind of music they deserve, no better and no worse. It is the other 10 percent—the cream of the cinematic crop—with which the hope of better movie music lies."[32]

Episode and the Piano Sonata

In the summer of 1940 Copland wrote a short piece for organ as part of a series commissioned by William Strickland and the H. W. Gray Company. For this work—first entitled *Improvisation* and later retitled *Episode*—he essentially transcribed Emily's dream sequence from *Our Town*. Although his only work for solo organ, it commanded relatively little attention after Strickland premiered it on 9 March 1941. Copland himself apparently did not take the piece very seriously; he failed even to mention it in his memoirs.[33]

In contrast, he devoted considerable time and energy to his only acknowledged Piano Sonata, completed in the fall of 1941. (He never included his student piano sonata, composed under Goldmark, in his catalog.) His first serious instrumental work in seven years, it took three years to complete, a long time, especially when compared to the few weeks set aside for *Of Mice and Men* or *Our Town*. A mishap during its composition slowed completion further. In June 1941, a thief stole two of Copland's valises, one packed full of music, including two movements of the nearly completed sonata. The music was never recovered, despite a widespread search and the eventual capture of the thief; Copland had to reconstruct the movements from memory with the help of surviving sketches.[34]

The Piano Sonata recalls the *Piano Variations* in its dramatic severity. Every note counts. At the same time, due in part to its larger size, it is a more expansively dramatic work; Leonard Bernstein, a Mahler devotee, significantly declared it his "favorite piece of Aaron's," adding, "I adore it." The sonata tradition itself carried some expectation of high drama for Copland, who compared the genre to a play; one wonders, in this context, about the role of Clifford Odets, who commissioned the work (at Copland's suggestion) and to whom it is dedicated. And, finally, with Europe plunged into a horrific war and America awaiting military involvement, the times lent themselves to expressions of this sort, especially from so public-minded an artist as Copland; the work certainly is a wartime work: grim, nervous, elegiac, with pervasive bell-like tollings of alarm and mourning. All these factors found common ground in the making of this remarkable piece.[35]

Much of the Piano Sonata's drama derives from its harmonic contrasts and ambiguities. Such conflicts appear at the very opening, as suggestions of both B-flat major and B-flat minor provide an ambivalent coloring that might be called bimodal. Although the resulting dissonances are very much like those found in the *Variations*, the bimodal context provides a different resonance, one not so much tragic and anguished as sorrowful and bittersweet. Bimodality remains something of a norm as the work proceeds, making the more purely minor-mode music that much more poignant and the more purely major-mode music that much more serene—or at least hopeful. The sonata exploits many other such contrasts, including exploitation of the instrument's highest and lowest registers.

The sonata's three movements form a slow-fast-slow design. The first movement is in sonata form, complete with an exposition of two themes, a development section, and a recapitulation. The first-theme group itself contains two principal ideas, the first highly dramatic, the second, slightly slower and more intimate. For all its songlike contrast, the second theme, marked "with sentiment," derives from the first-theme group and features similarly dissonant harmonies. The transition that connects these two theme groups—including an explosive scale running the length of the piano—recalls Copland's discussion of sonata form in *What to Listen For*: "You cannot very well go from one mood that is powerfully dramatic to another that is lyrically expressive without some kind of transition."[36]

The development successively unfolds the first theme and both impassioned and playful versions of the second theme. After growing tension and two dramatic pauses, Copland climactically recapitulates the main theme, triple forte, suggesting a move to the major mode but falling back into bimodality. The second theme, briefly recalled, also heads toward the major mode but concludes with an echo of the first theme, now decidedly in minor.

The second movement is a scherzo, marked "delicate, restless," with the pianist directed to play "half staccati." The six-note principal motive has often been described as wedgelike (or wedge shaped) because the intervals zigzag in a progressively outward fashion. The ensuing development of this material offers a particularly vivid illustration of the "additive" technique widely associated with Copland, in which a germinal motive is continuously repeated, becoming longer each time, eventually giving rise to a new germinal motive to be similarly developed; the first movement of the Violin Sonata provides another good example of this technique.

The rhythms of this scherzo are striking; although the frequent changes of 5/8, 6/8, 7/8 and other meters recall earlier scores, the beats fly by remarkably quickly, this "vivace" movement calling for the highest metronome marking possible. The resulting rhythmic vitality, while still related to jazz, seems derived as well from Latin-American music, which Copland heard much of while at work on the sonata. The influence of Latin music seems further suggested by the parallel sixths that regularly appear throughout this movement, but such connections are subtle; few of the work's commentators take any notice of them. Nearly all, however, mention the brief songlike, slightly folksy episode, often likened to a trio section, that provides a brief respite from the hectic scherzo proper, though even here little staccato hiccups maintain an atmosphere of suspense.[37]

Copland described the slow finale as "free in form." It puts forth, after a prefatory section derived from the first movement's first theme, two principal ideas: a funereal declamatory idea (derived from the scherzo's trio) and a slightly slower hymnlike idea (derived from the first movement's second theme). The declamation basically moves from major to minor; the hymn, from minor to a luminous major. A melody derived from a jagged bass line in the declamatory section harshly intrudes on the hymn, leading to a reprise of the first movement's main theme and another harrowing outburst of the jagged bass line. The hymn reappears, recapitulating its movement from minor to major. The jagged bass line returns, too, eventually subsiding into a sublime transformation of the hymn, full of bell-like sounds and faint echoes of the first movement's main theme. The hymn, resolved to major, has the last word, quadruple piano. John Kirkpatrick and Julia Smith argue that this finale movement "exhibits the main features of sonata-form," with the declamatory element constituting a first theme and the hymnlike idea, a second theme. But as both themes constantly alternate with each other, and both further derive from earlier movements, one can also think of this finale as an extended epilogue.[38]

Many listeners and performers, including John Kirkpatrick, Wilfrid Mellers, Douglas Young, Robert Silverman, and Dika Newlin, have been especially struck by the last movement's extraordinary coda. Silverman thought it deserved comparison with the finale of Beethoven's Sonata, op. 111, and the coda to Schumann's *Dichterliebe*: "Despite their great differences, each in its own way depicts a serenity far beyond normal human experience—a serenity which is achieved only after an intense struggle earlier in the work." Newlin also cited op. 111, as well as Copland's later *Piano Fantasy*, another example of "wide-flung sonorities gradually dissolving into nirvana." For Mellers, the music's "serenity is the more impressive and (to most of us) moving because Copland is not a mystic like Ruggles, or a primitive like Harris."[39]

This emphasis on the coda's "serenity"—including its frequent description as "immobile"—although endorsed by Copland himself, tells only part of the story. As Douglas Young notes, up to the very last moment, the "disturbing" opening theme throws its shadow on the music's "Apollonian calm." For this listener, even the music's calm has a prayerful quality that is not entirely restful, its bell-like sonorities posing a challenge like Hemingway's For Whom the Bell Tolls (1940). And the very final sonority, a widely spaced open fifth, offers only the most tremulous resolution.[40]

This remarkable coda derives some of its power from the simple tolling of two notes in the bass voice. Such tolling or at least rocking gestures permeate and unify the entire work from its very opening three-note motive. The first movement's principal themes all involve just such a rocking back and forth between two harmonies. The entire first page of the scherzo movement similarly alternates two harmonies in the left hand. And the passage just before the finale's coda features a fourfold repetition of the jagged bass line. For Arthur Berger, such "skeletonized" repetitiveness suggested a certain poverty of imagination; but the degree to which the Piano Sonata can draw new meanings out of repeated ideas constitutes one of its most astonishing features.[41]

When the sonata was first performed, it received the same sort of, in Copland's words, "sourpuss criticisms" that had long greeted his more ambitious efforts. At the same time, such friends as John Kirkpatrick, Arthur Berger, and David Diamond breathed a collective sigh of relief that he had not, after all, sold out. Kirkpatrick even argued that the work represented an advance over the earlier Piano Variations, in that it assimilated his more popular idiom, leading to a "humbler simplicity." Berger agreed that the sonata softened the "severity" of the Variations with the "wholesome atmosphere" of Our Town. Wilfrid Mellers continued this line of thought, evoking, like Berger, both the Variations and the "more relaxed" manner of Our Town in his discussion of the work. Copland himself more or less subscribed to this idea.[42]

Whatever its merits, this now commonplace idea that the sonata reconciled the severe and the popular sides of Copland seems a bit misleading. As far as this author can tell, the work partakes very little of Kirkpatrick's "humbler simplicity," Berger's "wholesome atmosphere," or Mellers's "relaxed manner." On the contrary, it is in its own way every bit as challenging and intense as the *Piano Variations*. One finds, it is true, a vaguely folklike quality to the first movement's second theme and the scherzo's trio, some choralelike harmonies at the start of the finale, and, more generally, something of the dramatic pacing and atmosphere found in the stage and screen works. But most listeners will find such connections remote. At the same time, one need not exaggerate the differences between the sonata and the popular ballet and film scores either.[43]

As with the *Variations*, the Piano Sonata became a celebrated dance; this time the choreographer was not Martha Graham but her distinguished rival Doris Humphrey (1895–1958). Like Graham, Humphrey had studied and taught with Ruth St. Denis and Ted Shawn in Los Angeles and established a dance troupe of her own in New York. She first used Copland's music (part of *Music for the Theatre*) for her extravaganza *Decade* (1941); and she choreographed *El Salón México* (1943) as well. Forced to stop dancing because of arthritis, in 1946 she became artistic director of the José Limón Dance Company, for which she choreographed Copland's Piano Sonata as *Day on Earth* (1947), a work quickly hailed as her masterpiece and an important landmark in American dance.[44]

Choreographed for four dancers (a man, a woman, a young woman, and a girl), *Day on Earth* suggests, in an abstract way, one man's life story. The work begins with a man at what appears to be manual labor (first movement: first theme); he dances playfully with a young woman, at the end of which section they fight, she leaving (first movement: second theme and development); a more serious, older woman becomes his companion (first movement: recapitulation); they have a child, all three dancing together (scherzo), during which the man and girl dance by themselves (scherzo: trio); waving good-bye, the girl leaves the man and the woman (finale); toward the very end, the young woman and girl solemnly join them (finale: coda). Archival footage of this powerful work documents how deeply Humphrey absorbed the music's complex tone and structure. But although widely admired by critics, the work won only a fraction of the popularity of Graham's in some ways not so different *Appalachian Spring*, paralleling the history of their musical scores. It is not known whether Copland even saw *Day on Earth*; he was in Hollywood when Humphrey invited him to the premiere.[45]

As a concert piece, the sonata enjoyed a rich performance history, if not as rich as it deserved. After premiering it in Buenos Aires on

21 October 1941, Copland let the work take wing with the many pianists eager to perform it, including John Kirkpatrick, Leonard Bernstein, Leo Smit, Andor Foldes, Radu Lupu, Noël Lee, Easley Blackwood, William Masselos, Leon Fleisher, and William Kapell, who declared it "the only true great piano composition to come from our country." Smit (1946) and Bernstein (1947) issued recordings of the work now considered authoritative, in part because of their personal closeness to the composer. Bernstein, however, found all performances of the sonata disappointing, even Kapell's, arguing that the work was uniquely suited to Copland's alternately delicate and harsh pianism.[46]

Many pianists seem to have special trouble finding the right tempo for the scherzo movement, either playing it too quickly, making it nearly impossible to produce the half-staccati as requested, or so slowly that its perpetual motion sounds labored. Some of the work's many challenges can be solved simply by more careful consideration of Copland's meticulous dynamic and tempo markings; significantly, the best performances—like Robert Silverman's fine recording of the work (1972)—pay closer attention to such details than most. Also outstanding is Easley Blackwood's distinctive reading (1991), a lean, dark interpretation that establishes the music's kinship to the *Piano Variations* and that well reveals how deeply probing the work is.[47]

20

From *Lincoln Portrait* to *Danzón Cubano*

(1942)

Lincoln Portrait and Fanfare for the Common Man

Soon after Pearl Harbor, the conductor André Kostelanetz, in preparation for a 1942 summer tour, commissioned Copland, Virgil Thomson, and Jerome Kern to write three works for orchestra based on national personages that, taken together, would present a "musical portrait gallery of great Americans." Kern picked Twain, Thomson selected Mayor Fiorello La Guardia and journalist Dorothy Thompson, and Copland chose Whitman; but when Kostelanetz suggested a statesman as opposed to another literary figure, he opted for Lincoln. He was especially impressed with Lord Charnwood's biography of Lincoln (1917), finding it surprising "that an English lord would want to write about Lincoln."[1]

Copland began work on *Lincoln Portrait* for orchestra and speaker in early 1942 to a text of his own devising, including some Lincoln quotes culled from the Charnwood book. He completed it three months later, a few weeks before its premiere by Kostelanetz and the Cincinnati Symphony Orchestra, with William Adams, on 14 May 1942. Copland dedicated the score to Kostelanetz.[2]

Although Copland's work turned out to be extraordinary, his attraction to Lincoln was not. An interest in America's sixteenth president had yielded in the course of the century famous poems by Vachel Lindsay (1914) and Stephen Vincent Benét (1928), a monumental biography by Carl Sandburg (1926–39), a ballet by Martha Graham (1938), a Pulitzer Prize–winning Broadway play by Robert Sherwood (1938) later adapted to the screen (1940), and another Lincoln motion picture, this one by John Ford (1939). As for music, Copland himself could recall Goldmark's *Requiem Suggested by Lincoln's Gettysburg Address* for orchestra (1918), composed during the previous world war; since then, other composers inspired by Lincoln included Robert Russell Bennett (1929), Daniel Gregory Mason (1936), Jacob Weinberg (1936) (another *Gettysburg Address*, which Copland apparently heard at an American Music Festival), Elie Siegmeister (1937), and Jaromir Weinberger (1941). In 1942 alone, Earl Robinson, Morton Gould, and Robert Palmer joined Copland in composing musical Lincolniana. The Popular Front in particular proclaimed Lincoln a great national hero, but his appeal—especially as a symbol of democracy in action—transcended partisan politics.[3]

There had also been some precedent for works for orchestra and speaker, including John Alden Carpenter's widely performed *Song of Faith* for speaker, chorus, and orchestra (1931), which also featured spoken quotations from an American president (George Washington). The growing dissemination of sound recording and amplification made such a medium that much more feasible. In this regard, Copland naturally benefited from his film work to date, including the need to write music to accompany dialogue and voice-overs; one wonders whether such experiences helped inspire the whole idea in the first place.[4]

Lincoln Portrait comprises a slow-fast-slow ABA form, with the second A section featuring the spoken recitation. This recitation contains five short quotes punctuated with narrative remarks in keeping with the idea of portraiture, noting Lincoln's background, giving his height, sketching his temperament, and citing his achievements in the briefest possible manner. These quotes—in expressing the urgent need for responsible action, defining the democratic principles at stake, and offering thanks and remembrance to the fallen dead and hopes for a "new birth of freedom"—clearly bore on the current crisis.[5]

The work's A sections feature two principal melodic ideas: a dirgelike, dotted-rhythm idea (in minor) and the American folk tune "Springfield Mountain" (in major). Copland knew "Springfield Mountain" not only from a recording by the Old Harp Singers of Nashville, which he'd reviewed in 1939, but from S. Foster Damon's collection, which contained two versions of the song: the original eighteenth-century ballad, an "elegy" for a twenty-two-year-old fellow who died from a snake bite, and "Pesky Sarpent," a popular burlesque of the same text. Copland seemingly had the original version in mind, given the nature of his setting and its context. He also might have noticed Bernard Herrmann's prominent use of the tune in his Oscar-winning film score to *The Devil and Daniel Webster* (1941), where the melody underscores the noble words of Daniel Webster; Herrmann even reportedly raised the charge of plagiarism, though the two settings differ considerably, not least in the fact that Herrmann rewrote the tune in a minor mode.[6]

That both the dirgelike idea and "Springfield Mountain" appear during the final oration helps clarify their meanings for Copland. The former is associated with national resolve and democratic ideals, the latter with death and remembrance. The work as a whole alternates these contrasting ideas—one terse and grim, the other lyrical, simple, and very American—for full emotional effect; and many listeners, no doubt, have been deeply moved by the final statement of "Springfield Mountain" for solo trumpet, beginning with the words "that from these honored dead we take increased devotion to that cause for which they gave the last full measure of devotion."

The fast middle section provides further dramatic contrast. It ostensibly aims to portray Lincoln's life, from its humble beginnings to its military climax, represented by snare drums and brass calls—music that "depicts a battlefield as accurately as a military painter," wrote Léon Kochinitzky in an early review. In the midst of this battle music, "Springfield Mountain" appears in three-part canon; this heightens the dramatic tension while providing a transition back to the A material.[7]

The principal theme for this fast middle section derives from Stephen Foster's "Camptown Races" (1850); the resemblance is unmistakable even though Copland quotes only a snippet of Foster's melody. This allusion not only establishes Lincoln's time and place but makes the connection between horse racing and political races. Did Copland know that political rallies of the time often made use of the tune, or that it sometimes was sung to words expressing abolitionist sentiment, or that Foster himself rewrote the text as a campaign song for two gubernatorial candidates? As in Copland's previous use of another campaign song, "The Sidewalks of New York," nasal sounds and dissonant bass lines convey an ironic edge.[8]

Later in 1942 Copland took part in another morale-boosting project, writing one of eighteen fanfares for brass and percussion for conductor Eugene Goossens and the Cincinnati Symphony. "It is my idea," explained Goossens, "to make these fanfares stirring and significant contributions to the war effort." Besides Copland and Goossens, the eighteen composers included Felix Borowski, Henry Cowell, Paul Creston, Anis Fuleihan, Morton Gould, Howard Hanson, Daniel Gregory Mason, Harl McDonald, Darius Milhaud, Walter Piston, Bernard Rogers, Leo Sowerby, William Grant Still, Deems Taylor, Virgil Thomson, and Bernard Wagenaar. Each concert in the Cincinnati Symphony's 1942–43 season opened with one or another fanfare; Copland's *Fanfare for the Common Man* premiered on 12 March 1943.[9]

After receiving the score, Goossens wrote to Copland, "Its title is as original as its music." A comparison with the nine other fanfares selected by Goossens for publication underlines this originality. As Goossens noted, even the title was unique, the other composers dedicating their fanfares to either a military unit or an ally. Copland had considered other unusual titles for the work, including *Fanfare for the Spirit of Democracy*, *Fanfare for Four Freedoms* (a reference to Roosevelt's 1941 State of the Union Address that called for freedom of speech, of religion, from want, and from fear), and *Fanfare for the Rebirth of Lidice* (a Czech town that had been destroyed by the Nazis in 1942). All of these titles bespoke his concern for the poor and downtrodden. Late in life he said, "I sort of remember how I got the idea of writing 'A Fanfare for the Common Man'—it was the common man, after all, who was doing all the dirty work in the war and the army. He deserved a fanfare."[10]

The music is of equal—and related—distinction. While the other fanfares are moderate to fast in tempo, Copland's tempo marking reads "very deliberate." And whereas the other fanfares quickly arrive at full-bodied sonorities, Copland takes his time. After a short, almost violently dramatic introduction for percussion, three trumpets put forth the principal theme, in unison and unaccompanied. The trumpets and horns then restate the theme in two-part harmony. A third statement expands the texture to three parts, the added part played by two trombones. About two-thirds of the way through, Copland introduces a kind of refrain scored, finally, for the full brass contingent: four horns, three trumpets, three trombones, and tuba, massively spaced.

The theme itself stands out. Whereas the other Goossens fanfares derive from bugle calls, folk songs, or the triplets, staccati, and repeated notes associated with the traditional fanfare, Copland's music is distinctively declamatory, with big leaps strongly accented, not all that different, in this sense, from the openings of some of his most serious and severe pieces. The work's harmonic language shows individuality as well, essentially alternating tonic and subdominant harmonies until the full brass group enters, at which point the harmonies become more complex; some exciting tonal shifts ensue and the work concludes dramatically in a distant key, a device Copland had honed in Hollywood.

Although Copland intended both *Lincoln Portrait* and *Fanfare* largely as occasional works composed in response to a national emergency, they became, to his astonishment, two of his best-known pieces. Scores of famous politicians, actors, musicians, and celebrities spoke the words to *Lincoln Portrait*, including Carl Sandburg, whose reading, accompanied by André Kostelanetz and the New York Philharmonic, remains one of the best on record. For his own recording, Copland selected for the speaking part Henry Fonda, who played the young Abe Lincoln in the John Ford film. Other famous reciters ranged from the expected—Eleanor Roosevelt, Gregory Peck, Adlai Stevenson, Charlton Heston, Edward Kennedy, General Norman Schwarzkopf—to the unexpected—Edward G. Robinson, Eartha Kitt, Zero Mostel, and André Watts. Copland himself recited the text from time to time.[11]

At Copland's request, Coretta Scott King recited the narration in a 1969 performance with the National Symphony Orchestra. After the performance, she wrote Copland, "Again I was impressed with how very relevant are the words you have chosen and how effectively you have set them. Along with many other people, I am glad that you wrote this unusual composition." She enjoyed, too, their discussions in which they shared their "common concerns and aspirations"; she hoped that he would consider composing a work based on her husband's words. Copland never wrote such a work, but he made financial contributions to the Martin Luther King Memorial Center and invited Coretta King to join with him on other performances of *Lincoln Portrait*.[12]

The dissemination of *Fanfare* proved even more diverse and widespread. It appealed to all brass players. Television and film producers found it useful for shows about sports, space travel, and other heroic topics. Politicians and radio pundits co-opted it in order to advance their own agenda. In part because of its strong rhythms and its modal harmonies, jazz and rock bands gravitated toward it as well; the touring

Rolling Stones at one point adopted its opening theme as their entrance music, while Woody Herman's New Thundering Herd used this same phrase, as arranged by tenor saxophonist Gary Anderson, as the basis for a funky jazz improvisation, including a brief coda added to reinforce Copland's modulation. In 1977 Keith Emerson more respectfully arranged the whole for synthesizer (himself), guitar (Greg Lake), and drums (Carl Palmer), before proceeding to a free improvisation and reprise of the material, thus expanding the work from three to nearly ten minutes.[13]

Meanwhile, higher opinion tended to belittle or ignore these works from the start. The great love William Schuman felt for *Lincoln Portrait* and the *Fanfare* was unusual. More typically, elite musicians and artists found them disturbingly bombastic. Even so staunch an advocate as Arthur Berger was of two minds, early on praising the "eloquence, vividness and beauty" of *Lincoln Portrait*, while decrying its "aura of good-boy sentiment." In his survey of Copland's music, Wilfrid Mellers pointedly omitted any mention of *Lincoln Portrait* or the *Fanfare*. Many of Copland's closest friends likewise chose to overlook or downplay just those works that appealed to the greatest numbers of people.[14]

Copland kept a sense of perspective and humor about all this. To a complimentary note about *Lincoln Portrait* from Boulanger, he answered, "It is a work, written to order, for a great crowd of people, on a patriotic subject. Think how fortunate I am, if it can also interest *you*!" Years later, when he heard a tape of *Lincoln Portrait* engineered by Phillip Ramey and John Corigliano in which the revamped text ("That's vat he said it!") was declaimed in a heavy Yiddish accent (allegedly by Isaac Bashevis Singer but actually by a friend of theirs, the pianist Sheldon Shkolnik), he exploded with laughter, falling to the floor of his studio, kicking his legs in the air and crying, "This is wonderful. It's a *Lincoln Portrait* that will offend absolutely *every*one!" In 1971 he himself wrote a parody of the piece for Virgil Thomson's seventy-fifth birthday ("We here highly resolve that these artists shall not have performed in vain: and that this nation shall have a new burst of Music and that encomiums of Virgil Thomson, by Virgil Thomson, and for Virgil Thomson shall not perish from the earth"). As for the *Fanfare*, he blithely attributed its success to its title. But he made no apologies for either work. He had set out to rally Americans at a critical historical moment and had done so beyond his wildest expectations. At the very least, both pieces helped establish him as one of the most versatile musicians of the twentieth century.[15]

Rodeo

In early 1942, the Ballet Russe de Monte Carlo, a transatlantic ballet company that nearly ten years earlier had assumed the mantle of Diaghilev's Ballets Russes, initiated a search for a choreographer to stage a new ballet for their 1943–44 season. Esconced in New York for the duration of the war, the company was without a resident choreographer, Léonide Massine having left to work for their principal rival, Lucia Chase's Ballet Theatre. Feeling the need for a bold countermove, the director of Monte Carlo, Sergei Ivanovitch Denham, decided to hire, for the first time in the company's history, an American choreographer. On the recommendation of friends, he asked Agnes de Mille, a respected but still largely unknown choreographer, to submit a scenario.[16]

Born in New York in 1905, Agnes de Mille was descended from theater people on her father's side and an esteemed economist and political reformer on her mother's. At age ten, the de Milles moved to Hollywood, where her father, William, and uncle, Cecil B. (who retained the capital D in DeMille, a telling distinction in Agnes's eyes), pursued careers in the motion-picture industry. Cecil's halfhearted attempts to help his niece's fledgling dance career ended badly; she considered him a philistine and a sham and resented his unwillingness to acknowledge the Jewish origins of his mother, whom she resembled. After her parents divorced in 1927, Agnes found herself back in New York with her devoted mother and eking out a living as a dancer.[17]

In the late 1920s, de Mille began performing her own solos and duets in small avant-garde dance recitals. Her unique style derived principally from ballet but incorporated aspects of popular and modern dance, especially in its emphasis on gesture to convey new kinds of dramatic and psychological meanings. In a number of these dances, she drew upon the de Mille family's well-known tendency toward sexual candor, playing a sex-starved young girl and depicting fantasies of rape and seduction. Dance critic John Martin compared these early dances to Charlie Chaplin: "She leaves you with the same sort of wistful laughter on your lips and the same sort of lump in your throat." In the 1930s, her work profited through study with Anthony Tudor in London. By the end of the decade, she had started to win important commissions; but she was considering giving up dancing altogether when she received the Monte Carlo commission, which she recognized as the opportunity of a lifetime.[18]

For this new ballet, de Mille expanded a movement, "Rodeo," from her ballet *American Street* (1938), which had used gestures and movements derived from horseback riding (a dance created without knowledge of Eugene Loring's comparable choreography for *Billy the Kid*, which she came to admire). She cast her scenario (later revised) in two scenes, the action taking place on a Saturday afternoon and evening on a ranch in the Southwest (eventually specified as Texas) around 1900. Scene one opens with folks strolling around a corral during the intermission of a local rodeo. The Cowgirl dresses and acts like a man in an attempt to stay close to the Head Wrangler, with whom she is infatuated. Other girls, including the frilly Ranchowner's Daughter, enter and flirt with the cowboys. The rodeo resumes, the cowboys displaying their skills. In the hopes of getting the attention of the Head Wrangler (who is smitten with the Ranchowner's Daughter), the Cowgirl attempts to ride a bronco but just gets in the way. Finally, the exasperated cowboys order her away and complete their show.[19]

As twilight approaches, sweethearts move in and out of the encroaching darkness as the Cowgirl, alone and lonely, finds herself moved by the spaciousness of the sky and the land. Out of the darkness, a small group of dancers perform a square dance, not to music but rather to the sounds of clapping hands, beating feet, and the cries of a caller.

Scene two takes place at night outside the ranch house. While some dance inside, others flirt, smoke, and drink stage front. An elderly Mexican man yearns for home. The Head Wrangler, accompanied by a fiddler, brings the dancing outside. A waltz follows. Unable to find a partner, the Cowgirl tearfully leaves with the Mexican, who tries to console her. In the midst of the waltz the men are suddenly called away to return a stray cow to the corral, leaving the women alone. The men, mopping their brows, return to finish the waltz. At the start of a vigorous hoedown, a young Buck seeks a woman equal to his passion (the hoedown, according to de Mille's scenario, being a competitive dance of sexual aggression and submission analogous to flamenco). Soon after the hoedown begins, the Cowgirl appears, wearing a dress and a bow in her hair. Everyone gapes. Only the Cowgirl can stand up to the Buck, who kisses her. "He grabs her, forces her to dance his way and wears her out by sheer brute strength. That's all she's wanted. She has met her master." The ballet ends as all join hands for a grand promenade.[20]

Copland worked largely from this scenario. However, before the premiere on 16 October 1942, de Mille modified the dance somewhat, occasionally in ways that subverted Copland's intentions. She fleshed out the subplot of the Head Wrangler and the Ranchowner's Daughter, giving them a pas de deux during the twilight episode. In addition, she combined the character of the Mexican with that of the Buck in order to create a new role, the Champion Roper; he buoys the Cowgirl up during that part of the waltz originally meant for the women alone and claims her while she and now the Head Wrangler dance the hoedown—just at the moment when the latter attempts to kiss her. These revisions made the ballet less of a Cinderella story and more of a love triangle.

"The theme of the ballet is basic," de Mille stated. "It deals with the problem that has confronted all American women, from earliest pioneer times, and which has never ceased to occupy them throughout the history of the building of our country: how to get a suitable man." The rodeo serves not merely as a display of cowboy skills but as a courtship ceremony, a rite of spring. At one point de Mille even titled the ballet *The Courting at Burnt Ranch*, which she changed to *Rodeo* (pronounced "ro-DAY-oh") only at the urging of the impresario Sol Hurok, who wanted something shorter. The cowboys, strutting and showing off, and the women, enticing and flirting, pair off and dance, alternately tenderly and passionately. Such a vehicle fitted the atmosphere of a mobilized America; like cowboys on the range, many of the country's young men were away from home. During rehearsals of the ballet, de Mille admitted thinking of "the men leaving, leaving everywhere—generation on generation of men leaving and falling and the women remembering." This sentiment apparently animated the idea of having the cowboys leave en masse in the midst of the waltz.[21]

Although such attitudes spoke deeply to wartime audiences, they later irked feminist critics. "I don't know why *Rodeo* hasn't been denounced and picketed by women's liberationists," wrote Marcia Siegel in 1979. It might help to realize, however, the extent to which the Cowgirl was a self-portrait of de Mille. For years she thought her features unattractive and her body ungainly, especially for a dancer. On stage, she put such feelings to good comic use, but it affected her private life in negative ways, leaving her dowdy in her dress and prim in her relations with men. In 1941 Martha Graham invited her to meet her concert manager, William Prude, with the admonition, "Wear your prettiest dress." De Mille dutifully donned her best dress, fixed her hair, and put on makeup; she and Prude met and soon after became engaged. De Mille seems to have thought of her dress, like the Cowgirl's, as representing her readiness to enter into a mature relationship, as a symbol not of docile conformity but of empowerment. Significantly, she created *Rodeo* shortly after she became engaged to Prude, who had grown up on ranches in West Texas and who reminded her of that famous Hollywood cowboy Gary Cooper. On one level she may have intended *Rodeo* as a patriotic celebration of social harmony, but at the same time it expressed her own joyous self-realization.[22]

During de Mille's initial interview with Monte Carlo, when asked what composer she wanted for her ballet, she responded, "The best, Aaron Copland." In one of her books, she later recalled her reaction when asked for a second choice: "I had fifteen dollars in the bank, and I was now shopping for the world's great composers. I adjusted my sister's hat with a languorous gesture and drawled, 'Let us decide that when Copland definitely refuses.' And I put my heels hard on the floor to keep my knees from trembling."[23]

De Mille and Copland had known each other at least casually since the early 1930s. They both frequented Kirk Askew's famous salon; according to Oliver Smith, Copland, unlike most of the Askew circle, took her seriously. De Mille, meanwhile, based her confidence in Copland largely on the strength of his score to *Billy the Kid*.[24]

De Mille arranged a meeting in her studio with Copland in order to discuss a possible collaboration. After she finished detailing the scenario, Copland was silent. "Well," de Mille added, "it isn't Hamlet [Copland giggled], but it can have what Martha Graham calls an 'aura of race memory.' " Copland burst out laughing and slyly asked, "Couldn't we do a ballet about Ellis Island?" De Mille threw a pillow at him, saying, "You go to hell!" Wary of undertaking another cowboy ballet, he hesitated and asked to think it over. But the following day, he accepted the $1,000 commission, rightly realizing that *Rodeo* promised to be a very different work from *Billy the Kid*.[25]

Before Copland composed a note, de Mille blocked out the entire dance for him. In contrast to Loring's more stylized adaptation of film, she created movements cinematic in their very essence; as Siegel notes, "Loring uses film techniques. De Mille uses film sensibility." The effect was one of enormous verisimilitude. Margaret Lloyd early on observed, "She told a human interest story in dance, movement, and gesture—movements, not only of riding a bucking broncho, but of the emotions of the rider; gestures, not only of roping and showing off, flirting, or meditating alone in the twilight hour, but of what is going on under the surface motions; dance steps, not only of country-dancing, but of disappointment or glee." Some of these movements approached farce, reminding one of Copland's attraction to Fanny Brice.[26]

In addition to sketching out the action, de Mille provided Copland with a detailed "time plot" that included not only specific timings—as Page and Loring had also done—but, in some instances, actual measure numbers, such as "girl rides alone—twelve measures." She also suggested various moods and techniques, including "fiddle-tune hit hard," "brass yells and whoops," and, for the top of the second scene, "Dance music inside. Night music outside." Copland heeded all these requests. Consequently, the completed score reflected much of de Mille herself—her personality, her movements, her dramatic and musical ideas—thus helping to explain, in the context of Copland's oeuvre, its unique character.[27]

Following the scenario, Copland divided his score into five sections: "Buckaroo Holiday," "Corral Nocturne," "Ranch House Party," "Saturday Night Waltz," and "Hoe-Down." (He also added a very brief transition between sections one and two.) More so than in *Billy the Kid*, he used folk tunes throughout: "Sis Joe" and "If He'd Be a Buckaroo" in "Buckaroo Holiday"; "I Ride an Old Paint" (also known as "Houlihan") in "Saturday Night Waltz"; and the fiddle tunes "Bonyparte" (better known as "Bonaparte's Retreat"), "McLeod's Reel," and (as only recently uncovered by Jessica Burr) "Gilderoy" and "Tip Toe, Pretty Betty Martin" in "Hoe-Down." De Mille supplied Copland with her own version of "I Ride an Old Paint" scribbled on a piece of paper, while he found "Sis Joe," "If He'd Be a Buckaroo," and "Bonyparte" (as transcribed by Ruth Crawford) in John and Alan Lomax's *Our Singing Country*, and "McLeod's Reel," "Gilderoy," and "Tip Toe, Pretty Betty Martin" in Ira Ford's *Traditional Music of America*.[28]

Unlike the folk songs in *El Salón México* and *Billy the Kid*, these tunes typically appear in their entirety and in relatively traditional settings. Moreover, the score features some original music in a folk style, to the point that one cannot be sure, without consulting the original sources, where a folk tune leaves off or resumes. In "Saturday Night Waltz," for example, a folklike melody smoothly bridges two verses of "I Ride an Old Paint." Entirely Copland's own—or nearly so (Leonard Bernstein offered a hand here)—is the piece of honky-tonk found in "Ranch House Party," which functions like the source music in Copland's film scores (and which derives, in fact, from the saloon scene in *Of Mice and Men*). Similarly, one might assume that Copland based the plaintive oboe melody found at the center of "Corral Nocturne" on folk song had he not assured us other-wise. The score's folklike character even extends to its orchestration, which suggests vernacular music making: the harp like a guitar, the wood-winds like a harmonium, the violins like country fiddles, and so on.[29]

Such folkloric qualities mirrored de Mille's intentions. "What underlies her best work," says one critic, thinking specifically of *Rodeo*, "is folk feeling, a genuine feeling for the folk." And yet, for all its folkishness, the score reveals Copland's inimitable personality at each turn, including a brilliant orchestration that demonstrates how timbre can dramatize the most homespun musical ideas. Copland no doubt shared de Mille's excite-ment about the commission; writing a ballet for the Ballets Russes had been one of his dreams since his Paris days. In any case, he provided her with a polished and ingenious score, one whose blend of irony and "genuine feeling for the folk" perfectly suited her aims and objectives.[30]

The largest and most complex of the ballet's five sections, "Buckaroo Holiday" opens with a short overture featuring the rodeo theme, a descending scalar idea in the strings and winds answered by syncopated chords in the brass. Without knowing that Copland sketched out this theme the previous year (1941) in Santiago—or his penchant for absorb-ing Latin-American musics—one might not discern the music's vaguely Hispanic profile; given the Mexican heritage of the American Southwest, the mingling of American and Latin-American styles works neatly here.

As the curtain rises, a softer, slower theme depicts the strolling about on stage. Like the overture, this ambling music features a unison melody (this time just in the winds) answered by chords in the brass, at once pro-viding a variation on the rodeo theme and possibly meant to suggest the courtship between the girls and the boys. The unison melody speeds up as the Cowgirl mounts her horse. A still faster passage accompanies her on horseback; this humorous Cowgirl music—more vamping than a theme per se—uses static harmonies (and cymbals) to portray her fal-tering efforts, and woodwind hiccups (and wood block) to depict her bumpy ride.

After this, the orchestra loudly announces the arrival of the rodeo cow-boys ("like thunder," instructed de Mille, which helps explain the rim shots in the snare drum). Copland marks this entrance with "Sis Joe," a railroad work song. The jagged rhythms might lead one to think that he had fragmented or otherwise distorted the tune, but, in fact, it closely approximates its transcription by Crawford. The use of a railroad song to represent the cowboys—an unusual choice—underscores de Mille's idea of the cowboys as real people, as workers, as opposed to mythic figures. After "Sis Joe," the rodeo theme returns, now developed more extensively, including an inversion of its basic scalar idea.

The music suddenly subsides into a droll gesture for bassoon and horns. Copland apparently intended this music to portray the Cowgirl as she prepares to ride a bronco, and meant the ensuing statements of "If He'd Be a Buckaroo" (the words of obvious aptness) to depict her attempts to do so, including little woodwind figures, marked "perky," that reflect her "cocky" attitude. De Mille, however, wound up staging this passage for the entrance of some girls, a brief solo for the Champion Roper, and some dancing for the entire corps—one of those moments in the ballet when the seeming intentions of composer and choreographer mismatch.

After a brief reprise of the Cowgirl theme, the entire orchestra explodes with "If He'd Be a Buckaroo" in three-part canon. The music continues smoothly as the cowboys display their skills; the Cowgirl's "perky" woodwind theme now appears "gracefully," with glockenspiel. The rodeo theme returns once more, followed by "Sis Joe," as the cowboys rebuke the meddling Cowgirl. After a grand pause for the Cowgirl's disgraced exit, "Buckaroo Holiday" concludes with a climactic restatement of "If He'd Be a Buckaroo," supported by "Sis Joe" in the bass, and a grandiose coda recalling something of *Billy*'s monumentality ("lift the skies," commanded de Mille).

All this diverse music forms a compelling whole, to the extent that "Buckaroo Holiday" imparts something of the dramatic coherence of a symphonic first movement. Copland accomplishes this through a variety of means, including alternating the themes associated with the Cowgirl and the cowboys. Compared to the similarly impressive "Street in a Frontier Town" that opens *Billy the Kid*, "Buckaroo Holiday" reveals perhaps an even more integrated and subtle handling of dramatic form.

The other four sections are shorter and simpler. "Corral Nocturne" reflects the Cowgirl's bittersweet twilight musings (Copland apparently had no thought of the pas de deux that de Mille eventually interpolated here). Strings of simple triads—suggesting a Western version of the Grover's Corners music from *Our Town*—suggest her attachment to home, while the forlorn duet for oboe and bassoon heard toward the end emphasizes her loneliness. The duet's rough-hewn counterpoint, with its marvelous parallel sevenths, captures something of her vulnerable awkwardness as well.

In "Ranch House Party," Copland rose to the challenge of de Mille's request for "Dance music inside. Night music outside." The scene opens with honky-tonk music for unaccompanied barroom piano; a contrasting section follows in which the orchestra plays the honky-tonk bass softly, while the clarinet freely varies its melody, suggesting the night outside. For the subsequent pantomime, the strolling music from "Buckaroo Holiday" returns, now in a more nighttime guise, with delicate pizzicati and staccati. This section concludes with a reprise of the plaintive duet from "Corral Nocturne" as the Cowgirl finds herself without a partner.

Given the staged folk dances that follow, the score's last two movements, "Saturday Night Waltz" and "Hoe-Down," stay understandably close to their folk sources: the former to the folk song "I Ride an Old Paint," the latter to the fiddle tunes "Bonyparte," "McLeod's Reel," "Gilderoy," and "Tip Toe, Pretty Betty Martin." To convey even greater realism, both movements open with passages that, in an elegantly stylized way, evoke the tuning of instruments.

In setting "I Ride an Old Paint," a waltzlike herding song, Copland may have been aware of Tex Ritter's popular recording of the tune (1933); he presumably was familiar with the transcriptions by Hazel Felman and Elie Siegmeister in the collections by Carl Sandburg and S. Foster Damon, respectively; and he definitely knew Virgil Thomson's setting in The Plow That Broke the Plains. But he stayed closest to de Mille's own transcription, which used one hypermeasure of 3/4 for every two measures of the standard 3/4, and which featured its own melodic variants, including a couple of measures of bridge that Copland further expanded. De Mille's unusual transcription—compounded by Copland's syncopated accompaniment—imparted a somewhat formal quality in keeping with her request for a "Texas minuet."[31]

As the men are called away, as specified by the original script, the waltz suddenly moves to a foreign key, accompanied by high repeated notes, like a distant call. The girls, left alone, dance to a syncopated melody in the cellos; this contrasting section, with its languid melody and static pedal, depicts the girls' ennui while functioning like the trio of a traditional minuet or scherzo. When the men return, the violins sweep back with the waltz's original key and texture, but with a new melody of heightened expressivity, before returning to the folk tune. This romantic outpouring both satisfies a dramatic requirement and provides the movement with a natural climax, yet another example of Copland's ability to shape stage action into cohesive musical forms. It is regrettable, in this sense, that de Mille overhauled this scene the way she did. Perhaps she decided that having the men leave in the middle of the waltz would confuse an audience, or perhaps she felt it necessary to more fully develop the Cowgirl's relationship with the Roper.

For the concluding "Hoe-Down," Copland provided music of a brash vitality that reflected de Mille's conception of the moment as one of tremendous release—of dance steps, as one critic put it, that "cannot contain themselves." He further accommodated de Mille's instructions for various vamps, pauses for tap-dance improvisations, and "eight measures of frenzy." Toward the end of the section, as the Buck (or later the Head Wrangler) seductively approaches the Cowgirl, the vamp becomes progressively softer and slower, a trombone moving downward chromatically to a moment of repose for the kiss on an E-flat-major triad, the tonality of the waltz and romance. The hoedown instantly resumes (just prior to which, in the eventual ballet, the Rope Champion intervenes, declaring the Cowgirl his own). Many of these dramatic requirements defeated the kind of formal wholeness Copland achieved in the ballet's other parts, but he managed a brilliant concluding stroke, namely, a triple-forte recitation on a single pitch that recalls "Sis Joe" from the first scene; this gesture not only rounds off the work but provides dramatic resonance, given the tune's association with working Americans.[32]

In getting ready for the premiere, de Mille had her hands full trying to teach the international Monte Carlo company to walk and gesture like American cowboys. "I made these men really use their backs, the way a tennis player does, the way a pitcher does in baseball," recalled de Mille. "They're not just hobby horse movements. They use the whole body the way any athletic exercise uses the entire body. And, by the way, I think that's one of the things the Americans do." "Don't plier. Sit your horse," she would order the Russians. In the end she wound up using fewer than twenty members of the company as one dancer after another gave up. But the members of varying nationalities who stuck it out amazed everyone with their characteristically American movements. "Oh Aaron," she wrote to Copland about a month before the premiere, "maybe I've done something good. I can't believe it yet. There's so much that seems crude."[33]

Meanwhile, at Copland's suggestion, Monte Carlo hired designer Oliver Smith, who created marvelously atmospheric sets that evoked large expanses of earth and sky. De Mille intensified this impression by, for example, positioning a few isolated figures at the rear of the stage during the twilight episode. Copland's music further intimated open spaces, as de Mille pointed out: "He struck certain cold, rather penetrating and evocative intervals that suggest space to us." Working together, de Mille, Copland, and Smith successfully conjured an ambience strongly suggestive of a vast and sparsely settled land.[34]

The 16 October 1942 premiere of *Rodeo* at the Metropolitan Opera was a sold-out event, its illustrious audience including Copland, Martha Graham, Edwin Denby, and the new Broadway team of Richard Rodgers and Oscar Hammerstein. Monte Carlo programmed it as the last of three one-act ballets. To the management's consternation, de Mille insisted on dancing the role of the Cowgirl herself. The Yugoslavian Casimir Kokich played the Head Wrangler, and the Englishman Frederic Franklin played the Champion Roper. "This was not a great performance; we gave better later," said de Mille of opening night. "Neither was it a great ballet. The style, as I always feared, did break. But it was the first of its kind, and the moment was quick with birth." Among other mishaps attending the first performance, Kokich forgot an entrance, leaving de Mille alone on the stage of the Met to improvise for sixty-four measures of music.[35]

Nonetheless, the premiere was an enormous success. The audience laughed and applauded throughout. "The painstakingly crafted, evocative gestures—the cowboys squinting in the sun, the Cowgirl stopping herself from hitching up her skirt as she had her pants—appeared improvised, and their meaning was clear," writes de Mille's biographer. "The jaunty, bowlegged male dancers lurching across the stage on their imaginary horses were so sexy, Agnes's sister noted, that you could smell them in the tenth row." The company received a standing ovation, even from some of the orchestra members, and some twenty curtain calls. "I never heard so friendly an enthusiasm as on the opening night," Denby wrote. It was a great moment for Copland, who joined de Mille on the stage of the Met for all the acclaim. Rodgers and Hammerstein immediately decided to hire de Mille to choreograph *Oklahoma!*[36]

Rodeo enjoyed similar success on national tour (1942–43). "*Rodeo* is a smash hit," wrote Claudia Cassidy from Chicago. The ballet became a fixture of the American Ballet Theatre's repertory, but over the course of the 1940s, productions of it grew increasingly slipshod. Among other things, de Mille's performance of the Cowgirl had set a standard hard to meet. As Copland noted, she had given "depth to the role, while still being hilariously funny." Morton Gould similarly observed, "Agnes gave the Cowgirl an edge. She never became too coy or arch; you felt sympathy, liked her, and smiled with her, were sad with her." De Mille candidly criticized her immediate successors, and when she gave ABT exclusive rights to the ballet in 1950, she insisted on a contractual prerogative to approve the casting; to the dismay of the company, this sometimes meant hiring a Broadway dancer for the part of the Cowgirl. In later years, the Boston Ballet, the Joffrey Ballet, and other dance companies also staged the work, which became, along wit the Copland-Loring *Billy the Kid,* one of the first American ballets to achieve repertory status.[37]

In 1943 Copland extracted a suite from the work, entitled *Four Dance Episodes from Rodeo* ("Buckaroo Holiday," "Corral Nocturne," "Saturday Night Waltz," and "Hoe-Down") for a somewhat larger orchestra than that used for the ballet. He hardly changed a note of "Buckaroo Holiday" and "Corral Nocturne" (though he removed the brief transition between them); "Saturday Night Waltz" and "Hoe-Down" he only slightly tightened. Consequently, aside from the music for the "Ranch House Party," the suite contained practically the entire score. The omission of "Ranch House Party" enhanced the score's symphonic qualities, the four episodes resembling the first movement, slow movement, minuet, and finale of a classical symphony. As a suite, Rodeo enjoyed tremendous success—greater even than the ballet—ever since its partial premiere on 28 May 1943 by Arthur Fiedler and the Boston Pops. It became—and remains—one of Copland's most recognizable and beloved achievements.

As with *Lincoln Portrait* and *Fanfare for the Common Man,* Rodeo also alienated a number of artists and intellectuals from the start. De Mille relates a telling anecdote about Ted Shawn's refusal to attend a rehearsal of *Rodeo* at Jacob's Pillow during the summer of 1942 after he and his dancers overheard Copland and a young Leonard Bernstein playing the score at the piano. De Mille confronted Shawn in an adjoining room and reported the following exchange:

"For God's sakes," I said, "I asked you to come down. Weren't you interested?" And Ted Shawn said, "Agnes, it's because of music like that that we are having war." "You're joking," I said. And he looked at me and said, "no." And I looked around at the company and asked, "He's making fun of me, isn't he?" The cast said, "Oh no." And all of them dead serious. Shawn said, "I find this the reverse of music. It is a step backwards." I said, "Well, they're [Copland and Bernstein] downstairs, can they have a drink or something to eat? What shall I do—tell them they've caused a war and reversed civilization?" Shawn said, "I repudiate their music. But I welcome them as human beings."

De Mille attributed Shawn's disdain to jealousy; she did not like Shawn, and she respected him less. But Shawn represented an attitude, in exaggerated fashion, shared by others in the arts community. Even sympathetic listeners, like Robert Ward, frequently compared the score unfavorably to *Billy the Kid*. Although he found the construction of "Buckaroo Holiday" astonishing, Arthur Berger similarly regretted the music's popularity. Less friendly critics simply dismissed the work as so much fluff.[38]

Rodeo remains widely misunderstood and underrated, not only because it is often heard piecemeal (especially "Hoe-Down," which among other things became the basis for a 1952 animated short, *Abstronic,* by the early master of abstract animation, Mary Ellen Bute [1906–1983]) and has fallen prey to rather unrelenting commercial exploitation but also because its intentions—as a whimsical comedy—are often only vaguely apprehended. Copland's own sensitivity toward the music's dramatic context helped make his recording of the work by and large the most amusing and touching of the many to date.

Las Agachadas and Danzón Cubano

Side by side with such Americana as *Lincoln Portrait* and *Rodeo,* Copland composed two works of Hispaniana: "Las Agachadas" for chorus and *Danzón Cubano* for two pianos (both 1942).

Copland wrote "Las Agachadas" at the request of the choral conductor Hugh Ross, with whom he had worked on the Copland-Sessions Concerts and more recently on the Tanglewood faculty. Ross commissioned the piece for a 25 March 1942 memorial concert by the New York Schola Cantorum in honor of composer, conductor, and ethnomusicologist Kurt Schindler (1882–1935). Schindler had founded the Cantorum in 1909 and directed it for over fifteen years; its concerts, which featured both contemporary works (including important premieres) and folk-song settings (including his own), had greatly enriched New York's musical life. When Schindler resigned from the Cantorum in 1926 in order to devote more time to the study of folk music, Ross succeeded him. For this memorial concert, Copland, Juan José Castro, Carlos Chávez, Henry Cowell, Pedro Sanjuan, Deems Taylor, and Bernard Wagenaar each agreed to arrange for chorus one of the many folk tunes Schindler had collected over the years.[39]

Copland chose the Spanish dance tune "Las Agachadas" (translated as "The Shake-Down") as found in Schindler's monumental *Folk Music and Poetry of Spain and Portugal*, published posthumously in 1941. He retained the original Spanish, "Las Agachadas" thus becoming his only mature work in a foreign language. Using the two verses reproduced in the Schindler volume, he composed somewhat contrasting music for both verses and then reprised the first verse in more or less its original form, thus creating an ABA design. The entire work lasts only about three minutes, with each verse roughly a minute in length.[40]

Aside from the addition of a guitarlike refrain of Copland's own devising ("drun de dun"), the tune appears much as Schindler transcribed it. The restrained accompaniment, avoiding all accidentals, plays with rhythmic ambiguities inherent in the tune itself, bringing out, as it were, various ways of feeling the song. Most striking is the way in which the a cappella eight-voiced mixed choir and four-voiced solo group continually weave their way through the work's kaleidoscopic textures. Spirited fun, "Las Agachadas," rather than mourning Schindler's death, celebrates his life.[41]

Claire Reis and the League of Composers commissioned Copland's *Danzón Cubano* for two pianos in celebration of the league's twentieth anniversary. Copland dedicated the piece to Rudy Burckhardt, a friend who had entertained Copland and Kraft during their stay in Havana in the spring of 1941, and who admired Copland's earlier essay on Latin-American themes, *El Salón México*.[42]

Copland had wanted to write a piece based on Cuban music ever since this trip to Havana; in a letter he told Leonard Bernstein,

> I'm bringing back a few records, but they are only analogous to Guy Lombardo versions of the real thing. I've sat for hours on end in 5¢ a dance joints, listening. Finally the band in one place got the idea, and invited me up to the band platform. "Usted musico?" Yes, says I. Thirteen black men and me—quite a piquant scene. The thing I like most is the quality of voice when the Negroes sing down here. It does things to me—it's so sweet and moving. And just think, no serious Cuban composer is using any of this. It's awful tempting, but I'll try to control myself.

Rosamund Bernier, in Havana at the same time, remembered accompanying Copland to a particularly large dance hall, a kind of Cuban Salón

México in which an orchestra played at either end of the hall; he positioned himself in the middle so that he could listen to both bands at once.[43]

Such enthusiasm for Cuban dance music was familiar enough; many midcentury American popular and jazz musicians exploited Cuban sounds and rhythms. But whereas much of this music commercialized Cuban folk sources, Copland hoped, in *Danzón Cubano*, to establish contact with "the real thing." He emphasized this distinction by basing his work not on one of the popular Cuban ballroom dances but on the *danzón*, which he described as "a stately dance, quite different from the rhumba, conga, and tango, and one that fulfills a function rather similar to that of the waltz in our own music, providing contrast to some of the more animated dances. The special charm of the danzón is a certain naive sophistication. Its mood alternates between passages of rhythmic precision and a kind of nonsentimental sweetness under a nonchalant guise."[44]

According to Copland, the six-minute *Danzón Cubano* uses "four simple Cuban dances" in the course of its "two contrasting sections." He never specified these four "dances" as they appear in the piece, but it seems that two occur in the first half—the opening idea featuring a fourth-beat accent not unlike the conga ("nonchalant, but precise") and a more lyrical idea ("naive and non-sentimental")—and two in the second half—the music with an exposed, slightly irregular bass and, heard shortly thereafter, the syncopated modal idea, related to the rumba, that uses the characteristic rhythmic grouping 3+3+2. The work's AB form reflects, according to Copland, the *danzón's* typical construction "in two parts which are thematically independent," but he unifies all of the work's material by means of a few key intervals. In addition, the lyrical "naive" idea from the first half reappears in the middle of the second half, and the music's opening gesture serves as its final one.

Copland considered a number of titles for the work—including *Tio Sam (Uncle Sam)*, *The Cuban Danzón*, and *Birthday Piece (on Cuban Themes)*—before settling on *Danzón Cubano*. He used *Birthday Piece* as the title for the 9 December 1942 premiere at Town Hall in New York, with Bernstein and himself at the two pianos. The birthday in question apparently started out as Rudy Burckhardt's, though he no doubt had the premiere's occasion—the league's twentieth birthday—in mind as well. In any case, the very opening theme suggests, both in its melodic shape and its harmonic structure, a pun on "Happy Birthday to You." The piece features other Americanisms, perhaps explaining the *Tio Sam* title; at one point, for example, it breaks out into a kind of swing chorus, complete with blues progression. In short, the work represents an artful integration of American and Latin-American elements, as also achieved in *El Salón México* and *Three Latin-American Sketches*.

The medium of two pianos suits the percussive and highly rhythmic nature of the material, permitting simulation of the dense polyrhythms and elaborate responsorial textures of Cuban dance music. The music occasionally even nears a kind of unrestrained jumble, perhaps reflecting Copland's fascination with the Havana dance hall and its orchestras playing simultaneously at either end. His colorful and sharp orchestration of the work (1946) clarified such rhythmic and textural intricacies, helping to make this later version immensely more popular than the original.

For this orchestral version, first performed by Reginald Stewart and the Baltimore Symphony on 17 February 1946, Copland specified a slightly slower tempo than in the two-piano original. Bernstein more or less adhered to this slower metronome marking in his recording with the New York Philharmonic, while Copland took an even slower tempo in his with the London Symphony Orchestra. Antal Dorati and the Minneapolis Symphony maintained a still slower beat in the work's very first recording, an early outing that remains particularly winsome.[45]

In 1978, Eliot Feld stylishly choreographed *Danzón Cubano* as a ballet of the same name for three women and one man. At a televised rehearsal, Copland asked Feld if he had ever been to Cuba, to which he responded:

No, I haven't been to Cuba, but in a sense I feel that even though I haven't been there directly, I've been there indirectly or through you and through your music. When I started to choreograph to the music, my strongest feeling was almost a kind of cubist feeling, some combination of Picasso sculptures in the sense of a sophisticated primitivism. It's what developed as I choreographed. It may not show when you look at the dance, but that's what I felt.[46]

21

From *The North Star* to *Appalachian Spring*

(1943–44)

The North Star

Copland spent most of 1943 in Hollywood in connection with *The North Star*, a motion picture produced by Samuel Goldwyn; because the film contained songs, choruses, and dances, he needed to be on hand before, during, and after production. He felt somewhat stranded in Hollywood, but he enjoyed socializing with friends like Lawrence Morton and Jerome Moross, and having the opportunity to hobnob with Stravinsky and movie stars like Farley Granger and Groucho Marx. His work on the picture also provided, he told Boulanger, "excellent preparation for operatic writing!" And during down times in the production schedule, he made progress on some other projects, including a ballet for Martha Graham.[1]

The North Star was—along with *Song of Russia* and *Mission to Moscow*—one of three major 1943 Hollywood films specifically aimed at fostering pro-Soviet sentiment. The brainchild of playwright Lillian Hellman and director William Wyler, it started life as a documentary about the Nazi invasion of the Soviet Union to be shot on location; but producer Samuel Goldwyn opted for a musical set on one of his studio lots. Goldwyn assembled a dazzling array of talent, not only Hellman and Copland (he came close to getting Stravinsky) but director Lewis Milestone (who replaced Wyler, now in the service), cinematographer James Wong Howe, set designer William Cameron Menzies, lyricist Ira Gershwin, choreographer David Lichine, and an all-star cast, including Anne Baxter, Dana Andrews, Farley Granger, Walter Huston, Dean Jagger, Walter Brennan, and Erich von Stroheim. The production cost over $3 million, the most lavish of Goldwyn's entire career. Copland earned $10,000 for about five months' work, far more money than he then customarily made in an entire year.[2]

Set in June 1941 in the North Star, a fictional communal farm near Kiev in the Ukraine, *The North Star* traces the fates of three families in the days just prior to and following the German invasion of the Soviet Union: the commune's doctor, Dr. Kurin (Walter Huston), and his grandchildren Clavdia (Jane Withers) and Grisha; Boris and Nadja and their sons Kolya (Dana Andrews) and Damian (Farley Granger); and Rodion (Dean Jagger) and Sophia and their daughters Marina (Anne Baxter) and Olga. Kolya is a bombardier in the Soviet air force; Damian is graduating from high school; Marina and Clavdia are a class behind; Grisha is in his early teens; and Olga is a child of about seven. Damian and Marina are in love, and Clavdia has a schoolgirl crush on Kolya. On the last day of school, the commune holds an evening celebration, with food, music, and dancing. The next day, Damian, Marina, Clavdia, and Grisha leave on a two-week holiday under Kolya's supervision; they plan to hike to Kiev and spend a few days there.

On their second day, as they meet up with some local villagers, including an elderly pig farmer, Karp (Walter Brennan), the Germans invade the country, and the hikers and villagers, exposed on an open road, find themselves the targets of German airplanes. Witnessing the death of a young boy in the attack deeply affects them all.

The planes strike the North Star as well, killing little Olga. Boris rallies the people, organizing a guerrilla force comprised of the commune's younger men under Rodion's supervision, and instructing the remaining comrades to destroy their crops and property when the Germans arrive.

Boris then leaves for a neighboring town in order to requisition additional guns for the guerrillas. Attacked and fatally wounded by a German fighter plane on the return trip, he drives his wrecked truck off the road just where the hikers and Karp happen to be; before he dies, he asks that they deliver the ammunition for him. Kolya, who needs to report for duty, hands this mission over to Karp and the others.

As the invading army approaches, the North Star residents attempt to burn down their commune. In retribution, the German commandant tortures Sophia. Under the supervision of Dr. von Harden, a cynical collaborator (Erich von Stroheim), and Dr. Richter, a hardened Nazi, the Germans turn the local hospital into a field clinic for their wounded soldiers; as they begin using the local children as a source of blood, a boy dies. In order to rescue the children, the guerrillas attack.[3]

Meanwhile, Karp and the young people make their way by wagon back home with the ammunition. Damian acts as a decoy to allow the others to get by German troops; unexpectedly, Clavdia joins him in the maneuver. Clavdia is killed and Damian, blinded. Kolya goes to his death in a kamikaze attack on German tanks. The surviving children, including the blind Damian, reach the commune in time to aid the triumphant guerrillas. During the melee, Dr. Kurin shoots the two German doctors. As the film ends, the comrades—now refugees—leave the North Star.

Much as *The City* (1939) reflected the attitudes of New York's leftist intelligentsia toward their own country, so *The North Star* revealed how a similar group viewed the Soviet Union. Unlike the Nazi doctors, with their harsh German accents, the Soviets speak at nearly all times nobly and gently. They are also exceptionally brave: Boris, Clavdia, Kolya, and the school principal sacrifice their lives; Sophia endures torture; Kolya has never even known fear. Dr. von Harden finds their resistance different from that encountered in Western Europe; these are, he tells Dr. Richter, "a strong people . . . a hard people to conquer."

The Soviets are superior in their very way of life. They play chess on their hayrides and the young people apply themselves diligently at school. Damian places his love for Marina in the context of education and citizenship, whereas the romantic Clavdia is derided as a "throwback," as someone who does not belong to this "new world" (this includes her wanting a campfire on the hiking trip); at a crucial moment, she even gives in to prayer (though without mentioning God). All this tells us, of course, much more about Hellman and Milestone than about the Soviet Union. Copland himself regarded the film, at least in retrospect, as so much bunkum, but he no doubt identified with its basic objective of inspiring sympathy and admiration for the average Soviet citizen; his music, in any case, showed a sensitivity to the movie's finer moments.[4]

The collaboration was not a happy one. Feeling that Goldwyn and Milestone had trivialized her script, Hellman eventually denounced the film as a "big-time, sentimental, badly directed, badly acted mess." For his part, Milestone complained that Hellman "knew nothing about Russia" (and, in fact, although Hellman had visited a Soviet collective in 1937, she derived much of her script from Russian novels and *Pravda*). Goldwyn thought the picture, in a word, "lousy."[5]

When *The North Star* opened, it horrified both reactionaries like William Randolph Hearst, who considered it bolshevik propaganda, and liberals like Mary McCarthy and James Agee, who reproved its treatment of war. Many Soviet viewers simply thought it a joke. But contrary to Copland's own remembrance, the film actually received good notices in most major newspapers (including, to Hearst's dismay, his own New York *Daily Mirror*—a review that he quickly replaced with a hostile one). It was nominated for six Oscars, including best musical score. The political climate, however, changed so quickly that within a few years the film seemed only slightly short of treasonous. In 1957, Goldwyn sold the rights to National Telefilm Associates, which bizarrely reedited it and rereleased it as *Armored Attack*, complete with a voice-over condemning Soviet aggression and newsreel footage of the 1956 Hungarian uprising. When *The North Star* finally resurfaced again in original form, Pauline Kael derided it as a "Second World War monstrosity" and a "slick piece of propaganda" that "romanticizes the Russians so fondly that they're turned into Andy Hardy's neighbors."[6]

The music, which tended to get lost amid all the political controversy, included four songs by Copland and Ira Gershwin: "No Village like Mine," a kind of theme song meant to be sung early in the film but heard only in part when the children meet up with Karp on their way to Kiev; "Jingles" ("Chari, vari"), a dancelike number sung at the commune party; "The Younger Generation," sung by the children while hiking; and "Song of the Guerrillas," sung by the North Star partisans on horseback as they prepare for battle.

In order to provide regional color, Copland consulted at least four collections of Russian folk and revolutionary songs. Considering that the film was set in the Ukraine, not Russia, this was not entirely apropos, but few Americans were likely to know the difference (Soviets, on the other hand, spotted this discrepancy immediately). He based all four original songs on tunes found in these collections, although he rewrote them to varying degrees; he and Gershwin also adapted Isaak Dunayevsky's "Song of the Fatherland," which the students sing in a school assembly. For instrumental music broadcast over the commune loudspeaker, Copland further arranged Dmitry and Daniel Pokrass's "My Moscow" (heard when we first meet Kolya) and Pierre Degeyter's "Internationale" (played after the German bombardment of the village). Finally, he adapted two other traditional Russian tunes: "We Have Sown Our Wheat," for the "Going to School" cue, and "And Who Knows" for the background choral singing during the party.[7]

Copland heightened the Russian ambience by developing some of these tunes for other parts of the film; by featuring such instruments as the accordion, balalaika, and harmonica in his orchestrations; and by cultivating a harmonic language sometimes reminiscent of Mussorgsky and Shostakovich. At the same time, his own voice could be heard even in the more folkloric moments; in his view, he suggested rather than emphasized the Russian flavor.[8]

The North Star required much more music than had his previous movies; in particular, the film's first half—the peacetime idyll—necessitated a practically continuous flow of songs, dances, and incidental music. And while the movie's second half featured less music (Copland deliberately refrained from scoring the scenes with bombers), it had a number of the more interesting cues, including the sequence for Damian awakening alone in the woods, "Damian Is Blind": this cue begins with a cluster in the very high strings as Damian confusedly squints; when he realizes his blindness, the brass enter with sharply biting chords. As bold in its own way as Lennie's crushing of Curley's hand in *Of Mice and Men*, such music marked yet another step in Hollywood's adoption of a more contemporary musical vocabulary.

Copland shaped the film's individual cues with growing mastery. In the two-minute "Waiting" episode, as the children spend a sleepless night before their hiking trip, a slightly restless clarinet solo, slowly unfolding against E-minorish harmonies, finally settles on a luminous G-major cadence as Marina and her parents say good-bye to one another. In another gemlike miniature, "Death of the Little Boy," in which the children for the first time come to grips with war, the music forms a kind of tiny sonata movement, with an introduction, an exposition of two themes, a development, a recapitulation, and a coda that effectively cadences in an unexpected relative minor at the very moment of the boy's death.

Copland attempted some remarkable larger forms as well, for example, for the children's hike, a long sequence imaginatively constructed from the opening phrase of "The Younger Generation." The final battle scene and its aftermath, however, constitute the most ambitious set piece, one almost symphonic in its construction, although an important transition (after Dr. Kurin confronts the German doctors) unfortunately got lost in the dubbing room. Copland seemed fairly resigned to such things—more than Hellman, who broke with Milestone and Goldwyn over changes in the script. But in fact, he had, for a Hollywood composer, little cause for complaint: nearly all of his score was used and could be heard—at least to some extent. So far, his own good judgment along with some luck had stood him well in this regard. It helped, too, that he orchestrated and conducted the music himself.

Although some critics have heaped scorn on the movie's musical numbers—Bernard Dick described them as sounding like the rejects from a "second-rate operetta"—Copland's music arguably ennobled the problematic *North Star*. He certainly won the appreciation of his collaborators, not only Gershwin and Hellman, with whom he remained on friendly terms, but Milestone and Goldwyn, both of whom independently wanted him for subsequent projects. The score also earned the admiration of his Hollywood colleagues in the form of another Oscar nomination. Many years later, film composer Laurence Rosenthal, who had consciously avoided imitating Copland's Western idiom, remembered *The North Star* when writing his Emmy-winning scores for televised miniseries about Peter the Great (1986) and Anastasia (1987): "Copland's way of treating Russian music appealed to me so much, I never forgot it." Meanwhile, the new-music community back East took a keen interest in the music, which won kudos from Elliott Carter, Robert Palmer, Lukas Foss, and Louise Talma. In a published review, Carter singled out, among others, the "Going to School" and "Scorched Earth" cues. "At every point," he concluded, "the intelligence and the personal elevation of Copland's music is recognizable, even in his arrangement and orchestration of the 'Internationale.' " Copland subsequently arranged "Song of the Guerrillas" for chorus and sanctioned choral arrangements of "The Younger Generation," but otherwise seems to have left the score alone.[9]

The Violin Sonata and *Letter from Home*

One might say of Copland's Sonata for Violin and Piano (1943) what is more often and less accurately said of the Piano Sonata: that it represents a middle ground between his difficult and his accessible pieces. A tender work, alternately reflective and exuberant, it stands as one of his most Apollonian achievements; each of its three movements (fast-slow-fast) ends with some variety of a quiet major triad. In its own way—in its intermittent elegiac passages, for example—the work is very much a wartime piece; but whereas the nervous, tragic Piano Sonata seems a harrowing prognosis of war, the Violin Sonata suggests the values at stake: peace, civility, and freedom. The opening directive to the violin is "freely singing."

The dedication to Lieutenant Harry H. Dunham (1910–1943), a friend shot down in the Pacific, underscores its connection with the war. Copland had known Dunham since 1931, when the well-to-do twenty-one-year-old Princetonian joined him and Paul Bowles in Morocco. Dunham subsequently became a much admired member of the Copland-Thomson circle. David Diamond remembered him as "the most adorable, good-looking boy." Dunham's death naturally shocked the New York arts community.[10]

While working on the piece in Hollywood, Copland studied and played the violin and piano sonata literature. Such preparation—reminiscent of the *Piano Variations*—seemingly worked its way into the score as a kind of neoclassicism, for one finds echoes of the European masters and, in general, a polished elegance of a type associated with the likes of Honegger and Piston. Indeed, its premiere occasioned an editorial by Olin Downes in the *New York Times* that bemoaned "the persistence" of the "rearward vision" of contemporary composers and a corresponding "absence . . . of any consciousness of a new age or a changing order."[11]

The work strikes a particularly neoclassical profile in its lean textures and extended contrapuntal play—notably, the first two movements' three-part canons and the finale's superimposition of one theme in the violin with a two-voice canon of another theme in the piano. The piece accordingly warrants as attentive listening as does Copland's most daring score, notwithstanding its relatively consonant surface.

And even the music's largely diatonic harmonic language poses unusual challenges. For instance, the opening of the slow movement, without one accidental, suggests shifting tonal centers in the turn of one or another note. This type of ambiguity—derived largely from Stravinsky but made Copland's own—helps provide, in Vincent Persichetti's words, the "thin thread of tragedy, suppressed but strong" that underlies the music's surface "gaiety."[12]

Even in this rather neoclassical outing, Copland avoids any real reliance on traditional schemes. The work moves along like a spontaneous improvisation; tempos speed up and slow down as the music goes every which way. However, the first movement—like the Piano Sonata's—

adapts sonata form to its own ends: it puts forth a slow introduction that gradually evolves into a vigorous first-theme group; a simple second theme, punctuated by plain triads in the piano, that forms a kind of calm oasis; a hectic development that climaxes in a triple-forte passage; a brief recapitulation, including a mere hint of the second theme (by means of a bare cadence in the movement's principal key); and a reprise of the introductory material as a coda. As for the utterly succinct "Lento" that follows—more interlude than movement per se—it in particular fits Colin McPhee's description of the Sonata as "both recherché and baffling in its simplicity, understatement and Stein-like syntax. For some this style will be warm and revealing, but to many it must remain an enigma."[13]

Annotators have interpreted the finale variously, though it seems best described as a binary (or perhaps binary sonata) form (AA'). The movement's first half successively states a scherzolike theme; a slower and more intimate melody; a fast, spirited tune; a short folklike interlude (over a static harmony); and a poignant closing theme. All this material derives—to various degrees of explicitness—from the first two movements. The finale's second half more or less recapitulates its first half, with the exception of the folklike section, an omission balanced by the unexpected reappearance of that episode's sauntering accompaniment in the otherwise somber coda. This coda—a brief reprise of the work's very opening—comes to rest on a stunning sonority involving harmonics in the violin and widely spaced intervals in the piano.[14]

After the 17 January 1944 premiere by violinist Ruth Posselt and Copland, violinists far and wide took up the sonata, making it very possibly the best-known American work of its kind (despite the feeling among some professional violinists that the work lacked bravura, that it was "a little withdrawn, a little pastoralish, a little on the Fauré Second side," as David Diamond characterized Isaac Stern's reaction). Early recordings included those by Louis Kaufman and Copland, Joseph Fuchs and Leo Smit, Fredell Lack and Leonid Hambro, and (playing only the slow movement) Yehudi Menuhin and Marcel Gazelle; in the 1970s, Copland recorded the work again, this time with Isaac Stern. Both Stern and Lack hoped to commission a violin concerto, but Copland demurred, saying that he felt wary about writing a virtuoso violin part; for the sonata, he relied on the help of Kaufman and Diamond for bowings and fingerings.[15]

More recent recordings include an insightful reading by a German duo, violinist Hans Maile and pianist Horst Göbel; a wholly compelling performance by violinst Anne Akiko Meyers and pianist André-Michel

Schub; and a particularly vigorous account by violinist Glenn Dicterow and pianist Israela Margalit. According to Larry Starr, the Maile recording had the particular virtue of deemphasizing the sonata's pastoral elements in favor of its "linear, directional qualities," reminding us "that linear tension should never be absent from Copland's music, even at its most restful, if the true quality of musical invention in his scores is to flower in performance." For sheer eloquence, the early Kaufman-Copland recording still holds its own against the very best.[16]

In the late 1970s, clarinetist Timothy Paradise arranged the sonata for clarinet and piano and played it for Copland, who later transcribed it himself in consultation with Paradise and another clarinetist, Michael Webster. Aside from transposing the work down a major third, Copland made only the slightest alterations. This transcription presents certain drawbacks, including the inevitable thickening of the piano part caused by transposing it downward, and the inability of the clarinet to play double notes. On the other hand, the new scoring brings a revealing clarity to the work's carefully etched melodies and a brilliant verve to its jazzy rhythms. Webster gave a preliminary performance of the work with Barbara Lister-Sink in 1983 and the official premiere with Barry Snyder on 10 March 1986; Boosey & Hawkes published it in 1988; and Victoria Soames and Julius Drake released the premiere recording in 1992, writing, "We have performed the Sonata many times and have no doubt that it is a wonderful addition to the repertoire for both performer and listener alike."[17]

Paul Whiteman (1890–1967) commissioned Copland's *Letter from Home* (1944) as a short work for radio to be played by his popular dance band. Over the years, Whiteman had ambitiously commissioned and performed a number of such concert works, including Gershwin's *Rhapsody in Blue* (1924) and Ferde Grofé's *Grand Canyon Suite* (1931); most of these crossover attempts were stillborn, but the extraordinary success of the Gershwin and the Grofé kept him hopeful. In the early 1940s, although past his heyday, he still drew large audiences, and the idea of a concert repertory for dance band hovered about yet.

In 1944, as musical director for a large radio network, the Blue Network, Whiteman established the Creative Music Fund for the commissioning of short (five- to six-minute) "symphonettes" for a new radio show, *Music out of the Blue,* to be played by his own orchestra and aired at midnight ("So if they are too bad," Whiteman explained to his superiors, "few people will know it"). A number of composers welcomed the opportunity (among other incentives, it paid $1,000—a good sum for so short a piece): not only Copland but Leonard Bernstein, Paul Creston, Peter De Rose, Duke Ellington, Morton Gould, Ferde Grofé, Roy Harris, Erich Wolfgang Korngold, Richard Rodgers, David Rose, Victor Young, and even Igor Stravinsky, who submitted his *Scherzo à la Russe*. Whiteman hoped to make *Music out of the Blue* an ongoing series, but the Blue Network canceled the program upon becoming the American Broadcasting System (ABC) in 1945.[18]

The precise makeup of the Whiteman Orchestra fluctuated but typically consisted of between twenty and thirty players, an assortment of strings, brass, woodwinds, and percussion not unlike a chamber orchestra. Copland scored *Letter from Home* for flute, oboe, four saxophones, French horn, three trumpets, three trombones, tuba, guitar, piano, harp, percussion, and strings. Whiteman premiered this original version (since lost) on 7 October 1944 and recorded it some time later, "much too fast from beginning to end," as Copland remembered. Copland subsequently arranged the work for full orchestra (1947) and eventually revised and shortened it for chamber orchestra as well (1962), recording this latter version with the London Symphony Orchestra (1975).[19]

In discussing the title, Copland said, "I meant only to convey the emotions that might naturally be awakened in the recipient by reading a letter from home"; the opening directive of this, by Copland's admission, "very sentimental" work calls for "simple warmth." He completed the piece in Mexico toward the end of the summer of 1944—often working by candlelight, since the town of Tepoztlán had no electricity—and the music reflected not only general wartime conditions but his own homesickness, as expressed in letters to Leonard Bernstein and Arthur Berger. Throughout the spring and summer, he'd received a series of letters from his sister Laurine full of urgent and sad news: about their mother's heart attack and death (too late for him to attend the funeral), about difficulties attending their father's senility, and about their brother Ralph in the army and Laurine's son Burton in the air force. Copland felt bereft and lonely, but he remained in Mexico, partly in order to complete *Letter from Home*. One cannot help but suppose that some of his feelings about the death of his mother and other family matters made their way into this score.[20]

Not surprisingly, the music resembles those homey passages in *Our Town* and *Rodeo*, but thrust, so to speak, into the urgent present. However, for all the sweet sentiment, the work retains a characteristic detachment. In addition, toward the end, the music turns progressively unsettled, reaching a dissonant climax, triple forte, before calming down again; the piece would be a lesser one without this outburst.

Letter from Home was Copland's last work composed specifically for radio. The genre—like symphonic jazz itself—had run its course. As with his earlier radio pieces (*Prairie Journal* and *John Henry*), the work, for all its accessibility, failed to find a following. Perhaps in all three cases, the music was too wedded to the medium to persuasively accommodate other venues.

Appalachian Spring

Since its premiere, *Appalachian Spring* (1944) has been more closely associated with Copland's name than any of his other works. Other pieces rival, if not surpass, it in familiarity; some enjoy greater critical cachet, boast bigger ambitions, or can be said to be more profound or perfect. But none holds the kind of emblematic stature of *Appalachian Spring*, a work admired by critics as well as by the average listener—something of a rarity in Copland's career—and one, furthermore, that evokes a special kind of admiration, even love. Chávez referred to it as the hit of a lifetime, like his own *Sinfonía India*. William Austin highlighted a passage from the score as the centerpiece of his article on Copland for the *New Grove Dictionary* (1980). The music was endlessly performed, arranged, imitated, exploited.[21]

In considering its iconic status, we have a helpful clue: Martha Graham, the choreographer for whom he composed the work. "When I wrote *Appalachian Spring*," he stated, "I was thinking primarily about Martha and her unique choreographic style, which I knew well. Nobody else seems quite like Martha: she's so proud, so very much herself. And she's unquestionably very American: there's something prim and restrained, simple yet strong, about her which one tends to think of as American." While composing the piece, Copland used the working title *Ballet for Martha*, later to become the ballet's subtitle.[22]

Martha Graham (1894–1991) grew up in Allegheny, Pennsylvania, near Pittsburgh, a doctor's daughter. She inherited her father's expert knowledge of the psychological implications of bodily movement and the austerity of both parents' strict Presbyterianism. In 1908 she moved to

Santa Barbara with her mother and two younger sisters, and in 1916 began studies in Los Angeles with Ruth St. Denis and Ted Shawn. The diminutive Graham—she stood all of five feet, two inches—soon was teaching at their school herself. From St. Denis she absorbed a lifelong fascination with fabrics and ancient cultures; from Shawn, a respect for American folk and vernacular styles. In 1926 she founded her own school in New York and formed an ensemble of devoted women dancers. "Not since the Middle Ages and the years of cloistered religious," observed Agnes de Mille, "have people banded together to work with similar dedication, faithfulness, and sacrifice."[23]

In the late 1920s, Graham refined an influential dance vocabulary now known as the "Graham technique," one that involved torso movement and percussive, angular gesture, including stomach spasms; this technique permitted innovative movement in kneeling and sitting positions. During these years—until 1948, in fact—she collaborated with her sometime lover, the pianist, conductor, and composer Louis Horst, who introduced her to modern scores, including, apparently, Copland's *Piano Variations*, choreographed in 1931; such music complemented her own development. She quickly established a small, enthusiastic following; Fanny Brice satirized her *Revolt* (1927) in the Ziegfeld Follies as "Rewolt." The starring role in the League of Composers' *The Rite of Spring* (1930) and her own ballet inspired by Native American ritual, *Primitive Mysteries* (1931), furthered her preeminence in New York dance circles. Each passing year brought fresh triumphs and new converts.[24]

In the 1930s Graham began commissioning scores, which allowed her greater control over the final product. She typically provided composers with detailed scripts, from which she felt free to deviate during the choreographic process (though apparently she never, in her long career, cut a composer's score). Some favored early collaborators, aside from Horst, included Henry Cowell, Hunter Johnson, Paul Nordoff, and Wallingford Riegger. In 1935 she similarly initiated associations with the sculptors Alexander Calder and especially Isamu Noguchi, whose sets brought a distinctive spaciousness to her work.[25]

Starting with *Primitive Mysteries* and continuing with such dances as *American Provincials* (1934), *Frontier* (1935), *American Document* (1938), and *Letter to the World* (1940), Graham began exploring America's past, including not only Indian ritual but colonial history, Mexican culture, frontier life, and minstrelsy. Descended from New England Puritans and pioneer stock, she felt deeply about her heritage. "She talked endlessly about the American folk roots, about Appalachia," remembered one of her dancers, Anna Sokolow. In 1932 Graham prophesied that American dance—whose rhythms, "rich, full, unabashed, virile," derived from the contrasting rhythms of the Native American and the African-American—will "contain a heritage from all other nations, but it will be transfigured by the rhythm, and dominated by the psyche of this new land." Her Americanism was not so much decorative or political (though she and her mostly Jewish dancers, sympathetic to the left, danced at a *New Masses* benefit in 1938) as spiritual, her aim nothing less than "the revelation of a people's soul" in dance. "She seemed an incarnate question of everything we fear and hope for in our daily lives," wrote Lincoln Kirstein in 1938.[26]

In that same year, Erick Hawkins, a disillusioned ballet dancer, became, after only a few weeks of study with Graham, the first man to join her company; other men soon after followed, including Merce Cunningham in 1939. As Graham's lover and the company's leading male dancer, Hawkins quickly gained ascendancy; he partnered with Graham, managed the company, and launched his own dances. Although the other dancers strongly resented Hawkins, they acknowledged that he not only strengthened their precarious financial base but allowed Graham to broaden her range and tackle such themes as relations between the sexes.

Graham married Hawkins, fifteen years her junior, in 1948; two years later they separated, the great personal tragedy of her life. Her work subsequently turned more psychological, her inclination toward Jungian symbolism that much more pronounced. She danced into her eighties, and choreographed and taught into her nineties, becoming a kind of national treasure. At the same time, she grew increasingly depressed and alcoholic. Those who intimately knew and admired her work, like Agnes de Mille and Arlene Croce, bemoaned a perceived decline in the company's artistic integrity and purpose in these later years.[27]

The careers of Graham and Copland paralleled each other in many ways. Moreover, their basic techniques and styles similarly owed an enormous debt to the American vernacular. Yet as much as he admired her, Copland seemed a bit cool about Graham's work, sometimes using the word *severe* in a vaguely critical way. Significantly, their collaboration resulted in one of her warmest and most tender creations; Copland's score, claimed Virgil Thomson, thwarted her "Germanic approach to theater." Nor did they ever, in spite of the success of *Appalachian Spring*, work together on another project (though in 1974 she proposed one based on Hawthorne's *The Scarlet Letter*—a dance about "tormented love" in which "certain hebraic melody lines could be employed" to communicate "the austerity and terror of the Hymns of the Puritans which are reminiscent in feeling at least of the teachings of the Old Testament"). Of course, the differences between them may help account for the special success of their one collaboration.[28]

Graham had long wanted a score from Copland. In February 1941, she proposed a "bitter, sardonic, murderous, despairing" dance about Medea, offering to pay as much as she could: $100 in advance and $150 in royalties. Copland declined. The following year, in June 1942, Hawkins approached Elizabeth Sprague Coolidge, America's premier patron of chamber music, about commissioning scores from Copland and Hindemith for Graham. Because Coolidge could budget only $500 per commission, she hesitated; but after consulting Harold Spivacke, head of the Music Division of the Library of Congress, she gave the Hawkins proposal her full consideration.[29]

After discussing the matter over the summer, Graham and Coolidge decided in favor of Copland and Carlos Chávez, both of whom accepted the commission, happy at the prospect of having their Graham ballets premiered together. Coolidge specified a work of about a half hour in length and a chamber orchestration for no more than twelve musicians. At first intended for the Pittsfield Festival in Massachusetts, the premieres were rescheduled for performance at the Library of Congress on Coolidge's birthday, 30 October 1943, in celebration of her twenty-five years of musical patronage.

As early as July 1942, even before the commissions had officially gone out, Graham sent Copland a script entitled "Daughter of Colchis," a Medea-inspired story set in nineteenth-century New England. Copland thought the script "too severe" and proposed something like a cross between it and *Our Town*. Graham subsequently sent Chávez a version of the Colchis script (purged of its New England references) and spent months brooding over the Copland dance. Finally, in May 1943, she sent him a new script, "House of Victory," which he generally liked, though he suggested various revisions; by the time an acceptable version reached him over the summer, he was thick in the midst of *The North Star*. In the meantime, not a note of Chávez's score had yet appeared, though he had received his script in November of the previous year. Given further complications imposed by wartime conditions, all the parties concerned agreed to postpone the premiere until the spring of 1944. Coolidge was "rather vexed" with both Copland and Chávez and might have canceled the commissions altogether had not Archibald MacLeish, head of the Library of Congress, counseled otherwise.

Although Coolidge and Spivacke set December 1 as the new deadline, only bits and pieces came dribbling in throughout the year. Graham at least liked the Copland she heard—"clear and open and very moving," as she described it—as opposed to the Chávez, which she thought lacked "stage awareness." The premieres now had to be rescheduled for the fall of 1944. In late January, an exasperated Coolidge decided to schedule the Chávez for a later time and offer a fresh commission to another composer. At first Graham once again proposed Hindemith, but after talking to Copland, she suggested Stravinsky instead. Whatever the reason—probably the unlikelihood of getting a Stravinsky ballet for $500—Coolidge and Spivacke commissioned Hindemith, as Hawkins had originally proposed. In March, to fill out the program, they decided to ask Milhaud for a score as well, possibly because, as Wayne Shirley suggests, he needed the money and could be counted on to deliver music quickly.

After some hounding by Graham, Copland finally completed his condensed score in June 1944 and proceeded to orchestrate it. Back in July 1943, he had imagined an instrumentation of double string quartet and piano, but then he'd decided to add a double bass and three woodwinds (flute, clarinet, bassoon) for a total of thirteen musicians, in part because he knew these instruments would be on hand for the Chávez (and, later, the Milhaud). This was one player more than Coolidge's limit of twelve, and four more than the Graham Company would have liked, considering that they could tour with at most nine musicians. But Coolidge obliged him in this matter.[30]

Over the summer of 1944, orchestral scores began turning up at the Library of Congress, Copland's *Ballet for Martha* in early August. On 30 October, Graham presented the Hindemith as *Mirror Before Me* (later retitled *Hérodiade*), the Milhaud as *Imagined Wing*, and the Copland as *Appalachian Spring*. In January 1946 she premiered the Chávez as *Dark Meadow*.[31]

Copland wrote most of *Ballet for Martha* at some geographical distance from its choreographer; he composed much of the reduced score in Hollywood and Cambridge and the orchestration in Mexico. This made him all the more reliant on the material Graham sent him: the "House of Victory" script received in May 1943 and two later revisions—both simply entitled "Name"—sent to him over the next few months. Copland drew upon all three scripts, creating a kind of composite scenario of his own.[32]

Whereas Ruth Page, Eugene Loring, and Agnes de Mille had similarly provided Copland with a rigorous outline, Graham's scripts, while more detailed in terms of mood and character analysis, rarely specified precise action and only hesitantly suggested music of one sort or another. In addition, as mentioned, she freely reinterpreted her original scripts any way she saw fit; and, in fact, *Appalachian Spring* deviated considerably from the scripts Copland worked from. According to Marta Robertson, costume listings compiled in the early summer of 1944 reveal that even by this late date, the dance still conformed more to the scripts than to its eventual rendering. Graham must have thoroughly revised the entire concept in the course of the summer as she became more familiar with the completed rehearsal score.[33]

Copland, who first saw the dance only days before the premiere, was surprised to find that "music composed for one kind of action had been used to accompany something else. . . . But that kind of decision is the choreographer's, and it doesn't bother me a bit, especially when it works." This characteristically even-tempered response contrasted with that of, say, Menotti, who upon seeing his Graham dance (*Errand into the Maze*, 1947) angrily complained to Copland that she had wholly ignored the script she had provided him with; Copland assuaged him by saying, "Oh Gian Carlo, she does that all the time." However, he was somewhat less sanguine in a letter to Chávez about *Dark Meadow* (1946): "What Martha did was often in direct contrast to what the music was doing—with the result that a special and interesting atmosphere was created—a kind of counterpoint between music and dance. She is becoming more and more psychoanalytic in her motifs which made a very strong contrast with your very unpsychoanalytical music! Such is the fate of a ballet composer." Perhaps this is how Copland felt about *Appalachian Spring*: that Graham did "extraordinary things," that her departures from the music's aims created "a special and interesting atmosphere," and that the choreographer had the final word in any case.[34]

Meanwhile, the Graham scripts he worked from can at least shed light on his original intentions. This means beginning with the rejected "Daughter of Colchis," for it provided the basis and some context for the later "House of Victory" scripts. A domestic psychodrama set in New England "about the time of a tale by Poe or Hawthorne," this script featured five characters: the Woman and the Man; the Fury, representing the Woman's emotions; the Muse, representing the Man's work; and the Passer-by, the "detached" and "heroic" New Englander who functions as a kind of Greek chorus. The essential conflict between Man (and his work) and Woman (and her emotions)—a theme thought by Graham to be "universal in its suffering"—permeated the script.

"House of Victory" moved the locale westward. Although these later scripts never actually identified time or place, all indications pointed to the years just before and during the Civil War and a small town in the North, presumably on the frontier, but not necessarily far west. "This need in no sense be western in feeling," explained Graham. "My own great Grandmother went into Pennsylvania when it seemed a frontier." At some point Graham actually specified the locale as western Pennsylvania—the region where she had grown up. She further imagined a set that would simply contain the bare bones of a home and that would divide the stage space into an inside and an outside area.

Like "Daughter of Colchis," the original "House of Victory" featured four principals: the Mother, a gentle but strong matriarchal figure whom Graham associated with early American portraits, Shaker furniture, Grant Wood, and her great-grandmother; the Daughter, a valiant "Pioneer Woman"; the shy, fanatical, and heroically tragic Citizen, a fighter for civil rights and a figure associated with the Puritans, Thoreau, and the abolitionist John Brown; and the persecuted Fugitive, "the slave figure of the Civil War," who should have "a broader meaning as well." The cast also included a "headlong" Younger Sister, who "suggests today"; Two Children; and Neighbors, the men being "a little like the Mark Twain figures." The principal roles of the Daughter and the Citizen (naturally intended for herself and Hawkins) recalled the Woman and the Man from "Daughter of Colchis."

In the two revised "Name" scripts, Graham added the Indian Girl, a character representing the land and associated with the myth of Pocahontas as found in Hart Crane's The Bridge. Graham, who wanted nothing authentically Indian about the Indian Girl, either in dance or music, imagined her interacting with the entire company throughout the piece, including a "pietà" with the Fugitive. She even thought that the dance might end with the Indian Girl running "strongly and quietly around the stage in a beautiful free run." Rightly suspecting that Copland might not approve of this new character, she argued for its potential as "a supremely theatrical device"; but she jettisoned the idea after he voiced objections.

"House of Victory" eventually coalesced into eight parts—"Prologue,"
"Eden Valley," "Wedding Day," "Interlude," "Fear in the Night," "Day
of Wrath," "Moment of Crisis," and "The Lord's Day"—interspersed
with planned spoken excerpts from the Book of Genesis for the Mother,
"not in a religious sense so much as in a poetic sense." Concerning the
"Prologue," Graham wrote, "If you think it best to have one, I feel it
should not be long. Perhaps there could be a sense of simple celebration
such as in the hearts of people at the beginning of a town. This might even
be a fanfare but not militant in feeling." As the lights go up during the
"Prologue," the Mother looks out "over the land she has helped to stake
and claim and win." In "Eden Valley," the Daughter dances a "joyous"
solo; the Citizen enters and he and the Daughter engage in a "duet of
courtship."

Graham divided "Wedding Day" into two parts, separated by spoken
text (in his rehearsal score, Copland specified these as "part one" and
"part two"). The Younger Sister opens the scene by running "across the
stage in an excited adolescent way" and dancing with the Two Children.
The Citizen dances a solo that "is like an exhibition of strength." At the
finish, he carries the Daughter across the doorway. In the second part,
two scenes develop simultaneously: a love scene for the Daughter and
Citizen within the house, and an "old fashioned charivari" for the others
outside the house. The charivari, states one of the later scripts, "develops
from a bridal party in a rough little town into something wilder and infi-
nitely older." The "Interlude" that follows, associated with spring
planting, depicts the town's daily life: "It should have the feeling of a telescoped day with such simple things as take place in times of peace, children playing, women talking, men in some feats of strength, a party at
night, dinner, perhaps, and a pattern of work." For this possible "core" of
the work, Graham suggested songlike music that might consist of a
"theme and variations in rondo form."

In "Fear in the Night," the hunted Fugitive slave enters with his solo,
"awkward with the tragic awkwardness of the hopeless," hiding in the
Mother's skirts. In "Day of Wrath" (originally, "Day of War"), the Citizen dances an "angry, violent, possessed" solo "reminiscent of Harper's
Ferry and John Brown," while the Children act out a charade of war.
Graham intended this scene to depict "the state of war at any time, with
its timeless tragedies of separations, bewilderment, loneliness, loss and the
quiet, simple agony of uneventful lives torn asunder." (For this episode
she requested that—although the music need not be folklike—Copland

emphasize the Civil War period and evoke "some sense of the negro in the scene. It will be played in such a light as not to need that make-up but the movement will need to be reminiscent of the negro body.")

In "Moment of Crisis," the women gather with movements suggesting "a barely suppressed hysteria." Graham meant the concluding scene, "The Lord's Day," to suggest a remembrance of "Sabbath in a small town." Like the second part of "The Wedding," it features a double scene, with the Daughter and Citizen now outside the home in a love duet, and the company inside as at a revival meeting, standing "in orderly rows facing offstage as though facing a preacher. . . . This could have the feeling of either a Shaker meeting where the movement is strange and ordered and possessed or it could have the feeling of a negro church with the lyric ecstasy of the spiritual about it." Near the end, the congregants gradually file out; when all have left, the Citizen lifts the Daughter through the doorway as on their wedding day "but without the sense of newness."

The very first "House of Victory" script also contained, just after the "Interlude," an "Episode" meant to feature a "show boat stage" and a dramatic telling of "crucial scenes" from Uncle Tom's Cabin, thus representing the critical events precipitating the Civil War. Graham apparently intended this pantomime to mark the work's transition from peace to war, as well as to elucidate its Civil War context, but at Copland's urging she omitted it from her revised scripts. Otherwise, the three drafts differed most in their endings. The initial script concluded not with "The Lord's Day," but with "Time of Return," another double scene, with the reunion of the Daughter and Citizen within the house and the "excitement of return" outside. The second draft ended "quite simply," with "the feeling of the town settling down for the night"; just before the curtain falls, the Daughter "goes to the fence, standing waiting." The third draft put forth "The Lord's Day" as related above. In short, the first draft concluded happily with war's end; the more melancholy second draft, with expectancy for the Citizen's return; and the third—a kind of compromise—with remembrance and hope.

Copland's score—unlike the eventual Graham dance—adhered closely to the "House of Victory" scripts. His intentions, clear enough from the music itself, are clarified further by the condensed piano score, which includes a few stage instructions. For example, it specifies that the curtain rise in silence at the opening half-note rest and a light shine on the

Mother's face at the solo in measure eight, the work's first dynamic louder than mezzo piano. This entire slow introduction, corresponding to Graham's "Prologue," suggests the Mother's nostalgic memories of youth and the land; its repeated-note introduction, its rising three-note motive, and its famous telescoping of simple triads may have derived specifically from Graham's idea of a nonmilitant fanfare (like *Fanfare for the Common Man* heard from an enormous distance away). A remarkable opening (one that contains, incidentally, not a single accidental), this "Prologue" epitomizes, in music, that combination of "vastness" and "clarity" that art critic Robert Hughes finds so characteristic of American painting in all its phases.[35]

As the Daughter enters from within the house, a forceful, energetic melody—derived from the opening pastoral, but full of action rather than dreaming—issues forth. The solo that follows and that begins the "Eden Valley" episode expresses the Daughter's "joy" in rhythms possibly related to the old-fashioned swing mentioned at this point in the script. Midway through the solo—in response to Graham's request that it occasionally have "the quality of a psalm"—Copland juxtaposes these swinging rhythms with a more solemn, hymnlike melody (the psalm theme). The Citizen enters, his strength and "awkward grace of action" depicted by block triads that move jaggedly, not unlike the Cowgirl's music from *Rodeo*. Copland twice interrupts this music with a tender melody, related to the psalm theme, presumably meant to express the Citizen's shy feelings of love (the love theme). For the courtship duet, Graham imagined music like *Quiet City* or the softer parts of *Lincoln Portrait*, but Copland composed an intense passage whose taut expressivity and bold dissonance reflect his more severe side; perhaps, given the Eden imagery, he had in mind man's fall. Near the end of the duet, he "tenderly" brings back the love theme in the clarinet, now answered by the flute, plausibly representing the Citizen and the Daughter, respectively.[36]

For the music for the Younger Sister and the Two Children that initiates the first part of the "Wedding Day," Copland subtly transforms the Daughter's melody into a theme of childlike playfulness that has, as Graham hoped, "the feeling of quicksilver." Meanwhile, the music's folklike qualities, which include some evocation of country fiddling, heeded Graham's request for "a little sense of a County Fair, a little of a revival meeting, a party, a picnic." A "pesante" section brings back the Citizen's jagged triads for his solo, exhibiting those Davy Crockett qualities spoken of in Graham's script. After a brief pause, the scene climaxes with a slower, "eloquent" passage as the Citizen sweeps the Daughter across the doorway; one can even faintly discern the outline of Mendelssohn's "Wedding March." A reprise of the love theme closes this first part of "Wedding Day."

Most of the second part of the "Wedding Day" portrays the "old fashioned charivari" identified by Graham with Merrymount. The music suggests the rustic merrymaking through repeated notes, scalar melodies, parallel fourths, and rhythmic jolts. After the charivari winds down, the music depicts the newlyweds inside the house by way of an extended treatment of the psalm theme. As the stage fades into darkness, the light illuminating only the Mother's face, Copland brings back the music from the opening "Prologue." This reinforces the sense that this entire exposition is a kind of reminiscence from the Mother's perspective.

For the "Interlude" portraying a routine day, Copland adopted Graham's suggestion for a songlike theme and variations, writing a set of variations on the then obscure Shaker song "Simple Gifts." He presumably chose the tune early on in the compositional process; the opening prologue anticipates it. Dating from 1848 or possibly earlier, the tune helped establish period atmosphere (as do the variations themselves, including one reminiscent of a horse's clip-clop); in addition, the (unsung) text—" 'Tis the gift to be simple, 'tis the gift to be free"—had connotations relevant to the work's larger themes of peace, war, remembrance, and national identity. Copland apparently recognized the tune's potential for canonic treatment as well. He set forth the theme more or less as found in Edward D. Andrews's study of Shaker song and dance (1940) but touched it up here and there; the subsequent variations put forth this slightly revised melody essentially intact, the variety primarily involving the other musical elements. This entire set piece fitted Graham's objective of alternately depicting children, women, and men at their daily tasks (the "vigoroso" variation no doubt representing the men and their "feats of strength") in a scene comprising "a warmth and a kind of sweetness that need in no sense be sentimental. It almost serves as a Greek chorus in its function."[37]

Because Copland eventually omitted the "Fear in the Night," "Day of Wrath," and "Moment of Crisis" episodes from his popular ballet suite, the public has far less familiarity with this music. "Fear in the Night" (derived from some incidental music to *Quiet City*) is a brief and nervous interlude, full of the kind of violent twitchings found in the "Gun Battle"

from *Billy*. The "Day of Wrath" opens with the Mother rising "in disturbance of spirit and deep anger," her pastoral music now transformed into
a noble declamation reminiscent of *Lincoln Portrait*. The Citizen's
"Harper's Ferry" solo that follows features the love theme also in a
declamatory context, this one sadder and more anguished than the
Mother's. For the Two Children's charade of war, the playful "Wedding
Day" music returns, now accompanied by toy-soldier bugle calls. The
scene concludes with a reworked version of the "Harper's Ferry" music,
perhaps mindful of Graham's stage direction: "The Children exit and the
Citizen follows them as though in a trance, using their childish rhythm."

For the anxious dance of the women, "Moment of Crisis," the music
explodes into an agitated perpetual motion. The arrival of the psalm
theme soothes the prevailing anxiety; this in turn leads to a reprise of
"Simple Gifts," now juxtaposed with the psalm, marking the start of
"The Lord's Day." Such transition from agitation to calm recalls
Graham's comment, "At the moment of greatest tension when it seems
that the whole thing will become a scourge of violence the Daughter
breaks the spell."

The score moves on to a climactic, fortissimo restatement of "Simple
Gifts," no doubt in response to Graham's saying, "There is a return to the
feeling of the Interlude with its warmth and simplicity. The relationships
established earlier make themselves felt again. There is a certain peace and
sense of order, a kind of suppressed gayety, and over all a shimmer of
living with eagerness." This leads directly into a soft hymn, representing
the "Shaker meeting" or "negro church" and meant "to give again the
American feeling of place." After the hymn reaches its final cadence, the
psalm theme reappears as first heard in the Daughter's opening solo (but
stripped of its lively counterpoint), music apparently meant to accompany
the Citizen and Daughter as they solemnly reenter the house. In the
work's final measures, the Mother's music returns for her final spoken
line, "In the Beginning God Created the Heaven and the Earth." Copland
wanted the slowly fading final chord to accompany the continuing dance
until the descent of the curtain in silence.[38]

The entire score represents an astonishing absorption of the
vernacular—suitable to a script so steeped in a wide range of American
myth and folklore. It often gives the impression of folk music, so much so
that listeners are often surprised to discover that it uses only one folk
tune. One source for this remarkable achievement lies with the culture of
the Shakers and their belief " 'Tis the Gift to Be Simple."

Copland's jottings on the initial "House of Victory" script suggest that he intended to use one or another Shaker song as early as this. Because Graham's script refers to the Mother's "Shaker rocking chair," it might seem that this one prop pointed him in this direction, and in part it may well have. But Copland had wanted to write a one-act opera about the Shakers at least as early as 1941. The Depression era generally witnessed, especially among artists, a notable interest in the Shakers, a group that for many decades had been the object of persecution and ridicule. Doris Humphrey, for instance, enjoyed considerable success with her dance *The Shakers* (1931). Throughout the 1930s, Charles Sheeler painted and photographed Shaker buildings and collected Shaker artifacts. During these same years, Edward Andrews published two texts—a book on Shaker furniture (1937) and a study of Shaker song and dance (1940)—that further helped popularize the Shakers (in 1938 Lincoln Kirstein even compared Graham's work to Shaker furniture). The second Andrews publication not only provided Copland with "Simple Gifts" but presumably influenced his thoughts on the Shakers and helped inspire the idea of a Shaker opera.[39]

A Protestant sect related to the Quakers, the Shakers emigrated to America in the late eighteenth century, establishing communities in upstate New York, western Massachusetts, and eventually New England and the Midwest (though never in Pennsylvania). They lived simple, industrious, and communal lives, practicing celibacy, denouncing private property, and extolling pacifism. Officially known by 1823 as the United Society of Believers, this "heretical group" conferred on its founder, Mother Ann Lee, a status approaching Christ's and avowed a male-female Godhead; their services, which featured ecstatic singing and dancing, were similarly notorious. By the 1930s, their numbers had dwindled to a few old-timers, but their legacy—including their reputation as America's first communistic society (in the words of Friedrich Engels, the "first people to set up a society on the basis of community of goods in America, indeed in the whole world")—clearly suited some of the time's trends and ideals.[40]

Copland apparently thought of "House of Victory" as taking place in a Shaker community; his use of "Simple Gifts" would indicate as much, as does this admission: "My research evidently was not very thorough, since I did not realize that there never have been Shaker settlements in rural Pennsylvania!" Graham's early scripts presumed no such connection—

indeed, the absence of Shakers in Pennsylvania seems a less glaring inconsistency than the notion of a celibate, temperate, pacifist community hosting a wedding, engaging in wild revelry, and preaching militant abolitionism; but intrigued by Copland's intended use of a Shaker song, Graham began investigating the Shakers, adding, in her third draft, "The Lord's Day" episode, with its possible "Shaker meeting."[41]

Even so, Graham and Copland responded to the Shakers differently. She understandably recognized a conflict between her preoccupations—as expressed by the Daughter and the Citizen—and those of the Shaker religion, which she thought of as a "cult." "There are so many cults here," she explained to Copland, obliquely referring to the Shakers. "There is something in the very soil that seems to make them flourish. There are over two hundred small ones in America." In her third draft of "House of Victory," when the church members leave the house, they regard the Daughter and the Citizen "as though these two were the symbols of themselves and their hidden desires." In this one gesture, buried in her twelve-page revised script, lay the kernel for a whole new slant for the ballet: the lovers pitted against religious orthodoxy. Graham vigorously pursued this direction in the dance she created from Copland's score, including an alternately satirical and admiring portrayal of a religious cult that drew upon elements of Shaker dance. Significantly, *The Scarlet Letter* (1975), for which she hoped Copland would furnish her a score, became her only subsequent work of Americana.

On 3 October 1944, some weeks before the premiere, Erick Hawkins wrote to Harold Spivacke informing him that Graham had entitled the Copland ballet *Appalachian Spring*. She had found the phrase in the poem "The Dance," from Hart Crane's cycle of poems about America, *The Bridge*. In context, Crane meant "spring" as in a natural source of water, though he may have intended a pun on the season as well. In any case, Graham apparently thought of "spring" in the latter sense, because her synopsis for the ballet provided at the premiere read, in toto:

> Part and parcel of our lives is that moment of Pennsylvania spring when there was "a garden eastward in Eden."
> Spring was celebrated by a man and woman building a house with joy and love and prayer; by a revivalist and his followers in their shouts of exaltation; by a pioneering woman with her dreams of the Promised Land.[42]

Copland often related the story of how he heard about the ballet's title from Graham just days before the premiere, as in this 1981 telling:

> The first thing I said to her when I came down to the rehearsal here in Washington was, "Martha, whatdya call the ballet?" She said, "Appalachian Spring." "Oh," I said, "What a nice name. Where'd'ya get it?" She said, "It's the title of a poem by Hart Crane." "Oh," I said, "Does the poem have anything to do with the ballet?" She said, "No, I just liked the title and I took it." And over and over again, nowadays people come up to me after seeing the ballet on stage and say, "Mr. Copland, when I see that ballet and when I hear your music I can just *see* the Appalachians and just *feel* spring." I've begun to see the Appalachians myself a little bit.

Copland could elicit roars of laughter from nearly every line of this anecdote, and would join in the laughter himself. But he and Graham—both similarly reluctant to expound on their work—were somewhat disingenuous or at least cagey about the matter. Graham had been thinking about *The Bridge* early on in their collaboration, as evident from the script in which she compared her Indian Girl to Crane's Pocahontas; she very well may have associated the Mother with the narrator of another of the cycle's poems, "Indiana." In general, her panoramic use of mythic figures to create a work about America paralleled and perhaps derived from *The Bridge*. Copland—who knew both Crane and his work—was at least somewhat aware of this.[43]

As a dance, *Appalachian Spring* both deviated from and conformed to the "House of Victory" scripts. Graham scrapped not only the Indian Girl but the Younger Sister, the Two Children, and the Neighbors, settling on a cast of eight: three familiar characters—the Daughter (now the Bride), the Citizen (now the Husbandman), and the Mother (now the Pioneer Woman)—and five new ones—the Revivalist and his four women Followers. Although many dance critics, from Edwin Denby to Jack Anderson, took Graham's sketchy scenario at its word, as a realistic tale of settling the frontier, the full scripts and the choreography itself suggest the use of these characters as symbolic archetypes, including the Pioneer Woman as the noble American dream, and the Revivalist and his Followers as an ascetic, resolute puritanism.[44]

Even with those characters and other ingredients retained from the "House of Victory," the choreographic action rarely corresponded to the music's designs; aside from the opening solo for the Husbandman and the courtship duet, little of the dance conformed to those indications noted by Copland in his rehearsal score. At times Graham virtually inverted his intentions, for instance, staging the charivari as a solo for the Bride and the ensuing love duet as a dance for the Revivalist and his Followers.[45]

Still, *Appalachian Spring* stayed closer to its original intentions than a casual viewer might suspect. It still divides into two parts that seemingly portray peace and war, respectively. The crucial transition, the "Fear in the Night" episode originally meant for the runaway Fugitive, now features a hellfire sermon by the Revivalist, widely thought to signify, in Marcia Siegel's words, "the demons that will prey on the couple." But one can arguably see this solo as still representing the spirit of John Brown and Harper's Ferry; if the Bride hates the Revivalist, as she does, it is in part because he embodies those forces that will take her husband away to war. One can similarly surmise that the ensuing scene, "Day of Wrath," depicts the Husbandman's departure for war; this helps account for the telltale waves good-bye at the end of the scene. As in the original scripts, "Moment of Crisis," now a solo for the Bride, can be viewed as an expression of wartime anxieties, and the "Lord's Day," a remembrance of and prayer for peace. And while critics assume that the dance concludes with the Husbandman comforting the Bride, the final "House of Victory" script suggests that he is there as a figment of the Bride's imagination; indeed, during the dance's finale, Graham reprises some of the choreography from "Wedding Day," which more than hints at a flashback. At the sublime end, the Husbandman—or rather his spirit—stands behind the Bride, as she stretches her arm out toward the horizon, a remarkable gesture conjoining private and public destinies.[46]

This interpretation can help address the puzzlement, voiced by Siegel and others, over the alleged uniqueness of *Appalachian Spring*, Graham's only dance in which she "is more nearly the equal of other characters. . . . Increasingly she kept herself at the center of her dance by surrounding herself with one-dimensional characters who always did or represented the same things, whose actions referred to the Graham-character's thoughts, and who in that way acted for her while she watched or paced up and down remembering." For in the light of "House of Victory," *Appalachian Spring* itself appears something of a psychological monodrama, with the non-Graham characters as visions, archetypes, and alter egos of one sort or another.

From its very first performance on 30 October 1944, critics and public alike greeted *Appalachian Spring* warmly (despite Copland's own reservations about Louis Horst's conducting). Throughout 1945, as the Graham Company took it on the road—continually reworking it, including revisions suggested by Copland—it found appreciative audiences in Boston, Rochester, Cincinnati, Cleveland, New York, and elsewhere. By the end of the year, everything about the ballet was famous: the cast (Martha Graham as the Bride, Erick Hawkins as the Husbandman, May O'Donnell as the Pioneer Woman, Merce Cunningham as the Revivalist), Graham's choreography and costumes, Isamu Noguchi's set, and Copland's score, which won both a New York Music Critics' Circle Award and a Pulitzer Prize within a few weeks in May. The dance remained in the Graham Company repertory as, in the words of Agnes de Mille, "one of Martha's signature pieces," with dance critics debating the relative merits of the many dancers who over the years assumed the principal parts. For a remarkably long time, Graham herself danced the Bride; among other interpreters, de Mille singled out Jeanne Ruddy, Yuriko Kimura, and Terese Capucilli for bringing "new dimensions" to the role. In its most celebrated performance, Mikhail Baryshnikov and Rudolf Nureyev—dancing the Husbandman and the Revivalist, respectively—joined Capucilli in an October 1987 gala performance that Copland was too ill to attend. "The audience crackled with excitement," remembered de Mille, "and broke, as the curtain fell, into shouts and cries."[47]

In May 1945 Copland arranged a suite from the ballet for orchestra. He principally omitted one large eight-minute section by joining the end of the "Interlude" and its variations on "Simple Gifts" with the tune's climactic restatement in "The Lord's Day," which now sounded like a culminating variation; consequently, the suite highlighted the work's more idyllic side. In addition, Copland made a few smaller cuts elsewhere in the score and reordered the variations on "Simple Gifts." In deference to the original scoring, he employed a relatively small orchestra for the suite, but the larger palette provided a new grandeur and brilliance to the work nonetheless. Some of the episodes, like the courtship duet, acquired a whole new richness with full strings and brass; wonderful new colors could be heard throughout, such as the final three notes, not for flute as in the original but for glockenspiel and harp harmonics, one of Copland's most magical endings.[48]

Serge Koussevitzky, Pierre Monteux, Artur Rodzinski, Antal Dorati, Eugene Ormandy, Leonard Bernstein, and many others quickly took up the suite. Its enormous success in turn helped further the dance's fame, and went far in establishing both Copland and Graham as not only esteemed but celebrated artists.

The suite's popularity led to still other versions and arrangements, including an orchestrated version of the complete score in 1954, so that Eugene Ormandy and the Philadelphia Orchestra could accompany a performance by the Graham Company; first recorded by Ormandy and more recently by Leonard Slatkin, this orchestrated version incorporated some revisions introduced in the suite, such as the reordered variations on "Simple Gifts." In what appears to have been a sheer concession to popular taste, Copland also arranged "Simple Gifts" and its variations as *Variations on a Shaker Melody* for band (1956) and for orchestra (1967). For many years, despite the urging of friends—notably Lawrence Morton—he refused to put forth any concert version of the work in its original instrumentation, telling Morton in 1954, "When the sound of the full orchestra is so present in people's minds, I feel certain it can only suffer by comparison." But Morton persevered and Copland eventually prepared arrangements of both the suite and the complete score for chamber group. The former incorporated some of the orchestral suite's fuller textures and offered the option of expanded strings; the latter, like the complete concert version for full orchestra, adopted some of the cuts and alterations from the suite as well.[49]

Consequently, not counting the two versions of *Variations on a Shaker Melody,* five separate versions of *Appalachian Spring* exist: the original ballet score for chamber group, a revised version of the complete ballet for both orchestra and chamber group, and a suite for both orchestra and chamber group. (Some recordings of the latter four are misleadingly advertised as the "original version" or the "original complete version.") The orchestral suite remains the best-known version, with a long and distinguished performance history, including early recordings by Koussevitzky and the Boston Symphony and Antal Dorati and the London Symphony. Current opinion, however, rates two recordings from the early 1970s—Copland's with the London Philharmonic and Bernstein's with the New York Philharmonic—as the benchmarks for all such recordings. In his performances of the work, Copland was particularly careful to keep the lines moving and to avoid mawkish sentiment. "I have often admonished orchestras, professional and otherwise, not to get too sweet or too sentimental with it," he once wrote.[50]

Copland also recorded the revised complete score for chamber group with the Columbia Chamber Orchestra in 1973, while Hugh Wolff and the St. Paul Chamber Orchestra released the original version in 1991. Meanwhile, the suite for chamber group—usually with additional string players, as authorized by the composer—has become increasingly popular in recent years. A particularly lovely recording by the Orpheus Chamber Orchestra occasioned John Wiser to remark, "That it is only the suite and not the complete score is the only occasion for regret." Today's critics widely prefer the chamber scoring in whatever guise to that for full orchestra; even Copland, reluctant to take a stand, admitted late in life, "I have come to think that the original instrumentation has a clarity and is closer to my original conception than the more opulent orchestrated version."[51]

22

From "Jubilee Variation" to *Four Piano Blues*

(1945–48)

The "Jubilee Variation" and *The Cummington Story*

Copland spent most of 1945 at work on his monumental Third Symphony, completed the following year, but took some time off in order to compose the "Jubilee Variation" for the joint-authored *Jubilee Variations* (later, *Variations on a Theme by Goossens*) and the score for a documentary film, *The Cummington Story*.

Commissioned by Eugene Goossens and the Cincinnati Symphony Orchestra in celebration of its Golden Jubilee, the *Variations* was another of Goossens's collaborative ventures—not a series of fanfares as before, but a set of variations by distinguished American composers on a lively theme of his own making. In addition to Copland, he garnered contributions from Ernest Bloch, Paul Creston, Anis Fuleihan, Howard Hanson, Roy Harris, Walter Piston, Bernard Rogers, William Schuman, and Deems Taylor; he subsequently devised an ordering of these pieces and rounded off the whole with a finale. The project was not explicitly patriotic, but generally so—as an embodiment of the solidarity of the American composer. "To the best of my knowledge," stated Goossens in program notes, "no group of eminent composers has ever before collaborated on the writing of a work for orchestra (with the possible exception of a small group of Russians—'Les Vendredis')."[1]

Concerned that any accompaniment "would set too fixed a harmonic pattern at the outset and prove cramping to the idiomatic peculiarities of the composers themselves," Goossens provided an unharmonized melody. To ensure variety, he specified to each contributor a desired mood or tempo indication along with a particular tonal center or key: in Copland's case, "spirited in feeling and in A major." Copland remembered his three-minute variation as "similar in style" to *Fanfare for the Common Man*, but the music seems closer still to the scherzo of the Third Symphony. *Jubilee Variations* premiered on 23 March 1945; reviewers noted resemblances between the Copland and Piston variations, the work's two scherzo movements. The piece has been revived as a novelty from time to time, especially by the Cincinnati Symphony.[2]

Copland's score to *The Cummington Story* represented a more direct contribution to the war effort. Produced by Frank Beckwith, directed by Helen Grayson and Larry Madison, and written by Howard Smith Southgate for the Office of War Information (OWI) for overseas distribution, this fifteen-minute pseudodocumentary (more a staged propaganda film than a documentary per se) traces the temporary settlement of a group of Eastern European refugees in a quintessentially American town, namely, Cummington, Massachusetts, the home of William Cullen Bryant. As narrated by the town's minister, the Reverend Sangree, the locals at first treat the refugees coolly, but relations improve as the refugees make valued contributions to town life; for their part, the refugees come to appreciate America and its traditions. At harvesttime, all celebrate together at a county fair. When the refugees move on after six months, the townspeople are sad to see them go. Copland quoted the film's last line as summing up the picture's message: "Strangeness between people breaks down when they live and work and meet together as neighbors."[3]

Critics have spoken well of the film. Arthur Knight describes it as "true and touching," Richard Barsam as "a beautiful and moving evocation of the American Dream," one that "remains a true and intimate variation on the 'melting-pot' theme," and Erik Barnouw as recording "touchingly the sometimes painful integration of a group of war refugees into a Connecticut town."[4]

Copland composed the condensed score quickly (in the last week of June), completed the orchestration three weeks later, and recorded the music the following week. The film lent itself even more than *The City* to a continuous stream of music; the only extended silence is a pointed one, when Joseph, newly arrived in town, gets the silent treatment from some men hanging around the general store. Otherwise, the music unfolds with impressive shape and continuity, notwithstanding a few later cuts that naturally impeded its flow.

The first part of the score puts forth two basic ideas: a noble theme, like the tolling of bells, for the church-centered town of Cummington, and a more plaintive theme for the refugees, related to a Polish lullaby hummed by one of them. As the refugees begin their involvement in town life, the score develops a vigorous new theme, subjected to subtle changes depending on circumstances; for Peter in the library of William Cullen Bryant, for example, it takes the form of a fugal exposition—an allusion apparently intended to delineate Peter as a European intellectual.

The county fair scene contains some festive, circuslike music, an intriguing contrast to Richard Rodgers's film musical *State Fair* (also 1945); for all its marked comic relief, this episode features a tune derived from the sober Cummington theme, one that reappears at the very end of the film, as the refugees depart by bus. The film also features some source music: the hymn "Wilmot" for shots of a Sunday-morning church service (at one point, Copland considered using "At the River") and some Mozart arranged for piano trio for a local musicale.[5]

The OWI considered Copland's contribution to the film its major asset. He received the film's only billing, and efforts were made to edit it in line with his specifications. Neil Lerner, who located a Hungarian copy of the film in the National Archives, believes that the picture was shown to refugees in Eastern Europe; however, no evidence reveals that it was ever shown in the States.[6]

As with other unpublished and unfamiliar scores, Copland recycled portions of *The Cummington Story* over time. He used the plaintive refugees' theme in the contrasting middle section of the Clarinet Concerto's first movement and some of the county fair music for the lively chorus "Stomp Your Foot," from *The Tender Land*. In the 1960s, he returned to the music for two commissioned piano pieces for students: *Down a Country Lane* (1962), commissioned and published by *Life* magazine; and *In Evening Air* (1966), commissioned by the Scribner Music Library. He based *Down a Country Lane* on the noble Cummington theme, while *In Evening Air* drew once more on the refugees' music, which he used still again—in its more original guise (1944)—for another piano piece, *Midday Thoughts* (1982). Whereas the titles "Down a Country Lane" and "Midday Thoughts" fitted the music's association with the film, the title "In Evening Air" more elaborately came from a poem of the same name by Theodore Roethke (1964); the piece even appended the poem's last two lines at its end. The relation between the Cummington refugees and Roethke's melancholy ruminations on life and death seems one of general mood. In any case, Roethke's appeal squared with the attraction Copland felt in his later years toward Emily Dickinson, George Meredith, and Gerard Manley Hopkins.[7]

The Third Symphony

After a few decades of relative neglect, the symphony, especially in its more epic guise, made a vigorous comeback in America in the late 1930s and 1940s. Copland's growing legion of friends hoped that he, too, would write a symphony, a genre which practically took the form of a patriotic gesture during the war. He met the challenge by writing his Third Symphony in the two-year period from the summer of 1944 to the summer of 1946, a large undertaking made possible by money earned from *The North Star* and a commission from the Koussevitzky Foundation; he dedicated the score to the conductor's late wife, Natalie.

Copland's Third Symphony—a big four-movement work lasting forty minutes, with a dramatic first movement, a scherzo, a slow movement, and a rousing finale—came closer to popular expectations of a symphony than had his earlier ones. It would be by far his longest orchestral composition. Copland attributed its unique character to Koussevitzky, explaining, "I knew exactly the kind of music he enjoyed conducting and the sentiments he brought to it, and I knew the sound of his orchestra, so I had every reason to do my darndest to write a symphony in the grand manner." At the same time, he also admitted, "The conditions for the writing of such a piece had been in place for some time."[8]

Copland provided succinct program notes for the piece at the premiere, paraphrased later in his autobiography. "If I forced myself," he stated, "I could invent an ideological basis for the Third Symphony. But if I did, I'd be bluffing—or at any rate, adding something ex post facto, something that might or might not be true but that played no role at the moment of creation." He went only so far as to say that the work "intended to reflect the euphoric spirit of the country at the time."[9]

Two helpful analyses of the Third Symphony followed soon after its premiere: a published one by Arthur Berger and an unpublished one by William Austin, who observed,

> Aaron Copland's Third Symphony is his largest work, and the favorite work of some of his closest students, such as Arthur Berger and Lawrence Morton, though not yet a favorite of the large audiences that enjoy his ballets and film scores, or of the adventurous musicians who prefer the Piano Variations, Piano Sonata, and perhaps the chamber music. The Third Symphony seems to its admirers the kind of work that could be and should be a favorite of all these people, for it is rich in tunes and in orchestral color, and at the same time original and intricate in its forms. The tunes, however, may need to be pointed out to some listeners, since the forms do not throw them into obvious relief. Likewise some listeners may benefit from an analysis of the forms, which have very little in common with those of Beethoven or Berg, and cannot be grasped in a superficial glance at the score or a single listening. To be sure, nothing can persuade a listener to enjoy the piece if he is altogether out of sympathy with its rather New-Dealish spirit of hopeful resolution and neighborliness. But if he can entertain such a spirit for a moment, Copland offers him a priceless opportunity to enter into it more deeply.

Although still not as popular as the ballets, the work has established itself as a cornerstone of the American symphonic repertory. "The Symphony has become an American monument," stated Leonard Bernstein, "like the Washington Monument or the Lincoln Memorial or something."[10]

For many concertgoers, the Third's incorporation of the popular *Fanfare for the Common Man*—heard first at the very beginning of the finale and subsequently used as one of that movement's principal themes—represents its most intriguing feature; for others it is a letdown. Berger, for instance, felt "a little uneasy" about the inclusion of music whose "pomp and overstatement were calculated to stir the most inattentive listener." In any event, it is important to realize that Copland did not simply arrive at the fourth movement and fall back on the *Fanfare* for want of another idea. Rather, he apparently intended to use the *Fanfare* from the very start, at least as early as the summer of 1944, when David Diamond wrote to him, "Make it a really KO symphony. And do, please use the fanfare material." Nor was his objective to capitalize on the piece's popularity; when he set about to work on the symphony, the *Fanfare* was an obscure little commission that he had every reason to expect would soon be forgotten. Rather, he wanted a noble finale that would reflect upon the war's victorious struggle, and the *Fanfare* suited such intentions.[11]

And while the *Fanfare* did not provide the genesis of the other themes per se—Elizabeth Bergman traces some of the symphony's main ideas to sketches dated 1940—it complements the kinds of other melodic materials found elsewhere in the work; this includes the main theme of the second movement, which originated, as Bergman has also discovered, as a discarded fanfare idea for the same Goossens commission that gave rise to the *Fanfare*. Typically, symphonies present short themes suitable for development; in some contrast, the Third presents long themes that, to an extraordinary degree, keep their shape, the score moving from one long theme to another. Many of the symphony's favored formal methods—such as juxtaposing, refiguring, or rescoring themes or subjecting them to canon or augmentation—allow Copland to keep his themes, as it were, intact. At times, especially when the themes are augmented, it takes pages and pages of orchestral score—perhaps a minute or two of music—to get from the beginning of a particular theme to its end. Such intensely thematic writing gives the Third an astounding breadth and monumentality, and makes the work, as Austin notes, challenging to grasp.[12]

For instance, in the ABA first movement, the entire first A section essentially states two lengthy themes, so closely related that the listener may well think of them as one extended theme. Like others in the work (including the fanfare itself), the opening theme, a melody of extraordinary repose, has struck many listeners as hymnlike; Berger writes that the entire symphony evokes the "general character of a glorified and expansive hymn—of prayer, of praise, of sorrow, of patriotic sentiment." This particular first theme—the work's motto, slowly put forth by the strings in unison—especially recalls the opening of Harris's Third Symphony, a work deeply admired by both Copland and Koussevitzky and one whose sweep may well have influenced the Third's own long-lined grandeur; but the sweetly calm and caring tone is Copland's own. With the slightly faster second theme, for violas and woodwinds, the music turns more expressive and urgent, becoming even more intense as the violins and horns put forth the melody in canon.

This canon leads directly into the movement's still faster—and dramatically brassy—contrasting middle section, built largely on a thirteen-note theme initially declaimed by two trombones. In contrast to the sedate previous material, this trombone melody makes a kind of circle, its last notes reiterating its first notes but at a different pitch level, so that in effect it modulates. Copland fully exploits this feature, restlessly moving from key to key; the sense of conflict intensifies until a climactic return of the motto theme, initiating the return of the A section.

As the music quickly subsides, the trombone and flute simultaneously recapitulate the first and second themes, the dramatic difference in timbre highlighting the juxtaposition; the presence of the trombone ineluctably retains some flavor of the middle section as well. The midsection's trombone theme subsequently appears (in counterpoint with fragments of the motto theme), remarkably transformed by its brittle scoring and cheerful tags in the major mode. A somber brass chorale follows, foreshadowing the finale's fanfare and dramatically reestablishing (via a brief arrival in C minor) the movement's tonal center, E. The motto theme, now rhythmically augmented and modally ambiguous, returns, slowly weaving its way back to the original major modality; the movement concludes with an exquisitely luminous E-major triad. The movement somewhat conforms, consequently, to the spirit if not the letter of sonata form, with its ABA sections corresponding to the exposition, development, and recapitulation, respectively.

The second movement comprises an ABA scherzo movement, with a bustling scherzo and a pastoral trio. The scherzo has a marchlike main theme stated, in the first A section, three times. In the first two statements, the French horns round the tune off with a tag that incorporates, at its end, the opening phrase of the main theme; in the third, augmented statement, the trumpets shrill out this same tag, at the end taking a brief detour before reaching their mark. The scherzo does not state its main theme immediately; rather, it opens with an unusual two-part introduction: a brassy section that breaks up the aforementioned cadential tag into brilliant splinters, and a perky section that explores an even smaller bit from the main theme. In other words, the movement's longish introduction constitutes a kind of development of a theme not yet heard. The perky material in particular seems to have a life of its own, either as a counterpoint to the main theme or in episodes separating the statements of the theme, to the extent that some ambiguity exists as to the relation of the parts to the whole; the main theme seems as much a kind of refrain as a principal theme per se. Austin notes, in this context, "how radically the structures of his music depart from classic conventions, from the very principle of classical reserve, as if he wanted to expose the way his mind actually works with musical ideas, rather than the stylized finished product of its working."13

The trio conforms to traditional expectations in its tender quiet, its folklike ambience, its triple meter, and its emphasis on woodwinds. In particular it recalls Copland's Western idiom, a rare instance of his incorporating this style, for all its popularity, into a nonprogrammatic context. It made sense to use it here, as a means of distinctively honoring the rustic associations of the traditional symphonic trio while at the same time making some small place for this, the composer's most familiar trademark; it also serves as a natural foil to the somewhat mechanistic scherzo proper. Even so, the music—whose two themes form a tiny ABA design—is considerably more complex than that found in the cowboy ballets, in terms of both the melodies themselves and their highly contrapuntal settings.

The scherzo proper returns with the main theme strikingly presented in the piano's highest register, the tag amusingly scored for oboes and clarinets. After an intervening episode, music similar to the second statement of the main theme appears, but Copland does not complete the theme and proceed to a third statement as before; rather, he puts forth a climactic statement of the trio's gentle theme, now in canon and gigantically scored for full orchestra. This climax leads directly into the cadential tag that it had interrupted, but in the augmented guise that had concluded the earlier A section. This ending is even bigger, with rim shots in the snare and tenor drums, and all the players reaching upward to the tonic pitch in their highest registers.

Like the first movement, the arched third movement progressively speeds up and slows down; even more symmetrical, its formal design can be described as ABCBA, with C the fastest section and the B sections serving in a transitional capacity. This movement thematically mirrors the opening movement: its A sections put forth a rather fatigued and brooding version (subjected as well to inversion) of the first movement's trombone melody, while the B and C sections derive from the first movement's motto theme. The A sections are introspective and later impassioned; the waltzlike B sections, nostalgic and bittersweet; and the vigorous middle section, whimsical and dancelike, with those quicksilver metrical changes often associated with Copland but in rather scant evidence elsewhere in the score.14

The dramatic opposition between this movement's outer and middle sections corresponds to the kind of dialectical thinking found in the previous two movements; and although there is precedence for slow movements with fast middle sections, this heightened internal contrast strikes a peculiar note. On a first listening, even an experienced listener might guess that the middle section marks the start of the finale. Adding to possible confusion is the fact that the movement eventually does lead directly into the finale, which begins with a statement of the fanfare for flutes, pianissimo; consequently, the opening of the finale provides in some ways less contrast than that found within the slow movement itself. It may help to remember that the first movement also begins with a slow melody; indeed, three of the work's four movements start slowly and move on to faster sections, which imparts to the piece, like its many augmented themes, a certain ponderous quality.

Adding to this sense of massiveness is the fact that this finale—like that of Beethoven's Ninth—is the longest of the work's four movements; in opening the movement with a quiet anticipation of the fanfare, Copland may even have been thinking of the "Ode to Joy." After a full statement of the fanfare for brass, Copland—who described this movement as a kind of sonata form—introduces a new theme, a fast toccatalike burbling that alternately resembles bird warblings and Latin-American dance, in particular, the rumba. Copland occasionally interrupts this jubilant outpouring with little brass figures that recall the fanfare.

A development section pits the fanfare theme, in canon and augmentation, against the toccata theme; this includes, after a dramatic pause, an ethereally scored passage featuring two harps, celesta, and piano. Most of the development, however, is given over to a new theme, a noble hymnlike tune that, as Austin points out, features congalike rhythms. The rumba-toccata returns, accompanied, eventually, by an augmented version of itself; the music grows more and more frenzied, until it is suddenly stopped dead in its tracks by a loud, strident chord, reminiscent of the music for Curley's crushed hand in *Of Mice and Men*. The piccolo tentatively resumes the toccata (shades of Mahler's Second), marking the start of the recapitulation.[15]

As in the first movement, this recapitulation quickly juxtaposes the two principal themes from its A section, namely, the fanfare (now in canon as in the development) and the toccata. At a climactic point, Copland reintroduces the hymn (with its congalike syncopations ironed out) accompanied at first by both the toccata theme and the motto theme, then by the fanfare and motto theme. The recapitulation proper concludes with a restatement of the fanfare's last phrases, now scored for full orchestra. A coda puts forth final statements of the hymn and the motto (and between them, in the uncut version, the toccata theme as well), accompanied all the while by fragments of the fanfare.

Some have pointed out that the Third Symphony as a whole represents a study in contrast. Virgil Thomson early on saw the work as a conflict between the pastoral and the military, resolved in the finale. Hugh Wolff likened it to songs of innocence and experience, of lightness and darkness. In each of the first three movements, the outer and middle sections present particularly stark contrasts: between repose and strife in the first movement, military-industrial activity and pastoral tranquillity in the second, and elegy and joy in the third. Moreover, in all four movements the recapitulations incorporate aspects of the contrasting section to the point that these final sections represent a synthesis. Consequently, each movement can be said to constitute a kind of Hegelian thesis, antithesis, and synthesis; it is not impossible that Copland was actually thinking of the Marxist dialectic.[16]

Of the work's many interesting details, the use of palindrome might be mentioned; some years earlier, Copland's discussion of music's most famous palindrome—the second theme from the first movement of Schubert's *Unfinished Symphony*—revealed no small fascination with this device. Here his own use of palindrome operates on a number of levels, from having motives and melodies to whole movements end as they begin. All this equating of ends and beginnings only contributes further to the work's grandeur.[17]

More readily apparent are the work's imaginative and varied colors; from the spacious doublings of its opening to the brilliantly rich tuttis of its final moments, the symphony constitutes a dazzling tour de force of virtuoso orchestral writing. This includes some striking passages that variously employ the top registers of the brightest instruments; even the warm and expressive string writing veers toward the upper ranges. Although critics have understandably compared the Third to Shostakovich's Fifth, the sound worlds of these two works actually stand poles apart; Copland characteristically tends toward the very highest registers, Shostakovich to rather dark sonorities.

From its premiere on 18 October 1946, the symphony was greeted as a major achievement. Reviewing its first performance in the *Boston*

Globe, Cyrus Durgin rated it and Harris's Third "as the two finest works in the form by American composers." Koussevitzky declared it simply the greatest American symphony ever written. It won some prestigious awards, including the New York Music Critics' Circle Award of 1947.[18]

Many regarded it as a culminating accomplishment. Arthur Berger referred to it as "a kind of panorama of all the musical resources that have through the years formed his musical language," while Leonard Bernstein went further, deeming it the epitome of a decades-long search by many composers for a distinctly American music; as he explained to a Young People's audience in 1958, the work contained "a lot of these American qualities we've been talking about: jazz rhythms, and wide-open optimism, and wide-open spaces, and the simplicity, and the sentimentality, and a mixture of things from all over the world, a noble fanfare, a hymn, everything!" In 1987 K. Robert Schwarz described the Third as one of those works that "every so often in a nation's history . . . captures the mood of a people, that speaks a shared language of hope, conviction, and affirmation."[19]

And yet a sense of dissatisfaction hovered about from the start. Even Copland's friends faulted aspects of the work: Fine took a dim view of its "populist tendencies," Berger winced at the "blatant" fanfare, and Shaperio criticized, among other things, the first movement's trombone melody. Virgil Thomson, who felt it necessary to assure readers of the work's sincerity, alternated blame and praise throughout his lengthy 1946 review, finding problems especially with the orchestration.[20]

Two days after giving the European premiere in Prague in 1947, Bernstein wrote Copland a rather grim letter in which he went from complaining about the work's coda, as had Thomson, to criticizing three of its four movements; he also reported negative reactions from Shostakovich ("too eclectic") and Walton ("not up my street"). Bernstein himself only warmed up to the work after conducting it a few times in Israel in 1948 in his own revised version that included "a sizable cut near the end." (Though offended by this unauthorized action, Copland eventually agreed to omit ten measures of the coda.)[21]

Some of the harsher complaints that the Symphony was "an example of grandiloquence hiding sheer emptiness" or a work defeated by "a busy web of contrapuntal academicism" recalled the invective typically leveled at the composer's more serious orchestral works; Copland himself described the piece, significantly, as "being closest in feeling" to the highly unpopular *Symphonic Ode*. But the Third elicited its own kind of respectful belittlement: *Time*, for instance, claimed that Copland had achieved "a kind of popularity that seemed to keep him too busy to be a great composer"; and *Fanfare* opined, "There is no real depth to the work . . . but as a picturesque filmscore in symphonic form it is quite delightful." Wilfrid Mellers's omission of the work from his 1964 survey—even more glaring than his neglect of *Lincoln Portrait* and the *Fanfare*—suggested that he thought the Third simply a grander version of these other secondary pieces.[22]

Nonetheless, the piece attracted enough conductors and listeners to make it the best-known American symphony of the century, more often performed and recorded than any other. Antal Dorati, Eduardo Mata, Leonard Slatkin, Yoel Levi, and Neeme Järvi all recorded the work, as did Copland and Bernstein, both twice. The Bernstein recordings—especially the second, a live performance with the New York Philharmonic from December 1985—demonstrate unequaled control over this treacherous score; on the other hand, the conductor's magniloquence tends to underline just those aspects of the music that have consistently put some people off. In this respect, Slatkin's more straightforward performance makes for a refreshing alternative. But even in Slatkin's ingratiating hands, the Third remains formidable in its intricate monumentality and frank in its social connotations.[23]

In a retrospective of a number of these recordings, William Malloch discussed as well live performances he had heard, including an "exemplary" performance by George Szell and a "beautifully proportioned" one by Pierre Monteux. Of Copland's renditions, his favorite was a 1968 performance with the New York Philharmonic: "It had all the dash and brio of his best intentions, magnificently brought off by the orchestra." Malloch urged a commercial release of the archival tape. He also hoped that conductors would reinsert the cut bars near the end of the finale: "Even as it stands, the ending is clearly overwritten. The cut did not solve the problem, and as long as it's going to be overwritten anyway, it might as well be *good* and overwritten."[24]

Christopher Rouse and other informed admirers similarly maintained that the cut should be reinstated. "It certainly would be interesting to hear the work performed as I originally conceived it," conceded Copland. Sympathetic to this general viewpoint, Hugh Wolff decided in favor of the cut after performing it both ways: "I found it to be one too many endings."

As in all recordings of the work to date, Leonard Slatkin preserved the cut in his release with the St. Louis Symphony, but then restored it to good effect on his 1997 European tour with the National Symphony. However this matter is resolved, it is important to note that the cut passage not only provides additional grandeur, as Malloch notes, but offers a glorious culmination of the toccata theme.[25]

In a lecture on the symphony, Hugh Ottaway regarded the Third as pertinent to no less a question than the very future of the genre:

> Some, no doubt, will consider it perverse to end with a reference to Copland's Third Symphony. True, this composer is neither a born symphonist nor the heir to a symphonic tradition; his imagination is much inclined towards a terse, epigrammatic mode of expression. But this is precisely the point. The fact that a composer such as Copland, as he enlarged and opened out his vision, sought fulfillment in a large-scale symphonic work is not the least of answers to those who say the form is "worn out." In reality a form does not wear out, for it has no physical existence; so long as there are artists prepared to grapple with experience, not merely to reflect it, the idea of the symphony—dynamic, constructive, expansive—will remain a great creative challenge.[26]

Tragic Ground

In early 1945 Copland signed a contract to write the score for a "dramatico-musical," *Tragic Ground,* after the novel of the same name by Erskine Caldwell (1944). The contract specified a fee of $2,000, not including royalties. His planned collaborators included producer Schuyler Watts, set designer Oliver Smith, choreographer Agnes de Mille, and playwright Lynn Riggs, who was to complete both the book and lyrics by August.[27]

De Mille and Smith—apparently the prime movers—had previously worked together on *Rodeo* (1942) and *Oklahoma!* (1943), the latter based on Riggs's play *Green Grow the Lilacs* (1931). They originally wanted to adapt Caldwell's bawdy novel about a poor Georgia family, *Tobacco Road* (1932), which, dramatized, had enjoyed a remarkable seven-year run on Broadway; but, unable to secure the rights, they settled on the similar but more recent *Tragic Ground.*

Set during the then current war, *Tragic Ground* tells the story of

Spence Douthit, a poor, middle-aged, shiftless, and good-natured "hill-billy," lured to a big oil city on the Gulf (presumably Houston) from his native Beasley County by a job he has since lost. Douthit's world is crumbling: his nagging wife, Maud, is sick and alcoholic; his older daughter, Libby, off whose earnings he and Maud live, is about to leave their shack in Poor Boy Town with Jim Howard, her soon-to-be soldier-husband; his thirteen-year-old daughter, Mavis, seduced by their next-door neighbor, has become a prostitute at a local brothel; and his closest friend, Floyd Sharp, teeters on the verge of violent despair. Spence wants to return to Beasley County, but when a social worker provides him with the means to do so, he ingenuously mishandles the whole affair: he squanders the money on gifts and brings home as a prospective husband for Mavis a pimp, whom Floyd murders when he discovers him in flagrante with his twelve-year-old daughter. Social services subsequently place Mavis in a juvenile home, and Spence and Maud return to Beasley County with Libby and Jim.[28]

The novel bespeaks Caldwell's communist affiliations in its suggestions that the degrading conditions of modern life create misfits like Spence; it sharply satirizes liberal social planning and careerist welfare bureaucrats and empathizes with Floyd's nascent revolutionary desire to burn down Poor Boy Town. However, critics generally consider Caldwell not so much a social critic as a fanciful storyteller with a keen appreciation for the speech and folkways of the South's poorest denizens.[29]

Although faithful to his source, Riggs's adaptation lost much of the novel's flavor by toning down or eliminating the pathetic absurdities that give the story its zest; in aiming for greater plausibility, he took some of the fun out of the book. Still, his script contained, especially for a prospective musical comedy, some pretty strong stuff, including Caldwell's colorful vulgarities: "You come around here doin' good again, babe," Maud tells one of the social workers, "and I'll slap those fluffy tits of yours to hell and gone!"[30]

Copland sketched out at least four songs: "Figgerin' on a Way to Git Home" for Floyd and the men of Poor Boy Town, "Alone at Night" for Libby and Jim, the folk song "I Bought Me a Cat" for the little girls of Poor Boy Town, and "A Man's Got to Live Someway" for Floyd. He learned "I Bought Me a Cat" from Riggs, who remembered it from his childhood in Oklahoma. "Figgerin' on a Way to Git Home" contained another folk tune, "The Cottage by the Sea," taken from the collection *Hill Country Tunes*.[31]

All this music featured an ultradiatonic, vaguely folkish idiom. Years later Paul Moor (Riggs's lover at the time) reminded Copland that he altered nearly every line of text: "As you can imagine, at first he [Riggs] was fit to be tied, but your reputation intimidated him and he set about rewriting his lines to fit the prosody of your melodies, even though he'd counted on its going the other way round. Even to begin with, he had hardly given you memorable lyrics, and your truncations and so on certainly did them no good."[32]

The producers hoped to get Walter Brennan for the show, presumably for the part of Spence, but unable to find backers, de Mille and the others abandoned the musical in late 1946. Copland regretted that the project had to be scrapped, and in the years that followed, he looked for ways to utilize the work he had already done; this included using "I Bought Me a Cat" for his first set of *Old American Songs* (1950) and "The Cottage by the Sea" for the chorus "Stomp Your Foot" from *The Tender Land* (1954).[33]

In the Beginning

Copland composed *In the Beginning* (1947), his most ambitious choral work, for Harvard University's Symposium on Music Criticism. Organized by musicologist A. Tillman Merritt, the symposium took place on the first three days of May 1947 and featured papers, panel discussions, teas, and three concerts: the Walden String Quartet playing string chamber works by Piston, Schoenberg, and Martinu on May 1; Robert Shaw conducting the Harvard University Collegiate Chorale in choruses by Hindemith, Malipiero, and Copland on May 2; and the Martha Graham Company performing ballets by Chávez and Schuman on May 3.[34]

Merritt requested from Copland an extended, a cappella choral work, possibly in Hebrew. Although Copland at first expressed a preference for a spot on the chamber-music concert, he ultimately agreed to the conditions, choosing as his text the opening chapter and the first seven verses of the second chapter of Genesis from the King James Version of the Bible.[35]

Certain factors led Copland to this text over and above Merritt's request for something Hebrew. Its grandeur, optimism, and humanism—emphasized by its ending with the creation of man—accorded with the tenor of his music from this period. The imagery also allowed for imaginative musical touches; and the stylized repetitions of certain words and phrases suited his own propensity for mobilelike forms, raising the question of whether such rhetoric shaped his musical style in the first place (he used similar formulas in his text for *Lincoln Portrait*). Finally, he had given the text serious thought since 1943, when Martha Graham used portions of it for her original scripts to *Appalachian Spring*. (Not surprisingly, some striking musical resemblances can be found between *In the Beginning* and the Graham ballet.)

The choice of text was an unusual one, nonetheless. Although composers have set portions of the Bible for chorus for centuries, they usually have either chosen a few verses for any given section or else rearranged or otherwise revamped the text. In contrast, *In the Beginning* uses a whopping thirty-eight verses of text verbatim (aside from updating a few archaic meanings) in a single sixteen-minute, through-composed movement. This gives, in conjunction with the music's long-lined melodies, a somewhat impenetrable, monolithic quality to the work not unlike that found in the Third Symphony. Remarkably, in Copland's skillful hands, the text comes across clearly and expressively; only occasionally do the circumlocutions of King James threaten to defeat him, as in the mouthful "and every tree, in the which is the fruit of a tree yielding seed."

Copland scored the piece for mezzo-soprano solo and four-part chorus. The solo generally declaims God's statements while the chorus comments on His actions, but often enough they reverse these roles or share them. All the music derives from the soloist's opening unaccompanied phrase, even more specifically, from the single gesture "In the beginning." Moreover, Copland literally repeats small, related motives for the text's ever recurring phrases; the intense similitude of the work's melodic material further enhances its blocklike character.

Symbolic and picturesque gestures abound, however, providing variety and contrast. The remarkably austere opening for unaccompanied soloist—sung, Copland writes, "in a gentle, narrative manner, like reading a familiar and oft-told story"—suggests the formless and dark earth, while the descending lines for alto and tenor that follow evoke "the Spirit of God" moving "upon the face of the waters." One can go through the entire work this way, savoring its subtle text painting phrase by phrase— text painting not necessarily obvious on a first hearing. For instance, a two-voiced duet for soprano and tenor in contrary motion depicts the division of light and dark. Similarly, the second day's separation of the waters features a wavelike three-voice canon, and the third day's "herb yielding seed" contains motives that organically grow and expand.

Copland's joyous setting of the fourth day's "lights in the firmament," with its jazzy melodies, its sustained notes in the chorus (like so many heavenly lights), and its brilliant use of choral divisi, constitutes one of the piece's highlights. Similarly vivid is the fifth day's creation of fish and fowl, with its circular melodies in canon that suggest a world alive with swimming and flying movement; the same melody, augmented in the bass, no doubt represents the "great whales." The sixth day's creation of earthly creatures recalls the music for the third day. For the creation of man, the chorus puts forth the first extended unison passage, though at the phrase "So God created man in his own image," the music neatly turns canonic.

The depiction of God's rest on the seventh day stands out for its remarkable calm; set for only the chorus, this beautiful section consists almost entirely of simple major triads. The soloist enters, soon after accompanied by the tenors in a poignant canon, explaining that God had yet to bring his creation to life. The work concludes with a slowly swelling passage for divisi chorus (expanded to as many as eight parts) for the verse in which God waters the earth and breathes life into man. At the final climactic word, "soul," the chorus sings a blazing major triad in its highest register, quadruple forte, an ending no less grand in its own way than the conclusion of the Third Symphony.

In the Beginning travels through a number of distantly related keys that do not seem to have any symbolic significance or hierarchical relationship; in fact, no single key stands out as particularly central. Rather, the work alternates a handful of favored keys, much as certain musical motives appear and reappear. These tonal shifts, sometimes quite jolting, make it hard for an unaccompanied chorus to stay in tune, but Copland writes the work so as to minimize such difficulties.

In the Beginning has been recorded numerous times, not always ideally. Copland's own recording features a chorus taxed by the work's considerable demands; the Gregg Smith Singers take some uncomfortably fast tempos; and Stephen Cleobury and the Choir of King's College (with boys and countertenors substituting for sopranos and altos) render a lovely but perhaps overly genteel account. The most persuasive recording to date is probably that by the Corydon Singers under Matthew Best, an elegant, warm performance that should further advance the work's reputation. As it is, *In the Beginning* remains a highly moving and personal account of the biblical creation and an acknowledged masterpiece of the choral repertory.[36]

The Clarinet Concerto and *Four Piano Blues*

In the 1940s, the bandleaders Benny Goodman (1909–1986) and Woody Herman (1913–1987), following in the footsteps of Paul Whiteman, straddled the worlds of jazz and classical music by commissioning works from concert composers. However, whereas Herman wanted music for his Thundering Herd band, Goodman commissioned concertos and chamber music (including Bartók's *Contrasts*) for his own use away from jazz bands. Coincidentally, both Herman and Goodman approached Copland for a work at about the same time, Herman in the summer of 1946, Goodman at the beginning of the next year. Unable to accept both offers, Copland accepted Goodman's (as, a few months earlier, had Hindemith, and for the same fee of $2,000). "I had long been an admirer of Benny Goodman," explained Copland, "and I thought that writing a concerto with him in mind would give me a fresh point of view."[37]

Copland scored the Clarinet Concerto for solo clarinet, strings, harp, and piano. After completing this seventeen-minute work in the fall of 1948, he revised the solo part in deference to Goodman's concerns about some high notes and other difficulties. Familiar with Goodman's playing from recordings, Copland was in some instances skeptical, but he made the necessary changes. To his further disappointment, Goodman did not premiere the concerto until a full two years later, on 6 November 1950, on a radio broadcast with Fritz Reiner conducting the NBC Symphony Orchestra. Goodman and Copland subsequently performed the concerto together and recorded it twice: first in 1950 shortly after the premiere and then in the early 1960s.[38]

Considering that Goodman and Copland were the outstanding Jewish-American figures in their respective fields of jazz and concert music, it would be interesting to know more about their relationship. But neither had much to say about the other. Their brief published recollections—Goodman's mention of "a little fracas" in particular—suggest a not altogether easy collaboration. Phillip Ramey observed that they were "perfectly friendly" and that Goodman "revered Copland," but that Copland found Goodman dull company. At the least, they appreciated the fact that their collaboration occasioned a great success.[39]

Much like Copland's Piano Concerto, his only other such work, the Clarinet Concerto is in a slow-fast two-movement format, its two movements linked by a cadenza for the soloist. The slow movement, which creates an astonishing lushness with the most economical of means, is famous as one of Copland's most romantic efforts, something he himself realized: "I think it will make everyone weep," he predicted to Victor Kraft. The main theme of this ABA slow movement originated from sketches for a "Pas de deux," which helps explain its special ambience. At the same time, the A music, scored for solo clarinet, strings, and harp, suggests something of the world of *Our Town*, while the B section, contrastingly scored for just clarinet and strings, derives literally from the score to *The Cummington Story*; such associations relate the entire movement to his film idiom.[40]

The cadenza that links the concerto's two movements effects the transition from dreamy nostalgia to jazzy vitality, or, as clarinetist Richard Stoltzman puts it, "from classic chalumeau to licorice stick." While concerto cadenzas usually explore and develop ideas near the conclusion of a movement, Copland had the happy idea, as in the Piano Concerto, of standing tradition on its head by having the cadenza introduce the material to follow.[41]

After the cadenza, the orchestra enters with its own introductory music, recalling the double introduction of the Third Symphony's scherzo. Though unified motivically, the concerto's two movements present a startling contrast: the second movement is as spiky and fragmented as the first movement is warm and lyrical. For added contrast, the finale introduces the piano, its potential for "crude" and other sharp sounds exploited.

Copland described this complex second movement as "a free rondo form." More specifically, one might chart its design as ABACDBDCA/B. A puts forth a jaunty, "staccattissimo" melody for the clarinet against a jazzy vamp in the lower strings; B contains two ideas, a syncopated chromatic lick and a singable, folklike fragment; C features faster, more frenetic syncopations; D, marked "with humor, relaxed," offers contrast. As suggested by the alphabet-soup diagram above, the main A theme makes its final appearance accompanied by the B material. The exciting coda concludes with a rollicking series of chords, huge leaps for the solo clarinet, and, at the very end, perhaps in recognition of Gershwin's *Rhapsody in Blue* as well as jazz band practices, a mighty clarinet glissando punctuated by a single note for the full orchestra.[42]

The finale's obvious references to jazz have tended to obscure its more subtle connections to South American music, in particular to the folk music of northern Brazil. Copland composed some of this movement while touring South America for the State Department, and he himself identified one of the movement's subsidiary themes—apparently the "relaxed" theme from the D section—as Brazilian. One can find other rhythms, melodies, and sounds in the work related to South American musics, smoothly integrated though they may be; composed at the very height of his enthusiasm for Latin-American music, the Clarinet Concerto is the work that perhaps most fully embodies Copland's Pan-American sensibilities.

Although Goodman felt lucky to get Reiner for the premiere, this first performance, broadcast over the radio and preserved on tape, was somewhat stilted; not surprisingly, the work's immediate reception was "lukewarm." Goodman's subsequent recordings with Copland (1950, 1963) fared much better. The latter, as Copland recalled, "really launched" the piece, though David Hamilton preferred Goodman's playing in the original as more "flexible" and "sure-footed" than in the remake. The Clarinet Concerto is now standard repertory, especially in the States.[43]

In its early days, the work's popularity also owed something to Jerome Robbins's choreographic adaptation, The Pied Piper (1951), a ballet that has little to do with the folktale of similar name aside from the general idea of young people responding viscerally to music. As part of the action, the solo clarinetist takes his place on a high stool at the corner of the stage, tuning up with the orchestra. During the first movement, a pair of dancers perform—appropriately enough—a romantic pas de deux, with other dancers watching and joining in. As the lovers disappear and the clarinet begins its cadenza, the corps members, listening, begin to twitch and shake to the music. The dancing becomes more and more frenetic in the course of the finale, and soon, writes Balanchine in his discussion of the ballet, "the whole group is dancing, responding to the music with spontaneous and spasmodic jerkings and jivings as it becomes brisker and hysterically carefree." At the final glissando, the dancers "dash across the stage toward the piper" and "fall at his feet in a wave."[44]

The Pied Piper was a hit—the "big surprise of the season," wrote Nik Krevitsky in 1952—both at home and abroad, where critics often noted its unmistakable American qualities. Arthur Berger claimed that its "clownish excesses" failed to do the music justice, but Copland himself thought it "a delightful ballet."[45]

As with other Copland scores that flirt with jazz, the Clarinet Concerto poses the question of how far performers might go in jazzing it up. Copland requested that musicians play the rhythms as written (he seems to have expected more freedoms with his symphonic jazz from the 1920s) and yet thought it advantageous for players to have "some feeling and knowledge of jazz." The Copland-Goodman renditions offer one solution to this seeming paradox; they adhere to the notated rhythms while maintaining a lilt that has some relation to swing. When Richard Stoltzman took additional freedoms in the direction of real jazz, his interpretation elicited both praise and censure. At the very least, Stoltzman's approach was commendable for its careful and imaginative attention to timbre, dynamics, and attack.[46]

While working on the Clarinet Concerto, Copland also composed, in 1947 and 1948, respectively, two short, moody piano pieces jazzy enough to suggest some connection with the concerto. After completing the second piece, he decided to group them with two earlier pieces—namely, "Blues No. 2" (1926) and "Hommage à Milhaud"/"Dove Dance" from *Hear Ye! Hear Ye!* (1926/1934)—as *Four Piano Blues*. He arranged these 1947, 1926/1934, 1948, and 1926 pieces in that order and dedicated them, respectively, to four pianist friends: Leo Smit, Andor Foldes, William Kapell, and John Kirkpatrick.

All four blues are highly personal, with—aside from certain characteristic modal inflections—rather remote stylistic connections to either folk or commercial blues. It seems that the blues, for Copland, basically betokened lonely or wistful feelings. The two new pieces are especially introspective. One practically has to go back to his juvenilia, to those piano pieces composed before Boulanger and inspired by Debussy and Scriabin, to find a comparable intimacy, albeit now tempered by a masterful restraint. After so many years of children's pieces and big public statements, such subjective expression signaled a change in the air and forewarned of developments to come.[47]

23

From *The Red Pony* to
the Piano Quartet
(1948–50)

The Red Pony and *The Heiress*

Having won Academy Award nominations in quick succession for three very different kinds of films, by 1944 Copland found himself in considerable demand by the film industry. Producer Lester Cowan wanted him for a number of projects, including *Tomorrow the World* (1944), directed by Leslie Fenton. Samuel Goldwyn and William Wyler approached his agent about *The Best Years of Our Lives* (1946), David Selznick and Alfred Hitchcock about *The Paradine Case* (1947). But Copland's preoccupation with the Third Symphony (1944–46) prevented him from seriously considering these and other offers.[1]

In early 1948, however, he returned to Hollywood to score the film version of John Steinbeck's *The Red Pony* for producer-director Lewis Milestone. He accepted the commission only after reading the novella, which he admired. He had worked with Milestone on two of his three previous Hollywood films—including another Steinbeck adaptation—and knew to expect better-than-average working conditions; this included a fee of $15,000 and a full ten weeks to complete the job. Moreover, the project enabled him to resume his affair with Erik Johns, back in Los Angeles.[2]

The novella *The Red Pony* (1945) comprises four short stories, originally published between 1933 and 1938, about a young boy, Jody Tiflin, who lives with his parents, Carl and Ruth, and the cowhand Billy Buck on a ranch outside of Salinas, California, in the years around 1910. In the first story Jody's beloved pony, Gabilan, dies, in part due to Billy's negligence; in despair, Jody kills one of the buzzards feeding on the pony's carcass. In the second story Jody meets an old Mexican peasant born in the area who has returned there to die. In the third Billy, regretful over the pony's death, kills his mare while she is in labor, so that he can save the foal for Jody. The fourth concerns an awkward visit by Jody's grandfather, whose frontier yarns bore everyone but the young boy.[3]

The screenplay, written by Steinbeck himself, omitted the story about the old Mexican and interwove elements of the other three, with both the death of the pony and the birth of the foal appearing climactically near the film's end. Carl, Ruth, and Jody are renamed Fred, Alice, and Tom; Grandfather now lives on the ranch. More significant, Billy only prepares to kill Rosie, the mare; as it turns out, she successfully delivers, thus providing the film with a happy ending, one a far cry from the startling original that has Billy tear the foal from the dead mare's womb. Steinbeck also interpolated a new subplot in which Fred questions his relations with his son and with his community, finally coming to terms with both; this subplot—marked by Fred's feelings of paternal ineffectiveness and social isolation—bespoke a postwar malaise that distinguished the film from the novella.

Milestone assembled a solid cast for the film: Shepperd Strudwick and Myrna Loy as Fred and Alice Tiflin, Robert Mitchum as Billy Buck, Louis Calhern as Grandfather, and Peter Miles as Tom. Tony Gaudio supervised the fine cinematography for this, Milestone's first color film, and Nicholas Remisoff designed the set around the identical ranch used in *Of Mice and Men*. Copland initially described the film, privately, as "awfully dull," but he later remembered it, publicly, as "moving in a quiet way." Steinbeck conversely liked the film at first but took a dim view of it in later years. Critics widely agree that Copland's music constitutes the picture's outstanding feature; Joseph R. Millichap writes, "As in his earlier work with Milestone, Copland's score perfectly matches the mood of the visuals, and in this case often surpasses them in evoking the lyric naturalism of Steinbeck's original work."[4]

Copland wrote nearly an hour's worth of music for this slowly paced, atmospheric film, making *The Red Pony* one of the largest works of his career. For most sequences, he provided his customary stopwatch and verbal cues, but for two episodes, "Walk to the Bunkhouse" and "Dream March," he employed, for the first time, the more precise click-track. He also meticulously indicated the orchestration, creating bright and delicate sonorities that reflect the youthful protagonist's viewpoint as well as, perhaps, the glistening Technicolor. Among sonorities unusual for Hollywood, he used a toy trumpet in "Dream March," a clarinet quartet at the end of "The Operation," and a stunningly brief vibraphone chord at the moment when Tom accuses Billy of letting Gabilan die. However, for the most part, he created the film's unique, memorable sounds—including passages that twang like a mouth harp—with a conventional orchestra.[5]

Even before the film's release in 1949, Copland prepared a suite in six movements: "Morning on the Ranch," "The Gift," "Dream March and Circus Music," "Walk to the Bunkhouse," "Grandfather's Story," and "Happy Ending." Dedicated to Erik Johns and premiered by Efrem Kurtz and the Houston Symphony Orchestra on 30 October 1948, the *Red Pony Suite* enjoyed widespread popularity; along with Prokofiev's *Lieutenant Kije* (1934), which it resembles in many ways, it became one of the few truly successful concert works so adapted from a film score.

Although the suite alters the chronological order of the various episodes as they appear in the movie, the movements themselves match the original cues to a surprisingly close degree. The two movements that frame the suite, "Morning on the Ranch" and "Happy Ending," contain two principal themes, one swaying, the other at a faster gallop. Each of these outer movements adapts music from both the beginning and end of the film: "Morning on the Ranch" contains the music just prior to the title, in which the swaying theme accompanies early stirring animals; the music just after the title, in which the galloping melody accompanies the Tiflin family at their morning routine; and a playfully transformed version of the same galloping music for the birth of the colt at the very end. The "Happy Ending" similarly comprises the galloping melody as it appears during the title; the tense passage in which Tom anxiously chases Billy, who is intent on killing Rosie; and a reprise of the baby colt music.

"The Gift" contains music for two consecutive sequences: the presentation of the red pony to an astonished Tom, and Tom's displaying Gabilan to his school friends. Its tender opening evokes Tom's love for the pony, while the ensuing waltzlike music underscores Billy's additional gift of a saddle, its allusions to circus music prompted by the mention of the circus from which Fred bought the pony. As Tom anticipates showing Gabilan to his friends, a theme introduced earlier in the film and associated with Tom the schoolboy and his schoolmates appears, embedded in the waltz. Almost immediately after, this theme appears in its more original guise as his friends rush to the barn to see the new pony. Consequently, the use of the schoolboy theme in the waltz section not only signifies Tom's thoughts but anticipates the following episode. After interpolating some material from a later cue, Copland arrives at a grand pause and a reprise of the opening tender theme as the school chums gawk speechlessly at the pony, thus rounding out the whole.

Copland extracted "The Dream March and Circus Music" (sometimes programmed as separate movements) from two episodes depicting Tom's daydreams. In the first, on his way to school Tom imagines that he and Billy lead a column of armored knights on horseback; in the second, while feeding the chickens he imagines the hens turned to white circus horses and himself a ringmaster, whip in hand. Both musical cues derive—appropriately enough—from those themes associated with school and ranch life, respectively; and both feature the kind of broad, satiric humor long Copland's trademark: toward the conclusion of "The Dream March," as Tom awakens from his glorious reveries, the march slowly falls apart; when he espies a little friend shuffling through the dust where he had imagined a knightly cavalcade, the music reduces to a mere piccolo tooting against the ubiquitous tuba. The harmonic dissonances of "Circus Music" are similarly droll. Because Milestone cut both of these episodes sizably (especially the circus fantasy), only preserved outtakes can fully reveal the imagery this music was meant to accompany.

"Walk to the Bunkhouse" contains two distinct musical ideas: a bow-legged theme of alternating meters for Billy Buck (at the shot of pinups in his bunkhouse, some amusing, bluesy grace notes slyly allude to his sexual life), and a more lyrical theme underscoring Tom's admiration for Billy and his mare. Whereas in the movie, music and dialogue alternate with razor-sharp clarity for comic effect, in the suite, clarinet figuration fills in the silences. "Grandfather's Story" similarly contains two elements: quietly sad music that represents Grandfather, and soft, slightly dissonant trumpet music that depicts his remembrances of crossing the plains.

The film contains a good deal more music than found in the suite. Copland was not the kind of film composer inclined to repeat large sections of music or even particular themes; each episode—the training of the pony, the thunderstorm, the sick pony, the fight with the buzzard, Tom's eventual recovery—evoked a fresh response. For the scene where Alice amuses herself at the piano after the troubled Fred leaves for San Jose, trenchant use is made of source music. At first Alice plays a Schubert duet arranged for solo piano; taunted by her father, who mischievously notes the absent piano partner, she launches into "Für Elise" (the apparent pun on her name a little private joke); finally, all alone, she plays the hymn "Shall We Gather at the River?" a prayer for the impending family crisis. For much of the film, Copland leaves Fred in chilly silence, thus emphasizing his presence as a distant husband and father; this only enhances the lyrical outburst when, after his return from San Jose, he embraces his son.

The film achieves an impressive musical continuity throughout, often by having one cue pick up—tonally or melodically—where the last left off. The cues themselves are ingeniously shaped, making it possible, as mentioned, for Copland to adapt some of them for concert purposes with only minor alterations. To some extent, these musical forms derive from Milestone's direction, but Copland also imposes his own architecture on various scenes, resulting in a give and take between director and composer not unlike that between librettist and composer. For instance, the introduction and opening credits form a prologue that vaguely approximates the traditional French overture. In "Walk to the Bunkhouse," Copland, subtly catching shifts in the action, creates a charming little ABABA rondo. "Grandfather's Story" provides another example, this one an ABA form, with the A sections portraying Grandfather and the B section delineating his story.

For the climactic episode "The Buzzard Flight," Copland tried something different, creating, in response to Milestone's direction at this point, a corresponding musical montage, with little alternating bits associated with Tom, the buzzards, Gabilan's tracks, and, eventually, Fred and Billy. He may have omitted this particular sequence from the suite precisely because it was so tightly tailored to the imagery.

Had *The Red Pony* been released in 1948 as planned, the work very likely would have earned Copland an Academy Award nomination and possibly an Oscar; but because of its delayed release date, it ran into competition with his score to *The Heiress*, which the academy honored instead, in part, no doubt, because the film itself was a much stronger one. Nonetheless, expert critics quickly recognized the music for *The Red Pony* as masterful—"the most elegant," wrote Virgil Thomson, "in my opinion, yet composed and executed under 'industry conditions,' as Hollywood nowadays calls itself." The only weak spot, ventured Thomson, was one true of all Hollywood music, namely, its inability to interpret the feelings of the American cinema's mythic "goddesses," in this case, Myrna Loy. Thomson chose an odd vehicle for airing this provocative idea, considering that Copland purposefully curtailed musical representation of Tom's parents for dramatic reasons; this thesis would be better tested in—and arguably refuted by—Copland's next film, *The Heiress*.[6]

In 1964 Copland approached Steinbeck about writing a narrative that might accompany a recording or performance of the suite. Steinbeck, who admired Copland's "beautiful" music, gladly provided one of about three hundred words; but when Copland specifically requested a "children's version," Steinbeck respectfully but forcefully declined. "Children have nearly always understood my work—and yours," he pointed out. "It is only critics and sophisticates who do not." Copland reprinted the bulk of this letter in his autobiography, tactfully omitting Steinbeck's contention that children's literature engendered homosexuality. Not dissuaded, Copland approved a narration for children devised by Katherine Rosen, subtitling the work " 'a suite for children,' since the music and action were intended to come from a child's point of view."[7]

In late 1948 Copland completed another Hollywood picture, director William Wyler's film version of Ruth and Augustus Goetz's stage play *The Heiress*, itself an adaptation of Henry James's novella *Washington Square*. Set in antebellum New York, *Washington Square* tells the story of a plain and shy heiress, Catherine Sloper, who falls in love with a handsome and charming fortune hunter, Morris Townsend. While her meddlesome aunt Lavinia Penniman encourages the romance, Catherine's disdainful father, Dr. Austin Sloper, threatens disinheritance. Realizing that her father despises her, Catherine willingly disinherits herself, only to have Morris jilt her. The emotionally battered Catherine resigns herself to a quiet, dignified spinsterhood; when Morris, still impoverished, turns up twenty years later to take up where they left off, she sends him away. The tale reads as an ironic indictment of America's nineteenth-century bourgeoisie, with its men obsessed by the bottom line and its women deluded by romantic sentimentality; its sharp but subtle critique of American culture surely made it attractive to social critics like Wyler and Copland, already under the gun of McCarthyism.

The Goetzes dramatized the story, adding two thwarted elopements. They also altered the story's moral thrust by making Morris less cunning and Sloper, in turn, that much more culpable. In the novella, for instance, Morris's sister, Mrs. Montgomery, warns Sloper against her brother, whereas in the play she is evasive and, at a crucial point, mute. The film softened Morris's character still further, portraying him largely from Catherine's romanticized perspective.

Wyler considered the musical score of fundamental importance to the film and insisted on offering the job to Copland over the objections of Paramount production chief Y. Frank Freeman, who was concerned about the composer's involvement with the pro-Soviet *The North Star*, which had become the target of congressional investigations. By this point, Wyler's film *The Best Years of Our Lives* itself had been attacked as communist propaganda; but as an acclaimed director he enjoyed a certain immunity, and as an honorable man he did what he could to break the cycle of fear gripping Hollywood. Copland signed a contract in July 1948 and spent the last six weeks of the year in Hollywood working on *The Heiress*.[8]

Copland, who had read the novella and seen the play on Broadway, with Wendy Hiller as Catherine, liked the black-and-white film, which starred Olivia de Havilland as Catherine, Montgomery Clift as Morris, Sir Ralph Richardson as Sloper, and Miriam Hopkins as Aunt Penniman. Once again, he prepared a condensed score in four staves with meticulous directives regarding orchestration, then passed it on to his assistant at Paramount, Nathan Van Cleave. And as with *The North Star* and *The Red Pony*, he conducted the music himself.[9]

Even before viewing the film, Copland knew, based on the script, that *The Heiress* would require relatively little music, for it had few of the kinds of extended outdoor or action sequences that he considered particularly suitable for musical treatment. Here he thought the music needed to provide psychological nuance as much as anything else. As a result, the score turned out to be, if one of his shorter Hollywood scores, his most complex and subtle one, the one that most resembled his serious concert work. Indeed, his use of a discarded variation from the *Piano Variations*—for the painful scene following Morris's desertion—perfectly fitted the score's overall tone and fabric.

No doubt in response to the film's psychological focus, Copland more thoroughly relied on a smaller number of musical ideas than he had in his earlier films; he himself referred to its "leitmotiv style." The score's five principal themes are stated in the picture's first few minutes. These include two motives—descending chords alternating with a sweeping declamatory melody above—associated with Catherine's love for Morris (heard during the opening title); a series of chromatic triads associated with the Sloper residence (heard at the first glimpse of Washington Square); Catherine's theme, a four-note idea that moves up through a triad and then descends the interval of the seventh (heard at Catherine's entrance); and Sloper's theme, a darker, more stately melody that often moves by fourths (heard at Sloper's entrance).

Some of the ways in which the score employs these ideas—the reappearance of a theme in a new harmonic context or as a reminiscence (as when Catherine walks through the courtyard recalling Morris's proposal five years earlier)—are traditional enough. However, these leitmotivs do not always appear as recognizable tags in the typical Hollywood manner but occur more as themes might in a Copland symphonic work—a topic that, notwithstanding a pioneering article by Frederick Sternfeld, awaits critical scrutiny. Who can easily identify Sloper's theme merged with the love music as he broods over Catherine's engagement, or his theme in retrograde as he examines himself, or his theme juxtaposed with Catherine's as she stonily sits in the park during his death, their themes altered to express her ascendancy over her father? Especially striking is the metamorphosis of Catherine's theme from innocence to love to painful awareness to final triumph.[10]

The film posed new challenges for Copland. For the impetuous and starry-eyed Catherine, he had to write love music of a sort he had never before attempted. More generally, the portrayal of upper-class New York required an urbane touch distinct from his familiar depictions of small towns and ranches. Taking his cue from the "special atmosphere inherent in the James original," one that "would produce a music of a certain discretion and refinement in the expression of sentiments," he found the right tone, even in expressive passages containing the harshest dissonance. In this respect, the depictions of Grover's Corners from *Our Town* (also set largely in a doctor's home) and Washington Square offer a striking contrast; both employ a similar texture—arpeggiated figures accompanied by simple triads—but what a difference between the unadorned simplicity of the former and the delicate, slightly enervated elegance of the latter.

Copland heightened this Jamesian ambience by using a smaller-than-average orchestra and emphasizing the violins, flutes, clarinets, and harp. In addition, he experimented with a technique known as "sweetening," in which a smooth sheen can be obtained by dubbing a string orchestra over a full orchestra; one example comes at the very end of the garden party, where Copland pits an ominous "sweetener," depicting Morris, against the concluding measures of a waltz.

Even before Copland began work, the studio, under music department head Louis Lipstone's direction, had decided on certain period music to be used in the film: a string of polkas, waltzes, and mazurkas arranged by Van Cleave for the garden party, and the Johann Schwartzendorf–Jean Florian song "Plaisir d'Amour," sung by Morris to Catherine. Copland took advantage of click-track technology to change some of the dances, composing a mazurka and waltz in period style and arranging François-Joseph Gossec's popular *Gavotte*. As for "Plaisir d'Amour," he complied with Wyler's request to work it into his score, and did so three times: immediately after Morris plays the song; after he proposes to Catherine and takes his leave, where it signifies Catherine's thoughts; and again as Morris sees Catherine and Sloper off on their way to Europe. (For additional atmosphere, he arranged the folk song "Ching-a-Ring Chaw" for a sequence, "Fortune Hunting," that was eventually cut from the film.)[11]

After Copland recorded the score, Wyler pleaded for further changes when, at a sneak preview, audiences snickered at the jilted Catherine; he accordingly substituted a more dissonant passage in lieu of the "very romantic kind of music" he had originally composed. It worked; audiences stopped laughing. Copland and others frequently cited this incident as illustrating the subliminal power of film music.

Copland learned a moral of another kind when Wyler asked him to rewrite his bold title music to incorporate "Plaisir d'Amour." When he refused, the studio simply had Van Cleave do it. The resulting pastiche consisted of Copland's original three opening bars, Van Cleave's arrangement of "Plaisir d'Amour," and a return to the original just as Copland's name appears in the title. This naturally destroyed the integrity of the opening "Prelude." To add insult to injury, Van Cleave provided a maudlin arrangement of the tune; André Previn likens the return of the original Copland on the heels of Van Cleave to "suddenly finding a diamond in a can of Heinz beans." All this was standard Hollywood procedure, but Copland, feeling that an important issue was at stake, publicly disowned the opening title.[12]

What has not been noted is the fact that the studio also decided to replace Copland's love music with a sweeping statement of "Plaisir d'Amour" for the scene in which Morris and Catherine are reunited. It is unlikely that Copland sanctioned this change either, but in any case, the score once again suffered by it. Even aside from these major alterations, Wyler did not serve the score as well as, say, Milestone had—a good deal of the music was cut and unevenly dubbed. "Willie Wyler was a wonderful man," recalls David Raksin, "but he didn't know anything about music. He screwed up score after score. He came close to ruining my score for *Carrie*." Nonetheless, Copland's music survived as one of enormous distinction, earning him his only Academy Award.[13]

Copland never adapted this particular film score as a suite, though he recycled one episode for *Dance Panels* (1959). After his death, however, Arnold Freed arranged an *Heiress Suite* (1990), subsequently recorded by Leonard Slatkin and the St. Louis Symphony (1994). That Freed managed to shape many of the more interesting episodes into one eight-minute movement gives proof of the score's remarkable economy. Had Copland created a suite himself, he presumably would have expanded and shaped the individual episodes to create larger, more coherent movements; medley was not his style. But the suite has its attractions, demonstrating, for example, the majesty of the love music and the brilliance of the embarkment scene. Moreover, the cut music from the "Prelude" and "Reunion," now restored, reveals what the film lost to Hollywood's boorishness.[14]

For whatever reason, *The Heiress* was Copland's last Hollywood film. Producers in the 1950s may have been reluctant to hire him because of his outspoken criticism of studio policies, or because of his problems with McCarthy, or because of his high fee of $25,000 per film. David Raksin suggests that producers and directors were simply too ignorant to recognize his distinction. But he still received offers during the course of the 1950s, especially from William Wyler, who wanted Copland for *Carrie* (1952), his adaptation of Dreiser's *Sister Carrie*; his film about Quakers, *Friendly Persuasion* (1956); and his Western *The Big Country* (1958).[15]

For his part, Copland no longer had to score films for financial reasons, which made him, perhaps, even more choosy than he had been in the past. He complained, for instance, that Wyler's *Friendly Persuasion* "seemed to falsify [the Quakers'] ideas as I understand them." The only Hollywood project that intrigued him, apparently, was director Fred Zinnemann's adaptation of Hemingway's *The Old Man and the Sea*. "The story lends itself so wonderfully to musical treatment," he wrote to Zinnemann, "or so it seems to me, that I can't resist the temptation of telling you how much I would enjoy working on such a film, especially with you at the directorial helm." (The assignment went to Dimitri Tiomkin, possibly because Zinnemann learned of Copland's interest in the film too late.) In fact, Copland composed one more film score, *Something Wild* (1961), but for an independent and somewhat avant-garde producer-director.[16]

Copland's movie career—while perhaps unexceptional in the context of world film history—proved unique in the States; he became by far the most distinguished American-born composer to work so extensively and successfully in Hollywood. This says much about his character, his abilities, and his aspirations. But as the controversy surrounding *The Heiress* reveals, Hollywood remained in many ways alien to his values and sensibilities.

Preamble for a Solemn Occasion and *Twelve Poems of Emily Dickinson*

NBC commissioned Copland's *Preamble for a Solemn Occasion* (1949) for orchestra and narrator for a 10 December 1949 concert commemorating the first anniversary of the United Nations' Universal Declaration of Human Rights, which had been approved by the General Assembly the previous year. For his text, Copland adapted about half of the Preamble to the Charter of the United Nations (1945): "We the peoples of the United Nations, determined to save succeeding generations from the scourge of war, which twice in our lifetime has brought untold sorrow to mankind, and to reaffirm faith in fundamental human rights, in the dignity and worth of the human person, in the equal rights of men and women of all nations large and small, and to promote social progress and better standards of life in larger freedom, have resolved to combine our efforts to accomplish these aims." Such sentiments recalled those "four freedoms" of President Roosevelt that had earlier inspired Copland and can be seen, like the creation of the United Nations itself, as an extension of the New Deal.[17]

The six-minute *Preamble* comprises four small sections. The first section—declamatory, dissonant, sad—evokes the "scourge of war" and "untold sorrow" later mentioned in the narration; this music, which represents as direct a response to the horrors of the Second World War as Copland may ever have made, could accompany newsreel footage of Auschwitz or Hiroshima. The trumpets, supported by brass, woodwinds, and timpani, introduce a contasting section whose noble, hymnlike, much more diatonic music reflects "faith in fundamental human rights." The narration follows, quietly underlined by the opening music, after which the affirmative hymn brings the work to a close on a brilliant C-major triad. At the premiere, Sir Laurence Olivier delivered the narration, accompanied by Leonard Bernstein and the Boston Symphony Orchestra.

Copland privately dismissed the *Preamble* as a "pot boiler," but in a review of the piece, Ingolf Dahl praised its tone as "one of great elevation, breadth, and power." For comparable sweep, one needs to look to the likes of Beethoven or Shostakovich, both, significantly, represented on the same commemorative concert at which the *Preamble* premiered. The form and rhetoric of the *Preamble* also recalls *Lincoln Portrait*, but as Copland himself pointed out, "the musical style is quite different." For one thing, as a tribute to the United Nations, it naturally avoids any overt American-isms; in this respect, it strikes a note closer to the *Fanfare*. But the *Pre-amble* does not have the same morale-boosting qualities of either of the two earlier, wartime works; rather, it reflects more solemnly on the sor-rows of the past and the challenges of the future.[18]

The *Preamble* enjoyed a few performances over the years, including one with Duke Ellington as narrator. But for all its effectiveness, Ameri-cans never took to it as they did to *Lincoln Portrait* or *Fanfare*; on the contrary, it remains one of Copland's most obscure works. One imagines that skepticism about the United Nations—emanating from all sides of the political spectrum—deprived the work of the attention it deserved. Copland attempted to salvage it by omitting the narration and arranging it, in various guises (for orchestra, for band, for organ), as *Preamble for a Special Occasion*. He also approved substituted narrations—as in a per-formance during the 1976 bicentennial celebration with Jimmy Stewart reading from the Preamble to the United States Constitution. But consid-ering how well the music embodies the spirit of its original text, *Preamble for a Solemn Occasion* warrants, at the least, a premiere recording and the occasional revival.

In March 1949 Copland started work on a setting of Emily Dickinson's celebrated poem "The Chariot." As work progressed, he considered a group of three songs, then six. By March 1950 he had composed twelve songs, arranging their order only after their completion, a time-honored procedure dating back to the song cycles of Schubert and Schumann. The soprano, Alice Howland, premiered the set, entitled *Twelve Poems of Emily Dickinson* (and commonly known as the *Dickinson Songs*), on 18 May 1950 with the composer at the piano.[19]

In the larger context of his career, the *Dickinson Songs* can be seen as part of a trend away from public statements toward more private ones; in some contrast to his earlier work, his postwar music seems more preoccupied with personal—one might even say existential—issues of nature, death, love, and self-realization. One can relate this development to the times—the shock of the Holocaust, the disillusion with the Soviet Union, the grisly specter of nuclear war, the flight to suburbia—as well as to Copland's personal life, including his own move out of Manhattan and his growing involvement with Erik Johns. Such tendencies appear related as well to his adoption of the twelve-tone method in the Piano Quartet, which was composed in tandem with the *Dickinson Songs*. In discussing these two works of 1950, Copland himself alluded to a shift of some sort, writing, "I have always had an aversion to repeating myself."[20]

Copland seemed born to set Dickinson, whose ability to succinctly traverse a wide emotional and intellectual range bespoke a sensibility like his own. Noting many other similarities between these two artists, Helen Didriksen dates his interest in the poet as far back as Martha Graham's Dickinson dance *Letter to the World* (1940, to music by Hunter Johnson); the *Dickinson Songs* even contain one of the poems recited as part of the ballet, namely, "Dear March, Come In." But Dickinson generally made a strong appeal to Americans in the 1950s. "Can one think of anyone who did less with her *outer* life than Emily Dickinson?" asks Didriksen by way of explanation. "I believe that Dickinson retreated to her room because she had to, to preserve a painfully heightened sensibility. And I believe the American people were doing much the same thing in the 1950s." Copland characteristically noted, however, that even from the confines of her Amherst home, Dickinson could at least observe "the outside world."[21]

That Copland began the cycle so soon after completing *The Heiress* might be considered as well. Emily Dickinson and the film's heroine, Catherine Sloper, would have been contemporaries; indeed, the similarities between the two—including a deep respect for a distant father and a subsequent withdrawal from the world—are striking. Copland may well have realized that with his music for *The Heiress* he had created a style that could accommodate Dickinson's poetry and her world. One can even find specific parallels between the two works: "Heart, We Will Forget Him" and Catherine's love music; "When They Come Back" and her planned elopement; "Going to Heaven!" and the wait for Morris; "The Chariot" and Sloper's death. Something of Copland's film work seems to hover about generally, as if the songs were the individual sequences of a motion picture. In any case, *The Heiress* nurtured a romantic delicacy and refinement, as well as a sympathy for a woman's point of view, that helped ready Copland for this new adventure.

Copland consulted at least two volumes of Dickinson's verse and, assertions to the contrary, set her poetry exactly as found. The editions he used, however, were corrupt to various degrees (no complete critical edition appeared until 1955). Among other things, they smoothed over her trademark dashes, leaving one wondering whether Copland's settings would have been more jagged had he worked from more faithful sources. In addition, they contained more substantive corruptions, from a few altered words to omitted stanzas. Such changes tended to conventionalize and sometimes obscure Dickinson's verse; in the case of "Heart, We Will Forget Him," Copland's setting—taken to task by one critic for its "slightly oversweet quality"—might well have been less sweet otherwise. On the other hand, Wayne Shirley, citing as one example the cycle's very first vocal line, points out that some of the revisions served Copland's purposes quite well. In any event, most of the texts closely approximate the original Dickinson; aside from punctuation, not a few appear exactly as they do in Thomas Johnson's critical edition.[22]

With over a thousand poems at his disposal, Copland seriously considered over twenty before deciding on the twelve he eventually set. He avoided some of Dickinson's more aphoristic verse in favor of well-shaped poems of, for the most part, two to four stanzas, though the gloriously expansive first song, "Nature, the Gentlest Mother," uses a six-stanza poem. Perhaps the cycle's only obscure metaphor is "doom's electric moccasin" for lightning, a reference to the Indian slipper, the water moccasin, or perhaps both.[23]

The poems selected concern life and death, nature as an alternately benign and destructive force, and the poet's own struggle between faith and despair. The first two songs exemplify the poet's—and the composer's—bifocal vision: "Nature, the Gentlest Mother" pictures nature as a loving mother, whereas "There Came a Wind like a Bugle," depicts it as brutal. "Why Do They Shut Me out of Heaven?" introduces the matter of the poet's problematic faith; she imagines herself turned out of heaven for her too-loud singing, a symbol for her noncomformity. "The World Feels Dusty" maintains that, in view of death, only love offers solace. In "Heart, We Will Forget Him," the poet conspires with her heart to forget the either deceased or departed beloved. "Dear March, Come In!" celebrates springtime, whimsically portrayed as a house caller.

"Sleep Is Supposed to Be," the cycle's central kernel, affirms an exalted, messianic vision of life and death. "When They Come Back" addresses the transience of spring in a highly personal way. The next two songs, "I Felt a Funeral in My Brain" and "I've Heard an Organ Talk Sometimes," feature another dichotomy: in the former, the poet imagines her own funeral service, a symbol, some have argued, of psychic breakdown and depressed withdrawal; in the latter, she gains consolation from a church organ, whose musical language manifests mysterious faith. "Going to Heaven!" contains both faith and doubt; after jubilantly picturing her ascent to heaven, the poet proclaims her own disbelief, taking comfort, however, in the fact that two deceased friends (or relatives) had faith. In the final poem, "The Chariot," the poet envisions her own funeral ride to the cemetery, observing the life cycle from childhood to death and beyond.

Although some of the songs are interconnected—"Sleep Is Supposed to Be" and "The Chariot," for instance, begin almost identically (their dotted rhythms related to the very opening song)—the cycle is extraordinarily varied, the music alternately melancholy, sardonic, wistful, and so on. Copland expressed a special liking for "Sleep Is Supposed to Be" and "The Chariot," probably the cycle's two most gripping songs; the luminous "Nature, the Gentlest Mother" and the poignant "The World Feels Dusty" also stand out. But the whole is larger than the sum of its parts; the work comprises a compelling and multifaceted portrait of what Copland, who researched the poet for months while composing the cycle, called Dickinson's "unique personality." He even considered such working titles as *Emily's World* and *Amherst Days*.[24]

Copland dedicated each of the twelve songs to composer friends: David Diamond, Elliott Carter, Ingolf Dahl, Alexei Haieff, Marcelle de Manziarly, Juan Orrego-Salas, Irving Fine, Harold Shapero, Camargo Guarnieri, Alberto Ginastera, Lukas Foss, and Arthur Berger. "At the time, something about each song felt right for each person," avowed Copland, though systematic attempts to explain these dedications have been far from conclusive.[25]

From the moment the *Dickinson Songs* first appeared, critics have consistently commented on the distinctive vocal writing, with the composer's declamatory rhythms, imposing range, bold leaps, and jagged shapes now provocatively applied to solo voice. Virgil Thomson and others complained of Copland's "cruelty" to singers. The cycle certainly requires an uncommon ease in both the soprano and mezzo ranges; and Copland duly offered mezzos a few optional lower notes (as heard in the Martha Lipton and Jan DeGaetani recordings), while for sopranos he sanctioned specified transpositions for six of the songs (confirming a certain freewheeling attitude toward large-scale tonal design). More demanding than any leap or high note, perhaps, is the cycle's final, sustained pitch on the last syllable of the word "eternity"—quite uncharacteristically, an almost superhuman demand on Copland's part. Most performers cut the note short, hurry through the accompaniment, or take the optional lower note. But when someone like Roberta Alexander can sing the ending as written, the effect is indescribably ethereal.[26]

Critics and musicians now agree that it is precisely the work's unusual prosody that gives the music much of its authentic flavor and authority (as could also be said of the solo mezzo-soprano part depicting God's utterances in *In the Beginning*). Soprano Phyllis Curtin observes, "It is my conviction, after having sung these songs hundreds of times, that nobody has ever understood her as Aaron does. . . . It was Aaron who found the musical voice for Emily Dickinson, and the times when I sang them best, I had the feeling that she was speaking." And Michael Tilson Thomas writes, "I actually learnt to love Emily Dickinson, my whole entry into her world of poetry was through Aaron's songs. I think he made, for a whole generation of Americans, the cadential intent of the actual words very clear in the way he set them."[27]

If the vocal part captures the poet's voice, the piano part, itself rather challenging, functions as metaphor, reflecting on the poetry's vivid imagery. Copland himself mentions the birdlike flutterings (related, perhaps, to both Mahler and Messiaen) that open "Nature, the Gentlest Mother" and the bugle melody in "There Came a Wind like a Bugle." One similarly can find musical descriptions of a "summer afternoon," "doom's electric moccasin," "the bell within the steeple wild," and numerous other images. In "Heart, We Will Forget Him," Copland practices another strategy, writing a walking countermelody in the piano to suggest the dialogue between the poet and her heart. Similarly, to introduce the phrase "The carriage held but just ourselves and Immortality," he unfurls a short, three-voice canon, presumably to symbolize the three riders. On occasion, the dramatic pacing of such ideas recalls his film scores, as in the way the dotted-note motive depicting death's carriage in "The Chariot" becomes childlike for the playing children, descends for the setting sun, turns ominous for the cemetery, and broadens for eternity.[28]

Although the musical community was slow to fully appreciate the *Dickinson Songs*, composer-critics like Stravinsky, Thomson, Cowell, Fine, and Flanagan quickly recognized its enormous distinction. Its reputation has only increased over time, and it now commands a central position in the vocal repertory. It has won the attention of a number of critics and scholars as well. In a 1961 discussion of the work deemed by William Austin "uniquely penetrating," Joseph Kerman praised some of the music as "finer than anything Copland had ever done," and yet criticized not only "harmonic clichés" akin to popular music (specifically, opulent dissonances and sliding parallelisms) that made certain songs sound "enervating," "tawdry," even "obnoxious" but a general tendency toward "deflection and what amounts to an announcement of withdrawal." In a similar vein, Douglas Young wondered whether Copland's "reticence" could encompass the "metaphysical immensity" of such poems as "I Felt a Funeral in My Brain" and "The Chariot." Robert Michael Daugherty responded by arguing that these two songs made their full impact only in the context of the entire cycle. Larry Starr further cautioned that Copland's restraint should not obscure the "risks" taken throughout the cycle, including the "breathtaking conclusion" of "The World Feels Dusty." There is surely nothing reticent about "Sleep Is Supposed to Be" and the setting of its climactic phrase, "East of Eternity," with its triple forte on a high B-flat for the voice, resounding sympathetically in the piano even after the singing stops.[29]

As can be seen, critical evaluation of the work often hinges on the question of whether or not the music does Dickinson full justice. At the least, critics widely consider the work the finest of the many musical realizations of Dickinson to date. Moreover, it is astonishing to observe how so many of Copland's characteristic gestures—the clangorous vitality, ironic humor, biting severity, heroic grandeur, and resigned sadness—can accommodate, with barely a nod to older musical styles, the verse of this mid-nineteenth-century poet. However, like settings of Goethe by Schubert, or Verlaine by Debussy, the *Dickinson Songs* ultimately must be taken on its own terms.

In 1958 Copland began orchestrating some of the songs; twelve years later, in 1970, he completed the eight deemed suitable as such—"Nature, the Gentlest Mother," "There Came a Wind like a Bugle," "The World Feels Dusty," "Heart, We Will Forget Him," "Dear March, Come In!" "Sleep Is Supposed to Be," "Going to Heaven!" and "The Chariot"—as *Eight Poems of Emily Dickinson*. The chamber orchestration helps clarify the music's contrapuntal structure and dramatize its text painting; the colorful "Nature, the Gentlest Mother," for instance, more fully than the original, reveals Copland as a composer of woodlands, not only of prairies and deserts. Douglas Young claimed that the orchestrations in general enhanced the work, while Curtin, who performed both versions, stated a strong preference for the original.[30]

For a few decades, the composer's two recordings of the *Twelve Poems*—first with mezzo-soprano Martha Lipton (1957) and then with soprano Adele Addison (1967)—filled out the work's slender discography. But recent years have witnessed a number of excellent new recordings of both piano and orchestral versions, including performances of the *Twelve Poems* by Jan DeGaetani, Roberta Alexander, and Barbara Bonney, and of the *Eight Poems* by Marni Nixon, Helene Schneiderman, Dawn Upshaw, and Barbara Hendricks. Consequently, the work is as well represented on disc as practically any Copland—an astounding development, considering its relative difficulty for both performers and audiences. These recorded interpretations, ranging from the poignant intensity of Alexander (with Roger Vignoles) and Hendricks (with Michael Tilson Thomas and the London Symphony Orchestra) to the cool sophistication of Bonney (with André Previn) and Upshaw (with Hugh Wolff and the St. Paul Chamber Orchestra), differ in many respects, but similarly illuminate the music's extraordinary range of nuance.[31]

The Piano Quartet

Copland composed the Piano Quartet, commissioned by Elizabeth Sprague Coolidge, in the summer and early fall of 1950, completing it a mere nine days before its 29 October premiere at the Library of Congress by members of the New York Quartet and himself at the piano. He dedicated the score to Coolidge, who had also commissioned *Appalachian Spring*.

With the Piano Quartet, a three-movement work in a slow-fast-slow format, Copland created a stir in music circles by adopting Schoenberg's twelve-tone method of composition. He was at first skeptical of the vogue for such "serial" techniques among the postwar avant-garde, expressing his doubts to Roque Cordero at Tanglewood in 1946. "Now they have come up with the Schoenberg twelve-tone system," he observed somewhat scornfully in April 1948, " 'discovering' it as if it were something quite new." But after encountering the music of Pierre Boulez while in Europe in 1949, he more fully realized that the technique could be divorced from the "old Wagnerian" aesthetic, a lesson confirmed by a growing familiarity with late Webern as well as with the tonal twelve-tone pieces by the Swiss Frank Martin and the Italian Luigi Dallapiccola. Much as he had absorbed neoclassical, jazz, and folkloric resources, so he absorbed dodecaphony, in the expectation that it might "freshen and enrich my technique." "As I see it," he explained further in 1957, "twelve-tonism is nothing more than an angle of vision. Like fugal treatment, it is a stimulus that enlivens musical thinking, especially when applied to a series of tones that lend themselves to that treatment. It is a method, not a style; and therefore it solves no problems of musical expressivity."[32]

Jennifer DeLapp also argues that the adoption of the twelve-tone method in the Piano Quartet marks a conscious rapprochement between "the mass-appeal music of a Shostakovich and the musical radicalism of a Schoenberg," a dichotomy that Copland viewed as emblematic of Cold War tensions. In 1952 Copland himself wrote, "The twelve-tone composer . . . is no longer writing music to satisfy himself; whether he likes it or not, he is writing it against a vocal and militant [communist] opposition." That the twelve-tone technique had acquired for Copland such political and sociological resonance may have contributed to its allure. But it would be simplistic to view his use of the method as representing in any way a retreat from his long-held ideals. One might more accurately say that Copland adopted the twelve-tone technique for his own purposes, of which both the affirmation of an American sound in the context of world trends and the observation of the world in which he lived—including its music—had always taken high priority.[33]

And although hardly the first American composer to employ the twelve-tone method—notwithstanding his brief flirtation with it in "Poet's Song" (1927) and the "quasi-serial" or "proto-serial" or "crypto-serial" techniques found in the Piano Variations (1930)—it should also be noted that, far from jumping on any bandwagon (as is widely alleged) Copland adopted the method before most of his friends or colleagues; this includes Stravinsky and Roger Sessions, both of whom are often credited as principal disseminators of the technique in America. Nor did the quartet represent a so-called conversion to the method; he used it only sporadically afterward. Consequently, in 1970 Leonard Bernstein did Copland a grave disservice with the notorious remark, "The truth is that when the musical winds blew past him, he tried to catch up—with twelve-tone music, just as it too was becoming old-fashioned to the young." Copland attempted to clarify the matter in his own way, stating, "It never occurred to me that by adopting a method that so many other people were working with that I was ... somehow betraying myself, my chosen path."[34]

One might add, too, that Copland remained consistently critical of the twelve-tone method as found in certain works by Schoenberg and many of his followers. He believed, rather, in expanding the method to permit more spontaneous procedures; he liked in particular to see it accommodate tonal resources. All this could be deduced from his own use of the method.[35]

The Piano Quartet, with typical economy, employs a single tone row for all three of its movements, thus ensuring the kind of unity so characteristic of its composer; indeed, the amenability of the twelve-tone method to Copland's customary procedures no doubt constituted some of the method's appeal in the first place. As often the case with Schoenberg, he presents the series as a theme rather than, more abstractly, a collection of pitches, though the actual row theme, immediately stated by the unaccompanied violin, is very unlike Schoenberg in its lyrical, even singable, contour, one that moves largely by step and with tonal implications. Indeed, this row derived in part from a melody from *The Red Pony* (one heard at the point when Grandfather says, "No, that isn't the worst. Westering has died out of the people"). Moreover, the theme contains only eleven, not twelve, pitches, something more than an academic detail.

Copland's actual use of the row marks an even greater divergence from twelve-tone orthodoxy. Schoenberg typically structured his twelve-tone music around statements of the tone row, using one of its four shapes— forward ("prime" or "original"), reversed ("retrograde"), inverted, or reversed and inverted ("retrograde inversion")—in any of twelve transpositions, for a total of forty-eight tone rows or row forms. In contrast, Copland states a complete tone row only rarely, as a structurally important event, comparable to the exposition of what, in more traditional contexts, might be called a principal theme. This includes the prime row and a reversed row as the two main themes of the first movement, respectively, and a row in retrograde inversion for the main theme of the second movement. The last movement does not even feature a row statement per se.[36]

Aside from these few major row statements, the work consists, rather, of melodies and harmonies derived from bits of the row (usually two to six notes). This method hardly differs from Copland's standard working operation, and one might rightly ask, to what extent are we justified in calling the Piano Quartet "twelve-tone" in the first place? But it is not as

---

if Copland's row contained, say, the sort of fragmented diatonic or modal scale that could produce an *Appalachian Spring* or even a *Piano Variations*. On the contrary, Copland felt precisely the potential for the kinds of densely rich harmonies such a theme could generate—harmonies that, given the row's stepwise motion, would naturally be comprised of clusters of seconds and their inversions. "The attraction of the method for me was that I began to hear chords that I wouldn't have heard otherwise," he told Edward Cone. Similarly, when Leonard Bernstein asked him why he adopted the method, he replied, "Because I need more chords. I've run out of chords."[37]

As it turns out, the quartet's harmonies resemble Bartók enough to suggest that it responded as much to the Hungarian's stunning rise in prominence as to the vogue for the twelve-tone method. Certainly, this new adventure did not lead to the renunciation of tonality. "The feeling of tonality or of tonal center is rarely missing," Copland himself said of the work. At times, for dramatic effect, he even manipulates motives and harmonies derived from the series in order to create frankly diatonic passages, as at the opening of the last movement, though much of the work could be fairly described as highly chromatic.[38]

David Conte further notes that the adoption of the twelve-tone technique led Copland to simplify other aspects of the score: regularizing meters and phrase lengths, slowing the harmonic rhythm, and utilizing sequences. In this way, Conte suggests, Copland compensated for some of the other complexities occasioned by the method. At the same time, the quartet reveals a new interest in unusual colors: having the strings, for instance, play without vibrato, or at the frog, or muted and pizzicato; or having the piano periodically produce "glassy" sounds or declaim a series of widely spaced notes with the pedal down. As with the work's harmonic language, some of these coloristic devices recall Bartók, though the interest in "glassy" sonorities points to Boulez as well.[39]

In short, the quartet combines familiarly Coplandesque gestures and moods (the slow-fast-slow format itself recalls such works as the Piano Sonata) with fresh ideas and feelings. Harold Clurman immediately recognized this newness when, in a comparison with the *Piano Variations*, he wrote, "The Piano Quartet of 1950 is even more disquieting, as if it described the quiet preceding or following an atom bomb attack. The work is the voice of our inner fear, an echo of the secret trepidation in all our hearts as we look out upon the bleak horizon of a world in bondage to its illusions." This hardly describes the work in its totality, for the quartet travels a wide emotional range; but one can perceive an unusually dark and unsettled quality throughout the piece.[40]

The quartet's drama hinges on the conflict between just such darkness and moments of hopefulness, humor, and calm. The first movement's exposition, for example, moves from its desolate first theme, presented in fugal fashion by the strings, to a hopeful second theme, initially stated by the cello, the piano following in canon. The ensuing development, brusquely halting such hopefulness, features clangorous, angry music followed by a dramatic exploration of the main theme, marked "eloquente." This in turn leads to a climactic, triple-forte return of the main theme (initially in the piano, though completed by the violin), grandly accompanied by various row fragments. The piano returns to the development's clangorous theme, eventually subdued by soft strings. As the strings sustain a harmony, the movement ends with a forlorn statement of the main theme in the piano, including, finally, the row's missing twelfth pitch.[41]

The second movement scherzo is in a kind of rondo form, statements of the jaunty main theme alternating with various episodes. Two such episodes contain static bass lines, recalling the traditional trio section. In the first of these, the mood grows restive as the strings, playing at the frog, argue among themselves against a fidgety piano; in the second, the music becomes broadly humorous. At two points, the action climaxes with an outburst of the first movement's clangorous music, introducing into the proceedings a characteristic note of grotesquerie. In the coda, the clangorous music, in the piano, dissipates, as the main theme, in the strings, eerily vanishes into thin air.

Like the first movement, the last movement comprises a compressed sonata form, except that its recapitulation more conventionally puts forth both principal themes. Moreover, the emotive qualities of their respective themes are reversed: the first theme now is vaguely pastoral and calm, or at least resigned, while the second theme is weary and sad, with chimings in the piano. The development section explores the more optimistic first theme, which, as in the first movement, returns in its entirety in the strings just prior to the formal recapitulation in the piano, a variant of the false recapitulations found, for example, in Haydn. The sad second theme promises to have the last word, but it serenely resolves into a major harmony; against this, the piano restates the work's very opening theme, not in full, as at the end of the first movement, but using only its first six notes. This remembrance explicitly reveals the opening theme as the source for the chiming music; it also throws the resolution of the strings into question.

That Copland continued to compose twelve-tone works was hardly due to the quartet's reception. The press was largely unsympathetic, and even friends like Bernstein, Diamond, and Berger quibbled about this and that aspect of the work. Few aside from Clurman seemed cognizant of the work's strong emotional power. But by this time, Copland was well accustomed to being misunderstood.[42]

24

The Changing Scene

Inquisition at Home

One can only guess at Copland's astonishment upon reading the lead piece of *Life* magazine's 4 April 1949 issue, "Red Visitors Cause Rumpus." A stinging attack on the World Peace Conference held the previous week in New York, the article featured a two-page spread with photographs of fifty of the conference's best-known participants—including not only Copland (his name misspelled with an *e*) but Leonard Bernstein, Charlie Chaplin, Albert Einstein, Lillian Hellman, Thomas Mann, Arthur Miller, and Harvard professor F. O. Matthiessen—under the banner headline "Dupes and Fellow Travelers Dress Up Communist Fronts." "They are not the most notorious 50," the magazine allowed, "but a representative selection ranging from hard-working fellow-travelers to soft-headed do-gooders who have persistently lent their names to organizations labeled by the U.S. Attorney General or other government agencies as subversive."[1]

This article marked the beginnings of Copland's victimization by the hysteria now known as McCarthyism, after the anticommunist crusader Senator Joseph McCarthy. Although the "red-baiting" that transpired during this period might well seem absurd in retrospect, it was no laughing matter at the time. On the contrary, it took a devastating toll, including, at the least, emotional stress, but also hate mail, obscene phone calls, passport and visa difficulties, broken friendships, destroyed marriages, ruined careers, damaged reputations, public boycotts, deportations, jail sentences, and even, in some instances, suicide (Matthiessen killed himself following publication of the aforementioned piece). More subtly, McCarthyism eroded traditional American optimism and idealism, something keenly felt in the arts community.[2]

A year after the *Life* article, three former FBI agents included Copland in the notorious *Red Channels: The Reports of Communist Influence in Radio and Television*, a compendium of 151 artists and their alleged communist associations. This publication, along with more clandestine FBI investigations, led to still further ostracism. On 3 January 1953, Illinois Representative Fred Busbey, a strident anticommunist, protested on the floor of the House a planned performance of the *Lincoln Portrait* (with the National Symphony, Walter Pidgeon narrating) at the January 18 Eisenhower inaugural concert, on the grounds of the composer's suspect political affiliations. The chairman of the inauguration's arrangements committee immediately dropped the Copland piece from the program "because we didn't want to do anything to bring criticism."[3]

The January 16 public announcement of this cancellation prompted immediate protest. Claire Reis, on behalf of the League of Composers, led the charge with a telegram sent that very day to the inaugural concert committee: "As an organization that has devoted itself for more than thirty years to the advancement of musical culture in this country," the telegram read in part, "we urge you to reconsider your action and to restore to the inaugural concert a composition recognized everywhere as great American music by the greatest American composer." Copland issued his own statement, noting, "This is the first time, as far as I know, that a composition has been removed from a concert program in the United States because of alleged political affiliations of a composer." Denying any political party membership, he admitted sponsoring

causes which seemed to me to have merit—sometimes mistaken ones like Henry Wallace, but I have never at any time lent my name to any organization except as a loyal and liberal American.

In a Brooklyn public school I was taught to believe that an American took pride in his right to speak his mind on controversial subjects, even to protest when some action seemed unworthy of our great democratic traditions. In doing precisely that, I believe I was doing my civic duty, keeping alive the finest of American traditions. Having been encouraged to speak openly as a free American, it now appears that I am in danger of being penalized for so doing.

He at least took comfort in the fact that his work had been banned on political as opposed to artistic grounds: "My 'politics'—tainted or untainted—are certain to die with me, but my music, I am foolish enough to imagine, might just possibly outlive the strictures of a member of the Republican party." He expressed himself similarly in a letter sent directly to President Eisenhower.[4]

Meanwhile, Busbey took the offensive, defending his actions in the *Congressional Record*. Acknowledging that his "passing knowledge of music" prevented him from commenting "on the quality of Mr. Copland's work," he based his protest "on but one thing—the known records of Aaron Copland for activities, affiliations, and sympathies with and for causes that seemed to me to be more in the interest of an alien ideology than the things representative of Abraham Lincoln." Why perform Copland, he asked, given "all the music of fine, patriotic and thoroughly American composers available to the concert committee of the Inaugural Committee." Busbey concluded with a long list of Copland's alleged ties with the Communist Party and its front organizations. "I agree that any person could have been affiliated with or supported one of the many Communist fronts that have mushroomed over a period of years without being aware that he was giving aid and comfort to the Communist Party," Busbey interjected, "but I insist that as the number of such activities or affiliations increase, any presumption of the innocence of such a person must necessarily decrease."[5]

The press—Paul Hume in the *Washington Post*, Howard Taubman in the *New York Times*, Bruce Catton in the *Nation*, and the editors of the *New Republic*—ridiculed the cancellation. When Hume personally confronted Busbey, facetiously asking why stop at the inauguration, why not ban Copland from the military's bands and orchestras, the congressman responded, "Indeed, that is something we would have to consider." Hume was appalled: "Every American musician and music lover has a vital concern in this matter. It was through such machinery as the Congressman advocates that the music of Mendelssohn and a dozen others was silenced in Germany. It is by such means that the music of the Coplands and who knows how many others could be stilled in America. Can it happen here?"[6]

The protests of newspapers and musicians were, however, to no avail. The inauguration went forward without *Lincoln Portrait*, "and if this was in the end something less than a fatal blow to the evil designs of the men in the Kremlin," wrote Bruce Catton, "it at least saved the assembled Republicans from being compelled to listen to Lincoln's brooding words: 'Fellow-citizens, we cannot escape history. We of this Congress and this Administration will be remembered in spite of ourselves.' " Notwithstanding Busbey's rhetoric about all the "fine, patriotic and thoroughly American composers," the inauguration concert contained no American music whatsoever, prompting Hume to provide a list of native works that could be performed at the next inauguration, assuming "that by 1957 we will have surmounted the idea that music by various American-born composers is to be banned if Congressmen protest."[7]

In April, Copland suffered another blow. Senator McCarthy frightened the State Department into stringent security hurdles for sending music and recordings to libraries abroad; any "derogatory" allegation made against a composer—whether substantiated or not—meant an immediate barring of the composer's work from any of the 196 official American libraries around the world. Such allegations could include a signature in defense of Republican Spain. Of a list of prominent American composers, the State Department could clear only one; they blacklisted not only Copland but Gershwin, Sessions, Thompson, Harris, Thomson, and Bernstein.[8]

Then, on Friday, May 22, Copland received the dreaded telegram summoning him to appear that coming Monday before the Senate Permanent Subcommittee on Investigations, chaired by McCarthy, in Washington. The hearing was delayed one day in order to allow him time to find legal representation. He arrived in Washington the night before the hearing accompanied by Victor Kraft and his lawyers, Oscar Cox, Charles Glover III, and Herbert Packer; Cox, his principal attorney, had supervised his perforce hasty preparation, but Glover, for political reasons, represented him at the hearing.

This Senate subcommittee was one of a number of congressional organs, including the House Un-American Activities Committee (HUAC), charged with identifying and researching alleged subversives, who then could be called to testify (some privately, others publicly). The committees cast their net wide and, until curtailed by the Supreme Court in the mid-

1950s, felt free to subpoena any American citizen or resident. Anyone even remotely involved with government or politics (say, a professor teaching a course on Marx) could come under scrutiny. In part because of its newsworthiness, the committees zealously targeted the arts community, especially Hollywood.

Persons called before these committees were deemed either "friendly" or "unfriendly" witnesses. Friendly witnesses typically expressed contrition for "subversive" activities and named other Communists or communist sympathizers. Unfriendly witnesses either questioned a committee's legitimacy or invoked the Fifth Amendment's privilege against self-incrimination. Those who denounced a committee were often cited with contempt and sent to jail, while pleading the Fifth was taken as a confession of guilt, the punishment (which usually meant being fired and blacklisted) meted out by the government or the highly cooperative private sector. (Lillian Hellman's unusual offer to testify about herself but take the Fifth when it came to others apparently disarmed HUAC, narrowly sparing her a jail sentence.)[9]

Copland's private hearing was held at the Capitol at 2:30 and lasted two hours. Chaired by McCarthy, the committee also included Senators Karl Mundt and John McClellan, both of whom heard only portions of Copland's testimony. Also in attendance were three government lawyers, including chief counsel Roy Cohn, and a representative from the State Department.

The principal reason or at least rationale for the hearing concerned Copland's three stints as a lecturer abroad (in Latin America in 1941 and 1947 and in Italy in 1951) under government auspices. This was part of an ongoing Republican attempt to discredit and possibly punish members of the formerly Democratic-controlled State Department. McCarthy even made a point of telling Copland that belonging to a communist front organization was, in itself, not an illegal activity; he was only interested in knowing why the government selected him "when we have many other people available as lecturers." He showed not the least recognition of Copland's enormous distinction as composer, lecturer, and cultural ambassador. One cannot help recalling the words of Chile's foremost composer, Domingo Santa Cruz, who told a group of American diplomats, "Out of this country [the United States] he [Copland] alone means more than twelve senators when he steps in."[10]

McCarthy and Cohn dominated the hearing. While the former was condescendingly cordial, the latter, alert to any inconsistency in Copland's testimony, was poised to attack. McCarthy even occasionally restrained Cohn, an old police tactic that he apparently cultivated in order to win over the confidence of his witnesses. Mundt and McClellan simply asked a few questions about how much money Copland earned for his three trips abroad.

Copland came before the hearing as a friendly but not particularly cooperative witness. He stated categorically, "I have not been a Communist in the past and I am not now a Communist." Otherwise, he smoothly talked his way around most questions and avoided naming names. When asked he if he had ever been a "Communist sympathizer," he answered, "I am not sure that I would be able to say what you mean by the word 'sympathizer.' From my impression of it I have never thought of myself as a Communist sympathizer." And again, "I have never sympathized with Communists as such." Here follows a typical exchange:

COHN: Do you feel Communists should be allowed to teach in our schools?

COPLAND: I haven't given the matter such thought as to come up with an answer.

COHN: In other words, as of today you don't have any firm thought?

COPLAND: I would be inclined to allow the faculty of the University to decide that.

MCCARTHY: Let's say you are on the faculty and are making a designation, would you feel Communists should be allowed to teach?

COPLAND: I couldn't give you a blanket decision on that without knowing the case.

MCCARTHY: Let's say the teacher is a Communist, period. Would you feel that is sufficient to bar that teacher from a job as a teacher?

COPLAND: I certainly think it would be sufficient if he were using his Communist membership to angle his teaching to further the purposes of the Communist Party.

Even under two hours of insistent interrogation, Copland maintained his customary aplomb.

Confronted with a long list of alleged associations with communist fronts, Copland acknowledged ties with only three: membership in the National Council of American-Soviet Friendship, sponsorship of a concert in support of Hanns Eisler (1948), and participation in the World Peace Conference (1949). As for the many other affiliations, he responded time and again with variations on "I don't remember," "I don't know," "I may have," and so on. He also reminded the committee that he had been subpoenaed only days earlier and had had little time to verify all of the charges. McCarthy seemingly sympathized with this but made it clear that he expected Copland to be better prepared at his next hearing. Cohn closed the proceedings by telling Copland, "You are reminded that you are still under subpoena and will be called again within the next week I would assume."

Whether or not Copland prevaricated under questioning, he clearly was not altogether forthcoming, sometimes even answering a committee question with one of his own. He was not about to divulge information about his friends that might prove injurious or to admit that he himself had written a "communist song" and preached "revolution" in 1934. In any case, his disarming manner seems to have prevailed.

The day after the hearing, Copland jotted down his impressions of McCarthy as "a man who doesn't really expect his luck to hold out," presciently writing, "When he touches on his magic theme, the 'Commies' or 'communism,' his voice darkens like that of a minister. He is like a plebian Faustus who has been given a magic wand by an invisible Mephisto—as long as the menace is there, the wand will work. The question is at what point his power grab will collide with the power drive of others in his own party. *A voir.*" He also released yet another statement that stated in part, "To the extent that I lent my name in the late 1930's and 1940's to organizations or causes, I did so without the knowledge or intention of supporting communist or communist front organizations. When in 1949 there was sufficient knowledge available to me to know that certain organizations might be communist or communist front and that any association by me with them might lead to the erroneous view that I was a communist—which I never was—I no longer would lend my name."

Expecting another hearing any day, Copland and Kraft quickly went to work researching his alleged affiliations, uncovering a total of $73.70 in contributions to four groups. Copland also prepared a defense, writing, "The committee should recognize that during the period under examination, roughly 1936–1951, persons prominent in artistic and intellectual fields were bombarded almost daily—with a continual flow of letters—mostly in mimeographed form and of greatest urgency concerning matters of great interest to intellectuals and artists—matters of personal liberty, the right to be non-conformist, thought control, racial, religious, and political oppression." Meanwhile, Cox reviewed the transcript of the hearing, discovering a number of factual and typographical errors.[11]

On June 5, Copland submitted a detailed follow-up to the committee, arguing that some of the alleged associations were demonstrably false while others represented unauthorized use of his name. All other connections, he further argued, represented such "good causes" as civil rights and antifascism. In response to the committee's request that he furnish the names of Americans who attended the World Peace Conference, he once again finessed, referring them to the *New York Times* and a *House Report*, stating, "I do not personally remember having seen anyone at the Conference who is not listed in those published sources." He presumed he would be called to testify at a June 9 public session on the State Department's exchange programs, but, for whatever reason, he fortunately was spared another hearing.[12]

Like most targets of McCarthy's probes, however, he subsequently faced difficulties securing a passport. In compliance with Glover's advice, he submitted to the State Department affidavits by Olga Koussevitzky (representing the Koussevitzky Foundation) and Henry Moe (representing the Guggenheim Foundation) testifying to his "pro-American position on various current issues." After considerable jumping through hoops and endless paper work, he managed to secure a passport, but such bureaucratic hassles continued into 1954. "The irony of Copland's passport difficulties," notes Vivian Perlis, "is that they coincided with his appearances as the major representative of American music in Europe and South America during 1954!"[13]

Moreover, the FBI continued investigating Copland's past and monitoring his current activities. Because of an informant's sworn testimony (1952) that he belonged to the Communist Party, in 1955 they conducted a wide-ranging investigation with the intent of possibly charging him with perjury and fraud against the government. However, on 30 November 1955, after months of research, the assistant attorney general, William Tompkins, concluded that there was "insufficient evidence to warrant prosecution."[14]

All this naturally drained Copland of time, energy, and money. What psychological and emotional stress he endured can only be imagined, because he rarely discussed the matter seriously; on the contrary, he made light of it, writes Vivian Perlis, "imitating McCarthy's deadly seriousness and Roy Cohn's way of repeating the word *Cooooommunist.*"

In terms of his career and reputation, he luckily came through relatively unscathed. His livelihood did not depend on a government job, a university post, or a studio contract. Only a few isolated problems occurred, all in 1953. Under pressure from conservative boards, both the University of Alabama and the University of Colorado canceled planned lectures. In addition, the Los Angeles Chamber Symphony reneged on Lukas Foss's suggestion that Copland conduct the orchestra. "Stupid, sinfully complacently stupid, that is what they are, and afraid," exploded Foss in a letter to the composer. There may well have been other lost opportunities. But as Cox wrote to Copland, "Non-conformists in any field—particularly the ones who are the salt of the earth—are the ones who at intermittent periods are the key targets of the political demagogues. But after someone like you has gone through the long, slow, hard road of public acceptance in your primary field—with the growth of public stature which goes with it—you tend more and more to be less and less vulnerable to unfounded political attacks." Indeed, Copland's "public stature" may have been at the heart of Congress's decision not to subject him to a public hearing.[15]

In a letter to Gurney Kennedy, who had arranged the revoked lecture at the University of Alabama, Copland himself wrote that after the Busbey incident, he "had no unpleasantness to complain of." His greatest sadness about the Alabama cancellation concerned the "loss of academic independence that such an action implies. It makes clear that freedom of thought is endangered in America if a large university such as yours can be intimidated by the allegations of a single individual, even though he be an elected public servant."[16]

For the most part, Americans, especially in the arts community, recognized the attacks on Copland for what they were: a sham. The American Academy of Arts and Letters awarded him membership (1954) and their prestigious Gold Medal (1956). Princeton, Brandeis, and other universities granted him honorary doctorates in the mid-1950s. Aside from the incidents already mentioned, symphony orchestras and educational institutions firmly defended him against the occasional threats and crank protests from the John Birch Society and the American Legion that plagued him as late as 1968.[17]

In the meantime, official Washington itself rehabilitated his reputation.

Beginning with the Kennedy administration and continuing through those of Johnson, Nixon, Ford, Carter, and Reagan, he regularly received invitations to White House inaugurations, dinners, and concerts. He joined, for instance, that dazzling assembly of artists and intellectuals who gathered to hear Pablo Casals perform at the Kennedy White House on 13 November 1961. Moreover, his music became a regular feature of state occasions, including the 1973 inauguration of President Nixon, a onetime McCarthyite. Kennedy congratulated him on his MacDowell Medal (1961), while Johnson awarded him the Presidential Medal of Freedom (1964), Carter, a Kennedy Center Honor (1979), and Reagan, a Medal of the Arts (1986). "You have set a magnificent example of what we Americans can accomplish by sharing our talents and energies with each other," wrote Carter in 1977. "Your love of our country, your awareness of the unique and vital heritage which is American, courses through every measure of your music," wrote Vice President Walter Mondale in 1980. "Your music is a very special part of the musical heritage of our great nation," wrote Reagan in 1981. A televised concert series from the early 1980s, *In Performance at the White House,* used a theme from *The Red Pony* as its signature music. Finally, in 1986, the House of Representatives, who some decades earlier had smeared Copland as "un-American," made amends, awarding him their highest civilian honor, the congressional Gold Medal.[18]

New Trends in Music

In the spring of 1949, Copland returned to Europe after an absence of twelve years, spending two months in England, France, Italy, and Belgium. He specifically wanted to catch up on the new generation of composers that had emerged from formerly Nazi-occupied Europe.

In Paris he found the new-music scene divided into a contingent of neoclassicists, led in part by his former teacher Nadia Boulanger, and a more radical group, dominated by the imposing Pierre Boulez. He apparently heard Boulez play parts of his Second Piano Sonata on two occasions: at Boulez's place and at Ned Rorem's. At the latter, Rorem recalled, "Aaron sat down and played his [own] *Variations,* no doubt to prove he was just as hairy as Boulez, but the effect was one of terrific force and form, and, yes, inspiration, thrown at the hostile chaos of the enfant terrible."[19]

Recalling the soiree at Boulez's apartment, Copland told Barbara Kolb, with typical self-effacement, "Well, I know Boulez didn't like my music, but since I managed to walk up those four floors, he treated me with respect." In fact, upon receiving from Copland a complimentary copy of the *Variations* in 1950, Boulez expressed his admiration of the piece to John Cage: "It is the best work I know of him. It is evidently under the Strawinsky's [sic] influence. But it is good Strawinsky, i.e. a good influence. And there was a 'violence' which seems to me very good (once more!)." Boulez apparently retained some fondness for the music, because in the mid-1970s, as director of the New York Philharmonic, he conducted performances of Copland's orchestrated version of the work, the *Orchestral Variations*.[20]

Boulez surprised and fascinated Copland—especially his rejection of "the Satie line" and his attachment to Webern. "The French are obviously unpredictable," he remarked. Notwithstanding his allegiance to Boulanger, he sympathized with Boulez, whose sonata he found somewhat "monotonous," yet impressive in its "conviction, particularly when Boulez himself plays it. How another pianist might do it is hard to say, and public reaction impossible to predict. Anyhow it's new, and therefore exciting." Boulez's "keen mind" and his abilities as a polemicist and organizer impressed him as well. He found himself in the "odd position" of having to defend Boulez to the Boulangerie.[21]

Copland also noted the prominence of Boulez's teachers: the theorist René Leibowitz, a champion of the twelve-tone method, and Olivier Messiaen, the organist-composer related, in Copland's estimation, to the religiosity of Bruckner and Franck, the spiritualism of Scriabin, the sensuality of Debussy, and the Catholicism of Paul Claudel and François Mauriac. At a reception hosted for him by his friend Rosamund Bernier, Copland met the French composer and later attended one of his church services, where he "was shocked to hear him improvise everything from the 'Devil' in the bass to what sounded like Radio City Hall harmonies in the treble. I couldn't understand how the church allowed it!"[22]

In addition, Copland visited Pierre Schaeffer's Musique Concrète studio, where composers produced taped music based on the manipulation of natural and electronically generated sounds. And in Florence he befriended Luigi Dallapiccola, whose tonal twelve-tone music, which had catapulted him to the forefront of the European music scene, was more to Copland's liking. He renewed his friendship with Dallapiccola while in Italy on a Fulbright Fellowship during the first half of 1951, and then at

Tanglewood during the summers of 1951 and 1952. "I found him person-ally charming," remembered Copland, "but became less interested in his music the more I heard of it."[23]

After returning from Europe in 1949, Copland published a review of Leibowitz's *Schoenberg and His School*, acknowledging the book's importance but criticizing, among other things, "its fanatical tone and dense prose style." Messiaen was hardly Copland's "dish of tea" either, as he confessed to Irving Fine, but he understood and respected his "attrac-tions for others." He duly brought Messiaen to Tanglewood that summer and lectured about his music at Tanglewood the following year; whatever his doubts about Messiaen's music, he clearly felt that America's young composers should be familiar with such an influential figure.[24]

Copland discussed both Messiaen and Boulez in his Norton lectures (1951–52), obliquely voicing concerns about Europe's postwar avant-garde in general. First, in contrast to Schoenberg, Webern, and Berg, who often incorporated "classicalizing principles" derived from tonality or old forms, the new "serial" music threatened to collapse into "near-chaos." Second, the music had "little hope of reaching a popular audience." But such caveats paled before the music's suppression in the communist bloc, for that denied "the immemorial right of the artist to be wrong. A crea-tor often learns as much from his miscalculations as he does from his successes."[25]

From April through September 1955, Copland traveled again through Europe, further exploring new music. One highlight was a performance of Boulez's *Le Marteau sans Maître*, which he heard as an ISCM jury member in Baden-Baden; he thought its "striking sounds and peculiar rhythms" deserved a prize. Later that year, in Munich, he also listened to tapes of music by contemporary German composers. Whereas he found Hartmann's "brooding" Sixth Symphony relevant to the times, Zimmer-mann's *Symphony in One Movement* he thought "Too German 'seriös,' too unsympathetic as expression to hold the audience of any country, too old-fashioned, fundamentally, despite all the modern sounds." Nor did Henze's Third Symphony or his *Ode to the West Wind* particularly appeal to him: "It is all vaguely impressionist in aesthetic. Hard to see how it could manage to hold one's attention after repeated hearings. Yet he is generally thought of as the white hope of young German music. This tells more about the state of German music than about Henze."[26]

As for the two Stockhausen pieces he heard, he preferred *Kreuzspiel* to *Kontra-Punkte*, but he found both problematic:

Here is an end to continuity in the old sense and an end of thematic relationships. In this music, one waits to hear what will happen next without the slightest idea of what *will* happen, or why what happened did happen once it has happened. Stockhausen's only chance is to mesmerize the listener. Failing that, one gets bored. Perhaps one can say modern painting of the Paul Klee variety has invaded new German music. . . . But one thing is sure—whatever the listener may think, it is without doubt the most frustrating music ever put on a performer's music stand.

In later years, he acknowledged Stockhausen's preeminence in avant-garde circles, showing familiarity with some other works, including the electronic *Gesang der Jünglinge*, deemed by him "the best of its kind."[27]

Copland's 1955 travels also took him to Scandinavia. In Helsinki, he attributed the provincialism of Finland's composers to the overwhelming figure of Sibelius, writing in his journals, "Things will probably get better when the old man dies." In Stockholm, he encountered a variety of young composers, including Ingvar Lidholm ("a gifted fellow"), Gustaf Allan Pettersson ("a violent, primitive talent"), and Karl-Birger Blomdahl ("a certain explosive-angry personality which makes him the most interesting of the newer Scandinavian composers"). In Copenhagen, his happy discovery of Carl Nielsen's Clarinet Concerto (1928) overshadowed his enthusiasm for more recent scores, though he commended Vagn Holmboe's Third String Quartet as "well-made" and "exportable." And in Oslo, he again listened to a handful of representative works, including Fartein Valen's Third Symphony, Harald Saeverud's *Psalm* for orchestra, and Klaus Egge's Violin Concerto; he criticized Valen's "sameness of texture," Saeverud's "none too easy handling of materials," and Egge's "disparity in harmonic style" (which reminded him of Arnold Bax and William Walton).[28]

Copland also kept abreast of European developments through Tanglewood, where Roberto Gerhard, Goffredo Petrassi, Witold Lutoslawski, Iannis Xenakis, and Luciano Berio taught in the late 1950s and early 1960s. He befriended all these composers; they came to Tanglewood at his invitation or at least with his consent. He began conducting some of their music as well, including Xenakis's *Pithoprakta* for orchestra (1956) and Lutoslawski's *Funeral Music* for strings (1958); one can imagine, in the context of the postwar avant-garde, the brash vigor of Xenakis and Lutoslawski attracting Copland. In the case of Xenakis especially, a cordial friendship ensued, Xenakis appreciative of Copland's guidance and touched by his interest in his work.[29]

Meanwhile, a tour of the Soviet Union and Japan in 1960 brought him into contact with many composers hardly known in the West. In the Soviet Union, he heard not only the music of Shostakovich and Andrey Balanchivadze (George Balanchine's brother) but that of such younger and less established composers as German Galïnin, Kara Karayev, Karen Khachaturian (Aram's nephew), Arvo Pärt, Alfred Schnittke, Rodion Shchedrin, Andrey Volkonsky, and Galina Ustvol'skaya, all of whom he thought talented to varying degrees. He seemed especially attracted to Galïnin's Piano Concerto (1946), regretting that "a bad accident" in 1948 had cut short his career (or so he was told: Galïnin had actually gone underground because of political pressures). In general, however, for all its high level of technical competence, Copland complained about the "official" sound of most Soviet music, with its "occasional 'modernisms' borrowed from Ravel and Hollywood." In conversation with a group of teachers and students at the Moscow Conservatory, he even ruffled a few feathers by frankly complaining that Russian composers "knew *too* well what style to write in."[30]

In Japan, Copland listened to the music of Yosiro Irino, Kazuo Fukushima, Michio Mamiya, Yoritsune Matsudaira and his son Yoriaki, Toshiro Mayuzumi, Makoto Moroi, Toru Takemitsu, Akio Yashiro, and others. He sympathized with the senior Matsudaira and, to a lesser degree, Yashiro, but his admiration for Takemitsu in particular grew in the course of his visit. "He has the 'pure gold' touch, he chooses his notes carefully and meaningfully. . . . I was pleased also by his personality— typically Japanese and yet a character of his own." In contrast, he thought most other Japanese music "repetitious as to phraseology and too slow-moving in mood development." In a lecture for the BBC (1960), he emphasized the need for Japanese composers to "adapt their special temperament" to Western traditions.[31]

Copland and Takemitsu subsequently exchanged letters and scores. Their friendship recalled those between Copland and younger Latin Americans like Ginastera, this partly due to the fact that Takemitsu reciprocated his admiration. Upon receiving a tape in 1967 of some recent Copland work (presumably *Inscape*), he wrote to the composer, "It is a strong and an honest piece; I am very much impressed. Today, we have much new music like houses which . . . have no rooms people can live inside of. Your music transmits your voice into us. I am very happy to stay in your room with [its] beautiful sonore." For his part, Copland found in Takemitsu something he felt largely missing from contemporary music from any nation—personality; he included the composer's *The Dorian Horizon* in his conducting repertoire.[32]

While on tour in Warsaw in November 1965, Copland had the opportunity to investigate the "new Polish school" as represented by Tadeusz Baird, Henryk Górecki, Wojciech Kilar, Witold Lutoslawski, Krzysztof Penderecki, and Kazimierz Serocki. He showed little enthusiasm for what he heard, including Serocki's *Symphonic Frescoes*, which he criticized as "rather too much in the new style," and Penderecki's *Threnody*, which he described as "effects music" (though in 1978, he recommended Penderecki for honorary membership to the American Academy of Arts and Letters). The principal exception was Lutoslawski's *Three Postludes* for orchestra, which he thought "a lovely piece."[33]

By the time of his last major statement on the subject of contemporary trends—the three added chapters for his revised text of *The New Music* (1968)—Copland struck a considerably less sanguine note than he had in his Norton lectures. In the first chapter, "The Generation of the Fifties," he attributed the "impressive flood of interest" in the Second Viennese School that followed the Second World War to years of Nazi censorship. "Young people have a determined will to learn about precisely those things which they are told are not for them." As for the "serial" works composed by Boulez and others, such music "produced a chaotic impression" and "left a confusing impression," marked by "a certain static quality," "a lack of variety of mood," "a seeming lack of personal profile," and "an overuse of glassy timbres," while making "extreme demands on the technical abilities of even the best interpreters."[34]

The chapter on John Cage and his influence, "The Music of Chance," similarly regarded such developments as appealing to those "who enjoy teetering on the edge of chaos" as opposed to those "who envisage art as a bulwark against the irrationality of man's nature." He also observed, with apparent concern, the "babel of graphic notations" that characterized this movement. In the 1970s, he somewhat more positively confessed to liking "the idea of introducing chance" and acknowledged that aleatoric techniques added "a resource to a score that wouldn't be there if no use were made of it." For himself, however, chance composition held little personal appeal: "I've spent most of my life trying to get the right note in the right place. Just throwing it open to chance seems to go against my natural instincts."[35]

In the chapter "New Electronic Media," Copland criticized electronic music as having "a depressing sameness of sound" and, in the absence of live performers, a "built-in monotony." In 1974, he reiterated this latter objection, writing, "I find one of the drawbacks of the electronic medium is the fact that every time you play it it's the same darn tape and it's playing exactly the same thing. It removes from music one of its most valuable assets which is that of interpretation." At the same time, he allowed, "You can do things with an electronic tape that you couldn't do with human hands; you're getting a whole new world of possibilities and that's very valuable, of course." And he suspected that composers working in the area would make "a real contribution to musical art in the end." When asked—as he often was—whether he himself ever felt tempted to compose electronic music, he routinely replied that he had no "mechanical talent" and felt lucky if the light went on when he flipped a switch.[36]

Copland found much of the newer music of the century's third quarter disappointingly dull and impersonal or, rather, dull because it was impersonal. He also regretted the growing difficulties for the performer and the loss of accessibility to the larger public. At the same time, he welcomed the promise of fresh techniques and resources and willingly gave the avant-garde the benefit of the doubt. "I am a great believer in the salutary effects of error," he affirmed. "By making mistakes we find the right way."[37]

25

From *Old American Songs* to the *Piano Fantasy*

(1950–57)

Old American Songs

During the winter of 1950, Copland interrupted work on the *Dickinson Songs* in order to set five traditional American songs for voice and piano: "The Boatmen's Dance," "The Dodger," "Long Time Ago," "Simple Gifts," and "I Bought Me a Cat." Peter Pears and Benjamin Britten premiered this cycle of *Old American Songs* at the Aldeburgh Festival on 17 June 1950, while baritone William Warfield gave the American premiere with Copland at the piano on 28 January 1951. The work's warm reception prompted an immediate sequel, *Old American Songs II* (1952), comprising settings of "The Little Horses," "Zion's Walls," "The Golden Willow Tree," "At the River," and "Ching-a-Ring Chaw," and first performed by Warfield and Copland on 24 July 1953. Copland subsequently transcribed both sets for voice and orchestra, while Irving Fine and others arranged them for chorus and piano and for chorus and orchestra. These songs became extremely popular, but they elicited little critical comment, as if Copland's part in their large success was little more than incidental.[1]

The songs themselves are quite varied, including three theater songs (the comic minstrel numbers "The Boatmen's Dance" and "Ching-a-Ring

Chaw" and the sentimental love song "Long Time Ago"), three religious songs (the Shaker tune "Simple Gifts," the camp-meeting spiritual "Zion's Walls," and the gospel hymn "At the River"), three folk songs (the children's song "I Bought Me a Cat," the lullaby "The Little Horses," and the ballad "The Golden Willow Tree"), and one political satire ("The Dodger"). As a whole they provide a diversified portrait of America itself, held together by the unity of Copland's style.

Except for the three folk songs, whose origins are unknown, all of the songs date from the period 1830–65, including "The Dodger," which, though composed during Grover Cleveland's presidential campaign (1884), parodies a glee published in 1844. Four can be ascribed to particular authors: "The Boatmen's Dance" (1843) to Dan Emmett of "Dixie" fame; "Long Time Ago" (1837) to Charles Edward Horn (music) and George Pope Morris (text); "Zion's Walls" to John G. McCurry, the compiler of *The Social Harp*; and "At the River" (1864) to the Baptist minister Robert Lowry. Whereas Copland discovered "I Bought Me a Cat" through his friend Lynn Riggs and "The Golden Willow Tree" by way of a recording, he found the bulk of these songs in various published collections. Moreover, he had used—or considered using—at least six of these songs in the past, so in some respects the project represented a cleaning house of sorts.[2]

What drew Copland to certain folk tunes? When asked the question in 1982, he answered, "It's very strange and I've often remarked upon this—give me a book of tunes and I'll immediately know what tune attracts me and what one doesn't. . . . I can play a tune out of a book and think: 'Gee, this is a good tune—but I could never work with it.' I can't tell you why exactly." The ten tunes here are, for all their differences, similarly direct, vigorous, void of chromatic elaborations and (with the exception of "The Little Horses," which might be described as dorian, and "The Golden Willow Tree," which is modally ambiguous) in a major mode. Most of them also prominently feature the falling interval of the third, a trait identified by Arthur Berger and others as characterizing Copland's own melodic style. The fact that he gravitated toward the era of Emerson and Whitman also seems significant.[3]

As always, however, Copland refashioned these tunes as he saw fit, from a few changed notes in order to smooth out a melody, as in "Simple Gifts," to entirely rearranging a song, as in "The Golden Willow Tree." His setting of "Zion's Walls" contains a special novelty: a contrasting section based on his own countermelody to the original tune.

Copland largely limited himself to two or three verses per song. In "The Dodger," for example, he used the stanzas satirizing the political candidate, the preacher, and the lover, and not those about the lawyer, the doctor, the merchant, or the farmer; in "Long Time Ago," he omitted the maudlin final stanza even at the cost of forgoing the ballad's denouement. Moreover, he revised some texts, for instance, changing "the praises of Jesus" to "the praises of Zion" in "Zion's Walls." Sensitive about the racial implications of the two minstrel songs, he purged "The Boatmen's Song" of its Negro dialect and thoroughly rewrote (with the exception of its nonsense chorus) "Ching-a-Ring Chaw"; originally about African-American immigration to Haiti, it became, in his hands, a more generally utopian fantasy—his one effort as a lyricist.

The genius of the *Old American Songs* lies in their settings, from the stunning river landscape (complete with echo) in "The Boatmen's Dance," to the evocation of banjo playing in "The Dodger" and "Ching-a-Ring Chaw," to the dramatic grandeur of "At the River" (a setting utterly unlike Charles Ives's), to the full-scale tone painting in "The Golden Willow Tree." As with the *Dickinson Songs*, the orchestrated versions arguably lose more than they gain, though William Warfield expressed a slight preference for these more opulent settings, especially "I Bought Me a Cat," with its barnyard sounds in the orchestra.[4]

During Copland's lifetime, the *Old American Songs* was widely associated both with Warfield, who frequently sang them and who recorded both the piano and orchestral versions with the composer, and with Pears, who not only gave the world premiere of the first set but became the first to record it (Pears was still singing the *American Songs* in 1975, arranged for voice and harp). Over time the songs became favored vehicles as well for such singers as Grace Bumbry (who premiered the orchestrated second set), Marilyn Horne, Teresa Stratas, Thomas Hampson, and Samuel Ramey, all of whom, like Warfield, preferred singing them with orchestra; we have Copland to thank, consequently, for the amusing spectacle of opera stars imitating barnyard animals. Meanwhile, soprano Roberta Alexander, accompanied by pianist Roger Vignoles, issued a particularly winsome recording of both sets in their original version.[5]

The Tender Land

American composers took a revitalized interest in opera during the postwar period, thanks partly to the successes of Britten and Menotti but even more so to the emergence of alternative venues to the great opera houses, such as regional companies and universities. "In the United States opera has held an uncertain and precarious position," wrote John Brodbin in an early review of Copland's only opera without spoken dialogue, *The Tender Land* (1954), "but is now meeting an unprecedented and revolutionary tide of awareness from composers, performers and laymen."[6]

Copland had thought about writing an opera throughout the 1940s. He seemed to have all the makings of a successful opera composer, but he cautiously recognized the genre's many potential pitfalls, including the problem of securing a suitable libretto, the risk of investing so much time in a single project, the unpredictability of production values, and the difficulties of finding a contemporary vocal idiom that had dramatic thrust. In his own estimation, his tentativeness distinguished him from the "born" opera composer, but he nonetheless hoped to try his hand at what he described as a "very problematical form—la forme fatale."[7]

His ambition to write an opera intensified in the early 1950s as he pursued possible collaborations with Thornton Wilder, Clifford Odets, and Arthur Miller. He also entertained the idea of adapting Theodore Dreiser's *An American Tragedy* (1925) or Frank Norris's *McTeague* (1899) as an opera, both tales of greed and corruption. Between 1950 and 1953, plans on a *McTeague* opera went as far as the drafting of a detailed scenario with librettist Arnold Sundgaard and the successful obtaining of rights from the Norris estate. But Copland eventually abandoned the idea.[8]

Meanwhile, in early 1952, he accepted a commission from the League of Composers to write an opera for television with a $1,000 grant provided by Rodgers and Hammerstein. For this venture, he decided to compose a relatively small work, something appropriate not only to television but to the "college trade," as he put it to Victor Kraft, a work meant to further prepare him for the big opera that, as it turned out, he never wrote. Whereas before the war only a handful of schools annually mounted operas, now over a hundred did. Moreover, their repertory featured far more contemporary opera than did America's few professional houses. Much as the nation's flourishing high school music programs inspired *The Second Hurricane* (1937), so developments in higher education helped shape this new project; both operas, consequently, shared a somewhat didactic impetus.[9]

For his libretto, Copland turned to his lover, the young, multitalented Erik Johns. "Since Erik Johns and I had been talking about working on a project together," explained Copland, "we decided to give it a try. I wanted a simple libretto, and it appealed to me to work with someone I knew without having to worry about changing a famous writer's work or doing damage to a preconceived play or story." He suggested something based on James Agee's *Let Us Now Praise Famous Men* and, in particular, the accompanying photographs by Walker Evans. As Johns (using the pseudonym Horace Everett) began drafting a libretto in early 1952, Copland remained closely involved with its progress—"fussy and not decisive," complained Johns in his diary—frequently making cuts and revisions of his own. "Aaron is mildly enthusiastic," noted Johns after showing him his completed second draft in May, "which I hope means he is saving his wild excitement for the score." After Harold Clurman deemed, that same month, that the book had the makings of "a charming and delicate opera," Copland began work, completing the opera in the spring of 1954. It took only two years to write, a relatively short time, especially considering that he had McCarthy to contend with during this period.[10]

Although they anticipated a television premiere, Copland and Johns failed to find an interested network; and so the New York City Opera launched *The Tender Land* at City Center on 1 April 1954. Thomas Schippers conducted, Jerome Robbins staged the work, Oliver Smith designed the sets, and John Butler choreographed the dances. The cast featured Rosemary Carlos as Laurie, John Crain as Martin, Jean Handzlik as Ma Moss, and Norman Treigle as Grandpa Moss. Because the opera was in a short two acts, the City Opera concluded the evening with a one-act opera, one also composed for television, Menotti's *Amahl and the Night Visitors*.

In the months following the premiere, Copland and Johns revised *The Tender Land* as a three-act work, partly in response to adverse critical reaction and partly to make the work a full-evening show. This revamped version premiered to better reviews in Tanglewood on 2 August 1954. After Copland made a few additional revisions, Oberlin College gave the work's final version its first performance on 20 May 1955.[11]

Agee's *Let Us Now Praise Famous Men*—the opera's starting point—began life in 1936 as a planned photo-essay (with Walker Evans) for *Fortune* magazine about tenant farmers in the Deep South. Agee and Walker spent three weeks in a small Alabama town, interviewing and photographing three very impoverished families. After *Fortune* turned down Agee's first draft, he expanded it into a sprawling book, published with Evans's photographs in 1941. Both men, critics now agree, brought a moving humanity to the subject of poverty in the rural South.[12]

Copland gravitated toward the book—still an obscure and controversial publication in 1952—not only because he liked it but because he thought that in this way he might be able to use some of the music from his abandoned musical after Erskine Caldwell's *Tragic Ground*; both concerned poor southerners. Johns never read the Agee book but rather adapted its basic premise of "two men from an outside world 'invading' the inside world of a provincial family." He further based two characters, Ma Moss and Laurie, on Evans's photographs of a "passive and stony" mother and her daughter "not yet hardened by the grim life" (in Agee's book, the twenty-seven-year-old Annie Mae Gudger and her ten-year-old daughter, Maggie Louise). He retained the period of the 1930s but switched the locale from the South to the Midwest. He also reversed the class tensions: the two intruding men are now poor migrant workers, while the family, identified as "lower-middle-class," owns a farm. "These changes shifted the emphasis from difference of class to difference of individual personality," he wrote.[13]

The action takes place in the spring, in the front yard of the Moss family farm. Grandpa Moss, Ma Moss, and her two daughters, Laurie and Beth, are about to celebrate both Laurie's graduation from high school and the spring harvest. As Act I opens, on the afternoon of the day before graduation, Ma Moss reflects on a mother's responsibilities and sorrows as Beth, about ten years old, daydreams, dancing. Mr. Splinters, the postman, arrives with a mail-order dress for Laurie, warning Ma Moss about two drifters who have sexually assaulted some neighboring girls. Laurie, about eighteen years old, enters, contemplating the life awaiting her after graduation. She complains to her mother about Grandpa, who a few months earlier had broken up a blossoming romance between her and a local boy. Ma Moss promises that Laurie will have her own life if she obeys Grandpa until graduation. Top and Martin, two hoboes, enter, teasing Laurie and offering to help with the harvest. Top is outspoken and somewhat uncouth, Martin more sensitive. Grandpa warily hires them and Laurie invites them to her graduation party that evening. The Moss family, Martin, and Top sing of the joys of work and neighborly love, of "the promise of living."

Act II takes place later that night. Friends and neighbors have gathered at the Mosses' to celebrate Laurie's graduation. Grandpa toasts Laurie, who admits to confusion at this critical moment of her life. Country dancing follows. Convinced that Top and Martin are the wanted molesters, Ma Moss sends Splinters to get the sheriff. Top, amusing everyone with a bawdy folk song, plies Grandpa with liquor in the hopes of having his way later with Laurie. As Martin and Laurie dance together, they draw closer, sharing their dreams; Martin speaks of settling down with her, and both confess their love. Discovering Martin and Laurie kissing, a drunk Grandpa accosts Martin, ignoring Laurie's protestations of love. As Ma Moss publicly accuses the two men, Splinters returns, reporting that, in fact, the molesters had been caught earlier that afternoon. "They're guilty all the same," declares Grandpa, who insults Laurie and orders Top and Martin to leave by daybreak. The party breaks up and all drift off.

Act III takes place the following morning. Martin and Laurie meet just before dawn and agree to elope. As Laurie packs her things, Martin ponders this move. When Top hears about the elopement, he warns Martin that Grandpa Moss will quickly catch up with them; besides, what sort of life could a tramp offer Laurie? Martin regretfully hurries off with Top. When Laurie realizes that they have gone without her, she resolves to leave anyway; saying her farewells to her mother and sister, she exits. Ma Moss reconciles herself to Laurie's departure, musing on the cyclical nature of life in which ends mark beginnings. Beth dances and peers off into the horizon.

Although Johns gleaned some motifs and themes from Copland's popular films and ballets, his libretto differed most dramatically from those earlier works in the fact that Laurie leaves at the end. For close to two decades, Copland's work had emphasized communal solidarity or at least some kind of social accommodation; "The Promise of Living" itself arguably constitutes a culmination of such idealism. But the promises are not fulfilled; the love scene is interrupted before its final resolution, and Laurie, ultimately, packs her bags and goes. The irrational fears of Grandpa and Ma Moss—a mixture of xenophobia and sexual anxiety—also strike a new note. Copland and Johns in part derived these ideas from personal experiences, including Johns's departure from home at an early age and Copland's ordeals with Congress. But such features more generally reflect the changing times; one finds almost identical elements in William Inge's play *Picnic* (1953).[14]

Although Copland and Johns saw *Picnic* on Broadway in early 1953, long after the libretto's completion, the similarities are such that Copland's friends used to joke that Inge could have sued him for royalties. Set in America's heartland, both works are about a young woman who is "strange inside," who is a "puzzle" to her mother, who dreams of distant horizons, and who falls in love with an outsider who wants to settle down as much as she wants her freedom. Both climax with a drunken party at which truths—largely about hidden fears and desires—unfold, and both conclude with the outsider, falsely accused, run out of town and the young heroine leaving voluntarily. Both ultimately concern, in large part, sexual identity and individual freedom.[15]

At the same time, Johns brought a unique dimension to their parallel stories, highlighting, more in the tradition of opera, and more in line with his own spiritual leanings, certain mythic qualities. Moreover, the opera contained a liberating message different from *Picnic*'s. Whereas Inge's heroine, Madge Owen, follows her male lover at the play's end, Laurie goes on her own, "with a secret knowledge of who she is, her authentic self newly emerged," in the words of Daniel Mathers, who also noted, in a paper aimed at "decoding" the opera's homosexual subtext, Laurie's telling rebuke to her grandfather: "No one can stop the way I feel! No one can ever tell me I can't love." The opera's underlying theme of sexual self-acceptance even makes some contact with the nascent feminist and gay movements of the time; in retrospect, Johns realized that in this sense Laurie was more a child of the fifties than of the thirties, writing, "I can imagine she might have gone on to become a 'flower child,' a war protestor, or a worker in a civil rights campaign."[16]

Johns and Copland decided on an operatic form in which set pieces—solos, duets, and so forth—are embedded within a continuous flow. The first act presents in succession two solos for Ma Moss ("Two Little Bits of Metal" and "This Is Like the Dress I Never Had"), two solos for Laurie ("Once I Thought I'd Never Grow" and "Remember the Boy That Used to Call"), a duet for Martin and Top ("We've Been North"), a trio for Martin, Top, and Grandpa ("A Stranger May Seem Strange That's True") and a quintet for all five leads ("The Promise of Living"). The second act contains Grandpa's toast ("Hear Now Mr. Jenks"), another solo for Laurie ("Thank You, Thank You All"), a chorus ("Stomp Your Foot"), a solo for Top ("Oh, I Was Goin' A-Courtin' "), and a solo for Martin ("I'm Getting Tired of Travellin' Through") that leads into a duet for Martin and Laurie ("The Plains So Green"). The third act includes a duet for the lovers ("Daybreak Will Come"), a solo for Top ("Hoppin' the Freight"), two solos for Laurie ("The Sun Is Coming Up" and "Perhaps I Did Love!"), and a concluding solo for Ma Moss ("All Thinking's Done"). Some of these set pieces are longer and more self-contained than others, but none ends conclusively enough to induce applause (except for "Stomp

Your Foot," and even here Copland apparently hoped to minimize any interruption by eliding into the next section). The fact that these set pieces are often stylistically indistinguishable from the surrounding dialogue—and sometimes from one another—contributes further to the work's blocklike structure, one comparable to Copland's instrumental forms and described by Johns as "in the nature of an operatic tone poem."[17]

Except for "Remember the Boy That Used to Call," the original two-act version of *The Tender Land* contained all of these set pieces; indeed, the two-act and three-act versions are remarkably alike. Johns and Copland basically divided the original second act into two acts; the second act's first scene became Act II, and its second and third scenes became Act III. Among the more substantive revisions, they interpolated a confrontation between Laurie and Ma Moss in the first act and a shorter one between Laurie and Grandpa at the end of the second act (also adding, at Copland's suggestion, the McCarthy-inspired line for Grandpa, "They're guilty all the same"). In addition, they expanded and rewrote the elopement scene; whereas Martin had been the assertive one, now Laurie pleads that he take her away. "This immediately gives her more passion and at the same time makes his decision to leave alone more clear," explained Johns to Copland. "This is more like the situation in *The Heiress*." Johns hoped by such means to "slip in a bit more urgency," and Copland duly wrote some new, rather anxious music for the scene. All of these revisions amplified and elucidated Laurie's character without disturbing the opera's basic structure and flavor.[18]

Copland used three folk tunes in the opera: "Zion's Walls" (along with his own countermelody as developed in *Old American Songs*) for "The Promise of Living," "Cottage by the Sea" for "Stomp Your Foot," and "If You Want to Go A-Courting" for Top's second act solo. He had planned to use the first two in *Tragic Ground* (which ultimately yielded very little else to the opera); the third—whose text helps delineate Top's character, thereby furthering Ma Moss's suspicions—he arrived at only after some consideration.[19]

The opera reveals a profoundly American profile hardly explained by its occasional references to folk melody. At early performances, this quality struck casual operagoers, accustomed to Italian and German opera, more forcibly than reviewers, who generally took it for granted. One exception was John Brodbin, who, though familiar with operas by Thomson, Blitzstein, Menotti, Moore, and Weill, thought the work's Americanism noteworthy and laudable: "When necessary, he has set the flavor and humor of colloquial speech to a music that itself might be called colloquial; he has used speech rhythms as an indigenous musical element, handling them with control and flexibility. The quality is so thoroughly American, that even when sung in translation it would be certain to retain its strong American inflexion."[20]

Although critics typically noted similarities to *Appalachian Spring*, another work set in the American heartland (Johns had Kansas in mind), *The Tender Land* has its own distinctive ambience, like the calm of a sun-baked cornfield; Michael Fleming described it as comprising "the essential musical speech of Middle America; plain, hard, wary of exaggeration or excess." Naturally this distinguished the work from much European opera, known precisely for a certain theatrical extravagance. But Copland made some concessions to such traditions, most obviously in the occasional fermatas on high notes for the singers, but more generally in the work's "sustained lyrical writing," thought by Mathers to be "unprecedented in Copland's oeuvre."[21]

The score also features, for all its understatement, some musical highlights, including the tender second-act love music, the exhilarating "Stomp Your Foot," and the moving "The Promise of Living"—the three episodes Copland selected for his three-movement *Tender Land Suite* for orchestra (1958). One might add to these Laurie's poignant "Once I Thought I'd Never Grow" (which has enjoyed a life of its own as "Laurie's Song"), Top's compelling "Hoppin' the Freight," Laurie's grand "The Sun Is Coming Up," and Ma Moss's Mahleresque "All Thinking's Done," a transcendent finale that incorporates the score's opening much as its text equates ends and beginnings. The work's often unrelieved wistfulness wants, perhaps, for greater variety and liveliness, but the score has, for all that, enormous eloquence and beauty.

Copland recorded the suite with the Boston Symphony (1960), as well as operatic highlights, shortened from the opera's full length of one hour and forty minutes to about an hour's worth of music, with the New York Philharmonic (1966); the former earned him his only Grammy Award. A complete recording of the opera had to wait until 1990, when conductor Philip Brunelle issued one with soloists, chorus, and orchestra of the Plymouth Music Series of Minnesota.[22]

From the start, critical opinion about the work tended to focus on the book. Reviewing the premiere, Olin Downes roundly condemned it as so unconvincing as to make it impossible for Copland to bring the characters to life. Ronald Eyer similarly thought that the dramatically weak story failed to provide "a satisfactory catharsis." On the other hand, John Brodbin thought it "convincing theater," and Israel Citkowitz, taking direct issue with Downes, wrote, "The much-criticized libretto, in spite of some structural weakness and a somewhat facile language, is serviceable enough, and provides a cohesive framework for Copland's music." William Flanagan similarly thought that whatever its strengths and weaknesses, the libretto "falls into its properly subordinate place and the music moves in—a phenomenon that has occurred with many works in the standard operatic repertory. And this music is almost without question the finest composed for an American opera."[23]

Meanwhile, Virgil Thomson, who saw one of the early performances, and Wilfrid Mellers, who attended the European premiere (1962) given by the Cambridge University Opera Group, took a different tack, arguing that the libretto was perfectly fine but that the music's lack of the kind of "continuing dynamicism" (Thomson) and "expansive vocal lyricism" (Mellers) necessitated by opera made this one of Copland's least successful and representative scores. Even so, Thomson concluded that "the Copland catalog has good stuff under every heading, including that of opera," and Mellers was at least willing to give the work the benefit of the doubt, writing, "Adequate performance might, indeed, reveal that the opera's high-lyrical moments are its high-successes, as Copland intended them to be."[24]

More recent productions have not clarified the work's stature. "The music misses out on one of the key elements, the sheer attraction between this sheltered girl ready to be carried off and the opportunistic young man whose arousal briefly persuades him to feel, or seem, sincere," wrote Will Crutchfield reviewing a production by the Long Wharf Theater that featured conductor Murry Sidlin's own reduced orchestration for thirteen players. And yet, continued Crutchfield, the opera succeeded in "other of its aims," so much so that, in his opinion, it clearly merited revival. Asking, "What exactly is the problem with *The Tender Land*," in his review of a performance by the Bronx Opera Company (1995), Alex Ross cited its inability to capture the story's "darker side," as when Grandpa insults Laurie in the second act. "Still," Ross admitted, "that golden-hued melancholy makes a strong impact by the end of the opera." Such ambivalence typified most critical response to the work.[25]

At the least, *The Tender Land* is a fragile work, aside from the Act I finale, which is seemingly indestructible. The work requires clear singing and natural, understated acting; the least affectation can jeopardize an entire scene. Only with a really fine cast, sensitive direction, and the proper venue (including perhaps television, for which the work was originally intended) can a more assured evaluation of the work be possible. For all this, *The Tender Land* has established itself as one of only a few American operas in the repertory; the early 1990s alone witnessed over fifteen separate productions, mostly among music schools and regional companies.

The *Tender Land Suite*—a viable work in its own right and one that should be much better known—was staged for the Oakland Ballet in 1978 by Eugene Loring, the original choreographer of *Billy the Kid*. Loring used the opera's scenario as his basic framework; the ballet seemed to work despite the fact that the music only occasionally matched the appropriate dramatic situation.[26]

In the years following *The Tender Land*, Copland's interest in opera continued undiminished. He appreciated the high workmanship of Britten's *A Midsummer Night's Dream*, the accessibility of Douglas Moore's *Wings of the Dove*, and the daring of Hugo Weisgall's *Six Characters in Search of an Author*. And he regretted the conventionality of the opera scene at home, wishing he could see such works as Schoenberg's *Moses und Aron*, Henze's *Elegy for Young Lovers*, and Nono's *Intolleranza*. For a number of years, he hoped to compose another piece for the lyric stage but could not find a libretto that suited him. "I admit that if I have one regret," he stated in his memoirs, "it is that I never *did* write a 'grand opera.'"[27]

A Dirge, a Canticle, and Music for Television

Copland's output for voice continued with a song for high voice and piano, "Dirge in Woods" (1954), commissioned by Nadia Boulanger in celebration of her fiftieth year of teaching, and a work for chorus and orchestra, *Canticle of Freedom* (1955, revised 1965), commissioned by MIT for the dedication of Kresge Auditorium. "Dirge in Woods" was premiered at Fontainebleau in the summer of 1954 and received its first American performance at Carnegie Hall on 28 March 1955 with Adele Addison, soprano. Klaus Liepmann led the MIT chorus and orchestra in the premiere of *Canticle of Freedom* on 8 May 1955. These would be Copland's last vocal compositions.

"Dirge in Woods" takes its text from a poem of the same name by

George Meredith (1828–1909), an English poet and novelist contemporary with Emily Dickinson. Published in 1888, the poem contrasts images of swaying pine trees and moving clouds, symbolic of life, with fallen pinecones on the still, moss-covered ground, symbolic of death.

Copland's setting comprises four discrete sections: a quiet introduction for the opening nature imagery (upward piano figuration depicting life, downward figuration reflecting death); a slower, dirgelike section for the fallen pinecones; a "stormy" passage for the billowing clouds and the poet's moral; and a remembrance of the song's opening for the repeated moral, with a coda that briefly recalls the dirgelike music.

Composed largely for Boulanger's delectation, "Dirge in Woods" presupposes a sophisticated listener. The vocal line is more jagged than even the craggiest of the *Dickinson Songs*, and the piano part is correspondingly more adventurous, with delicate clusters of unusual harmonies. Though it is one of his most abstruse songs, Copland admirers will want to know it nonetheless, because, thanks to the Meredith text, it takes us close to some of his most intimate thoughts: his serene love of nature, his affirmation of the active life, and his melancholy but calm acceptance of death—all condensed in a three-minute piece.

The *Canticle of Freedom* is something else again, a big public statement in the tradition of *Lincoln Portrait* and *Preamble for a Solemn Occasion*. The work consists of three sections: a prologue for orchestra, a more urgent section also for orchestra, and a finale for chorus and orchestra. For his text, Copland used an excerpt from an epic poem by John Barbour (c. 1320–1395) about Scotland's struggle for independence from England in the early fourteenth century, *Book of the Deeds of the Illustrious Prince, the Late Lord King Robert de Bruce*; he no doubt discovered it by way of Carlos Chávez's own setting, *A! Fredome* (1947), whose modern English adaptation by Willis Wager may have provided the basis for his own. Copland apparently called the piece a canticle not only to reflect the text's medieval provenance and psalmlike structure but to underline the sacred nature of freedom.[28]

Whereas *Lincoln Portrait* and *Preamble* addressed the exigencies of World War II and the Cold War, respectively, the *Canticle* stared McCarthyism squarely in the face. Copland even joked about dedicating the work to his nemesis, Fred Busbey. One passage in particular gave him the opportunity to vent: "Nor he that aye have lived free / May know well the misery, / The anger, and the wretched doom / That is coupled to foul thralldom." In writing this work Copland also may have had the civil rights movement in mind, given the association of "freedom" with that struggle.[29]

Although he had set some English Renaissance verse in 1923, the use of a Scottish medieval poem for this kind of vehicle proclaimed his desire to try something new; along with the Meredith setting, it can even be said to signal the end of an over thirty-year involvement with almost exclusively American materials. The *Canticle*'s musical style itself seems related to Scottish idioms, including the "Scotch snap" (associated with the rhythm of the word "freedom") that imbues the entire score. Even more remarkable is the work's pungent evocations of medieval music, from its unusual colors and its quirky asymmetrical rhythms to its parallel fifths and austere counterpoint, including choral writing restricted to unison and two-voice textures.

This assimilation of medieval music was not incidental, for Copland carried it onward, if more subtly, to the *Piano Fantasy* and other late works; like the twelve-tone method, neomedievalism was a trend of the times. In such works, Copland accommodated medieval idioms to his own voice and personality, translating their bright sounds and rhythmic jags into the recognizably Coplandesque, including, in the *Canticle*, an ending even louder than *Lincoln Portrait* or the *Preamble*. Copland characteristically found in the Middle Ages more an era of earthy vigor than of pious retreat.

Even so, the *Canticle* projects a different, less confident tone from the optimism of *Lincoln Portrait* or the weathered hopefulness of the *Preamble*. Rather, it presents a face of wounded dignity and troubled defiance. And in some ways, this makes the work all the more courageous and perhaps all the more relevant to our own times.

Copland showed a more familiar profile in his incidental music for a televised adaptation of Hemingway's Nick Adams stories entitled *The World of Nick Adams*, broadcast live on 10 November 1957 for a series, *The Seven Lively Arts*, produced by John Houseman and Robert Herridge. Copland had admired Hemingway since the 1920s and had hoped to collaborate on some dramatized version of his work at least as far back as Sam Wood's film adaptation of *For Whom the Bell Tolls* (1943). Moreover, he liked the idea of writing for television, much as radio had appealed to him in the 1930s; both mediums seemed, in their early years, fresh and full of promise. He had, after all, composed *The Tender Land* for television, too.[30]

A. E. Hotchner skillfully devised the Hemingway teleplay by weaving together five Nick Adams stories. The play opens with Nick Adams, wounded during the First World War, lying sleepless in an Italian hospital ("Now I Lay Me") and recalling various events from his youth in Michigan: a broken romance ("The End of Something"), a drunk with a good friend ("The Three-Day Blow"), and encounters with some prostitutes and a homosexual in a railroad station ("The Light of the World") and two hoboes along the railroads ("The Battler"). As he recollects these incidents in the light of his wartime experiences, Nick grows wiser, more mature.[31]

Copland's substantial score for chamber orchestra (without oboes) makes his attraction to Hemingway crystal clear; his hard rhythms, open textures, bittersweet lyricism, and noble declamations perfectly match Hemingway's depictions of war, quiet nights, failed romance, and personal growth. For all its strengths, however, he never adapted the score for concert purposes, perhaps because the music resembled his somewhat outmoded incidental and film music from previous decades, in particular *Quiet City*. As a result, *Nick Adams* remains virtually unknown.

The *Piano Fantasy*

The *Piano Fantasy* (1957) is possibly Copland's most challenging work. It combines the monumentality of the Third Symphony with the brooding introspection of the *Piano Variations*, a formidable combination. Moreover, it poses challenges unique to itself, especially concerning form and sonority. Many first-time listeners, even those at home with the *Variations*, might not even immediately recognize it as the work of Copland, despite its many familiar gestures: the booming declamations, the jazzy scamperings, the sonorous tollings, and so forth. Nor will closer inspection diminish the work's freshness and daring.

The *Fantasy* took Copland an arduously long time to write, probably longer than any other composition in his career. It started life in 1951 as a concerto for piano and orchestra, commissioned by the Louisville Symphony Orchestra, for the brilliant young pianist William Kapell (1922–1953). When the commission fell through, Copland decided to write a solo piano work—as early as 1952, a "fantasy"—for Kapell based on the concerto sketches. In the meantime, he had received another commission in 1951, this one from William Schuman, president of Juilliard, for a work celebrating the school's fiftieth anniversary in 1954; Copland started work on a choral cantata to words by Walt Whitman but made little headway with it. When Kapell died in an airplane crash in 1953,

Copland decided to finish the piano piece for Juilliard and dedicate it to his memory. But it took him longer than he expected—he had trouble especially with the fast music. After repeated but sympathetic nudgings on Schuman's part, he finally submitted the completed score in February 1957. Remarked Copland, "Lucky for me that the president of Juilliard was a composer!"[32]

As with the Piano Quartet, Copland freely adapted the twelve-tone method for the *Fantasy*, here using a ten-note rather than an eleven-note row, reserving the last two notes as a tonal resolution and anchor. The piece states this ten-note series at the start "in a very bold and declamatory manner," the first four notes descending (and then repeated), the next six notes ascending. In contrast to the quartet's row, with its many major seconds, this one moves primarily by thirds and fourths, yielding correspondingly more vaulting melodies and spacious harmonies. The *Fantasy* also differs from the quartet in its more extensive use of the full row, as opposed to bits of the row, which results in a more thoroughgoing chromatic texture throughout and a form closer to the Schoenbergian concept of continuous variation.[33]

Still, Copland turned the method somewhat on its head by creating a long one-movement fantasy lasting over half an hour that suggests, as befits its title, spontaneous improvisation. Elliott Carter hailed the work as "a further step" in the evolution of Western musical thought, one distinguished from comparable trends in European music, which depended more on "number systems" and "numerological formula." Arthur Berger and Peter Evans were similarly impressed. Observed Berger, "The Fantasy . . . is like an adventure. Though each event brings some skillful reference to the basic idea, the listener feels as if he is let loose in a new big city with fresh rewards at every turn of the corner. Once caught up in the adventure he finds it hard to drop out. What will be next? What will be the dénouement? There are just a few familiar landmarks." And Evans wrote, "This is no simple conflation of sonata types but an accumulation of varied textures of unequal lengths. Yet a real unity is felt to develop from within. One idea, of figuration or harmonic distribution, suggests the next and when, towards the end, restatements or reworkings appear, their effect is not arbitrary for the thread has been continuous."[34]

From their analyses, one cannot say to what extent Berger's "landmarks" coincide with Evans's "ideas," for both writers, respectful of the work's elusive form, hesitate to impose a formal scheme on the music. However, with Copland's earlier work in mind (in particular, the Piano

Sonata), one can at least make a few suggestions toward this end. To begin with, one can identify six principal thematic ideas: the opening bell-like, "declamatory" theme; a slow, lyrical theme, marked "cantabile"; a dirgelike theme, marked "crystalline"; a vaguely medieval theme, marked "delicate, 'uncertain' "; a "light and playful" theme; and a jazzy theme to be played "with humor." Without too much difficulty one can follow these six ideas as they unfold throughout the piece's largely slow-fast-slow format.

Moreover, one can even interpret the *Fantasy* as a "conflation" (though admittedly not a "simple" one) of two of the composer's most favored formal designs: the slow sonata movement (with a fast development section) and the slow-fast-slow three-movement form (consisting of a slow sonata movement, a fast scherzo, and a slow epilogue). The opening slow section (one might argue) comprises a motto-introduction (the declamatory theme), a first theme (the lyrical theme), a transition (the dirgelike theme), and a second theme (the delicate theme). The fast section puts forth an ABA scherzo (the A corresponding to the playful theme, the B to the humorous theme), followed by a free working of previous material that seems to function as both interlude and development section. The concluding slow section, after a recapitulation of the motto-introduction, expands the dirgelike theme into a finale proper, followed by restatements of the declamatory and the lyrical themes that round things off. The final statements of the dirgelike and declamatory themes, against a static E-major background, function clearly as a coda. As complex as this schematic outline is, it is further complicated by, among other things, the similarities between all the themes, thanks to their derivation from the same series of pitches.

The work takes its impetus as much from the sheer sound potential of the piano as from melodic ideas per se. This is what Evans has in mind when he speaks of the work's form as an "accumulation of varied textures" and what pianist William Masselos means when he refers to the work's "Lisztian-Copland style." Many of these sonorities—in the tradition especially of the Piano Sonata—tend toward the bell-like: some evoke great big tollings, others more delicate chimings, while one curious passage near the end sounds remarkably like a hand-bell choir. Even the occasional tuneful moments are accompanied or articulated by bell-like sounds. But the work explores many other, mostly percussive sounds, covering the whole range of the piano. Some suggest harps, xylophones, snare drums, bass drums, and gongs; others more vaguely might evoke busy traffic or birdsong; still others defy description. The *Fantasy* is the culminating pianistic expression of a composer whose piano style stands, along with those of Debussy and Bartók, as one of the most original of the century.

Some of the more avant-garde pianistic gestures—for instance, the dwelling among the extreme registers, the unusual trilling figuration, and certain glassy sonorities (in particular, the passage marked "cool and crystalline")—possibly owed something to Pierre Boulez, whose music Copland had discovered just before setting out on this piece in 1951. Copland no doubt liked Boulez's music and could readily assimilate something of his style because, whatever the differences between them, the hard, lean qualities of Boulez's piano idiom had some resemblance to his own.

The *Fantasy*'s form and sonorities naturally serve expressive purposes (Copland originally subtitled the work *The Music Within*). Like clues, the score lays out a series of directives that help us decipher its composer's intentions, such as "restless, hesitant," "urgent," "brooding," "hurried and tense," "agitated," "uncertain," "light and playful," "violent," "furiously," "musingly," "insistent," "assertive." The mood is predominantly dark, and even the more playful sections periodically give way to violence. In a letter to the composer, Lawrence Morton wrote, "I rejoice that you have been able to deliver yourself of a work so tragic as this." Still, as in classical tragedy, not all is darkness: the delicate theme contains something akin to Copland's pastoral, nostalgic side; the scherzo introduces, in its allusions to jazz and Latin music, a touch of levity; the concluding dirge has its hopeful moments; and the work concludes in a state of amazing calm (though as Terri Gailey Everett points out, the evocative addition of the piano's lowest note at the final sonority questions the coda's "serenity").[35]

William Masselos premiered the *Fantasy* at Juilliard on 25 October 1957 on a program devoted solely to the work, playing it both before and after intermission. The audience, described by Howard Taubman as "one of the most knowledgeable that could be assembled in New York," hailed it with cheers and bravos, notwithstanding a few boos from Morton Feldman—who presumably found the work not avant-garde enough. The reviews were highly laudatory and remained so as Masselos took the work on tour from coast to coast. Paul Henry Lang called it "an outstanding addition to his [Copland's] own oeuvre and to contemporary piano literature"; Alfred Frankenstein thought it "a tremendous achievement"; and Alexander Fried detected "the earmarks of a lasting masterpiece." "This is a new Copland to us," wrote Jay Rosenfeld, "an artist advancing with strength and not building on the past alone." Such enthusiastic response—something of a rarity for one of Copland's more ambitious works—clearly challenges the received wisdom that his adoption of the twelve-tone method in the 1950s damaged his powers and prestige.[36]

After its premiere, a number of other distinguished pianists performed the piece, including Noël Lee, Leo Smit, Andor Foldes, and Shura Cherkassky; Masselos, Lee, and Smit recorded it as well. More recently, Nina Tichman and Ramon Salvatore issued recordings imaginatively detailing the music's rich shadings and subtleties; Tichman delivered a particularly compelling account, one of the best on record to date.[37]

26

From *Dance Panels*
to *Connotations*
(1959–62)

Dance Panels and the Nonet

Jerome Robbins (1918–98) commissioned Copland's *Dance Panels* (1959) for his short-lived company Ballets: U.S.A. (1958–59). He had wanted to collaborate with Copland since 1944, when, fresh from the success of *Fancy Free*, he proposed a "ballet-play" about a Brooklyn boy who joins the Navy, *Bye-Bye Jackie*. But not until 1958 did it appear that he and Copland would finally produce a ballet together. "I enjoy all his work," Copland said about Robbins. "It has a certain authenticity about it. . . . It might be a little too long, or too short—you know you could make the usual objection of one kind or another—but it's basically the work of an enormously gifted man."[1]

Robbins proposed either a nonprogrammatic ballet or one based on *The Dybbuk*; after Copland expressed a preference for the former, Robbins outlined something tentatively entitled *Theatre Waltzes*.

The originating idea is to do a ballet which presents the style, youth, technical competence, theatrical qualities and personalities of the company [Ballets: U.S.A.] in pure dance terms. The technique is essentially classic ballet (in the way that Americans employ it) and to make the whole ballet a declarative statement—open, positive, inventive, joyous (rather than introspective)—a parade; a presentation; perhaps elegant, witty, tender and with a sure technique.

The ballet should be a chamber work in effect, both on stage as well as in the pit: the form, number of people and the quality of the atmosphere intimate and clear. It should say, this is Dance; it's the way we use our European heritage (classic technique) in America.

Robbins went on to suggest over twenty different types of waltzes, including "circus waltz" and "tea room waltz"; at the same time, he recognized the advantages of working with "more abstract and evocative" forms. He envisioned a simple opening with "basic 3/4 rhythm and waltz steps," and, in the light of Copland's "*terribly* unfounded" resistance to "a finale waltz," an ending that would mirror the work's opening.[2]

Copland composed the ballet in early 1959 with the expectation that it might be premiered at that summer's Spoleto Festival. In deference to Robbins's request for an intimate chamber work, he scored it for a small orchestra requiring only six woodwinds and five brass.[3]

Entitled at various times *Music for J.R.*, *Music for a Ballet*, *Ballet in Seven Movements*, *Dance Panels in Seven Movements*, and, finally, *Dance Panels: Ballet in Seven Sections*, the piece contains seven contiguous movements—"like the panels of a screen," Copland once remarked—lasting just under a half hour. Although these individual panels tend toward some waltz type or other, enough so that the work can be seen as a kind of "Valses Nobles et Sentimentales," Copland's highly stylized approach rarely evokes traditional waltzing, in part because syncopations and fermatas often obscure and halt the music's flow. William Austin also points to fluctuations of tempo within the individual panels, "where a waltz is more a lingering memory or shy hope than a whirling dance."[4]

The enigmatic preludial movement explores a characteristic waltz rhythm, one favored by Brahms, that unifies the entire piece. At first, the orchestra, lingering on a single pitch, puts forth, barely articulated, this elemental idea, which seems to emerge from the void. Other voices subsequently enter with the same motive in jarring counterpoint, eventually reaching a dissonant climax before subsiding back into pristine simplicity. After a long pause, a trumpet heralds a noble motto theme (incorporating the elemental idea) that functions like a refrain in the course of the work; it reappears at the end of the second, third, and seventh movements. In all cases, it dissolves back into the elemental rhythm, which in turn serves, in the first three panels, as a transition to the next movement and, in the final panel, as the last word. This unusual structure recalls the recurring "Promenade" in Mussorgsky's *Pictures at an Exhibition*; given their similar titles, this might well have been intentional.

The second movement suggests, in Copland's words, "charm and delicacy, involvements, hesitations and swirlings"; a stream of quarter notes produces the "swirlings," when not interrupted by fermatas, which create "hesitations." The delightful, scherzolike third movement shares its basic material with an episode from *The Heiress* in which the heroine giddily tries on a new red party dress. The slow, romantic fourth movement, a pas de trois marked "somewhat hesitant, melancholy and naïve," is more ballet adagio than waltz per se; an alto flute, two muted trumpets, and a trio of flute and two clarinets—representing one, two, and three dancers, respectively—successively state the tune, described by the composer as having "the plainness and directness of a song without words, evoking a somewhat 'lost' and nostalgic mood." Vaguely reminiscent of Copland's cowboy waltzes, it has a sweetly tentative quality all its own.[5]

The fifth movement, another scherzolike section, is cast largely in a jazzy duple meter, though the periodic appearance of the elemental idea retains the connection with the waltz. Copland described this panel, which highlights the percussion battery and concludes with an extended snare drum solo that softly fades out, as "carefree, snappy, sharp, 'knowing'"; some of its ideas resemble—and possibly derive from—Falstaff's music from *The Five Kings* (1939).[6]

The brief sixth panel, a tense and somewhat sorrowful interlude marked "menacing," and later "eloquent," leads into a finale that begins, writes Copland, "by suggesting flight and hectic emotions." The music, alternately violent and joyful, becomes increasingly frenetic until, after a sudden pause, the motto theme returns, says Copland, in "triumphant songfulness"; this refrain subsides into the vaguely articulated rhythms heard at the very start of the work. Like the ending of *Music for the Theatre*, the final note for French horn is a jazzy added sixth, except that here no major triad enters to contextualize it; rather, the lone dissonance simply dies away, suggesting the continuing dance.[7]

One of the more accessible scores of his later years, *Dance Panels* recalls some of Copland's earlier pieces for stage and screen, sometimes, as we have seen, literally so. At the same time, the work's nonprogrammatic framework distinguishes it from his earlier ballets. Moreover, its thicker and more dissonant moments bespeak some connection with his later twelve-tone scores. Similarly, the music contains rhythmic novelties, though they tend not so much toward irregular and changing meters as toward flux and fluidity within regular meters. Finally, with its evocative backstage brass, glassy string harmonics, and vibrant percussion writing, the ballet features its own sound world. Although Bayan Northcott thought the work represented "the exhaustion of that side of his musical personality," *Dance Panels* seems at least a valiant acclimation of the composer's ballet idiom to changing times.[8]

A good comparison in this respect might be made with Stravinsky's *Agon* (1957), which similarly accommodated new trends to a personal dance style. However, unlike *Agon*, which but for Balanchine's choreography might have met the same dismal reception as did most late Stravinsky, *Dance Panels* suffered a major setback when Robbins decided not to stage it—a lost opportunity, for the music's wistfulness and verve were tailor-made for the choreographer.[9]

By way of explanation, Robbins claimed that he could not remember the music after hearing Copland play it at the piano and decided, instead, to use its "counts," independent of its notes, for a dance without music, *Moves*. That *Dance Panels* provided, in Robbins's words, the "accidental genesis" of *Moves* was surely cold comfort for Copland, who typically showed no dismay but rather puzzlement and impatience as Robbins equivocated.[10]

When in 1962 the Bavarian State Opera offered to mount *Dance Panels in Seven Movements* (as it was then called), Copland revised the score (a mere cut of four measures, it seems), still hoping, as did the opera management, that Robbins could be induced to choreograph it. But when Robbins once again declined, Heinz Rosen, music director of the Opera House, decided to stage it himself, with guest dancers Arthur Mitchell of the New York City Ballet and Liane Daydé of the Paris Opera. The ballet premiered on 3 December 1963, sandwiched between ballets by Orff and Hartmann. "Up until recently," Copland told the press, "the United States imported art and music—now we export it. I am proud to be performed at the Munich Opera Festival together with Strauss, Beethoven, Wagner, and the local composers Orff, Hartmann, and Egk." He himself conducted the premiere, which, reported Thea Dispeker, "was greeted with great applause," the capacity audience bringing back the composer for eight solo bows. Copland was disappointed, however, with Rosen's choreography, made all the more faltering by an injured Mitchell, who needed, at the premiere, a last-minute replacement for the ballet's first half; Rosen did not have, he remembered, "too much feeling for the American quality of the music."[11]

The ballet still awaited an American premiere. Balanchine considered choreographing it himself, but the task fell to his assistant, John Taras, a former New York City Ballet dancer. Aware that Copland was willing to have the work produced either with or without a story, Taras used a scenario devised by Scott Burton: Two lovers meet in a cemetery, their dancing interrupted by episodes depicting the lives of those buried therein, including a devoted couple, a boating party in which all drowned, a grieving widow who found another love, and soldiers killed during the First World War; at the end, the lovers entomb themselves in the cemetery's mausoleum. Mounted as *Shadow'd Ground* (1965) in the company's brand-new home at Lincoln Center, the production featured multiple-screen slide projections designed by John Braden.

Although Lincoln Kirstein liked it, the ballet was neither a critical nor a popular success. The production seemed overblown; the slides (which regularly malfunctioned) overwhelmed the dancers; and the poetic epitaphs printed in the program struck many as gratuitous. Taras's choreography was taken to task as well. "Listening to the wonderfully danceable music," wrote Walter Terry, "one wished for choreography which would capture folk energies, and dramatic actions which would reveal the very hearts of those who had lived and were now at rest beneath the stones." Taras himself added, "There was a great deal of opposition to Copland at the time—it was fashionable not to like him. I think the audience was interested in the ballet visually, but the idea that it was set in a cemetery and full of dead people was not appealing. *Giselle* is the only cemetery ballet that works." If Copland saw the ballet, it failed to make much of an impression; he could not remember it in 1975.[12]

As a concise, plotless, beautifully crafted ballet, however, *Dance Panels* easily accommodated itself to concert format. The composer-conductor Ingolf Dahl and the Ojai Festival Orchestra premiered it as such on 24 May 1966. In this way it enjoyed, in spite of Copland's own concerns, considerably more success than it had on the stage. Copland recorded the work, as have, more recently, Leonard Slatkin and Dennis Russell Davies. For his own recording, Copland took two tiny cuts amounting to hardly a minute's worth of music, whereas Slatkin and Davies rendered the score in its entirety.[13]

In 1960 Copland composed his *Nonet* for strings (three violins, three violas, and three cellos) on a commission from the Dumbarton Oaks

Research Library in honor of the fiftieth wedding anniversary of the library's principal donors, Mr. and Mrs. Robert Woods Bliss. He completed the score on 28 December 1960, dedicating it to Nadia Boulanger "after forty years of friendship" and conducting its first performance on 2 March 1961 in Washington, D.C., with members of the National Symphony Orchestra.

Copland based the one-movement, fifteen-minute *Nonet* on a three-chord progression heard at the work's start and immediately expanded into an eight-measure theme for the three cellos. This kind of germinal idea—involving a stepwise, three-note melody supported by rich harmonies—was thoroughly characteristic, going back at least as far as *Music for the Theatre*. But the emphasis on the harmonic (as opposed to the melodic) represented a new twist; Copland even spoke of the work's relation to the "chaconne," a form he once described as having a "harmonic bias."[14]

This harmonic proclivity suggested some rapport with Copland's twelve-tone scores, and early analyses by Eric Salzman and Paul Des Marais placed the work in just such a context. At the same time, much of the work is frankly diatonic, with key signatures scattered throughout. Leon Kirchner even assailed Salzman's analysis to Copland; for him, the *Nonet* fell squarely in the tradition of the Piano Sonata.[15]

In any case, the real novelty of the *Nonet* resided not so much in its harmonies per se as in its textures. In composing a work for such an unusual ensemble, Copland apparently took his cue from Bach's Brandenburg Concerto No. 3 and Stravinsky's *Dumbarton Oaks*, which, given the circumstances of the commission, was natural enough. But the music even exceeds Bach in terms of sheer textural complexity. Although it has moments, especially near its center, when the lines thin into three-voice counterpoint, more typically each part goes its own way, with many passages characteristically sounding series of rich six-note harmonies.

The resulting denseness—at a climactic point, Copland even writes octaves for the first violin and first viola, with double-stops for nearly everyone else—contrasts not only with Bach and Stravinsky but with his own customary "transparency," as Salzman points out. Judging from the complex interweaving of crossed voices, he may have had in mind the six-part viol consort music of, say, William Lawes and Henry Purcell, an association that squares with his frequent conducting of Purcell's fantasias during these years and his growing interest in early music generally. Whatever its roots and sources—and one cannot rule out, either, the vogue for thick string writing as found in the work of Xenakis and Penderecki—the *Nonet*'s unwieldy textures pose significant challenges for listeners and performers alike, though they neatly match the autumnal and somber qualities that, for all its moments of gaiety, seem very much part of its essential makeup.

The work's shape, which unfolds spaciously with frequent climaxes and unexpected turns, can be roughly described as in slow-fast-slow ABA form. Stephen Plaistow thought the middle section "a shade incongruous stylistically when set against the opening and closing sections, despite all the thematic correspondences and developments and the masterly way in which Copland integrates the rhythmic momentum of the middle section into the work as a whole." Of course, Copland typically inclined toward just such strong antitheses. Moreover, as in the slow movement of the Third Symphony, which it resembles, the *Nonet* only slowly works to and from its fast, joyous music, so that its form more closely resembles an arch than a strict three-part design.[16]

On the *Nonet*'s flyleaf, Copland made specific recommendations for larger groups of twenty-four, thirty-six, and forty-eight strings (12-6-6, 18-9-9, and 24-12-12), advising against performance by "a string orchestra as normally constituted." He hoped that Balanchine might use one of these larger versions for a ballet; he seems to have had the music's dance potential in mind from the start. Although Balanchine never choreographed it, this highly atmospheric score may yet find wider exposure as a dance. For the moment, though a favorite of a small group of aficionados, it remains one of the least-played of Copland's major chamber works.

Something Wild / Music for a Great City

In 1961 Copland composed the music for his eighth and final motion picture, an independent production entitled *Something Wild*. He had become somewhat hesitant about film work; but after previewing the picture at the urging of its thirty-one-year-old director, Jack Garfein, he was won over. "I found it extraordinarily vivid—even now—I've not much visual memory," he explained a few months later. "It grips the imagination. . . . The picture is so basic it lends itself naturally to music." Moreover, Garfein obliged Copland's working preferences, letting him compose at home with a Moviola and giving him control over the end product—no small matter after his last film, *The Heiress* (1949). And, in fact, *Something Wild* became his only feature film score to make it from paper to final edit intact.[17]

Born in Czechoslovakia in 1930, Jack Garfein survived eleven Nazi concentration camps before his liberation at Auschwitz. After immigrating to the States, he studied at the New School of Social Research with directors Lee Strasberg and Erwin Piscator and devoted most of his career to stage direction and teaching. His friend the writer Henry Miller described him as "not only most affable, charming, exciting, but a great raconteur who holds you spellbound," "a perfectionist" with "the endurance of a giant and the knowledge of an encyclopedist," someone "deeply religious without belonging to church or synagogue."[18]

In 1955 Garfein married Carroll Baker, whose performance the following year in Elia Kazan's *Baby Doll* (1956) made her a star. After directing his first film, a military-school drama called *The Strange One* (1957), he founded, with Baker, Prometheus Enterprises, a company aimed at producing quality, low-budget motion pictures. With $100,000 advanced to him by United Artists, he made *Something Wild*—his second and, to date, last feature film. He considered both Shostakovich and Morton Feldman for the music, but then gravitated toward Copland; he knew and loved *The Tender Land*, a work that, like *Something Wild*, concerned a young girl's self-discovery. Realizing how much the film stood to benefit from Copland's music, Baker offered her services to United Artists as collateral in order to cover his $42,500 fee—a hefty figure even by Hollywood standards and a huge percentage of the film's relatively small budget. Because the picture lost money, Carroll wound up having to go to Africa to film *Mr. Moses*. "But at the time," she recalled, "I was very happy to find a way for Copland to do it."[19]

Garfein based *Something Wild* on *Mary Ann*, the first published novel of Alex Karmel (b. 1931), a New York–born author Garfein's age who had spent some years in Paris during the 1950s. Garfein and Karmel cowrote the screenplay, which closely adhered to the novel, an existentialist beauty-and-the-beast tale. On her way home from choir rehearsal, Mary Ann Robinson, an innocent high school girl, is raped in a New York public park. She immediately exhibits neurotic tendencies: washing herself compulsively, flinching from any bodily contact, and wearing a coat throughout the hot summer months, during which most of the story transpires. Unable to discuss the rape with her self-absorbed mother (Mrs. Gates) and ineffectual stepfather, she leaves home and disappears into the city, renting a tiny room in a rundown tenement and taking a part-time job in the local five-and-dime. Withdrawn from her miserly landlord, the vulgar prostitute who rents the room next to hers, and the catty shopgirls at work, she attempts to jump off a bridge, only to be prevented at the last moment by a passing auto mechanic, Mike.

Accepting Mike's offer to rest in his secluded basement apartment, she finds herself locked up as a virtual prisoner. Mike's behavior wavers between tenderness and brutality. Early on, when he returns home drunk, Mary Ann kicks him in the face, blinding him in one eye; when he awakens, he thinks his injured eye the result of a bar brawl. He hopes Mary Ann will eventually agree to marry him, but after she confesses that she blinded him, he lets her escape. After wandering about the city, Mary Ann spends the night in a park; she awakens transformed, reconciled to the world. She returns to Mike, who now seems attractive to her. Mrs. Gates visits her at Christmastime and learns that she and Mike, now married, are expecting a baby.[20]

The film, produced by George Justin, starred Carroll Baker as Mary Ann, Ralph Meeker as Mike, Mildred Dunnock as Mrs. Gates, and Jean Stapleton as the prostitute. Garfein shot the film on location in New York, emphasizing the city as wasteland: squalid apartments, crammed subways, excavation rubble, looming billboards, homeless beggars, and so on, all baking in the summer heat. Assisted by Eugen Shuftan's gritty black-and-white cinematography, such direction recalled the photographs and films about New York (including *The City*) that emanated from the Stieglitz circle; this surely constituted some of the picture's appeal for Copland. At the same time, the picture resembled Europe's neorealist cinema, the connections heightened by the vague malaise of its two main characters, withdrawn to the point of silence, suicide, drunken stupor, frigidity, fatigue, claustrophobia, and nausea. All this enabled Copland to revisit, in a fresh light, his longstanding inclination toward urban realism and social criticism.

Indeed, the film score, with its music for New York's skyscrapers and apartment buildings, its subways, its crowded streets, its bridges and factories, and its playgrounds, as well as for Harlem and Times Square, can be viewed as Copland's culminating cityscape. Even in the two scenes depicting Mary Ann walking through a city park, he attempted "pastoral sounds that are edged with a steely quality, hoping thereby to suggest the country in the midst of the city," a sound partly achieved through accented chimings in the glockenspiel and vibraphone.[21]

Significantly, he originally intended to title his suite from the film *Music for New York* but changed it to *Music for a Great City* in deference to the London Symphony Orchestra, whose sixtieth season the piece commemorated. The "great" in the title, he explained, "meant large and noisy." When the work was premiered in London on 26 May 1964, he noted, with evident satisfaction, that "every critic mentioned that the precise locale of the 'great city' in the title was Manhattan, not London."[22]

Copland's penchant in his later years for dense, dissonant harmonies, chromatic (sometimes twelve-tone) melodies, and percussive sonorities served him well in this regard. The main title, for instance, immediately announces a somewhat strident seven-note harmony that evokes, in Copland's own words, "a sense of power and tension. I worked on that chord to make it sum up what the picture is all about." When a depressed Mary Ann slowly walks down the stairs of her tenement on her way to the bridge, a descending twelve-tone melody in canon ably captures her utter defeat. And in many episodes, the score accentuates its enormous percussion battery, as in Mary Ann's crowded subway ride to school. Copland even hoped to collaborate with his secretary, David Walker, on electronic sounds for the scene at the bridge, but monetary considerations precluded this.[23]

The music not only heightens the film's atmosphere but helps delineate character, especially that of Mary Ann, the movie's principal figure by far (though there are distinct themes for Mrs. Gates and Mike as well). Copland took advantage of Mary Ann's appearance in nearly every scene (often by herself) to paint a vivid portrait of a rape victim—forlorn after her rape, anxious as she decides to leave home, dazed on her way to the bridge, fearful and confused when she finds herself prisoner. The music becomes more psychologically complex—wavering between fear and love—as Mary Ann begins to develop romantic feelings toward Mike. Copland also faced the critical and daunting task of elucidating Mary Ann's overnight transformation, but it was a challenge for which he was particularly well suited; so many of his works contain affirmative gestures that rise up from the prevailing gloom. Here he states a poignant melody, one neatly introduced during the title, so that the viewer has some foreshadowing of Mary Ann's coming rebirth.

Copland also made incisive use of silence, withholding music, for example, at the film's two most violent moments: the rape of Mary Ann and the kick in Mike's face. Garfein had his one disagreement with Copland over the absence of music for the rape scene, but he later acknowledged this decision as "absolutely masterful." Copland also avoided writing music for the first few scenes between Mary Ann and Mike, the silence pointing up the ambiguity of their relationship; he apparently felt that even the most neutral music would somehow color the drama in a way that might dissipate the tension. And at the end of the film's one short love scene, the music fades out just prior to the climactic moment when Mary Ann and Mike kiss. "Music, when it speaks, tells too much," he noted while working on the score. "In this film we must wonder what is going on, and not really know."[24]

Garfein found the music moving and effective; Copland, he thought, had not only brilliantly depicted the crushing impact of modern life on a vulnerable girl but had revealed, seemingly hidden in the film, his own attempts to break through the isolation and violence of his traumatic past: "It is not too much to say that Aaron made me realize things about my life I had not confronted." For her part, Baker was "ecstatic at what the music added to the film," telling Copland, "Your music makes me a wonderful actress."[25]

Something Wild received mixed reviews in the press; the critics liked its offbeat qualities but found the story somewhat dull and confusing. General audiences took little interest in it, at least until it appeared on television a year or two after its release. Although the music was in some ways the most arresting of Copland's eight film scores, United Artists chose not to issue the soundtrack and Hollywood ignored it at Oscar time—in large part, one imagines, because the film was neither a studio production nor a box-office hit. Even today, most studies of film music overlook this towering achievement.[26]

Copland had better success with the score's concert adaptation, *Music for a Great City* (1964). In contrast to earlier such suites, for this work he stitched together, in three of the four movements, large sections from disparate parts of the film. The first movement, "Skyline," even resembles, to one familiar with the film score, something of a crazy quilt: it comprises the main title, "New York Profile"; part of Mary Ann's "Escape Through the City" (the rumba); an interpolation of "The Park at Night"; Mary Ann's "Nightmare" (the celesta solo); and, after a pause, a return to "New York Profile." The second movement, "Night Thoughts," more narrowly focuses on those moments depicting the reflective Mary Ann but similarly conjoins separate episodes: "Mary Ann Resigned," "Incarceration" (the swaying 6/8 meter), the opening portion of "Escape Through

the City" (the English horn solo), and a reprise of "Mary Ann Resigned."
The third movement, "Subway Jam," consists simply of that one sequence,
a study in claustrophobia. The final movement, "Toward the Bridge,"
comprises nearly all of "The Bridge," yet more untapped music from
"Escape Through the City" that ushers in the same rumbalike music as
found in the first movement, and a final reprise of "New York Profile."
Considering its juggling of varied materials, *Music for a Great City* makes
a surprisingly taut and coherent whole.[27]

Copland used approximately half of the film score for this suite. He left
out both the more sentimental and the more upbeat portions of the score,
including Mrs. Gates at the police station, Mary Ann's morning walk, the
love scene between Mary Ann and Mike, and the final reconciliation
between Mary Ann and her mother. Some years later, however, a little
snippet of the happy morning walk (at that moment when Mary Ann
passes a playground) turned up as the jaunty climax of the first movement
of his *Duo* for flute and piano (1971).

Although *Something Wild* was the last motion picture that Copland
scored, his music made its way into later movies. A short excerpt from the
opening of the Clarinet Concerto, for example, turned up in an erotic
thriller, *Love & Money* (1982), by James Toback (b. 1944), all too briefly
elevating the film above the mediocre.

In *He Got Game* (1998), director Spike Lee (b. 1954) made far more
extensive and serious use of a wide variety of Copland scores, including
*John Henry, Appalachian Spring, Rodeo, Down a Country Lane, The
Red Pony, Music for the Theatre, Our Town, The City, Orchestral Variations, Fanfare for the Common Man, Dance Panels, Lincoln Portrait,* and
Billy the Kid. Moreover, he used large portions, even whole movements of
these works, which he only briefly interspersed with songs by the rap
group Public Enemy. The film honored Copland in the way that Woody
Allen's *Manhattan* paid homage to Gershwin; the differences between
these two pictures underscores those between the composers themselves.

Set in contemporary Brooklyn, *He Got Game* is about Jake Shuttle-
worth (Denzel Washington)—imprisoned for the unintentional murder of
his wife, Martha (Lonette McKee)—and his relationship with his
daughter, Mary (Zelda Harris), and especially his son, Jesus (Ray Allen),
who, six years after the murder, has still not forgiven him. Jake is released
from prison for a week and promised an early parole if he can persuade
Jesus, a superstar basketball player graduating from high school, to attend

the governor's alma mater. Jake helps Jesus, beset by a variety of temptations, find his way; in a related subplot, Jake also befriends a beleaguered prostitute, Dakota Burns (Milla Jovovich).

The film's mythic intentions—the main title, accompanied by *John Henry*, comprises shots of men and women of various ethnicities playing basketball all across rural and urban America—helped lead Lee to Copland. Moreover, Copland's music had long traced the ideals and fears of everyday New Yorkers, and the appearance of, say, the "Interlude" from *Music for the Theatre* for little Mary's dream of a home on Long Island, or the *Orchestral Variations* for the wrenching episode leading up to Martha's death, seem unexceptional from that standpoint.

More unexpected is Lee's use of *Appalachian Spring* for men shooting hoops at public housing projects and correctional facilities; the "Hoe-Down" from *Rodeo* for the exhilaration of a neighborhood basketball game; *Our Town* for romantic moments between Jake and Dakota in a Coney Island flophouse; and *Lincoln Portrait* for a pivotal one-on-one match between Jake and Jesus. At the least, such recontextualizations support the idea that Copland's pastoralisms reflect common aspirations for freedom and dignity. At the same time, the film highlights the tension that underlies even Copland's more serene and hopeful music.

Connotations

Connotations was one of the most exciting commissions of Copland's career: the featured premiere at a gala concert by Leonard Bernstein and the New York Philharmonic inaugurating the orchestra's new home in Lincoln Center's Philharmonic (later Avery Fisher) Hall. Copland, who dedicated the score to Bernstein and the members of the Philharmonic, clearly felt the need to write something special for the occasion and worked assiduously throughout 1961 and 1962 to get it done in time for the scheduled performance on September 23.

A sold-out crowd of about twenty-six hundred attended the white-tie gala; another thirty-five hundred gathered outside the new hall in order to glimpse the star-studded audience, which included First Lady Jackie Kennedy, Secretary of State Dean Rusk, Governor Nelson Rockefeller, Mayor Robert Wagner, U.N. General Secretary U Thant, and leading figures in the arts, from Rudolf Bing and Lucia Chase to Isaac Stern and Merle Oberon. A number of prominent composers also turned up, including Samuel Barber, Henry Cowell, Roy Harris, Walter Piston, Richard

Rodgers, William Schuman, and Roger Sessions. The evening's program presented the "Gloria" from Beethoven's *Missa Solemnis* and Copland's *Connotations* on the first half, followed after intermission by Vaughan Williams's *Serenade to Music* and the first movement of Mahler's Eighth Symphony. The concert was televised and later broadcast nationwide.[28]

In the tradition of the *Symphonic Ode* (1929) and the Third Symphony (1946), Copland composed for this august event the third and last of his orchestral works in the grand manner. *Connotations* in particular recalls the *Ode*, not merely because both are one-movement works lasting just under twenty minutes but because both feature intense strings, piercing winds, blaring brass, pounding percussion—in short, the same kind of hard-edged (as opposed to the Third Symphony's more exultant) look at contemporary life. In a program note for the premiere, Copland wrote, "After some consideration, I concluded that the classical masters would undoubtedly provide the festive and dedicatory tone appropriate to such an occasion. For my own part, I decided to compose a work that would bring to the opening exercise a contemporary note, expressing something of the tensions, aspirations and drama inherent in the world of today."[29]

Also like the *Ode*, *Connotations* explores its basic idea—here a twelve-tone row (specifically, three four-note harmonies)—in a series of alternating fast and slow sections, thereby creating a complex variation form related as well to the *Piano Variations*. (*Connotations* even contains a prominent motive strongly reminiscent of that piano piece.) Its title, according to the composer, refers both to the music's "primary meaning" (namely, the tone row) and its "subsequent treatment," which "seeks out other implications—connotations that come in a flash or connotations that I might have only gradually uncovered." Some of the other titles he considered, such as *Pregnancies*, imply similar notions.[30]

At the same time, as a twelve-tone work, his first for orchestra, *Connotations* struck a distinctive stylistic profile. Explained Bernstein, "*Connotations* is Copland looking back at earlier works from the vantage of 1962—and the 1962 point of view is a twelve-tone one." Some of the music's thorny sonorities also bespoke new perspectives. In addition, the emphasis on harmony, already noted in the *Nonet*, represented a departure of sorts, requiring a different kind of listening, for one does not always have the sharply etched unifying melodic phrase or fragment to hang on to. Virgil Thomson exaggerated when he remarked that "counterpoint was totally lacking in *Connotations*"; but as with the *Nonet*, Copland himself referred to the harmonically oriented "chaconne" in discussions of the work.[31]

Connotations' straightforward ABCBA arch also resembles the *Nonet*. These sections yield long-familiar moods: the A sections are prophetic, tragic; the B sections, jazzy, frenetic; and the brief middle section, pastoral, reflective. But a new darkness hangs over the whole. The outer portions are grave; the jazzy sections rather cheerless; the pastoral contrast more weary than peaceful. The music often seems lost, uncertain, trapped; this includes the ending, a series of crashing twelve-tone chords that offer nothing like the *Ode*'s valiant resolution. Along with its twelve-tone language, its spiny orchestration, its harmonic structure, and its arch-like form, such solemnity made *Connotations* a particularly complete, if unusually severe, summation of the composer's late work.[32]

At the premiere, the bewildered gala audience responded, in Copland's words, with "a confused near silence." Robert J. Landry reported in *Variety*,

> For the majority of the audience, all over 35, if the ladies don't object to the sweep of the statement, it was totally evident that Copland represented an assault on their nervous systems which they resented. Seldom has this reviewer heard such outspoken comment in the lobbies after such dull response in the auditorium. It is strictly accurate to declare that an audience paying $100 a seat and in a mood for self-congratulation and schmaltz hated Copland's reminder of the ugly realities of industrialization, inflation and cold war—which his music seemed to be talking about.

After the performance, Jackie Kennedy, looking radiant, found herself tongue-tied with the composer, unable to utter more than, "Oh, Mr. Copland." (When he asked his companion for the evening, Verna Fine, what to make of this, she answered, "Oh, Aaron, it's obvious. She hated it!") Aside from a very few critics, such as Louis Biancolli—who called it "a turning point in his career, a powerful score in 12-tone style that has liberated new stores of creative energy"—most reviewers did not care for the piece either. Everett Helm deemed it "unnecessarily strident," Harriet Johnson thought it "too long for its content," and Richard Franko Goldman found it "completely without charm," while Paul Henry Lang and others used the occasion to bemoan, in Lang's words, Copland's "yield to the conformism of 12-tone music."[33]

When Bernstein brought the work to England in early 1963, the reviews contained similar talk of "mere din" and "dodecaphonic deserts," though the English cautioned against hasty judgment. A recording of the world premiere released in 1963 brought a similarly bleak outpouring, Robert Marsh finding the work "dreary" and "dull," and Irving Kolodin calling it "rather relentlessly grim." "*Connotations* for Orchestra sounded rather strident on September 23," wrote Everett Helm; "on the disc it becomes ear-piercing." Through it all Copland remained typically unperturbed and philosophical. "I hope that you and I will turn out to be justified in enjoying that kind of music," he wrote in response to an appreciative letter from the very young Christopher Rouse.[34]

What audiences and critics failed to realize was that Bernstein's rather harsh and overblown performances, preserved on record, may have played some part in the work's poor reception. In contrast, revivals by Pierre Boulez and the New York Philharmonic (1973), Edo de Waart and the San Francisco Symphony (1979), and Sixten Ehrling and the student Juilliard Orchestra (1987) brought cheering ovations and raves in the press. "The work is beautifully put together: full of energy, variety, thought," said Desmond Shawe-Taylor of the Boulez performance. Reviewing the piece as played by de Waart, Bartlett Naylor wrote of "a majesty hidden in this dark piece," and Michael Andrews spoke of Copland's "mammoth, anxious and angry vision." And after hearing Ehrling and the Juilliard Orchestra, Peter Davis praised the music's "pungent and exhilarating Coplandesque sonorities." Harold Schonberg specifically judged Boulez's rendition superior to Bernstein's, writing, like Shawe-Taylor, that the Frenchman seemed particularly well disposed to "this kind of music."[35]

One might have thought that Bernstein only needed time to digest the score, but when he revived *Connotations* in 1989 (in an unauthorized shortened version) the reviews were even worse than at the premiere (with again an occasional exception, such as Tim Page's). No one, apparently, considered the possibility that the limitations they perceived might have been Bernstein's, not Copland's. On the contrary, Donal Henahan, who thought that the work's "formulaic commonplaces" ground on "relentlessly," asserted that Bernstein played the Copland pieces on the concert "for all they were worth," and Bill Zakariasen guessed that Bernstein programmed the "boring" *Connotations* "out of a sense of duty to his old friend."[36]

One can only conclude that Bernstein, for all his brilliance as a Copland interpreter, could not persuasively put over this score. What made this especially regrettable was the fact that for nearly thirty years the only available recording of *Connotations* was the inelegant world premiere. A recording by the Juilliard Orchestra under Ehrling (1988), which incorporated a few revisions made prior to the score's publication, consequently offered a welcome alternative.[37]

The celebrated and controversial American-born choreographer John Neumeier, famous for his portentous ballets on literary themes, used *Connotations*, along with the *Piano Variations* and portions of the *Piano Fantasy*, for a *Hamlet* ballet for the American Ballet Theatre. Premiered on 6 January 1976, the production, which explored the play's principal characters rather than the drama per se, featured an international all-star cast, including Mikhail Baryshnikov as Hamlet, Gelsey Kirkland as Ophelia, Marcia Haydee as Gertrude, and Erik Bruhn as Claudius. Although the ballet received mostly poor reviews, Bob Micklin thought that Copland's "prickly, restless music" suited the ballet's basic concept.[38]

27

From *Emblems* to *Proclamation*

(1964–82)

Emblems and *Inscape*

For a number of years, conductors of America's many high school and college symphonic bands hoped that Copland might write an original composition for them (as did his publisher, who recognized its financial potential); in 1964 he accepted a commission from Keith Wilson, president of the College Band Directors National Association, for a piece for band that would be "representative of the composer's best work, and not one written with all sorts of technical or practical limitations."[1]

Copland composed the one-movement, eleven-minute *Emblems* for band during the summer and fall of 1964. As always with his music for young people, the piece makes an especially fresh and lively impression, perhaps that much more conspicuous in the context of his mostly elegiac late work. Although glad not to have any specified limitations, he imposed some on himself, writing a challenging but engaging work whose accessibility includes references to the hymn "Amazing Grace," as well as to jazz and Latin music.

The straightforward ABA form makes it all the more readily approachable. The slow outer portions are themselves ternary, with their framing parts issuing a kind of fanfare and their midsections comprising a waltzlike episode that concludes with "Amazing Grace." The fast and snazzy B section similarly has a subsidiary theme, one possibly related to medieval music. As in the *Nonet* and *Connotations*, the whole is unified by a germinal harmonic idea that unfolds somewhat in the manner of a chaconne, resulting in strings of rich six-note harmonies; but its basic motif—four stepwise ascending major triads—yields less dissonant and complex harmonies than those found in the previous two works.[2]

As Copland expanded his chaconne idea in the waltzlike section, he discovered that he could juxtapose each of the four phrases of "Amazing Grace" over his extended chaconne bass, not for a conventional setting of the tune but for a sweetly jazzy one. "It was only by chance perusal of an anthology of tunes," he wrote, "that I realized a connection existed between my harmonies and 'Amazing Grace'!" In contrast to his customary methods of quotation, he did not take the tune as a starting point but rather, to use his own word, "embedded" it into a preexisting structure. This technique, naturally related to the harmonic bias of his music from this period, bespoke his growing rapport with Ives as well.

Aside from the fact that the tune fitted his harmonies, what reason did Copland have for quoting "Amazing Grace"? The piece anticipated—as opposed to exploited—the tune's huge popularity that followed Judy Collins's recording (1971). One might at least say that the tune contained features that had long appealed to him, including its movements by thirds, its pentatonic complexion, and its flavor of pioneer America. But did the concept of "amazing grace" have some relation to the moralism of the traditional pictorial "emblem"? Or to the music's somewhat didactic purpose as a work for school bands? In any event, the quotation of a hymn tune in a nonprogrammatic work—highly unusual for Copland—again raised the specter of Ives.

William Schaefer and the Trojan Band of the University of Southern California gave the work's premiere in Tempe, Arizona, on 18 December 1964. As Copland's only piece for band, *Emblems* naturally entered the repertory, but it largely disappointed the band community. Many conductors, regarding it as overly percussive and fragmented, presumably presided over mediocre performances. David Whitwell, who thought the work "logical, not disjointed, and both lyric and expressive," held band directors responsible for the work's poor reception, partly for not carefully heeding the notation but, more generally, for not properly interpreting the music. Pointing especially to the opening directive, "in a bold and marked manner," he argued that conductors typically shortened the accented notes in ways that defeated not only the sense of line but the music's very essence; such lack of musicality helped mask the fact that Copland had very much delivered "the masterwork which was promised."[3]

Writers, understandably enough, often mention Copland's last major work for orchestra, *Inscape* (1967), in the same breath as *Connotations* (1962). Both are in one movement, of similar duration, and the composer's only orchestral scores to employ the twelve-tone method. In addition, he wrote both for Leonard Bernstein and the New York Philharmonic—*Inscape* for the orchestra's 125th anniversary season—and Bernstein issued recordings of both on the same disc.

Less recognized is the fact that *Inscape* is quite literally the flip side of *Connotations*, as intimate and reflective a work as *Connotations* is public and tragic. If *Connotations* recalls the *Ode*, *Inscape* looks back to *Quiet City*, though this mostly slow twelve-minute movement has no real precedent among Copland's oeuvre. Although it traces the characteristic outlines of a dramatic opening, a bustling scherzo, and a dirgelike finale, followed by a coda that reprises the opening, such schematic contrast is softened by the brevity of the individual episodes as well as by nearly constant fluctuations of tempo, so that the work communicates greater stream-of-consciousness than perhaps any other piece by Copland—at least until *Night Thoughts* (1972), its pianistic equivalent.[4]

The title *Inscape* derived from the writings of Gerard Manley Hopkins (1844–1889), the Victorian poet-priest whose life and work bore a striking resemblance to those of his American contemporary Emily Dickinson. Copland had long admired Hopkins, an enthusiasm possibly explained by his friendship with Britten, who was working on some Hopkins settings when he and Copland spent the summer together in 1939. Copland even considered writing a work for reciter and accompaniment, *Readings from Hopkins,* at about the same time he composed the *Dickinson Songs.* "Hopkins interested me because of his originality and his experiments with prosody and meter, language and structure," wrote Copland, who was also intrigued by the poet's musical interests and aspirations.[5]

Hopkins coined the word *inscape* to describe the essential qualities of things, which he contrasted with *instress*, meaning one's perceptions of things. In his flyleaf to the score, Copland quoted W. H. Gardner's explanation of *instress* (or the "sensation of inscape") as "a quasimystical illumination, a sudden perception of that deeper pattern, order and unity which give meaning to external forms." Hopkins himself used the words *pattern* and *design* interchangeably with *inscape*. Copland thought music particularly well matched to such ideas, in that the composer uses sounds as an "instress" that communicates a deeper inner essence, an "inscape." "What appealed to me was Hopkins' ability to see beyond the outward appearance of things to their innermost being and his genius in making the outer appearance itself reflect the inner reality," he wrote. "My idea was to write music that would attempt to do just that, music that seemed to be moving inward upon itself." He further recognized a connection between such aesthetics and Nadia Boulanger's emphasis on "order, unity, discipline," though he acknowledged that *Inscape* "set out to find a different way of expressing these principles."[6]

By a "different way," Copland alluded to the fact that *Inscape* employed the twelve-tone method, toward which Boulanger had a well-known antipathy. Here, in Copland's fourth and essentially last twelve-tone work, he used the row (or, rather, two rows) largely as in *Connotations*—that is, as a harmonic resource; the piece even opens with an eleven-note chord (to which he would "always jolt jokingly," recalled the composer David Conte, when the two of them listened to various recordings of the work together). But for the most part Copland extracted from the work's rows simple two-note harmonies, as opposed to the dense chords so characteristic of the earlier work, its leaner texture helping to make it more accessible. In addition, the prominence of harmonic thirds provides the work with a less dissonant, more tonal countenance; the music even poignantly settles, from time to time, into simple triads.[7]

Leonard Bernstein and the New York Philharmonic gave the world premiere in Ann Arbor, Michigan, on 13 September 1967 as part of the University of Michigan's sesquicentennial celebration. The first-night audience responded with a standing ovation; William Wolf wrote two days later of the work's "emotional intensity which is disturbing yet uncannily beautiful." However, in the ensuing months and years, as Bernstein and Copland conducted the work in New York and London, critics largely dismissed it as expert but unexciting and dry.[8]

In his memoirs, Copland turned a blind eye to the work's poor reception, selectively excerpting positive reviews by Irving Kolodin and Allen Hughes, and writing, "For once, the critics seemed to understand right off that my intention was to make a piece of music in my own way, with my own sound, using the twelve-tone method, instead of creating an example of a perfect serial composition." In fact, Hughes was unusual in arguing how well the twelve-tone method suited the composer, "as though it had been invented to create the Copland sound." More typically, Winthrop Sargeant (in the *New Yorker*) and Harold Schonberg (in the *New York Times*) criticized his adoption of the technique in ways that even exceeded the response to *Connotations*. "What impels composers to write this kind of thing is beyond me," wrote Sargeant of the New York premiere. "The method is fifty years old. The work makes no statement of any sort, except that Mr. Copland can turn out twenty minutes or so of twelve-tone composition with the greatest skill." "His serial works, of which 'Inscape' is an example, are unconvincing, " opined Schonberg after a performance by Copland in 1970. "He sounds unnatural here, and one suspects that he himself has no great confidence in this style." *Inscape* became a victim of shifting cultural winds.[9]

More recent reviews of performances by Larry Newland and Oliver Knussen saw no noticeable improvement in this regard; indeed, few were as harsh as one by Gavin Thomas (1993) that described "the late and distinctly dry *Inscape*" as containing "chunky chromatic chords, horribly orchestrated, and some pedantic atonal counterpoint."[10]

Inscape remains the enthusiasm of a small group of friends, who regard it as one of his crowning achievements. Further performances are needed to allow us to more fully gauge its stature and viability, but as a lovely if elusive distillation of some of the composer's most characteristic and touching moods and gestures, it may in time endear itself to a larger audience. Meanwhile, Copland's own "live" recording with the Orchestre National de France makes, for the most part, a more compelling case for the work than that by Bernstein and the New York Philharmonic.[11]

Three Latin-American Sketches and Smaller Works

Although *Inscape* has all the earmarks of a swan song, Copland's final work for orchestra was the youthful *Three Latin-American Sketches* (1971). He actually wrote the second and third movements—"Paisaje Mexicano" and "Danza de Jalisco"—while in Acapulco in 1959, on a commission by Gian Carlo Menotti for the Spoleto Festival, but only the latter was performed on that occasion. After Copland conducted both as *Two Mexican Pieces* in 1965, he withdrew them on account of their brevity. At the request of André Kostelanetz, he composed in 1971 an additional movement, "Estribillo," based on a melodic fragment heard in

Venezuela. Kostelanetz and the New York Philharmonic premiered the newly titled *Three Latin-American Sketches* on 7 June 1972.[12]

Three Latin-American Sketches uses a small orchestra of flute, oboe, clarinet, bassoon, trumpet, two pianos, percussion, and strings; the percussion battery forgoes the traditional timpani, snare drum, and bass drum in favor of claves, wood block, xylophone, ratchet, slap-stick, triangle, suspended cymbal, and conga drum, an instrument prominently featured in Copland's later scores. Both instrumentation and orchestration accentuate the music's relation to authentic folk practices.

Copland based all three movements on traditional melodies, fragmenting and developing them as was his wont. In "Estribillo" he repeats an ardently syncopated phrase through the different sections of the orchestra, thus reflecting the sort of responsorial volleying between soloist and chorus characteristic of the traditional *estribillo*, a refrainlike section associated with types of salsa and calypso music. A more carefree tune offers contrast. The movement's remarkably spiky sonorities throughout throw the lyrical warmth of "Paisaje Mexicano" ("Mexican Landscape") into relief. Very analogous to his rural American landscapes, this latter movement has, for all its serenity, a vaguely melancholy undertone; "soft and sad," states the opening directive. The work's vigorous finale, "Danza de Jalisco" ("Dance from Jalisco," a province in central Mexico) captures some optional hand-clapping for the pianists along with the alternating 6/8 and 3/4 meters characteristic of Mexican dance.

Even in the context of his more popular pieces, *Three Latin-American Sketches* is a light work, though "not so light," Copland once advised, "as to be pop-concert material." Indeed, at each turn one finds complex polyrhythms, biting dissonances, and intriguing colors. Yet in spite of its potential appeal to both a general and sophisticated audience, the work remains obscure. The chamber instrumentation—including the need for two pianos—has possibly discouraged its wider dissemination; but one imagines that it will eventually find the ever-growing audience for the similarly scored *Music for the Theatre*.[13]

Far from a deterrent, the work's chamber scoring recommended itself to dance companies, who quickly took the kind of interest in *Three Latin-American Sketches* that they had long shown *Music for the Theatre*. In 1991, a distinguished choreographer in the tradition of de Mille and Robbins, Donald MacKayle, used the piece, with *Danzón Cubano* as an introductory movement, for a four-scene ballet, *Sombra ye Sol*, inspired by four paintings of Frida Kahlo: *Viva la Vida*, *Wounded Flesh*, *Tree of*

Hope, and *Embrace of Love*. In associating the music with Kahlo, McKayle showed a rare sensitivity. As in decades past, choreographers generally remained refreshingly attuned to Copland's latest scores—whether it be John Neumeier's ballet to *Connotations* or Bella Lewitzky's dance to the *Duo*—at a time when such music sometimes struggled to make inroads into the musical community.

Copland also continued to write small occasional pieces. In 1966, he accepted a lucrative commission to write the theme music for the *CBS Playhouse* television series. Although he admitted that so much money for so little music was an inducement, he took the task seriously, composing a rather clangorous and arresting collage, with vague echoes of his *Piano Variations*, for the unusual ensemble of five trumpets, three trombones, three pianos, four percussion players, and strings. The result, which matched the modern sculptural images on the screen, earned him an Emmy nomination.[14]

In 1969 he composed three more short works: *Happy Anniversary* for orchestra; *Ceremonial Fanfare* for an eleven-piece brass ensemble; and *Inaugural Fanfare* for a twenty-four-piece wind ensemble.

The one-minute *Happy Anniversary*, a mere trifle, was one of twenty arrangements commissioned by the Philadelphia Orchestra on the popular tune "Happy Birthday," in honor of Eugene Ormandy's seventieth birthday. Copland's arrangement spotlights his own countermelody, soaring above in the upper instruments, against the familiar melody, stated three times in the bass. This countermelody is pure Copland: vigorous, lilting, sputtering merrily with big leaps and falling thirds, broadening at the very end. Also characteristic is the little introduction containing fragments that anticipate both melodies. Copland conducted its premiere on 24 January 1970 on the occasion of the Philadelphia Orchestra's seventieth anniversary concert (hence its title), and it subsequently was heard at birthday celebrations for Copland himself.

Despite their duration of less than four minutes each, the two fanfares are far more interesting, with exquisitely fashioned sounds, evocative chromatic melodies, and subtle ternary forms. The lovely *Ceremonial Fanfare*, commemorating the centennial of the Metropolitan Museum of Art and first performed on 14 November 1970, begins with a strong quasi-fugal declamation; moves, via a quiet transition, to a soft contrasting section featuring muted brass in canon; and abruptly returns to the loud declamation, subsiding poetically at the very end.

The more festive *Inaugural Fanfare* (revised in 1975) similarly alternates loud, stately music with a soft middle section (whose melody returns, triple forte, at the coda), the woodwind and percussion instruments allowing greater contrast. For instance, the transition to the middle section includes a striking passage for tenor drum, snare drum, and suspended cymbals that gradually fades out, uncoordinated with a trumpet that eventually enters "softly, as from a distance"—a nod once again in the direction of Ives.

Also Ivesian was Copland's suggestion, on the occasion of the premiere, that the two principal trumpets might "first be heard in the distance, preferably out of sight of the audience, and each one on opposite sides, outside the performing area. It should make the impression of a call from the distance. If this isn't practical, then I suggest muted trumpets on opposite sides of the stage, in the wings, possibly with stage doors open (if there are such)."[15]

The city of Grand Rapids paid $1,000 for *Inaugural Fanfare* as part of a public unveiling of an Alexander Calder sculpture, *La Grande Vitesse* (*Grand Rapids*), in a downtown plaza on 14 June 1969. A crowd of over two thousand heard the work performed by members of the Grand Rapids Symphony Orchestra under its conductor, Gregory Millar. Copland accepted this commission only because he "knew and admired Sandy Calder" and thought the enormous (fifty-five-foot-long, forty-foot-high) red *Grande Vitesse* "a spectacular sculpture." The *Fanfare*'s spatial play may have been as much indebted to Calder as to Ives. Some years prior to the work, William Austin had suggested a connection between Copland and Calder; this congruity presumably involved their lean textures and bright colors, their disarming whimsy and austere monumentality, and their absorption of both the European avant-garde and the American vernacular. Both were also two of the most influential American artists of their time.[16]

In 1971 Copland returned to the "Happy Birthday" melody, composing an unaccompanied version of the tune as a "salute" to the Music Library Association on the occasion of its fortieth birthday. He did not specify the instrumentation but apparently intended it for a single brass instrument (only a trombone can play it as written) or any number of brass players. Nor did he title this little effort; catalogers refer to it by its tempo indication, "Larghetto Pomposo," though it might as well be called "Happy Birthday." With its pitches displaced up and down octaves, Copland's version resembles Stravinsky's more familiar variation—or, rather, deconstruction—of the same tune. But Copland's similar leaps have a weight and gravity all their own.[17]

The *Duo* and Other Memorials with Flute

Copland wrote his last extended work, the *Duo* for flute and piano (1971), in memory of the first flutist for the Philadelphia Orchestra from 1921 to 1960, William Kincaid, at the behest of a large group of Kincaid's students and friends. When approached by one such student, John Solum, about a commemorative piece shortly after Kincaid's death in 1967, Copland said that he had been thinking of writing a work for flute for some time and that, as an admirer of Kincaid's, he regarded this as the right opportunity. Offered $2,000, he countered with $2,500, telling Solum that although he did not need the money, he was concerned that if he lowered or waived his fee, that might set a bad precedent for fellow composers. He resolved instead to use some of the money to commission a young composer to write another flute piece in Kincaid's memory, though apparently nothing came of this.[18]

It took Copland nearly four years to deliver the three-movement work. Usually hard-pressed by fast music, he spent most of the time in this case on the slow middle movement; the fast outer movements, derived from sketches from the 1940s, he completed relatively quickly. Solum had requested a "work like a sonata," and Copland took him at his word, writing a piece that is a sonata in all but name.[19]

With its pastoral first movement, elegiac slow movement, and vigorous finale, the work in particular recalls his Sonata for Violin and Piano (1943). Even the themes bear resemblances—this due, no doubt, to the fact that some of the *Duo*'s main ideas originate from the same period. The *Duo*, however, displays a more intense chromatic palette than does the Violin Sonata, especially its slow movement, which apparently relies less (if at all) on earlier sketches than do the others. In any case, the *Duo* feels like a late Copland work, reflective and autumnal.[20]

The first movement, marked "Flowing," forms an ABCBA arch in such a way as to suggest an inverted sonata, that is, a sonata whose recapitulation reverses the order of its two principal themes. It opens with a folklike main theme for flute; the piano subsequently introduces a somewhat faster, waltzlike secondary theme. A still faster, more modulatory development ensues. After a jazzy climax, the waltzlike music returns, followed by the folklike theme and a coda, the waltzlike theme having the last word.

The second movement, "Poetic, somewhat mournful," embraces, in Copland's words, "a certain mood that I connect with myself—a rather sad and wistful one, I suppose." The music contains gently undulating chromatic melodies, moving sinuously through changing meters, against static, bluesy harmonies—a rather sultry ambience that recalls his music of the 1920s. The movement unfolds an AABA form, with the outer A sections in one key, the second A section in another key, and the more unstable B section containing a poignant climax centered in yet a third key. Its expanded song form enhances the music's intense lyricism. "What can you do with a flute in an extended form that would not emphasize its songful nature?" he asked.[21]

In contrast, the whimsical finale, marked "Lively, with bounce," exploits the flute's more percussive possibilities. A kaleidoscopic exploration of a single interval (namely, the third), this ABA movement contains a jaunty, rather childlike main theme, a more jagged, argumentative middle section, and, after a recapitulation, an exciting coda that leads to a cogent and satisfying resolution.

One of Kincaid's most distinguished pupils, flutist Elaine Shaffer, the wife of the conductor Efrem Kurtz, premiered the *Duo* with pianist Hephzibah Menuhin on 3 October 1971. The work quickly established itself as one of Copland's most widely played chamber works and possibly his most popular instrumental composition since the Clarinet Concerto (1948). It entered the repertory of great flutists from around the world, including Jean-Pierre Rampal, James Galway, Doriot Anthony Dwyer, Harvey Sollberger, Paula Robison, and Carol Wincenc; and Shaffer and Copland became the first of a number of duos to record it. Critics, however, tended to minimize the work as "lightweight" or "slight." Even Copland sounded a defensive note, saying that he had composed it "for Kincaid's students, not for future generations." But as Peter Davis wrote in a review of the premiere, "Beneath the surface charm lies the composer's customary sophisticated sense of narrative development, rhythmic ingenuity and keen ear for instrumental color."[22]

In 1977 Copland approached Robert Mann about arranging the *Duo* for violin and piano. For many years a violinist with the Juilliard Quartet, Mann had recorded both the *Sextet* and the Piano Quartet with the composer. (Like other chamber players who performed with Copland, he was amused at the way Copland occasionally would get lost in his own scores.) Mann helped transcribe the *Duo* at no fee—"out of love for this man," he explained—and gave the work's premiere with pianist André-Michel Schub at the Library of Congress on 5 April 1978. Violinist Gregory Fulkerson and pianist Robert Shannon recorded this version three years later.[23]

Copland featured the flute in two other memorial pieces from these years, namely, two threnodies composed in 1971 and 1973, respectively: *Threnody I* ("In memoriam Igor Stravinsky") for flute, violin, viola, and cello, commissioned by Boosey & Hawkes for publication in their quarterly journal, *Tempo*; and *Threnody II* ("In memoriam Beatrice Cunningham") for the same instrumentation (except with the darker alto flute replacing the more conventional flute in C), commissioned by the Ojai Festival. (Beatrice Cunningham was a friend of Copland's and the sister of the critic Lawrence Morton, a lifelong devotee who directed the Ojai Festival for a number of years.) *Threnody I* premiered over the radio in England on 6 April 1972; *Threnody II*, at the Ojai Festival on 2 June 1973.[24]

Both threnodies are novel in technique and expression. Cast in a meter of 3/2, *Threnody I* pits a freely flowing chromatic melody in the flute against a modal, slower-moving ground bass in three-voice canon in the strings. Neil Butterworth speaks of the work as a "simple exercise of counterpoint," but to follow the shapely flute line, with its two fortissimo climaxes, and the hulking three-part canon below sets the kind of challenge posed by late Bach or, for that matter, late Stravinsky, which seems to have been something of the point of the piece to begin with.[25]

Freer in form, *Threnody II* has its own distinct profile, alternating or juxtaposing rather diatonic harmonies with chromatic melodies derived from a twelve-tone row. This particular kind of blend of tonal harmony and twelve-tone melody signaled a somewhat new slant on Copland's part, suggesting one direction he might have pursued had he continued composing.

Night Thoughts and Final Piano Pieces

In 1972 Copland composed an eight-minute piano piece, *Night Thoughts (Homage to Ives)*, for the 1973 Van Cliburn Competition, an international piano contest held quadrennially in Fort Worth, Texas. Beginning with the initial contest (1962), Van Cliburn instituted the practice of commissioning a new American work for each event; all contestants receive the piece a month prior to the competition (though only the semifinalists perform it) and the jury grants a special commissioned-work award. Samuel Barber wrote *Ballade* and Leonard Bernstein, *Touches* for the 1977 and 1981 competitions, respectively, making the Van Cliburn something of a repository for pianistic swan songs.[26]

These commissions specify no particular guidelines in terms of technical requirements, and far from writing a virtuosic showpiece, Copland composed a slow and pensive work in a rhapsodic, quasi-improvisatory manner. "My intention," he stated, "was to test the musicality and the ability of a performer to give coherence to a free musical form." Neil Butterworth aptly describes the work's rounded form as one in which episodes arise "naturally from the previous one with slight fluctuations of speed."[27]

Perhaps the piece's most striking feature is its piano writing. Whereas in the past Copland had offset his longstanding predilection for bell-like sounds with dry, lean passages, here dense clusters and murky dissonances, heavily pedaled, dominate to the point that everything chimes; even simple melodies and triads emerge against reverberant sonorities. These ringing harmonies generate a good deal of tonal ambiguity; one needs to listen hard to grasp all the overtones.

With its forlorn melodies set against the funereal sonorities, the piece creates a mood of deep melancholy. After John Kozar gave the work's European premiere in 1974, one review spoke of its "highly disturbing atmosphere." At the same time, at the very end, a lingering major triad, heard "very distant, but clear," suggests some repose.[28]

This "distant" harmony, along with other features, recalls Ives's *The Unanswered Question* and helps explain the work's subtitle. Copland claimed, however, that he had not thought of Ives during the work's composition and that the subtitle came as an afterthought. "By calling it that," he explained, "I stopped a lot of my friends from telling me how Ivesian it sounds." Paul Hume reasonably deemed the work "a singularly fragrant elicitation of thoughts shared by the two great American musicians."[29]

This connection with Ives betokened two related developments: first, the heightened interest in Ives during these years; and second, the contemporaneous movement toward an eclectic romanticism. One imagines that had Copland continued to compose, he would have put his personal stamp on the "New Romanticism" much as he had absorbed so many of the century's trends.

In the late 1970s and early 1980s, his compositional career essentially behind him, Copland published three short piano pieces, all based on earlier sketches, at the promptings of composer Phillip Ramey and pianist

Bennett Lerner: *Midsummer Nocturne* (1947, 1977), *Midday Thoughts* (1944, 1982), and *Proclamation* (1973, 1982). Ramey discovered the two-page *Midsummer Nocturne* among the composer's papers, headed by an intriguing list of tentative titles, including, in addition to the one eventually selected, *Pas de Trois*, *The Twilight Gathers*, and *Wordless Song*. Devoid of any accidentals, this gentle, pastoral piece comprises an AABA form reminiscent of popular song. Ramey notes that Copland intended the piece as part of a piano suite, possibly for children; the title *Pas de Trois*, combined with the fact that he based the first movement of the Clarinet Concerto (1948) on a sketch entitled "Pas de Deux," suggests that he might, too, have considered it for a ballet. As it was, its principal theme, considerably varied, found its way into the theater as Ma Moss's opening aria, "Two Little Bits of Metal," from *The Tender Land*. Leo Smit premiered the piece, dedicated to Ramey, on 13 January 1978 in Cleveland.[30]

Copland composed *Midday Thoughts* in 1944 as a sketch for a never completed *Ballade* for piano and orchestra. He subsequently used this same or similar music in his documentary film score *The Cummington Story* to depict the story's European refugees, and again for the Clarinet Concerto and another piano piece, *In Evening Air* (1966), making *Midday Thoughts* somewhat redundant.[31]

Proclamation, on the other hand, offers a valuable glimpse into Copland's final musical thoughts. Whether one goes by the earlier date of 1973 or the later one of 1982, the music is, apparently, the last he ever wrote. Vivian Perlis remembers that when she visited Copland in the early 1980s he often had the music, bearing the title *Improvisation*, on the piano stand and would occasionally play it upon request. At Ramey's urging, he completed it as the two-minute *Proclamation*, describing it as a "rather stern-sounding piece, in what has not inappropriately been termed my 'laying-down-the-law' style."[32]

Proclamation is a short, moody piece reminiscent of the *Four Piano Blues* but updated to allow for the kinds of tonal and formal ambiguity characteristic of the composer's late piano style. Although the piece contains a brief moment of nostalgic sweetness at its center, the overall mood is quite restless and dark; the work ends abruptly with a pounding note in the bass. Copland retained his strong, forceful musical personality to the very end.

Copland dedicated *Proclamation* to Ramey and *Midday Thoughts* to Bennett Lerner, who premiered both pieces at Carnegie Recital Hall on

28 February 1983. Whereas Lerner wisely placed them at different points in his program, Boosey, against Copland's advice (according to Ramey), published them as *Two Piano Pieces,* an incongruous pairing, considering their widely divergent musical styles. Copland also authorized Ramey's idiomatic orchestration of *Proclamation,* which Zubin Mehta and the New York Philharmonic premiered at a special eighty-fifth birthday program on 14 November 1985.[33]

Aside from these few late piano pieces and some arrangements, Copland produced no new score in the last seventeen years of his life. Never particularly prolific to begin with, his compositional career, which had begun to slow in the course of the 1960s, came to a virtual standstill after 1973. In the early 1970s, rumor spread about a new piece for the Juilliard Quartet; in 1974, he accepted a commission for a "major Bicentennial work" to be performed by six orchestras; and in 1978, Harry Haun, substituting for gossip columnist Liz Smith, reported a possible "short symphony" for Zubin Mehta and the New York Philharmonic for 1979. But none of these works materialized.[34]

Copland wanted to write new works, as his letters to Carlos Chávez document, but he had run out of fresh ideas. "It was exactly as if someone had simply turned off a faucet," he told Paul Moor. Although he could have ransacked his old sketchbooks, as he did to some extent for the *Duo* and some late piano pieces, this little appealed to him. "You have to get ideas that excite you," he explained to Phillip Ramey.[35]

To his displeasure, some friends and journalists dramatized this retirement from composition, as he preferred to think of it, often taking their cue from Leonard Bernstein, who in 1970 held that Copland's adoption of the twelve-tone method led to his halting output. "That lasted for four more pieces," Bernstein bemoaned, "and then he didn't write any more. How sad for him. How awful for us." Although Copland wrote other than twelve-tone music in his later years—not to mention the fact that he had yet to write the *Duo, Night Thoughts,* and some other pieces—this dubious idea that he could no longer compose because he was somehow out of sync with the times or with his true self gained ground in his final years.[36]

That the creative output of an elderly person—especially someone on the brink of senile dementia—should taper off hardly seems cause for surprise. In Copland's case, his ever expanding career as a conductor further limited his time and energy for composition. Of course some argued, as Copland himself did, that he pursued conducting as compensation for his slowing output, to keep "hopping," as he put it. And yet as early as 1958 Claire Reis warned him that his conducting was becoming an addiction. "I had to admit," he confessed, "that it was pretty heady stuff. Part of me would say, 'Stay home and compose,' and I would do so. But after a short time, particularly when fresh composing ideas were hard to come by, I would get bored and want to take off again." Agnes de Mille remembers meeting Copland in the 1970s and discussing the possibility of another collaboration:

> He said, "Agnes, I don't think I'm ever going to compose anything else. I'm having such a good time conducting." And I said, "Aaron, that's too bad because there are lots of good conductors and there will be more. There's only one of you as a composer. One. And it's you we need." He asked, "Have you ever conducted?" I looked at him and said, "You know, Aaron, I've been asked a lot of damned fool questions in my life, but this tops them all."

It certainly would not have been the first time a composer traded in paper and pencil for a baton. "There is such a need for conductors today," explained Pierre Boulez, "that if you are just a little bit gifted you get sucked into the machinery."[37]

In any case, Copland viewed the end of his compositional career with characteristic composure. Shrugging off Bernstein's pitying remarks, he told the *New York Times*, "Why he should seem unhappy for me, I don't know." When Phillip Ramey asked him, at age eighty, if he had "a comfortable feeling, a feeling of deserved rest, of having done enough," he answered:

> "Comfortable" is hardly the word; I don't feel as if I'm resting, and *nobody's* ever done enough. But, as a matter of fact, I'm amazed that I don't miss composing more than I do. You'd think if you had spent 50 years at it you'd have the feeling that something was missing, and I really don't. I must have expressed myself sufficiently. I certainly don't feel tortured or bitter, only lucky to have been given so long to be creative. And resigned to the fact that it appears to be over. I assure you that I do not sit around drooling with disappointment.[38]

28

Identity Issues

The Composer as Jew

Although Copland only occasionally used explicitly Jewish subjects or themes in his music, many listeners over the years perceived his music, in one or another way, as Jewish. This was especially so in the 1920s, not only because some of his pieces from that period suggested connections to Russian-Jewish styles but because they often conformed to the widespread association of Jewish composers with the avant-garde and with jazz.[1]

The connection with jazz in particular drew comment in this context. In a discussion entitled "Aaron Copland and His Jazz," for instance, Isaac Goldberg asserted that "the ready amalgamation of the American Negro and the American Jew goes back to something Oriental in the blood of both." In a related vein, Paul Rosenfeld noted, "Copland has a taste for hot colours and garish jazziness, perhaps a happy consequence of his oriental-American psyche." Later commentators paid less attention to this idea, though it caught the fancy of Wilfrid Mellers, who wrote, in connection with the *Piano Variations*, "It is significant that both Negro and Jew are dispossessed people who have become, in a cosmopolitan urban society, representatives of modern man's uprootedness."[2]

From time to time, listeners also noted correspondences between the alleged Jewishness of Copland and that of such other composers as Mahler, Schoenberg, Bloch, and Gershwin. Roger Sessions, for instance, thought it "interesting to note the occasional Jewish character of Copland's music, approaching in this respect the spirit of Bloch and even of Mahler, though with his own idiom and feeling." Mellers argued that Copland came closer to the more assimilated Mahler and Schoenberg than to Bloch, in that one could not distinguish the "loneliness" and "rootlessness" associated with both his Jewish and his national, that is, American, background.[3]

Most writers treated this matter parenthetically and discreetly, at least publicly (E. B. Hill, for instance, might privately describe *Music for the Theatre* as the "usual clever Hebraic assimilation of the worst features of polytonalité," but he never said anything like that in print). Daniel Gregory Mason, Henry Cowell, Lazare Saminsky, and Virgil Thomson, however, were among those visibly preoccupied with Copland's Jewishness.[4]

Mason claimed that Copland's Jewish background precluded him from writing genuine American music, arguing, in an oft-quoted passage, that "the speciousness, the superficial charm and persuasiveness of Hebrew art, its brilliance, its violently juxtaposed extremes of passion, its poignant eroticism and pessimism" were diametrically opposed to the American character, marked, as it was, by the "poignant beauty of Anglo-Saxon sobriety and restraint . . . the fine reserve so polar to the garrulous self-confessions, the almost indecent stripping of the soul." The prominence of Copland, a "cosmopolitan Jew," made Boston Symphony concerts more "European" and "exotic" and "a little less representatively American" than Chicago Symphony concerts, he opined.[5]

Although coming from an entirely different place, Henry Cowell shared Mason's view of Copland as an outsider amid a fundamentally Anglo-Saxon culture. He publicly vented such thoughts in a series of articles in 1930 for the German journal *Melos*, in which he grouped Copland, Gershwin, and Louis Gruenberg as leaders of a group of Jewish-American concert composers who employed jazz, which he defined as "Negro music seen though the eyes of [Tin Pan Alley] Jews." This prevented Copland—like Negro jazz musicians themselves—from composing genuinely American music, in contrast to Ives and Ruggles, who both descended from old New England stock. Although principal spokespersons for the old guard and the avant-garde, respectively, Mason and Cowell sounded a remarkably similar racial note when it came to Copland.[6]

Writer and composer Lazare Saminsky also found Copland's Jewishness problematic, though for different reasons. An expert in Jewish music and himself Jewish, Saminsky denounced Copland's work as "Judaic," that is, rooted in ghetto experience and assimilationist aspirations, as opposed to "Hebraic" music based on ancient tradition. Although he liked the "wistful, earnest and delicate" slow movements of *Music for the Theatre* (1925), he had only contempt for *Vitebsk* (1928), whose "Jewishness" he declared "musically shallow" and "opportunistic." Copland ultimately deserved comparison with Mahler, another Judaic composer of similar stripe: "Copland is of an observing, an absorbing nature, rather than a creative one. In this he is a sort of miniature Mahler; this kinship in mentality is perhaps the reason for Copland's Mahler-worship."[7]

Saminsky's disdain, reiterated in numerous publications, climaxed with a bitter five-page diatribe (1949), drenched in anti-Semitic and homophobic innuendos, that remains perhaps the most scathing attack on Copland ever penned. "A small, cool creative gift," wrote Saminsky, "but an ego of much frenetic drive, a devious personality with a feline *savoir faire*, with his fine commercial acumen and acute sense of the direction of today's wind, Aaron Copland is a shrewd manager of *musique à succès*." The "suave," "clever," "feeble," and "impotent" Copland, with his "tricks of orchestration," Saminsky argued, cannot really create but can only give "an excellent imitation of a creator"; he "exploits" the American scene, but unlike Ives, his "shrewdly used nationalism" reveals no genuine feeling for the folk. For Saminsky, the composer's presumed Americanisms sound Eastern European, whether it be the "faint Slavonic colors" of *Music for Radio*, the "Appalachian cossacks" of *Appalachian Spring*, or the "faintly Russian contour" of the Third Symphony's opening theme. With *Lincoln Portrait*, Copland has "the audacity to trade in things sacred."[8]

Although far more sympathetic than Mason, Cowell, or Saminsky, Virgil Thomson also emphasized the supposed Jewish character of Copland's work; he would often utter to friends, after hearing some piece or other, "very Jewish music." His references to Copland's famed economy of means sometimes even assumed an anti-Semitic edge, as in the comment "Musically, he knows how to make five cents perform the services of a dollar." (One imagines that Thomson was the unnamed wag who told Theodore Chanler, "Aaron Copland's musical ideas are like pennies shrewdly invested rather than pearls advantageously set.")[9]

Thomson also helped popularize the notion of Copland as prophet or rabbi, pulling out all the stops in a landmark article on the composer

(1932) that began, "Aaron Copland's music is American in rhythm, Jewish in melody, eclectic in all the rest."

> He is a prophet calling out her sins to Israel. He is filled with the fear of God. His music is an evocation of the fury of God. His God is the god of battle, the Lord of Hosts, the jealous, the angry, the avenging god, who rides upon the storm. . . . The gentler movements of his music are more like an oriental contemplation of infinity than like any tender depiction of the gentler aspects of Jehovah.

While tempering such remarks in later years, Thomson maintained that Copland's lifelong social concerns constituted a kind of latent Jewishness: "He's the Jewish preacher telling people right and wrong."[10]

Beginning with the *Symphonic Ode* (1929), a number of listeners besides Thomson associated Copland with biblical prophecy or rabbinical law; one early review, for instance, viewed the work in terms of "the August Prophets" (and "their descendants on Broadway"). Paul Rosenfeld referred to some of Copland's material as "fine Hebraic, harsh and solemn, like the sentences of brooding rabbis." Discussing the Piano Sonata (1941), John Kirkpatrick felt "a strong contact with the Old Testament, which evidently operates quite without the composer's knowledge." "That voice, the Mosaic voice," exclaimed Leo Smit. ". . . The first time I heard the opening of the Piano Concerto, I thought of Moses blasting away on the mountaintop." Even so sober a critic as Arthur Berger related some declamatory passages to "the psalmodic chants for the synagogue with their biblical air of prophecy and gloom."[11]

Some thought of Copland himself as a "prophet" or "patriarch." Leonard Bernstein pictured him, on the strength of the *Piano Variations*, as "a cross between Walt Whitman and an Old Testament prophet." Eric Salzman likened him at age eighty to "a cross between an Old Testament patriarch and some gentle, lyrical bird of prey," while Donal Henahan referred to him as "the Moses of the modern-music movement."[12]

Meanwhile, Arnold Dobrin related Copland's pastoral impulses to his Jewish background. Reasoning that his music "is not an expression of the great prairies as much as it is the *urban longing* for the pastoral life of a different period," Dobrin concluded that such yearning derived specifically from the Jewish experience of enforced ghetto life in Europe: "Perhaps Copland's music speaks also for the longing for the open country felt by a people who were for centuries forbidden by law from ownership of

AARON COPLAND

land." (In her memoirs, Ruth Gay, on the other hand, suggests that the "positive reverence" for "open spaces" among New York's Jewish immigrants derived from their new overcrowded tenement life and "nostalgia for the landscape of [their] youth.")[13]

Although few writers, in this context, discussed actual notes, harmonies, or rhythms, one could reasonably ask, for instance, whether it is mere coincidence that the principal idea of the Piano Concerto suggests the calls of the shofar. Or that the pas de trois from *Dance Panels* opens with a theme akin to a popular setting of the Sabbath hymn "Lecha dodi." Or that some of Copland's proselike declamations resemble Jewish cantorial singing. Investigation along these lines needs to be pursued.

In any case, Copland never intended his music, aside from a very few works, to have any particular Jewish style or content. "I accepted, never questioned my religion," he stated in an attempt to clarify the relation of his music to his Jewish roots. "The Eastern European thing was merely a matter for my parents. It was background atmosphere, but it didn't exist for me in the sense of the life that I was then living in Brooklyn. What preoccupied me was the fact that America had not found its voice as Germany and then France had in producing composers in the music world. The Jewish national aspect had never preoccupied me."[14]

Copland did not seem particularly concerned with the Jewishness of other composers either. In a lecture, he might passingly refer to Schoenberg as a "talmudic student" (an idea possibly borrowed from Rosenfeld) or briefly place Messiaen in the context of French Catholicism, but he rarely dwelt on any composer's religious affiliations, with the principal exception of Milhaud; for in discussions of the French-Jewish composer, he viewed his "nostalgia," "subjectivism," "violence," and "strong sense of logic" as indicative of his "Jewish blood" and "Jewish spirit."[15]

Copland even expressed wariness about explicitly Jewish idioms in a letter to Leonard Bernstein on receipt of sketches to the *Jeremiah Symphony*:

There are certain drawbacks, of course, to adopting a Jewish melos. People are certain to say—"Bloch." But more serious, the general "ambience" is bound to sound familiar to most ears. As far as I can judge by your music thus far, you are hopelessly romantic as a composer. It was clever to have adopted the "Jewish" manner in this piece and thereby justify the romanticism of the piece. (I don't mean to imply that this was more than sub-conscious.) But

522

somehow, someday, that richness of feeling that I call romantic will have to be metamorphosed so that it comes out more new-sounding, more fresh.

Here, as in his remarks about Bloch, he identified the "Jewish melos" with a worn "romanticism."[16]

In 1951 Copland gave a rare lecture in Jerusalem on the subject of Jewish composers, only notes of which survive. While granting that the notion that "the artist of Jewish race" who affirms his Jewishness in his art "comes off best" might be an appealing one—expecially to an Israeli audience—he offered a less dogmatic viewpoint: "A man doesn't create Art because he is a Jew, but because he is a Man. His creative Nature is influenced by his temperament and his environment. If by temperament he is deeply racial, [his] art will come out Jewish. If his environment [is] non-Jewish, that will mix with [his] temperament."

The lecture continued with a profile of some well-known Jewish composers, beginning with Mendelssohn and (or so Copland thought) Saint-Saëns; what he said about them on this occasion remains unknown, though decades earlier he had contrasted their "talent" with the "genius" of Bach and Fauré. In this 1951 lecture, he apparently referred to Mahler as "the assimilated Jew par excellence"; summarized Schoenberg's "Jewish side" with the words "idealist—fighter—purist—intransigent"; described Bloch as a symbol of "Jewish inspiration" (though he criticized a "lack of freshness" in some of the music); and praised Milhaud as the "best example of a Jewish composer." One wonders what Copland in this respect thought of Paul Dukas, a performance of whose *Ariane et Barbe-Bleue* had so "engrossed" him while a student in Paris.[17]

Aside from citing the use of a Jewish folk song in *Vitebsk* and the influence of Jewish chant in *Quiet City*, Copland only occasionally discussed his own music in a Jewish context. For instance, he offered this telling aside while speaking about certain stylistic changes that accompanied his 1930 *Piano Variations*:

In addition to the sense of the Americanness, the need to find a musical language that would have American quality, I had also a-shall we say Hebraic—idea of the grandiose, of the dramatic and the tragic, which was expressed to a certain extent in the Organ Symphony, and very much in the Symphonic Ode. . . . I think now, however, that the Variations was another version of the grandiose, except that it had changed to a very dry and bare grandiosity, instead of the fat grandiosity of a big orchestral work that lasted twenty minutes.

These remarks not only confirm his association of the "Jewish spirit" with the "dramatic and the tragic," but acknowledge such features in his own music as distinct from its "American quality."[18]

Copland's remarks about the "Jewish spirit" resembled his characterization of German art, which he similarly described as "emotional" and "logical," though, in a telling distinction, he contrasted Jewish "grandiosity" with German "bombast," and the Jew's "deep sense of tragedy of all life" with the German's "pessimism." In contrast to both, American, French, and Russian music tended, he thought, to be more "simple" and "natural," the Americans "optimistic," the French "gay," and the Russians "objective." In describing the "bare grandiosity" of his *Piano Variations*, he consequently created an apt metaphor for his Jewish-American identity, in that bareness and grandiosity were, for him, quintessentially American and Jewish traits, respectively.[19]

For Copland, however, the essential point was that a composer could be true to his Jewish heritage without necessarily sounding Eastern European or Middle Eastern; on the contrary, he could and should assimilate his own time and place. This is what drew him time and again to the example of Milhaud: "In Milhaud's compositions," he wrote, "we have proof that a composer can remain profoundly national and at the same time profoundly Jewish."[20]

The Composer as Homosexual

Discussions of Copland's music in the context of gender or sexuality did not publicly surface during the composer's lifetime. Of interest, though, is the fact that some critics described his music as "masculine" and "manly." Copland himself once critically associated Debussy's "curiously feminine nature" with "the realm of feeling as it was understood and reflected by the Romantic artist." From this and other evidence it appears that Copland's identity as a homosexual included conventional notions of gender attributes. Indeed, the concept of a restrained and humane "manliness" seems to have had no small appeal and importance to many American male artists of Copland's generation.[21]

The relation of Copland's gender and sexuality to his work remains largely unexplored. One idea that gained currency in recent years avers that this country's twentieth-century homosexual composers in general wrote, in the words of K. Robert Schwarz, the "tonal, lyrical, more conservative music America wanted to hear," as opposed to its "macho modernists." "There was almost a kind of self-selection in American music," notes Susan McClary. "The straight boys claimed the moral high ground of modernism and fled to the universities, and the queers literally took center stage in concert halls and opera houses and ballet, all of which are musics that people are more likely to respond to." Identifying Copland, Thomson, Barber, Blitzstein, and Bernstein as gay men without long-standing academic affiliations, Mark Levine, in a related vein, asks, "Could it be that the music [in the postwar era] that nevertheless continued to claim ready access to emotional life—tuneful, harmonically secure music—was in some sense *gay* music?"[22]

However intriguing such notions may be, they failed to illuminate the wide variety of styles and aesthetics among gay and straight composers alike. In Copland's case, accessibility was, indeed, a strongly valued aspect of musical communication, but his work as a whole could hardly be described as the "lyrical, more conservative music America wanted to hear" or "tuneful, harmonically secure music."

Copland rarely spoke of sexuality in his own music or anyone else's. When Phillip Ramey suggested to him that the "bittersweet lyricism" heard in the first movement of the Clarinet Concerto had something to do with his homosexuality, or at least with "growing up a loner," he simply responded, "You might have something there." As a reflective artist, he gave the matter some thought—he admitted to Rosamund Bernier that he occasionally wondered whether his homosexuality in any way limited his range—but, as with his Jewishness, his homosexuality largely appeared as a background element to his work. According to Erik Johns,

> Aaron felt that his sexuality was there in the music, that it was represented, but also that it was incidental to his major theme. He also knew that homosexual themes may be there in the music, but in a way so abstract that it is very difficult to pinpoint. This musical way contrasts with the literary, where one can deal with all in a fashion much more direct. Copland felt his sexuality to be there by virtue of general outlook, in breadth of outlook. Indeed, this scope made him a good teacher, sympathetic to all types of musical inflections, to

musicians, to their different backgrounds. There was in Copland the general idea of acceptance—of accepting life and the world as it is—and of making the most of these potentials.

Moreover, romantic tenderness clearly inspired some of his work. Once after a good-looking student walked by him at Tanglewood, he remarked to a friend, "There goes my Fourth Symphony."[23]

Homosexual subtexts in Copland's oeuvre arose most clearly in his texted and dramatic works. This would include the macabre eroticism of *Grohg*, the portrait of a rebel of *Billy the Kid*, the acceptance of difference in *The Second Hurricane*, and the male bonding in *Of Mice and Men* and *The Tender Land*. Moreover, *Rodeo*, *The Heiress*, *The Tender Land*, and *Something Wild*, all of which concern a young woman's sexual and emotional self-discovery, could be seen as "coming out" tales of one kind or another.[24]

Daniel Mathers pioneered such investigation in a paper on *The Tender Land* that treated its composer's sexuality in relation to the more general issues of personal identity and freedom that inform his work, including a correlation between Copland's acceptance of homosexuality as natural and his attraction to the pastoral—an interesting counterpoint to those who found the same trait reflective of his Jewish or American background. More generally, the dialectical complexities of Copland's work arguably incorporate not only a Marxist perspective but the kinds of "binarisms" characteristic of modernist homosexual-identified literature as explored by Eve Kosofsky Sedgwick.[25]

The presence of Copland's music on recent recordings devoted to the work of composers "who just happen to be gay" asks us to consider his courage and his humanity in this particular context. Such new perspectives and added meanings can only enrich our appreciation of his work.[26]

The Composer as American

Although recent studies by Barbara Tischler and Carol Oja have endeavored, with some justification, to place at least Copland's earlier work in the context of "internationalism" and "neoclassicism," the fact remains that from the start of his career, Copland set out to compose music that was "recognizably American" and that reflected "the American scene . . . in musical terms." He had been leaning in this direction at least since writing "Jazzy" (1921), but meeting Rosenfeld and others in the Stieglitz circle no doubt helped reinforce such intentions. "This desire to be 'American' was," he stated in a discussion of his music from the 1920s, "symptomatic of the period."[27]

Although the Americanisms of Copland's output, as he tirelessly pointed out, varied from work to work according to the circumstances of each composition, he remained faithful to the goal of a recognizably American idiom, thus providing some continuity to changes of style and technique over the years. And while in 1941 he argued that "American individuals will produce an American music, without any help from conscious Americanisms," in 1952 he emphasized the constancy of his desire "to find a musical vernacular."[28]

The impetus for Copland's Americanism can be summed up in two words: character and relevance. These two related ideas coalesced while he was a student in Paris; the French music he encountered there "sounded so French," while, he says, its relation "to the life around me became increasingly manifest." From there, the desire to write music that would both sound distinctively American and reflect American life naturally followed. He recognized that such preoccupations were "not so very different from the experience of other young American artists, in other fields, who had gone abroad to study in that period; in greater or lesser degree, all of us discovered America in Europe."[29]

In fact, not every American musician who went abroad during these years came to these same conclusions; certainly, Roger Sessions and Walter Piston reached different ones. Copland's aesthetics had roots in his own temperament; for example, his marked preference for distinctive national styles—the English madrigalists, Mussorgsky, Fauré, the early Stravinsky, Bartók, and Chávez. As with Paul Rosenfeld, music often evoked for him a strong sense of place: Schoenberg with Vienna, jazz with New York, the Poulenc *Mass* with "a sunny church in southern France." In listening to Latin-American and Japanese music, he typically noted the presence or absence of a distinctly national profile. He even admitted a "deep psychological need" for listeners like himself to find "the note" that makes music "characteristically itself," especially as concerned "nations whose music is still unformed." "This attitude may be narrow and wrong," he conceded, "but it is an unpremeditated reaction which rightfully should be balanced by the realization that not all the composers of any country are to be limited to an obviously indigenous expression." On the contrary, he expressed exasperation with "the European music lover who wants our music to be all new, brand-new, absolutely different."[30]

Moreover, he realized that the search for a national style was loaded with pitfalls. Would it result in the kind of "provincial imagination" that he criticized in Smetana, Sibelius, Vaughan Williams, and others? The artist's "emotional states" and the "meaning" and "moral purpose" of music, he argued, transcended questions of style; the vernacular provided a means, not an end.[31]

As for the relation of music to life, he recalled as a young man singing the songs of Hugo Wolf in a world described as "industrial," "commercially minded," "workaday," "crude," and "grim." He did not consider this in itself reprehensible, for music provided "meaning to my own existence, where the world outside had little or none"; but how desirable, he implied, for Americans to have a music that might make contact with and stand up to the real world—as a means, if nothing else, of "revolt."[32]

Copland achieved his ambitions with resounding success; by his life's end, countless listeners found his work "recognizably American" and reflective of "the American scene." William Schuman argued that his more "popular" music could "be perceived as a national American sound." Samuel Lipman similarly stated, "He has succeeded in fixing in the mind of a large public an aural image of what America, and therefore American music, sounds like." Leighton Kerner even admitted the "heresy" of thinking the music of Ives, Harris, Thomson, and Schuman "identifiably American . . . only insofar as it resembles Copland's." Both Kerner and André Previn compared Copland in this regard to Elgar (Kerner also to Vaughan Williams and Mussorgsky). Most recently, director Spike Lee, explaining why he used Copland's music for a film about basketball, stated, "When I listen to his music, I hear America, and basketball is America."[33]

Listeners far and wide felt similarly. "For musicians throughout the world," stated the Englishman Neil Butterworth, "Aaron Copland represents all that characterises the United States." Another Englishman, Kenneth Dommett, claimed that his "sound" was "synonymous" with "the voice of America." Many Latin-American composers especially valued this accomplishment, such as the Argentinian Alberto Ginastera, who observed, "Copland has created American music in the same way Stravinsky did Russian music, or Falla Spanish, or Bartók Hungarian, because he's an artist with a great personality."[34]

Such tributes, which could be duplicated many times over, perhaps overstated the case, for others made similar claims for Foster, Sousa, Carpenter, Ives, Thomson, Gershwin, and Harris, not to mention jazz artists. But Arthur Berger rightly observed that Copland's Americanism had an extraordinary influence on younger composers, partly, he guessed, because he provided such a persuasive intermediary to the American vernacular. In any event, in her *A History of Musical Americanism*, Barbara Zuck concluded, "Copland's musical language, perhaps more than any other . . . has come to be identified as 'American.' " Both she and Alan Howard Levy, author of *Musical Nationalism: American Composers' Search for Identity*, strategically placed Copland at the end of their surveys, suggesting, as Leonard Bernstein did in another context, the composer's Americanism as a kind of culmination.[35]

In discussing what made Copland's music "recognizably American," critics typically mentioned the allusions to and quotations of American popular and folk musics, the jazzy polyrhythms and irregular meters, the vigor and angularity of some melodies, the lean and bare textures and the favored extremes of closely knit harmonies and widely spaced sonorities, and the distinctively brittle piano writing and brassy and percussive orchestrations.

The music further evoked, for many, pictures or feelings associated with New York City and the great open plains and prairies, that is, the "urban congestion and rural expansiveness" that some thought typified America all over the world. Certain works usually smacked of either one or the other, though some suggested both, even at once, the common denominator being the sense of something particularly expansive—either towering skyscrapers or endlessly flat country. "He catches the emptiness of the city and the quiet of the land," wrote Samuel Lipman, as if, perhaps, they were the same thing.[36]

In his 1964 book on American music, Wilfrid Mellers featured this dichotomy in his chapter title "Skyscraper and Prairie: Aaron Copland and the American Isolation." This particular discussion paid more attention to form and harmony than was usual in this context, Mellers noting two distinctive and recurring traits: the music's fragmentary, cubistlike forms and the static, nonmodulatory harmonies. Such features, he argued, underscored the music's essential uprootedness and disintegration, reflective of American alienation. And yet the cubist forms ultimately represented a personal reintegration, like the improbable order of the New York skyline; and the immobile harmonies captured a serenity of sorts, not a religious one, but an affirmative one nonetheless, related to America's geographical immensity.[37]

Arthur Berger also singled out Copland's "immobility," a characteristic, he argued, that critics had long found salient in the poetry of Dickinson and the novels of Faulkner. Other opinions on the matter were voiced: Milhaud spoke, in this nationalist context, of the music's "tremendous sadness," its "underlying distress," and its "sturdy strength"; Michael Tilson Thomas, of its "clangorous defiance"; and Samuel Adler, of its "bigness of heart" and "generosity of spirit."[38]

Although Copland only occasionally discussed the Americanism of his own music, he often spoke about what generally seemed distinctively American in music. He maintained, for instance, that certain rhythmic features—the presence of polyrhythms, the fondness for percussion—most readily distinguished the musics of the Americas from those of Europe. "If there is a school of American composers," he further ventured in 1952, "optimism is certainly its keynote." In 1956, discussing a wide range of American symphonies, he described their general character as "vigorous, bouncy, optimistic, noisy; at other times it may be intricate or brooding, or even plainly sentimental and direct as a hymn tune." And in 1961, when asked in an interview what made a work characteristically American, he mentioned "the optimistic tone," "the love of rather large canvases," "a certain directness in expression of sentiment," and "a certain songfulness."[39]

In the 1970s, even as he granted that the goal of a distinctly American music had become unfashionable, he reasserted, "I would hope that my music is distinctly American because I want to write music that's an expression of the life we live—a zippy rhythm that nobody but an American would dream up, or a largeness of utterance that only a large country can produce, as the end of my symphony evokes a large landscape." He now added the concept of "healthy-sounding" to other long familiar notions:

It's very hard to define the kind of American national music we created. We used actual American musical materials, and jazz-derived things were a strong part of it. But more important was a kind of atmosphere, a very direct singing quality suggestive of a very big country and expansive emotions. No little miniatures. We attempted to write big-sounding, healthy-sounding music somehow reflective of that aspect of America.[40]

While Sessions, Piston, and other colleagues early on challenged the advisability if not the legitimacy of such aims, others more skeptically questioned Copland's motives. Some wondered whether he exploited

American themes for personal fame and fortune, or whether he intended his Americanism as a cover for his Jewishness or his homosexuality. Lazare Saminsky and Paul Rosenfeld voiced such suspicions as early as the 1940s. Even Zuck suggested that Copland "may have felt more compelled to prove himself 'American' because of his ethnic heritage." More recently, Richard Taruskin asserted that Copland, a "left-leaning homosexual Jew from Brooklyn," cashed in on nationalism by creating "an ingratiating white-bread-of-the-prairie idiom that could be applied ad libitum to the higher forms of art." Arthur Berger, meanwhile, contested such allegations, writing, "It took courage to stem the tide of a world inclined towards internationalism, and for this Brooklyn-born Jew and passionate New Yorker it took imagination to surmount parochialism and encompass the whole of America."[41]

One needs to remember that the basic premises for the ballets and films that lay at the heart of this debate originated not from Copland but from the distinguished writers, choreographers, and film directors with whom he collaborated. But such discussion at least raises the intriguing question (surely of interest to Copland himself) of whether an artist—in particular, one belonging to a religious, ethnic, sexual, or political minority—is bound or obliged to remain an outsider.

In his panoramic study of Americanism and the arts (1980), Charles C. Alexander concluded, "The history of cultural nationalism in twentieth-century America is ultimately a story of failure—the failure of an idea and a belief to sustain themselves in the face of swift intellectual and social change. . . . Americans . . . still seemed a long way from their regeneration—through art or otherwise." Yet however far Copland may have succeeded in helping to effect America's "regeneration," he had more modest hopes that were undeniably fulfilled; his music, in all its phases, was recognized as American around the world; and it was not indifferent to the world around him but, on the contrary, looked out onto the land.[42]

29

The Later Years

Copland as Conductor

Although Copland studied conducting briefly in 1921 at Fontainebleau with the composer-conductor Albert Wolff, he was essentially self-taught in that area. He wielded a baton only periodically until he emerged, in the 1950s, as a viable conductor in his own right—and one, moreover, in international demand due not only to his reputation as a composer but to his growing authority as an interpreter of his own and other modern scores.[1]

For many years he conducted exclusively his own music, beginning in 1926, when he tried out an arrangement of the scherzo movement of the *Organ Symphony* in France with an amateur orchestra. In 1930 he took over a rehearsal of his *Symphonic Ode* with the Boston Symphony in order to prove to Koussevitzky that the work could be conducted as written; and although he failed to get through the work's fast sections, the experience marked an important step in his development as both a composer and a conductor.[2]

Other than espousing the idea that composers should be able to conduct their own music, however, Koussevitzy did little to promote Copland's conducting. He did not think much of Copland's abilities as such and was further concerned about him wasting his time. ("You must stay home and compose," he would say, wagging a finger.) "He always seemed to have an image of how a conductor should look," explained Copland, "and that image was much more like Leonard Bernstein than me." Perhaps greater stimulus came from the example of Chávez. In any case, his earliest conducting jobs arose from practical exigencies: conducting *Music for the Theatre* for a Copland-Sessions concert (1931), presiding over the New York performances of *Hear Ye! Hear Ye!* (1934), and leading a WPA orchestra in an all-Copland concert (1936).[3]

Copland's conducting activities intensified in the 1940s. Beginning with *The North Star* (1943) he assumed responsibility for recording his own film scores. On his trips to Latin America, he took advantage of the opportunity to try out his music with professional orchestras in Lima, Santiago, and Havana in 1941, and in Montevideo, Mexico City, and Buenos Aires in 1947, these latter performances including the challenging Third Symphony. Another turning point came in 1946, when he realized he could not substitute for an ailing Eugene Goossens and conduct *Appalachian Spring* with the Cincinnati Symphony. "I date from that episode a determination to learn how to conduct at least my own works," he wrote, adding that Stravinsky's counsel—"My dear, you *should* conduct your own music, every composer should"—furthered his resolve. In 1948 he conducted a Ballet Theatre production of *Billy the Kid* at the Metropolitan Opera.[4]

Reluctant to bother Koussevitzky, Copland occasionally turned to Bernstein for advice. "Lenny, how do you do this?" he would ask. "How do you conduct this part?" Copland enjoyed these informal lessons with Bernstein, who welcomed being able to teach something to his mentor. Observing one such session over the dinner table, Robert Cornell recalled Bernstein saying, "Aaron, you have to loosen up."[5]

In 1951 Copland reached new milestones. On May 1 he made his official European premiere in Rome with a program that included, for the first time, another composer's music—David Diamond's *Rounds*. In Israel, he took choruses through *In the Beginning*. And he began to record his orchestral music: the Piano Concerto with Leo Smit and the Clarinet Concerto with Benny Goodman.

In the following two years such activities subsided, due to work on *The Tender Land* as well as to McCarthy-related difficulties, but 1953 found him conducting not only his own music but Chausson's and Harris's with the National Symphony Orchestra. "I am learning a lot about conducting," he wrote to Victor Kraft. In 1955 he broke new ground by premiering his own music: the orchestrated second set of *Old American Songs* and the final revision of *The Tender Land*. That same year he undertook his first real tour, conducting seven European orchestras: "I was beginning to feel out of the amateur class as far as conducting was concerned," he reflected. More assured, he began programming Ives's *The Unanswered Question*.[6]

Copland's confidence increased further in 1956 as he performed with some major American orchestras, including the Chicago Symphony Orchestra in an all-Copland concert at the orchestra's Ravinia Festival that included the Third Symphony. In 1957 he initiated a long-standing affiliation with the Ojai (California) Festival Orchestra with two concerts that contained more rounded programs than had hitherto been his custom: in addition to his own music, one contained selections by Purcell, Diamond, Britten, and Grieg, the other, by Haydn, Fauré, and Stravinsky. Then, on 30 January 1958, he made his debut with the New York Philharmonic—again conducting the Third—and his television debut with the same orchestra, playing the Third's finale.

After this television appearance, his conducting career, under the management of Arthur Judson, really took off, including a 20 August 1958 debut with the orchestra with which he would become most associated, the London Symphony Orchestra. He toured extensively over the next twenty-five seasons, averaging between ten and twenty orchestras (and consequently twenty to thirty concerts) a year, not including studio sessions, continued film work, appearances with bands and choruses, and engagements with opera and dance companies. As a climax to all this activity, he conducted a free outdoor concert with the National Symphony on Memorial Day 1979 to a crowd estimated at twenty-two thousand.

A natural performer since age five, when he'd recited a poem in the pulpit of his synagogue, Copland found the attractions of conducting many. "It's tempting. It's fun. It's well paying. And you get applauded at the end. The orchestra does all the work and you turn around and take the bow. If you want to be nice, you ask the musicians to stand up, too, the poor dears." Conducting also enabled him to keep active and stimulated; he often referred to an "elderly and wise woman" (namely, Minna Lederman) who had once advised him, "Aaron, it is very important, as you get older, to engage in an activity that you didn't engage in when you were young, so that you are not continually in competition with yourself as a young man."[7]

Moreover, he wanted to demonstrate "how my music should go" and liked the idea of forging such a legacy for posterity, though he had no desire to "establish a definitive version." On the contrary, he relished the unpredictability of each performance. "Even the same orchestra playing the same piece twice never plays it exactly the same way," he once noted. Finally, he welcomed the opportunity to disseminate the music he admired to audiences all over the world. "Conducting puts one in a very powerful position," he explained. "Best of all, it is a use of power for a good purpose."[8]

Although he received offers for permanent conducting positions, he turned these down, preferring to tour. As a guest conductor, he could play a limited repertory week after week, and he could travel widely, an especially attractive perquisite to someone who had a streak of wanderlust. Indeed, he conducted in such places as Istanbul, Prague, Edinburgh, Madrid, San Salvador, and Honolulu specifically because he wanted to visit them. Freelancing also enabled him to accept engagements with student ensembles, something he very much enjoyed. Over the years, he appeared with most of the major and many of the minor orchestras around the globe—not only all over North and South America and Europe but in Russia, Turkey, Israel, Japan, the Philippines, Australia, and New Zealand. This included such novelties as an all-American program with the Berlin Philharmonic.[9]

In his own words, he developed "three types of programs: all-Copland; all-American; American with standard repertoire." Nearly every program contained at least one of his own works, and over time he conducted nearly his entire orchestral output; he recorded much of it as well. Although he regularly brought out his less familiar work (one concert in 1976, for example, included *Statements*, *Inscape*, and the Piano Concerto), he most frequently programmed his more popular pieces. He especially liked conducting *Rodeo* and often concluded concerts with that or another similarly accessible work.[10]

At least until the late 1970s, he only rarely programmed all-Copland concerts, and he ultimately conducted the work of more than eighty composers (mostly from the twentieth century), with a core repertory more extensive than he suggested in his autobiography. Sometimes he had to honor management's request for a work like Rachmaninoff's First Piano Concerto that he would not have scheduled otherwise; but for the most part, he was free to devise his own programs.[11]

Copland's repertoire included a wider variety of works than one might expect, either in view of the style (Wagner's *Siegfried Idyll*) or in terms of sheer size (Mahler's Fourth Symphony). At the same time, there were some notable gaps, including hardly any Beethoven or Debussy. And notwithstanding the fact that Copland promoted a few protégés— particularly Edward Miller and David Del Tredici—and occasionally performed, especially in the late 1960s, some fairly cutting-edge scores— including works by Varèse, Lutoslawski, Xenakis, Henze, Takemitsu, and Feldman—he devoted most of his mixed programs to the work of established twentieth-century composers, filled out by a piece or two from earlier times. As in all things, he sought balance.

Although Copland acknowledged that noncomposing conductors could shed light on a piece by fine-tuning a work (thereby offering the composer a service comparable to that provided by a stage director to a playwright or an editor to a writer), he also believed that, as someone who tended to "relive" a piece as an insider, the composer-conductor uncovered subtleties not necessarily discerned by others. More negatively, this same sensitivity limited the range of works a conductor-composer would want to conduct (except for the likes of Leonard Bernstein and Lukas Foss, "from the inception of their careers, equally adept as performers and composers").[12]

As for the great composer-conductors of his time, including Strauss, Schoenberg, Stravinsky, Hindemith, Chávez, and Britten, he observed that they were all unusually forthright in their conducting. He mentioned Strauss's "markedly cool detachment," Schoenberg's downplaying the "latent hysteria" of *Pierrot Lunaire*, Stravinsky's avoidance of sentimentality, Hindemith's "business-like approach," Britten's simplicity of gesture, and Chávez's "no nonsense" leadership. He felt very much part of this tradition—he acknowledged learning his trade, to some extent, from watching Stravinsky and Hindemith—and reviewers often found his own conducting distinguished for its precision and clarity. "He is not the sort of conductor who insists on imposing his personality upon all music at all times," wrote Martin Bernheimer. "He may even concern himself more with the shape of a composition than with its content. . . . His beat epitomizes clarity, his interpretations reflect analytical intelligence, his manner oozes no-nonsense authority, and the orchestra plays beautifully for him."[13]

Copland handled himself unpretentiously in other ways. In rehearsal he was direct, but typically in a charming way, sometimes indulging in a kind of collegial humor. He took an unpatronizing tone with student groups and he accommodated dancers and singers from the pit. Soloists like Benny Goodman enjoyed playing under his baton, much as soprano Phyllis Curtin liked singing with him at the piano. Remembering his own adolescent shyness before the composer-conductor Henri Rabaud, he gladly welcomed aspiring musicians in the green room after concerts. "As might be expected," remarked David Del Tredici, "he had none of the typical conductorial vanities."[14]

Some record of his rehearsal techniques survives, thanks not only to newspaper reportage but to a commercial release of a rehearsal of *Appalachian Spring* (1974). He rehearsed with the full score spread before him, even for works of his own that he had conducted numerous times. Sitting for the most part, rising for climactic moments, he paid special attention to rhythmic accuracy. In his own music, he strove for a clean, clear sound, warning against overly expressive and sentimental playing, including too much vibrato. "It's too much on the Tchaikovsky side" (or "the Massenet side") became a familiar admonition. He further explained, time and again, that Americans (or Mexicans, when rehearsing *El Salón México*) did not wear their hearts on their sleeves, did not display their feelings in public.[15]

For all his restraint, he cut a boyishly vigorous figure on the podium, one that belied his advancing years and one, further, that distinguished him from many of the composer-conductors he admired. In an early appearance, performing *An Outdoor Overture* with the Boston Pops in 1944, he looked so much like "a modern dancer" that his friends Irving and Verna Fine sat in the audience laughing uncontrollably. Even later descriptions emphasized, often in a humorous way, his verve and élan. "Copland's left toe went a-tapping like a trippy metronome," observed Bernheimer; "his long arms swooped down in angular beats like the awesome wings of some gaunt, giant-size bird; the tails of his podium uniform flew about as if they had a syncopated life of their own; his smiling, bespectacled head bobbed up and down like a happy Halloween apple." Vivian Perlis similarly described "the lean figure with the wide grin, the long arms akimbo, the informal stance on the podium, a kind of running jump on and offstage at the end of a piece," gestures which had become "part of the American consciousness." A videotaped appearance on a Young People's Concert (1958) makes it possible for today's viewer to so observe him—at least at the start of his conducting career.[16]

Copland rarely recorded any music but his own, so a fuller knowledge of his conducting will have to wait until archival tapes of his concerts become more widely accessible. From all accounts, he cultivated a long lyrical line and leisurely tempos that fluctuated slightly. This placed him, according to some observers, in a somewhat romantic tradition. At the same time, critics noted historically sensitive performances of Mozart and Haydn, including significantly reduced forces, carefully balanced sections, and grace notes on the beat. In general, reviews praised his reading of other composers, including a "moving" account of Stravinsky's *Symphony in C* and a "glowing" reading of Fauré's *Pelléas et Mélisande*. "I can remember few more electrifying performances of Walton's *Portsmouth Point* overture than one which Copland gave in London several years ago," reported Andrew Keener in *Gramophone*.[17]

Copland's conducting earned the respect of his colleagues as well. Leonard Slatkin, for instance, remembered some "extraordinary performances." And although Bernstein occasionally joked that Copland should have conducted his own works "a little better," he noted continual technical improvements and thought him, as opposed to Stravinsky and Hindemith, a naturally gifted conductor. He further observed,

> I know that he learned a lot from watching Koussevitzky over the decades, but his conducting is nothing like Koussevitzky's. Nor is it, I think, like mine. It is very personal, his own brand, and it relies a great deal on facial expression, on grins and grimaces. It is very clear conducting and, pragmatically speaking, it's fine. But it is based mainly on Aaron's own charm and personality and on his amiable relationship with the orchestra he happens to be working with.[18]

Orchestra members tended to evaluate his conducting more severely. While they liked his friendly, modest persona and his enormous enthusiasm, and rated him higher than Stravinsky, Hindemith, and most other conductor-composers, they widely characterized his beat as unsteady, his flailing body movements as awkward and ineffective, his podium manner as mechanical, and his interpretations as unexciting. Moreover, his tendency to talk his way through a piece, rather than exact what he wanted through movement, struck some as pedantic. A few also remembered that he could be surprisingly caustic in rehearsal.[19]

And while his amiability, stature, musicality, and, perhaps above all, brilliance as an orchestrator typically won over players in performances of his own music, where he carried obvious authority, when it came to other composers' music, many felt that they carried him along rather than the other way around. As soloists in the Schumann Cello Concerto and the Griffes *Poem* for flute and orchestra, respectively, Laszlo Varga and Donald Peck marveled at his difficulty in simply getting through the work; they assumed that he had not done his homework. Peck also claimed that Copland's "zest" failed him in a work like Ravel's *Mother Goose* suite, while Ray Fliegel, concertmaster of the Houston Symphony, remembered some heavy-handed gestures in Brahms's *Haydn Variations*. Still, orchestral musicians generally enjoyed Copland's guest appearances. "The orchestra didn't take him too seriously," recalled Newton Mansfield, violinist with the New York Philharmonic. "It was like going out to a nice lunch."[20]

For Copland, the experience was not always so nice. The Boston Symphony and the New York Philharmonic occasionally gave him a hard time, notwithstanding his close, lifelong involvement with both orchestras. On a 1959 tour with the BSO, the musicians, unenthusiastic about his conducting and exhausted by the tour's strenuous demands, acted mischievously during a rehearsal of Tchaikovsky's Fifth, putting down their instruments and applauding at that point in the finale when audiences sometimes do so by mistake. Meanwhile, Copland found the New York Philharmonic a "tough" group that resisted playing modern music. Some of the problems with these orchestras stemmed from the fact that Koussevitzky and Bernstein had established standards for playing his own music that he had difficulty meeting. Moreover, both orchestras knew him so well that they tended to take him for granted. In any case, during the regimes of Seiji Ozawa and Pierre Boulez, relations grew even more aloof, in part because neither director was that close to his music. "Aaron was having a wonderful time conducting all over the world," recalled Harry Kraut, "and it may have been hard for him to understand why Boston and New York did not pay the same attention to him as a conductor."[21]

This was something of an exaggeration. Copland also had problems with other orchestras, as Kraut well knew, having witnessed a Parisian orchestra's behaving so rudely to him that Kraut had Bernstein upbraid the manager of the orchestra. Copland himself criticized the "reluctant cooperation" of some German radio orchestras, the lack of sympathy for American music among French and Italian orchestras, and the Turkish orchestras who similarly showed "only a mild sign of interest in the new music they were reading." In contrast, he developed mutually satisfying relationships with major orchestras in upstate New York, the Midwest, Texas, California, and Great Britain.[22]

In appraising orchestras, Copland often mentioned rhythmic precision and ease, especially in playing American music, and a show of involvement and cooperation. Rhythmically, he thought American orchestras the world's best, the British running a close second—perhaps, he guessed, because of "a kind of Anglo-Saxon connection there." But in terms of involvement, he preferred the London Symphony Orchestra, the Mexico Symphony Orchestra, and even student groups to America's "business-like" professional orchestras.[23]

An enthusiastic attitude and careful preparation combined to make the London Symphony Orchestra one of his favorites. They played, he once said, "as though they still loved music." For close to two decades, he conducted the London Symphony nearly every season, and it was with the LSO that he did most of his studio work. He liked English orchestras quite generally, "because the players are such *gentlemen*. They are inclined to help you in any way they can to get the job done."[24]

Concurrently—and no doubt relatedly—English journalists and audiences received Copland as conductor far more warmly than did their American counterparts. Whereas American critics acknowledged his "competent" conducting in respectful and sometimes patronizing language, the English much more affectionately praised his vigor and charm. One would have to look far among American reviews for the likes of this review from the *Sunday Telegraph* (1968): "His style on the rostrum is relaxed, economical and attractively informal, the audience being immediately caught up by his zest and vitality, by his concentration and physical enjoyment of the music. Above all his performances possessed an exhilarating rhythmic energy which can be traced to his own style of composition." Or this one from the *Financial Times* (1968): "Copland conducted as if his sixty-eight years were hardly more than thirty-five. He has a wiry, precise vigour and a hugely engaging manner. . . . The LSO clearly found his high spirits infectious, and followed every jubilant nuance with enthusiastic attention." Such reviews highlight the fact that by the late 1960s he was, in some ways, more deeply revered in England than in the United States; although he attributed this to his having a London-based publisher, other factors seem to have been at work.[25]

Copland conducted his last concert on 7 December 1982 with the New Haven Symphony. That he maintained his career as long as he did was amazing, especially considering that he had slowly been losing his memory since the mid-1970s. Ned Rorem reacted with wonder that "the elderly Aaron Copland, who drew blanks from one five-minute period to the next, was nonetheless able to conduct his half-hour *Appalachian Spring* from start to finish—though on leaving the stage he could not recall what he had just performed; he had been wafted by the rote, by the inertia, by the programmed kinetics of his own creation." During his last few years on the road, orchestras often indulged him, but his appearances became increasingly embarrassing, as he would absentmindedly ask players to repeat certain passages in rehearsal or would lose his place in performance. Eventually he simply had to give it up.[26]

Copland rarely spoke about the future of orchestras and orchestral music. He expressed some concern that as orchestras played less contemporary music, the institution threatened to become antiquated. He also pondered, especially in the 1960s and early 1970s, the low ebb of interest in the orchestra among younger composers. Nonetheless, he believed in the viability of the orchestra as both institution and medium. "The orchestra is too glamorous, with too many opportunities, to ignore completely," he observed. "Anyway, the orchestra has always been about ten years behind what is going on musically."[27]

At Home

After he separated from Erik Johns in 1952, Copland felt the need for professional secretarial assistance; he had the financial wherewithal to pay someone, and with his newfound fame came greater demands on his time. Samuel Barber recommended a young composer, David Walker (b. 1919), who had studied at the Manhattan School with Vittorio Giannini and had then worked for Gian Carlo Menotti in nearby Mount Kisco. Copland met Walker at Barber's home and hired him.[28]

Walker worked for Copland three and a half days a week for over thirty years (1952–85). He would stay at Shady Lane Farm and later Rock Hill from Tuesday to Friday (Copland provided him with a bedroom) and then for the weekends return to his apartment in Greenwich Village, where he pursued his own career as a composer of electronic music. A soft-spoken, discreet, and efficient assistant, Walker made phone calls, screened appointments, filed letters and scores, and copied music. Even after Copland's official retirement, he continued to help arrange his affairs right through the composer's 1991 memorial concert. "I think possibly the reason that Aaron and I had such a long and workable relationship is that we tended naturally to, so to speak, stay out of each other's way," Walker told Vivian Perlis. "By that, I mean that we shared whatever work was to be done without any intrusions of a personal nature."[29]

At first, Walker prepared meals as well—"Copland couldn't open a can of soup," he joshed—but eventually a local woman from Ossining came in to clean and cook. With the move to Rock Hill, guest quarters made it possible to lodge full-time domestics, and in the 1960s and early 1970s, a Belgian couple, Mireille and Gaston Vanaertenryck, sporadically lived on the premises in that capacity.[30]

Around 1974, Copland hired a handsome and charming young friend, Sophronus Mundy (b. 1940), to live at Rock Hill and supervise the household. Copland had first met Mundy around 1960 through the artist Richard Schiff. As Mundy pursued a master's degree in social work, he and his then current lover, the painter and critic Richard Hennessy (b. 1941), frequently traveled up from New York to Rock Hill on weekends, staying even for entire months during the summer. Still in their twenties, they enlivened the atmosphere; Mundy, a talented cook, would supervise "fabulous" parties and get the abstemious Copland, giggling with delight, to drink a whiskey sour. He and Hennessy helped out with the gardening and interior design, persuading Copland to install recessed lighting and purchase a glass-and-chrome Mies van der Rohe coffee table; in addition, Copland acquired two of Hennessy's paintings. Mundy and Hennessy independently remained friends with Copland after they broke up around 1970; when Mundy moved to Rock Hill permanently in the mid-1970s, his new lover, Paul Manow, also visited on weekends. [31]

Once established at Rock Hill, Mundy became somewhat imperious, all the more emboldened by Copland's growing senility. "Remember, you're not working for Aaron, you're working for me!" he told Chris Cole, a local painter who helped out with odd jobs and gardening. "Sophronus took advantage of Aaron in every conceivable way," recalled Walker. "People saw that, I saw that, but I didn't meddle." David Conte, living at Rock Hill for an extended visit, was shocked at the way Mundy bullied Copland. "He was a very mentally unstable person and became progressively more so as he got older," noted Hennessy, who, recalling Copland's friendship with Victor Kraft and others, detected a pattern. At the same time, Hennessy realized that Mundy had "a huge investment in

Aaron's distinction" and felt threatened by his deterioration, whereas others "were all too eager to sweep it under the rug." Mundy finally left Rock Hill in 1982 after sounding an ultimatum similar to the one made by John Kennedy in the 1950s; he threatened to quit unless Copland fired Chris Cole. "Well, go," responded Copland.[32]

By the mid-1970s Copland had begun to have trouble with his short-term memory. "My memory isn't as hot as it used to be," he told a reporter in 1975. For many years he had enjoyed good health, aside from the dental problems that plagued him his entire life and occasional spells of dizziness, loss of vision, and headaches—diagnosed as migraines—that dated back to the 1950s. His loss of memory scared him, because his father and his sister Laurine had both succumbed to dementia in their later years, a fate he hoped he would be spared. He consulted specialists—one doctor prescribed vitamins—but nothing really could be done. He typically made light of the situation, saying that his doctor had told him, upon hearing about his memory problems, "Just forget about it."[33]

In the late 1970s his memory noticeably worsened. While dining out in a restaurant with Christopher Rouse in 1978, he repeatedly asked the same question in a loud voice, evoking disdainful looks from other patrons. At Christmas dinner that same year, John Kenworthy-Browne found that "already he had largely lost his memory." And in 1980 he startled Sam Adler by phoning him, unable to remember why. The public began to take note as well; an eightieth-birthday newspaper tribute mentioned his confusion about his age. Although the symptoms resembled those of Alzheimer's, his primary physician at the time, Arnold Salop, could not make a definitive diagnosis as to the kind of dementia he suffered from.[34]

Copland handled the situation as well as could be hoped for. He curtailed public appearances and learned to keep his remarks to a minimum—"Thank you very much, ladies and gentleman" was his entire speech upon receiving an honorary doctorate from the State University of New York at New Paltz. When attending symposiums or radio interviews, he often brought Phillip Ramey along to help ameliorate his dazed lapses and disturbing repetitions. For his last radio interview—a New York Philharmonic intermission feature in 1985—he and Ramey actually read their questions and answers over the air, a sadly stilted affair. Michael O'Connor, who worked for Copland in the mid-1980s, admired the way he cultivated various strategies to help defuse awkward moments: "And how do we *know* this Mrs. [Geraldine] Ferraro?" he would ask in his roguish singsong, or, upon learning the current year, he might say, "1986! Why it was *just* 1926 the other day!" David Conte similarly recalled Copland's response in 1982 when he had to be reminded, upon settling into his seat at a Graham recital, that he was to conduct *Appalachian Spring* on the concert's second half: "Well, young man, it's a good thing you're here to tell me, or I would have wandered off at the intermission to have a cigarette!" Remarked Verna Fine, "Even in his senility he was a very sweet man."[35]

Copland became that much more dependent on Sylvia Goldstein at Boosey & Hawkes; Ellis Freedman, his lawyer since 1973; Sidney Korsch, his accountant; and eventually his niece Felice's son Roger Levey, who became his executor. Some friends were alarmed in particular at the large role that Freedman began to play in Copland's life, in part because of his persona as a high-powered attorney and in part because Copland seemed sadly neglected.[36]

In the meantime, Victor Basso succeeded Mundy as caretaker, managing the household, cooking meals, and keeping track of nurses from 1982 to 1987. Basso, who had worked as a cook for Lincoln Kirstein and came recommended by Copland's old friend Robert Cornell, brought on board as cohelpers his friends Michael O'Connor, Irene Wiley (and her boyfriend Elliott Goldenthal, later a successful film composer), and eventually Patrick O'Shea. They were young, lively people in their twenties and thirties, all aspiring to theatrical careers; O'Connor was somewhat taken aback when Copland offered to help him rehearse "Zip-a-Dee-Doo-Dah" for an upcoming audition.[37]

Under Basso's regime, the atmosphere at Rock Hill became even more chaotic than it had been under Mundy. Basso began moving furniture, buying appliances, painting rooms, and hiring and firing staff, including O'Connor. Finally, after hearing of some dubious activities, Ellis Freedman fired him.[38]

Even Basso's detractors acknowledge, however, that all the commotion stimulated the increasingly isolated Copland, explaining in part why he tolerated this "madhouse" for the years he was still able to do something about it. And Copland seemed genuinely fond of Basso and the other young people in his employ. The vivacious Wiley especially amused everyone with her risqué stories, sometimes prompting Copland, with mock offense, to exclaim, "And I thought this was a *respectable* household!"[39]

Another diversion came in the way of his collaboration with Vivian Perlis on an autobiography. Copland first met Perlis, then a reference librarian at Yale, sometime around 1969 on a visit to the university's Ives collection. He subsequently agreed to write the foreword for her published oral history of Ives (1974) and then, in 1976, to relate his life's story for the Oral History, American Music Project at Yale that she directed. After numerous interviews, he "was amazed to see the transcripts of the interviews, which in size resembled nothing less than two very large Manhattan telephone books." He and Perlis decided to use these transcripts—along with other interviews Perlis had conducted—as the basis for a book (a procedure reminiscent of his three previous books, each similarly based on a series of lectures). They also collaborated on a documentary, *Aaron Copland: A Self Portrait* (1979), coproduced by Perlis and Ruth Leon, directed by Allan Miller, and first broadcast by PBS in 1985 as part of their *American Masters* series.[40]

Copland and Perlis published their completed manuscript in two volumes: *Copland: 1900 Through 1942* (1984) and *Copland Since 1943* (1989). These books included not only Copland's first-person narrative but eleven separate "interludes" by Perlis and excerpted conversations with friends and colleagues. That Copland agreed to have others join in the telling of his life says much about the man.[41]

Both volumes met with good reviews, though some, like John Rockwell and Robin Holloway, criticized what seemed to be an overreliance on previously published writings. In fact, Copland and Perlis compiled the work, especially the second volume, at a time when he was losing his memory, leaving them little choice but to rely increasingly on old documents. But throughout they also made extensive and trenchant use of letters and other unpublished sources. And in any case, such a masterful compilation of so much material was invaluable.[42]

A related but more widely expressed criticism concerned the books' reticence; readers missed, among other things, intimate portraits of the composer's family, friends, and romantic relationships. In addition, Copland steered away from any distressing incidents, telling Perlis, "Agonizing is not my thing." A few readers and friends spoke of Copland coming across as "entombed" or "embalmed." One wonders, however, why anyone would expect Copland to unburden himself in print when he avoided discussing personal matters with his closest friends. The more pertinent question remains how such discretion contributed to his achievement as both a man and an artist. Nor are the books as impersonal as has been occasionally alleged; on the contrary, they richly reveal Copland's warmth and wit.[43]

As the 1980s wore on, Copland's condition deteriorated further. He became extremely disoriented, not recognizing people or places. His hearing, which had been bad for a while, became much worse. He also developed borderline diabetes and ischemia and suffered a series of small strokes, making him all the more frail.

After a colostomy in 1985, a nurse, Donal Morrison, moved into the house. That same year Walker, disturbed by Copland's decline as well as by those taking charge of his life, resigned his position. His replacement, Ronald Caltabiano (b. 1959), was a composer in his twenties who had studied at Juilliard with Persichetti and Carter. Like Walker, he filed and helped answer letters, and made and answered telephone calls. During his first years at Rock Hill, he remembered that Copland spent most of his time reading the newspaper, magazines, or such favored authors as Gide, Bowles, and Paul Goodman or listening to recordings, often something by Stravinsky, Schuman, or Bernstein, though open to Caltabiano's own suggestions.[44]

For a few years, Copland had enough lucidity, especially in the morning, to help direct business affairs. As late as October 1986, he reviewed a list of possible candidates for a proposed revision of *What to Listen for in Music* (he named, in preferential order, Schuman, Bernstein, and Andrew Porter, nixing other suggestions). But by 1987 his faculties had so declined that Caltabiano had to turn to Walker, Perlis, and Freedman for guidance on a variety of matters.[45]

After Basso's dismissal in 1987, Freedman and Roger Levey arranged for nurses, working in three shifts, to care for Copland and the house. In 1989, Caltabiano left Rock Hill in order to pursue his own career, and another young composer, Christopher Culpo, replaced him as secretary. Copland spent his last four years—from 1987 through 1990—in poor shape, reading and rereading the same newspaper or simply staring at the television set. However, at no time did those responsible consider placing him in a nursing home, feeling that at-home care was more dignified.

Unfortunately, he was rather isolated in Cortlandt. He had no really close family, and many friends found it painful or disturbing to spend time with him, especially after that point at which he seemed unable to recognize people. "Painful or not, his friends should have paid more rather than less attention," notes Vivian Perlis; Perlis, Verna Fine, and Phillip Ramey were among the few who regularly continued to visit. Fine thought Copland's care particularly slipshod and careless after Donal Morrison left. When Perlis and her husband drove up to Rock Hill on Copland's ninetieth birthday—coincidentally the same day as the Bernstein memorial concert at Carnegie Hall—they found no other visitors, nor any special provisions, such as a cake. At the same time, Perlis felt that the nurses on staff tried to make his final years as comfortable and peaceful as possible. To the end, Copland maintained a certain poise and confidence, showing some presence before guests, reacting positively to music, and—the old pianist's habit—drumming his fingers.[46]

Copland died at Phelps Memorial Hospital in North Tarrytown, New York, on 2 December 1990, some weeks after his ninetieth birthday. His physician, Charles Starke, reported that he died of respiratory failure brought on by pneumonia and that he had suffered two strokes in the preceding weeks. As specified by his will, he was cremated, his ashes eventually buried on the grounds at Tanglewood in a private, nonreligious ceremony without eulogy, as also specified. His will further requested that any possible memorial service be a purely musical one, and pursuant to his wishes, David Walker helped organized a concert in his honor on 20 April 1991. Lukas Foss, Fenwick Smith, Gilbert Kalish, Leo Smit, Roberta Alexander, David Del Tredici, Isaac Stern, William Warfield, and the Harvard Glee Club performed a wide range of his works before a large assembly, including such friends as Arthur Berger, John Cage, David Diamond, Verna Fine, and Vivian Perlis. "Not every memorial concert ends with a standing ovation," reported John Rockwell in the *New York Times*. "This one did, not only for the quality of the music-making, but also for the continuing affection with which Copland's memory is held by the musical public."[47]

Copland drew up one will in 1970 with his attorney Abraham Friedman as sole executor, and another in 1984 with Ellis Freedman, his grandnephew Roger Levey, and Citibank as joint executors. Both wills were much the same, differing only in a few details. He left larger amounts—ranging from $7,500 to $50,000—to family members, his godson Jeremy Kraft, David Walker, and (in the earlier of the two wills, before their deaths) Victor Kraft and Harold Clurman, and smaller amounts of a few thousand dollars to other friends and more distant relatives. He also left donations to the MacDowell Colony, the Henry Street

Settlement Music School, and the Lili Boulanger Memorial Fund, as well as a complete set of his published works to selected university libraries. The balance of his large estate he bequeathed to the creation of the Aaron Copland Fund for Composers. He originally intended for the fund to financially assist composers under the age of forty and to sponsor as well fellowships that would allow foreign composers to study in the States; but the revised will cited its mission more generally as encouraging and improving "the public knowledge and appreciation of serious American contemporary music," with the aid to younger composers part of the larger picture.[48]

Copland requested that some eminent composer friends—Berger, Bernstein, Carter, Druckman, Smit, Schuman, and Del Tredici—serve, along with Freedman and Perlis, on the fund's board of directors. As Bernstein died shortly before Copland, the board voted Lukas Foss in his stead and made a place, too, for another composer, John Harbison. Faced with hundreds of applications requesting literally millions of dollars, the fund, in 1992, began granting over $600,000 a year to performing groups, in mostly small grants averaging about $4,000 apiece. About one-third of these moneys were earmarked for performing groups playing contemporary American music as part of the Performing Ensembles Program, and about half went more specifically to the recording of such music through the fund's Recording Program, the balance covering supplementary expenses. The fund's directors, however, decided not to extend grants and fellowships to composers per se; the executors even changed the organization's name (as Copland's will permitted) to the Aaron Copland Fund for Music, Inc.[49]

Meanwhile, other institutions helped promote Copland's name and ideals. The American Music Center, which Copland had cofounded in 1939, continued its work of collecting and distributing composers' scores on a non-profit basis. The music department at Queens College, CUNY, became the Aaron Copland School of Music in 1981. In 1993 the Copland Heritage Association of Cortlandt was established in the hopes of restoring and maintaining Rock Hill as a retreat for younger composers. (The Aaron Copland Fund aided the association by providing the town of Cortlandt wiht a long-term lease to the house for a token annual fee of one dollar.) And in 1996 the Copland Society formed to help garner nationwide support for the association's fund-raising objectives.[50]

Copland left his musical manuscripts, letters, photographs, recordings of his music, and other personal materials to the Library of Congress;

his scores of North and South American composers to the New York Public Library; and, aside from a few books and records that went to friends, the remainder of his library to the Brooklyn Library. As a result, the Library of Congress became custodians of the mammoth Copland Collection, containing approximately four hundred thousand items, including scores, sketches, books, articles, clippings, pamphlets, lecture notes, letters, diaries, cards, programs, certificates, medals, recordings, pamphlets, financial statements, contracts and other legal papers, photographs, and more, making it one of the largest collections devoted to a single musician in the world. It took ten library staff members a few years to process this collection, which opened to the public in late 1995 and which stands as a remarkable monument to the man and his music.[51]

Conclusion

Success came neither quickly nor easily to Aaron Copland. As a young and impoverished composer in his twenties and thirties, he faced for the most part a hostile public, an unsympathetic press, and an indifferent musical establishment. He survived during these difficult years thanks to the help of a small circle of patrons, friends, and relatives, as well as to some crucial institutional support.

Throughout the 1940s, his popularity and fame grew, largely due to the success of his ballets and film scores. By the early 1950s, the concert-going public widely considered him the time's foremost serious American composer. His reputation survived the smears of McCarthyism better, perhaps, than the stigma of popularity itself; by the 1960s, even as his name had become enshrined among the global audience for modern dance, motion pictures, and symphony concerts, sophisticates sometimes adopted a condescending attitude. Still, he died tremendously revered, as both man and composer.

The enormous fame of the ballets and the relative neglect of the piano and chamber pieces gave rise to the notion that there were two Coplands: one popular, the other serious. Copland himself liked telling the following anecdote: While out in Hollywood scoring *The North Star* for Samuel

Goldwyn, he met Groucho Marx at a recital that included his Piano Sonata. When during the intermission Marx expressed surprise at the work's modern language, Copland explained, "Well, you see, I have a split personality." "It's okay, Copland," responded Marx, "as long as you split it with Sam Goldwyn."[1]

Copland undeniably had tremendous versatility, often gauging a work's ambition and complexity in terms of not only targeted performers and audiences, but particular genres and venues. But such range cannot be reduced to two large categories; between the extremes of *Fanfare for the Common Man* and the *Piano Fantasy* one encounters a broad spectrum of work, with many pieces falling, so to speak, between the cracks. Moreover, all of Copland's works feature, for all their differences, the highest standards of craftsmanship and integrity and the same unmistakably individual stylistic voice. Those who knew his work best, such as Harold Clurman, William Schuman, Elliott Carter, Leonard Bernstein, and William Austin, often emphasized this point.

Because Copland composed many of his most popular pieces around the time of the Second World War, commentators have further assumed that his career forms an arch, with the most accessible scores clustered at the center. In the late 1930s and early 1940s, Copland admittedly wrote an unusually large number of works intended (for a variety of reasons) for a more general audience. But works of varying accessibility alternate throughout his entire career.

More subtle but similarly problematic is the widely held view that Copland's career divides into four stylistic periods: a "jazz" period (1920s), an "abstract" period (early 1930s), an "Americana" period (late 1930s and 1940s), and a "twelve-tone" period (1950s and 1960s). This paradigm took root from the composer's own autobiographical sketch (1941) and Julia Smith's early monograph (1955). But whatever its general validity, it has spawned many misunderstandings.[2]

Copland grew up hearing and liking American popular music, ragtime, and early jazz, and this general repertory influenced his music throughout his career, at least as early as *The Cat and the Mouse* (1920) and, more explicitly, *Three Moods* for piano (1921)—that is, independently of the famous "jazz" pieces by Milhaud and Gershwin. Although he more fully came to appreciate the potential of the American vernacular while in Europe in the 1920s, his assimilation of it was hardly an affectation inspired by European trends, but rather a natural development for a composer growing up in Brooklyn in the early years of the twentieth century and one, moreover, eager both to strike a distinctive note and to make contact with the world in which he lived. He himself could not play jazz; and his "symphonic jazz" of the twenties should not be misconstrued as inferior jazz but rather should be seen as concert music that parodies some of jazz's techniques and moods for its own purposes.

Nor did Copland ever renounce jazz, a misconception fostered especially by his 1941 remark "With the [1926] Piano Concerto, I felt I had done all I could with the idiom." Such statements alluded to symphonic jazz of a certain sort, not to jazz per se, which continued to inform his work, sometimes explicitly, though more typically indirectly as a pervasive background element. As for his personal admiration and respect for real jazz, it only increased over the years; in the late 1930s he became an outspoken Ellington enthusiast, and his interest in jazz peaked in the 1950s in the wake of such artists as Lennie Tristano, Charles Mingus, and Billy Taylor. He always acknowledged that the most characteristically distinctive rhythms of the Americas—in and out of the concert hall—had their origin in African-American culture.[2]

The argument that the period 1929–35 constituted an "abstract" period usually cited one or more of four works: the *Symphonic Ode*, the *Piano Variations*, the *Short Symphony*, and *Statements*. Aside from the fact that, in these same years, Copland wrote a piano trio inspired by a play, incidental music to another play, a ballet, and a chorus, these four works belie the concept of abstraction, not only in some of their titles (especially the six subtitles for *Statements*), but in their expressive markings and stylistic allusions, including quotations of and references to other works. Nor have writers explained how the presumed abstraction of these works differs from that of, say, the *Organ Symphony* (1924), the Piano Sonata (1941), the *Nonet* (1960), or the *Duo* (1971).

By "Americana," commentators have in mind the appearance of Anglo-American folk music in Copland's music dating from *The Second Hurricane* (1937) and *Billy the Kid* (1938). Such usage involved a number of factors, including musicodramatic exigencies, the dissemination of folk song in leftist circles, and possibly the example of Virgil Thomson and others, including writers and photographers.

Still, the notion of an "Americana" period seems misleading for a number of reasons. The bulk of Copland's compositions from the late 1930s and 1940s makes the most tenuous use, if any, of American folk music. At the same time, he used, throughout his career, not only American folk and popular music—from "The Sidewalks of New York" (in

1925) to "Amazing Grace" (in 1964)—but musical materials from Jewish Eastern Europe, Austria, Germany, France, England, Mexico, Israel, Spain, Russia, Poland, Cuba, Brazil, Venezuela, and no doubt elsewhere.

The notion of a late "twelve-tone" period is likewise riddled with difficulties, not the least involving Copland's free and personal use of the twelve-tone method itself. Moreover, he essentially wrote only four twelve-tone works—the Piano Quartet (1950), the *Piano Fantasy* (1957), *Connotations* (1962), and *Inscape* (1967). While this includes some of the more ambitious works of his later years, he concurrently wrote other works that did not use the twelve-tone method.

A related cliché contends that the twelve-tone works represented a futile attempt to stay current. In fact, Copland adapted the method prior to its widespread popularity among American composers. One might add, too, that these twelve-tone works achieved a success comparable to Copland's more challenging chamber and orchestral scores from previous years. The *Piano Fantasy* in particular enjoyed the kind of critical acclaim that only occasionally greeted his more adventurous work.

All this is not to say that one cannot detect stylistic trends in Copland's work over time. Indeed, he had an uncanny ability to absorb a wide variety of styles, techniques, and ideals and respond to a variety of stimuli without sacrificing his own authentic, inimitable voice. From his assimilation of the European classics and Jewish music in his youth; to Debussy, Scriabin, and ragtime in his teenage years; to Mahler, Stravinsky, Milhaud, and jazz in Paris; to Harris and Chávez in the late 1920s; to Blitzstein, Thomson, swing jazz, and Anglo-American and Mexican folklore in the 1930s; to South American and Caribbean musics in the 1940s; to Boulez, cool jazz, and medieval music in the 1950s; to Ives in the 1960s, Copland's art continually grew and developed as he made contact with a great range of musics and opinions. This remarkable adaptability helped keep his music fresh and relevant.

Even before Copland completed his last compositions in the early 1970s, the press reported that he had stopped composing because of some supposed antipathy toward the times. It would seem, however, that such assertions had little foundation. Copland always balanced a sharply critical view of the world with a determination to go on and do one's best. Although some clearly presumed that Copland shared their bitterness and despair, he did not. He only admitted that he had difficulty, as he entered his seventies, getting new ideas and that he would rather not compose at all than merely repeat himself. Moreover, by the mid-1970s he was experiencing memory loss. So in fact, not much time transpired between his final compositions and the onset of the dementia that afflicted his final years.

Admittedly, in the course of the 1950s and 1960s, Copland came to occupy a less central position than he had held in the 1940s, at least among large numbers of composers, critics, and historians. Many of his most esteemed contemporaries shared a similar fate, including Hindemith, Prokofiev, Milhaud, Harris, and Piston. Even those for whom Copland remained an important figure could better evaluate the limitations of his work. Such reappraisal involved not only a natural swing of the pendulum and the kinds of discontinuities especially characteristic of the history of American concert music, but the sheer difficulty of meeting standards set by Bach, Beethoven, Stravinsky, and others. Still, Copland continued to reach a wider and more varied audience than virtually any American successor, an achievement, however, that presumably afforded him only a limited satisfaction, as his ultimate ambition concerned not so much his own fame as the growth and development of serious music in the Americas.

Complementing misconceptions about Copland's career were those about his person. Some suggested, for instance, that he disavowed his Jewish background and his homosexuality, assumptions derived partly from his disinclination to talk about his personal life. But he calmly and unapologetically accepted both his ethnicity and his sexuality.

The occasional allegations of prejudice against women composers were similarly specious. While discussing the apparent lack of great women composers, he sometimes wondered aloud whether musical composition was uncongenial to women; but in drawing attention to such remarks, commentators have unfairly neglected his very real assistance, as both friend and mentor, to numerous women composers throughout his life.

Some in the musical community—especially rival composers—promoted the idea that Copland's support of American music was in other ways partisan. Such perceptions, often fueled by frustration and resentment, sometimes imagined him heading up a powerful cabal variously populated by New Yorkers, Jews, homosexuals, Communists, Boulanger students, populists, modernists, nationalists, or some combination thereof. Copland would have been the first to admit that his personal taste veered away from music he thought experimental, academic, reactionary, hackneyed, or commercial and toward well-crafted pieces with personality. But he shunned sectarianism; and as a concert organizer, publisher, administrator, advocate, writer, conductor, teacher, and friend, he made unparalleled contributions to his profession as a whole.

Still, it is Copland's music that represents his greatest achievement. He wrote about one hundred works large and small, not a huge output but one exceptional in its diversity, embracing opera and ballet, chorus and song, orchestra and band, chamber ensemble and solo piano, radio, film, and television—music, moreover, for a wide range of players, from schoolchildren to virtuosi, and music of consistently fine quality, practically all of it currently in print. Virgil Thomson had this extraordinary versatility in mind when he approvingly quoted Leonard Bernstein's remark "It's the best we've got." "The Copland catalog," he explained, "has good stuff under every heading, including that of opera."[3]

Moreover, a large number of these works have become part of the standard American repertory, including, for orchestra, *Music for the Theatre*, *El Salón México*, *An Outdoor Overture*, *Quiet City*, the suites from *Billy the Kid*, *Rodeo*, and *Appalachian Spring*, *Danzón Cubano*, *Lincoln Portrait*, the Third Symphony, the Clarinet Concerto, and the *Red Pony Suite*; for band, *Emblems*; for chamber ensemble, *Vitebsk*, *Fanfare*, the Violin Sonata, and the *Duo*; for voice, *In the Beginning*, the *Dickinson Songs*, the *Old American Songs*, and *The Tender Land*; and much of the solo piano music. His less popular work is at least regularly revived, and his place in the repertory continues to expand; it is not at all unusual to find in a given year, somewhere in the world, a performance of the Piano Concerto, *Statements*, the *Nonet*, or *Connotations*.

One cannot simply cite as reasons for this extraordinary accomplishment Copland's use of jazz or folk music or the twelve-tone method; others have exploited such resources with far less success. Nor did he forge any strikingly original techniques, notwithstanding his absorption of a variety of new methods. Rather, one must look to his individual voice, one that in part bespoke a twenties sensibility—lean, incisive, ironic—but one with its own unforgettable personality. Indeed, Copland had perhaps the most distinctive and identifiable musical voice produced by this country so far, an individuality—in some part fashioned by vaulting melodies, jazzy polyrhythms, bright colors, open textures, bluesy harmonies, and collagelike structures—that helped define for many what American concert music sounds like at its most characteristic and that exerted enormous influence on multitudes of contemporaries and successors.

Further elucidating Copland's achievement are the startling dichotomies embodied by both the man and his work: his output encompasses nervous violence and utter calm, austere severity and childlike whimsy, knowing sarcasm and naive tenderness, wistful loneliness and civic solidarity.

Earthy, daring, expressive, and personal, his music is also elegant, restrained, objective, and humane. A participant in the avant-garde, he wrote works of popular appeal; respectful of the great European traditions, he embraced the musics and cultures of the Americas; a private individual, he took to heart the health of his profession and the fears and aspirations of the average person; a Jewish, homosexual, liberal New Yorker, he created an American musical language; sensitive to life's "tragic reality," he remained resiliently optimistic. To America and the world he left this paradoxical legacy.

Appendix:
List of Works

All works are published unless stated otherwise; all arrangements are by the composer.

OPERA

The Second Hurricane (school play–opera, 2 acts, Edwin Denby), 1936, New York, 21 April 1937, Henry Street Settlement Music School, cond. Lehman Engel

The Tender Land (opera, 2 acts, Horace Everett, pseudonym for Erik Johns), 1952–54, New York, 1 April 1954, New York City Opera, cond. Thomas Schippers; rev. 3 acts, 1955, 2 August 1954, Tanglewood, cond. Frederic Waldman; final rev., Oberlin, OH, 20 May 1955, cond. Copland; orch suite, 1958, Chicago, 10 April 1958, Chicago SO, cond. Fritz Reiner

BALLET

Grohg, 1922–25, rev. 1932, London, 20 June 1992, London Sinfonietta, cond. Oliver Knussen (rev. version); "Dance of the Adolescent," arr. 2 pf, 1933; excerpt *Cortège Macabre* and *Dance Symphony,* see Orchestral

Hear Ye! Hear Ye!, 1934, Chicago, 30 Nov 1934, cond. Rudolph Ganz

Billy the Kid, 1938, Chicago, 6 Oct 1938 (with 2 pf); New York, 24 May 1939, cond. Fritz Kitzinger; orch suite, 1939, New York, 9 Nov 1940, NBC SO, cond. William Steinberg; arr. 2 pf, 1946; excerpts arr. chamber orch, 1946, vn, pf, 1950, vc, pf, 1952

Rodeo, 1942, New York, 16 Oct 1942, cond. Franz Allers; 4 dance episodes, orch, 1942, Boston, 28 May 1943, Boston Pops Orch, cond. Arthur Fiedler (3 episodes only); New York, 22 June 1943, New York PO, cond. Alexander Smallens; arr. pf, 1946; "Hoe-Down" arr. string orch, 1946, vn, pf, 1946

Appalachian Spring, fl, cl, bn, pf, 4 vn, 2 va, 2 vc, db, 1943–44, Washington, DC, 30 Oct 1944, cond. Louis Horst; suite, orch, 1945, New York, 4 Oct 1945, New York PO, cond. Arthur Rodzinski; complete ballet, orch, 1954; suite, 13 instruments, n.d.; excerpt *Variations on a Shaker Melody,* see Orchestral and Symphonic Band

Dance Panels, 1959, rev. 1962, Munich, 3 Dec 1963, cond. Copland; arr. 2 pf, 1959; arr. pf, 1965

FILM SCORES

The City, dir. Ralph Steiner and William Van Dyke, 1939, unpubd; excerpt "Sunday Traffic" incl. in *Music for Movies,* see Orchestral

Of Mice and Men (after John Steinbeck), dir. Louis Milestone, 1939, unpubd; excerpt incl. in *Music for Movies,* see Orchestral

Our Town (after Thornton Wilder), dir. Sam Wood, 1940, unpubd; orch suite, 1940, Boston, 7 May 1944, Boston Pops Orch, cond. Leonard Bernstein; arr. vn, pf ("Story of Our Town"), 1940; 3 excerpts arr. pf, 1944; excerpt incl. in *Music for Movies,* see Orchestral

The North Star (after Lillian Hellman), dir. Louis Milestone, 1943, unpubd; excerpt "Song of the Guerrillas," see Choral

The Cummington Story, 1945, unpubd

The Red Pony (after John Steinbeck), dir. Louis Milestone, 1948 (released 1949); orch suite, 6 scenes, 1948, Houston, 30 Oct 1948, Houston SO, cond. Efrem Kurtz; sym band suite, 4 scenes, 1966

The Heiress (after Henry James, *Washington Square*), dir. William Wyler, 1948 (released 1949), unpubd

Something Wild (after Alex Karmel, *Mary Ann*), dir. Jack Garfein, 1961, unpubd; excerpt *Music for a Great City,* see Orchestral

INCIDENTAL MUSIC

Miracle at Verdun (Hans Chlumberg), chamber orch, 1931, 16 March 1931, unpubd

The Five Kings (after Shakespeare), v, cl, tpt, gui, org, perc, 1939, unpubd

Quiet City (Irwin Shaw), cl, sax, tpt, pf, 1939, unpubd; suite for tpt, Eng hrn, strings, 1940, New York, 28 Jan 1941, Saidenberg Little SO, cond. Daniel Saidenberg

From Sorcery to Science (*Music for a Puppet Show*), orch, 1939, New York World's Fair, 12 May 1939, unpubd

The World of Nick Adams (teleplay after Hemingway), orch, 1957, Columbia Television Network, 10 Nov 1957, cond. Alfredo Antonini, unpubd

CBS Playhouse, signature theme, brass, perc, 1967, CBS television, 29 Jan 1967, unpubd

Appendix: List of Works

ORCHESTRAL

Organ Symphony, org, orch, 1924, New York, 11 Jan 1925, Nadia Boulanger, New York SO, cond. Walter Damrosch; arr. without org as Symphony no. 1, 1926–28, Berlin, 9 Dec 1931, Orchestre de la Suisse Romande, cond. Ernest Ansermet; "Prelude," arr. chamber orch, 1928, pf trio, n.d., unpubd

Cortège Macabre, 1923 (from ballet *Grohg*), Rochester, 1 May 1925, cond. Howard Hanson

Music for the Theatre (Suite in Five Parts), chamber orch, 1925, Boston, 20 Nov 1925, Boston SO players, cond. Serge Koussevitzky

Piano Concerto, 1926, Boston, 28 Jan 1927, Copland, Boston SO, cond. Serge Koussevitzky

Symphonic Ode, 1927–29, Boston, 19 Feb 1932, Boston SO, cond. Serge Koussevitzky; rev. 1955, 3 February 1956, Boston SO, cond. Charles Munch

Dance Symphony, 1929 (from ballet *Grohg*), Philadelphia, 15 April 1931, Philadelphia Orch, cond. Leopold Stokowski

Short Symphony (Symphony no. 2), 1932–33, Mexico City, 23 Nov 1934, Orquesta Sinfónica de México, cond. Carlos Chávez; arr. as *Sextet,* see Chamber

Statements: "Militant," "Cryptic," "Dogmatic," "Subjective," "Jingo," "Prophetic," 1935, Minneapolis, 9 January 1936, Minneapolis SO, cond. Eugene Ormandy (last two movements only); New York, 7 Jan 1942, New York PO, cond. Dimitri Mitropoulos

El Salón México, 1932–36, Mexico City, 27 Aug 1937, Orquesta Sinfónica de México, cond. Carlos Chávez

Prairie Journal (formerly *Music for Radio: Saga of the Prairie*), 1937, retitled 1968, New York, 25 July 1937, CBS RO, cond. Howard Barlow

Signature, 1938, New York, 23 February 1938, High-Low Chamber Orch, cond. Ivor Karman, unpubd

An Outdoor Overture, 1938, New York, 16 Dec 1938, High School of Music and Art Orch, cond. Alexander Richter; arr. sym band, 1942, New York, 22 June 1942, Goldman Band, cond. Copland

John Henry, chamber orch, 1940, New York, 5 March 1940, CBS RO, cond. Howard Barlow; rev. full orch, 1952

Lincoln Portrait, speaker, orch, 1942, Cincinnati, 14 May 1942, William Adams, Cincinnati SO, cond. André Kostelanetz

Music for Movies (from film scores for *The City, Of Mice and Men, Our Town*), 1942, New York, 17 Feb 1943, Saidenberg Little SO, cond. Daniel Saidenberg

"Jubilee Variation on a Theme of Goossens," 1 of 10 *Jubilee Variations* (later, *Variations on a Theme by Goossens*) (each by a different composer), 1945, Cincinnati, 23 March 1945, Cincinnati SO, cond. Eugene Goossens, unpubd

Letter from Home, dance orch, 1944, New York, 17 Oct 1944, cond. Paul Whiteman; arr. full orch, 1947; rev. chamber orch, 1962

Danzón Cubano (arr. of 2 pf piece), 1946, Baltimore, 17 Feb 1946, Baltimore SO, cond. Reginald Stewart

Appendix: List of Works

Symphony no. 3, 1944–46, Boston, 18 Oct 1946, Boston SO, cond. Serge Koussevitzky

Clarinet Concerto, cl, str, harp, pf, 1947–48, New York, 6 Nov 1950, Benny Goodman, NBC SO, cond. Fritz Reiner

Preamble for a Solemn Occasion, speaker, orch, 1949, New York, 10 Dec 1949, Laurence Olivier, Boston SO, cond. Leonard Bernstein; arr. as *Preamble for a Special Occasion* for orch; org, 1953; sym band, 1973

Orchestral Variations (arr. of *Piano Variations*), 1957, Louisville, 5 March 1958, Louisville Orch, cond. Robert Whitney

Connotations, 1962, New York, 23 Sept 1962, New York PO, cond. Leonard Bernstein

Music for a Great City (from film score *Something Wild*), 1964, London, 26 May 1964, London SO, cond. Copland

Down a Country Lane (arr. of pf piece), school orch, 1964, London, 20 Nov 1964, London Junior Orch, cond. Ernest Read

Variations on a Shaker Melody (from ballet *Appalachian Spring*), 1967

Inscape, 1967, Ann Arbor, 13 Sept 1967, New York PO, cond. Leonard Bernstein

Happy Anniversary, 1969, Philadelphia, 24 January 1970, Philadelphia Orch, cond. Eugene Ormandy, 24 January 1970

Three Latin-American Sketches: "Estribillo," "Paisaje Mexicana" (1959), "Danza de Jalisco" (1959), 1971, Spoleto, Italy, July 1959 ("Danza" only); Washington, DC, 20 April 1965, Pan-American Union, cond. Copland ("Paisaje" and "Danza" as *Two Mexican Pieces*); New York, 7 June 1972, New York PO, cond. André Kostelanetz; "Danza" arr. pf, 1959, 2 pf, 1963, see Keyboard

SYMPHONIC BAND AND BRASS ENSEMBLES

Fanfare for the Common Man, brass, perc, 1942, Cincinnati, 12 March 1943, Cincinnati SO, cond. Eugene Goossens

Variations on a Shaker Melody, sym band (from ballet *Appalachian Spring*), 1956

Emblems, sym band, 1964, Tempe, AZ, 18 Dec 1964, Trojan Band of the Univ. of Southern California, cond. William Schaefer

Inaugural Fanfare, wind ens, 1969, Grand Rapids, MI, 14 June 1969, Grand Rapids SO, cond. Gregory Millar; rev. 1975

Ceremonial Fanfare, brass, 1969, Metropolitan Museum of Art, New York, 14 November 1970

"Larghetto Pomposo" ("Happy Birthday"), unspecified brass, 1971

CHAMBER

Capriccio, vn, pf, 1916; *Poème,* vc, pf, 1918; *Lament,* vc, pf, 1919 (arr. pf trio, incomplete, 1919); *Preludes I and II,* vn, pf, 1919, 1921; *Sonata Movement on a Theme by Paul Vidal,* str qt, 1921; all unpubd

Movement, str qt, c1923, New York, 18 Oct 1984, Alexander Qt

Two Pieces, str qt: "Rondino," 1923; "Lento Molto," 1928, Fontainebleau, September 1924 ("Rondino" only), New York, 6 May 1928; arr. str orch, 1928, Boston, 14 December 1928, cond. Serge Koussevitzky

Two Pieces, vn, pf: "Nocturne," "Ukelele Serenade," 1926, Paris, 5 May 1926, Samuel Dushkin, Copland; "Nocturne" arr. cl, pf, 1976

Vitebsk (Study on a Jewish Theme), pf trio, 1928, New York, 16 Feb 1929, Walter Gieseking, Alphonse Onnou, Robert Maas

Elegies, vn, va, 1932, New York, 2 April 1933, Charlotte Karman, Ivor Karman, unpubd

Sextet (arr. of *Short Symphony*), cl, pf, str qt, 1937, New York, 26 Feb 1939

Sonata for Violin and Piano, 1942–43, New York, 17 Jan 1944, Ruth Posselt, Copland; arr. cl, pf, 1983, rev. 1986, Rochester, 10 March 1986, Michael Webster, Barry Snyder (rev. version)

Piano Quartet, 1950, Washington, DC, 29 Oct 1950, Alexander Schneider, Milton Katims, Frank Miller, Mieczyslaw Horszowski

Nonet, 3 vn, 3 va, 3 vc, 1960, Washington, DC, 2 March 1961, cond. Copland

Duo, fl, pf, 1971, Philadelphia, 3 Oct 1971, Elaine Shaffer, Hephzibah Menuhin; arr. vn, pf, 1977, Washington, DC, 6 April 1978, Robert Mann, André-Michel Schub

Vocalise (arr. of song), fl, pf, 1972, 6 April 1973, Doriot Anthony Dwyer, Robert Levin (hpd); ob, pf, 1972

Threnody I ("In memoriam Igor Stravinsky"), fl, str trio, 1971, London, 6 April 1972, London Sinfonietta

Threnody II ("In memoriam Beatrice Cunningham"), G-fl, str trio, 1973, Ojai, CA, 2 June 1973

KEYBOARD
(for one piano unless otherwise specified)

Moment Musicale, 1917; *Waltz Caprice,* 1918; *Sonnet I,* 1918; *Sonnet II,* 1919 (New York, 26 Oct 1985, Bennett Lerner); *Sonnet III,* 1920 (Paris, 23 Sept 1921, Copland); all unpubd

Humoristic Scherzo: The Cat and the Mouse (Scherzo Humoristique: Le Chat et la Souris), 1920, Fontainebleau, 21 Sept 1921, Copland

Piano Sonata [in G], 1921, Washington, DC, 21 May 1995, Ramon Salvatore

Three Moods: "Embittered," "Wistful," "Jazzy," 1920–21, Paris, 23 Sept 1921

Petit Portrait, 1921

Passacaglia, 1921–2, Paris, Jan 1923, Daniel Ericourt

"Blues No. 1" (pub. as *Sentimental Melody: Slow Dance*), 1926, 1927, Copland

"Blues No. 2" (pub. as *Four Piano Blues,* no. 4), 1926, 7 May 1942, Hugo Balzo

Piano Variations, 1930, New York, 4 Jan 1931, Copland; orchd as *Orchestral Variations,* 1957, see Orchestral

Sunday Afternoon Music, 1935, New York, 24 Feb 1936, Copland

The Young Pioneers, 1935, New York, 24 Feb 1936, Copland

Piano Sonata, 1939–41, Buenos Aires, 21 Oct 1941, Copland

Episode, org, 1940, 9 March 1941, William Strickland

Danzón Cubano, 2 pf, 1942, New York, 9 Dec 1942, Copland, Leonard Bernstein; orchd 1946, see Orchestral

Midday Thoughts, 1944/1982, New York, 28 Feb 1983, Bennett Lerner

Midsummer Nocturne, 1947, 1977, Cleveland, 13 January 1978, Leo Smit

Four Piano Blues, 1947, 1926/1934, 1948, 1926, New York, 13 March 1950, Leo Smit; nos. 1 and 2 arr. chamber orch, 1978–1979

Piano Fantasy, 1952–57, New York, 25 Oct 1957, William Masselos

Down a Country Lane, 1962

In Evening Air, 1966

Danza de Jalisco (arr. of orch piece), 2 pf, 1963

Night Thoughts (Homage to Ives), 1972, Fort Worth, 30 Sept 1973, Vladimir Viardo

Proclamation 1973/1982, New York, 28 Feb 1983, Bennett Lerner

CHORAL

Four Motets (Bible), SATB, 1921, Fontainebleau, fall 1924, Paris-American-Gargenville Chorus, cond. Melville Smith

"The House on the Hill" (E. A. Robinson), SSAA, 1925, New York, 24 April 1925, Women's Univ. Glee Club, cond. Gerald Reynolds

"An Immorality" (Pound), S, SSA, pf, 1925, New York, 24 April 1925, Women's Univ. Glee Club, cond. Gerald Reynolds

"Into the Streets May First" (Alfred Hayes), unison vv, pf, 1934, New York, 29 April 1934, Workers' Music League

"What Do We Plant?" (Henry Abbey), SSA, pf, 1935, New York, Henry Street Settlement Girls' Glee Club

"Lark" (Genevieve Taggard), Bar, SATB, 1938, New York, 13 April 1943, Collegiate Chorale, cond. Robert Shaw

"Las Agachadas" ("The Shake-Down Song") (Sp. trad.), SSAATTBB, 1942, New York, 25 May 1942, Schola Cantorum, cond. Hugh Ross

"Song of the Guerrillas" (Ira Gershwin), Bar, TTBB, pf, 1943 (from film score *The North Star*)

In the Beginning (Genesis), Mez, SATB, 1947, Cambridge, MA, 2 May 1947, Nell Tangeman, Harvard University Collegiate Chorale, cond. Robert Shaw

"The Promise of Living" (from opera *The Tender Land*), SATBB (also TTBB), pf duet, 1954; arr. chorus, orch, 1954

"Stomp Your Foot" (from opera *The Tender Land*), SATB, pf duet, 1954; arr. chorus, orch, 1954

Canticle of Freedom (John Barbour), 1955, Cambridge, MA, 8 May 1955, Chorus and Orch of MIT, cond. Klaus Liepmann; rev. 1965, Atlanta, 19 Oct 1967, Atlanta SO, cond. Robert Shaw

SONGS

(for one voice and piano unless otherwise stated)

"Melancholy" (Jeffrey Farnol), 1917; "Spurned Love" (T. B. Aldrich), 1917; "After Antwerp" (Émile Cammaerts), 1917; "Simone" (Rémy de Gourmont), 1919; "Music I Heard" (Conrad Aiken), 1920; all unpubd

Three Songs: "My Heart Is in the East," "A Summer Vacation," "Night" (Aaron Schaffer), 1918, Austin, Darlene Wiley, David Garvey, 4 November 1986

"Old Poem" (Arthur Waley, trans.), 1920, Paris, 10 Jan 1922, Charles Hubbard, Copland

"Pastorale" (E. P. Mathers, trans.), 1921, Paris, 10 Jan 1922, Charles Hubbard, Copland

"Une Chanson" (Victor Hugo), 1921, unpubd

"Reconnaissance" (Fernand Gregh), 1921, unpubd

"Alone" (E. P. Mathers, trans.), 1922, New York, 4 Dec 1985, Jan DeGaetani, Gilbert Kalish

"As It Fell upon a Day" (Richard Barnefield), S, fl, cl, 1923, Paris, 6 Feb 1924, Ada MacLeish, J. Boulze, René Verney

"Jazz Song," c. 1924, unpubd

"Poet's Song" (E. E. Cummings), 1927, New York, 11 Oct 1935, Ethel Luening, Copland

"Vocalise," S/T, pf, 1928, New York, 11 Oct 1935, Ethel Luening; arr. for fl, pf, and ob, pf, see Chamber

"We've Come" ("Banu") (Isr. trad.), 1938

"Song of the Guerrillas" (Ira Gershwin) (from film score *The North Star*), 1943

Twelve Poems of Emily Dickinson, 1950, New York, 18 May 1950, Alice Howland, Copland; *Eight Poems* arr. v, chamber orch, 1970, New York, 14 Nov 1970, Gwendolyn Killebrew, Juilliard Orch, cond. Michael Tilson Thomas

Old American Songs I (arrs.): "The Boatmen's Dance" (Dan Emmett, 1843), "The Dodger" (c. 1884), "Long Time Ago" (C. E. Horn and G. P. Morris, 1837), "Simple Gifts" (attrib. Joseph Brackett, c. 1848), "I Bought Me a Cat" (trad), 1950, Aldeburgh, 17 June 1950, Peter Pears, Benjamin Britten; arr. v, orch, 1954, Los Angeles, 7 Jan 1955, William Warfield, Los Angeles PO, cond. Alfred Wallenstein

Old American Songs II (arrs.): "The Little Horses" (trad), "Zion's Walls" (attrib. J. G. McCurry), "The Golden Willow Tree" (trad), "At the River" (Robert Lowry, 1864), "Ching-a-Ring Chaw" (trad), 1952, Ipswich, MA, 24 July 1953, William Warfield, Copland; arr. v, orch, 1957, Ojai, CA, 25 May 1958, Grace Bumbry, Ojai Festival Orch, cond. Copland

"Dirge in Woods" (George Meredith), 1954, Fontainebleau, summer 1954

"Laurie's Song" (from opera *The Tender Land*), 1954

Notes

To help reduce clutter, the numbers for notes are consistently placed at the ends of paragraphs. Where the source for quotations may not be self-evident, I have added short cues.

Sources are cited in full the first time they appear in each chapter; subsequent references within each chapter appear in abbreviated form. "Marginalia" refers to readers' written comments on manuscript drafts. In addition, I have used the following abbreviations throughout:

BCLC: Leonard Bernstein Collection at the Library of Congress
BCUW: Marc Blitzstein Collection at the University of Wisconsin
BHCF: Boosey & Hawkes Clipping File
CCLC: Copland Collection at the Library of Congress
C-P I: Copland and Vivian Perlis, *Copland: 1900 Through 1942* (London: Faber and Faber, 1984)
C-P II: Copland and Vivian Perlis, *Copland Since 1943* (New York: St. Martin's Press, 1989)
FCLC: Irving Fine Collection at the Library of Congress
NYPL: New York Public Library (Music Division, unless otherwise indicated)
SCNY: William Schuman Collection at the New York Public Library

Introduction

1 Donald Jay Grout, *A History of Western Music* (New York: W. W. Norton, 1960), pp. 623–24; Otto Deri, *Exploring Twentieth-Century Music* (New

York: Holt, Rinehart and Winston, 1968), pp. 470–72. The latest edition of Grout (5th ed., 1996) includes, in its American unit, musical examples for Billings, Joplin, Handy, Varèse, Thomson, Still, Sessions, Carter, Babbitt (two), Reich, Rochberg, and Del Tredici, but none at all for Copland, who now gets about the same amount of text as Cowell, Carter, and Babbitt and less than Ives and Cage.

2 Copland, *Our New Music* (New York: McGraw-Hill, 1941); *The New Music 1900–1960* (New York: W. W. Norton, 1968); Arthur Berger, *Aaron Copland* (New York: Oxford University Press, 1953); Julia Smith, *Aaron Copland: His Work and Contribution to American Music* (New York: Dutton, 1955); Neil Butterworth, *The Music of Aaron Copland* (New York: Universe Books, 1986); C-P I; C-P II.

3 Larry Starr, "Ives, Gershwin, and Copland: Reflections on the Strange History of American Art Music," *American Music* 12.2 (1994): 186.

1. A Copland Portrait

1 John Gruen, interview with Copland, 9 July 1975 (transcript), Dance Division, NYPL; Lederman quoted in C-P I, p. 112; Ned Rorem, *Knowing When to Stop: A Memoir* (New York: Simon and Schuster, 1994), p. 183; Ned Rorem quoted in Joan Peyser, *Bernstein: A Biography* (New York: William Morrow, 1987), pp. 54, 56 ("stunningly"); Paul Moor, interview by author, 26 July 1995 ("endearingly"); Robin Holloway, review of C-P II, *Tempo* (March 1990): 33, BHCF ("wonderful").

2 C-P I, p. 52; Verna Fine, interview by author, 7 May 1994; Phillip Ramey, interview by author, 6 May 1994; David Diamond, interview by author, 15 May 1994.

3 Harold Clurman, *All People Are Famous (Instead of an Autobiography)* (New York: Harcourt Brace Jovanovich, 1974), p. 27; Juan Orrego-Salas to Copland, 23 October 1981, CCLC; Richard Hennessy, interview by author, 27 July 1995; Copland, interviewed on *Soundings*, BBC Radio, Michael Oliver, narrator (24 November 1991).

4 Copland to Leonard Bernstein, 26 July 1944, BCLC; Leonard Bernstein, interviewed by Phillip Ramey, 14 November 1975, *Copland Conducts Copland* (Columbia M 33586); C-P II, pp. 198, 356; C-P I, pp. 243, 334.

5 Jean-Pierre Marty, interview by author, 8 August 1995; Copland, Diaries, CCLC; see also Copland, *Copland on Music* (New York: Norton, 1963), p. 137.

6 Virgil Thomson, *American Music Since 1910* (New York: Holt, Rinehart and Winston, 1970), p. 49; C-P I, p. 351; Marjorie Loggia and Glenn Young, eds., *The Collected Works of Harold Clurman* (New York: Applause Books, 1994), p. 960.

7 C-P I, p. 192; Ramey, interview.

8 Vivian Fine, interview by author, 27 September 1996; Verna Fine, interview by author, 18 March 1997; Minna Lederman, "To Aaron at Eighty," *Perspectives of New Music* 19 (1980): 38.

Notes

9 Jeffrey Miller, ed., *In Touch: The Letters of Paul Bowles* (New York: Farrar, Straus and Giroux, 1994), p. 111; Leonard Bernstein to Copland, 1941, CCLC.

10 Chard Powers Smith to Eva Goldbeck, 3 May 1930, BCUW; Rorem, pp. 182, 285.

11 C-P I p. 114; Robert Cornell, interview by author, 29 July 1995; Sylvia Goldstein, interview by author, 8 July 1996.

12 C-P I, p. 18; Mildred Copland to Copland, 22 June 1968, CCLC.

13 John J. O'Connor, "TV: Copland in Limelight on Two PBS Programs," *New York Times* (17 March 1976), p. 83:1, BHCF; Rosamund Bernier, interview by author, 21 January 1996; C-P I, p. 136.

14 David Walker, quoted by Helen Didriksen, "Strange Company: Aaron Copland, Emily Dickinson, and America at Mid-Century," unpublished paper (May 1988), p. 7, courtesy of Helen Didriksen; Miller, p. 73; Arnold Dobrin, *Aaron Copland: His Life and Times* (New York: Thomas Y. Crowell Co., 1967), p. 62.

15 Oscar Levant, *A Smattering of Ignorance* (New York: Doubleday, Doran and Co., 1940), p. 236.

16 C-P I, pp. 269, 335 ("Can you"); Dobrin, p. 107; Bernier, interview; Hennessy, interview.

17 C-P I, p. 335 ("It was"); Clurman, *All People*, p. 27; Kennedy, interview.

18 C-P II, p. 136; Hennessy, interview; Levant, p. 239.

19 C-P II, pp. 401, 407.

20 David Walker, interview by author, 27 July 1995; Dobrin, p. 87; John Kennedy, interview by author, 10 May 1994.

21 C-P I, p. 72; Vladimir Havsky, "What Makes It Great? A Conversation with Aaron Copland" (Winthrop Laboratories, Dec. 1970), CCLC. Early in his career, Copland worked largely at Steinway grands, but in the early 1950s he entered into an agreement with Baldwin in which they regularly loaned him new grand pianos.

22 Cole Gagne and Tracy Caras, *Soundpieces: Interviews with American Composers* (Metuchen: Scarecrow Press, 1982), p. 104 ("Somehow, suddenly"); Joe Stevenson, "A Conversation with Aaron Copland," *Your Musical Cue Quarterly* (Indiana University) (Spring 1973), BHCF ("You might").

23 Copland, *Music and Imagination* (Cambridge, MA: Harvard University Press, 1952), p. 33.

24 Robert S. Hines, "William Schuman Interview," *College Music Symposium* 35 (1995): 140; William Malloch, "Copland's Triumph," *Opus* (February 1988): 22–25.

25 One can find portions of *Grohg* in the *Dance Symphony* and *Hear Ye! Hear Ye!*; the "Nocturne" in the *Ode*; *Elegies* in *Statements*; "An Immorality" and "Ukelele Serenade" in *Miracle at Verdun* and *Hear Ye! Hear Ye!*; *The Five Kings* in *Dance Panels*; *Hear Ye! Hear Ye!* in *The City* and *Four Piano Blues*; *Quiet City* in *Our Town* and *Appalachian Spring*; *Signature* in *An Outdoor*

Overture; Our Town in *Episode; Fanfare for the Common Man* in the Third Symphony; *The Cummington Story* in the Clarinet Concerto, *The Tender Land, Down a Country Lane,* and *In Evening Air; The Heiress* in *Dance Panels.* The *Nonet, Something Wild,* and the *Duo* also share materials, though the chronology of these borrowings appears rather muddled. Daniel Mathers's Ph.D. dissertation in progress, *Fragments of Self: A Study of Aaron Copland's Self-Borrowed Music* (University of Cincinnati), in the author's words, "construes self-borrowing as pervasive in Copland's work and as affording rich critical, theoretical potential."

26 Kennedy, interview; David Diamond, interview by author, 10 February 1996; Ramey, interview; "Aaron Copland talks to Ates Orga," *Hi-Fi News and Record Review* 26.12 (1981): 77; BHCF ("The passage"). See also Joe Stevenson, "A Conversation with Aaron Copland" ("After two weeks of doing nothing, you come back and look at what you did before. You have a clearer picture of it than you have at the moment you're getting it down, in the heat of inspiration, so to speak. I think that's the reason why most of my pieces have been written over long periods of time. I need those intervals of getting away from it in order to more justly appreciate what I've gotten down when I was working").

27 Copland, *Music and Imagination,* pp. 14 ("Yes"), 41 ("self-expression," "self-discovery"), 46 ("superb").

28 C-P I, p. 180.

29 Copland, "Scores and Records," *Modern Music* 15.4 (1938): 245; Copland, *Music and Imagination,* p. 9.

30 The art historian John Kenworthy-Browne, who took Copland to see Chartres Cathedral, writes, "He did not mind sightseeing if someone was there to lead the way," Kenworthy-Browne, interview. On the other hand, another traveling companion, Donald Plotts, remembers how Copland gladly visited the homes of Emily Dickinson and Mark Twain. "Copland was not about to write a piece inspired by the Chartres Cathedral," explained Plotts, noting the difference, Donald Plotts, interview by author, 3 December 1995.

31 Meryle Secrest, *Leonard Bernstein: A Life* (New York: Knopf, 1994), p. 63.

32 Erik Johns, interview by author, 22 December 1996; Robert Cornell, interview by author, 29 July 1995; Michael O'Connor, interview by author, 4 July 1996.

33 Copland, *Music and Imagination,* p. 10; C-P I, p. 84; Humphrey Burton, *Leonard Bernstein* (New York: Doubleday, 1994), p. 456.

34 Erik Johns, interview by author, 23 May 1994; Plotts, interview; Ramey interviewed on *Soundings.* As for Muzak, it once sent him heading for the exit of a fashionable furniture store (Plotts, interview).

35 C-P I, p. 141; Copland to his parents, 5 July 1921, 24 April 1922, CCLC; Susan Watters, "Aaron Copland on the Sporting Life," *Women's Wear Daily* 6 September 1978, BHCF. According to Phillip Ramey, Copland once said, on the subject of his declining interest in novels late in life, "I don't have time for stories," Ramey, interview.

³⁶ Leonard Bernstein, letter to Copland, 6 September 1948; Humphrey Burton, *Leonard Bernstein* (New York: Doubleday, 1994), p. 456; C-P II, p. 423.

2. Background Matters

1 The dates of Copland family members cannot be definitively ascertained because of contradictory records, including a 1906 birth certificate for Aaron that gives a birthdate of 25 August, Aaron Copland, "Certificate and Record of Birth," 28 August 1906, No. 3018, Borough of Brooklyn (Copland's social security number, incidentally, was 551-20-4475); Edward T. Cone, "Conversation with Aaron Copland," *Perspectives of New Music* 6.2 (1968): 57.

2 Copland, transcript of interview with Vivian Perlis, CCLC; Arnold Dobrin, *Aaron Copland: His Life and Times* (New York: Thomas Y. Crowell, 1967), p. 3.

3 Copland, transcript.

4 Dobrin, pp. 7–8; Catharine Owens Peare, *Aaron Copland: His Life* (New York: Holt, Rinehart and Winston, 1969), p. 6; C-P I, pp. 15, 373n5; "Married 52 Years, the Coplands Still Enjoy Going Out Together," *Brooklyn Daily Eagle* (26 September 1937), Copland Clipping File, NYPL.

5 C-P I, pp. 15, 18 (some sources report Josephine as born in 1893, but the 1900 census says 1894); Burt Marcus, interview by author, 22 May 1994; John Kennedy, interview by author, 10 May 1994; Dobrin, pp. 10, 15; Trish Barnes, interview with Copland (unedited draft copy, November 1980), Copland Clipping File, NYPL ("the sort of baby"); Leo Smit, "A Conversation with Aaron Copland on His 80th Birthday," *Keyboard* 6.11 (1980), p. 9 ("I don't know").

6 C-P I, pp. 10–11, 17–18; Copland to his parents, 15 March 1922, 11 April 1922, CCLC; Copland, Diaries, CCLC.

7 C-P I, p. 18; for a gay perspective of the Lafayette Baths, see George Chauncey, *Gay New York: Gender, Urban Culture, and the Making of the Gay Male World, 1890–1940* (New York: Basic Books, 1994), pp. 217–21; J. R. Ackerley, *My Father and Myself* (New York: Harcourt Brace Jovanovich, 1968); Ramey, interview.

8 Smit, p. 9 ("blow"); Stuart Isacoff, "Copland at 80: A Birthday Interview," *Keyboard Classics* (Mar.-Apr. 1981): 6, BHCF; C-P I, p. 11; Laurine Marcus to Copland, 29 August 1944, CCLC. Decades later, when a single conducting appearance could bring him over two thousand dollars, Copland would remark to friends, "If only Papa could see me now!" C-P II, p. 389.

9 C-P I, pp. 4, 18 (Copland could not remember hearing his mother sing or play the piano, though Sarah's greatniece remembered her singing "The Battle Hymn of the Republic," pp. 4, 373), 131; "Married 52 Years"; Alice Cogan, "Musical Genius," Scrapbook, CCLC.

10 Dobrin, p. 1; for various accounts of this anecdote, see Herbert Kubly, "America's No. 1 Composer," *Esquire* April 1948: 143 and Gerald Nachman, "Closeup: 'Dean of Composers,'" *New York Post* (c. 1962), BHCF.

11 Copland to his parents, 28 June 1921, 25 July 1921, 23 August 1921, 27 September 1921, 18 October 1921, 18 December 1921, CCLC. He told them of being "willing to put down that $10,000 bet that I don't come home married, in spite of the fact that there are 50 girls at the school, all musicians," of missing spending the Jewish High Holidays at home, though "one needn't be religious to appreciate those things," and that he was not likely "to make any fortunes out of my compositions. Composition is not a business, but a luxury, which you are so good as to allow me to afford, for a little time anyhow."

12 "Married 52 Years"; Copland to his parents, 3 September 1932, 10 September 1932, 29 September [1932], CCLC; C-P I, p. 123.

13 C-P I, p. 20; Ralph Marcus, interview by author 21 May 1994; Burt Marcus, interview.

14 Laurine Marcus to Copland, 6 June 1944; 3 February 1951; 1961; 6 April 1964, CCLC.

15 Copland to Laurine Marcus, 31 October 1947, CCLC; Burt Marcus, interview.

16 C-P I, p. 20; Ralph Copland to Copland, 30 June 1947, 9 July 1947, 25 March 1950, CCLC.

17 Copland to Ralph Copland, 19 January 1922.

18 Interview with Martin Bookspan, 29 April 1980, CCLC; C-P I, p. 25; C-P II, p. 178; Dorothy ("Dot") Copland to Copland, undated, CCLC.

19 Copland, transcript; annotated family tree, courtesy of John Kennedy; Mildred Copland, letter to Norman and Ruth Peale, 27 November 1972.

20 Mildred Copland to Copland, 13 March 1968; 18 September 1968; 5 May 1970; 24 September 1970; 29 October 1972, CCLC.

21 Obituary for Percy Uris, New York Times, CCLC. The Uris family name remains a familiar one, thanks in part to the buildings on the Columbia and Cornell campuses that they helped underwrite.

22 Copland to Percy Uris, 6 May 1929; C-P I, p. 164; Donald Plotts, interview by author, 3 December 1995.

23 Robert Cornell, interview by author, 29 July 1995; Verna Fine, interview by author, 7 May 1994.

24 David Diamond, interview by author, 15 May 1994; Copland to his parents, 11 April 1922, CCLC.

25 Aaron Copland, The New Music 1900–1960 (New York: W. W. Norton, 1968), p. 151; Nathaniel Hawthorne, Complete Novels and Selected Tales (New York: Modern Library, 1937), p. 590.

26 C-P I, p. 17.

27 Eric Salzman, "Aaron Copland: The American Composer at Eighty," Stereo Review 80.2 (1981): 68.

28 David M. McCullough, Brooklyn . . . and How It Got That Way (New York: Dial Press, 1983), p. 198; see also Grace Glueck and Paul Gardner, Brooklyn: People and Places, Past and Present (New York: Harry N. Abrams, Inc., 1991).

Notes

29 Betty Smith, *A Tree Grows in Brooklyn* (1943; New York: HarperCollins, 1992).

30 Copland, transcript, pp. 15–16; Fine, interview; Julia Smith, *Aaron Copland, His Work and Contribution to American Music* (New York: Dutton, 1955), p. 321; Peare, p. 4.

31 C-P I, pp. 19–20, 24; Copland, Diaries, CCLC (although the Copland memoirs report that he spent 1915 at a YMHA camp, the diaries indicate that he spent 1914 at a YMHA camp and 1915 at a hotel, possibly the Breezy Hill Hotel, in the Catskills); Copland, transcript, p. 17; Karen Mittleman quoted by Peter Marks, "Bunk Beds and Cultural Identity," *New York Times* (27 May 1994).

32 Copland to his parents, 22 February 1922, CCLC; Ralph Marcus, interview, 21 May 1994; Bookspan, interview.

33 Israel Goldfarb, "Congregation Baith Israel Anshei Emes," souvenir pamphlet (1956, reprinted with amendments in the 1980s), courtesy of Judith R. Greenwald.

34 Harris Copland, 1908 Annual Address to Congregation Baith Israel Anshei Emes, courtesy of Judith R. Greenwald.

35 Israel Goldfarb, "Bar-Mitzvah Speech for Aaron Copland" (30 October 1913), "Bar-Mitzvah Toast for Aaron Copland" (10 November 1913), CCLC.

36 C-P I, p. 19; Bookspan, interview; Copland, "What Is Jewish Music?" *New York Herald Tribune* (2 October 1949); Diamond, interview.

37 C-P II, pp. 171–72. "Oy" turns up frequently in Copland's letters to Irving and Verna Fine, FCLC; Phillip Ramey to Copland, 8 May 1974, CCLC; Copland, last will and testament, 23 March 1984, courtesy of Verna Fine.

38 Thornton Wilder to Copland, 6 September 1948; C-P II, p. 215.

39 C-P II, p. 173 (Hitler); Copland to Irving Fine, 21 May 1951, FCLC (Mason); "Aaron Copland: A Visit to Israel," *Boosey & Hawkes Newsletter* 3.2 (1969).

40 Erik Johns, marginalia.

41 Phillip Ramey, interview by author, 6 May 1994; David Diamond, interview by author, 15 May 1994; Samuel Lipman, "Out of the Ghetto," *Commentary* 79 (March 1985): 56–61.

42 Fine, interview.

43 Copland to Carlos Chávez, 6 April 1947, CCLC; Diamond, interview; Dobrin, p. 196; Johns, interview; Kennedy, interview; Cornell, interview; Ramey, interview; Diamond, interview.

44 Bertrand Russell, *A History of Western Philosophy* (New York: Simon and Schuster, 1945); Diamond, interview; Loggia, p. 964; Copland, *Music and Imagination,* p. 111.

3. Early Education and First Works

1 Arnold Dobrin, *Aaron Copland: His Life and Times* (New York: Thomas Y. Crowell, 1967), p. 2; Julia Smith, *Aaron Copland: His Work and Con-*

tribution to American Music (New York: Dutton, 1955), p. 15; Horatio Alger, Jr., *Ragged Dick,* introduction by Carl Bode (New York: Penguin, 1985), p. xiv; Gary Scharnhorst with Jack Bales, *The Lost Life of Horatio Alger, Jr.* (Bloomington: Indiana University Press, 1985), pp. 149–56.

2 Copland, *The Home Coming,* CCLC.

3 Betty Smith, *A Tree Grows in Brooklyn* (1943: New York: HarperCollins, 1992), pp. 191–93.

4 C-P I, pp. 20–22.

5 C-P I, p. 17.

6 Trish Barnes, interview with Copland (unedited draft copy, November 1980), Copland Clipping File, NYPL ("great luck"); George Von Der Muhll, "Copland Discusses Career, Voices Approval of Federal Art Subsidies," *Oberlin Review* (18 February 1955), BHCF; Dobrin, p. 13.

7 C-P I, p. 23; Catharine Owens Peare, *Aaron Copland: His Life* (New York: Holt, Rinehart and Winston, 1969), p. 14; Copland, "Comments on Copland," *American Record Guide* 44 (1980): 4; Leo Smit, "A Conversation with Aaron Copland on His 80th Birthday," *Keyboard* 6.11 (1980): 8; marginalia, early programs, CCLC.

8 C-P I, p. 13, reproduces "Lola!" in facsimile; I am indebted to Wayne Shirley, marginalia, for bringing my attention to the connection with *Cavalleria Rusticana.*

9 C-P I, p. 23; Dobrin, p. 16; Von Der Muhll quotes Copland as saying, "It was only after I started studying theory that I knew I wanted to become a composer."

10 C-P I, p. 374n14.

11 Peare, pp. 34–44; Dobrin, p. 17; C-P I, p. 26.

12 Charles Schwartz, *Gershwin: His Life and Music* (London: Abelard-Schuman, 1973), pp. 55–56; Copland, "Rubin Goldmark: A Tribute," *Juilliard Review* Fall 1956: 16.

13 Copland, quoted by David Tomatz, "Rubin Goldmark, Postromantic: Trial Balances in American Music" (Ph.D. thesis, Catholic University, 1966), p. 88; Copland, "Rubin Goldmark," p. 16.

14 C-P I, pp. 27–28.

15 Tomatz, pp. 64–80, 95, 103; C-P I, p. 35.

16 Smith, pp. 24–31; for a rare admission of Copland's interest in Wagner's operas during his formative years, see Andrew Keener, "Aaron Copland," *Gramophone* February 1981: 1072, BHCF.

17 Smith, p. 24; C-P I, pp. 24–25.

18 Smith, pp. 31–34; C-P I, pp. 28–29; Aaron Schaffer to Copland, 5 August 1919, 14 August 1919, 3 October 1919, 20 October 1919. While in Paris, Copland asked his parents to send him some Bloch scores (songs and the Viola Suite) that he apparently had left behind in Brooklyn, Copland to his parents, 20 November 1921, 21 January 1922.

19 Smith, p. 34; Copland, Piano Sonata [in G Major], recorded by Ramon Salvatore (Cedille Records CDR 90000 021); C-P I, pp. 36, 81.

20 C-P I, pp. 24, 26, 33.

21 Copland, Diaries, CCLC ("first intellectual"); Florence Elberta Barns, *Texas Writers of Today* (Dallas: Tardy Publishing Co., 1935), p. 399; Aaron Schaffer, *Parnassus in France* (Austin: University of Texas, 1929); Schaffer, *The Genres of Parnassian Poetry* (Baltimore: Johns Hopkins, 1944).

22 Aaron Schaffer to Copland, 23 May 1918, 11 August 1916, 12 July 1918, 18 November 1918, 2 February 1919, 8 September 1919, 23 September 1919, CCLC; Leo Smit, "A Conversation," p. 9.

23 Aaron Schaffer to Copland, 23 May 1918, CCLC ("a deep impression"); Stefan Zweig, *Romain Rolland: The Man and His Work* (New York: Blom, 1921, 1972); David Sices, *Music and the Musician in Jean-Christophe: The Harmony of Contrasts* (New Haven: Yale University Press, 1968), p. 146; William Thomas Starr, *Romain Rolland: One Against All* (Paris: Mouton, 1971); David James Fisher, *Romain Rolland and the Politics of Intellectual Engagement* (Los Angeles: University of California Press, 1988); Romain Rolland, trans. Gilbert Cannan, *John Christopher* 3 (London: Calder and Boyars, 1966), p. 365.

24 David Fromkin, *A Peace to End All Peace* (New York: Avon Books, 1989), p. 300.

25 Aaron Schaffer to Copland, 30 June 1918 ("have won their way"), 2 February 1919 ("endless vistas"), 23 October 1919, 10 March 1919 ("I am sure"), CCLC; Smith, *Aaron Copland*, p. 32.

26 Aaron Schaffer to Copland, 28 June 1943 (this letter in the Moor file), CCLC; Paul Moor, interview by author, 26 July 1995.

27 Martha Dreiblatt to Copland, 21 October 1984, CCLC.

28 C-P I, p. 33; Phillip Ramey, liner notes to *Copland Piano Music* (Cedille CDR 90000 021); Irving Howe, *World of Our Fathers* (New York: Harcourt Brace Jovanovich, 1976), p. 323.

29 Clurman, *All People Are Famous (Instead of an Autobiography)* (New York: Harcourt Brace Jovanovich, 1974), pp. 26–28; Clurman to Copland, 14 July 1934, CCLC.

30 Copland, *Music and Imagination,* p. 99. The Stevens quote is "And thus it is that what I feel, / Here in this room, desiring you, / . . . Is music."

31 Peter Dickinson, "Copland: Early, Late and More Biography," *Musical Times* (November 1990): 582ff., BHCF.

32 C-P II, p. 250.

33 Smith, p. 24. Although vaguely modeled after such songs as "The Red Cross Spirit Speaks," which Copland kept among his papers, "After Antwerp" contains some remarkable dissonances.

34 The soprano Roberta Alexander and the pianist Roger Vignoles have expertly recorded some of these songs, *Copland Songs* (Etcetera KTC 1100, 1990).

35 Daniel Mathers, in conversation with the author, 9 November 1996, makes

the point that although Copland wrote many waltzes throughout his career, he is not thought of as a composer of waltzes—a fact Mathers attributes to Copland's highly idiosyncratic approach to the dance.

36 The quotes are as follows: *Sonnet II* ("Music I heard with you was more than music / And bread I broke with you was more than bread," Conrad Aiken, "Music I Heard"); *Sonnet III* ("I cried over beautiful things knowing no beautiful thing lasts," Carl Sandburg, "Autumn Movement"), *Prelude I* ("As though it mattered, / As though anything mattered— / Even laughter! / For in the end there shall be no one to tell / Whether it was laughter / Or weeping," Witter Bynner), *Prelude II* ("And thus it is that what I feel, / Here in this room, desiring you, / . . . Is music," Wallace Stevens, "Peter Quince at the Clavier"). Copland's music for *Sonnet II* and that for the song "Music I Heard" are altogether different.

37 C-P I, p. 51; Smith, pp. 299–300; Copland to his parents, 27 September 1921, CCLC.

38 *The Complete Fables of Jean de la Fontaine*, edited, with a rhymed verse translation by Norman B. Spector (Evanston: Northwestern University Press, 1988), pp. 609–10 ("La jeunesse se flatte, et croit tout obtenir; La vieillesse est impitoyable"). In the manuscript of *The Cat and the Mouse*, the opening six notes are accompanied by the phrase "on a beautiful night," in parenthesis.

39 Copland, perhaps following Julia Smith, mistakenly gives the completed date of "Jazzy" as 3 November 1921, confusing it with "Le Petit Portrait," a little piece composed in Paris and tacked on as a "supplement" to *Three Moods*, C-P I, p. 36.

40 "Embittered" also contains certain wedgelike harmonies that look ahead to Copland's later work (see, for example, the second movement of the Piano Sonata).

41 C-P I, pp. 51, 90.

4. Paris

1 C-P I, pp. 41–52; Edward T. Cone, "Conversation with Aaron Copland," *Perspectives of New Music* 6.2 (1968): 60; Copland to his parents, 28 June 1921; 30 August 1921, CCLC.

2 C-P I, pp. 50, 61–62, 68; Copland to his parents, 3 November 1921, CCLC; Léonie Rosenstiel, *Nadia Boulanger: A Life in Music* (New York: W. W. Norton, 1982), pp. 160–61. Rosenstiel claims that Marion Bauer, Richard Myers, Melville Smith, and others studied with Boulanger prior to Copland; while most of these students studied either organ or theory with Boulanger, David Diamond confirms that at least Bauer and Smith studied composition with her.

3 Andrew Keener, "Aaron Copland," *Gramophone* February 1981: 1072, BHCF.

4 Copland, "Nadia Boulanger: Mother of Modern Music" (the title not Copland's), unpublished 1981 lecture, CCLC.

Notes

5 Copland to Ralph Copland, 19 January 1922, CCLC; Copland, "Nadia Boulanger: An Affectionate Portrait," *Harper's* October 1960: 50.

6 Julia Smith, *Aaron Copland: His Work and Contribution to American Music* (New York: Dutton, 1955), pp. 46–47.

7 C-P I, pp. 65–66; *Elliott Carter: Collected Essays and Lectures, 1937–1995,* ed. Jonathan W. Bernard (University of Rochester Press, 1997), p. 288 (for *Wozzeck*); Copland, "Nadia Boulanger: An Affectionate Portrait," p. 50; Rosamund Bernier, interview by author, 21 January 1996.

8 C-P I, p. 65; Cone, p. 61; Rosenstiel, pp. 170, 177, 186–87.

9 Copland, "Nadia Boulanger: An Affectionate Portrait," p. 51; Leo Smit, interview by author, 4 May 1994; Rosenstiel, pp. 117, 172, 217; Alan Kendall, *The Tender Tyrant: Nadia Boulanger—a Life Devoted to Music* (Wilton, T: Lyceum Books, 1977).

10 Copland, "Nadia Boulanger." Elliott Carter also emphasized Boulanger's appreciation for "the big sense of rhythmic progress," writing, "Mlle. Boulanger taught us to feel an inexorable, constant beat, a push forward regularly like the march of time throughout the work. This gave the piece of music its forward motion and a great sense of continuity. There was no dwelling, so to speak, on beautiful moments, but these passed one after the other without being lingered upon, put into sharp focus by her beautiful sense of phrasing. This was one of the ways we were encouraged to play, hear, imagine, and appreciate music," pp. 285, 287.

11 C-P I, 81, 103; Minna Lederman Daniel to Copland, 16 April 1978, CCLC; Copland to Nadia Boulanger, 24 November 1950, and David Walker interview, both cited by Helen Didriksen, "Strange Company: Aaron Copland, Emily Dickinson, and America at Mid-Century," unpublished paper (May 1988), p. 13, courtesy of Helen Didriksen.

12 Verna Fine, interview by author, 18 March 1997; Jean-Pierre Marty, interview by author, 8 August 1995; Andrew Keener, "Aaron Copland," *Gramophone* February 1981: 1072 ("very inflexible"); C-P II, p. 146 ("rather"); Ned Rorem, *Knowing When to Stop: A Memoir* (New York: Simon & Schuster, 1994), p. 399; C-P I, p. 65; Rosenstiel, p. 198. Copland surely knew that his friend Harold Clurman had heard Boulanger say that Roy Harris "would go further than Copland because, unlike Copland, he was not handicapped by being a Jew," a comment that, however, can be read in different ways, Clurman, *All People Are Famous (Instead of an Autobiography)* (New York: Harcourt Brace Jovanovich, 1974), p. 33. When David Diamond denounced Boulanger's support of the right-wing French army leader Henri Pétain, Copland responded, "We have to accept her as she is," Diamond, interview by author, 15 May 1994.

13 Rosenstiel, p. 384.

14 Elia Kazan, *A Life* (New York: Alfred A. Knopf, 1988), p. 121.

15 Clurman, pp. 3–15; Marjorie Loggia and Glenn Young, eds., *The Collected Works of Harold Clurman* (New York: Applause Books, 1994), p. 955.

[16] C-P I, p. 57; Clurman, p. 73, 228; Loggia, p. 989; Robert Brustein, "The Vitality of Harold Clurman," *New Republic* 18 October 1980, p. 26; Kazan, p. 27.

[17] Harold Clurman to Copland, 24 May 1932, CCLC.

[18] In Fontainebleau, Copland rented a room at 195 Rue St. Merry. C-P I, pp. 44, 46, 59, 91; Smith, p. 53.

[19] The literature on American artists (in particular, writers) in Montparnasse in the 1920s is considerable. Two classic, firsthand accounts are Malcom Cowley, *Exile's Return: A Literary Odyssey of the 1920s* (New York: Viking Press, 1934) and Ernest Hemingway, *A Moveable Feast* (New York: Charles Scribner's, 1964). Two recent critical studies are Humphrey Carpenter, *Geniuses Together: American Writers in Paris in the 1920s* (Boston: Houghton Mifflin, 1988) and J. Gerald Kennedy, *Imagining Paris: Exile, Writing, and American Identity* (New Haven: Yale University Press, 1993). Two helpful street-by-street guides are Brian N. Morton, *American in Paris: An Anecdotal Street Guide* (Ann Arbor: Olivia and Hill Press, 1984) and Arlen J. Hansen, *Expatriate Paris: A Cultural and Literary Guide to Paris of the 1920s* (New York: Little, Brown and Company, 1990).

[20] Jerrold Seigel, *Bohemian Paris: Culture, Politics, and the Boundaries of Bourgeois Life, 1830–1930* (New York: Viking Press, 1986), p. 368; C-P I, pp. 75, 87; Morton, pp. 150–151; Copland to his parents, 18 October 1921, CCLC; Trish Barnes, interview with Copland (unedited draft copy, November 1980), Copland Clipping File, NYPL ("He had"). The Rotonde, the Dôme, and the Sélect all figure in Hemingway's *The Sun Also Rises*, the most celebrated depiction of American artists in Paris in the 1920s, Hemingway, *The Sun Also Rises* (New York: Charles Scribner's, 1926), pp. 42–51.

[21] Humphrey Burton, *Leonard Bernstein* (New York: Doubleday, 1994), p. 109; Rorem, pp. 281, 285 ("One can't make a habit of inviting students out," Copland told Rorem).

[22] Copland, Diaries, CCLC; reprinted in C-P I, pp. 140–41.

[23] Paul Valéry, *Selected Writings* (New York: New Directions, 1950); Cowley, pp. 126–32.

[24] William W. Austin, *Music in the 20th Century from Debussy through Stravinsky* (New York: W. W. Norton, 1966), p. 336; Copland, *Music and Imagination* (Cambridge: Harvard University Press, 1952), pp. 41, 45; Edmund Wilson, *Axel's Castle: A Study in the Imaginative Literature of 1870–1930* (New York: Charles Scribner's, 1931), pp. 297–298. Both Stravinsky and Valéry entrusted the musical education of their sons to Boulanger, whom Valéry described as arousing "enthusiasm through strictness," Rosenstiel, p. 226.

[25] Copland to Nadia Boulanger, 12 August 1923, CCLC; C-P I, p. 268.

[26] Gide, quoted by Wilson, p. 257; Thomas Corde, *André Gide,* updated ed. (New York: Twayne Publishers, 1993), p. 148.

[27] André Gide, *The Immoralist,* trans. Richard Howard (New York: Bantam,

1970), pp. 32, 106; Diamond, interview, claims that it was the "shock of recognition" that attracted Copland to *The Immoralist*, in particular, Michel's attraction to boys.

28 Loggia, pp. 1005–10.

29 Clurman, pp. 31, 251; Copland, Diaries, CCLC; Loggia, p. 958; *Harold Clurman: A Life in Theatre* (videocassette).

30 Hemingway, *A Moveable Feast*, p. 35; C-P I, pp. 75–76.

31 C-P I, p. 75; Copland, Diaries, CCLC; Clurman, *All People*, pp. 30–31.

32 Gerald Nachman, "Closeup: 'Dean of Composers,' " *New York Post* (c. 1962), BHCF ("I thought"); C-P I, p. 82 ("It's curious").

33 Copland to Leonard Bernstein, 23 March 1938, BCLC.

5. Copland and the Music of Europe

1 Copland to his parents, 28 November 1921, CCLC.; C-P I, pp. 81–92 ("insatiable," p. 90).

2 C-P I, pp. 81–92.

3 Copland, *Copland on Music* (1960; W. W. Norton, 1963); Copland, *What to Listen for in Music* (McGraw-Hill, 1939, rev. 1957); Copland, *Our New Music* (New York: McGraw-Hill, 1941), revised as *The New Music: 1900–1960* (New York: W. W. Norton, 1968). The most notable difference between the two versions of *What to Listen For* involves the addition of two chapters, "Contemporary Music" and "Film Music" (page citations below refer to the more available second edition). For the revision of *Our New Music* (retitled *The New Music*) Copland retained the original text punctuated with updated commentary in italics that assessed his earlier pronouncements (again, the citations below are from the more inclusive *The New Music* unless otherwise indicated).

4 Copland, letter to Clifford Odets, 11 September 1956, CCLC (upon receiving from Odets a recording of Machaut's *La Messe de Nostre Dame* earlier in the month, Copland wrote, "I've been hearing about that Mass for years, but never had heard it"); Copland, "Contemporary Trends in Music Today," unpublished 1962 lecture based on the 1959 lecture, "Pleasures of Music," CCLC, p. 9.

5 Copland, "Contemporary Trends," pp. 7–8 ("purity and serenity," "Americans," "What strikes me"), C-P II, p. 250; Copland, *What to Listen For*, pp. 110–11.

6 Copland, "At the Thought of Mozart," *Copland on Music*, pp. 105–08; *What to Listen For*, p. 43 ("purity"); Copland, "Gabriel Fauré, a Neglected Master," *Musical Quarterly* October 1924: 584 ("profundity"). Copland took a particularly keen interest in Mozart in the early 1930s; on a trip to Tangier in 1931, he brought with him a volume of the complete Mozart quartets and quintets, writing Israel Citkowitz, "I'm getting to know it well, all of it, and will leave Morocco understanding him 100% better," Copland to Israel Citkowitz, 22 September 1931, CCLC.

7 Copland, "Contemporary Trends," p. 8.

8 Vladimir Havsky, "What Makes It Great? A Conversation with Aaron Copland" (Winthrop Laboratories, 1970), CCLC.

9 Copland, *The New Music*, pp. 19–22; Copland, "Berlioz Today" and "Liszt as Pioneer," Copland, *Copland on Music*, pp. 108–25 ("too elegant," p. 118, "the feeling of," p. 110); Clifford Odets, *The Time Is Ripe: The 1940 Journal of Clifford Odets* (New York: Grove Press, 1988), p. 106; Arthur Berger to Copland, 2 October 1964, CCLC; Copland, "Gabriel Fauré," pp. 575–76 ("perfect"); Susan Watters, "Aaron Copland on the Sporting Life," *Women's Wear Daily* 6 September 1978, BHCF ("other than").

10 Leo Smit, interview by author, 4 May 1994; Phillip Ramey, interview by author, 6 May 1994; C-P II, p. 250; C-P I, p. 88.

11 Copland, *The New Music*, p. 27.

12 Copland, lecture notes on Verdi, CCLC.

13 Copland, *The New Music*, pp. 28–31.

14 Harold Clurman, *All People Are Famous (Instead of an Autobiography)* (New York: Harcourt Brace Jovanovich, 1974), p. 34; Copland, "Gabriel Fauré," pp. 585–86; Copland, *Our New Music*, p. 41 (*The New Music*, p. 38); Copland, "Fauré Festival at Harvard," *New York Times* 25 November 1945; Trish Barnes, interview with Copland (unedited draft copy, November 1980), Copland Clipping File, NYPL ("the rythmical").

15 Copland, notes for an autobiography, CCLC; Copland, "Copland Defends the Music of Mahler," *New York Times* 5 June 1925 (specifically, Copland praised the last movement of the Fourth, first movement of the Seventh, and the scherzo of the Ninth—ostensibly the "Burleske"); Copland, statement on Mahler, c. 1931, Koussevitzky Collection, LC. Copland, *The New Music*, pp. 32–34; Jack Diether, "Guide to Record Collecting," *Hi-Fi Music Magazine* March-April 1957, BHCF (here Copland reaffirmed his admiration for the last movement of the Fourth but singled out the first movement of the Ninth).

16 Copland, *The New Music*, pp. 34–40; Copland to Roger Sessions, 18 August 1927, Andrea Olmstead, ed., *The Correspondence of Roger Sessions* (Boston: Northeastern University Press, 1992), p. 79; John Kenworthy-Browne to author, 27 October 1995.

17 Copland, *The New Music*, pp. 54–59, 76–77; C-P II, p. 235; Copland, Diaries, 16 October 1955, CCLC; Copland to Clifford Odets, 11 September 1956.

18 When asked in 1951 to name those musicians he thought "the most potent musical forces of this century so far," he similarly named Debussy, Busoni, Mahler, Satie, Schoenberg, Bartók, Stravinsky, Hindemith, Ravel, Prokofiev, and Milhaud, *Etude* January 1951, clipping file, CCLC. Of the other musicians surveyed, seven included Copland in their lists, namely, Stokowski, Gould, Pelletier, Diamond, Sevitzky, Kastendieck, and Taubman. More than that included Gershwin, and almost as many, Barber.

19 Copland, *Our New Music*, pp. 56–57; *The New Music*, pp. 41–45, 85–89.

20 Copland, *Our New Music*, pp. 46–54; Copland, *The New Music*, pp. 41–45, 85–89 (Copland's discussion of the Second Viennese School in *Our New Music* was the only one he completely rewrote); Copland, notes for an autobiography, CCLC; Copland, "Playing Safe at Zurich," *Modern Music* 4.1 (1926): 28; Copland to Irving Fine, 30 November 1949, FCLC; Copland, "The World of A-Tonality," *New York Times* 27 November 1949.

21 Joe Stevenson, "A Conversation with Aaron Copland," *Your Musical Cue Quarterly* Spring 1973, BHCF.

22 Copland, *The New Music*, pp. 45–50; Watters; Copland, *Music and Imagination* (Cambridge: Harvard University Press, 1952), pp. 37–38; C-P I, pp. 72–73.

23 Copland, *The New Music*, pp. 73–74, 92–93; C-P I, pp. 72–75; Copland, "Stravinsky's 'Oedipus Rex,' " *New Republic* 29 February 1928: 68–69; Copland, "Stravinsky and Hindemith Premieres," *Modern Music* 9.2 (1932): 85–88; Copland, "Scores and Records," *Modern Music* 14.3 (1937): 168 ("somewhat cold-blooded"); Copland, "Scores and Records," *Modern Music* 15.1 (1937): 46 (Concerto and *Jeu de Cartes*); Copland to Irving Fine, 23 January 1946, FCLC (*Symphony in C*).

24 "Stravinsky—Darling of Moderns Lauds 2 Americans: Copland and Piston," *New York World Telegram* 10 February 1945; Igor Stravinsky and Robert Craft, *Dialogues and a Diary* (London: Faber and Faber, 1968), p. 100; Copland, interview with Glenn Plaskin, WNYC, 7 June 1983, courtesy of Phillip Ramey; David Matthews, "Copland and Stravinsky," *Tempo* 95 (1971): 10–14.

25 C-P I, p. 84; Copland, *The New Music*, pp. 50–51; Copland, "The Essence Remained," *New York Times* 3 May 1953.

26 Clurman, p. 34; Copland, *The New Music*, pp. 58–59, 69; Copland, "Scores and Records," *Modern Music* 15.4 (1938): 245 (for Poulenc).

27 Copland, *The New Music*, pp. 59–62; Copland, "The Art of Darius Milhaud," *Saturday Review of Literature* June 1948.

28 Francis Poulenc, *Selected Correspondence 1915–1963*, ed. Sidney Buckland (London: Victor Gollancz Ltd., 1991), p. 152; Darius Milhaud, *Notes Without Music* (New York: Knopf, 1953), p. 299.

29 C-P I, 83, 90, 124, 136; Copland, "Playing Safe," pp. 28–30 ("magical," p. 31); Copland, "Baden-Baden, 1927," *Modern Music* 5.1 (1927): 31–33; Eric A. Gordon, *Mark the Music: The Life and Work of Marc Blitzstein* (New York: St. Martin's Press, 1989), p. 48; Copland to Nadia Boulanger, 25 July 1923, CCLC (Vienna, Copland wrote, was " 'pas mal,'—beaucoup plus sympathique que Berlin, mais loin d'être Paris. It lacks, perhaps due to the war, a certain carefree atmosphere—'la joie de vivre' ").

30 Copland, *Our New Music*, pp. 47, 55–56; *The New Music*, pp. 89–92; Copland, "Contemporaries at Oxford," p. 18.

31 Copland, *The New Music*, pp. 69, 78–79, 80; Copland, "Playing Safe," p.

31; Copland, "Baden-Baden," pp. 32, 34; Copland, "Contemporaries at Oxford," p. 18.

32 Copland, "Stravinsky and Hindemith Premieres," *Modern Music* 9.2 (1932): 87; Leonard Bernstein to Copland, 1943, CCLC ("slick"); Rudy Burckhardt and Simon Pettet, *Talking Pictures* (Cambridge, MA: Zoland Books, 1994), p. 121; *Copland on Music,* p. 186; Copland, "A Note on Young Composers," *Music Vanguard* 1.1 (1935): 14–16.

33 Harold Clurman to Copland, 24 August 1942, 27 November 1944, CCLC (on Eisler); William W. Austin, "Aaron Copland's Music," unpublished draft, June 1986; Harold Shapero, interview with author, 3 January 1997; Luther Noss, *Paul Hindemith in the United States* (Urbana: University of Illinois Press, 1989), see also Kim H. Kowalke, "For Those We Love: Hindemith, Whitman, and 'An American Requiem,' " *Journal of the American Musicological Society* 50.1 (1997): 141–42, 166; John L. Steward, *Ernst Krenek* (Berkeley: University of California Press, 1991), p. 230.

34 *Arnold Schoenberg Letters,* edited by Erwin Stein (London: Faber and Faber, 1958), pp. 192, 234; Virgil Thomson, "Music in Review," *New York Herald Tribune* 11 September 1949.

35 Copland to Virgil Thomson, 11 September 1949, CCLC; published as "Music in Review," *New York Herald Tribune* 25 September 1949.

36 Arnold Schoenberg to Thomson, 25 September 1949; Copland to Schoenberg, 12 (first draft) and 13 February 1950; Schoenberg to Copland, 21 February 1950, CCLC.

37 Copland, "Stravinsky and Hindemith Premieres," p. 86; Copland, *The New Music,* pp. 83–85; Copland, tribute to Serge Prokofiev, 1961, CCLC.

38 Phillip Ramey, "You Didn't Want Even to Meet Prokofiev?" *Paul Bowles: Music* (New York: Eos Music Inc., 1995).

39 C-P II, pp. 183, 288; "Ear to the West" (3 July 1954), Copland Clipping File, NYPL; Dmitry Shostakovich to Copland, December 1969, CCLC.

40 C-P II, p. 182; Copland, birthday tribute to Dmitry Shostakovich, 1968, CCLC; Copland, Diaries, 1960, October 1961, CCLC; "Aaron Copland Talks to Ates Orga," *Hi-Fi News and Record Review* 26.12 (1981): 77, BHCF.

41 Copland, "Scores and Records," *Modern Music* 16.1 (1938): 51 ("stuffy," Bliss); Copland, "Scores and Records," *Modern Music* 15.2 (1938): 179 (Lambert); Copland, "Contemporaries at Oxford, 1931," *Modern Music* 9.1 (1931): 20 (Vaughan Williams).

42 Aaron Copland, "A Visit to Snape," CCLC, published in *Tribute to Benjamin Britten on His Fiftieth Birthday* (London: Faber, 1963); Humphrey Carpenter, *Benjamin Britten: A Biography* (London: Faber and Faber, 1992), p. 124.

43 Copland, "A Visit"; Carpenter, p. 124; Donald Mitchell, ed., *Letters from a Life: The Selected Letters and Diaries of Benjamin Britten 1913–1976. Volume Two: 1939–1976* (Los Angeles: University of California Press,

1991), p. 634; Christopher Headington, *Britten* (London: Eyre Methuen, 1981), p. 41.

44 Mitchell, pp. 634, 675; C-P I, p. 293.

45 Mitchell, pp. 685, 688; C-P I, p. 293; Interview with Geoffroy Millais, 24 November 1976, CCLC; Copland to Benjamin Britten, undated, CCLC; Benjamin Britten to Copland, 10 September 1939.

46 Mitchell, pp. 747, 817; Benjamin Britten to Copland, 15 August 1940, CCLC.

47 Carpenter, pp. 78, 163–64, 241–42, 478; Benjamin Britten to Copland, 28 October 1963, 8 January 1974; Peter Pears to Copland, 5 January 1975, CCLC.

48 Mitchell, pp. 772, 839; Arthur Berger, "Scores and Records," *Modern Music* 22.3 (1945): 199; Peter Evans, *The Music of Benjamin Britten* (London: J. M. Dent, 1979), p. 57 ("lonely prairie"); Wilfrid Mellers, "Paul Bunyan: The American Eden," *The Britten Companion*, ed. Christopher Palmer (New York: Cambridge University Press, 1984), p. 100; Copland, "A Visit."

49 Copland, review of Benjamin Britten's *The Rape of Lucretia*, *Notes* 4.2 (1947): 190; Copland, "Benjamin Britten," lecture notes, CCLC; Millais, interview ("a certain forthrightness").

50 Copland, Diaries, 18 May 1949, CCLC; Ian Kemp, *Michael Tippett: A Symposium on His 60th Birthday* (London: Faber and Faber, 1965), p. 53 (Copland originally titled this tribute "Cousin Michael," CCLC); David Matthews, *Michael Tippett: An Introductory Study* (London: Faber and Faber, 1980), p. 90; Kemp, p. 53.

6. From *Sonata Movement* to *Grohg* (1921–24)

1 C-P I, p. 375n19. Copland would also base a work on a name with his "Rondino" (1923), using the letters, *Gabriel Fauré*.

2 C-P I, p. 78.

3 Phillip Ramey, liner notes, Copland, *Old American Songs* (Columbia MK 42140); "Notes on the History of *Four Motets*," Copland, *Four Motets* (New York: Boosey & Hawkes, 1979); Julia Smith, *Aaron Copland: His Work and Contribution to American Music* (New York: Dutton, 1955), p. 48.

4 Smith, p. 48.

5 Copland, *What to Listen for in Music* (McGraw-Hill, 1939, rev. 1957), p. 172.

6 Neil Butterworth, *The Music of Aaron Copland* (New York: Universe Books, 1986), p. 21.

7 C-P I, p. 78.

8 C-P I, p. 90; Otto Luening, *The Odyssey of an American Composer* (New York: Charles Scribner's, 1980), p. 387.

9 Copland spelled out Fauré's name as follows: G (sol), A (la), B (si), R (re), I (si), E (mi), L (sol), F (fa), A (la), U (sol), R (re), É (mi), fudging primarily on the U and adding accidentals as he saw fit.

[10] Paul Rosenfeld, *An Hour with American Music* (Philadelphia: J. B. Lippincott and Co., 1929), p. 133.

[11] Roy Harris, "Problems of American Composers," in *The American Composer Speaks*, ed. Gilbert Chase (Baton Rouge: Louisiana State University Press, 1966).

[12] In 1966 Daniel Mathers discovered a pencil draft of the score at the Library of Congress, Mathers, marginalia.

[13] Copland, liner notes to the *Dance Symphony* (Columbia MS 7223). Roberta Lindsay, "Aaron Copland's *Grohg*: Its Place in Copland's Oeuvre" (Ph.D. diss., Ohio University, 1996), points out that the origins of the ballet can be found in some "petites valses" sketched out in late 1921; specifically, "Petite Valse No. 2" became the Dance of the Young Girl and "Petite Valse No. 3" became the Dance of the Streetwalker. Sources alternatively give the date of completion for the ballet as 1924 and 1925. Note, too, that only a piano reduction of the complete original 1925 ballet has as yet turned up among the composer's papers at the Library of Congress, though later sources make it possible to reconstruct a full orchestral score.

[14] Copland to Nadia Boulanger, 15 August 1922; C-P I, pp. 84, 86.

[15] Arthur Knight, *The Liveliest Art* (New York: New American Library, 1957), p. 56; Bram Stoker, *Dracula* (New York: Modern Library, 1897).

[16] Donald F. Glut, *The Dracula Book* (Metuchen: Scarecrow Press, 1975), p. 102.

[17] Copland and Harold Clurman, CCLC ("Sa figure, au long nez crochu, aux yeux géants, est tragique en sa laideur, tragique—et pitoyable").

[18] The ballet scenario uses both masculine and feminine articles to describe the adolescent; however, given that the original ballet also contains a solo for a "young girl"—and recalling, too, Nosferatu's opening scenes in the film—one might presume the adolescent to be male, or at least androgynous.

[19] A French sketch of the ballet scenario originally called for two other cadavers: "une femme du monde" and "un jeune artiste" were to have dances between the streetwalker and the young girl. Copland and Clurman first omitted the idea of the woman-of-the-world dance, then that for the young artist, reducing the number of cadavers to four. This same sketch refers to the "jeune-fille" as "belle."

[20] Peter Laki, *Cleveland Orchestra Program Notes*, Program 14 (1992–93): 41; Ronald Caltabiano and John Mugge, liner notes to *Grohg* (Argo 443 203-2), p. 7. That Copland himself misremembered *Nosferatu* is evident from his description of the film, C-P I, p. 84.

[21] Jack Kerouac quoted in John O. Barlow, *German Expressionist Film* (Boston: Twayne, 1982); Robin Wood, *Hollywood from Vietnam to Reagan* (New York: Columbia University Press, 1986), p. 76; Lotte H. Eisner, *The Haunted Screen: Expressionism in the German Cinema and the Influence of Max Reinhardt* (Los Angeles: University of California Press, 1969), p. 98; see also George E. Haggerty, "Gothicism," *The Gay and Lesbian Literary Heritage*, ed. Claude J. Summers (New York: Henry Holt, 1995), p. 335; Paul Coates,

The Gorgon's Gaze: German Cinema, Expressionism, and the Image of Horror (New York: Cambridge, 1991), p. 95; Lotte H. Eisner, *Murnau* (Los Angeles: University of California Press, 1964), pp. 17–23.

22 Gregory A. Waller, *The Living and the Undead: From Stoker's* Dracula *to Romero's* Dawn of the Dead (Chicago: University of Illinois Press, 1986), p. 189; Siegfried Kracauer, *From Caligari to Hitler: A Psychological History of the German Film* (Princeton: Princeton University Press, 1947), pp. 107–09.

23 Igor Stravinsky and Robert Craft, *Retrospectives and Conclusions* (New York: Knopf, 1969), p. 44; Copland, liner notes to the *Dance Symphony*; C-P I, pp. 90, 92; *The Cabinet of Dr. Caligari: Texts, Contexts, Histories*, ed. Mike Budd (New Brunswick: Rutgers University Press, 1990), pp. 73, 141.

24 C-P I, p. 86.

25 C-P I, pp. 164.

26 Copland, liner notes to the *Dance Symphony*; Oliver Knussen, "In Search of 'Grohg,' " *Tempo* 189 (1994): 7.

27 "Grohg Unveiled at Aldeburgh," *Boosey & Hawkes Newsletter* September 1992, courtesy of Sylvia Goldstein; Knussen, p. 7 (Knussen apparently made this assessment based on the reduced 1925 score, see n. 12); John Gruen, interview with Copland, 9 July 1975 (transcript), Dance Division, NYPL. Those portions of *Grohg* arrangéd as the *Dance Symphony* have been choreographed by Pauline Koner (as *Dance Symphony*) in 1963 at Jacob's Pillow, and by Tomm Ruud (as *Polyandrion*) for the American Ballet Theatre in 1973.

7. Return and Rediscovery

1 C-P I, p. 16.

2 Arnold Dobrin, *Aaron Copland: His Life and Times* (New York: Thomas Y. Crowell, 1967), pp. 58–60.

3 Copland to Nicolas Slonimsky, 18 October 1924, Koussevitzky Collection, LC; Dobrin, pp. 60–61.

4 C-P I, pp. 101, 112, 117; Dobrin, 61.

5 C-P I, p. 164; Catharine Owens Peare, *Aaron Copland: His Life* (New York: Holt, Rinehart and Winston, 1969), p. 98, reports that in 1935 Copland taught adults privately in his studio for the Henry Street Settlement.

6 Vernon Duke, *Listen Here! A Critical Essay on Music Depreciation* (New York: Ivan Obolensky, Inc.), p. 37; C-P I, p. 282; Harold Clurman to Copland, 12 February 1932, CCLC (Clurman had asked Copland for $150).

7 Gena Dagel Caponi, *Paul Bowles: Romantic Savage* (Carbondale: Southern Illinois University Press, 1994), p. 115.

8 C-P I, pp. 157, 247; David Metzer, "The League of Composers: The Initial Years," *American Music* 15.1 (1997): 54; Neil Butterworth, *The Music of Aaron Copland* (New York: Universe Books, 1986), p. 46. In 1938 Cos Cob merged with Arrow Press, and in 1956 both houses were acquired by Boosey & Hawkes, Copland's principal publisher since 1938.

[9] Copland, transcript of interview with David Markle, 25 February 1970, CCLC.

[10] Copland to Leonard Bernstein, fall 1939, BCLC; Copland to Abe Meyer, MCA correspondence, CCLC.

[11] C-P I, p. 349; C-P II, pp. 316, 439n41, 444n7; financial records, CCLC.

[12] Perhaps telling is the fact that neither President Truman nor his staff knew anything about Copland in the fall of 1946, when a young pianist played *The Cat and the Mouse* at the White House. Even as late as the summer of 1950, Truman claimed no familiarity with Copland, Elise K. Kirk, *Music at the White House* (Chicago: University of Illinois Press, 1986), p. 259; Anthony Leviero, "Harry Truman, Musician and Music Lover," *New York Times Magazine* 18 June 1950, Copland Clipping File, NYPL; Robert Sabin, "Survey of Our Orchestral Repertoire," *Musical America* September 1947, BHCF; Leslie R. Bell, "Musically Speaking," *Toronto Daily Star* 18 November 1950, Copland Clipping File, NYPL ("most significant"); Koussevitzky quoted at the premiere of Copland's Third Symphony, "There is no doubt about it, he is the greatest American composer," unidentified magazine article, 1950, Copland Clipping File, NYPL; a poll asking musicians who in their opinion "were the most potent musical forces of this century so far," *Etude* January 1951, Copland Clipping File, NYPL; Alan Penchansky, "Barber, Copland, Walton Win," *Billboard* 27 October 1979, BHCF.

[13] C-P II, p. 439n41.

[14] C-P II, pp. 389, 444n7; Copland, financial records, CCLC.

[15] C-P I, p. 247; Stuart Pope, interview by author, 9 July 1996.

[16] C-P II, p. 313; Ellis Freedman, interview by author, 5 April 1996. The appropriation of his music for, say, the television commercials produced by General Motors, Continental Airlines, the American Beef Association, and the U.S. Navy, among others, postdated his death.

[17] Pope, interview; Goldstein, interview by author, 2 March 1997; Verna Fine, interview by author, 2 March 1997. After Copland became senile, Citibank helped facilitate responsibility for his finances.

[18] C-P I, pp. 191, 244; Alex North to Copland, 10 October 1957, CCLC.

[19] Herbert Kubly, "America's No. 1 Composer," *Esquire* 29.1 (1948), p. 57; David Diamond, interview by author, 10 February 1996.

[20] C-P I, p. 252; C-P II, p. 25. The Empire still stands, but 115 West 63rd was demolished to make room for Lincoln Center.

[21] C-P II, pp. 73, 77; Linda Winer, "Copland at 80: Reflections of a Great Composer," Copland Clipping File, Dance Division, NYPL.

[22] Aaron Copland, "Always in My Thoughts," *Perfect Home* February 1953: 3.

[23] David Walker, interview by author, 18 July 1996.

[24] Copland, "Always in My Thoughts."

[25] *Soundings*, BBC Radio, Michael Oliver, narrator, 24 November 1991; Rick Pezzullo, "Copland Remembered as Great Teacher," *North County News* 23–29 August 1995, courtesy of Florence H. Stevens.

26 Winer.

27 C-P II, p. 316; Edward T. Cone, "Conversation with Aaron Copland," *Perspectives of New Music* 6.2 (1968): 72. Copland's summer retreats from 1925 to 1945 can be summarized as follows: 1925, MacDowell Colony (in Peterborough, New Hampshire); 1926, rural France; 1927, rural Germany; 1928, Santa Fe and the MacDowell Colony; 1929, rural France; 1930, Yaddo (Saratoga Springs, New York); 1931, Tangier; 1932, Yaddo and rural Mexico; 1933, Friends Lake, New York; 1934, Bemidji, Minnesota; 1935, MacDowell Colony; 1939, Woodstock, New York; 1940–42, Tanglewood (the Stockbridge-Richmond area, Massachusetts); 1943, Hollywood (where he spent most of that year); 1944, rural Mexico; 1945, Bernardsville, New Jersey (spring and summer, the following winter and spring spent in Ridgefield, Connecticut). From 1945 to 1965, he spent most summers at Tanglewood; subsequent summers, at least until 1980, found him on world tours.

28 C-P II, p. 18; Copland, quoted by Mildred Norton, Los Angeles *Daily News* April 1948, CCLC.

29 Copland, "Memorial to Paul Rosenfeld," *Notes* 4 (1947): 147; C-P I, p. 32; Copland to his parents, 8 September 1921, CCLC.

30 Sherman Paul, "Portrait of Paul Rosenfeld," *Accent* 20 (1960): 99–111; Copland, "Memorial," p. 148.

31 Paul Rosenfeld, *Musical Portraits: Interpretations of Twenty Modern Composers* (New York: Harcourt, Brace and Co., 1920), pp. 3, 57, 206; Rosenfeld, *Musical Chronicle (1917–1923)* (New York: Harcourt, Brace and Co., 1923), p. 101; Rosenfeld, *Discoveries of a Music Critic* (New York: Harcourt, Brace and Co., 1936), p. 260.

32 Rosenfeld, *Musical Portraits*, pp. 155, 251.

33 Barbara A. Zuck, *A History of Musical Americanism* (Ann Arbor: UMI, 1980), pp. 6–7; Paul Rosenfeld, *By Way of Art: Criticism of Music, Literature, Painting, Sculpture and the Dance* (New York: Coward-McCann, 1928), pp. 64, 274; Rosenfeld, *An Hour with American Music* (Philadelphia: J. B. Lippincott and Co., 1929), p. 50; Rosenfeld, *Discoveries,* pp. 319–20, 327.

34 Paul Rosenfeld, "A Musical Tournament," *New Republic* 15 June 1932: 120 (in a revised version of the review, as published in *Discoveries,* Rosenfeld added, "Pretentious sterility and sterile lack of earnestness both took up too much place," p. 355).

35 Paul Rosenfeld, "Musical Chronicle," *Dial* 78 (1925): 258–59 ("Mr. Copland works a little too steadily"); "Copland Without the Jazz," *By Way of Art,* pp. 266–72; "Aaron Copland: George Gershwin," *An Hour,* pp. 126–43; "Aaron Copland's Growth," *New Republic* 27 May 1931: 46–47; "The New American Music," *Scribner's Magazine* 89 (1931): 624–32 (comparison with Harris, p. 628; observes third "austere" strain, p. 630); "A Musical Tournament," p. 121; "Copland," *Discoveries,* pp. 332–37, though Rosenfeld allowed, in the same review, "through much wrestling and travail [the

revolutions of machinery] break madly out of their separate cells and their isolation and find their way into a new day and union and harmony"; "Current Chronicle: Copland—Harris—Schuman," *Musical Quarterly* 25 (1939): 372–76 ("arbitrarily mosaical," p. 375).

[36] Paul Rosenfeld, "Aaron Copland's Growth"; "Current Chronicle" ("altogether innocent," p. 372).

[37] Rosenfeld, *Discoveries*, pp. 237–55; Copland, review of *Discoveries, New Republic* 15 April 1936: 291; Harold Clurman, "Paul Rosenfeld," *Modern Music* 23.3 (1946): 184–85.

[38] Clurman, "Paul Rosenfeld," p. 188.

[39] Richard Whelen, *Alfred Stieglitz: A Biography* (New York: Little, Brown, and Co., 1995), pp. 474–75.

[40] C-P I, p. 125; Leo Smit, "A Conversation with Aaron Copland," *Keyboard* 6.11 (1980): 9.

[41] Harold Clurman, *All People Are Famous (Instead of an Autobiography)* (New York: Harcourt Brace Jovanovich, 1974) pp. 54, 56, 58; see also, Waldo Frank, ed., *America & Alfred Stieglitz: A Collective Portrait* (New York: Farrar, Straus and Giroux, 1934, 1975).

[42] Sharon Denton, *Paul Strand Archive* (University of Arizona, 1980), pp. 5–10.

[43] David Diamond, interview by author, 15 May 1994; Frank, *America*, p. 275; Clurman, *All People*, p. 65; C-P I, pp. 125, 190; Georgia O'Keeffe to Copland, 19 July 1968, CCLC ("It is to me as if our worlds are so different that I don't seem able to get through the door into yours—I say it as it is—Thinking you will understand—and probably laugh as you lay down this sheet of paper"). After lunching with Dorothy Norman in 1934, Paul Bowles wrote Copland, "She held forth on your complete lack of sympathy for Stieglitz of course," Paul Bowles to Copland, 1934, CCLC.

[44] Ralph Steiner, *A Point of View* (Middletown: Wesleyan University Press, 1978); Denton; Elia Kazan, *A Life* (New York: Alfred A. Knopf, 1988), p. 105.

[45] Copland to Paul Strand, 6 August 1974, CCLC.

[46] Steiner, pp. 12, 14.

[47] Rudy Burckhardt, interview by author, 4 May 1994.

[48] C-P I, p. 258; Burckhardt, interview. One still of the film is reproduced in C-P I, p. 259; more can be found in Edwin Denby, *Miltie Is a Hackie* (Calais, VT: Z Press, 1973).

[49] Rosenfeld, "A Musical Tournament," p. 121; Hugo Cole, "Popular Elements in Copland's Music," *Tempo* 95 (1971) ("photographic realism"); Arthur Berger, *Aaron Copland* (New York: Oxford University Press, 1953), p. 57 ("virtually"); Denton.

[50] Copland, *Music and Imagination* (Cambridge: Harvard University Press, 1952), p. 100.

[51] Copland, "One Hundred and Fourteen Songs," *Modern Music* 11.2 (1934): 59–64.

52 Diamond, interview; Waldo Frank to Copland, undated, CCLC; Alan Trachtenberg, editor, *Memoirs of Waldo Frank* (Amherst: University of Massachusetts Press, 1973), p. 219.

53 Copland, "The Composers of South America," *Modern Music* 19.2 (1942): 75–82; Waldo Frank, *South American Journey* (New York: Duell, Sloan and Pearce, 1943). During World War II, Copland (1941) and Frank (1942) independently toured South America—including Argentina, Brazil, Chile, Uruguay, Peru, and Colombia—and published their reactions and discoveries.

54 Paul J. Carter, *Waldo Frank* (New York: Twayne Publishers, 1967), pp. 98–100; Trachtenberg, pp. 184–85; Clurman, *All People,* p. 61; Harold Clurman to Copland, 24 May 1932, CCLC.

55 C-P I, p. 191; Edmund Wilson, *The Thirties* (New York: Farrar, Straus and Giroux, 1980), p. 142 (Wilson's reasons for voting communist in the 1932 presidential election, pp. 208–14, shed light on this whole issue); Edmund Wilson, *The Forties* (New York: Farrar, Straus and Giroux, 1983), pp. 208, 309.

56 Mary Lescaze to Copland, 13 September 1933, CCLC; Lorraine Welling Lanmon, *William Lescaze, Architect* (Cranbury, NJ: Associated University Press, 1987).

57 C-P I, pp. 244, 258, 263; Copland to Mrs. Leonard Elmhirst, 13 March 1935, CCLC; Mary Lescaze to Copland, undated, CCLC; Copland to Mary Lescaze, various, CCLC.

58 Lola Ridge to Copland, 8 April 1931, CCLC.

8. The Usable Past

1 Copland, *Music and Imagination* (Cambridge: Harvard University Press, 1952), pp. 100, 102, and 106; "Composers' Conference—Yaddo," transcript, 2 and 3 May 1932, BCUW; Copland, "Making Music in the Star-Spangled Manner," *Music and Musicians* 8 (1960): 9; Gerald Nachman, "Closeup: 'Dean of Composers,' " *New York Post* (c. 1962), BHCF.

2 Copland, *Music and Imagination,* pp. 80–81. In a letter to Christopher Rouse, Copland further described Gottschalk as "lots of fun," a "minor composer" who "must be credited with having been the first American who had the bright idea of using Latin-American materials in his own music. In that sense, he is an ancestor of mine," Copland to Rouse, 11 September 1964, courtesy of Rouse.

3 Copland, *Music and Imagination,* pp. 100–01; Copland, "Making Music" ("over-reverence"), p. 8.

4 Edward T. Cone, "Conversation with Aaron Copland," *Perspectives of New Music* 6.2 (1968): 63 ("smoothly written"); C-P II, p. 178 ("varied in style"); Copland, *Music and Imagination,* p. 101; Copland, "Making Music," p. 9. See also "Lack of Tradition Blocks Musical Progress Here," *World* 7 July 1929, Scrapbook, CCLC, for an early pronouncement on MacDowell's individuality.

5 Copland, *Our New Music* (New York: McGraw-Hill, 1941); Copland, *The New Music: 1900–1960* (New York: W. W. Norton, 1968), p. 104 ("official").

6 Copland, *Music and Imagination,* p. 102.

7 "Lack of Tradition"; Copland, *Music and Imagination,* pp. 103–04. In " 'I'm an Indian Too': Creating Native American Identities in Nineteenth- and Early Twentieth-Century Music," *The Exotic in Western Music,* ed. Jonathan Bellman (Boston: Northeastern University Press, 1998), pp. 256–57, Michael V. Pisani suggests that the "pastoral simplicity based on the pentatonicism of folk tunes and the spaciousness of parallel chords and open fifths" associated with Copland and some of his contemporaries owed some lingering debt to the Indianist movement.

8 Copland, lecture notes, "American Music and the American Scene," given in October 1940 at Columbia University (at other times, Copland included Carpenter and Hill with Loeffler and Griffes as composers of "French influence," as opposed to Gruenberg, grouped with Gershwin as a jazz-related composer); William W. Austin, *Music in the 20th Century from Debussy through Stravinsky* (New York: Norton, 1966), p. 62; Howard Pollack, *Skyscraper Lullaby: The Life and Music of John Alden Carpenter* (Washington: Smithsonian Press, 1995), pp. 387, 392.

9 Copland, "Neglected Works: A Symposium," *Modern Music* 23 (1946): 7–8; Copland, *Music and Imagination,* p. 23; Copland, *The New Music,* p. 184 ("In the '20s"); see also Copland to Henry Brant, 1930, CCLC.

10 Copland, *The New Music,* pp. 109, 116; C-P I, p. 204; John Kirkpatrick to Copland, 17 September 1958, CCLC; Jan Swafford, *Charles Ives: A Life with Music* (New York: Norton, 1996), p. 386; Arthur Mendel, "The American Composer," *Nation* 18 May 1932: 579.

11 Copland, "One Hundred and Fourteen Songs," *Modern Music* 11 (1934): 59–64; *The New Music,* pp. 109–16.

12 Charles Ives to Copland, 24 May 1934, courtesy of William W. Austin; Copland, "A Businessman Who Wrote Music on Sundays," *Music and Musicians* 9 (November 1960): 18; C-P I, p. 204; Copland to Roy Harris, 10 May 1945, CCLC; Copland, "Neglected Works," p. 8.

13 Copland, *Music and Imagination,* pp. 92–94, 105–06.

14 C-P II, pp. 235, 383; Copland, *The New Music,* p. 117; Vivian Perlis, interview by author, 21 March 1996; Vivian Perlis, *Charles Ives Remembered* (New Haven: Yale University Press, 1974), xi–xiii.

15 Phillip Ramey, "Copland at 80," *Chicago* January 1981: 148, BHCF.

16 Gena Dagel Caponi, *Paul Bowles: Romantic Savage* (Carbondale: Southern Illinois University Press, 1994), p. 44; C-P I, p. 190 (this ISCM concert also featured works by Gruenberg and Sessions as well as the premiere of Copland's own First Symphony); Robert Jacobson, "Lincoln Center Spotlight," Lincoln Center Programs, BHCF (photograph); Malcolm Bessom, "Conversation with Copland," *Music Educator's Journal* 59.7 (1973): 44–45 ("an interesting"); Marilyn J. Ziffrin, *Carl Ruggles: Composer, Painter, and Story-*

teller (Urbana: University of Illinois Press, 1994), pp. 136, 191, 195, 243; Marilyn Ziffrin, interview by author, 3 April 1997.

17 Copland, quoted by Cone, pp. 62–63; Copland, "Making Music," p. 9.

18 Copland, "Jazz as Folk-Music," *Musical America* 43.9 (1925): 19.

19 Arnold Dobrin, *Aaron Copland: His Life and Times* (New York: Thomas Y. Crowell, 1967), pp. 80–81.

20 Leonard Feather, "Piano Giants of Jazz: Aaron Copland on Jazz," (transcript of 1958 Copland-Seldes interview), *Contemporary Keyboard* November 1980, BHCF ("You mustn't"); Julia Smith, *Aaron Copland: His Work and Contribution to American Music* (New York: Dutton, 1955), p. 60; David Diamond, interview (on the Weinberg Bar); Copland quoted in "World of Music," *Brooklyn Standard Union* 29 June 1924, Scrapbook, CCLC. Because of the paucity of recordings from the early 1920s, it is hard to know what kind of "jazz" Copland may have heard in Vienna or Paris; safe to say, most if not all of it consisted of "prejazz," "sweet" jazz, or European-jazz hybrids, as opposed to what current scholars refer to as "real" jazz, Vincent J. Panetta, "Le Jazz 'Hot'?" American Musicological Society Annual Meeting, 9 November 1996.

21 Copland, *Music and Imagination,* p. 81 ("He [Stephen Foster] was a song writer rather than a composer"); Trish Barnes, interview with Copland (unedited draft copy, November 1980), Copland Clipping File, NYPL ("You can only hear"). Discussing "Dance" from *Music for the Theatre,* for instance, Copland wrote, "It was an attempt to make jazz even more exciting," Don Gold, "Aaron Copland: The Well-known American Composer Finds Virtues and Flaws in Jazz," *Down Beat* (1 May 1958): 16. Like many writers, Copland used the term "serious music" to denote what is more commonly called "classical music."

22 Vivian Perlis with Aaron Copland, "Copland and the BSO," *The Boston Symphony Orchestra* (Boston: Boston Symphony Orchestra, 1981): 29; "Nightclubs," *New Grove Dictionary of Jazz,* ed. Barry Kernfeld, Vol. 2; Dobrin, p. 82; Gold, p. 40 ("He listened").

23 C-P I, p. 119.

24 Copland, *The New Music,* pp. 56, 60, 63, 67, 69, 141; "Lack of Tradition."

25 Copland, *The New Music,* p. 159 ("With the concerto"); Copland, "Jazz Structure and Influence," *Modern Music* 4.2 (1927): 9–14; Pollack, p. 199; F. Scott Fitzgerald thought that by 1927 the jazz age had, in the words of Ann Douglas, "lost its exhilaration," Douglas, *Terrible Honesty: Mongrel Manhattan in the 1920s* (New York: Farrar, Straus and Giroux, 1995), p. 482; Martha Bayles, *Hole in Our Soul: The Loss of Beauty and Meaning in American Popular Music* (New York: Free Press, 1994), p. 55; see also Copland to Roger Sessions, 18 February 1927, *The Correspondence of Roger Sessions,* ed. Andrea Olmstead (Boston: Northeastern University Press, 1992): 76.

26 Copland, "Jazz Structure and Influence," pp. 9–14.

27 Winthrop Sargeant, *Jazz: A History* (New York: McGraw-Hill, 1938, 1964); for a critique of Copland's article, see Vernon Duke, *Listen Here! A Critical Essay on Music Depreciation* (New York: Ivan Obolensky, 1963), p. 30; Copland, *Our New Music*, pp. 89–94; Copland, *Music and Imagination*, pp. 83–85.

28 *In Touch: The Letters of Paul Bowles*, edited by Jeffrey Miller (New York: Farrar, Straus and Giroux, 1994), p. 106; Copland, *What to Listen for in Music* (New York: McGraw Hill, 1939), pp. 19, 99–100; Copland, "Scores and Records," *Modern Music* 15.2 (1938): 109–11; Copland, "Scores and Records," *Modern Music* 16.3 (1939): 186.

29 Copland, "Scores and Records," p. 109; Copland, *Our New Music*, pp. 96–98 ("A few more years," p. 98).

30 Douglas Gilbert, "Brahms—Boogie-Woogie Envisioned for Carnegie Hall," *New York World-Telegram* 26 September 1945, Clipping File, CCLC; Gold ("The two fields").

31 Copland, *Music and Imagination*, pp. 83–90; Gunther Schuller, "Jazz and Musical Exoticism," *The Exotic in Western Music*, p. 287; John M. Conly, "Aaron Copland Looks Ahead," *Reporter* 12 August 1965: 56. BHCF.

32 Erik Johns, interview by author, 23 May 1994; John Kennedy, interview by author, 10 May 1994. It is not unreasonable to wonder whether, as America's most frequently performed concert composer of the 1950s, Copland had any influence on contemporary jazz.

33 Gold; Feather; see also Copland, "Contemporary Trends in Music Today," unpublished 1962 lecture based on the 1959 lecture "Pleasures of Music," CCLC.

34 Gold ("for the freedom," "erudition"); Pleasures ("Jazz does not," "free and untrammelled"); see also Feather.

35 Copland, *The New Music*, pp. 70–71.

36 William Clopton, "Audiences Need Shock Says Aaron Copland," *Washington Post*, 18 February 1967, CCLC ("The music," "more open"); "An Interview with Aaron Copland," *Sinfonian* 20.3 (1970): 5 ("Marvelous," "I can see"); see also Barnes; Copland, "An Uncertain Glimpse into the Musical Future," unpublished lecture (April 1972), CCLC ("I myself like to think that since our popular music is more complex and more subtle than ever it was, a broader public for music may be on the way to absorption of a more sophisticated, a more knowing appreciation of the many varieties of music's power"). Once again, Copland himself may have had some influence on such developments, as Eric Salzman argued, pointing to Judy Collins and other "folk rock" artists, Salzman, "Aaron Copland: The American Composer Is Eighty," *Stereo Review* 80.2 (1981): 69.

37 Barbara Kolb to Copland, 4 September 1982, CCLC; "Copland Finds Composers in Russia Co-operative," *New York Herald Tribune* 8 May 1960, BHCF; Guy Freedman, "A Copland Portrait," *Music Journal* 25.1 (1977): 8, BHCF (all quotes).

38 Edmund Wilson, "The Jazz Problem," *New Republic* 13 January 1926: 218;
E. B. Hill, "Copland's Jazz Concerto in Boston," *Modern Music* 4.4 (1927):
37; Paul Rosenfeld, "Musical Chronicle," *Dial* April 1927: 356–57;
Lawrence Gilman, "A New American Concerto at the Boston Symphony
Concert," *New York Herald Tribune* 4 February 1927: 15; Isaac Goldberg,
"Aaron Copland and His Jazz," *American Mercury* 12 (1927): 63–65 ("A
Brooklynite," p. 64); Henry Cowell, "Die kleineren Komponisten," *Melos*
12.9 (1930): 527; Henry Cowell, "The Development of Modern Music,"
Ohio State University Bulletin 36.3 (1931): 378–379; C-P I, pp. 121,
131–32.

39 R. D. Darrell and Constant Lambert, quoted in *The Duke Ellington Reader*,
ed. Mark Tucker (New York: Oxford University Press, 1993), pp. 60, 111;
Hall Overton, "Copland's Jazz Roots," *Jazz Today* 1 (1956): 40; Sidney
Finkelstein, *Composer and Nation: The Folk Heritage in Music* (New York:
International Publishers, 1960, 1989), p. 331; Wilfrid Mellers, *Music in a
New Found Land* (New York: Oxford University Press, 1964), p. 84; David
Ross Baskerville, "Jazz Influence on Art Music to Mid-Century" (Ph.D. diss.,
UCLA, 1965), p. 508; Hugo Cole, "Popular Elements in Copland's Music,"
Tempo 95 (1970–71): 6.

40 Elliott Carter, "The Rhythmic Basis of American Music," *Score* 12 (1955):
28–29 (Carter distinguished Copland's works or passages that sounded
a regular beat from those that avoided a regular beat—a feature he also
associated with Harris—and from those that dispensed with a regular
beat altogether); "Lack of Tradition"; Copland, *Music and Imagination*,
pp. 84–85.

41 Copland, *Music and Imagination*, pp. 83–84; see also Duke, who viewed
Copland's occasional fusion of three principal Americanist trends—
"folklorist," "urbanist," and "jazzist"—into "an 'All-American' whole" as
comparable to Ives, pp. 30–31.

9. From the *Organ Symphony* to "Vocalise" (1924–28)

1 C-P I, pp. 91–92.

2 Hugo Leichtentritt, *Serge Koussevitzky* (Cambridge, MA: Harvard University
Press, 1946), pp. 1–13.

3 Leichtentritt, pp. 158–70.

4 C-P I, pp. 108–09; Copland, "Serge Koussevitzky and the American Composer," *Musical Quarterly* 30 (1944): 255–69.

5 Julia Smith, *Aaron Copland: His Work and Contribution to American Music*
(New York: Dutton, 1955), pp. 111–12.

6 The situation vis-à-vis the New York Philharmonic changed dramatically
during the Leonard Bernstein and Zubin Mehta years, and by 1985 the
orchestra could claim to have performed, between 1925 and 1985, thirty-one
Copland works a total of 432 times, including five world premieres.

7 C-P I, pp. 123, 187; C-P II, pp. 49, 69; Copland to Serge and Natalie Kousse-
vitzky, 1938, Koussevitzky Collection, LC; for Copland on the Stokowski-
Koussevitzky rivalry, see Joe Stevenson, "A Conversation with Aaron
Copland," *Your Musical Cue Quarterly* Spring 1973, BHCF; Humphrey
Burton, *Leonard Bernstein* (New York: Doubleday, 1994), p. 255.

8 Harry Ellis Dickson, interview by author, 14 October 1996. For Koussevitzky's recordings of Copland, see Joann Skowronski, *Aaron Copland: A
Biobibliography* (Westport, CT: Greenwood Press, 1985); *Koussevitzky Conducts American Music* (Pavilion Records LTD, Pearl, GEMM CD 9492,
1991). For tapes of Koussevitzky's 78 rpm recordings of Copland as well as
radio broadcasts by Rodzinski and Monteux, see the Rodgers and Hammerstein Archives of Recorded Sound, Music Division, New York Public Library.

9 C-P II, p. 68; Arthur Berger, interview by author, 8 May 1995.

10 Natalie Koussevitzky to Copland, 20 January 1928; Copland to Natalie Koussevitzky, 11 November 1933; Olga Koussevitzky, sworn affidavit, November 1953, Koussevitzky Collection, LC.

11 Copland, quoted by Phillip Ramey, liner notes to Copland, *Symphony for
Organ and Orchestra* (Columbia MS 7985). John Alden Carpenter also
alluded to "Au Clair de la Lune" in his jazzy ballet *Skyscrapers* (1924), composed for the Ballets Russes.

12 Neil Butterworth, *The Music of Aaron Copland* (New York: Universe Books,
1986), pp. 28–29.

13 Copland, quoted by Ramey; Smith apparently misidentified one of the "four
main elements," p. 79; Butterworth, for his part, claimed, apparently
unaware of Copland's own analysis, that this movement *is* a passacaglia, Butterworth, p. 29.

14 C-P I, p. 92; Copland, *Organ Symphony,* conducted by Leonard Bernstein
(Columbia MS 7058) and Leonard Slatkin (RCA 09026-68292-2).

15 Copland, First Symphony, conducted by the composer (Etcetera KTC 1098).

16 C-P I, pp. 117–20; Claire R. Reis, *Composers, Conductors and Critics* (New
York: Oxford University Press, 1955), p. 65.

17 Rudy Burckhardt, interview by author, 4 May 1994; George Chauncey, *Gay
New York: Gender, Urban Culture, and the Making of the Gay Male World,
1890–1940* (New York: HarperCollins, 1994), pp. 147, 194.

18 Leo Smit, "A Conversation with Aaron Copland on His 80th Birthday,"
Contemporary Keyboard 6.11 (1980), p. 12.

19 C-P I, p. 120; Barbara W. Grossman, *Funny Woman: The Life and Times of
Fanny Brice* (Bloomington: Indian University Press, 1991), pp. xi ("manic
mimicry"), 124 ("Yes, yes, Armand").

20 C-P I, p. 120; Arthur Rimbaud, *Une Saison en Enfer,* translated by Enid
Rhodes Peschel (New York: Oxford University Press, 1973).

21 Harold Clurman, "What Was Broadway's All-Time Best Season?" *The Collected Works of Harold Clurman,* ed. Marjorie Loggia and Glenn Young
(New York: Applause Books, 1994), pp. 934–37.

22 Clurman, p. 934; C-P I, p. 127; Harold Clurman to Copland, [1934], CCLC; John Howard Lawson, *Processional: A Jazz Symphony of American Life in Four Acts* (New York: Thomas Seltzer, 1925).

23 Arthur Berger, *Aaron Copland* (New York: Oxford University Press, 1953), p. 28; Ethan Mordden, *The American Theatre* (New York: Oxford University Press, 1981), p. 99; C-P I, p. 106. In discussing his popular film and ballet scores, Copland himself claimed that they "gave me a chance to try for a home-spun musical idiom similar to what I was trying for in a more hectic fashion in the earlier jazz works," C-P I, p. 251.

24 C-P I, pp. 120.

25 Judith Chazin-Bennahum, *The Ballets of Anthony Tudor* (New York: Oxford University Press, 1994), pp. 106–09; John Martin, "City Ballet Group Begins on Its Own," *New York Times* 14 January 1948; see also Walter Terry, "The Ballet," *New York Herald Tribune* 14 January 1948.

26 Copland, *Music for the Theatre,* recorded by Leonard Bernstein and the New York Philharmonic (Columbia MS 6698); Bernstein and the New York Philharmonic (DGG 431 672-2); Dennis Russell Davies and the Orchestra of St. Luke's (Musicmasters MMD 60162L); Yoel Levi and the Atlanta Symphony Orchestra (Telarc CD-80201); Gerard Schwarz and the New York Chamber Symphony (EMI CDC 7 49095); Hugh Wolff and the St. Paul Chamber Orchestra (Teldec 2292-46314-2).

27 Larry Starr, "Copland on Compact Disc II: Music for Orchestra," *American Music* 10.4 (1992): 502; John Kennedy, interview by author, 10 May 1994.

28 C-P I, p. 130.

29 Copland exaggerated the concerto's use of changing meters, referred to, in his memoirs, as "a variety of highly unorthodox and frequently changing rhythms—7/8, 5/8, 9/8, 1/8, etc., that made the music polymetric," C-P I, p. 131. In fact, the work's dizzying polyrhythms largely unfold within the traditional meters of 2/4, 3/4, and 4/4.

30 C-P I, pp. 130–31.

31 Harold Shapero, interview by author, 3 January 1997.

32 Copland, Piano Concerto, Leonard Bernstein, conductor, Aaron Copland, piano (Columbia MS 6698); Aaron Copland, conductor, Earl Wild, piano (Vanguard OVC 4029); Aaron Copland, conductor, Noël Lee, piano (Etcetera KTC 1098).

33 Copland, Piano Concerto, Gerard Schwarz, conductor, Lorin Hollander, piano (Delos DE 3154); Michael Tilson Thomas, conductor, Garrick Ohlsson, piano (RCA 09026-68541-2).

34 Copland used the variant spelling of *ukelele* in both his manuscript and in his memoirs.

35 C-P I, p. 126.

36 Robert Citkowitz, interview by author, 28 April 1997.

37 Although Copland claimed that "An Immorality" was his "first real jazz piece" (C-P I, p. 116), that distinction would seem to belong to "Jazzy" from

Three Moods for piano of 1921. Smith (p. 81) and Butterworth (p. 32) both call attention to the use of lydian and phrygian modes in "The House on the Hill," although the music veers more to the aeolian and dorian modes; in any case, as with *Four Motets* the writing is not purely modal, but rather modal-chromatic. During the Second World War, performances of "An Immorality" became controversial because of Pound's support of fascist Italy. In 1942, William Schuman defended one such performance by writing to a concerned party, "May I say personally that if the Duce himself were a fine composer I would still want to see him shot but in the meantime I would perform his music," William Schuman to Robert A. Schmid, 16 February 1942, SCNY. When Copland read this letter, he responded to Schuman, "I thought your replique admirable, though I must say I'm rather relieved that the Duce doesn't compose anything. What will happen when somebody discovers all the anti-Semitic references in Chopin's letters??" Copland to Schuman, 25 February 1942, SCNY.

[38] Copland, "Playing Safe at Zurich," *Modern Music* 4.1 (1926): 29; Smith, p. 99; Copland, letter to Israel Citkowitz, 12 July 1926, CCLC; C-P I, pp. 127, 136.

[39] Andrea Olmstead, ed., *The Correspondence of Roger Sessions* (Boston: Northeastern Press, 1992), pp. 79, 86 ("My enthusiasm").

[40] Copland, *The New Music: 1900–1960* (New York: W. W. Norton, 1968), p. 75.

[41] C-P I, p. 143; Copland, "Baden-Baden, 1927," *Modern Music* 5.1 (1927): 33.

[42] C-P I, pp. 129, 143, 153.

[43] Olmstead, p. 97.

10. From *Vitebsk* to the *Piano Variations* (1928–30)

[1] C-P I, p. 162.

[2] C-P I, pp. 1, 5. At the same time, the reference to Chagall may have simply reflected the impressions of Julia Smith, *Aaron Copland: His Work and Contribution to American Music* (New York: Dutton, 1955), p. 123.

[3] Joseph C. Landis, *The Great Jewish Plays* (New York: Horizon Press, 1966), pp. 15–16; S. Ansky, *The Dybbuk*, trans. S. Morris Engel (Los Angeles: Nash, 1974), pp. 7–9. The Neighborhood Playhouse production moved to Broadway in 1926 and subsequently enjoyed a successful national tour.

[4] *Great Ages and Ideas of the Jewish People*, ed. Leo W. Schwarz (New York: Modern Library, 1956); Max I. Dimont, *Jews, God and History* (New York: Signet, 1962).

[5] Marjorie Loggia and Glenn Young, eds., *The Collected Works of Harold Clurman* (New York: Applause Books, 1994), pp. 212, 898 ("The play").

[6] Ansky, p. 19. Joel Engel published his incidental music to *The Dybbuk* as a suite entitled *Hadibuk*.

[7] Copland, *Vitebsk* (Columbia M 30376). Larry Starr expressed a preference for this particular recording of the work in "Copland on Compact Disc 1:

Chamber Music," *American Music* 10.3 (1992), p. 383. Other fine performances of the work include one by members of the Boston Symphony Chamber Players (RCA Victor LSC 6167).

8   Irving Howe, *World of Our Fathers* (New York: Harcourt Brace Jovanovich, 1976), pp. 562–63; Ann Douglas, *Terrible Honesty: Mongrel Manhattan in the 1920s* (New York: Farrar, Straus and Giroux, 1995), pp. 358–64.

9   *The Jazz Singer,* ed. with an introduction by Robert L. Carringer (Madison: University of Wisconsin Press, 1979).

10   For a variety of opinions on the similarities and differences between the black and Jewish experience in America, see *Blacks and Jews: Alliances and Arguments,* ed. Paul Berman (New York: Delta, 1994).

11   Arthur Berger, *Aaron Copland* (New York: Oxford University Press, 1953), p. 39; Smith, p. 121.

12   See C-P I, pp. 182, 209, on the quasi-serial aspects of the *Variations* and the *Short Symphony.*

13   C-P I, pp. 165–69; Copland to Marc Blitzstein and Eva Goldbeck, 13 February 1931, BCUW.

14   Copland, "Shop Talk: On the Notation of Rhythm," *Copland on Music* (New York: W. W. Norton, 1963), p. 280 ("likely"). In contrast, Copland barred his solo piano music as he liked, with the result that orchestral and piano reductions of the same Copland work are in some spots likely to look different to the eye.

15   C-P I, p. 166.

16   Berger, p. 25.

17   Irving Fine to Copland, 6 February 1956, CCLC.

18   Fine to Copland.

19   C-P I, pp. 169–70; Copland, *Symphonic Ode,* conducted by Gerard Schwarz (Delos DE 3154, 1995) and Michael Tilson Thomas (RCA 09026-68541-2).

20   Sketches exist for the opening two movements of the *Suite for Two Pianos,* CCLC. Copland provisionally entitled the first movement "Fantasie" and the second movement "Bagatelle." Copland seems to have derived some of *Vitebsk*'s fast music from the "Bagatelle" movement.

21   Arthur Mendel, "Music," *Nation* 134 (4 May 1932): 578; Berger, p. 25; Mellers, p. 84; H. Wiley Hitchcock, *Music in the United States* (Englewood Cliffs: Prentice Hall, 1969, 1988), p. 192.

22   Berger, p. 45.

23   Gerald Sykes, *The Perennial Avantgarde* (Englewood Cliffs: Prentice Hall, 1971), pp. 104–05; Mellers, p. 84; Smith, p. 129; see also Berger, p. 45. One should note, however, that the success of its form has not persuaded all critics. Paul Rosenfeld, for instance, felt that, like other Copland works, the *Variations* "lacked cohesion" and were "arbitrarily mosaical," Paul Rosenfeld, "Aaron Copland's Growth," *New Republic* 27 May 1931: 46–47; Paul Rosenfeld, "Current Chronicle: Copland—Harris—Schuman," *Musical Quarterly* 25 (1939): 375.

24 C-P I, pp. 179, 183; Paul Rosenfeld, "A Musical Tournament," *New Republic* 15 June 1932: 121; Wilfrid Mellers, *Music in a New Found Land* (New York: Oxford, 1964), pp. 84–86; Berger, p. 44; C-P I, p. 179.

25 Copland, *Piano Variations,* played by Gilbert Kalish (Elektra/Nonesuch 9 79168-2), Nina Tichman (Wergo 286 211–2), and Copland (New World Records NW 277).

26 C-P I, p. 183.

27 C-P I, p. 129; Gerald Sykes to Copland, 4 August 1926; 20 July 1926, 29 August 1926; 7 July 1928; 18 July 1928, CCLC.

28 C-P I, p. 172; Copland, letters to Eva Goldbeck, 1929, BCUW; Gerald Sykes to Eva Goldbeck, 18 October 1930, BCUW; Copland to Eva Goldbeck and Marc Blitzstein, 13 February 1931, BCUW; Copland to Gerald Sykes, 6 March 1931; 2 May 1979; CCLC. Sykes, who married the painter Buffie Johnson in 1950 (they later divorced), vainly tried to persuade Mark Rothko to listen to a recording of *Vitebsk* shortly before Rothko killed himself: "I thought that music from the place and the people whom he had known in childhood might help," he wrote Copland in 1979. In contrast, the artist Louise Nevelson, upon receiving a recording of *Vitebsk* from the composer, listened to it "with relish," Louise Nevelson to Copland, 30 October 1984, CCLC.

29 Gerald Sykes, *The Hidden Remnant* (New York: Harper and Brothers, 1962); Gerald Sykes, *The Cool Millennium* (Englewood Cliffs: Prentice Hall, 1967), p. 217 ("The vanguard no longer expects the regular army to catch up with it, except commercially. It knows that its discoveries will be exploited to the limit, and therefore tries to make them too 'far out' to be of any use").

30 Sykes, *Cool Millennium,* p. 215; Sykes, *Perennial Avantgarde,* pp. 101–03.

31 John Kirkpatrick, Jr., "On Copland's Music," *The Fontainebleau Alumni Bulletin* 1 (1928), CCLC; C-P I, p. 104 (Kirkpatrick also arranged the Prelude from the *Organ Symphony* for piano trio); C-P I, p. 104.

32 C-P I, p. 179; Elliott Carter, "The Changing Scene, New York 1940," *Modern Music* 17.4 (1940): 238; A. Lehman Engel, "American Fesival at Yaddo," *Musical Leader* 12 May 1932: 3. When asked for a list of neglected works in 1946, Bernstein mentioned both Copland's *Ode* and *Statements,* while Chávez, Shapero, and Ingolf Dahl (along with Rosenfeld) cited the *Short Symphony,* all works written about the same time as the *Variations,* "Neglected Works: A Symposium," *Modern Music* 23.1 (1946): 9, 11.

33 Christena L. Schlundt, *Tamiris: A Chronicle of Her Dance Career 1927–1955* (New York: New York Public Library, 1972), pp. 17, 19, 20–21.

34 Agnes de Mille, *Martha: The Life and Work of Martha Graham* (New York: Random House, 1991), pp. 172–73 (Whether or not de Mille knew anything about *Sentimental Dance,* she must have been aware of *Olympus Americanus,* because she shared the same February 3 program on which Tamiris premiered it; she apparently forgot about it, however, for she cited Graham's *Dithyrambic* as the first dance set to Copland's music); Schlundt ("to

weld"), p. 21; M.W., "Tamiris Joins Dancers Presenting New Ballet," Scrapbook, CCLC; John Martin, "Dancers' Group Gives Third of Its Series,"
Scrapbook, CCLC.

35 John Martin, "The Dance: Martha Graham's Art," *New York Times* 26
November 1933 ("orgiastic"); de Mille, p. 184, remembered the dance as a
"fifteen-minute solo," though other sources say ten minutes, which is about
the time it takes to play the *Variations*; John Martin, "Brilliant Dancing
by Martha Graham," *New York Times* 4 April 1932 ("Its emotional");
John Martin, "Martha Graham Hailed in Recital," *New York Times*
20 November 1933 ("ancestor") (all Martin articles found in the Martha
Graham Clipping File, Dance Division, NYPL); in later years, both Pauline
Koner (1953) and Daniel Nagrin (1978) choreographed and danced solos to
the *Variations*.

36 Edward Cushing, "Music of the Day," *Brooklyn Eagle* 13 October 1927,
BHCF; Warren Storey Smith, "Barbaric Music by Symphony," Scrapbook,
CCLC; William R. Trotter, *Priest of Music: The Life of Dimitri Mitropoulos*
(Portland, OR: Amadeus Press, 1995), pp. 120 ("It never touches"), 145
("such as we"); Linton Martin, "Musical Fireworks Feature Orchestra,"
Philadelphia Inquirer 5 November 1927, CCLC; Warren Storey Smith,
"Symphony Plays Ode of Copland," Clipping File, CCLC; C-P I, p. 131
("shows a shocking"); Nicolas Slonimsky, *Lexicon of Musical Invective*
(Seattle: University of Washington Press, 1953, 1965), pp. 86–87; Lawrence
Gilman, "Music," *New York Herald Tribune* 4 March 1932, Clipping
File, CCLC; "An Evening of Ballet," *Musical Leader* 8 December 1934:
20; Robert Sabin, "Dance at the Coolidge Festival," *Dance Observer* 19
(1944): 121.

37 For references to nose-thumbing, see Penfield Roberts, "Copland Heard at
Symphony Concert," *Boston Globe* 29 January 1927, Scrapbook, CCLC;
Jerome D. Bohm, *New York Herald Tribune,* 5 January 1931; and Paul
Rosenfeld, "Aaron Copland's Growth," p. 45. Frances Goldwater, "Huge
Crowd at Bowl to Hear Jazz Concerto," Scrapbook, CCLC; Pauline F.
Schindler, Scrapbook, CCLC; C-P I, p. 132 ("poking fun at America"); Philip
Hale, "Music," *Boston Herald* 15 December 1928, Scrapbook, CCLC ("anti-
Christ"); E. B. Hill, "Copland's Jazz Concerto in Boston," *Modern Music* 4.4
(1927): 36 ("a unique example"); Philip Hale, "Music," *Boston Herald* 29 Jan-
uary 1927; Richard Crawford, R. Allen Lott, and Carol J. Oja, eds., *A Celebra-
tion of American Music: Words and Music in Honor of H. Wiley Hitchcock*
(Ann Arbor: University of Michigan Press, 1990), p. 335 ("close to rotten").

38 David Metzer, "The New York Reception of *Pierrot Lunaire*: The 1923 Premiere and Its Aftermath," *Musical Quarterly* 78.4 (1994): 669–91; C-P I, p.
104 ("a kind"); R.M.K., "Copland and Strauss," *Musical America* 16 January 1926 ("a more cheerful"); Isaac Goldberg, untitled, undated article c.
1927, Scrapbook, CCLC; Bohm.

39 C-P I, p. 104 ("To the names"); Paul Rosenfeld, *By Way of Art* (New York:

Coward-McCann, Inc., 1928), p. 269; Rosenfeld, *An Hour,* p. 126; Rosenfeld, "The New American Music," *Scribner's Magazine* 89 (1931): 629. In this last piece, Rosenfeld outlined similarities between Copland and Varèse, including "a grandiosity which contrasts with the more popular, humble, homely quality of works of the others [American composers], simultaneously differing from the grandiosity of the European late-romanticists."

40 "Organist, Appears," *New York Times* 12 January 1925; Lawrence Gilman, "Music," *New York Herald Tribune* 12 January 1925, Scrapbook, CCLC. For a discussion of Damrosch's remark as a "ploy" that successfully defused audience "hostility," see Léonie Rosenstiel, *Nadia Boulanger: A Life in Music* (New York: W. W. Norton, 1982), p. 184. What Damrosch actually thought of the piece remains uncertain. In a letter to Howard Shanet, 13 December 1966, CCLC (courtesy of Wayne Shirley), Copland maintains that by making such a statement, Damrosch implied that he was on the "side" of the "elderly ladies in the audience, of whom there were plenty"; but he also mentions that Damrosch made some "complimentary remarks" about the *Symphony* in a recommendation to the Guggenheim Foundation a few months later, and that on more than one occasion Damrosch greeted him by saying, "*You* understood what I meant by that remark, didn't you?"

41 Lawrence Gilman, "Music," *New York Herald Tribune* 12 January 1925, Scrapbook, CCLC; C-P I, pp. 132, 216 ("whether"); "Mr. Copland Twice; Mr. Converse Anew; Handel for Viola," *Boston Transcript* 31 January 1926.

42 Henry F. Gilbert, "Notes on a Trip to Frankfurt in the Summer of 1927," *Musical Quarterly* 16 (1931): 27; C-P I, p. 163 ("For some reason").

43 C-P I, pp. 123 ("I never left," "bucking the tide"), 132; Aaron Copland to Nicolas Slonimsky, *Letters of Composers: An Anthology 1603–1945* (New York: Knopf, 1946), p. 401; Slonimsky, *Lexicon;* Copland to Serge and Natalie Koussevitzky, 3 September 1927 ("J'avais l'impression d'être un vrai 'pioneer.' "), Koussevitzky Collection, LC; Copland to Leonard Bernstein, 27 May 1950, BCLC.

44 C-P I, p. 206; Olin Downes, "American Composers and Critics," *New York Times* 8 May 1932; Smith, p. 155; for a helpful discussion of Copland's remarks at Yaddo, see Oscar Levant, *A Smattering of Ignorance* (Doubleday, Doran, and Co., 1940), pp. 226–29. Levant reports that these remarks constituted "the first public evidence of Copland's developing stature as a leader among the younger composers," p. 226.

45 Copland, *The New Music: 1900–1960* (New York: W. W. Norton, 1968), p. 81.

11. Copland Among His Peers

1 John Rockwell, "Copland, at 75, Is Still Copland the Kid," *New York Times* 12 November 1975, p. 40; Copland, *Copland on Music* (New York: W. W. Norton, 1963), p. 164.

2 Copland, *Copland on Music,* pp. 142–51.

3 Andrea Olmstead, ed., *The Correspondence of Roger Sessions* (Boston:

Northeastern University Press, 1992), p. 100; Phillip Ramey, "Copland at 80," *Chicago* January 1981, p, 148, BHCF.

4 Copland, *Copland on Music,* p. 159; Copland, "Scores and Records," *Modern Music* 15.1 (1937): 47–48; Catherine Parsons Smith, " 'Harlem Renaissance Man' Revisited: The Politics of Race and Class in William Grant Still's Late Career," courtesy of the author; see also Gayle Murchison, "Nationalism in the Music of William Grant Still and Aaron Copland Between the Wars: Style and Ideology" (Ph.D. diss. in progress, Yale University). Verna Arvey strained to treat Copland fairly and objectively in her impressively monumental study *Choreographic Music* (New York: E. P. Dutton and Company, 1941).

5 Henry Cowell, "Amerikanische Musik?" *Melos* 8-9.9 (1930): 362–65; Cowell, "Die beiden wirklichen Amerikaner: Ives und Ruggles," *Melos* 10.9 (1930): 417–20; Cowell, "Die kleineren Komponisten," *Melos* 12.9 (1930): 526–29; Frank R. Rossiter, *Charles Ives and His America* (New York: Liveright, 1975), pp. 222-23; Richard Crawford, R. Allen Lott, and Carol J. Oja, ed.; *A Celebration of American Music: Words and Music in Honor of H. Wiley Hitchcock* (Ann Arbor: University of Michigan Press, 1990), pp. 83–84; see also Jan Swafford, *Charles Ives: A Life with Music* (New York: Norton, 1996), p. 395. Copland may have had Sidney Cowell in mind when he told Art Buchwald, "The only person I've ever been insulted by during my professional career was the wife of a composer. I'm afraid she thought I was getting too many performances," Art Buchwald, "P.S. from Paris," *New York Herald Tribune* 12 June 1955: 5.

6 Henry Cowell, "The Development of Modern Music," *Ohio State University Bulletin* 36.3 (1931): 378–79; Rita Mead, *Henry Cowell's New Music 1925–1936: The Society, the Music Editions, and the Recordings* (Ann Arbor: UMI, 1981), pp. 44, 66, 89, 126, 147; Judith Tick, *Ruth Crawford Seeger* (New York: Oxford University Press, 1997), p. 153 ("clicked"); "Aaron Copland Talks to Ates Orga," *Hi-Fi News and Record Review* 1981: 75, BHCF; Matilda Gaume, *Ruth Crawford Seeger: Memoirs, Memories, Music* (Metuchen: Scarecrow Press, 1986), p. 198; Henry Cowell to Copland, 17 September 1937, CCLC.

7 Carol Oja, *Colin McPhee: Composer in Two Worlds* (Washington: Smithsonian Institution Press, 1990), pp. 98 ("vitality"), 117 ("I think"), 155, 164 ("eloquent"), 227.

8 Copland, *Copland on Music,* p. 146; C-P I, p. 75; George Antheil, *Bad Boy of Music* (New York: Da Capo, 1981): 132–41.

9 Copland, "George Antheil," *Modern Music* 2.1 (1925): 26–28; Oscar Levant, *A Smattering of Ignorance* (Doubleday, Doran, and Co., 1940), p. 240; Antheil, p. 208; C-P I, p. 127.

10 C-P I, pp. 157, 201 (Antheil was originally scheduled to perform at the 1932 festival, but after a last-minute cancellation, Copland substituted by playing his own *Piano Variations*).

11 Minna Lederman, *The Life and Death of a Small Magazine* (Brooklyn College:

ISAM Monographs, No. 18, 1983), pp. 16–17 (Wrote Antheil, "It appears as if Copeland [*sic*] is so anxious to score a point or two before I reach America that he has lost his last scruple and thrown overboard the last rules of sportsmanship. He does not neglect to disparage whatever statements I may have written about music as the not-to-be-taken-seriously statements of an otherwise very talented musical idiot"); Marc Blitzstein to Eva Goldbeck, 11 August 1930 (" 'recluse' "), BCUW; Copland, *Copland on Music*, p. 158; Copland, "Influence, Problem, Tone," *Stravinsky in the Theatre*, ed. Minna Lederman (New York: Da Capo, 1975), p. 121 ("a reductio"); David Diamond, interview by author, 15 May 1994; C-P I, pp. 271, 350; George Antheil to Copland 4 March 1946, CCLC.

12 Copland, *Copland on Music*, pp. 141, 158; Copland, *Our New Music* (New York: McGraw-Hill, 1941); *The New Music: 1900–1960* (New York: W. W. Norton, 1968), p. 70.

13 Joan Peyser, *The Memory of All That* (New York; Simon & Schuster, 1993), p. 99; C-P I, p. 130 ("nothing to say"); Joe Stevenson, "A Conversation with Aaron Copland," *Your Musical Cue Quarterly* Spring 1973, BHCF ("we weren't together"); Sam Kashner and Nancy Schoenberger, *A Talent for Genius* (New York: Villard, 1994), p. xi.

14 Carl Van Vechten (see Oja, below, p. 653); Lazare Saminsky, *Music of the Ghetto and the Bible* (New York: Bloch Publishing Company, 1934), p. 124; Virgil Thomson, "The Cult of Jazz," *Vanity Fair* June 1925: 54; Edmund Wilson, "The Jazz Problem," *New Republic* 13 January 1926: 218; Paul Rosenfeld, *An Hour with American Music* (Philadelphia: J. B. Lippincott and Co., 1929), p. 139; Henry Cowell, "Die kleineren Komponisten"; Carol Oja, "Gershwin and American Modernists of the 1920s," *Musical Quarterly* 78.4 (1994): 657; Isaac Goldberg, "Aaron Copland and His Jazz," *American Mercury* 12 (1927): 66–65; Vernon Duke, *Listen Here! A Critical Essay on Music Depreciation* (New York: Ivan Obolensky, Inc., 1963), a relatively late source, but one with roots in the 1920s: Duke had been friends with both Gershwin and Copland (comparing the Copland and Gershwin Piano Concertos, Duke wrote that the Copland "is still a fresh and electrifying farrago of jazz devices, technically far smoother than Gershwin's one effort in the genre, melodically less convincing," p. 36; in 1925, Thomson similarly wrote that Copland did not have "the melodic gift of Gershwin," Thomson, p. 54); John Kirkpatrick, Jr., "On Copland's Music," *Fontainebleau Alumni Bulletin* 1 (1928), CCLC (discussing Copland's *Sentimental Melody*, Kirkpatrick wrote, "if [it] contains an echo of George Gershwin's marvelous 'Someone to watch over me,' the idea has been so completely assimilated and reborn as to preclude all thought of 'lifting' "). Years later, in 1956, Sessions referred to Copland and Gershwin as "equally gifted," *Reflections on the Music Life in the United States* (New York: Merlin Press, 1956), p. 159; Copland to Serge Koussevitzky, 5 September 1932, Koussevitzky Collection, LC; Kashner, p. 114.

Notes

15 Peyser, pp. 98–101, 214–15, 223, 242 (these pages contain some erroneous remarks); Copland, *Copland on Music*, p. 141; Copland, "Jazz Structure and Influence," *Modern Music* 4.2 (1927): 12; Copland, "Contemporaries at Oxford, 1931," *Modern Music* 9.1 (1931): 20; C-P I, pp. 247, 271.

16 Roy Harris to Aaron Copland, 2 May 1945; Copland to Roy Harris 10 May 1945, CCLC; Stevenson ("He became ambitious"); John Kennedy, interview by author, 10 May 1994. Edward Jablonski, interview by author, 27 July 1997, confirms Copland's high regard for Gershwin.

17 Copland, "The American Composer Gets a Break," *American Mercury* 36.136 (1935): 488–92; Copland, *The New Music*; Virgil Thomson, *American Music Since 1910* (New York: Holt, Rinehart and Winston, 1970), p. 51; Copland himself referred to Thomson's phrase "America's up-and-at-'em commando unit," C-P I, p. 244.

18 Olmstead, *Correspondence*, pp. 25, 46n1, 474 (Olmstead, E-mail to author, 11 November 1997, believes that Copland and Sessions met one another earlier, citing a June 1924 letter from Sessions to his wife that refers to an "Aaron" familiarly); Andrea Olmstead, *Roger Sessions and His Music* (Ann Arbor: UMI Research Press, 1985); Sarah Chapin, "Sessions and Jean-Christophe," *Roger Sessions Society, Inc., Newsletter* 3 (1990): 2; Roger Sessions to Copland, 22 March 1929, CCLC. Sessions claimed not to have studied with Boulanger, but letters reveal that he at least showed her his scores and took her comments seriously.

19 Olmstead, *Correspondence*, pp. 65, 78.

20 Andrea Olmstead, "The Copland-Sessions Letters," *Tempo* 175 (1990): 2–5.

21 Olmstead, *Correspondence*, p. 66.

22 Olmstead, pp. 81, 93 ("You are"), 129 ("I am really"). Sessions himself had an Episcopalian background and referred to himself as "a closet Catholic," Olmstead, *Roger Sessions*, pp. 138, 179.

23 Olmstead, p. 91.

24 Carol J. Oja, "The Copland-Sessions Concerts and Their Reception in the Contemporary Press," *Musical Quarterly* 45 (1979).

25 Carol J. Oja, "Women Patrons and Activists for Modernist Music: New York in the 1920s," *Modernism/Modernity* 4.1 (1997): 132.

26 Marion Bauer and Claire R. Reis, "Twenty-Five Years with the League of Composers," *Musical Quarterly* 34.1 (1948): 1–14; Claire R. Reis, *Composers, Conductors and Critics* (New York: Oxford University Press, 1955); Louise Varèse, *Varèse: A Looking-Glass Diary* (New York: W. W. Norton, 1972); David Metzer, "The League of Composers: The Initial Years," *American Music* 15.1 (1997): 45–69; Donal Henahan, "He Made Composing Respectable Here," (1970), BHCF ("Either you were").

27 Carol Oja, *Experiments in Modern Music: New York in the 1920s* (New York: Oxford University Press, forthcoming); see also Rossiter, p. 223, and Marilyn J. Ziffrin, *Carl Ruggles: Composer, Painter, and Storyteller* (Urbana: University of Illinois Press, 1994), p. 136 (for anti-Semitism in the Pan-

American Association); Varèse, p. 186; Thomson quoted by Oja, "Women Patrons," p. 141. The subject of homophobia and anti-Semitism in New York's new-music circles remains cloudy. Oja cites Reis as pointing out, for instance, that Salzedo was Jewish and Varèse's best friend ("Women," p. 141); Oja further quotes a homophobic remark by Louis Gruenberg, one of the original founders of the league ("Women," p. 154n70).

28 "Composers' Conference—Yaddo," transcript, 2 and 3 May 1932, BCUW; C-P I, pp. 204, 207.

29 Olmstead, *Correspondence,* pp. 177–82, 190–93, 211–12, 226.

30 Olmstead, *Correspondence,* p. 241; Copland to Carlos Chávez, 30 September 1935, CCLC, in which he refers to Sessions' Violin Concerto as "extremely difficult—almost too difficult I should say," and recommends the slow movement of the First Symphony. William R. Trotter, *Priest of Music: The Life of Dimitri Mitropoulos* (Portland, OR: Amadeus Press, 1995), p. 457n8, reports that, according to a former Sessions student, David Cooper, Sessions was "particularly jealous and suspicious of Copland" in the late 1940s; Andrea Olmstead, E-mail to author, 1 April 1997, responds, "All I can say is that Sessions never said anything against Copland in my hearing, and he called me his 'confidante.' Jealousy and suspicions were not part of his personality at that stage of his life." David Diamond, a close associate of both Sessions and Copland, claimed that Sessions was jealous but not suspicious of Copland, interview by author, 7 April 1996.

31 C-P I, p. 242; Diamond, interview; Copland, "Neglected Works: A Symposium," *Modern Music* 23 (1946): 8; Copland, *The New Music,* pp. 127–31; Phillip Ramey, interview by author, 6 April 1997.

32 Olmstead, *Correspondence,* pp. 217, 267, 310; Roger Sessions, *Reflections on the Music Life in the United States* (New York: Merlin Press, 1956), pp. 146–66; Diamond, interview, 1997; Milton Babbitt, interview by author, 18 November 1996.

33 C-P I, p. 118–19 (the phrases "at that time" and "when I first knew him" intimate that, for Copland, Harris lost his "freshness" and "simple charm" by the time of this recollection); Phillip Ramey, interview by author, 6 May 1994; Neil Gould, interview by author, 26 March 1996.

34 Copland, *The New Music,* pp. 119–26; Stevenson.

35 Dan Stehman, *Roy Harris: An American Musical Pioneer* (Twayne Publishers, 1984), p. 52; Roy Harris to Copland, [1931], CCLC; Léonie Rosenstiel, *Nadia Boulanger: A Life in Music* (New York: Norton, 1982), pp. 228–29, 384; Diamond, interview; Copland, *The New Music,* pp. 121–26.

36 Roy Harris to Copland, undated [c. 1930], 28 March 1930, 22 September 1930, CCLC (Harris had, in particular, a running feud with Sessions and Israel Citkowitz over, among other things, the neoclassical Stravinsky, in particular, *Oedipus Rex,* which Harris loathed; it seems that underlying some of such conflicts was some rivalry between Citkowitz and Harris for Copland's attentions); Copland to Israel Citkowitz, 29 May 1930, CCLC.

37 Roy Harris to Copland, 26 June 1942, CCLC; Gould, interview; Copland to William Schuman, 22 September 1943, SCNY.

38 Ramey, interview; C-P I, p. 75.

39 Copland, *Copland on Music*, p. 151; Virgil Thomson, *Virgil Thomson* (New York: Da Capo, 1966), pp. 78–80, 208, 220; Julia Smith, *Aaron Copland: His Work and Contribution to American Music* (New York: Dutton, 1955), p. 109.

40 Tim Page and Vanessa Weeks Page, *Selected Letters of Virgil Thomson* (New York: Summit Books, 1988), pp. 100–01, 103–04; Anthony Tommasini, *Virgil Thomson: Composer on the Aisle* (New York: Norton, 1997), p. 349.

41 Virgil Thomson to Copland, 27 May 1932, CCLC; Thomson, "American Composers. VII: Aaron Copland," *Modern Music* 9.2 (1932): 67–72; Thomson, "The Cult of Jazz," *Vanity Fair* 24.4 (1925): 54; Thomson, *Virgil Thomson*, p. 207.

42 Theodore Chanler, "Aaron Copland," *American Composers on American Music: A Symposium,* ed. by Henry Cowell (New York: F. Unger, 1962), pp. 49–56; Theodore Chanler to Copland, August 1930, 20 August 1930, CCLC; Theodore Chanler, "The New Romanticism," *Modern Music* 19.1 (1941): 65–67; C-P II, p. 301.

43 Copland, *The New Music*, pp. 135–39; Copland to Leonard Bernstein, 4 June 1947, BCLC.

44 Page, pp. 127–29 (Thomson was particularly skeptical of Copland's discussion of sonata form); Copland, "Thomson's Musical State," *Modern Music* 7.1 (1939): 63–65; Phillip Ramey, interview by author, 6 May 1994.

45 C-P I, pp. 276–77, 199–200; Tommasini, p. 271; Thomson, *Virgil Thomson,* pp. 278–79.

46 Ned Rorem, *Knowing When to Stop: A Memoir* (New York: Simon & Schuster, 1994), pp. 207, 281; David Diamond, interview by author, 10 February 1996.

47 Tommasini, p. 443.

48 Thomson, *American Music*, pp. 53–55.

49 Harold Clurman to Copland, 4 March 1948, CCLC; see also Bernstein's 1989 obituary for Thomson, Tommasini, p. 563; C-P II, p. 123; Rorem, pp. 281, 322; Donald R. Vroon, *American Record Guide* 60.6 (1997): 300.

50 Copland to Roger Sessions [1928], CCLC; Copland, *Our New Music*, p. 132; Copland to Carlos Chávez, 30 September 1935, CCLC.

51 Copland, *Our New Music*, p. 133; Howard Pollack, *Walter Piston* (Ann Arbor: UMI Research Press, 1982), p. 181; Charles Mills, "Over the Air," *Modern Music* 18.3 (1941): 199–202.

52 Pollack, p. 174; William W. Austin, "Thoughts on Piston and Copland," unpublished, 1980, courtesy of the author.

53 Diamond, interview, 15 May; Walter Piston to Copland, c. 1938, CCLC; Walter Piston, *Orchestration* (New York: W. W. Norton, 1955), p. 312; Pollack, p. 174 (in contrast to *Orchestration*'s nine Copland examples, one finds

only two examples by William Schuman, one by Riegger, and a reference to Creston). Piston did not cite Copland, or any specific composer, in discussing the wood block, saying only that it "has been used orchestrally chiefly by American composers in the twentieth century"; but Copland—along with Ferde Grofé—clearly helped further that instrument's popularity among American concert composers.

54 Donald Fuller, "Style in Recent Chamber Music," *Modern Music* 21.3 (1944): 165; Robert Tangeman, "Variations for a Jubilee," *Modern Music* 22.4 (1945): 261; Pollack, pp. 104–05.

55 Diamond, interview, 15 May; Ronald Caltabiano to Ellis Freedman, 7 May 1986, CCLC; Olmstead, *Correspondence*, pp. 474, 484; Leo Smit, interview with author, 4 May 1994; Ramey, interview.

56 Malcolm Bessom, "Conversation with Copland," *Music Educator's Journal* 59.7 (1973): 47; Ramey, "Copland at 80," pp. 124, 148.

12. Copland and Younger American Composers

1 Roy Harris to Copland, 26 March 1933, CCLC.

2 Bernard Heiden, interview by author, 18 December 1996 (Copland arranged to have the parts copied through Philadelphia's Fleisher Library).

3 Arthur Berger, marginalia; Israel Citkowitz to Copland, 30 July 1926, 26 February 1928 ("tenderness"), CCLC; C-P I, p. 129; David Diamond, marginalia.

4 Israel Citkowitz to Copland, September 1926, 2 November 1930, 18 September 1934, CCLC; C-P I, p. 139.

5 C-P I, pp. 138, 153; Israel Citkowitz to Copland, 1 October 1927, 26 October 1929, 29 May 1930, 15 September 1934; Andrea Olmstead, ed., *The Correspondence of Roger Sessions* (Boston: Northeastern University Press, 1992), p. 147; Ned Rorem, liner notes, *But Yesterday Is Not Today* (New World Records NW 243), p. 5.

6 Eric A. Gordon, *Mark the Music: The Life and Work of Marc Blitzstein* (New York: St. Martin's Press, 1989), p. 46 ("infatuated"); Israel Citkowitz to Copland, 26 October 1929, 7 April 1931; Copland to Israel Citkowitz, 29 May 1930, 13 September 1933, CCLC.

7 C-P I, p. 333; C-P II, p. 156. In the late 1950s Citkowitz married the Irish aristocrat Lady Caroline Blackwood (1931–1996), a latter-day Alma Mahler whose other husbands included, before and after, the painter Lucian Freud and the poet Robert Lowell, "Lady Caroline Blackwood, Wry Novelist, Is Dead at 64," *New York Times* 15 February 1996.

8 Marc Blitzstein, unidentified letter, 16 November 1927, BCUW; Gordon, pp. 34, 46, 48–49, 461 (Moor); Marc Blitzstein to Eva Goldbeck, 30 September 1929, BCUW ("too young").

9 Marc Blitzstein to Eva Goldbeck, 18 September 1929, BCUW; Blitzstein scholar Mitchell Patton surmises that the two may have had sex during this trip, perhaps with an eye to even establishing a relationship, Patton, letter to author, 16 August 1996.

10 Marc Blitzstein to Eva Goldbeck, 13 January 1931, BCUW; Copland, "Neglected Works," p. 8; Eva Goldbeck to Lina ("Mutzi") Goldbeck, 26 August 1935 (Ruth Page); Gordon, p. 76; Copland, *The New Music: 1900–1960* (New York: W. W. Norton, 1968), pp. 139–40.

11 Copland, *The New Music,* pp. 139–44.

12 Marc Blitzstein, "New York Chronicle of New Music," *Modern Music* 8.2 (1931): 39–42; Marc Blitzstein, "Premieres and Experiments—1932," *Modern Music* 9.3 (1932): 121–27; Marc Blitzstein, "Composers as Lecturers and in Concerts," *Modern Music* 13.1 (1935): 47–50; Meryle Secrest, *Leonard Bernstein: A Life* (New York: Knopf, 1994), p. 304.

13 Christopher Sawyer-Lauçanno, *An Invisible Spectator: A Biography of Paul Bowles* (New York: Ecco Press, 1989), p. 87 ("He likes"); Gena Dagel Caponi, *Paul Bowles: Romantic Savage* (Carbondale: Southern Illinois University Press, 1994), p. 42.

14 Phillip Ramey, "You Didn't Want Even to Meet Prokofiev?" *Paul Bowles: Music* (New York: Eos Music Inc., 1995) ("wholeheartedly"); Gena Dagel, "A Nomad in New York: Paul Bowles 1933–1948," *American Music* 7.3 (1989); Jeffrey Miller, ed., *In Touch: The Letters of Paul Bowles* (New York: Farrar, Straus and Giroux, 1994); Jay Harrison, "Composer at Home Abroad," *New York Herald Tribune* 17 May 1953, Clipping File, CCLC; Caponi ("alert"), p. 42.

15 Sawyer-Lauçanno, p. 49 ("an exceedingly"); Eva Goldbeck to Cecil Goldbeck, 21 July 1931, BCUW.

16 Sawyer-Lauçanno, pp. 129–30 ("coy"), ("Aaron"), p. 148 (Bowles apparently spread a rumor that Copland had given him hemorrhoids); Virgil Thomson, *Virgil Thomson* (New York: Da Capo, 1966), p. 206; Miller, p. 63 ("When you"). In later years, when questioned about the nature of his relationship with Copland, Bowles remained elusive; although one piece of evidence points to physical intimacy—a 1933 letter from Bowles to Thomson expressing resentment of Copland's new lover, Victor Kraft ("Aaron of course has a new pet so there is no snuggling there")—Bowles told Phillip Ramey that he intended the remark metaphorically, Ramey, interview by author, 6 May 1994.

17 Miller, p. 364; Caponi, p. 45; Arnold Dobrin, *Aaron Copland: His Life and Times* (New York: Thomas Y. Crowell, 1967), pp. 106–07; Christopher Isherwood, *Christopher and His Kind* (New York: Avon Books, 1976), pp. 59–60.

18 Sawyer-Lauçanno, pp. 97–115 ("For Copland Morocco was a continual source of bewildering frustration, for Bowles a continual source of amazement," p. 111); Copland to Eva Goldbeck, 27 August 1931, BCUW ("If there is anything more unappetizing than a piano out of tune, I'd like to know it," he explained to Goldbeck); Phillip Ramey, "Aaron Copland: Genial Patriarch of American Music," *Ovation* November 1985: 13, BHCF

Notes

Notes

Notes

("Of course"); Copland to Eva Goldbeck, 7 October 1931, BCUW ("wonderfully regal"); Caponi, pp. 50–52.

19 Ramey, "You Didn't"; Sawyer-Lauçanno, p. 129 ("It"); Lawrence D. Stewart, *Paul Bowles: The Illumination of North Africa* (Carbondale: Southern Illinois University Press, 1974), p. 11.

20 Miller, p. 105; Paul Bowles to Copland, 20 February 1933; Copland to Paul Bowles, 24 October 1934, CCLC.

21 Lauçanno, pp. xii ("the world"), 153–282; Copland, *Copland on Music* (New York: Norton, 1963), p. 162; Ramey, "Paul Bowles: A Memoir," *Paul Bowles: Music* ("Don't be"); Ramey interview ("Oh, he was").

22 Copland to Ross Lee Finney, 25 February 1930, 28 June 1934, 2 November 1966, Ross Lee Finney Collection, NYPL.

23 C-P I, pp. 191–94; Arthur Berger, "The Young Composers' Group," *Trend* April-May-June 1933: 26–28.

24 Henry Brant, interview by author, 15 September 1996 ("Whatever"); Copland to Israel Citkowitz, 25 January 1930; Copland to Eva Goldbeck and Marc Blitzstein, 13 February 1931, BCUW; Cole Gagne and Tracy Caras, *Soundpieces: Interviews with American Composers* (Metuchen: Scarecrow Press, 1982), pp. 54–55; Copland to Henry Brant, letters 1930–33, CCLC; C-P I, p. 207.

25 Steven C. Smith, *A Heart at Fire's Center: The Life and Music of Bernard Herrmann* (Berkeley: University of California Press, 1991), pp. 30–33; C-P I, pp. 192–93; Arthur Berger, interview by author, 8 May 1995; Berger, "Young Composers" ("devout"), p. 26 (Berger claimed, at this point, only Moross and Heilner as Ivesians, though he added that Ives had been "taken up by the Group," p. 27); Carol Oja, "Composer with a Conscience: Elie Siegmeister in Profile," *American Music* 6.2 (1988): 165; Miller, p. 163.

26 Brant, interview; C-P I, p. 193; David Ewen, ed., *The Book of Modern Composers* (New York: Knopf, 1950), p. 466; Lehman Engel, *This Bright Day: An Autobiography* (New York: Macmillan, 1974), p. 39; Arthur Berger, *Aaron Copland* (New York: Oxford University Press, 1953), p. 21.

27 Sam Kashner and Nancy Schoenberger, *A Talent for Genius* (New York: Villard Books, 1994); Oscar Levant, *The Memoirs of an Amnesiac* (New York: G. P. Putnam's, 1965), p. 107; Oscar Levant, *A Smattering of Ignorance* (New York: Doubleday, Doran and Co., 1940), pp. 213, 222, 225, 230.

28 Kushner, p. 113; Levant, *A Smattering*, p. 213.

29 Copland to Henry Brant, 1932 and 1933, CCLC; Copland to Israel Citkowitz, September 1934; Copland to Paul Bowles, 8 January 1935 ("crib"), to which Bowles replied, "I shudder at the thought of all the good-sounding bad music that will fall on the backs of the people when Roger turns his classes out into the world," Bowles to Copland, January 1935, CCLC; Copland, *Copland on Music*, pp. 159–63.

30 Irwin Heilner to Copland, 10 March 1968; C-P II, p. 209.

605

31 C-P I, p. 350; C-P II, pp. 7–8; Alfred Williams Cochran, "Style, Structure, and Tonal Organization in the Early Film Scores of Aaron Copland" (Ph.D. diss., Catholic University, 1986), p. 202 (for Moross and *Our Town*); Johnny Green to Copland, 24 July 1947, CCLC.

32 Levant, *Smattering,* pp. 235–36; Kushner, p. 181.

33 Smith, p. 86n; Royal S. Brown, "An Interview with Bernard Herrmann," *High Fidelity* 26.9 (1976): 64–67; Bernard Herrmann, "The Contemporary Use of Music in Film: *Citizen Kane, Psycho, Fahrenheit 451,*" *University Film Study Center Newsletter Supplement* 7.3 (1977): 5–10; C-P II, p. 7; Alex North to Copland, 23 October 1946, 29 July 1947, 10 October 1957; Copland to North, undated, CCLC; see Christopher Palmer, *The Composer in Hollywood* (New York: Marion Boyars, 1990), p. 295, for Copland's influence on North.

34 Copland, review of Conlon Nancarrow's *Toccata* and *Prelude and Blues,* "Scores and Records," *Modern Music* 15.3 (1938): 180; in Kyle Gann, *The Music of Conlon Nancarrow* (New York: Cambridge University Press, 1995), the author writes, "It is easy to see why Copland gave the Prelude and Blues a flattering review; they are in the style of his early jazz works, and not well-written enough to pose competition," an unlikely assumption; Copland to John Kennedy, September 1953, courtesy of Kennedy.

35 In response to a 1945 request from Roy Harris (2 May 1945, CCLC) for "a list of the ten composers of symphonic and chamber music whom [*sic*] you think are most worthy to represent American culture to European nations," Copland (10 May 1945, CCLC) named Schuman, Barber, and Diamond along with such older composers as Gershwin, Harris, Ives, Piston, Sessions, Thompson, and Thomson. He added, however, that such a list would vary according to the purposes at hand: "For example, for a broad radio audience I would prescribe R[obert] R[ussell] Bennett or M[orton] Gould rather than R[oger] Sessions, altho from a purely cultural standpoint I think the latter more significant. But of course the significance would only be apparent to an elite public."

36 David Diamond to Copland, 15 June 1939, 20 March 1956, 19 August 1964, 16 November 1967, 24 March 1969, 20 October 1970, 16 June 1980, CCLC; although Diamond praised *Connotations* and *Inscape* to Copland, he was critical of these works in an interview by the author, 15 May 1994: "I hear noise music in the *Connotations*; when he [Copland] starts plunking around with the 12 notes, then we get real noise. And *Connotations* is unbearable. I really can't listen to it."

37 Copland, *Copland on Music,* p. 163; Copland, "Scores and Records," *Modern Music* 15.4 (1938): 246; Diamond, interview.

38 David Diamond to Copland, 22 October 1940, 24 June 1943, CCLC; C-P I, pp. 241–42; Copland to David Diamond, 17 February 1947. Though appreciative of Copland's intervention, Diamond defended himself to Vivian Perlis, saying, "I'd had two manhattans, no more," and "I was upset because I

could not find work." At the same time, Copland often enjoyed, in what John Kennedy calls "his sportively mischievous way," Diamond's outspokenness.

39 C-P I, p. 243; C-P II, pp. 173, 401.

40 Copland, "Scores and Records," p. 245; C-P I, pp. 282 ("What"), 351; Copland, "Current Chronicle," *Musical Quarterly* 37 (1951): 394–96.

41 William Schuman to Copland, 31 March 1943, CCLC; Laura Stanfield, "Orchestration in Time of War: American Responses to Pearl Harbor," Sonneck Society Annual Meeting, 7 March 1997; C-P I, pp. 348, 353–54.

42 C-P I, pp. 351–52.

43 William Schuman to Copland, 17 December 1945, 17 January 1946, SCNY; Copland to Schuman, 17 January 1946, SCNY; William Schuman, "Statement on Copland," 29 October 1965, SCNY; Phillip Ramey, "Copland at 80," *Chicago* January 1981: 148, 149, BHCF.

44 Copland, *Copland on Music*, p. 162; Barbara Heyman, *Samuel Barber: The Composer and His Music* (New York: Oxford University Press, 1992), p. 242 (Heyman quotes Mills as saying, "It [the Capricorn Concerto] exemplifies what a productive study of Copland will do for a young musician who has been brought up in the tradition of big, fat sounds and pompous effects"); Ramey, interview.

45 Heyman, p. 174; Samuel Barber to Copland, 28 August 1967, CCLC; Copland, radio broadcast (transcript), 1982, CCLC; Ramey, "Copland at 80," p. 149.

46 Samuel Barber to Copland, 12 August 1953; 17 June 1960, CCLC; Heyman, p. 414 ("contemporary").

47 Charles Turner, interview by author, 23 May 1998; Charles Turner, letter to author, 4 June 1998; Heyman, p. 294 ("rejected"); Harold Shapero, interview by author, 3 January 1997; see also John Gruen, *Menotti: A Biography* (New York: Macmillan, 1978), p. 117.

48 Secrest, pp. 43–44.

49 C-P I, p. 337; Secrest, pp. 70–71.

50 C-P I, pp. 335, 339; C-P II, pp. 129, 210; Howard Pollack, *Harvard Composers: Walter Piston and His Students, from Elliott Carter to Frederic Rzewski* (Metuchen: Scarecrow Press, 1992), pp. 105, 278; William Westbrook Burton, *Conversations About Bernstein* (New York: Oxford University Press, 1995), p. 13; Humphrey Burton, *Leonard Bernstein* (New York: Doubleday, 1994), pp. 50, 52, 134; Copland to Leonard Bernstein, September 1939, CCLC.

51 Vivian Perlis, transcript of conversation with Copland and Leonard Bernstein, CCLC.

52 Secrest, pp. 96, 180; Erik Johns, interview by author, 13 December 1994; Paul Moor, interview by author, 26 July 1995; Burton, pp. 43, 82; Leonard Bernstein to Copland, 26 June 1939, CCLC; Bernstein to Copland, 14 September 1943, BCLC.

53 Burton, pp. 96, 102, 109, 132.

54 Leonard Bernstein to Copland, 6 February 1948, 6 September 1948, 1959, CCLC; Humphrey Burton, p. 370. During these later years, Copland would

jokingly refer to Bernstein as a "PH" ("phony homo"), Phillip Ramey, interview by author, 6 May 1994.

55 Shapero, interview; Humphrey Burton, pp. 102, 107.

56 Copland, *Copland on Music,* p. 173 (based on "The New 'School' of American Composers," *New York Times,* 14 March 1948, sec. VI, p. 18); Copland to Irving Fine, 14 November 1944, FCLC; David Conte, letter to author, 12 November 1997.

57 C-P I, p. 334; Humphrey Burton, pp. 99; Joan Peyser, *Bernstein: A Biography* (New York: William Morrow, 1987), p. 56.

58 Virgil Thomson, *American Music Since 1910* (New York: Holt, Rinehart and Winston, 1970), p. 58; C-P I, p. 334; C-P II, pp. 69, 71.

59 Humphrey Burton, pp. 85, 165; C-P I, pp. 334, 359; C-P II, pp. 71, 154; Leonard Bernstein to Copland, 1952, CCLC.

60 C-P II, pp. 232, 353; Ramey, interview; Humphrey Burton, p. 458; Copland to Leonard Bernstein, 23 September 1958. Oscar Levant relates this relevant exchange with Bernstein: " 'Do you identify yourself with Mahler?' I asked Lenny. 'Only when I play Mahler,' he said. 'But you play Mahler all the time,' I rejoined," *The Unimportance of Being Oscar* (New York: G. P. Putnam's Sons, 1968), pp. 152–53.

61 C-P II, pp. 367–68; Verna Fine, interview with author, 7 May 1994; Humphrey Burton, p. 458; Ronald Caltabiano to Leonard Bernstein, 3 May 1988, BCLC; Lukas Foss, interview with author, 6 June 1995.

62 Copland, *Copland on Music,* pp. 164–75.

63 Copland, "Influence, Problem, Tone," *Dance Index* 6.10-12 (1947): 249, reprinted in *Stravinsky in the Theatre,* ed. by Minna Lederman (New York: Da Capo, 1975), pp. 121–22; Arthur Berger, "Stravinsky and the Younger American Composers," *Score* 12 (1955): 38–46; Pollack, p. 161.

64 Berger, "Stravinsky," p. 40; C-P II, p. 69 ("popularist tendencies").

65 C-P I, p. 235; Foss recently revealed that he was born not in 1922, as usually given, but in 1923.

66 Shapero, interview; C-P I, pp. 308, 311; C-P II, pp. 132, 284–85.

67 C-P II, pp. 132–33, 285; Pollack, pp. 140–41; Shapero, interview.

68 C-P I, p. 141; C-P II, p. 284 (*Billy the Kid* profoundly influenced Foss's *The Prairie*; Foss also quoted a tune from the score in a work from the 1970s, Lukas Foss to Copland, 26 June 1976, CCLC); Harold Shapero, "Neglected Works: A Symposium," *Modern Music* 23 (1946): 9; Leo Smit, interview with author, 4 May 1994; Foss to Copland, 6 August 1964, CCLC; Shapero to Copland, 5 January 1962, CCLC; C-P II, pp. 65, 287; Lukas Foss to Copland, undated [c. 1976?], CCLC ("Yours"); Harold Shapero to Copland, 18 May 1943, CCLC ("I liked").

69 Irving Fine to Copland, 1 February 1950, CCLC; Harold Shapero, 5 May 1943; Lukas Foss to Copland, 18 September 1965, CCLC; Copland, liner notes to *Music of Irving Fine* (Desto DC 7167); Foss, interview; C-P II, p. 285.

70 Copland, review of Stefan Wolpe's *Two Songs, Notes* 6 (1948): 172; Copland,

"Neglected Works: A Symposium," *Modern Music* 23 (1946): 8; Copland, review of Leon Kirchner's *Duo* for violin and piano, *Notes* 8 (1950): 434.

71 Easley Blackwood, interview by author, 4 December 1996.

72 Milton Babbitt, interview by author, 18 November 1996; Ralph Shapey, interview by author, 18 December 1996; Gunther Schuller, interview by author, 27 January 1997.

73 Shapey, interview; Schuller, interview; Samuel Adler, interview by author, 19 March 1996; Karl Korte, interview by author, 7 May 1997. Another airing of such resentments, without mention of Copland by name, can be found in Secrest, p. 256, as follows: "The composer Benjamin Lees claimed it was a disadvantage not to be a homosexual in the music world and that careers of many heterosexuals had suffered from a form of discrimination. He claimed to know a well-known composer who had deliberately changed his sexual orientation in order to improve his career prospects."

74 Albert Goldberg, "The Sound Board," 1957, BHCF; Copland, *Copland on Music,* pp. 175–78.

75 Copland, *Copland on Music,* pp. 175–78.

76 Else Stone and Kurt Stone, eds., *The Writings of Elliott Carter: An American Composer Looks at Modern Music* (Bloomington: Indiana University Press, 1977), pp. 13, 33, 46, 47 ("Each new"), 82, 96, 112, 187–88 ("emancipated").

77 Copland to Serge Koussevitzky, 25 September 1939, Koussevitzky Collection, LC; Copland to Ashley Pettis, Composers Forum Special Collection, NYPL; David Schiff, *The Music of Elliott Carter* (New York: Da Capo Press, 1983), pp. 113–15; Kennedy, interview.

78 Kennedy, interview; Copland, Diaries, December 1961, CCLC.

79 Ramey, interview; Korte, interview; "Copland on Carter," *New York Philharmonic Program Book* November 1978, CCLC; Nicholas Kenyon, "The Scene Surveyed," *Music and Musician* 24 (1975): 22–23.

80 David Walker, interview by author, 18 July 1996.

81 Copland, "America's Young Men of Music" (December 1960), BHCF; see also Copland, Diaries, October 1961, CCLC.

82 David Raymond, "His song expands our spirit," *City Times* (Rochester, NY), 15 November 1990, BHCF ("David"); John Cage to Copland, 20 January 1974.

83 Morton Feldman to Copland, 21 August 1968.

84 Hugo Leichtentritt, *Serge Koussevitzky: The Boston Symphony Orchestra and the New American Music* (Cambridge: Harvard University Press, 1946), pp. 171–76. Barber substituted for Honegger at the last minute in 1947 and Sessions took Copland's place in 1955, coteaching with Boris Blacher.

85 Herbert Kupferberg, *Tanglewood* (New York: McGraw-Hill, 1976); Erich Leinsdorf to Copland, 12 August 1963, CCLC. Although Perlis states that Copland suggested Schuller for the position, C-P II, p. 319, Kupferberg, Schuller, and David Diamond agree that the idea originated principally with

Leinsdorf; Schuller further contends that he was not Copland's first choice, Schuller, interview.

86 C-P II, p. 317; Kupferberg, p. 192.

87 C-P II, pp. 129–30; Cole Gagne and Tracy Caras, *Soundpieces: Interviews with American Composers* (Metuchen: Scarecrow Press, 1982), p. 109; Copland to William Schuman, 29 December 1979; composers who had previously won the medal included Copland (1961), Varèse (1965), Sessions (1968), Schuman (1971), Piston (1974), and Thomson (1977).

88 Joe Stevenson, "A Conversation with Aaron Copland," *Your Musical Cue Quarterly* Spring 1973, BHCF ("I think Mario Davidovski [*sic*] is an especially gifted man"); C-P II, pp. 281–82; Korte, interview, recalled, however, some disapproval of John Duffy's composing a piece for John Coltrane.

89 Ned Rorem, *Knowing When to Stop: A Memoir* (New York: Simon & Schuster, 1994), p. 282; Paul Hertelendy, "The Cabrillo Festival: Alert," *High Fidelity/Musical America* December 1978: MA-30, BHCF ("too much"); Ned Rorem, *Settling the Score* (New York: Harcourt Brace Jovanovich, 1988), p. 22; Ned Rorem, *Other Entertainment* (Simon & Schuster, 1996), p. 275.

90 Adler, interview; Raymond.

91 William Flanagan to Copland, 5 May 1956, 29 October 1962, 1 February 1963; Rorem, *Settling*, p. 36.

92 C-P II, pp. 319–21, 356; Robert Jacobson, "David Del Tredici," *After Dark* August 1973: 50; Peter Galvin, "Silent Nights," *Advocate* 22 August 1995: 50.

93 C-P II, p. 320; David Del Tredici, interview on *Soundings*, BBC Radio, Michael Oliver, narrator, 24 November 1991.

94 "David Del Tredici"; Ramey, interview; Robert Cornell, interview by author, 19 August 1996; David Del Tredici to Copland, 12 April 1982.

95 C-P II, pp. 259, 355–57; Ramey interview. Del Tredici and Ramey shared a special enthusiasm for *Inscape*, Phillip Ramey to Copland, 8 March 1969, CCLC ("I have decided that *Inscape* may be your masterpiece") and David Del Tredici to Copland, 7 October 1983, CCLC ("I love *Inscape*, contrary to what one silly little critic says. Your 12-tone music especially in *Inscape* is as fresh, poetic and beautiful as anything you've written. Grrrrrr!").

96 Phillip Ramey to Copland, [May 1969], 8 May 1974, CCLC.

97 Phillip Ramey to Copland, CCLC; Phillip Ramey, interview with author, 10 May 1996.

98 Carlisle Floyd, "Copland Remembered," *Opera News* 55.10 (1991): 33; Meryle Secrest, *Stephen Sondheim: A Life* (New York: Alfred A. Knopf, 1998), pp. 68, 86; Stephen Sondheim, letter to author, 26 March 1998.

99 Betty Auman, interview by author, 18 March 1998.

100 Kenyon, pp. 22–23.

101 Philip Glass, interview by author, 31 October 1997; Philip Glass, "Growing Bold in the Presence of a 'Great Man,'" *New York Times* 9 December 1990; Ronald Caltabiano, interview by author, 2 July 1996; Steve Reich to Cop-

land, 27 October 1980, CCLC; David Walker, interview by author, 5 May 1994.

[102] Ramey, interview; Phillip Ramey, "A Talk with John Corigliano," New World Records (NW 309); John Corigliano, interview by author, 2 August 1997.

[103] C-P II, p. 314; Barbara Kolb, interview by author, 23 August 1996; Barbara Kolb to Copland, 10 August 1972, 29 October 1980, 4 September 1982, CCLC.

[104] Copland, *Copland on Music,* p. 14.

[105] Copland, *Music and Imagination* (Cambridge: Harvard University Press, 1952), pp. 43–44; Copland, "Nadia Boulanger: An Affectionate Portrait," *Harper's* October 1960: 49 (another statement from this essay, namely, "in so far as she [Boulanger] composed at all she must of necessity be listed in that unenviable category of the woman composer," was misquoted in a recent publication to read, "But had she become a composer, she would of biological necessity have joined the automatically inferior ranks of the 'woman composer,' " Catherine Parsons Smith, " 'A Distinguishing Virility': Feminism and Modernism in American Art Music," *Cecilia Reclaimed: Feminist Perspectives on Gender and Music* [Urbana: University of Illinois Press, 1994], p. 92); Hertelendy, MA-30 ("Writing"); Chuck Thurston, "Straight Answers from Copland," *Detroit Free Press* 17 May 1978 ("Music), CCLC.

[106] For Copland as "implicated" in "the legendary misogyny of the [musical] profession," see Philip Brett, "Musicality, Essentialism, and the Closet," *Queering the Pitch: The New Gay and Lesbian Musicology* (New York: Routledge, 1994), p. 22; and for a misquote said to constitute an "infamous" misogynistic remark, see the previous footnote; Kolb, interview; Phillip Ramey, interview by author, 10 May 1996 (on Manziarly); C-P I, p. 201; Vivian Fine, interview by author, 27 September 1996 (according to Fine, Copland expressed some surprise that a woman would pursue composition, but he helped launch her career at Yaddo in 1932 and could not have been, she thought, more supportive or generous); Copland to Irving Fine, 19 November 1947, FCLC (on Sebastiani); Sheila Eastman and Timothy J. McGee, *Barbara Pentland* (Toronto: University of Toronto Press, 1983) (Copland apparently had a profound and lifelong influence on Pentland's music; see especially pp. 34–36, 45, 61, 63–64, 77, 109); Thea Musgrave to Copland, 8 February 1958; Musgrave remembered Copland as "very nice and encouraging"; she assumed that he helped her get a Koussevitzky Award, Musgrave, interview by author, 10 November 1996.

[107] Christopher (as a boy, "Chip") Rouse to Copland, 6 April 1962, 3 May 1966, 9 August 1966, 31 August 1967, 5 June 1970, CCLC.

[108] Copland to Christopher Rouse, 20 July 1968, 13 June 1971, courtesy of Rouse.

[109] Christopher Rouse to Copland, 1 June 1971, 17 June 1971, 16 April 1977, 27 May 1977, CCLC.

[110] Kupferberg, p. 228; C-P II, p. 357.

111 Virgil Thomson, presentation of the Gold Medal for Music by the American Academy of Arts and Letters, 1956, CCLC.

13. South of the Border

1 Robert L. Parker, "Copland and Chávez: Brothers-in-Arms," *American Music* 5.4 (1987): 434.

2 Robert Stevenson, *Music in Mexico: A Historical Survey* (New York: Thomas Y. Crowell, 1952); Robert L. Parker, *Carlos Chávez: Mexico's Modern-Day Orpheus* (Boston: Twayne, 1983).

3 Parker, pp. 4–6.

4 James W. Wilkie and Albert L. Michaels, *Revolution in Mexico: Years of Upheaval, 1910–1940* (New York: Alfred A. Knopf, 1969); John Mason Hart, *Revolutionary Mexico: The Coming and Process of the Mexican Revolution* (Berkeley: University of California Press, 1987).

5 Carlos Chávez, *Musical Thought* (Cambridge, MA: Harvard University Press, 1961), pp. 95–96; Diego Rivera, *My Art, My Life* (New York: 1960, 1991), p. 95.

6 Chávez, pp. 97–98; Copland to Carlos Chávez, 29 February 1929, CCLC.

7 Chávez, pp. 97–98.

8 Stevenson, p. 240; C-P I, p. 214.

9 Dore Ashton, "Mexican Art of the Twentieth Century," *Mexico: Splendors of Thirty Centuries* (New York: Metropolitan Museum of Art, 1990), p. 556; Philip Stein, *Siqueiros: His Life and Works* (New York: International Publishers, 1994), pp. 167, 214; Carlos Chávez to Copland, 18 January 1935, CCLC; Rivera, pp. 167–173.

10 J. H. Plenn, *Mexico Marches* (New York: Bobbs-Merrill Co., 1939), p. 343; Parker, *Carlos Chávez*, p. 126.

11 Parker, "Copland and Chávez," pp. 436–37. Copland thought of Chávez, surely, as Mexican, but also—as with the Canadian composer Colin McPhee—as simply "American," Howard Pollack, *Skyscraper Lullaby: The Life and Music of John Alden Carpenter* (Washington: Smithsonian Institution Press, 1995), p. 387. In *Our New Music*, he profiled Chávez alongside American contemporaries in the chapter "Composers in America," Copland, *Our New Music* (New York: McGraw-Hill, 1941).

12 C-P II, p. 448n19.

13 Copland, "Carlos Chávez—Mexican Composer," *New Republic* 2 May 1928: 322–23; reprinted in *American Composers on American Music: A Symposium*, ed. by Henry Cowell (New York: F. Ungar, 1962), pp. 102–06. Copland slightly altered this article for his chapter on Chávez in *The New Music* (New York: Norton, 1968), pp. 145–50. He toned down the language, replacing, for example, the "complete overthrow" of tyrannizing "Germanic Ideals" with the "rejection of German ideals." In *Our New Music*, he newly emphasized the Indian character of Chávez's Mexicanness, changing the phrase "distinctly Mexican flavor" to "distinctive Indo-American dogged-

ness," and replacing "sun-filled, naïve, Latin soul" with "naïve, stolid, *mestizo* soul." In a similar vein, he now described the Sonata for Four Horns as "Mexican-Indian—stoic, stark, and somber, like an Orozco drawing."

[14] Copland to Carlos Chávez, 6 May 1959, 28 July 1967, 26 September 1971, CCLC; Copland, *The New Music,* p. 150.

[15] Carlos Chávez, "Aaron Copland," *El Universal,* 4 September 1932, CCLC ("una obra de suprema inteligencia, de sensibilidad superior, de supremo cultivo"); Carlos Chávez to Copland, 1 December 1934, 4 May 1955, CCLC; Carlos Chávez, "Neglected Works: A Symposium," *Modern Music* 23.1 (1946): 5–6.

[16] Carlos Chávez to Copland, 7 September 1931, 18 January 1935; Copland to Chávez, 26 December 1931, c. 1931, CCLC.

[17] Copland to Chávez, 7 July 1931, 7 April 1933; Carlos Chávez to Copland, 1 December 1934, CCLC.

[18] Carlos Chávez to Copland 25 November 1933, 22 December 1951; Copland to Chávez, 28 August 1935, CCLC.

[19] C-P I, p. 213 (Copland recalled that he and Kraft drove down to Laredo, but letters from the time indicate otherwise).

[20] Copland to his parents, 3 September 1932, 10 September 1932, 29 September 1932, CCLC; Copland to Henry Brant, 16 November 1932.

[21] Copland to Carlos Chávez, 16 December 1933, CCLC.

[22] Copland to his parents, 10 September 1932, CCLC.

[23] Arnold Dobrin, *Aaron Copland: His Life and Times* (New York: Thomas Y. Crowell, 1967), p. 126.

[24] Copland to Chávez, 2 January 1933, 2 February 1933; Copland to Mary Lescaze, 13 January 1933, CCLC.

[25] C-P II, pp. 25–27; Copland to Leonard Bernstein, 11 August 1944; Copland to Irving Fine, 12 August 1944; Copland to Arthur Berger, 8 September 1944, CCLC.

[26] C-P II, pp. 71, 273, 335; Copland to Irving Fine, 29 August 1953, FCLC; John Kennedy, interview by author, 5 August 1995; Copland to Carlos Chávez, 13 February 1959, 1 January 1965, CCLC.

[27] C-P I, pp. 216, 266; Copland to Carlos Chávez, 4 September 1937; Copland to Leonard Bernstein, 25 August 1949, BCLC; C-P II, pp. 208–09, 379.

[28] Silvestre Revueltas to Copland, October 1933, CCLC; Copland, "Mexican Composer," *New York Times* 9 May 1937.

[29] Copland, "Mexican Composer"; Copland, *Our New Music,* p. 149; Copland to Arthur Berger, 8 September 1944.

[30] Copland to Carlos Chávez, 31 December 1934; C-P I, p. 324; Copland to Arthur Berger, 8 September 1944.

[31] C-P I, pp. 318, 323–29.

[32] Rosamund Bernier, interview by author, 7 January 1996; Copland to Leonard Bernstein, undated letters from Havana, BCLC.

[33] Copland to Leonard Bernstein, undated letter from Quito, BCLC; Copland

to Laurine Marcus, 7 November 1941, CCLC; Copland, "The Composers of South America," *Modern Music* 19 (1942): 75–82; reprinted in *Copland on Music* (New York: W.W. Norton, 1960): 203–17.

34 Copland, "The Composers," p. 211; Copland, "Festival in Caracas," *New York Times* 26 December 1954, sec. II, p. 9 ("the pride"); Copland, *Music and Imagination* (Cambridge: Harvard University Press, 1952), pp. 92–93 (comparison with Ives).

35 Copland, "The Composers," pp. 203–17.

36 C-P II, pp. 78–84; Copland, "Composer's Report on Music in South America," *New York Times* 21 December 1947.

37 Copland, "The Composers," p. 216; C-P I, p. 326; C-P II, pp. 83–84; Dobrin, pp. 169–70 (Copland also visited, still farther north, the town of Fortaleza); Copland, "Composer's Report"; Copland to Irving and Verna Fine, 19 November 1947, FCLC.

38 Copland, *Music,* p. 82.

39 Copland, "Festival in Caracas"; C-P II, pp. 231, 267–69.

40 Heitor Villa-Lobos to Copland, 25 April 1947; Julián Orbón to Copland, 3 December 1960; Juan Orrego-Salas to Copland, 23 October 1981; Roque Cordero to Copland, 6 December 1987, CCLC.

41 Undated tribute by Copland; Alberto Ginastera to Copland, 2 February 1943, 20 January 1951, 28 January 1953, CCLC.

42 Roque Cordero, interview by author, 25 September 1997; Juan Orrego-Salas, interview by author, 23 September 1997.

43 Orrego-Salas, interview.

14. Personal Affairs

1 Clurman, *All People Are Famous (Instead of an Autobiography)* (New York: Harcourt Brace Jovanovich, 1974), pp. 26–28; Clurman to Copland, 14 July 1934, CCLC.

2 André Gide, *Corydon,* translated by Richard Howard (New York: Farrar, Straus and Giroux, 1983); David Diamond, interview by author, 6 May 1994.

3 C-P I, p. 28; Havelock Ellis and John Addington Symonds, *Sexual Inversion* (London: Wilson and Macmillan, 1897), p. 140 ("predisposition"), p. 123 ("artistic aptitude"); Phillip Ramey, interview by author, 6 May 1994; Diamond, interview; Noel Annan, *Our Age: English Intellectuals Between the World Wars—a Group Portrait* (New York: Random House, 1990), p. 116.

4 Diamond, interview; Ramey, interview; John Kennedy, interviews by author, 10 May 1994, 29 July 1995; see also George Chauncey, *Gay New York: Gender, Urban Culture, and the Making of the Gay Male World, 1890–1940* (New York: Basic Books, 1994), pp. 106, 280, 344. Discussing homosexual culture in New York during the period 1890–1940, Chauncey writes, "The cultural stance of the queer embodied the general middle-class preference for

privacy, self-restraint, and lack of self-disclosure, and for many men this constituted part of its appeal. Similarly, one source of middle-class gay men's distaste for the fairy's style of self-presentation was that its very brashness marked it in their minds as lower class—and its display automatically preempted social advancement." Not only this, but even as late as the 1960s, the "fairy" could wind up in jail for "lewd and lascivious behavior" or "disorderly conduct" simply by acting or dressing effeminately. According to Diamond, however, Copland disapproved of the "fairy's style" primarily because it caricatured women. Such sensibilities explain why Copland and many other homosexuals of his generation rejected the term *gay* when that word gained currency as a catchall for homosexuals in the 1960s; for them, the word recalled the "fairies" and "pansies" that they had more or less distanced themselves from.

[5] Erik Johns, interviews by author, 13 December 1994, 3 May 1994.

[6] Johns, interviews.

[7] Johns, interviews; Kennedy, interviews.

[8] Marc Blitzstein to Eva Goldbeck, 18 September 1929, BCUW; undated, unattributed list of Japanese contacts for Copland, CCLC; Johns, interviews; Kennedy, interviews.

[9] Humphrey Burton, *Leonard Bernstein* (New York: Doubleday, 1994), p. 475.

[10] Erik Johns, interview by author, 22 December 1996; Harold Shapero, interview with author, 3 January 1997; Paul Moor, E-mail to author, 13 February 1997.

[11] C-P I, p. 377n29; Eric A. Gordon, *Mark the Music: The Life and Work of Marc Blitzstein* (New York: St. Martin's Press, 1989); Robert Cornell, interview by author, 29 July 1995; according to Ned Rorem, *Knowing When to Stop: A Memoir* (New York: Simon & Schuster, 1994), when Paul Goodman first met Copland at a party, Goodman said, "A lot of cute boys here, don't you think?" after which Copland walked away, leaving Goodman with the impression that Copland was hypocritical (p. 304).

[12] Michael O'Connor, interview by author, 4 July 1996.

[13] Kent Kennan, interview by author, 9 February 1997; C-P II, p. 180.

[14] Anthony Tommasini, " 'Outing' Some 'In' Composers," *New York Times* 6 August 1995 ("tortured"); David Del Tredici, interviewed on *Soundings*, BBC Radio, Michael Oliver, narrator (24 November 1991); Kennedy, interviews.

[15] Cornell, interview; Kennedy, interviews; Betty Auman, interview by author, 18 March 1998; David Diamond to Copland, 4 July 1936, CCLC.

[16] C-P I, p. 213; Victor Kraft, 1951 visa application, CCLC; Rheba Kraft, interview by author, 16 November 1994.

[17] Photographs, CCLC.

[18] Victor Kraft to Copland, 11 February 1937, CCLC.

[19] C-P II, pp. 19, 65.

[20] Copland to Leonard Bernstein, April 39, BCLC; C-P II, p. 65; Rudy Burck-

hardt, interview by author, 4 May 1994; David Jacobs, interview by author, 23 August 1994.

21 C-P II, p. 135; Diamond, interview.

22 C-P I, p. 268; C-P II, p. 135.

23 Paul Bowles to Copland, 24 December 1934, Victor Kraft to Paul Bowles, 5 November 1936, CCLC; Kraft, interview.

24 Paul Bowles to Copland, 18 December 1935, Victor Kraft to Copland, 2 February 1937; Copland to Leonard Bernstein, 24 August 1942, CCLC.

25 Leonard Bernstein to Copland, two 1943 letters, CCLC.

26 C-P II, pp. 64, 126; Kennedy, interviews.

27 Burckhardt, interview; David Diamond contends that Kraft was genuinely bisexual, interview by author, 10 February 1996.

28 Victor Kraft to Verna Fine, FCLC, 1947; C-P II, p. 174–75.

29 David Walker, interviews by author, 5 May 1994, 27 July 1995.

30 Kraft, interview; C-P II, p. 387.

31 Paul Bowles to Copland, 18 February 1973, 7 March 1973, CCLC.

32 Another private reflection, this one scribbled on a piece of cardboard, seems also to be about Kraft: "You have great difficulty balancing your simple cheque-book bank-statement. How much more difficult, then, is it then for you to even begin to balance life-statements, which deal with multi-level interacting contingencies, events, sets, and options," undated jottings, Kraft file, CCLC.

33 Burckhardt, interview; Verna Fine, interview by author, 7 May 1994; Richard Hennessy, interview by author, 29 July 1995; Johns, interviews; Kennedy, interviews; Ramey, interview; Walker, interviews.

34 Ramey, interview; Walker, interviews.

35 Ramey, interview; Paul Moor, "Aaron Copland: Fanfare for an Uncommon Man," *Advocate* 15 January 1991: 55; Hennessy, interview; Cornell, interview.

36 C-P II, p. 387; Ramey, interview; Richard Hennessy to Copland, 5 August 1976.

37 Copland, last will and testament, 23 March 1984, courtesy of Verna Fine.

38 Auman, interview; Vivian Perlis to Ellis Freedman, 11 July 1986, CCLC; Perlis, interview with author, 22 March 1998. Both Ellis Freedman and Roger Levey, Copland's executors, deny knowing anything about the fate of the Copland-Kraft correspondence.

39 Morris Golde, interview by author, 31 October 1995; "Alvin Ross, Artist and Educator, 55," *New York Times* 11 December 1975; Hilton Kramer, review of a Ross memorial exhibition, *New York Times* 25 January 1976.

40 Johns, interviews; Rorem, pp. 174, 187; Cornell, interview; Arthur Weinstein, interview by author, 29 July 1995.

41 Paul Moor, interview by author, 26 July 1995.

42 C-P II, p. 111; Moor, interview; Paul Moor to Copland, 13 August 1946, 9 November 1947, CCLC; Paul Moor, E-mail to author, 3 March 1997.

[43] Paul Moor to Copland, 1976 (letter addressed to "Schmaaron"), 1 January 1981, CCLC; Moor, "Fanfare," p. 55; Moor, E-mail to author, 13 February 1997.

[44] Johns, interviews.

[45] Diamond, interview, 15 May; Erik Johns to Copland, March 1947, CCLC.

[46] Johns, interviews; Erik Johns to Victor Kraft, July 1949.

[47] Erik Johns to Copland, 30 June 1951, 24 October 1951, 4 February 1952, CCLC.

[48] Erik Johns, letters to Copland, CCLC; Johns, interviews.

[49] After leaving Copland in 1952, Johns lived in New York and for a short time in California. In the 1970s, he began an interior design business and moved to Carmel, New York, where he built a summer residence, at which Copland was often a guest.

[50] Johns, interviews; Charles Turner, interview with author, 23 May 1998; Fine, interview; Copland to Victor Kraft, October 1955, CCLC; Diamond, interview, 15 May 1994. Recalling the *Tender Land* episode, Kennedy empathized with Charles Lamb's statement "Anything awful makes me laugh," letter to author, 1 March 1997.

[51] Kennedy, interviews; Copland to John Kennedy, courtesy of Kennedy.

[52] Cornell, interview.

[53] Hennessy, interview; Kennedy, interviews; Ramey, interview; Walker, interviews; John Kenworthy-Browne, letter to author, 21 February 1997.

[54] Hennessy, interview.

[55] James Montgomery to Copland, 22 July 1963 (Montgomery kept in casual touch with Copland, Montgomery to Copland, 17 August 1974, CCLC); Cornell, interview.

[56] John Kenworthy-Browne to author, 27 October 1995.

[57] Donald Plotts, interview by author, 3 December 1995.

[58] Ann Douglas, *Terrible Honesty: Mongrel Manhattan in the 1920s* (New York: Farrar, Straus and Giroux, 1995), especially pp. 217–53; Carol J. Oja, "Women Patrons and Activists for Modernist Music: New York in the 1920s," *Modernism/Modernity* 4.1 (1997): 144–49 (for misogyny specific to the new-music scene in New York in the 1920s); Copland, interview with Glenn Plaskin, WNYC, 7 June 1983, courtesy of Phillip Ramey ("all those").

[59] Ned Rorem, p. 182; Arthur Berger, interview by author, 8 May 1995; Robert Cornell, interview by author, 19 August 1996.

[60] "Nadia Boulanger: An Affectionate Portrait," *Harper's* October 1960: 50.

[61] Claire R. Reis, *Composers, Conductors and Critics* (New York: Oxford University Press, 1955); Oja, p. 139; Claire R. Reis, *Composers in America* (New York: Macmillan, 1947).

[62] Reis, p. 210; "Claire Reis (1889–1978)," *Musical Quarterly* 64.3 (1978): 386–88; Claire R. Reis Memorial Service, Rodgers and Hammerstein Archive of Recorded Sound, NYPL.

[63] Copland, "Claire Reis," p. 386; Reis to Copland, 3 October 1966, CCLC.

64 R. Allen Lott, "Minna Lederman (Daniel)," *New Grove Dictionary of American Music*, vol. 3, ed. H. Wiley Hitchcock and Stanley Sadie (New York: Macmillan, 1986), p. 23; Minna Lederman, *The Life and Death of a Small Magazine* (Brooklyn College: ISAM Monographs, no. 18, 1983), pp. 7, 198.

65 Reis, p. 211; David Metzer, "The League of Composers: The Initial Years," *American Music* 15.1 (1997): 52; Lederman, pp. 21, 123–25.

66 Reis, p. 211; Rorem, p. 210; see also Helen Didriksen, "Alma Wertheim of Cos Cob: Portrait of a Patroness," *Historical Society of the Town of Greenwich Newsletter* Winter 1994: 6–10, courtesy of the author; Minna Lederman to Copland, 17 August [c. 1980].

67 Reis felt that the league simply could no longer cover the journal's expenses; Lederman felt it the league's duty to do all that it could to keep it afloat, Oja, p. 148; Claire Reis to Copland, 3 October 1966; Minna Lederman to Copland, undated, 16 April 1978, CCLC.

68 Minna Lederman, "To Aaron at Eighty." *Perspectives of New Music* 19 (1980): 38; Carol Oja, E-mail to author, 27 April 1997.

69 Eva Goldbeck to Copland, 19 June 1929 ("sweep"), 6 March 1931 ("I seem to have"); Copland to Eva Goldbeck, 19 March 1931, BCUW.

70 Bernier was married three times: to Lew Riley, George Bernier, and John Russell; Rosamund Bernier, interview by author, 21 January 1996; C-P I, pp. 266–69.

71 Verna Fine, interview by author, 7 May 1994; C-P II, pp. 132–37.

15. Copland and the American Theater

1 Harold Clurman, *The Fervent Years: The Group Theatre and the Thirties* (New York: Da Capo, 1941, 1975), pp. 20, 29; Foster Hirsch, *A Method to their Madness: The History of the Actors Studio* (New York: W. W. Norton, 1984), pp. 71–72; David Garfield, *A Player's Place: The Story of The Actors Studio* (New York: Macmillan, 1980), pp. 27–28.

2 Copland to Israel Citkowitz, 29 May 1930, CCLC; Elia Kazan, *A Life* (New York: Alfred A Knopf, 1988), p. 153; Clifford Odets, *The Time Is Ripe: The 1940 Journal of Clifford Odets* (New York: Grove Press, 1988), p. 335.

3 Garfield, pp. 9–16; Kazan, p. 64.

4 Margaret Brenman-Gibson, *Clifford Odets, American Playwright: The Years from 1906 to 1940* (New York: Atheneum, 1981), p. 166; Clurman, p. 6; C-P I, pp. 60, 219–20.

5 Harold Clurman to Copland, 27 May 1937 (Adler), 24 May 1941 (Farmer), CCLC; Kazan, pp. 181 ("beautiful"), 659 ("geniuses").

6 Clurman, *The Fervent Years,* pp. 50, 93; Harold Clurman to Copland, 24 May 1932, 31 July 1934, 16 August 1934, CCLC.

7 Kazan, pp. 125–31.

8 Kazan, p. 85; Clurman, p. 166; Harold Clurman to Copland, 4 May 1935, CCLC.

9 Odets, pp. 155, 179, 303.

10 Brenman-Gibson, p. 381; Clurman, pp. 290–92; Kazan, p. 136.

11 Garfield, pp. 33–37.

12 Clurman, *All People Are Famous (Instead of an Autobiography)* (New York: Harcourt Brace Jovanovich, 1974), p. 244; Clurman, *Fervent Years*, p. 302; Harold Clurman to Copland, 20 May 1956, CCLC.

13 Marjorie Loggia and Glenn Young, eds., *The Collected Works of Harold Clurman* (New York: Applause Books, 1994), pp. 70, 289–90.

14 Loggia, pp. 97–99; compare with similar statements by Wilfrid Mellers, *Music in a New Found Land* (New York: Knopf, 1965), pp. 81–101, for instance, the description of *Statements* as "boldly lonely music, even though it was at bottom an affirmation of the human spirit" (p. 87) or "There is no music . . . which is more compassionately human in its acceptance of spiritual isolation: or which attains, through tension, a deeper calm" (p. 101).

15 Jack Garfein, interview by author, 17 October 1996; Clurman, *All People*, p. 28; David Walker, interview by author, 5 May 1994.

16 Kazan, p. 122; Copland to Clifford Odets, 18 October 1951, CCLC.

17 C-P II, p. 215.

18 Odets, p. xii; Gabriel Miller, *Clifford Odets* (New York: F. Ungar, 1989), p. 14; William W. Demastes, *Clifford Odets: A Research and Production Sourcebook* (New York: Greenwood Press, 1991), p. 9.

19 *Six Plays of Clifford Odets,* with a preface by Clifford Odets and an introduction by Harold Clurman (New York: Grove Weidenfeld, 1979), p. xi.

20 Brenman-Gibson, pp. 225, 409; Kazan, p. 27.

21 Miller, p. 202; Kazan, p. 273.

22 Kazan, p. 463 (Kazan noted a comparable decline in Orson Welles and Marlon Brando, p. 135).

23 Clifford Odets to Copland, [October] 1951, 13 September 1956, 12 March 1962; Copland to Odets, 18 October 1951, 11 September 1956, CCLC. The handwriting in question looks little different to this reader, though in the 1956 letter Copland had complained about life at the MacDowell Colony in uncharacteristically strong terms: "Perfect hide-away if you want to get work done. But it's the ascetic life, god dammit!"

24 Odets, pp. ix, 178; Clifford Odets to Copland, 30 August 1956, 13 September 1956; Copland to Odets, 11 September 1956, CCLC.

25 Clifford Odets to Copland, [February] 1943 ("has real"), 22 December 1945, 1951 ("strange"), CCLC; C-P I, p. 344 ("proud").

26 Jack Garfein, interview with author, 17 October 1996; Clifford Odets to Copland, 17 July 1956; Copland to Odets, 9 August 1956; C-P I, pp. 61, 238–39.

27 Gilbert A. Harrison, *The Enthusiast: A Life of Thornton Wilder* (New York: Ticknor & Fields, 1983), p. 204; Thornton Wilder to Copland, 26 August 1968. Years earlier, Wilder had used the word *plangent* in a letter to Copland that described the "wonderfully plangent" motets of Victoria as appropriate to Easter-morning processionals in Spain, Thornton Wilder to Copland, [April] 1950.

28 Opera Ideas, CCLC; Verna Fine, interview with author, 7 May 1994 (for *San Luis Rey*); Thornton Wilder to Copland, 6 September 1948; [April 1950] (the complete letter is reproduced in facsimile in C-P II, p. 214); Copland to Wilder, 28 March 1950; Rudolf Bing to Copland, 18 September 1950; Paul Moor, review of *Copland Since 1943, Musical America* May 1990: 52–53, BHCF; C-P II, p. 215.

29 William Inge to Copland, 12 May 1955, CCLC; 24 May 1955, Garfein, interview.

30 Arthur Miller to Copland, 23 March 1956, 3 April 1956, CCLC.

31 Edward Albee to Copland, 26 July 1958, 4 August 1958, 27 June 1959 ("Several"), CCLC; Edward Albee, interview by author, 22 April 1997 (Albee expressed a current preference for the more severe Copland, citing especially the *Piano Variations*).

32 Edward Albee to Copland, 27 June 1959, CCLC; David Adams, memo, 20 January 1959, BHCF.

33 R. H. Winnick, ed., *The Letters of Archibald MacLeish: 1907 to 1982* (Boston: Houghton Mifflin Co., 1983), p. 127; Elizabeth Bishop to Copland, 24 October 1956, CCLC; C-P II, p. 441n7.

16. An Engaged Citizen

1 Copland to Leonard Bernstein, 30 August 1938, BCLC; Copland to Victor Kraft, 28 November 1963, CCLC; Betty Auman, interview by author, 18 March 1998.

2 Aaron Copland, *Music and Imagination* (Cambridge: Harvard University Press, 1952), p. 111; Copland, transcript of hearing before a Senate Subcommittee on Investigations of the Committee on Government Operations, CCLC.

3 Copland to his parents, 3 September 1932, CCLC; C-P I, p. 17; Hugh Brogam, *The Pelican History of the United States of America* (New York: Penguin, 1985), p. 411; see also Betty Smith, *A Tree Grows in Brooklyn* (1943; New York: HarperCollins Perennial, 1992), pp. 161–62.

4 Julia Smith, *Aaron Copland, His Work and Contribution to American Music* (New York: Dutton, 1955), p. 120.

5 Arthur Weinstein, interview by author, 29 July 1995; Smith, p. 29.

6 Copland to his father, 25 July 1921; Harold Clurman to Copland, 24 May 1934, CCLC.

7 Harold Clurman to Copland, [1934], CCLC; C-P I, p. 162.

8 "I never was a member of the Communist Party or anything like that," Copland told Vivian Perlis in an unpublished interview, quoted by Helen Didriksen, "Strange Company: Aaron Copland, Emily Dickinson, and America at Mid-Century," unpublished paper (May 1988), courtesy of the author, p. 16; Copland, FBI file.

9 Elia Kazan, *A Life* (New York: Knopf, 1988), p. 131.

10 T. H. Watkins, *The Great Depression: America in the 1930s* (New York: Little, Brown and Company, 1993), pp. 91–107; Harold Clurman to Cop-

land, 24 May 1932, CCLC; Edmund Wilson, *The Thirties* (New York: Farrar, Straus and Giroux, 1980), pp. 206–14.

11 Barbara A. Zuck, *A History of Musical Americanism* (Ann Arbor: UMI Research Press, 1978, 1980), pp. 115–138. Seeger used the name Carl Sands; Siegmeister, the name L. E. Swift.

12 Ann M. Pescatello, *Charles Seeger: A Life in American Music* (Pittsburgh: University of Pittsburgh Press, 1992), p. 116; Eric A. Gordon, *Mark the Music: The Life and Work of Marc Blitzstein* (New York: St. Martin's Press, 1989), pp. 98–101; Zuck, pp. 121–34.

13 Mary Lescaze to Copland, 13 September 1933, CCLC.

14 Carl Sands [Charles Seeger], "Copeland's [sic] Music Recital at Pierre Degeyter Club," *Daily Worker* 22 March 1934, CCLC.

15 Ashley Pettis, "Marching with a Song," *New Masses* 11.15 (1934): 15; C-P I, p. 225.

16 Copland to Carlos Chávez, 30 September 1935, CCLC; Copland, McCarthy file, CCLC; Pettis.

17 Copland, "Workers Sing!" *New Masses* 11.9 (1934): 28–29.

18 C-P I, p. 223; Copland to Israel Citkowitz, [September] 1934; Copland to Harold Clurman, 16 August 1934, CCLC. Copland possibly appropriated the phrase "political struggle with the peasantry" from Clurman's letter.

19 Copland to Citkowitz.

20 Paul Bowles to Copland, 24 December 1934, CCLC.

21 Zuck, pp. 117, 308n78, 308n79; Pescatello, pp. 116–17; Manfred Grabs, ed., *Hanns Eisler: A Rebel in Music* (New York: International Publishers, 1976), p. 87; David Diamond, marginalia, remembered attending a collective meeting with Copland for about half an hour.

22 C-P I, p. 224; Copland, "A Note on Young Composers," *Music Vanguard* 1.1 (1935): 14–16; Copland, *Copland on Music* (New York: Norton, 1963), p. 160; Copland to Citkowitz.

23 Judith Tick, *Ruth Crawford Seeger* (New York: Oxford University Press, 1997), p. 196; Pescatello, p. 117.

24 Zuck, p. 146; see also R. Serge Denisoff, *Great Day Coming: Folk Music and the American Left* (Baltimore: Penguin, 1973); Irving Howe and Lewis Coser, *The American Communist Party: A Critical History* (New York: Da Capo Press, 1974); and Robbie Lieberman, *People's Songs, American Communism and the Politics of Culture, 1930–1950* (Urbana: University of Illinois Press, 1988).

25 Denisoff, pp. 57–58; Pescatello, p. 115.

26 Copland, "Workers Sing!" p. 28; Copland, *Copland on Music,* pp. 160–61; Copland, "Scores and Records," *Modern Music* 16.2 (1939): 124.

27 Copland to Citkowitz; Harold Clurman to Copland, 3 November 1934; Copland to Carlos Chávez, 28 August 1935; Harold Clurman to Copland, 2 May 1936, CCLC; C-P I, pp. 226, 230.

28 "Writers and Artists Aid Browder, Ford," *Daily Worker* 2 September 1936,

CCLC; Alan Trachtenberg, ed., *Memoirs of Waldo Frank* (Amherst: University of Massachusetts Press, 1973), p. 187; Victor Kraft to Paul Bowles, 5 November 1936, CCLC.

29 Copland to Carlos Chávez, 30 September 1935, 11 December 1936, 18 May 1937, CCLC; C-P I, p. 266; Copland, "A Note on Young Composers," *Music Vanguard* 1.1 (1935), p. 16; Copland to Virgil Thomson, 11 September 1949, CCLC.

30 Copland, "Scores and Records," *Modern Music* 16.2 (1939): 188; Harold Clurman to Copland, 24 October 1941 (in which Clurman writes of having "ranted against the C.P. line of 1940 to June 1941" to Copland, Kraft, and Odets); Bowles to Copland, [1940], CCLC; Marc Blitzstein to Copland, 22 January 1943, 17 April 1944, CCLC. According to Copland's FBI file, the military classified him as 3-A on 22 September 1942 and as 4-H on 16 January 1943. According to David Hogan, an army historian, the former classification signified hardship on dependents (presumably, in Copland's case, his parents), while the latter designated him as between thirty-eight and forty-five years of age, Hogan, interview by author, 3 November 1997.

31 According to government investigators, Copland defended the rights of political prisoners by supporting the National Committee for the Defense of Political Prisoners (1935) and the National Committee for People's Rights (1938); served on the advisory board of Frontiers Film, a progressive film company (1937); signed a petition against California's extradition of Sam Darcy, a prominent Communist Party official (1940); served on the executive committee of the musicians section of the American Committee for Democracy and Intellectual Freedom (1940); signed an open letter to President Roosevelt defending the rights of the Communist Party (1941); signed an open letter to President Roosevelt protesting the deportation of Harry Bridges, a communist labor leader (1942); sponsored a mass meeting of the Artists' Front to Win the War, which called for a second front in order to relieve the beleaguered Soviets (1942); signed an open letter to President Roosevelt urging a declaration of war against Finland (1942); signed a declaration in honor of George Dimitrov, a Comintern official (1943); petitioned the right of Puerto Rico to decide on its own status (1943); signed an open letter to President Roosevelt urging the forceful punishment of racial attacks (1943); offered to serve as vice-president for the Workers' Music Association (1944); signed a petition calling for the abolition of the Dies Committee (1944); signed a letter to Governor Thomas Dewey of New York in defense of Morris U. Schappes, a communist professor fired from City University (1944); sponsored a statement calling for the United States to break relations with Franco's Spain (1945); signed a letter urging the abolition of the Wood-Rankin Committee (1946); signed a petition protesting Hanns Eisler's deportation (1947) and sponsored a concert in his honor on the day before his enforced departure (18 February 1948); signed a letter urging the abolition of the House Un-American Activities Committee (1948); and sponsored

People's Songs, Inc. (1949). In addition, he allegedly supported an array of other leftist organizations, including the Non-Partisan Committee for Reelection of Congressman Vito Marcantonio (1936), the American League Against War and Fascism (1937), the Joint Anti-Fascist Refugee Committee (1943), the National Committee to Oust BILBO (1946), the American Committee for Yugoslav Relief, Inc. (1947), and, throughout the 1940s, the National Council of American-Soviet Friendship. "Films for Progressives Is New Company's Plan," *Daily Worker* 6 April 1937, p. 9; "Free Sam Darcy, Educators and Writers Urge Olson," *Daily Worker* [1940]; "List of Signers of Statement Defending the Communist Party," *Daily Worker* 5 March 1941; "Flay Biddle Attack upon Bridges, Communist Party," *Daily Worker* 19 July 1942; "For a Second Front," *Daily Worker* 7 October 1942; "The Fire That Has Been Burning for Ten Years," *Daily Worker* 22 December 1943; Will Sahnow to Copland 26 July 1944, CCLC; *Congressional Record* 16 January 1953, Appendix 178–80; Copland, FBI file.

32 William Howard Melish to Copland, 15 November 1946, CCLC; 24 January 1946 statement by Corliss Lamont, CCLC; for Copland's participation, see "112 Notables Ask U.S., Soviet Talks on Peace," *Daily Worker* 21 June 1948, p. 3.

33 Copland, FBI file; American-Soviet Music Society file, CCLC. The FBI file notes Copland's 1944 vice chairmanship of the committee, though other sources put their first meeting at 16 February 1946; perhaps Copland assumed this position for some time before the committee actually met. Siegmeister gave a lecture entitled "Life and Work of the Soviet Musician" and Bernstein, "The Soviet Influence in American Music"; Clurman gave his talk, "The Life and Work of the Soviet Theatre Artist," at the session on theater.

34 American-Soviet Music Society file, CCLC; Gordon, pp. 288, 290–92, 296–97, 309.

35 Copland, quoted by Mildred Norton, Los Angeles *Daily News* 5 April 1948; Gordon, p. 337.

36 Harlow Shapley to Copland, 21 February 1949; "Rival Rallies Debate Peace Policies," *New York Post* 27 March 1949; "Shostakovich Bids All Artists Lead War on New 'Fascists,' " *Daily Worker* 28 March 1949; Arthur Miller, *Timebends: A Life* (New York: Grove Press, 1987), pp. 234–36. The estimates of conference attendants range from eight hundred to three thousand.

37 "Rival Rallies"; "Red Visitors Cause Rumpus," *Life* 26.14 (1949): 39–43.

38 Copland, "Effect of the Cold War on the Artist in the U.S.," CCLC.

39 "Shostakovich Bids"; Senate transcript, p. 86, CCLC.

40 Richard Morford to Copland, 28 October 1949, 7 June 1950, CCLC; Will Sahnow to Copland, 12 April 1954, CCLC; Copland, *Music and Imagination*, p. 76.

41 Phillip Ramey, interview by author, 6 May 1994.

42 Ramey, interview; Erik Johns, interview by author, 13 December 1994; C-P I, p. 339. "May I take this opportunity," he told President Kennedy upon receiving the 1961 MacDowell Medal, "to assure you that the creative artists

in our country are greatly heartened by the warm interest in the arts of yourself, Mrs. Kennedy and your Administration," White House file, CCLC.

43 "The Composer in the U.S. and Russia: A Frank Talk Between Copland and Khachaturian," *ASCAP Today* 3.1 (1969): 22–25; Johns, interview; Ramey, interview.

44 C-P II, pp. 381, 398; Ramey, interview.

45 "A Leading Composer Looks at American Music Today," *U.S. News and World Report* 4 October 1976, CCLC; Jacob Javits, letters to Copland, CCLC; C-P II, p. 396.

46 Copland, "Is the University Too Much with Us?" *New York Times* 26 July 1970; Edward T. Cone, "Conversation with Aaron Copland," *Perspectives of New Music* 6.2 (1968): 68, 71–72; for a public rebuttal of "Is the University," see John Vincent, "Where It Is" (letter to the editor), *New York Times* 30 August 1970.

47 Copland, *Copland on Music*, pp. 51–60 ("Bureaucratic control," p. 59); George Von Der Muhll, "Copland Discusses Career, Voices Approval of Federal Art Subsidies," *Oberlin Review* 18 February 1955, BHCF ("It doesn't"); Chuck Thurston, "Straight Answers from Copland," *Detroit Free Press* 17 May 1978, CCLC ("The government").

48 "Aaron Copeland [*sic*] Supports ASCAP Versus Juke Ind. in House Talk," *Cashbox* 14 June 1975, BHCF (Copland pointed out that ASCAP's songwriters set aside 5 percent of their performing rights income for special rights to serious composers); Copland to Senator Howard Metzenbaum, 19 June 1986, CCLC.

17. From the *Short Symphony* to *A Prairie Journal* (1933–37)

1 C-P I, pp. 208–12.

2 Copland to Eva Goldbeck, 26 May 1931, BCUW; Gerald Sykes to Copland, 12 May 1960, CCLC; Joseph Kerman, "American Music: The Columbia Series (II)," *Hudson Review* 13.3 (1961): 441.

3 Copland to Marc Blitzstein and Eva Goldbeck, 16 August 1932, BCUW ("The Divertimento is now a Partita"); C-P I, p. 112; Copland to Israel Citkowitz, 22 September 1931, CCLC (studying Mozart); C-P I, p. 209.

4 Michael Steinberg, liner notes, Copland, *Sextet* (Elektra/Nonesuch 9 79168-2); Copland to Marc Blitzstein and Eva Goldbeck.

5 Arthur Berger, *Aaron Copland* (New York: Oxford University Press, 1953), p. 91.

6 Daniel Mathers, "Closure in the *Sextet* and *Short Symphony* by Aaron Copland: A Study Using Facsimiles and Printed Editions" (master's thesis, Florida State University, 1989).

7 Daniel Mathers, interview by author, 23 April 1995.

8 Kerman, pp. 410–11; C-P I, p. 212; Dennis Russell Davies, liner notes to Copland, *Short Symphony*, performed by Davies and the Orchestra of St. Luke's (MusicMasters 01612-67101-2), p. 6.

9 Copland, *Short Symphony*, performed by Copland and the London Sym-

phony Orchestra (Sony SM2K 47232); Copland, *Sextet* (Columbia 32 11 0042); Copland, *Short Symphony,* performed by Leonard Slatkin and the St. Louis Symphony Orchestra (RCA 09026-68292-2); Copland, *Short Symphony,* performed by the Orpheus Chamber Orchestra (DGG 427 335-2).

[10] C-P I, p. 233; John Martin, *Ruth Page: An Intimate Biography* (New York: Marcel Dekker, Inc., 1977), p. 89; Ruth Page, *Page by Page* (New York: Dance Horizons, 1978), p. 126.

[11] Martin; Page; Howard Pollack, *Skyscraper Lullaby: The Life and Music of John Alden Carpenter* (Washington: Smithsonian Institution Press, 1995).

[12] Marcia B. Siegel, *The Shapes of Change: Images of American Dance* (New York: Avon Books, 1979), pp. 109–13; Agnes de Mille, *America Dances* (New York: Macmillan, 1980), p. 186.

[13] C-P I, p. 234; Ruth Page, scenario to *Hear Ye! Hear Ye!,* CCLC.

[14] C-P I, p. 234.

[15] Page, *Page,* p. 127.

[16] C-P I, p. 235; Page, *Page,* pp. 126–27.

[17] Copland, *Hear Ye! Hear Ye!,* performed by the London Sinfonietta under Oliver Knussen (Argo 443 203-2); Bernard Holland, "In Witness of the New and Nothing but the New," *New York Times* 26 November 1996: B1; Julia Smith, *Aaron Copland: His Work and Contribution to American Music* (New York: Dutton, 1955), p. 187.

[18] C-P I, p. 236–37; Donald Fuller, "Winter to Spring, New York, 1942," *Modern Music* 79.3 (1942): 173; David Diamond, interview by author, 15 May 1994; Leonard Bernstein, "Neglected Works: A Symposium," *Modern Music* 23.1 (1946): 11.

[19] Copland to Marc Blitzstein and Eva Goldbeck.

[20] Diamond, interview; *Harold Clurman: A Life in Theatre* (videocassette).

[21] Hugo Cole, "Popular Elements in Copland's Music," *Tempo* 95 (1971), pp. 6–7.

[22] Copland, "The Story Behind *El Salón México,*" c. 1939 (an article written on the occasion of the 1939 Victor release of the work, with photographs by Victor Kraft), CCLC; this article became the basis of Copland's discussion of the work in C-P I; Arnold Dobrin, *Aaron Copland: His Life and Times* (New York: Thomas Y. Crowell, 1967), p. 125 (Dobrin asserts that Copland stayed at El Salón only till midnight).

[23] Inga Karetnikova in collaboration with Leon Steinmetz, *Mexico According to Eisenstein* (Albuquerque: University of New Mexico Press, 1991), pp. 169–71 (contrary to Copland's account, Eisenstein remembered the three halls as having different entrance fees); Ned Rorem, *Knowing When to Stop: A Memoir* (New York: Simon & Schuster, 1994), p. 147.

[24] Copland, "The Story Behind *El Salón México.*"

[25] Rubén M. Campos, *El Folklore y la Musica Mexicana* (Mexico City: Publicaciones de la Secretaria de Educacion Publica, 1928); Frances Toor, ed., *Cancionero Mexican* (Mexico City: Mexican Folkways, 1931); C-P I, p. 246

(Copland mistakenly wrote "La Malacate"). Toor categorizes "La Jesusita" as a "revolutionary" song, meaning that revolutionaries sang it, not that it has a political text (it is, in fact, a love song).

26 Gerald Abraham, notes to Copland's *El Salón México* (New York: Boosey & Hawkes, 1939). For "El Mosco," see rehearsal 4.

27 Eisenstein, p. 170.

28 Copland, "Nationalism in American Music," lecture notes, CCLC.

29 Abraham proposes a rough three-part design, whereas Julia Smith suggests a binary one (Smith, *Copland*), arguing that the work moves from G major to E major in the first half and vice versa in the second half; note, however, that the conflict between these two tonalities resolves at the end in favor of E.

30 Copland, "The Story Behind"; C-P I, pp. 246, 249.

31 Fred Karlin and Rayburn Wright, *On the Track: A Guide to Contemporary Film Scoring* (New York: Schirmer, 1990), p. 514.

32 Berger, p. 30; Cole, pp. 6, 8–9; Elliott Carter, "Once Again Swing; Also 'American Music,' " *Modern Music* 16.2 (1939): 102.

33 T. H. Watkins, *The Great Depression: America in the 1930s* (New York: Little, Brown and Company, 1993), p. 258; C-P I, p. 237.

34 Watkins, pp. 130–31.

35 Copland to Marc Blitzstein, 13 February 1931, BCUW; C-P I, p. 251; the Boosey & Hawkes score also refers to the work as an "operetta."

36 Jack Anderson, "Edwin Denby, Dance Critic, Dies at 80," *New York Times* 14 July 1983, sec. 2, p. 8; Jennifer Dunning, "Edwin Denby, Dance Critic, Is Remembered," *New York Times* 3 November 1983, sec. 2, p. 16; Rudy Burckhardt, interview by author, 4 May 1994.

37 Marc Blitzstein to Eva Goldbeck, 30 September 1929, BCUW.

38 Edwin Denby, "A Good Libretto," *Modern Music* 13.3 (1936): 14–21.

39 Denby, pp. 20–21.

40 C-P I, p. 261; "Composers' Conference—Yaddo," transcript, 2 and 3 May 1932, BCUW.

41 Copland to Carlos Chávez, 18 May 1937, CCLC (note, too, that the work's exhilarating final measures feature rising triads in first inversion, like the opening of Beethoven's Piano Sonata op. 10, no. 3); Edwin Denby to Copland, 1937, CCLC.

42 Virgil Thomson, *American Music Since 1910* (New York: Holt, Rinehart and Winston, 1970), claims, "*The Second Hurricane* . . . followed Blitzstein's lead into a city-style harmonic simplicity, rather than to my country-style one," p. 55. "Gyp's Song," in turn, clearly influenced the Bernstein of *On the Town* and *Wonderful Town*.

43 Edwin Denby to Copland, various letters, 1936 and 1937, CCLC; Wilfrid Mellers, "The Teenager's World," *Musical Times* 105 (1964): 504.

44 S. Foster Damon, *Series of Old American Songs* (Providence: Brown University Library, 1936), p. 453.

45 C-P I, pp. 257–61.

46 Virgil Thomson, "In the Theatre," *Modern Music* 14.4 (1937): 235; William Schuman, "Layman's Guide and Student Opera," *Modern Music* 16.2 (1939): 135–37; Paul Bowles, "Film and Theatre," *Modern Music* 20.2 (1945): 129–32; Marc Blitzstein, "On Writing Music for the Theatre," *Modern Music* 15.1 (1937): 82; Humphrey Burton, *Leonard Bernstein* (New York: Doubleday, 1994), pp. 98, 366.

47 Donald Mitchell, ed., *Letters from a Life: The Selected Letters and Diaries of Benjamin Britten 1913–1976. Volume Two: 1939–1976* (Los Angeles: University of California Press, 1991), pp. 634, 709; Mellers, p. 502.

48 Thornton Wilder to Copland, 6 September 1948, CCLC; Ethan Mordden, *A Guide to Opera Recordings* (New York: Oxford University Press, 1987), p. 282; C-P I, p. 265; Edwin Denby to Copland, 3 December 1939, CCLC.

49 Margaret Susan Key, " 'Sweet Melody over Silent Wave': Depression-Era Radio and the American Composer" (Ph.D. diss., University of Maryland at College Park, 1995), p. 134; Watkins, p. 305; Charles C. Alexander, *Here the Country Lies: Nationalism and the Arts in Twentieth-Century America* (Bloomington: Indiana University Press, 1980), p. 225; C-P I, p. 225.

50 Smith, p. 178; C-P I, p. 255; "This adaptation of a commercial device," wryly noted Oscar Levant in reference to the naming contest, "(almost suggesting that Copland was affiliating himself with 'Lucky Strike' or 'Old Gold') was evidence of a digression toward practicality that had begun to assert itself in American music generally at this time," Levant, *A Smattering of Ignorance* (Doubleday, Doran, and Co., 1940), p. 241.

51 C-P I, p. 255. Copland's sketches for *Prairie Journal* intimate that he thought of the work as having seven sections.

52 C-P I, p. 255; Key, p. 189; Copland to Eugene Ormandy, 23 September 1958, CCLC, courtesy of Jessica Burr.

53 Smith, p. 178; Levant, *A Smattering,* p. 241.

54 Arnold Rampersad, ed., *The Collected Poems of Langston Hughes* (New York: Knopf, 1944), pp. 188–89, 637; Watkins, pp. 89–91.

55 Wayne Shirley, interview by author, 7 March 1997.

56 Key, pp. 59–60, 140–41.

57 Copland, *Prairie Journal,* performed by Leonard Slatkin and the St. Louis Symphony Orchestra (RCA Victor 09026-61699-2).

18. From *Billy the Kid* to *John Henry* (1938–40)

1 Charles C. Alexander, *Here the Country Lies: Nationalism and the Arts in Twentieth-Century America* (Bloomington: Indiana University Press, 1980), pp. 237–39; Agnes de Mille, *America Dances* (New York: Macmillan, 1980), pp. 124–128. Kirstein's American Ballet is not to be confused with the Ballet Theatre (later American Ballet Theatre), founded in 1940 by Lucia Chase.

2 Nicholas Jenkins, "The Great Impresario," *New Yorker,* 74.8 (1998): 48–61; Lincoln Kirstein, "Crisis in the Dance," *North American Review* 243 (Spring

1937): 80–103; see also Kirstein, *Three Pamphlets Collected* (New York: Dance Horizons, 1967).

3 Lincoln Kirstein, "The Popular Style in American Dancing," *Nation* 146 (16 April 1938): 450–51.

4 Virgil Thomson, *Virgil Thomson* (New York: Da Capo, 1966), p. 275.

5 *Memorial Day* synopsis, CCLC.

6 Eugene Loring, taped interview with Richard Schottland, Dance Division, NYPL.

7 Alan Boehmer, interview by author, 28 October 1997; Patrice Whiteside, interview by author, 28 October 1997; "Eugene Loring, Choreographer" (www.execpc.com/~jjjurek/loring; some sources give 1914 as the year of Loring's birth).

8 Walter Noble Burns, *The Saga of Billy the Kid* (Garden City: Garden City Publishing, 1925).

9 Robert M. Utley, *Billy the Kid: A Short and Violent Life* (Lincoln: University of Nebraska Press, 1989), p. 200.

10 Loring, interview.

11 [Eugene Loring], scenario to *Billy the Kid,* CCLC; some sources credit Kirstein as the ballet's librettist, but statements by both Copland and Loring point to Loring's authorship, C-P I, p. 279.

12 Marcia B. Siegel, *The Shapes of Change: Images of American Dance* (New York: Avon, 1979), p. 125.

13 Eugene Loring, narration for Omnibus presentation of *Billy the Kid,* 8 November 1953, Loring Collection, Dance Division, NYPL.

14 C-P I, p. 279.

15 Copland took the Burns-Loring story at face value. He seemed rather uninterested in the historical Billy, maintaining even late in life that William Bonney was his real name (as opposed to an alias) and that he was born in Brooklyn (as opposed to Missouri). In these later years, he exchanged one mythic view for another, stating, "I thought of Billy the Kid as being part of the picturesque folklore of the Far West, a young innocent who went wrong, not the monster he was," Phillip Ramey, "Copland and the Dance," *Ballet News* 2.5 (1980): 11.

16 "The Old Chisolm Trail," "Whoopee Ti Yi Yo," and "Old Paint," collected by John A. Lomax and arranged by Oscar J. Fox (New York: Carl Fischer, Inc., 1924 [Chisolm], 1927 ["Whoopee," "Old"]); *Songs of the Open Range,* edited by Ina Sires (New York: C. C. Birchard and Co., 1928); and *The Lonesome Cowboy,* ed. by John White and George Shackley (New York: George T. Worth, 1930). The author is indebted to Elizabeth Bergman, who found the Lomax-Fox songs stitched into Copland's copy of the *Lonesome Cowboy,* and Jessica Burr, who discovered the Sires collection among Copland's possessions. The tunes set by Copland found in the Sires collection are: "Whoopee Ti Yi Yo," "The Dying Cowboy," and "The Old Chisholm Trail." In addition to the White-Shackley version of "The Dying Cowboy," Copland seems to have used Sires's second version of the same tune for the trumpet solo ("solo espressivo") in "Card Game at Night."

Notes

[17] Copland, "Notes on a Cowboy Ballet," CCLC. This reminiscence strongly recalls the composer's comments about his attraction to jazz after hearing it played in Europe.

[18] Loring, interview.

[19] Siegel, p. 119; Jessica Burr, "Open Fifths, Open Prairie, and the Opening of *Billy the Kid*," Sonneck Society Annual Meeting, 7 March 1997, points out that the ballet's opening bars—music that has come to epitomize Copland's "open-prairie sound"—owe as much to their extraordinary scoring for two high clarinets and low oboe as to the novelty (for Copland) of beginning a work with bare, parallel fifths.

[20] Arthur Berger, *Aaron Copland* (New York: Oxford University Press, 1953), p. 63.

[21] Edwin Denby, *Dance Writings* (New York: Knopf, 1986), p. 164; Siegel, pp. 118–25.

[22] Loring, interview; C-P I, p. 283.

[23] Whiteside, interview.

[24] Denby, *Dance Writings,* p. 119; C-P I, p. 284, quotes Kirstein as saying, "I don't recall much about Billy because I don't want to. I didn't like what the ballet became after I agreed to let Ballet Theatre do it"; *Billy the Kid* (film and video, 1938–1940, 194?, 1953, 1976, 1979), Dance Division, NYPL; Whiteside, interview.

[25] C-P I, p. 354; C-P II, p. 284.

[26] Paul Rosenfeld, "Current Chronicle: Copland—Harris—Schuman," *Musical Quarterly* 25 (1939): 372–76; David Diamond, interview by author, 15 May 1994; Lawrence Starr, "Copland's Style," *Perspectives of New Music* 19 (1980–81): 77–78.

[27] Copland, interviewed on *Soundings*, BBC Radio, Michael Oliver, narrator (24 November 1991) ("Jewish adaptability"); *Newsweek* (8 March 1976), CCLC.

[28] C-P I, pp. 285–86.

[29] Elliott Carter, "Once Again Swing; Also 'American Music,' " *Modern Music* 16.2 (1939): 102–03; C-P I, p. 286.

[30] C-P I, p. 286.

[31] Vernon Duke, program notes, High-Low Concert, 23 February 1938, CCLC ("similar"); Vernon Duke, *Listen Here! A Critical Essay on Music Depreciation* (New York: Ivan Obolensky, Inc., 1963), p. 37.

[32] Elaine Showalter ("a socialist") quoted by Jennifer Rector, *American Proletarianism in Two Collaborative Works by William Schuman and Genevieve Taggard* (master's thesis, University of Missouri at Kansas City, 1996), pp. 25, 38, courtesy of the author.

[33] Rector, pp. 28, 32.

[34] Irving Howe and Lewis Coser, *The American Communist Party: A Critical History* (New York: Da Capo Press, 1974), pp. 342–43.

[35] C-P I, p. 287. As it turned out, Copland had trouble collecting his fee for *The Five Kings*, which led to strained relations with the Mercury Theatre; as late as May 1941 he was still trying to collect $500 owed him; Copland

629

to John Houseman, 5 April 1939, CCLC; Copland to L. Arnold Weissberger, 20 May 1941, CCLC.

36 Norman Nadel, *A Pictorial History of the Theatre Guild* (New York: Crown, 1969), pp. 110–12; Roy S. Waldau, *Vintage Years of the Theatre Guild: 1928–1939* (Cleveland: Case Western Reserve University, 1972): 107–10 ("pompous," p. 108).

37 C-P I, pp. 286–87; Waldau, pp. 326–27; Orson Welles and Peter Bogdanovich, *This Is Orson Welles* (New York: HarperCollins, 1992), p. 259; James Naremore, *The Magic World of Orson Welles* (Dallas: Southern Methodist University Press, 1989), p. 217. According to Welles—for the matter remains one of some confusion—the play's first part combined *Richard II*, *Henry IV*, and *Henry V*, while the never-finished second part was to complete the cycle with adaptations of *Henry VI* and *Richard III*; Waldau's list of the "five kings"—Henry IV and Henry V (for part one) and Henry VI, Edward VI, and Richard III (part two)—accords more with Copland's remembrance. Copland used the Lully "Courante" found in Isidore Philipp's *Anthology* vol. 1 (Boston: Ditson, 1906).

38 Harold Clurman, *The Fervent Years: The Group Theatre and the 30's* (New York: Da Capo Press, 1945, 1983), pp. 237, 239–40, 247; Elia Kazan, *A Life* (New York: Knopf, 1988), p. 181. Clurman and Kazan disagree over the number of performances of *Quiet City*: Clurman says two, Kazan says six.

39 Irwin Shaw, *Quiet City* (Boston University Library).

40 *Schwann Opus* 8.3 (1997), p. 260; Copland, *Quiet City*, recorded by Gerard Schwarz and the New York Chamber Symphony (EMI CDC 7 49095 2); C-P I, p. 288.

41 Jack Anderson, "New York Newsletter," *Dancing Times* 76.910 (1986): 883.

42 Claire R. Reis, *Composers, Conductors and Critics* (New York: Oxford University Press, 1955), pp. 84, 137–38; John Bell, "*From Sorcery to Science: Remo Bufano and World's Fair Puppet Theater*," courtesy of the author; Donald Deskey to Copland, 5 May 1939, CCLC, specified $500 for the score, $200 for the orchestral score, and $150 for the copying of the orchestra parts; Copland surely made at least $500, while Brant presumably earned some if not all of the $200 fee and possibly the $150 fee as well. Although Copland referred to the work as *From Sorcery to Science*, the New York Public Library currently has a sketch score catalogued under Copland's working title, *Music for a Puppet Show*. According to this copy, Copland completed the reduced score in a mere five days, 4–8 May, 1939.

43 C-P I, p. 288; Bell.

44 Bell.

45 Wayne Shirley, interview by author, 15 March 1997.

46 C-P I, p. 291; Barbara Zuck, *A History of Musical Americanism* (Ann Arbor: UMI, 1980), p. 149; John and Alan Lomax, *American Folk Songs and Ballads* (New York: Macmillan, 1934), pp. 3–10; Judith Tick, *Ruth Crawford Seeger* (New York: Oxford University Press, 1997), p. 260.

[47] David Ewen, *All the Years of American Popular Music* (Englewood Cliffs: Prentice Hall, 1977), p. 418; Alexander, p. 223.

19. Music for the Movies and for Keyboard (1939–41)

[1] Roy M. Prendergast, *Film Music: A Neglected Art,* 2nd ed. (New York: W. W. Norton, 1977, 1992), pp. 45–48.

[2] Harold Clurman to Copland, 5 May 1937, CCLC; C-P I, pp. 270–71.

[3] Copland to Carlos Chávez, 2 June 1937, CCLC; Prendergast, p. 47.

[4] C-P I, p. 290.

[5] Leslie Squyres Calmes, *The Letters Between Edward Weston and Willard Van Dyke* (Tucson: Center for Creative Photography, 1992), pp. 37–40.

[6] C-P I, p. 290.

[7] Robert A. Simon, "Mr. Copland Here, There, and at the Fair," *New Yorker* 15.16 (1939): 58; Calmes, p. 40.

[8] Arnold Dobrin, *Aaron Copland: His Life and Times* (New York: Thomas Y. Crowell, 1967), pp. 145–46.

[9] Joseph R. Millichap, *Lewis Milestone* (Boston: Twayne Publishers, 1981); Phillip Ramey, interview by author, 10 May 1996.

[10] Copland to Leonard Bernstein, 12 November 1939, LBCL; C-P I, p. 297.

[11] C-P I, pp. 297–300.

[12] Fred Karlin, *Listening to Movies: The Film Lover's Guide to Film Music* (New York: Schirmer Books, 1994), p. 40.

[13] Copland, "Tip to Moviegoers: Take Off Those Ear-Muffs," *New York Times* 6 November 1949, sec. 6, p. 29.

[14] C-P I, p. 300; for a discussion of "source" (or "diegetic") music versus "narrative" (or "nondiegetic") music, see Claudia Gorbman, *Unheard Melo-dies: Narrative Film Music* (Bloomington: Indiana University Press, 1987), p. 22.

[15] C-P I, p. 298; Paul Bowles, "On the Film Front," *Modern Music* 17.3 (1949): 187.

[16] C-P I, p. 299.

[17] Copland lost "best score" to Alfred Newman (*Alexander's Ragtime Band*) and "original score" to Erich Wolfgang Korngold (*The Adventures of Robin Hood*) (during the years 1938–1940, the academy presented separate awards for "best score" and "original score"); Bowles; Léon Kochnitzky, "On the Film Front," *Modern Music* 19.3 (1942): 193–94; Virgil Thomson, *American Music Since 1910* (New York: Holt, Rinehart and Winston), p. 55.

[18] C-P I, p. 302.

[19] Linda Simon, *Thornton Wilder: His World* (Garden City: Doubleday, 1979), p. 139.

[20] Gilbert A. Harrison, *The Enthusiast: A Life of Thornton Wilder* (New York: Fromm International Publishing Corporation, 1986), p. 204.

[21] Paul Bowles, "On the Film Front," *Modern Music* 18.1 (1940): 61; Alfred Williams Cochran, "Style, Structure, and Tonal Organization in the Early Film Scores of Aaron Copland" (Ph.D. diss., Catholic University, 1986), p. 202 (for Moross and *Our Town*).

22 Stephen Raybould, "Evolution of Style: From *Our Town* to *The Red Pony*" (www.jmu.edu/libliaison/music/stopics/95.1/cophom.htm#), points out that Emily's love theme derives from the Grover's Corners music.

23 Marjorie Loggia and Glenn Young, eds., *The Collected Works of Harold Clurman* (New York: Applause Books, 1994), p. 386. Copland may have noticed, too, Herbert Stothart's more conventional use of "Home, Sweet Home" in *The Wizard of Oz* (1939).

24 Copland lost "best score" to Alfred Newman (*Tin Pan Alley*) and "original score" to Leigh Harline, Paul J. Smith, and Ned Washington (*Pinocchio*).

25 Copland, "Tip to Moviegoers," p. 32; Jennifer Dunning, "Bringing a Little Human Warmth to the Fireworks," *New York Times* 7 February 1997.

26 C-P I, p. 366.

27 Cochran; Alfred Cochran, "The Spear of Cephalus: Observations on Film Music Analysis," *Indiana Theory Review* 11 (1990): 65–80; Christopher Palmer, *The Composer in Hollywood* (New York: Marion Boyars, 1990), pp. 295, 303; André Previn, *No Minor Chords* (New York: Doubleday, 1991), p. 92; David Raksin, Los Angeles Philharmonic intermission tribute, broadcast 11 February 1986, courtesy of Phillip Ramey. Cochran uses Schenkerian analysis to investigate "long-range structural and tonal organization" in Copland's film scores.

28 Karlin, p. 273 (Friedhofer); Palmer, pp. 303 (Rosenman) and 315 (Moross).

29 Copland, "The Aims of Music for Films," *New York Times* 10 March 1940, sec. 11, p. 7; Copland, "Second Thoughts on Hollywood," *Modern Music* 7.3 (1940): 141–47; Copland, *Our New Music* (New York: McGraw-Hill, 1941), pp. 260–75; Copland, "Tip to Moviegoers," pp. 28–32; Copland, *What to Listen for in Music* (New York: McGraw-Hill, 1939, 1957), pp. 152–57.

30 Copland, lecture notes, CCLC.

31 C-P II, p. 8.

32 C-P I, p. 297; Copland, "Tip to Moviegoers," p. 32; Copland, "Second Thoughts," p. 146; Copland, "The Aims."

33 C-P I, p. 314.

34 C-P I, pp. 318–19, 330.

35 C-P I, pp. 330, 333.

36 Copland, *What to Listen for in Music,* pp. 116–17.

37 Wilfrid Mellers, *Music in a New Found Land* (New York: Oxford, 1964), p. 92.

38 John Kirkpatrick, "Aaron Copland's Piano Sonata," *Modern Music* 19.4 (1942): 246–50; Julia Smith, *Aaron Copland: His Work and Contribution to American Music* (New York: Dutton, 1955), p. 232.

39 Kirkpatrick, p. 250; Mellers, pp. 92–93; Douglas Young, "The Piano Music," *Tempo* 95 (1921): 21; Robert Silverman, liner notes, Copland's Piano Sonata (Orion ORS 7280); Dika Newlin, "The Piano Music of Aaron Copland," *Piano Quarterly* 111 (1980): 11.

40 Young, p. 21.

41 Arthur Berger, "Copland's Piano Sonata," *Partisan Review* 10 (1943): 189–90.

42 C-P I, p. 333; Smith, pp. 233–34; Joann Skowronski, *Aaron Copland: A Bio-bibliography* (Westport, CT: Greenwood Press, 1985), pp. 106 (B245) and 180 (B786); Kirkpatrick, p. 246; Berger, pp. 187–89; Mellers, pp. 91, 93.

43 Berger, p. 188; David Burge, *Twentieth-Century Piano Music* (New York: Schirmer Books, 1990), p. 122; William W. Austin, *Music in the 20th Century from Debussy Through Stravinsky* (New York: W. W. Norton, 1966), pp. 504–05.

44 Humphrey recast the "Prologue" from *Decade* (which apparently used only the Prologue movement from *Music for the Theatre*) as the 1943 *Prologue* (which also contained a *Fugue on a Theme of Copland* by Lionel Nowak).

45 Marcia Siegel, *The Shapes of Change: Images of American Dance* (New York: Avon Books, 1979), pp. 163–64 (Siegel's comparison of the ballet as "a sort of *Our Town* without any detail or sentiment" hints at the complex relationship between Copland's Sonata and his music to *Our Town*); Doris Humphrey, *Day on Earth* (1959 film), Dance Division, NYPL; Doris Humphrey to Copland, 1947, Humphrey Collection, Dance Division, NYPL.

46 C-P I, p. 333.

47 For a discography of the Copland Piano Sonata through 1985, see Skowronski, pp. 53–54; Copland, Piano Sonata played by Robert Silverman (Orion ORS 7280, 1972); and by Easley Blackwood (Cedille CDR 9000000 005, 1991).

20. From *Lincoln Portrait* to *Danzón Cubano* (1942)

1 C-P I, pp. 341–42; "Aaron Copland on Aaron Copland" (transcript), 9 February 1981, Copland Clipping File, NYPL ("that an English lord").

2 Donal Henahan, "He Made Composing Respectable Here," (1970), BHCF; Lord Charnwood, *Abraham Lincoln* (Garden City: Garden City Publishing Company, 1917); C-P II, p. 343.

3 Charles C. Alexander, *Here the Country Lies: Nationalism and the Arts in Twentieth-Century America* (Bloomington: Indiana University Press, 1980), pp. 194–95; Barbara Zuck, *A History of Musical Americanism* (Ann Arbor: UMI Research Press, 1980), p. 190. Copland conducted his First Symphony at the same festival at which Weinberg's work was premiered, "American Music Festival," *Musical Leader* 22 May 1936: 25.

4 Howard Pollack, *Skyscraper Lullaby: The Life and Music of John Alden Carpenter* (Washington: Smithsonian Institution Press, 1995), p. 294.

5 Copland, *Lincoln Portrait* (New York: Boosey & Hawkes, 1942).

6 The dirgelike idea and "Springfield Mountain" strongly recall, albeit in much more accessible guise, the two contrasting themes found in the finale to the Piano Sonata (1941). Copland, "Scores and Records," *Modern Music* 16.2 (1939): 186; S. Foster Damon, *Series of Old American Songs* (Providence: Brown University Library, 1936); Copland also may have been familiar with

the version of "Springfield Mountain" as found in S. Olin Downes and Elie Siegmeister, *A Treasury of American Song* (New York: Knopf, 1940, 1943), p. 38 (Downes and Siegmeister state, seemingly erroneously, that the song's victim was a Lieutenant Thomas Myrick, whereas according to Damon it was his son, Timothy Myrick).

7 Léon Kochinitzky, "Musical Portraits," *Modern Music* 20.1 (1942): 32.

8 William W. Austin, *"Susanna," "Jeanie," and "The Old Folks at Home": The Songs of Stephen C. Foster from His Time to Ours* (New York: Macmillan, 1975), p. 33; Downes and Siegmeister, p. 155.

9 Howard Pollack, *Walter Piston* (Ann Arbor: UMI Research Press, 1982), p. 75; *Cincinnati Symphony Orchestra 1994–1995 Handbook,* courtesy of the Cincinnati Symphony Orchestra.

10 C-P I, p. 368; "Aaron Copland on Aaron Copland."

11 C-P I, pp. 344–48, 388n16.

12 Coretta Scott King to Copland, 20 February 1969; Copland to King, 17 August 1971, CCLC.

13 Woody Herman: The New Thundering Herd, "Fanfare for the Common Man," *The 40th Anniversary, Carnegie Hall Concert* (Gryphon BGL2-2203); Emerson, Lake & Palmer, "Fanfare for the Common Man," *Works* (Atlantic SD 2-7000).

14 William Schuman to Copland, 31 March 1943, CCLC; William Schuman, "Aaron Copland," *Perspectives of New Music* 19 (1980–81), p. 52; Rudy Burckhardt, interview by author, 4 May 1994; Arthur Berger, "Scores and Records," *Modern Music* 23.4 (1946): 306; Arthur Berger, Aaron Copland (New York: Oxford University Press), pp. 29, 60–61, 76; Wilfrid Mellers, *Music in A New Found Land* (New York: Oxford University Press, 1964, 1987).

15 Copland to Nadia Boulanger, 23 April 1943, CCLC; John Corigliano, interview by author, 2 August 1997; Phillip Ramey, interview by author, 21 October 1997.

16 Agnes de Mille, *Dance to the Piper* (Boston: Little, Brown, 1952), pp. 205–07.

17 De Mille; Anne Edwards, *The DeMilles: An American Family* (New York: Harry N. Abrams, 1988).

18 De Mille; Edwards, p. 116.

19 De Mille later specified some of the girls as visiting from Kansas City.

20 Agnes de Mille, "American Ballet" (scenario), CCLC.

21 "Note," *Rodeo* (New York: Boosey & Hawkes, 1946); de Mille, *Dance,* p. 227.

22 Marcia Siegel, *The Shapes of Change: Images of American Dance* (New York: Avon Books, 1979), pp. 126–28; Agnes de Mille, *And Promenade Home* (Boston: Little, Brown, 1958), pp. 14, 16, 18.

23 De Mille, p. 208.

24 Carol Easton, *No Intermissions: The Life of Agnes de Mille* (New York: Little, Brown, 1996), p. 159. Easton writes, too, that Copland had accompa-

nied de Mille in a performance she gave on the Île de France en route to Europe in the fall of 1932, but Copland did not go to Europe that particular year (p. 188); perhaps this performance transpired at some other time.

25 De Mille, p. 210; *Aaron Copland: A Self-Portrait* (Films for the Humanities and Sciences, Inc., 1979); Copland, at a distance of many more years, remembered this meeting with de Mille somewhat differently, C-P I, p. 356.

26 Siegel, p. 126; Margaret Lloyd, *The Borzoi Book of Modern Dance* (New York: Dance Horizons, 1949), p. 332.

27 Agnes de Mille, "Time Plot" (*Rodeo*), CCLC.

28 Somewhat confusingly, Copland referred to the ballet's four—as opposed to five—"episodes," ostensibly because he did not consider "Ranch House Party" of equal stature; to avoid confusion, I accordingly refer to the ballet's five "parts" or "sections," reserving the word "episode" for the ballet suite. Jessica Burr, interview by author, 21 March 1996; C-P I, p. 257 (Thomson and others refer to the song as "Houlihan"); regarding "I Ride an Old Paint," de Mille had written to Copland, "This is a good riding rhythm and a nearly unknown tune as far as I can make out," Agnes de Mille to Copland, undated, CCLC; Ira Ford, *Traditional Music of America* (Hatboro, PA: Folkore Associates, Inc., 1965), pp. 31, 43, 58; John and Alan Lomax, *Our Singing Country: A Second Volume of American Ballads and Folk Songs* (New York: Macmillan, 1941), pp. 54, 249, 262. "Tip Toe, Pretty Betty Martin" does not appear in the suite from the ballet. As in the case of "Springfield Mountain" and *Lincoln Portrait*, the presence of "McLeod's Reel" in Bernard Herrmann's 1941 film score to *The Devil and Daniel Webster* (as in the harvest dance and the final credits) may have inspired Copland's adoption of this particular tune.

29 "Note," *Rodeo*.

30 Lloyd, p. 333.

31 Downes; Carl Sandburg, *The American Songbag* (New York: Harcourt Brace Jovanovich, 1927, 1990), pp. 12–13; Damon; Agnes de Mille to Copland, undated, CCLC.

32 Lloyd, p. 332.

33 Agnes de Mille, videotaped interview, *Dance in America* (1973), Dance Division, NYPL ("I made"); De Mille, *Dance*, pp. 212–20; Easton, p. 189; Agnes de Mille to Copland, 2 September 1942, CCLC.

34 De Mille, videotaped interview.

35 De Mille, *Dance*, p. 232.

36 Easton, p. 194; Edwin Denby, "With the Dancers," *Modern Music* 20.1 (1942): 53; C-P I, p. 362.

37 C-P I, p. 362; Lloyd, p. 332; Easton, pp. 193, 322–23. Fortunately, some film footage of de Mille's original performance survives in the Dance Division, NYPL.

38 C-P I, pp. 359–61; Robert Ward, review of *Rodeo*, *Notes* 4 (1947): 191; Berger, p. 57.

³⁹ C-P I, p. 355; Pollack, p. 84.

⁴⁰ Kurt Schindler, *Folk Music and Poetry of Spain and Portugal* (New York: Hispanic Institute, 1941), no. 202.

⁴¹ In a note to the work, Copland recommended approximately three or four voices for each part of the solo group but acknowledged that the appropriate number depends on the size of the larger choir.

⁴² Burckhardt, interview.

⁴³ Copland to Leonard Bernstein, [spring 1941], BCLC; Rosamund Bernier, interview by author, 7 January 1996.

⁴⁴ C-P I, p. 367.

⁴⁵ Copland, *Danzón Cubano,* performed by Bernstein and the New York Philharmonic (Columbia MS 6514); Copland and the London Symphony Orchestra (Columbia M 33269); and Antal Dorati and the Minneapolis Symphony Orchestra (Mercury MG 50172).

⁴⁶ Eliot Feld, *Dance in America* (video), Dance Division, NYPL.

21. From *The North Star* to *Appalachian Spring* (1943–44)

¹ C-P II, pp. 13–19.

² Crescent Productions to Copland, 4 September 1943, CCLC; Goldwyn's negotiations with Stravinsky broke down in January, 1943, after the latter had already begun to sketch out some music, Richard Taruskin, *Stravinsky and the Russian Traditions,* vol. 2 (Berkeley: University of California Press, 1997), p. 1624.

³ In his autobiography, Copland mistakenly stated that the Germans burned down the village, C-P II, p. 15.

⁴ C-P II, p. 15.

⁵ Toward the end of the shoot, Goldwyn called in Edward Chodorov to slightly doctor the script, though Hellman was more upset by Milestone's direction, Bernard F. Dick, *Hellman in Hollywood* (Teaneck: Fairleigh Dickinson University Press, 1982), pp. 97–103; William Wright, *Lillian Hellman: The Image, the Woman* (New York: Simon & Schuster, 1986), pp. 186, 188; Carl Rollyson, *Lillian Hellman: Her Legend and Her Legacy* (New York: St. Martin's Press, 1988), pp. 196–97; Joseph R. Millichap, *Lewis Milestone* (Boston: Twayne, 1981), p. 124 ("big-time").

⁶ Dick, p. 105; Wright, p. 188; Rollyson, p. 203; Millichap, p. 117; C-P II, p. 21 (oddly, on the following page, Copland-Perlis reprint a letter from Ira Gershwin to Copland, in which Gershwin says of the New York notices, "I thought, on the whole, they were very good"); Pauline Kael, *5001 Nights at the Movies: A Guide from A to Z* (New York: Holt, Rinehart and Winston, 1984), p. 418.

⁷ Among the songbooks Copland used were *Fifty Russian Revolutionary Songs* (Leningrad: Muzgiz, 1938); *Songs* (Moscow: Muzgiz, 1939); *Russian Folksongs from the Voronezh Region* (Moscow: Muzgiz, 1939); *Fifty Russian Folksongs,* edited By E. L. Swerkoff (Leipzig: J. H. Zimmermann, 1937).

[8] Copland, *Film Music Notes* 3.3 (1943); C-P II, p. 15.

[9] Dick, p. 101; Laurence Rosenthal, interview by author, 2 May 1998; C-P II, pp. 21, 65, 88; Elliott Carter, "Theatre and Films, 1943," *Modern Music* 21.1 (1943): pp. 51–52; Robert Palmer to Copland, 21 November 1940, 8 March 1944, CCLC (Palmer, who also admired Copland's previous film scores, did not, however, like the film itself; as he explained to Copland: "The Romanticizing of the idyllic life of the Russian Peasants was a little too much, and part of the same trend shown by the falsification of the facts of the frame-up trials in *Mission to Moscow*. I'm afraid I'm on the side of John Dewey when it comes to deliberate falsifications for propaganda purposes"); Lukas Foss to Copland, 8 November 1943, CCLC.

[10] Virgil Thomson, *Virgil Thomson* (New York: Da Capo Press, 1966), pp. 206, 280, 297; Anthony Tommasini, *Virgil Thomson: Composer on the Aisle* (New York: Norton, 1997), pp. 292–93; David Diamond, interview by author, 10 February 1996.

[11] Olin Downes, "Looking Backward," *New York Times* 23 January 1944, sec. 2, p. 5; see also Carole Rosen, *The Goossens: A Musical Century* (Boston: Northeastern University Press, 1993), p. 239.

[12] Vincent Persichetti, "Modern Chamber Music in Philadelphia," *Modern Music* 22.1 (1944): 47.

[13] Colin McPhee, "Scores and Records," *Modern Music* 22.1 (1944): 58.

[14] Julia Smith, *Aaron Copland: His Work and Contribution to American Music* (New York: Dutton, 1955), p. 237; Neil Butterworth, *The Music of Aaron Copland* (New York: Universe Books, 1986), p. 98.

[15] Diamond, interview; for an early discography of the Copland Violin Sonata, see Joann Skowronski, *Aaron Copland: A Bio-bibliography* (Westport, CT: Greenwood Press, 1985), pp. 63–64; Fredell Lack, interview by author, 9 February 1996; C-P II, p. 212.

[16] Copland, Sonata for Violin and Piano, performed by Hans Maile and Horst Göbel (Thorofon CTH 2012), p. 385; by Anne Akiko Meyers and André-Michel Schub, *The American Album* (RCA 09026-68114-2); and by Glenn Dicterow and Israela Margalit (EMI 7CDC 5 55405 2); Larry Starr, "Copland on Compact Disc, 1: Chamber Music," *American Music* 10.3 (1992): 385.

[17] Michael Webster, interview by author, 28 January 1998; Copland, Sonata for Clarinet and Piano, performed by Victoria Soames and Julius Drake (Clarinet Classics CC0001).

[18] Thomas A. DeLong, *Pops: Paul Whiteman, King of Jazz* (Piscataway: New Century Publishers, Inc., 1983), pp. 259–81.

[19] C-P II, pp. 28–29, 429nn11, 12, 13 (for the specific instrumentation of the three versions of *Letter from Home*).

[20] C-P II, pp. 27–28.

[21] Copland to Carlos Chávez, November 1971, CCLC; William W. Austin, "Aaron Copland," *The New Grove Dictionary of Music and Musicians*, vol. 4, Stanley Sadie, ed. (New York: Macmillan 1980), pp. 719–25.

22 Copland, liner notes, recording of *Appalachian Spring*, performed by Eduardo Mata and the Dallas Symphony Orchestra (RCA Red Seal ARL1-2862, 1978).

23 Agnes de Mille, *Martha* (New York: Random House, 1991), p. 126 (perhaps one could draw a comparison with the Group Theatre, established at around the same time); see also Ernestine Stodelle, *Deep Song: The Dance Story of Martha Graham* (New York: Schirmer Books, 1984); Marta Elaine Robertson, " 'A Gift to Be Simple': The Collaboration of Aaron Copland and Martha Graham in the Genesis of Appalachian Spring" (Ph.D. diss., University of Michigan, 1992).

24 Martha Graham, *Blood Memory: An Autobiography* (New York: Doubleday, 1991), p. 125 (Brice satire).

25 De Mille, p. 210; Graham, *Blood Memory*, p. 225.

26 De Mille, p. 148; Martha Graham, "The Dance in America," *Trend* 1.1 (1932), pp. 5–7; Charles C. Alexander, *Here the Country Lies: Nationalism and the Arts in Twentieth-Century America*, p. 235; Lincoln Kirstein, "Martha Graham at Bennington," *Nation* 147 (1938): 231.

27 De Mille, pp. 405, 419; Arlene Croce, "The Blue Glass Goblet, and After," *New Yorker* 50 (1974): 130–37.

28 De Mille, p. 98; C-P II, p. 30; Graham, *Blood Memory*, p. 127; Virgil Thomson, "Two Ballets," *New York Herald-Tribune*, 20 May 1945; Martha Graham, notes on *The Scarlet Letter*, mailed to Copland by Francis Mason, 26 August 1974, CCLC.

29 Wayne D. Shirley, "Ballet for Martha: the Commissioning of *Appalachian Spring*," *Performing Arts Annual* 1987 (Library of Congress): 102–23; Wayne D. Shirley, "Ballets for Martha: The Creation of *Appalachian Spring*, *Jeux de Printemps*, and *Hérodiade*," *Performing Arts Annual* 1988 (Library of Congress): 40–69; Robertson, pp. 122–72; Martha Graham to Copland, 17 February 1941; 7 July 1942, CCLC. Graham was able to supplement the $500 commission with $15 in royalties per performance.

30 Early on, Chávez decided to score his ballet for string quartet and woodwind quartet (to the concern of Graham and Spivacke, who both worried about the lack of a piano or percussion part).

31 In May, 1946, Graham finally launched her Medea ballet, *Cave of the Heart*, with music by Samuel Barber.

32 Martha Graham, "House of Victory," "Name.," and "Name?" (Graham punctuated the title of the first "Name" script with a period, the second "Name" script with a question mark), CCLC.

33 Robertson, p. 145.

34 C-P II, p. 34; Graham, *Blood Memory*, p. 232; Copland to Carlos Chávez, 7 February 1946, CCLC. Marta Robertson's ongoing work specifically addresses parallel and nonparallel relationships between the "kinesthetic" qualities of Graham's choreographies and their musical scores.

35 Robert Hughes, *The Shock of the New* (New York: Knopf, 1995), p. 311.

36 Marta Robertson writes that this "Love" theme "undoubtedly depicted the whistling that announced the Citizen's presence in Graham's script," that is, the first "Name" script ("From a distance there seems to come someone whistling"). She accordingly refers to this theme as the Citizen's "whistle" solo, Robertson, pp. 239ff.

37 Edward D. Andrews, *The Gift to Be Simple: Songs, Dances and Rituals of the American Shakers* (New York: J. J. Augustin Publisher, 1940), p. 136. Because *Appalachian Spring* made "Simple Gifts" famous, Copland's—not Andrews's—is the version by which the melody is generally known. For more on "Simple Gifts" see Roger Hall, "Joseph Brackett's 'Simple Gifts,' " *Sonneck Society Bulletin* 23.3 (1997): 72–73.

38 The third "House of Victory" draft ended with the Mother's line as well as a short solo for the Indian Girl; whether or not Copland had the Indian Girl in mind while composing the work, his final directive implies some such stage action as described by Graham.

39 Edwin Denby to Copland, 1941, CCLC ("I go around telling all the poets I meet you are looking for a Shaker one acter, it's like planting cherry pits in the yard"); Stephen J. Stein, *The Shaker Experience in America: A History of the United Society of Believers* (New Haven: Yale University Press, 1992), pp. 376–77, 383.

40 Stein, p. 217.

41 C-P II, p. 33.

42 Shirley, "Ballets," p. 67; Robertson, p. 155.

43 Copland, recorded interview at the Coolidge Auditorium of the Library of Congress, 14 November 1981 (Bridge Records BCD 9046). Copland at first assumed the common pronunciation of "Appalachian" (the third *a* as in *pay*) as opposed to a more authentically regional pronunciation (with the third *a* as in *pat*); in later years, he used both.

44 Edwin Denby, "Appalachian Spring," *Dance Writings* (New York: Knopf, 1986), pp. 313–14 (originally 15 May 1945); Jack Anderson, "Dance: Copland Conducts for Graham," *New York Times* 18 June 1982, p. C8.

45 Martha Graham, *Appalachian Spring* (videocassette, 1958).

46 Marcia Siegel, *The Shapes of Change: Images of American Dance* (New York: Avon Books, 1979), p. 145.

47 Robertson, pp. 156ff.; Copland to Carlos Chávez, 7 February 1946 (about Horst's ineptitude); Martha Graham to Copland, 1 May 1945, CCLC; de Mille, p. 419.

48 Studying letters and sketches, Marta Robertson concludes that Copland anticipated such a version of the work from the very beginning, notwithstanding some statements to the contrary, Robertson, pp. 164–65.

49 See Skowronski, pp. 29–32, for a discography of *Appalachian Spring* up through 1992 (an impressive thirty-eight entries in all); notable releases since then include the suite for chamber group by the Orpheus Chamber Orchestra (Deutsche Grammophon 427 335-2, 1989), the complete ballet score for

chamber group by Hugh Wolff and the St. Paul Chamber Orchestra (Teldec 2292-46314-2, 1991), and the complete ballet score for orchestra by Leonard Slatkin and the St. Louis Symphony Orchestra (Angel CMS 7 64315 2, 1992); Copland to Lawrence Morton, 11 November 1954 (and other correspondence between Copland and Morton, 1954–70), Ojai Festival Archives, courtesy of Betty Izant.

50 Skowronski, pp. 29–32; Leslie Gerber, review of a recording of Copland's *Appalachian Spring*, Fanfare 11.6 (1988): 147–48; 12.3 (1989); 149; C-P II, p. 50.

51 John Wiser, review of a recording of Copland's *Appalachian Spring*, Fanfare 13.2 (1989): 180; C-P II, p. 49.

22. From "Jubilee Variation" to *Four Piano Blues* (1945–48)

1 Eugene Goossens, quoted by F. M. Blasing, *Cincinnati Symphony Orchestra Program Book* 9 June 1995: 12.

2 Goossens, p. 11; C-P II, p. 61.

3 C-P II, p. 62.

4 Arthur Knight, *The Liveliest Art* (New York: Mentor Books, 1957), p. 254; Richard Meran Barsam, *Nonfiction Film* (New York: E. P. Dutton, 1973), p. 213; Erik Barnouw, *Documentary: A History of the Non-Fiction Film* (1974; New York: Oxford University Press, 1993), p. 164; Neil Lerner, "Music and Documentary Film, 1936–1945: Style, Rhetoric, and Ideology in Scores by Virgil Thomson, Aaron Copland, and Louis Gruenberg" (Ph.D. diss., Duke University, 1997).

5 Neil Lerner identifies the music as an arrangement of the finale to Mozart's Fifth Violin Concerto, K. 219, Lerner, E-mail to author, 8 April 1996.

6 Lerner, E-mail.

7 C-P II, p. 259.

8 Phillip Ramey, "Copland at 80," *Chicago* (January 1981): 123, BHCF; C-P II, pp. 66–67.

9 Copland, program notes, reprinted as liner notes, Symphony No. 3, conducted by Antal Dorati (Mercury MG50018).

10 Arthur V. Berger, "The Third Symphony of Aaron Copland," *Tempo* 9 (1948): 20–27; William Austin, "Copland's Third Symphony: An Analysis," unpublished paper, c. 1957, courtesy of the author; C-P I, p. 341.

11 Berger, p. 26; David Diamond to Copland, 27 August 1944, CCLC, courtesy of Elizabeth Bergman.

12 Elizabeth Bergman, letter to author, 15 September 1997.

13 Austin.

14 David Hiram Robertson, "An Analysis of Aaron Copland's Third Symphony" (master's thesis, Eastman School, 1965), refers to my B and C sections as B' and B", thus emphasizing the basic similarity between these two sections.

15 Austin.

16 Virgil Thomson, "Copland as Great Man," *New York Herald Tribune* 24 November 1946, sec. 5, p. 6; Hugh Wolff, interview by author, 27 April 1997.

17 Copland, *What to Listen for in Music*, rev. ed. (New York: McGraw Hill, 1957), p. 44.

18 Cyrus Durgin, "Symphony Hall: Boston Symphony Orchestra," *Boston Daily Globe* 19 October 1946, p. 10.

19 Arthur Berger, *Aaron Copland* (New York: Oxford University Press, 1953), p. 72; Leonard Bernstein, "What Is American Music?" videotape (CBS Inc., 1990): K. Robert Schwarz, "Copland's Third: Language of Hope," *New York Times* 19 April 1987, p. H27.

20 C-P II, pp. 69, 432n5; Berger, p. 77; Thomson.

21 C-P II, pp. 70–71.

22 S.B., "Copland's Third Symphony," *Musical Times* 99 (1958): 29; John Rockwell, "Philharmonic: Copland," *New York Times* 21 November 1980, sec. 3, p. 25; C-P II, p. 69; *Time* 48 (1946): 55, reprinted in William Malloch, "Copland's Triumph," *Opus* (February 1988): 22–25; Walter Simmons, *Fanfare* 10.4 (1987): 101–02; Wilfrid Mellers, *Music in a New Found Land* (New York: Oxford University Press, 1964).

23 Phillip Ramey, interview by author, 10 May 1996. According to Ramey, Copland did not want his 1978 recording of the symphony with the New Philharmonia Orchestra (Columbia M 35113) released, because of the lack of sufficient rehearsal time.

24 Malloch.

25 Copland to Christopher Rouse, 3 December 1971, courtesy of Rouse; Wolff, interview.

26 Hugh Ottaway, "Prospect and Perspective," *The Symphony, Volume II*, ed. by Robert Simpson (New York: Penguin Books, 1967), p. 277.

27 Contract for *Tragic Ground*, February, 1945, CCLC; Copland to Marc Blitzstein, 24 April 1945, BCUW.

28 Erskine Caldwell, *Tragic Ground* (New York: Duell, Sloan and Pearce, 1944).

29 Caldwell, p. 236; Scott MacDonald, "Introduction," *Critical Essays on Erskine Caldwell* (Boston: G. K. Hall, 1981).

30 Lynn Riggs, *Tragic Ground: A Music-Play*, 15 June 1946, CCLC.

31 *Tragic Ground* sketches, CCLC; C-P II, p. 166; the verse of "Alone at Night" exists in Copland's hand, whereas the refrain was transcribed from memory by Paul Moor in 1982, Moor to Copland, 26 June 1982, CCLC; Samuel Preston Bayard, ed., *Hill Country Tunes* (Philadelphia: American Folkore Society, 1944), no. 70.

32 Moor.

33 Schuyler Watts to Copland, 21 September 1945, CCLC; Arnold Dobrin, *Aaron Copland: His Life and Times* (New York: Thomas Y. Crowell, 1967), p. 179.

34 Elliot Forbes, *A History of Music at Harvard to 1972* (Cambridge, MA: Harvard University, Department of Music, 1988), pp. 103–10.

35 C-P II, p. 73; Forbes, p. 105.

36 For a discography for *In the Beginning*, see Joann Skowronski, *Aaron Copland: A Bio-bibliography* (Westport, CT: Greenwood Press, 1985), pp. 44–45; see also *In the Beginning*, Stephen Cleobury conducting the Choir of King's College, Cambridge (EMI CDC 7 54188 2); and Matthew Best conducting the Corydon Singers (Hyperion CDA 66219).

37 C-P II, pp. 76–77, 93; James Lincoln Collier, *Benny Goodman and the Swing Era* (New York: Oxford University Press, 1989), p. 338; Ross Firestone, *Swing, Swing, Swing: The Life and Times of Benny Goodman* (New York: W. W. Norton, 1993), p. 250.

38 C-P II, p. 93.

39 C-P II, p. 94; Phillip Ramey, interview by author, 10 May 1996. The "fracas" alluded to concerned a passage just prior to the cadenza, one that consequently became the source of a misunderstanding about the piece. Copland originally concluded the concerto's slow movement with a repeated four-note phrase, the last long-held note of which leads directly into the cadenza. Because Goodman wanted some relief before launching into the cadenza, Copland provided two alternatives: replacing the long-held note with some optional harp music or, for even greater respite, in addition to the harp music, having a solo viola play the whole last four-note phrase in lieu of the clarinet. In early performances, Goodman used this second option, admitting that he was "a little sticky about leaving it [the phrase] out," while in later performances he went the first route. However, even in performances where soloists play the phrase as originally written—such as those by David Shifrin and Richard Stoltzman—conductors leave the harp music in, perhaps due to force of habit. It would seem, however, that if the soloist can handle the long note, omitting the harp *ossia* would make for a more effective transition to the cadenza.

40 C-P II, p. 434n43.

41 Richard Stoltzman, liner notes, *The Essential Clarinet* (RCA 09026-61360-2).

42 C-P II, p. 93.

43 David Hamilton, "The Recordings of Copland's Music," *High Fidelity/Musical America* 20.11 (1970): 72.

44 Julia Smith, *Aaron Copland: His Work and Contribution to American Music* (New York: Dutton, 1955), p. 198; George Balanchine, *Balanchine's New Complete Stories of the Great Ballets* (Garden City: Doubleday and Company, 1954, 1968): 304–06; Nancy Reynolds, *Repertory in Review: 40 Years of the New York City Ballet* (New York: The Dial Press, 1977), pp. 134–35.

45 Nik Krevitsky, *Dance Observer* 19.1 (1952): 9; Reynolds (for the ballet's critical reception); Berger, p. 83; John Gruen, interview with Copland, 9 July 1975 (transcript), Dance Division, NYPL.

46 Larry Starr, "Copland on Compact Disc, II: Music for Orchestra," *American Music* 10.4 (1992): 503–04.

47 For a discussion of the third of the *Four Piano Blues* as "an expansion" of a "single sonority," see Allen Forte, *Contemporary Tone Structures* (New York: Teachers College, Columbia University, 1955), pp. 63–73, 161–66.

23. From *The Red Pony* to the Piano Quartet (1948–50)

[1] Abe Meyer to Copland, MCA Artists Ltd., correspondence file, CCLC.

[2] C-P II, p. 88.

[3] John Steinbeck, *The Red Pony* (New York: Bantam, 1955), p. 91; Jackson J. Benson, *The True Adventures of John Steinbeck, Writer* (New York: Viking Press, 1984), p. 483.

[4] Copland, p. 90; Copland to Irving Fine, 3 February 1949, FCLC; Benson, p. 629; John Steinbeck to Copland, 22 September 1964, CCLC; Joseph R. Millichap, *Lewis Milestone* (Boston: Twayne, 1981), p. 160.

[5] In composing *The Red Pony*, Copland made some small use of his sketches for the incomplete *Tragic Ground*, C-P II, p. 88.

[6] Lawrence Morton, "*The Red Pony*: A Review of Aaron Copland's Score," *Film Music Notes* February 1949: 2–8; Virgil Thomson, "Hollywood's Best," *A Virgil Thomson Reader* (Boston: Houghton Mifflin, 1981), pp. 324–26.

[7] C-P II, pp. 90–91, 434n40; Donald V. Coers, Paul D. Ruffin, and Robert J. DeMott, eds. *After the Grapes of Wrath: Essays on John Steinbeck in Honor of Tetsumaro Hayashi* (Athens: Ohio University Press, 1995), pp. 64–66; John Steinbeck to Copland 22 September 1964, CCLC; Steinbeck's unpublished narrative, meanwhile, can be found in Columbia University's Butler Library.

[8] Jan Herman, *A Talent for Trouble: The Life of Hollywood's Most Acclaimed Director, William Wyler* (New York: G. P. Putnam's Sons, 1995), pp. 298–305, 311–13; C-P II, pp. 100–01.

[9] C-P II, p. 98; see p. 104 for a facsimile of one page of the original score.

[10] Frederick W. Sternfeld, "Copland as a Film Composer," *Musical Quarterly* 37 (1951): 161–75, an article summarized by Roy M. Prendergast in *Film Music: A Neglected Art* (New York: W. W. Norton, 1977), pp. 89–95; C-P II, p. 100.

[11] William Wyler to Copland, 24 July 1948, CCLC.

[12] André Previn, *No Minor Chords* (New York: Doubleday, 1991), p. 92.

[13] David Raksin, interview by author, 29 May 1997.

[14] Copland, *The Heiress Suite*, performed by Leonard Slatkin and the St. Louis Symphony Orchestra (RCA 09026-61699-2); listeners to this recording might appreciate the timings of the individual sections, which are not provided by the liner notes: "Prelude" (with "Reunion" at 1:15), "Catherine's Engagement" 3:37 (preceded by the Washington Square music at 3:22), "Cherry Red Dress" (in which Catherine happily tries on a new party dress, only to have her father compare her unfavorably to her mother) 4:34, "Departure" 5:38 (which incorporates "Plaisir d'Amour"), "The Proposal" 6:03 (with the end credits at 7:41). The liner notes also list "Morris Suggests Love," but this is the title of an omitted episode, one that consists of an arrangement of "Plaisir d'Amour."

[15] Abe Meyer to Copland, MCA Artists Ltd., correspondence file, CCLC; Raksin, interview.

[16] Copland to Victor Kraft, c. 1955, CCLC; L. Arnold Weissberger to Copland, 11 November 1954, CCLC; Karlin, p. 199.

17 *Charter of the United Nations: Commentary and Documents,* 3rd. ed., ed. Leland M. Goodrich, Edvard Hambro, and Anne Patricia Simons (New York: Columbia University Press, 1969), pp. 19, 377; C-P II, p. 148.

18 Copland to Irving Fine, 18 September 1949, FCLC; Ingolf Dahl, review of Copland's *Preamble for a Solemn Occasion, Notes* 11 (1954): 276–77; C-P II, p. 148.

19 Arnold Dobrin, *Aaron Copland: His Life and Times* (New York: Thomas Y. Crowell, 1967), p. 178.

20 C-P II, p. 159.

21 Helen Didriksen, "Strange Company: Aaron Copland, Emily Dickinson, and America at Mid-Century," unpublished paper (May 1988), pp. 2–5, 34–37, courtesy of the author; notes Didriksen, "Copland's environment is not quite so urban, nor Dickinson's quite so rural, as has been supposed," p. 2; C-PII, p. 158.

22 C-P II, p. 438n20 (for alleged changes of text). Copland consulted *Emily Dickinson Poems: First and Second Series,* ed. Mabel Loomis Todd and T. W. Higginson (New York: World Publishing Company, 1948), at least for "The Chariot," which conforms to their version; and *Poems by Emily Dickinson,* ed. Martha Dickinson Bianchi and Alfred Leete Hampson (Boston: Little, Brown and Company, 1947); Didriksen, pp. 38–40, who found both volumes among the composer's possessions, guesses that Copland also knew, at the time he composed the *Dickinson Songs,* George Frisbie Whicher, *This Was a Poet: A Critical Biography of Emily Dickinson* (New York: Charles Scibner's Sons, 1938); for the first critical edition of Dickinson's poetry, see *The Complete Poems of Emily Dickinson,* edited by Thomas H. Johnson (Boston: Little, Brown and Company, 1955). This explains the missing stanzas from "I Felt a Funeral in My Brain" and "The Chariot." Also compare, in "There Came a Wind like a Bugle," the original "And Rivers where the Houses ran / Those looked that lived—that Day—" with "And rivers where the houses ran / The living looked that day"; in "The World Feels Dusty," the original "Mine be the Ministry / When thy Thirst comes— / and Hybla Balms— / Dews of Thessaly, to fetch—" with "Mine be the ministry / When thy thirst comes, / Dews of thyself to fetch / And holy balms"; and in "Heart, We Will Forget Him," the original "When you have done, pray tell me / That I may straight begin! / Haste! lest while you're lagging / I remember him!" with "When you have done, pray tell me, / that I my thoughts may dim; / haste! lest while you're lagging, / I may remember him!" Douglas Young, "Copland's Dickinson Songs," *Tempo* 103 (1972): 36 ("slightly oversweet"); Wayne Shirley, marginalia.

23 Didriksen, p. 41, mentions seven poems considered but not set by Copland as follows: "A Bird Came Down the Walk," "Could I But Ride Indefinite," "Heart Not So Heavy as Mine," "I Died for Beauty, but Was Scarce," "I Should Not Dare to Leave My Friend," "It Was Not Death, For I Stood Up," "On Such a Night, or Such a Night," "The Moon Is Distant from the Sea," "To Make a Prairie It Takes a Clover and One Bee," and "Will There Really Be a Morning?"

[24] C-P II, pp. 157–59, 162.

[25] C-P II, p. 438n26; Didriksen, pp. 27–32. Copland apparently thought of Lukas Foss for "Going to Heaven!" because "it was so jumpy." Juan Orrego-Salas similarly guessed that his dedication of "Dear March, Come In!" had something to do with the fact that Copland "always said I was high spirited and humorous." Shapero contended a connection between himself and his song's text: "The poem 'When they come back' contains references to the past, along with hopes that some of the past might be repeated or regained. . . . I always assumed that Aaron dedicated that particular song to me because of my 'neo-classic' preferences, and interest in the music of the past." It seems hardly coincidence, either, that Copland dedicated "Heart, We Will Forget Him" to the one woman of the group. On the other hand, Diamond and Berger apparently just picked their own songs.

[26] C-P II, p. 165, p. 438n23; Copland, *Twelve Poems of Emily Dickinson,* performed by Martha Lipton and the composer (Columbia ML 5106); Jan DeGaetani and Leo Smit (Bridge Records BCD 9046); Roberta Alexander and Roger Vignoles (Etcetera KTC 1100).

[27] C-P II, p. 163; Michael Tilson Thomas, liner notes, *Eight Poems of Emily Dickinson,* performed by Barbara Hendricks, Thomas conducting the London Symphony Orchestra (EMI 7243 5 55358 2 5).

[28] C-P II, p. 159.

[29] Didriksen, pp. 23–26; Igor Stravinsky and Robert Craft, *Dialogues and a Diary* (London: Faber and Faber, 1968), p. 100; William W. Austin, *Music in the 20th Century from Debussy Through Stravinsky* (New York: W. W. Norton, 1966), p. 577; Joseph Kerman, "American Music: The Columbia Series (II)," *Hudson Review* 13.3 (1961): 411–18; Young, pp. 33–37; Robert Michael Daugherty, "An Analysis of Aaron Copland's *Twelve Poems of Emily Dickinson*" (DMA thesis, Ohio State University, 1980), pp. 4–5; Larry Starr, "Aaron Copland, Emily Dickinson, and the Aesthetics of Risk," Annual Sonneck Society Meeting, 21 March 1996, courtesy of the author.

[30] Young, pp. 36–37; C-P II, p. 166.

[31] Copland, *Twelve Poems of Emily Dickinson,* performed by Martha Lipton; Adele Addison (Columbia M 30375); Jan DeGaetani; Roberta Alexander; and Barbara Bonney (London 289 455 511-2); *Eight Poems of Emily Dickinson,* performed by Marni Nixon, Keith Clark conducting the Pacific Symphony Orchestra (Reference Recordings RR-22CD); Helene Schneiderman, Dennis Russell Davies conducting the Orchestra of St. Luke's (MusicMasters 01612-67101-2); Dawn Upshaw, Hugh Wolff conducting the St. Paul Chamber Orchestra (Teldec 9031-77310-2); Barbara Hendricks.

[32] Roque Cordero, interview by author, 25 September 1997; Copland, quoted by Mildred Norton, Los Angeles *Daily News* 5 April 1948; Copland, *Music and Imagination* (Cambridge: Harvard University Press, 1952), p. 73; Edward T. Cone, "Conversation with Aaron Copland," *Perspectives of New Music* 6.2

(1968): 67; C-P II, p. 151; Copland, "Fantasy for Piano," *New York Times* 20 October 1957, BHCF.

33 Jennifer DeLapp, "Copland in the Fifties: Music and Ideology in the McCarthy Era" (Ph.D. diss., University of Michigan, 1997), courtesy of the author.

34 Lawrence Starr, "Copland's Style," *Perspectives of New Music* 19 (1980–81): 82n13; Bayan Northcott, "Copland in England," *Music and Musicians* 18 (1969): 35; Howard Pollack, *Harvard Composers: Walter Piston and His Students, from Elliott Carter to Frederic Rzewski* (Metuchen: Scarecrow Press, 1992), p. 150; Leonard Bernstein, "Aaron Copland: An Intimate Sketch," *High Fidelity* 20.11 (1970): 55; Donal Henahan, "He Made Composing Respectable Here" (1970), BHCF ("It never occurred"). For an example of misconceptions surrounding Copland's adoption of the twelve-tone method, see Joan Peyser, *Boulez* (New York: Schirmer, 1976), p. 89.

35 Copland, *Music and Imagination*, pp. 68–73.

36 While composing this work, Copland used the term *reversed* rather than *retrograde*.

37 Cone, p. 67; Bernstein, "Aaron Copland," p. 55 (this confirmed by Verna Fine, interview by author, 7 May 1994).

38 C-P II, p. 151.

39 David Joseph Conte, "Aaron Copland's Piano Quartet: An Analysis" (master's thesis, Cornell University, 1982), p. 64, courtesy of the author.

40 Marjorie Loggia and Glenn Young, eds., *The Collected Works of Harold Clurman* (New York: Applause Books, 1994), p. 261.

41 Peter Evans, "The Thematic Technique of Copland's Recent Works," *Tempo* 51 (1959): 7.

42 C-P II, p. 152; Leonard Bernstein to Copland, 1952, BCLC; David Diamond to Copland, 11 October 1952, CCLC; Arthur Berger, *Aaron Copland* (New York: Oxford University Press, 1953), p. 85.

24. The Changing Scene

1 "Red Visitors Cause Rumpus," *Life* 26.14 (1949): 39–43.

2 Richard M. Fried, *Nightmare in Red: The McCarthy Era in Perspective* (New York: Oxford University Press, 1990), pp. 71–72, 95, 136, 150, 161; Lillian Hellman, *Scoundrel Time* (New York: Bantam Books, 1976), pp. 109–10; Arthur Miller, *Timebends: A Life* (New York: Grove Press, 1987), pp. 334, 341, 456.

3 Fried, p. 157; C-P II, p. 185; Bruce Catton, "Maharajah in the White House," *Nation* 31 January 1953, CCLC.

4 The League of Composers to the Inaugural Concert Committee, 16 January 1953; Copland, undated statement (revised version of the one quoted in C-P II, p. 186); Copland to President Eisenhower [1953], CCLC.

[5] Fred E. Busbey, "Aaron Copland and Inaugural Concert," *Congressional Record—Appendix* 16 January 1953, p. A178, CCLC.

[6] Paul Hume, "Music Censorship Reveals New Peril," *Washington Post* 18 January 1953, CCLC; C-P II, p. 187; Catton; "Wicked Music," *New Republic* 26 January 1953: 7, CCLC.

[7] Catton; Paul Hume, "American Music Is Comfortably of Age," *Washington Post* 25 January 1952, CCLC.

[8] Frederick Kuh, "Top American Composers' Works Barred at U.S. Libraries Abroad," *Chicago Sun-Times* 26 April 1953, CCLC.

[9] Hellman.

[10] Transcript, Copland hearing before the Senate Permanent Subcommittee on Investigations of the Committee on Government Operations, 26 May 1953, CCLC; Domingo Santa Cruz to Copland, 10 April 1961, CCLC.

[11] McCarthy file, CCLC.

[12] McCarthy file, CCLC; Copland to Joseph McCarthy, 5 June 1953; C-P II, p. 197.

[13] Charles Glover to Copland, 5 October 1953; C-P II, p. 199.

[14] Copland, FBI file.

[15] C-P II, pp. 200–01; Lukas Foss to Copland, 21 May 1953; Oscar Cox to Copland, 14 February 1956, CCLC.

[16] Copland to Gurney Kennedy, 12 March 1953.

[17] C-P II, pp. 201–02; when the Dallas Symphony engaged Copland as a guest conductor in 1960, the John Birch Society threatened to bomb the podium, Samuel Adler, interview by author, 19 March 1996.

[18] Jimmy Carter to Copland, 3 April 1977; Walter Mondale to Copland, 14 November 1980; Ronald Reagan to Copland, 13 November 1981; Elise K. Kirk, *Music at the White House* (Chicago: University of Illinois Press, 1986), pp. 290, 308, 350.

[19] Ned Rorem, *Knowing When to Stop: A Memoir* (New York: Simon & Schuster, 1994), p. 283.

[20] Barbara Kolb, interview by author, 23 August 1996; Jean-Jacques Nattiez, ed., *The Boulez-Cage Correspondence* (New York: Cambridge University Press, 1993), pp. 51 ("It is"), 55, 91. Cage only went so far as to agree that the *Variations* was Copland's best work.

[21] C-P II, p. 146; Copland, *Music and Imagination* (Cambridge: Harvard University Press, 1952), p. 72.

[22] C-P II, p. 147.

[23] Copland, *Music and Imagination*, p. 76; C-P II, pp. 171, 233.

[24] C-P II, p. 146; "Olivier Messiaen—Pro and Con," lecture notes, CCLC; Copland, "The World of A-Tonality," *New York Times* 27 November 1949; Copland to Irving Fine, 23 January 1953, FCLC; C-P II, p. 147.

[25] C-P I, p. 146; Copland, *Music and Imagination*, pp. 61–77 ("classicalizing," p. 65; "near-chaos," p. 69; "little hope," p. 75; "immemorial," p. 76).

26 C-P II, p. 234; Copland, Diaries, 20 September 1955, 26 September 1955, CCLC.

27 Copland, Diaries, 26 September 1955, CCLC; Copland, "Compositional Techniques in the 20th Century," lecture notes, CCLC.

28 Copland, Diaries, October 1955, CCLC.

29 Iannis Xenakis to Copland, letters, CCLC.

30 Copland, Diaries, 1960, CCLC.

31 C-P II, pp. 289–91; Copland, Diaries, 1960, CCLC; Copland, "Japan's Composers," lecture notes, CCLC.

32 Toru Takemitsu to Copland, 16 March 1967, CCLC.

33 Copland, Diaries, 1965, CCLC; Copland to William Schuman, 16 August 1978, SCNY.

34 Copland, *The New Music: 1900–1960* (New York: W. W. Norton, 1968).

35 Christopher Ford, "Conducting Keeps Him Young" (September 1972), BHCF; Cole Gagne and Tracy Caras, *Soundpieces: Interviews with American Composers* (Metuchen: Scarecrow Press, 1982), p. 108; Joe Stevenson, "A Conversation with Aaron Copland," *Your Musical Cue Quarterly* Spring 1973, BHCF ("I've spent most").

36 "Copland and His Music . . . ," *San Diego Union* November 1974, CCLC; Gagne, p. 108 ("a real contribution"); Neil Butterworth, *The Music of Aaron Copland* (New York: Universe Books, 1986), p. 191.

37 Copland, *The New Music* p. 188.

25. From *Old American Songs* to the *Piano Fantasy* (1950–57)

1 C-P II, pp. 166–68.

2 Copland found "The Boatmen's Dance," "Long Time Ago," and "Ching-a-Ring Chaw" in S. Foster Damon, *Series of Old American Songs* (Providence: Brown University Library, 1936) (Copland changed the titles, however: "De Boatman's Dance" to "The Boatmen's Dance"; "On the Lake Where Dropped the Willow" to "Long Time Ago"; and "Ching A Ring Chaw" to "Ching-a-Ring Chaw"); "The Dodger" in John A. Lomax and Alan Lomax, *Our Singing Country* (New York: Macmillan, 1949), pp. 289–90, and perhaps, too, Alan Lomax, *The People's Song Book* (New York: Boni and Gaer, 1948), p. 14; "The Little Horses" in John A. Lomax and Alan Lomax, *Folk Song: USA* (also published as *Best Loved American Folk Songs*; New York: Grosset and Dunlap, 1947), pp. 14–15; "Simple Gifts" in Edward D. Andrews, *The Gift to Be Simple: Songs, Dances and Rituals of the American Shakers* (New York: J. J. Augustin Publisher, 1940), p. 136; and "Zion's Walls" in George Pullen Jackson, *Down-East Spirituals and Others* (Locust Valley NY: J. J. Augustin, 1932, 1953), p. 211. And he apparently consulted one or another hymnal for "At the River" (which usually appears as "Shall We Gather at the River?"). Allegedly sung by supporters of Grover Cleveland to ridicule his corrupt Republican opponent Senator James G. Blaine, "The Dodger" parodies, as Wayne Shirley informs the author, "We are all

noddin'," *The Boston Glee Book* (Boston: J. H. Wilkins and R. B. Carter, 1844). Copland had used "Simple Gifts" in *Appalachian Spring*, "Ching-a-Ring Chaw" in *The Heiress*, and "At the River" in *The Red Pony*. He had also considered using "At the River" for *The Cummington Story* and planned on using "Zion's Walls" and "I Bought Me a Cat" for *The Tragic Ground*.

3 "Aaron Copland—an Interview with Roger Hall," *Journal of Church Music* 24 (1982): 6.

4 C-P II, p. 168.

5 Peter Pears to Copland, 5 January 1975, CCLC; for the early discography of *Old American Songs*, see Joann Skowronski, *Aaron Copland: A Bio-bibliography* (Westport, CT: Greenwood Press, 1985), pp. 49–50; see also *Copland Songs*, Roberta Alexander, soprano, with Roger Vignoles, piano (Etcetera KTC 1100).

6 John Brodbin, "The Tender Land," *Opera News* 18.22 (1954): 15, 28.

7 C-P II, pp. 211–15.

8 Opera Ideas, CCLC; C-P II, p. 215; see also chapter 15; Legal Files, CCLC (for correspondence from L. Arnold Weissberger concerning *McTeague*).

9 C-P II, pp. 179; Richard RePass, "Opera Workshops in the United States," *Tempo* 27 (1953): 10–18.

10 C-P II, p. 216; Johns, interview by author, 6 August 1997.

11 C-P II, pp. 221–23.

12 James Agee and Walker Evans, *Let Us Now Praise Famous Men*, with an introduction by John Hersey (1939; Boston: Houghton Mifflin, 1988).

13 Horace Everett [Erik Johns], "Notes on 'The Tender Land,'" *Tempo* 31 (1954): 13–16.

14 Erik Johns, interview by author, 13 December 1994.

15 *Four Plays by William Inge* (New York: Grove Press, 1958).

16 Daniel Mathers, "Against the American Grain: Sexuality and the Rezoning of *The Tender Land*," paper delivered at the University of Cincinnati, 13 November 1995, courtesy of the author; Erik Johns, "More Notes on *The Tender Land*" (December 1994), courtesy of the author.

17 Erik Johns to Copland, undated [1954], CCLC.

18 Erik Johns to Copland, undated [1954], CCLC.

19 Everett, p. 14; Copland found these three songs in collections by George Pullen Jackson, Samuel Preston Bayard, and Cecil J. Sharp, respectively: Jackson; Samuel Preston Bayard, ed., *Hill Country Tunes* (Philadelphia: American Folklore Society, 1944), no. 70; Cecil J. Sharp, *English Folk Songs from the Southern Appalachians*, vol. 2 (New York: Oxford University Press), pp. 6, 9 (Copland used the tune of version A but the text of version D); Copland also seems to have derived "Two Little Bits of Metal" from a piano sketch (1947) published in 1977 as *Midsummer Nocturne*.

20 Brodbin, p. 15.

21 Michael Fleming, "Introduction," Copland, *The Tender Land*, conducted by Phillip Brunelle (Virgin Classics VCD 7 91113-2); Mathers.

22 Copland, *The Tender Land*, conducted by Copland (Columbia MS 6814); Copland, *The Tender Land*, conducted by Phillip Brunelle; Larry Starr, "Copland on Compact Disc, III: Opera and Songs," *American Music* 11.2 (1993): 256–61.

23 Olin Downes, "Music: Premiere of One-Act Opera," *New York Times* 2 April 1954; Ronald Eyer, "New Copland Opera," *Musical America* 74.5 (1954): 5–8; Brodbin, p. 28; Israel Citkowitz, "Current Chronicle," *Musical Quarterly* 40 (1954): 394–97; W.F. [William Flanagan], *Musical America* 74.11 (1954): 29. Copland himself had doubts about the opera, especially the libretto: "It doesn't have a strong libretto; the libretto is too conventional, perhaps, too full of conventional circumstances. . . . I knew I didn't have a great libretto but I did think it was at least adequate for the purpose," Phillip Ramey, "Copland at 80," *Chicago* January 1981: 123, BHCF.

24 Virgil Thomson, *American Music Since 1910* (New York: Holt, Rinehart and Winston, 1910), pp. 55–57; Wilfrid Mellers, "Cambridge: *The Tender Land*," *Musical Times* 103 (1962): 245–46.

25 Will Crutchfield, "Opera: Copland's 'Tender Land,' " *New York Times* 3 May 1987: 76; Alex Ross, "Small Company Finds Copland Piece in Compatible Size," *New York Times* 9 January 1995.

26 Copland-Loring, *The Tender Land* (video), Dance Division, NYPL; Stephanie Von Buchau, "San Francisco Bay Area," *Ballet News* 1.1 (1979); Loring also choreographed the *Organ Symphony* for the Oakland Ballet as *American Gothic* (1979).

27 John W. Freeman, "The Reluctant Composer: A Dialogue with Aaron Copland," *Opera News* 26 January 1963: 9–12, BHCF; C-P II, p. 221.

28 Carlos Chávez, *A! Fredome* (New York: G. Schirmer, 1947), modern English by Willis Wager, courtesy of Wayne Shirley. A few of the *Canticle*'s gestures— including exposed major sevenths—suggest the possible influence of Chávez's setting.

29 C-P II, p. 231.

30 C-P II, p. 270.

31 A. E. Hotchner, "The World of Nick Adams," manuscript of teleplay, CCLC; Ernest Hemingway, *The Nick Adams Stories* (New York: Charles Scribner's Sons, 1972).

32 C-P II, pp. 238–40; Arthur Berger, *Aaron Copland* (New York: Oxford University Press, 1953), p. 33.

33 This includes a more systematic use of a technique explored in the Piano Quartet, namely, reversing consecutive pitches of the row; see Jennifer DeLapp, "Copland in the Fifties: Music and Ideology in the McCarthy Era" (Ph.D. diss., University of Michigan, 1997), p. 198, and Terri Gailey Everett, "Beyond Serialism: An Analysis of Gesture, Form and Serial Relationships in Aaron Copland's *Piano Fantasy*" (master's thesis, University of Texas at Austin, 1997), courtesy of the authors.

34 Dika Newlin, "The Piano Music of Aaron Copland," *Piano Quarterly* 111

(1980): 6–12 (*Fantasy* discussed on pp. 11–12); Elliott Carter, "A Further Step," *The Writings of Elliott Carter: An American Composer Looks at Modern Music,* ed. Else and Kurt Stone (Bloomington: Indiana University Press, 1977), pp. 185–91; Arthur Berger, "Aaron Copland's 'Piano Fantasy,' " *Juilliard Review* 7.2 (1972): 13–27; Peter Evans, "The Thematic Technique of Copland's Recent Works," *Tempo* 51 (1959): 2–13.

35 C-P II, p. 246; Terri Gailey Everett, p. 59.

36 Howard Taubman, "Copland Fantasy for Piano Heard," *New York Times* 26 October 1957; Paul Henry Lang, "On Copland's 'Piano Fantasy,' " *New York Herald Tribune* 26 October 1957; Alfred Frankenstein, "Rich New Music for S.F.," *San Francisco Chronicle* 16 December 1957; Alexander Fried, "Music Gourmets Enjoy Novelties," *San Franciso Examiner* 16 December 1957; Jay C. Rosenfeld, "New Copland Work Played at Fromm Concert in Chicago," *Berkshire Eagle* 5 March 1958, BHCF.

37 For an early discography of the Copland *Fantasy,* see Joann Skowronski, *Aaron Copland: A Bio-bibliography* (Westport, CT: Greenwood Press, 1985), pp. 52–53; see also *Aaron Copland: Works for Piano, Vol. II,* Nina Tichman, piano (Wergo WER 6212-2); *Copland Piano Music—Romantic and Modern,* Ramon Salvatore, piano (Cedille Records CDR 900000 021).

26. From *Dance Panels* to *Connotations* (1959–62)

1 Jerome Robbins to Copland, 1 June 1944, CCLC; John Gruen, interview with Copland, 9 July 1975 (transcript), Dance Division, NYPL.

2 Jerome Robbins to Copland, 1 December 1958 ("nonprogrammatic"); [early 1959], ("The originating idea") CCLC.

3 David Adams, memo, 20 January 1959, BHCF.

4 Gruen ("like the panels"); William W. Austin, "Aaron Copland," *The New Grove Dictionary of Music and Musicians,* vol. 4, ed. by Stanley Sadie, (New York: Macmillan, 1980), p. 723.

5 Copland, "Music for a Ballet," BHCF.

6 Copland, "Music for a Ballet."

7 Copland, "Music for a Ballet."

8 C-P II, p. 276; Bayan Northcott, "Composers of the Sixties," *Music and Musicians* 18.5 (1970): 36; Reynolds, p. 231.

9 C-P II, p. 274.

10 C-P II, pp. 274–75. Robbins went on to stage other collections of waltzes, including *Dances at a Gathering* (1969) after Chopin and *An Evening's Waltzes* (1973) after Prokofiev; he also created a *Dybbuk* ballet (1974) in collaboration with Leonard Bernstein.

11 C-P II, pp. 275–76; Thea Dispeker, review of *Dance Panels,* *Music Journal* 22.1 (1964): 112; Gruen ("too much feeling").

12 Reynolds, pp. 230–31; Gruen.

13 Copland, *Dance Panels,* recorded by Copland (Sony SM2K 47236), Leonard Slatkin (EMI CDC 7 49095 2; also Angel CMS 7 64315 2), and Dennis

Russell Davies (MusicMasters 01612-67101-2); see C-P II, p. 445n15 for Copland's cuts.

14 Copland, *What to Listen for in Music,* rev. ed. (New York: McGraw-Hill, 1957), p. 102.

15 Eric Salzman and Paul Des Marais, "Aaron Copland's Nonet: Two Views," *Perspectives of New Music* 1.1 (1962): 172–79; Leon Kirchner to Copland, 17 January 1963, CCLC.

16 Stephen Plaistow, "Some Notes on Copland's Nonet," *Tempo* 64 (1963): 11.

17 Howard Thompson, "Copland Accepts Film Assignment," *New York Times* 15 March 1961; C-P II, pp. 327–32.

18 Henry Miller, *My Bike and Other Friends* (Santa Barbara: Capra Press, 1978), pp. 69–74.

19 Jack Garfein, interview by author, 17 October 1996; C-P II, p. 332; Contract between Prometheus Enterprises, Inc., and Aaron Copland, 12 April 1961, CCLC.

20 Alex Karmel, *Mary Ann* (New York: Viking Press, 1958).

21 C-P II, p. 328; see also Copland, "Composing for *Something Wild,*" unpublished article (December 1961), CCLC.

22 C-P II, pp. 333, 335.

23 C-P II, p. 329.

24 C-P II, p. 331; Copland, "Notes on Making a Movie Score" (March 1961), CCLC.

25 Garfein, interview; C-P II, pp. 331 ("It is"), 332 ("ecstatic").

26 Reviews of *Something Wild,* BHCF; see also Vernon Young, *On Film: Unpopular Essays on a Popular Art* (Chicago: Quadrangle Books, 1972), pp. 168–70. Copland slightly misremembered Bosley Crowther's review, writing, "He claimed it was hard to believe that a girl like Mary Ann would not find one person to sympathize with her in the whole city of New York" (C-P II, p. 332), whereas Crowther wrote, "We wouldn't know whether a young person, especially one as pretty and bright and clearly used to normal associations with other people as Carroll Baker makes the girl in this film, would report her violation, would turn so into herself and would fall into such a deep depression that she would finally attempt suicide," Crowther, "The Screen: A Shattering Experience," *New York Times* 21 December 1961.

27 The "Mary Ann Resigned" music is actually an extension of the earlier "Mary Ann Awakens" music; the new tender theme with grace notes foretells Mary Ann's attachment to Mike.

28 For the inaugural concert, see the *Connotations* file, BHCF, especially Nick Lapole, "Spectacle Awes Jackie," *New York Journal-American* 24 September 1962.

29 Copland, program notes for *Connotations,* BHCF.

30 Copland, program note; C-P II, pp. 448n9.

31 C-P II, pp. 341–42; Copland, program note ("Structurally the composition comes closest to a free treatment of the baroque form of the Chaconne").

32 For discussions of the form of *Connotations*, see Peter Evans, "Copland on the Serial Road: An Analysis of *Connotations*," *Perspectives of New Music* 2.2 (1964): 141–49; and Robert Matthew-Walker, "Aaron Copland's Symphonic Legacy," *Musical Opinion* February 1991: 48–51, BHCF.

33 Robert J. Landry, "Philharmonic Hall's Historic Preem: Glam, Traffic Jam and Copland Capers," *Variety* 26 September 1962, BHCF; Louis Biancolli, "Philharmonic Debuts in Own Hall at Center," *New York World-Telegram and Sun* 24 September 1962; Everett Helm, "Lincoln Center Opening," *Musical America* November 1962; Harriet Johnson, "Philharmonic Hall Opens with Bernstein on Podium," *New York Post* 24 September 1962; Richard Franko Goldman, "Current Chronicle," *Musical Quarterly* January 1969; Paul Henry Lang, quoted in "Showcase Music Clubs," (1963); see also "Music," *Time* October 1962.

34 London *Sunday Times* 17 February 1963 ("mere din"); K. F. C., "Leonard Bernstein: February 13th," *Musical Opinion* April 1963: 392 ("dodecaphonic"); Robert C. Marsh, "The First Recordings from Philharmonic Hall," *High Fidelity* February 1963; [Irving Kolodin], "Recordings in Review," *Saturday Review* 45.51 (1962): 54; Everett Helm, " 'Tis True, 'Tis Pity," *Musical America* (1963) BHCF; Copland to Christopher Rouse, 25 October 1962, courtesy of Rouse.

35 Desmond Shawe-Taylor, "Copland at the Philharmonic," *New Yorker* 7 January 1974; Bartlett Naylor, "Check It Out," *The Little Paper* (Foster City, CA) 12 December 1979; Michael Andrews, *Peninsula Times Tribune* 19 December 1979; Peter Davis, "Voices of Import," *New York* 16 February 1987; Harold C. Schonberg, "Music: A Storm No More," *New York Times* 22 December 1973, BHCF.

36 Tim Page, "Genius²: Bernstein Conducts Copland," *Newsday* 24 October 1989; Donal Henahan, "A Bernstein Celebration of Copland," *New York Times* 21 October 1989; Bill Zakariasen, "A Copland Ball at Fisher Hall," *Daily News* 21 October 1989; see also Shirley Fleming, "Bernstein's Red, White and Blues," *New York Post* 21 October 1989, BHCF.

37 For the Bernstein recordings, see Joann Skowronski, *Aaron Copland: A Bio-bibliography* (Westport, CT: Greenwood Press, 1985); Copland, *Connotations*, performed by Sixten Ehrling and the Juilliard Orchestra (New World Records NW 368–1).

38 Bob Micklin, "Hamlet as Nightmare"; Clive Barnes, "The Dance: 'Hamlet' from Neumeier," *New York Times* 7 January 1976; Bill Zakariasen, "Players Are the Thing," New York *Daily News* 8 January 1976, BHCF.

27. From *Emblems* to *Proclamation* (1964–82)

1 C-P II, p. 343.

2 C-P II, p. 343.

3 David Whitwell, "The Enigma of Copland's *Emblems*," *Journal of Band Research* 7.2 (1972): 5–9.

4 David Conte, "A Study of Aaron Copland's Sketches for *Inscape*" (DMA thesis, Cornell University, 1983), p. 42.

5 C-P II, pp. 157, 348.

6 W. H. Gardner, *Poems and Prose of Gerard Manley Hopkins* (New York: Penguin Books, 1953, 1985), pp. xx–xxi; C-P II, pp. 348–49.

7 David Conte, letter to author, 12 November 1997.

8 William Wolf, "Copland's 'Inscape' Uncannily Beautiful at World Premiere," *Detroit Free Press* 15 September 1967.

9 C-P II, p. 351; Winthrop Sargeant, "Musical Events," *New Yorker* [1967]; Harold C. Schonberg, "Music: Copland Salute," *New York Times* 31 October 1970, BHCF.

10 Gavin Thomas, "Back to the Future," *Musical Times* June 1993: 357; see also *Inscape* file, BHCF.

11 Copland, *Connotations*, performed by Leonard Bernstein and the New York Philharmonic (Columbia MS 7431); performed by Copland and the Orchestre National de France (Etcetera KTC 1098).

12 Phillip Ramey, liner notes, *The Copland Collection: Orchestral Works 1948–1971* (Sony SM2K 47236).

13 Neil Butterworth, *The Music of Aaron Copland* (New York: Universe Books, 1986), p. 177.

14 C-P II, pp. 346–48; video of CBS *Playhouse* titles courtesy of Daniel Mathers.

15 Copland to Gregory Millar, 29 May 1969, CCLC.

16 C-P II, p. 360; William W. Austin, *Music in the 20th Century from Debussy Through Stravinsky* (New York: W. W. Norton, 1966), p. 505.

17 C-P II, p. 375. The Institute for Studies in American Music published "Larghetto Pomposo" (*"Happy Birthday"*) in their *Newsletter* 10.1 (1980): 1.

18 John Solum, interview by author, 27 September 1996; Richard Wyton, "The Copland-Solum Correspondence, 1967–1975," *Flute Quarterly* 27.1 (1992): 33–43.

19 Wyton, p. 33.

20 C-P II, p. 376; Copland, letter to Christopher Rouse, 28 October 1971, courtesy of Rouse ("aura of the past"); Daniel Mathers, interview by author, 8 November 1996, discovered that those snippets of the *Duo*'s first movement also found in the *Nonet* and *Something Wild* derive from these earlier sketches.

21 C-P II, p. 376.

22 For the Shaffer, Padorr, and Bryan recordings, see Joann Skowronski, *Aaron Copland: A Bio-bibliography* (Westport, CT: Greenwood Press, 1985); Copland, *Duo* for flute and piano, performed by Martin-Ulrich Senn and Horst Göbel (Thorofon CTH 2012); Fenwick Smith and Randall Hodgkinson (Northeastern NR 227-CD); Jeanne Baxtresser and Israela Margalit (EMI CDC 5 55405 2); Michael Steinberg, "Aaron Copland's Double Surprise," *Boston Globe* 24 January 1972, BHCF ("lightweight"); John Rockwell, "Copland, Kraft Works Premiered at Museum," *Los Angeles Times* 22

March 1972 ("slight"), BHCF; C-P II, p. 376; Peter G. Davis, "Hephzibah Menuhin and Miss Shaffer Play Copland's Duo," *New York Times* 12 October 1971, BHCF.

23 Robert Mann, interview with the author, 23 April 1998; Copland, *Duo* for violin and piano, played by Gregory Fulkerson and Robert Shannon (New World Records NW 313).

24 C-P II, p. 381.

25 Butterworth, p. 176.

26 Dolores Fredrickson, "The Cliburn Commissions," *Clavier* May–June 1003: 28–29 BHCF.

27 C-P II, p. 262; Butterworth, p. 180.

28 D.A.W.M., "Rich Tone Suits Brahms's Sonata" *Daily Telegraph* 22 May 1974, BHCF.

29 C-P II, p. 262; Paul Hume, "The Marvel of Copland," *Washington Post* 10 September 1981, B1, B8. At the point in the score marked "mark the lower line," the melody (coincidentally?) resembles that famous five-note phrase from Stephen Foster's "Massa's in the cold, cold ground"—"Down in de cornfield [/ Hear dat mournful sound]"—prominently featured in the "Thoreau" movement of the *Concord Sonata* and other works by Ives.

30 Phillip Ramey, liner notes, *Copland Piano Music—Romantic and Modern*, played by Ramon Salvatore (Cedille CDR 90000 021).

31 Ramey.

32 C-P II, p. 262; Copland, composer's note, *Two Piano Pieces* (New York: Boosey & Hawkes, 1984).

33 Ramey, marginalia.

34 Copland apparently began work on a string quartet for the Juilliard in 1969, "An Interview with Aaron Copland," *Sinfonia* 20.4 (1971): 7, hoping to have it ready by 1973; Max Loppert, "Night Thoughts," London *Financial Times* 22 May 1974, BHCF; C-P II, p. 386; Harry Haun, "The Whos, Whats, Wheres and When," 31 November 1978, BHCF.

35 Copland to Carlos Chávez, 22 August 1970, 25 December 1971, CCLC; Paul Moor, review of *Copland Since 1943, Musical America* May 1990: 52–53, BHCF; Phillip Ramey, "Copland at 80," *Chicago* January 1981: 149.

36 Leonard Bernstein, "Aaron Copland: An Intimate Sketch," *High Fidelity* 20.11 (1970): 53–55; C-P II, pp. 367–68.

37 C-P II, pp. 271, 387 ("hopping"); C-P I, p. 362; Joan Peyser, *Boulez* (New York: Schirmer Books, 1976), p. 148.

38 Phillip Ramey, "Aaron Copland at 80," *Ovation* November 1980: 43.

28. Identity Issues

1 Macdonald Smith Moore, *Yankee Blues: Musical Culture and American Identity* (Bloomington: Indiana University Press, 1985), pp. 128–68.

2 Isaac Goldberg, "Aaron Copland and His Jazz," *American Mercury* 26, September 1927: 63; Paul Rosenfeld, *An Hour with American Music* (Philadel-

phia: J. B. Lippincott and Co., 1929), p. 132; Wilfrid Mellers, *Music in a New Found Land* (New York: Oxford University Press, 1964,), p. 85.

3 Roger Sessions, "An American Evening Abroad," *Modern Music* 4.1 (1926–27): 34; Julia Smith, *Aaron Copland: His Work and Contribution to American Music* (New York: Dutton, 1955), suggested the influence of Bloch, p. 59; Wilfrid Mellers, review of Aron Marko Rothmüller's *The Music of the Jews: An Historical Appreciation*, in *Musical Times* August 1954, CCLC.

4 Richard Crawford, R. Allen Lott, and Carol J. Oja, eds., *A Celebration of American Music: Words and Music in Honor of H. Wiley Hitchcock* (Ann Arbor: University of Michigan Press, 1990), p. 335 ("usual clever").

5 Daniel Gregory Mason, "Is American Music Growing Up?" *Arts and Decoration* November 1920; Daniel Gregory Mason, *Tune In, America* (New York: Knopf, 1931), pp. 28, 161. Ironically, Copland, who thought of American music as typically "plain and bare," and full of "simplicity and naturalness" and "optimistic vitality," struck a similar note in *Music and Imagination* (Cambridge: Harvard University Press, 1952), pp. 81, 94–95. One wonders what reaction Mason might have had to Copland's statement, made late in life, that English orchestras seemed to have "a special feeling" for his own music because of "a kind of Anglo-Saxon connection," C-P II, p. 394.

6 Henry Cowell, "Amerikanische Musik?" *Melos* 8-9.9 (1930): 362–65; Cowell, "Die beiden wirklichen Amerikaner: Ives and Ruggles," *Melos* 10.9 (1930): 417–20; Cowell, "Die kleineren Komponisten," *Melos* 12.9 (1930): 526–29.

7 Lazare Saminsky, *Music of the Ghetto and the Bible* (New York: Bloch Publishing, 1934), pp. 92, 100, 118, 123–25; Saminsky, *Music of Our Day: Essentials and Prophecies* (Freeport, NY: Books for Libraries Press, 1939, 1970), pp. 163, 166; Saminsky, *Living Music of the Americas* (New York: Howell, Soskin and Crown, 1949), p. 119.

8 Lazare Saminsky, *Music of Our Day*, p. 154; Saminsky, "American Phase of International Music Festival Revealed New Talent," *Musical Courier* July 1941: 19; Saminsky, *Living Music*, pp. 123–27.

9 Rudy Burckhardt, interview by author, 4 May 1994; Rudy Burckhardt and Simon Pettet, *Talking Pictures* (Cambridge, MA: Zoland Books, 1994), p. 120; Harold Clurman, *All People Are Famous (Instead of an Autobiography)* (New York: Harcourt Brace Jovanovich, 1974), p. 27; Theodore Chanler, "Aaron Copland," *American Composers on American Music*, ed. by Henry Cowell (New York: F. Ungar, 1933), p. 48.

10 Virgil Thomson, "Aaron Copland," *Modern Music* 9.2 (1932): 67; Virgil Thomson, *Virgil Thomson* (New York: Da Capo, 1966): 276–77; C-P I, p. 199. Others in Copland's circle expressed similar ideas about the relation of political activism and Judaism; see, for example, Alan Trachtenberg, *Memoirs of Waldo Frank* (Amherst: University of Massachusetts Press, 1973), p. 196, and Edmund Wilson, *The Thirties* (New York: Farrar, Straus and Giroux, 1980), p. 379.

[11] Smith, p. 138; Paul Rosenfeld, *Discoveries of a Music Critic* (New York: Harcourt, Brace and Co., 1936), p. 334; John Kirkpatrick, "Aaron Copland's Piano Sonata," *Modern Music* 19.4 (1942): 246–47; C-P II, p. 251 ("That voice"); Arthur Berger, *Aaron Copland* (New York: Oxford University Press, 1953), p. 52.

[12] Leonard Bernstein, "Aaron Copland: An Intimate Sketch," *High Fidelity* 20.11 (1970): 53; in reference to Clurman's Group Theatre, Mary Lescaze informed the merely thirty-three-year-old composer, "You're not a Grouper. You're a Patriarch," Mary Lescaze to Copland, 25 July 1933, CCLC; Salzman, p. 66; Donal Henahan, "This Aaron Is a Musical Moses," *New York Times* 9 November 1975: 20–21, BHCF.

[13] Dobrin, pp. 194–95; Ruth Gay, *Unfinished People: Eastern European Jews Encounter America* (New York: W. W. Norton, 1996), pp. 144, 156, 166.

[14] Interview with Martin Bookspan, 29 April 1980, CCLC.

[15] Copland, lecture notes on Arnold Schoenberg, CCLC; Copland, "The Lyricism of Milhaud," *Modern Music* 6.2 (1929): 14–19 (Copland reiterated this discussion almost verbatim in *The New Music*, p. 60; he significantly omitted a passage concerning Milhaud's nostalgia in relation to tragedy and yearning).

[16] Copland to Leonard Bernstein, September, 1939, BCLC.

[17] Copland, "Jewish Composers in the Western World, Lectures," CCLC; Copland, "Gabriel Fauré, a Neglected Master," *Musical Quarterly* October 1924: 574–75 (Mendelssohn and Saint-Saëns); Smith, p. 50 ("engrossing"). Copland's distinction between "talent" and "genius" regrettably, if unintentionally, recalled anti-Semitic discourse; see Sander Gilman, *The Jew's Body* (New York: Routledge Press 1991); in his recent *Modern American Music* (Teaneck: Fairleigh Dickinson University Press, 1996), p. 48, Otto Karolyi coincidentally distinguishes Stravinsky's "genius" from Copland's "talent."

[18] Berger, p. 52; Edward T. Cone, "Conversation with Aaron Copland," *Perspectives of New Music* 6.2 (1968): 64.

[19] Paul Rosenfeld first brought attention to Copland's "leanness, slenderness of sound, sharpened by the fact that it is found in connection with a strain of grandiosity," something, however, that he compared to Varèse and which he thought of as an entirely American phenomenon, Paul Rosenfeld, *An Hour with American Music* (Philadelphia: Lippincott, 1929), p. 128 ("leanness, slenderness"); Paul Rosenfeld, "The New American Music," *Scribner's Magazine* 89 (1931): 629 (comparison with Varèse).

[20] Copland, "What Is Jewish Music?" *New York Herald Tribune* 2 October 1949.

[21] Copland, *The New Music: 1900–1960* (New York: W. W. Norton, 1968): 28–31.

[22] K. Robert Schwarz, "Composers' Closets Open for All to See," *New York Times,* BHCF (including McClary quote); Mark Levine, "The Outsider," *New Yorker* 26 August and 2 September 1996: 157. Levine himself points

out, "Other gay composers, among them Cowell, Cage, and Harry Partch, had never really moved in mainstream musical channels."

23 Ramey, interview; Rosamund Bernier, interview by author, 21 January 1996; Johns quoted by Daniel Mathers, "Against the American Grain: Sexuality and the Rezoning of *The Tender Land*," paper delivered at the University of Cincinnati, 13 November 1995, courtesy of the author; Erik Johns, interviews by author, 13 December 1994, 3 May 1994.

24 *The Dybbuk* (which inspired *Vitebsk*) is also thought by some to have a homosexual subtext.

25 Mathers; Eve Kosofsky Sedgwick, *Epistemology of the Closet* (Berkeley: University of California Press, 1990).

26 *Out Classics* (RCA 09026-68261-2); *Out Classics II* (RCA 09026-68430-2); *Gay American Composers II* (CRI CD 750).

27 Barbara L. Tischler, *An American Music: The Search for an American Musical Identity* (New York: Oxford University Press, 1986); Carol Oja, *Experiments in Modern Music: New York in the 1920s* (New York: Oxford University Press, forthcoming); Copland, "Making Music in the Star-Spangled Manner," *Music and Musicians* 8 (1960): 8 ("recognizably"); Copland, *The New Music: 1900–1960* (New York: W. W. Norton, 1968) ("symptomatic of the period"), p. 158.

28 Copland, quoted by Oscar Thompson, *Great Modern Composers* (New York: Dodd, Mead, 1941), p. 44; Copland, *Music and Imagination,* p. 109.

29 Peter J. Rosenwald, "Aaron Copland Talks About a Life in Music," *Wall Street Journal* 14 November 1980: 31; Copland, *Music and Imagination,* pp. 99–100. See also Edward Rothstein, "Fanfares for Aaron Copland at 80," *New York Times,* 9 November 1980: D22: "I was very conscious of how French the French composers sounded in comparison with the Germans, and how Russian Stravinsky was."

30 Copland, "Scores and Records," *Modern Music* 15.4 (1938): 245; Copland, *Music and Imagination,* p. 95.

31 Copland, *Our New Music,* p. 39; *Music and Imagination,* p. 111.

32 Copland, *Music and Imagination,* pp. 96–99.

33 William Schuman, "Aaron Copland," *Perspectives of New Music* 19 (1980–81): 52; Samuel Lipman, "Copland as American Composer," *Commentary* 61 (1976): 72; André Previn, *No Minor Chords* (New York: Doubleday, 1991), p. 92; Leighton Kerner, "Aaron Copland's Time and Place," *Village Voice* 25 (10 December 1980): 95; Spike Lee, "Why Aaron Copland?" liner notes to *Spike Lee Presents: The Music of Aaron Copland* (Sony SK 605930). Oscar Levant used to quip that in American music, B.C. stood for "Before Copland," Levant quoted by Kubly, p. 57.

34 Neil Butterworth, *The Music of Aaron Copland* (New York: Universe Books, 1986), p. 8; Kenneth Dommett, Copland at 80," *Hi-Fi News* 25.11 (1980): 103; Alberto Ginastera, quoted in C-P II, p. 114.

35 Berger, p. 93; Barbara Zuck, *A History of Musical Americanism* (Ann Arbor:

UMI Research Press, 1980), p. 272; Alan Howard Levy, *Musical National-*
ism: American Composers' Search for Identity (Westport, CT: Greenwood
Press, 1983), pp. 105–27; Leonard Bernstein, "What Is American Music?"
Young People's Concert, 1958.

[36] Paul Rosenfeld, "A Musical Tournament," *New Republic* 15 June 1932:
121; Lipman, p. 72.

[37] Wilfrid Mellers, *Music in a New Found Land* (New York: Oxford University
Press, 1964), pp. 81–101. Copland's 1980 remark to Edward Rothstein—
"Agony I don't connect with. Not even alienation"—contradicts Mellers's
basic thesis.

[38] Arthur Berger, "Aaron Copland 1900–1990," *Perspectives of New Music*
30.1 (1992): 297; Darius Milhaud, *Notes Without Music* (New York: Knopf,
1953), p. 299; Chris Culwell, "Mr. Transcendental," *Bay Area Reporter* 26.8
(1996): 37; Samuel Adler, interview by author, 19 March 1996.

[39] Copland, *Music and Imagination,* pp. 78–95 ("If there," p. 95); Copland,
"America Is Unfamiliar with Music by Its Own Many Superb Composers,"
Topeka Daily Capital 15 July 1956, BHCF; J.D.G., "An Interview with
Aaron Copland," *Delaware Dateline* June 1961: 44, CCLC (in this same
article, Copland noted that American music, as in Sessions and Schuman,
could be quite "pessimistic" and that, in any case, "interest in nationalism
had died down in America").

[40] Cobey Black, "Eternal Spring of Aaron Copland," *Honolulu Advertiser* 3
December 1974, CCLC; Robert Jones, "Aaron Copland: Musician of the
Month," *High Fidelity/Musical America* 25 (1975): MA-7.

[41] Zuck, p. 270; Richard Taruskin, " 'Nationalism': Colonialism in Disguise?"
New York Times 22 August 1993; Berger, "Aaron Copland: 1900–1990."

[42] Charles C. Alexander, *Here the Country Lies: Nationalism and the Arts in*
Twentieth-Century America (Bloomington: Indiana University Press, 1980),
p. 276.

29. The Later Years

[1] Paul Hume, "Copland," *Washington Post* 9 February 1969: K2.

[2] C-P I, pp. 108, 166.

[3] C-P II, pp. 116, 338; Vivian Perlis, transcript of interview with Copland and
Leonard Bernstein, CCLC ("You must stay home"); Hume ("He always").

[4] Copland, *The New Music: 1900–1960* (New York: W. W. Norton, 1968), p.
164; C-P II, p. 389 ("My dear").

[5] C-P I, p. 340; Perlis, transcript; Robert Cornell, interview by author, 29 July
1995.

[6] C-P II, pp. 208, 234.

[7] C-P II, pp. 388–92; Randy Banner, "Fanfare for the Composer," BHCF;
Copland, *The New Music,* p. 165 ("Aaron, it is").

[8] Andrew Keener, "Aaron Copland," *Gramophone* February 1981: 1072,
BHCF ("how my music"); Hugo Cole, "Copland: Clash of Contrasts," *Los*

Notes

Angeles Times 17 October 1965, BHCF ("establish"); Susan Watters, "Conducting Is Sport for Aaron Copland," *Los Angeles Herald Examiner* 15 October 1978: E2, BHCF ("Even"); C-P II, 271 ("Conducting").

9   C-P II, pp. 383, 392.

10   C-P II, p. 392.

11   Works programmed with special frequency included *Three Fantasias* by Purcell, Haydn's Symphony no. 95, Mendelssohn's Symphony no. 4, Berlioz's *Royal Hunt and Storm*, Smetana's Overture to *The Bartered Bride*, Brahms's *Variations on a Theme by Haydn*, Tchaikovsky's *Romeo and Juliet*, Busoni's *Rondo arlecchinesco*, Fauré's Suite from *Pelléas et Mélisande*, Ravel's *Le Tombeau de Couperin*, Roussel's Third Symphony and *Suite in F*, Ives's *The Unanswered Question* and *Decoration Day*, Ruggles's *Portals*, Stravinsky's *Ode* and *Symphony in C*, Walton's *Portsmouth Point*, Tippett's Concerto for Double String Orchestra, Chávez's *Sinfonía India*, Shostakovich's Ninth Symphony, Harris's Third Symphony, Diamond's *Rounds*, Barber's Overture to *The School for Scandal* and *Capricorn Concerto*, Schuman's *New England Triptych*, Carter's *Holiday Overture*, Fine's *Serious Song*, and Bernstein's Overture to *Candide*.

12   Copland, "When Private and Public Worlds Meet," *New York Times* 9 June 1968, sec. 2, p. 17.

13   Copland, "When Private Worlds"; C-P II, p. 392 ("I may have been influenced by Stravinsky, whose conducting seemed to me dry and precise, and I thought that Hindemith had been admirably businesslike when conducting"); Martin Bernheimer, "Copland Enlivens Concert," *Los Angeles Times* 25 March 1972, BHCF.

14   C-P I, p. 33; C-P II, pp. 57, 76, 95, 163, 321 ("As might").

15   Copland, rehearsal of *Appalachian Spring*, with the Columbia Chamber Orchestra (Columbia BTS 34); Christopher Ford, "Aaron's Rod," *Arts Guardian* 30 May 1072, BHCF; Keener.

16   C-P II, pp. 133 ("modern dancer"), 293 ("the lean"); Bernheimer; Perlis, transcript. In the tapes and recordings of Copland's conducting of other composers' music that I have heard—including the commercial release of a concert with the Czech Philharmonic Orchestra (Romantic Robot RR1973), courtesy of Phillip Ramey—he obtained mixed results but showed a special flair for the American repertory, including a stirring account of Schuman's *New England Triptych*.

17   John Warrack, "American Accent," *Sunday Telegraph* 7 November 1965, BHCF ("moving"); Bill Zakariasen, "Copland Does Them All Well," *Daily News* 7 February 1980, Copland Clipping File, Dance Division, NYPL ("glowing"); Keener; C-P II, p. 389; Perlis, transcript.

18   Paul A. Harris, "All-American: 2 Great Composers," *St. Louis Post-Dispatch* 17 February 1991, BHCF ("extraordinary," "a little better"); Leonard Bernstein, interview by Phillip Ramey, 14 November 1975, *Copland Conducts Copland* (Columbia M 33586).

19   Harry Ellis Dickson, interview by author, 14 October 1996; Stanley Drucker,

interview by author, 18 October 1996; Ray Fliegel, interview by author, 19 October 1996; Adolph Herseth, interview by author, 29 September 1996; Donald Koss, interview by author, 27 September 1996; Luis Leguia, interview by author, 20 September 1996; Jeffrey Lerner, interview by author, 12 September 1996; Newton Mansfield, interview by author, 7 October 1996; Edgar Muenzer, interview by author, 16 March 1996; Leo Panasevich, interview by author, 26 September 1996; Donald Peck, interview by author, 27 September 1996; Laszlo Varga, interview by author, 19 October 1996; Gottfried Wilfinger, interview by author, 25 September 1996. Dickson, Leguia, Panasevich, and Wilfinger played with the Boston Symphony; Fliegel and Lerner with the Houston Symphony; Herseth, Muenzer, Peck, and Koss with the Chicago Symphony; and Mansfield, Drucker, and Varga with the New York Philharmonic.

20 Varga, interview; Peck, interview; Fliegel, interview; Mansfield, interview.

21 Hume; C-P I, p. 134; C-P II, pp. 73 ("tough"), 318 ("Aaron").

22 C-P II, pp. 358 ("reluctant"), 384, 392 ("only"), 394.

23 C-P II, pp. 379, 394 ("a kind"); Jack Frymire, "Copland 68," *Music and Artists* (November 1968), BHCF ("businesslike"); Alan M. Kriegsman, "Aaron Copland at Intersection of American Musical Currents," *Los Angeles Times* 20 May 1973, BHCF ("It's [conducting Ruggles's *Portals*] often fun with a university orchestra; the response is often fresher").

24 Cole ("as though"); Frymire ("because").

25 Donal Henahan, "Music: Aaron Copland as Conductor," *New York Times* 8 December 1975, BHCF ("Mr. Copland is hardly a virtuoso conductor, but he led admirably clear performances"); C-P I, p. 201 (Virgil Thomson: "Aaron's quite a good conductor—not a star but very competent"); "The Conducting Bug," *Sunday Telegraph* 27 October 1968, BHCF ("His style"); Dominic Gill, "Copland," *Financial Times* 25 October 1968, BHCF ("Copland conducted").

26 Ned Rorem, *Knowing When to Stop: A Memoir* (New York: Simon & Schuster, 1994), p. 36.

27 Ainslee Cox, "Copland on the Podium," *Music Journal* 29.2 (1971): 50.

28 David Walker, interviews by author, 5 May 1994, 27 July 1995.

29 C-P II, p. 405. Copland paid Walker a good salary and provided health coverage as well; in 1983, his salary amounted to about $34,000.

30 Richard Hennessy, interview by author, 27 July 1995, claims that Copland had trouble keeping domestics for very long because he appeared rather impersonal and distant.

31 Hennessy, interview.

32 Chris Cole, interview by author, 30 April 1996; David Conte, letter to author, 12 November 1997; Walker, interviews; Hennessy, interview.

33 Robert Jones, "Aaron Copland: Musician of the Month," *High Fidelity/ Musical America* November 1975: MA-6, BHCF; Sidney M. Greenberg to Copland, 3 January 1961, CCLC; Walker, interviews.

34 Interview with Christoper Rouse, 26 September, 1996; John Kenworthy-Browne, letter to author, 27 October 1995; Samuel Adler, interview by author, 19 March 1996; Walker, interviews; Arnold Salop, interview by author, 15 July 1997.

35 Adler, interview; Michael O'Connor, interview by author, 4 July 1996; Conte; Verna Fine, interview by author, 7 May 1994.

36 Over the years, Copland retained primarily four attorneys: L. Arnold Weissberger in the 1940s, Oscar Cox in the 1950s, Abraham Friedman in the 1960s, and, after Friedman's death in 1972, Ellis Freedman; Walker, interviews; Fine, interview.

37 Robert Cornell, interview by author, 29 July 1995.

38 Cole, interview; O'Connor, interview; Walker, interviews.

39 O'Connor, interview.

40 C-P II, p. 398, 404; Vivian Perlis, interview by author, 21 March 1996; Copland had wanted to write an autobiography at least as early as 1965, Herbert Weinstock to Copland, 27 December 1965, CCLC. In the early 1970s, Copland also asked Phillip Ramey to collaborate with him on an autobiography. "On reflection," writes Ramey, "I decided that the project was more suited to an academic than a composer and, to Copland's disappointment, bowed out," Ramey, marginalia.

41 C-P, I and II.

42 John Rockwell, "Copland: 1900 Through 1942," *International Herald Tribune* 24 September 1984; John Rockwell, "Aaron Copland's Reticence About Himself and His Art," *New York Times* 25 December 1989; Robin Holloway, review of *Copland Since 1943*, *Tempo* March 1990: 33, BHCF.

43 Rockwell; Virgil Thomson, "Copland on Copland," *Vanity Fair* September 1984: 107–08; Paul Moor, review of *Copland Since 1943*, *Musical America* May 1990: 52–53, BHCF; C-P II, p. 415; Holloway ("entombed"); John Kennedy, interview by author, 10 May 1994 ("embalmed"). Virgil Thomson described the first volume to Phillip Ramey as "a fake," saying, "That's not Aaron's voice or tone," Ramey, marginalia.

44 Ronald Caltabiano, interview by author, 2 July 1996.

45 Copland, marginalia, Ellis Freedman to Copland, 23 October 1986, CCLC.

46 Walker, interviews; Fine, interview; Vivian Perlis, marginalia; Vivian Perlis, interview by author, 16 September 1997.

47 John Rockwell, "Copland, the Dean of U.S. Music, Dies at 90," *New York Times* 3 December 1990; Copland, last will and testament, 15 July 1970, and 23 March 1984, CCLC; John Rockwell, "A Memorial Concert Celebrates Aaron Copland's Musical Legacy," *New York Times* 21 April 1991: 38.

48 Copland, Last Will and Testament.

49 Tim Page, "Grants Through Copland Fund," *Newsday* 25 June 1992, BHCF; press releases, Aaron Copland Fund for Music, Inc., courtesy of the American Music Center; "Chronicle," *New York Times*, 6 August 1996.

50 C-P II, pp. 277–78. Rick Pezzullo, "Copland Remembered as Great Teacher,"

North County News 29.35 (1995); this and other press materials are courtesy of Florence H. Stevens. Although Copland considered himself a resident of Peekskill, Rock Hill is located in Cortlandt (Westchester County, New York).

51 In 1970, Copland willed only his manuscripts to the Library of Congress, leaving his letters and so forth to the New York Public Library; however, by 1984 he'd decided that it made sense to keep all of these materials in one place. Wilda Heiss, E-mail to author, 8 October 1996, states that the collection "consumes 306 linear feet of shelf space and consists of 564 boxes, one map case drawer, and 386 books on open shelves"; in the library's Music Division, only the Serge Koussevitzky, Irving Berlin, and Leonard Bernstein Collections contain more items.

Conclusion

1 C-P II, p. 18.

2 Copland, *Our New Music* (New York: McGraw-Hill, 1941); Julia Smith, *Aaron Copland: His Work and Contribution to American Music* (New York: Dutton, 1955).

3 Virgil Thomson, *American Music Since 1910* (New York: Holt, Rinehart, and Winston), p. 58.

Selected Bibliography

WRITINGS BY COPLAND
What to Listen for in Music. New York: McGraw-Hill, 1939. Rev. and enl., 1957.
Our New Music. New York, McGraw-Hill, 1941. Rev. and enl. as *The New Music: 1900–1960,* New York: W. W. Norton, 1968.
Music and Imagination. Cambridge, MA: Harvard University Press, 1952.
Copland on Music. New York, Doubleday, 1960. New York: W. W. Norton, 1963. (Selected essays.)
   For lists of articles by Copland consult Smith (1955, under "Life and Works"), Gleason and Becker (1980), and Skowronski (1985, both under "Bibliographies and Discographies").

BIBLIOGRAPHIES AND DISCOGRAPHIES
Hamilton, David. "Aaron Copland: A Discography of the Composer's Performances." *Perspectives of New Music* 9.1 (1970): 149–54.
————. "The Recordings of Copland's Music." *High Fidelity/Musical America* 20.11 (1970): 64–66, 70–72, 116.
Gleason, Harold, and Warren Becker. "Aaron Copland." *20th-Century American Composers, Music Literature Outlines* 4th ser. 2nd ed. Bloomington: Frangipani Press, 1980. 33–57.
Oja, Carol. "Aaron Copland." *American Music Recordings.* Brooklyn: ISAM, 1982. 62–72.

Skowronski, Joann. *Aaron Copland: A Bio-bibliography*. Westport: Greenwood Press, 1985.

LIFE AND WORKS

Thomson, Virgil. "Aaron Copland." *Modern Music* 2.2 (1932): 67–73.

Kubly, Herbert. "America's No. 1 Composer." *Esquire* Apr. 1948: 57, 143–45.

Berger, Arthur. *Aaron Copland*. New York: Oxford University Press, 1953. (Reviewed by Harold Clurman, *Saturday Review* 28 Nov. 1953: 36.)

Smith, Julia Frances. *Aaron Copland: His Work and Contribution to American Music*. New York: Dutton, 1955.

Goldman, Richard Franko. "Aaron Copland." *Musical Quarterly* 47 (1961): 1–3.

Mellers, Wilfrid H. *Music in a New Found Land*. London, 1964. New York: Alfred A. Knopf, 1965. 81–101.

Cole, Hugo. "Aaron Copland." *Tempo* 76 (1966): 2–6; 77 (1966): 9–15.

Dobrin, Arnold. *Aaron Copland: His Life and Times*. New York: Thomas Y. Crowell, 1967.

Peare, Catharine Owens. *Aaron Copland: His Life*. New York: Holt, Rinehart and Winston, 1969.

Northcott, Bayan. "Copland in England." *Music and Musicians* 18.3 (1969): 34–36, 68.

Thomson, Virgil. *American Music Since 1910*. New York: Holt, Rinehart and Winston, 1970.

Bernstein, Leonard. "Aaron Copland: An Intimate Sketch." *High Fidelity/Musical America* 20.11 (1970): 53–63.

Dickinson, Peter. "Copland at 75." *Musical Times* 116 (1975): 967–70.

Rosenberg, Deena, and Bernard Rosenberg. "Aaron Copland." *The Music Makers*. New York: Columbia University Press, 1979. 31–38.

Kerner, Leighton. "Aaron Copland's Time and Place." *Village Voice* 10 Dec. 1980: 95–96.

Rothstein, Edward. "Fanfares for Aaron Copland at 80." *New York Times* 9 Nov 1980: D 21, 24.

Schuman, William. "More Comments on Copland." *American Record Guide* 44.1 (1980): 6–7. (With other articles: 5–11, 58–59.)

Silverman, Robert. "Aaron Copland: Happy Birthday." *Piano Quarterly* 111 (1980): 5–6.

Hitchcock, H. Wiley. "Aaron Copland and American Music." *Perspectives of New Music* 19 (1980–81): 31–33. (With tributes by many composers and colleagues, including Berger, Bernstein, Del Tredici, Diamond, Kirchner, Lederman, Orrego-Salas, Persichetti, Ramey, Rorem, Shapero, Talma, and Thomson, 3–95.)

Dommett, Keith. "Copland at 80." *Hi-Fi News and Record Review* 25.11 (1980): 103–05, 109. (Includes discography.)

Salzman, Eric. "Aaron Copland: The American Composer Is Eighty." *Stereo Review* 46.2 (1981): 66, 68–69.

Copland, Aaron, and Vivian Perlis. *Copland: 1900 Through 1942*. London: Faber and Faber, 1984. (Reviewed by Arthur Berger, *New York Review of Books* 32.3 (1985): 21–22.)

Butterworth, Neil. *The Music of Aaron Copland*. London: Toccata Press, 1985. New York: Universe Books, 1986.

Copland, Aaron, and Vivian Perlis. *Copland Since 1943*. New York: St. Martin's Press, 1989.

Moor, Paul. "Aaron Copland: Fanfare for an Uncommon Man." *Advocate* 15 Jan. 1991: 54–55.

Berger, Arthur. "Aaron Copland 1900–1990." *Perspectives of New Music* 30.1 (1992): 296–98.

INTERVIEWS

Gold, Don. "Aaron Copland: The Well-Known American Composer Finds Virtues and Flaws in Jazz." *Down Beat* 25 (1958): 16, 39–40.

Cone, Edward T. "Conversations with Aaron Copland." *Perspectives of New Music* 6.2 (1968): 57–72.

Mayer, William. "The Composer in the U.S. and Russia." *ASCAP Today* 3.1 (1969): 22–25.

Havsky, Vladimir. "What Makes It Great? A Conversation with Aaron Copland." Winthrop Laboratories, 1970.

Stevenson, Joe. "A Conversation with Aaron Copland." *Your Musical Cue Quarterly* (Indiana University) 1(1973): 21–22.

Bessom, Malcolm E. "Conversation with Copland." *Music Educator's Journal* 59.7 (1973): 40–49.

Kenyon, Nicholas. "The Scene Surveyed: Nicholas Kenyon Talks to Aaron Copland." *Music and Musicians* 24.3 (1975): 22–23.

Smit, Leo. "A Conversation with Aaron Copland on His 80th Birthday." *Keyboard* 6.11 (1980): 6–35. (With musical tributes by twelve composers.)

Ramey, Phillip. "Copland and the Dance." *Ballet News* 2.5 (1980): 8–12, 40.

———. "Copland at 80." *Chicago* 30.1 (Jan 1981): 122–24, 148–49.

Orga, Ates. "Aaron Copland Talks to Ates Orga." *Hi-Fi News and Record Review* 26.12 (1981): 75, 77.

Gagne, Cole, and Tracy Caras. "Aaron Copland." *Soundpieces: Interviews with American Composers*. Metuchen: Scarecrow Press, 1982. 101–16.

WORKS: GENERAL STUDIES

Kirkpatrick, John. "On Copland's Music." *Fontainebleau Alumni Bulletin* 1 (1928): 1–2, 6–7. (Includes list of works.)

Rosenfeld, Paul. "Copland Without the Jazz." *By Way of Art*. New York, 1928. Freeport: Books for Libraries Press, 1967. 266–72.

———. "Aaron Copland; George Gershwin." *An Hour with American Music.* Philadelphia: J. B. Lippincott and Co., 1929. 126–43.

———. "Current Chronicle." *Musical Quarterly* 25 (1939): 372–76.

Chanler, Theodore. "Aaron Copland." *American Composers on American Music* ed. by Henry Crowell. Stanford, CT, 1933. New York: F. Ungar, 1962. 49–56.

Sternfeld, Frederick. "Copland as Film Composer." *Musical Quarterly* 37 (1951): 161–75.

Overton, Hal. "Copland's Jazz Roots." *Jazz Today* 1 (1956): 40–41.

Cole, Hugo. "Popular Elements in Copland's Music." *Tempo* 95 (1971): 4–10.

Kay, Norman. "Aspects of Copland's Development." *Tempo* 95 (1971): 23–29.

Matthews, David. "Copland and Stravinsky." *Tempo* 95 (1971): 10–14.

Young, Douglas. "The Piano Music." *Tempo* 95 (1971): 15–22

Newlin, Dika. "The Piano Music of Aaron Copland." *Piano Quarterly* 111 (1980): 6–12.

Northcott, Bayan. "Notes on Copland." *Musical Times* 122 (1980): 686–89.

Starr, Lawrence. "Copland's Style." *Perspectives of New Music* 19 (1980–81): 68–89.

STUDIES OF PARTICULAR WORKS

Rosenfeld, Paul. "Musical Chronicle." *Dial* 78 (1925): 258. (*Organ Symphony.*)

Wilson, Edmund. "The Jazz Problem." *New Republic* 13 Jan 1926: 217–19. (*Music for the Theatre.*)

Goldberg, Isaac. "Aaron Copland and His Jazz." *American Mercury* Sept. 1927: 63–64. (*Music for the Theatre*, Piano Concerto.)

Rosenfeld, Paul. "Aaron Copland's Growth." *New Republic* 27 May 1931: 46–47. (*Piano Variations.*)

Berger, Arthur. "The Piano Variations of Aaron Copland." *Musical Mercury* 1 (1934): 85–86.

Carl Sands [pseud. of Charles Seeger]. "Copeland's [sic] Recital at Pierre Degeyter Club." *Daily Worker* 22 March 1934: 5. (Several pieces.)

Kirkpatrick, John. "Aaron Copland's Piano Sonata." *Modern Music* 19 (1942): 246–50.

Berger, Arthur. "Copland's Piano Sonata," *Partisan Review* 10 (1943); 187–90.

Morton, Lawrence. "*The Red Pony*: A Review of Aaron Copland's Score." *Film Music Notes* Feb. 1949: 2–8.

Forte, Allen. *Contemporary Tone Structures.* New York: Teachers College, Columbia University, 1955. 63–73. (*Piano Blues* No. 3.)

Berger, Arthur. "Aaron Copland's *Piano Fantasy*." *Juilliard Review* 5.1 (1957): 13–27.

Evans, Peter. "The Thematic Technique of Copland's Recent Works." *Tempo* 51 (1959): 2–13. (Piano Quartet, *Piano Fantasy*.)

Kerman, Joseph. "American Music: The Columbia Series (II)." *Hudson Review* 13.3 (1961): 408–18. (*Sextet, Dickinson Songs*.)

Mellers, Wilfrid H. "Cambridge *The Tender Land*." *Musical Times* 103 (1962): 245–46.

Selected Bibliography

Salzman, Eric, and Paul Des Marais. "Aaron Copland's Nonet: Two Views." *Perspectives of New Music* 1.1 (1962): 172–79.

Plaistow, Stephen. "Some Notes on Copland's *Nonet*." *Tempo* 63 (1963): 6–11.

Evans, Peter. "Copland on the Serial Road: An Analysis of *Connotations*." *Perspectives of New Music* 2.2 (1964): 141–49.

Mellers, Wilfrid H. "The Teenager's World." *Musical Times* 105 (1964): 500–05 (*The Second Hurricane*.)

Robertson, David Hiram. "An Analysis of Aaron Copland's Third Symphony." Master's thesis. University of Rochester, 1965.

Whitwell, David. "The Enigma of Copland's *Emblems*." *Journal of Band Research* 7.2 (1972): 5–9.

Young, Douglas. "Copland's *Dickinson Songs*." *Tempo* 103 (1972): 33–37.

Salzman, Eric. "Copland's *Appalachian Spring*." *Stereo Review* 34.4 (1974): 108.

Stone, Else, and Kurt Stone, eds. *The Writings of Elliott Carter: An American Composer Looks at Modern Music*. Bloomington: Indiana University Press, 1977. (Several pieces.)

Daugherty, Robert Michael. "An Analysis of Aaron Copland's *Twelve Poems of Emily Dickinson*." Diss. Ohio State University, 1980.

Conte, David. "Aaron Copland's Piano Quartet: An Analysis." Master's thesis. Cornell University, 1982.

———. "A Study of Aaron Copland's Sketches for *Inscape*." Diss. Cornell University, 1983.

Cochran, Alfred. "Style, Structure and Tonal Organization in the Early Film Scores of Aaron Copland." Diss. Catholic University, 1986.

Shirley, Wayne D. "Ballet for Martha: The Commissioning of *Appalachian Spring*." *Performing Arts Annual* (Washington, DC, 1987): 102–23.

———. "Ballets for Martha: The Creation of *Appalachian Spring, Jeux de Printemps*, and *Hérodiade*." *Performing Arts Annual* (Washington, DC, 1988): 40–69.

Mathers, Daniel. "Closure in the *Sextet* and *Short Symphony* by Aaron Copland: A Study Using Facsimiles and Printed Editions." Master's thesis. Florida State University, 1989.

Wyton, Richard. "The Copland-Solum Correspondence, 1967–1975: The *Duo for Flute and Piano* Commission." *Flutist Quarterly* 17.1 (1992): 33–43.

Robertson, Martha E. " 'A Gift to Be Simple': The Collaboration of Aaron Copland and Martha Graham in the Genesis of *Appalachian Spring*." Diss. University of Michigan, 1992.

Starr, Larry. "Copland on Compact Disc." *American Music* 10.3 (1992): 381–86; 10.4 (1992): 501–06; 11.2 (1993): 256–61. (Several pieces.)

Lindsay, Roberta. "Aaron Copland's *Grohg*: Its Place in Copland's Oeuvre." Diss. Ohio University, 1996.

Everett, Terri Gailey. "Beyond Serialism: An Analysis of Gesture, Form and Serial Relationships in Aaron Copland's *Piano Fantasy*." Master's thesis. University of Texas, Austin, 1997.

DeLapp, Jennifer. "Copland in the Fifties: Music and Ideology in the McCarthy Era." Diss. University of Michigan, 1997. (Piano Quartet.)

Lerner, Neil. "Music and Documentary Film, 1936–1945: Style, Rhetoric, and Ideology in Scores by Virgil Thomson, Aaron Copland, and Louis Gruenberg." Diss. Duke University, 1997. (*The Cummington Story.*)

OTHER LITERATURE

Thomson, Virgil. "The Cult of Jazz." *Vanity Fair* 24.4 (1925): 54, 118.

Cowell, Henry. "Amerikanische Musik?" *Melos* 8–9.9 (1930): 362–65.

Rosenfeld, Paul. "A Musical Tournament." *New Republic* 71 (15 June 1932): 119–21.

Levant, Oscar. *A Smattering of Ignorance.* New York: Doubleday, Doran & Co., 1940.

Thomson, Virgil. *The Musical Scene.* New York: Knopf, 1945. New York: Greenwood Press, 1968.

Leichtentritt, Hugo. *Serge Koussevitzky.* Cambridge, MA: Harvard University Press, 1946.

de Mille, Agnes. *Dance to the Piper.* Boston: Little, Brown, 1952.

Reis, Claire R. *Composers, Conductors and Critics.* New York: Oxford University Press, 1955.

Sessions, Roger. *Reflections on the Music Life in the United States.* New York: Merlin Press, 1956.

Thomson, Virgil. *Virgil Thomson.* New York, 1966. New York: Da Capo Press, 1977.

Clurman, Harold. *All People Are Famous (Instead of an Autobiography).* New York: Harcourt Brace Jovanovich, 1974.

Oja, Carol J. "The Copland-Sessions Concerts and Their Reception in the Contemporary Press." *Musical Quarterly* 65 (1979): 212–29.

Siegel, Marcia B. *The Shapes of Change: Images of American Dance.* Boston: Houghton Mifflin, 1979.

Alexander, Charles C. *Here the Country Lies: Nationalism and the Arts in Twentieth-Century America.* Bloomington: Indiana University Press, 1980.

Zuck, Barbara. *A History of Musical Americanism.* Ann Arbor: UMI Research Press, 1980.

Pollack, Howard. *Walter Piston.* Ann Arbor: UMI Research Press, 1981.

Lederman, Minna. *The Life and Death of a Small Magazine: Modern Music, 1924–1946.* Brooklyn: ISAM, 1983.

Levy, Alan Howard. *Musical Nationalism: American Composers' Search for Identity.* Westport: Greenwood Press, 1983.

Meckna, Michael. "Copland, Sessions, and Modern Music: The Rise of the Composer-Critic in America." *American Music* 3.2 (1985): 198–204.

Parker, Robert. "Copland and Chávez: Brothers-in-Arms." *American Music* 5.4 (1987): 433–44.

Gordon, Eric A. *Mark the Music: The Life and Work of Marc Blitzstein.* New York: St. Martin's Press, 1989.

Olmstead, Andrea. "The Copland-Sessions Letters." *Tempo* 175 (1990): 2–5.

Carpenter, Humphrey. *Benjamin Britten: A Biography*. London: Faber and Faber, 1992.

Pollack, Howard. *Harvard Composers: Walter Piston and His Students, from Elliott Carter to Frederic Rzewski*. Metuchen, NJ: Scarecrow Press, 1992.

Clurman, Harold. *The Collected Works of Harold Clurman*. Ed. Margorie Loggia and Glenn Young. New York: Applause Books, 1994.

Rorem, Ned. *Knowing When to Stop: A Memoir*. New York: Simon & Schuster, 1994.

Burton, Humphrey. *Leonard Bernstein*. New York: Doubleday, 1994.

Index

Index

Baird, Tadeusz, 465
Baker, Carroll, 493, 494, 496
Balanchine, George, 314–15, 426, 464, 489, 490, 492
Balanchivadze, Andrey, 464
Ballet Caravan, 314–16, 323
Ballet Russe de Monte Carlo, 363
Ballets Russes, 57, 363
Barber, Samuel, 92, 123, 189, 207, 254, 332, 498, 514, 525, 541
Barbour, John, 479
Barnefield, Richard, 79
Barnouw, Erik, 408
Barsam, Richard, 408
Bartók, Béla, 57, 424; Copland on, 60, 64, 66, 68, 75, 201, 221; compared with Copland, 85, 92, 119, 145, 448, 484, 528; and Copland, 69, 140, 527; Bernstein, 194; Boulanger, 48; Clurman, 54; Rosenfeld, 97–98
Baryshnikov, Mikhail, 404, 502
Baskerville, David Ross, 119–20
Basso, Victor, 544, 546
Bauer, Marion, 89, 212
Bauman, Mordecai, 110
Bax, Arnold, 463
Bayles, Martha, 115
Beach, Amy, 36
Beach, Sylvia, 55
The Beatles, 118
Beaton, Cecil, 239
Beckwith, Frank, 408
Beethoven, Ludwig van, Copland on, 12, 60, 61, 63, 72, 287; compared with Copland, 307, 353, 411, 415, 439; and Copland, 32, 33, 228, 237, 432, 489, 536, 554; Goldmark, 35; Rolland, 37; Ross, 245; Odets, 265
Béjart, Maurice, 302
Bennett, Richard Rodney, 75, 358
Bennett, Robert Russell, 86, 164
Berezovsky, Nicolai, 34
Berg, Alban, 47, 57, 68, 187, 201, 245, 411, 462
Berger, Arthur, 179, 186–88, 194, 227, 262, 273, 387, 547, 548; on Copland, ix, 149, 150, 151, 187, 199, 252, 290, 303, 323, 354–55, 362, 374, 411, 412, 417, 426, 450, 468, 482, 521, 529–30, 531; on Copland's influence, 74, 199, 528–29; and Copland, 61, 153, 201, 387, 442

Bergman, Elizabeth, 412, 628 n. 16
Bergman, Josephine, 16, 19
Bergman, Louis, 19, 22
Bergsma, William, 198
Bergson, Henri, 29
Berio, Luciano, 206, 463
Berkeley, Lennox, 75
Berlin, Irving, 113, 114, 115–16
Berlioz, Hector, 60–61
Bernheimer, Martin, 536, 537
Bernier, Rosamund, 7, 54, 240, 255–56, 375, 525
Bernstein, Elmer, 347
Bernstein, Leonard, 55, 74, 91, 172, 182, 190, 226, 228, 237, 245, 270, 290, 296, 346, 387, 446, 448, 454, 514, 516, 525, 547, 548, 555; on Copland the man, 4, 5, 8, 13, 28, 244, 521; on Copland's music, 14, 135, 174, 197, 296, 302, 351, 356, 411, 417, 446, 450, 516, 529, 551, 555; on Copland's conducting, 538; Copland on, 196, 207, 522–23, 536, 546, 608 n. 54; Copland's influence on, 7, 136, 194, 324, 348, 626 n. 42; and Copland, 6, 53, 92, 123, 146, 153, 176, 193–98, 211, 236, 241, 367, 376, 533, 660 n. 11; as conductor, 127, 133–34, 136, 299, 310, 326, 377, 404, 405, 439, 501–02, 506, 507, 539
Berrigan, Bunny, 116
Best, Matthew, 423
Biancolli, Louis, 500
Bible, 27, 28, 77, 395, 421
Biggs, E. Power, 127
Billings, William, 108
Bing, Rudolf, 267, 498
Bishop, Elizabeth, 138, 268–69
Bishop, Henry, 346
Blackwood, Easley, 202, 203, 356
Bliss, Arthur, 72
Bliss, Mr. and Mrs. Robert Woods, 491
Blitzstein, Marc, 58, 102, 148, 255, 274, 281, 289, 296, 304, 305, 307, 329, 475, 525; on Copland, 182, 244, 309; Copland on, 120, 181–82; and Copland, 68, 124, 152, 164, 173, 180–82, 216, 236, 254, 307, 350, 533; Eisler, 279
Bloch, Ernest, 36, 41, 58, 85, 86, 97, 194, 407, 519, 522–23, 571 n. 18

Index

Chávez, Carlos, 59, 94, 124, 175, 206, 216–26, 239, 256, 276, 280, 337, 374, 391, 392, 393, 421, 516, 527, 533, 553; on Copland, 219, 221–22, 388; compared with Copland, 156, 219, 222, 301–02, 333, 479, 650 n. 28; conducts Copland, 220, 288, 301; Copland on, 221, 227–28, 231, 536; Copland performs, 164; Rosenfeld, 97–99

Chekhov, Anton, 54, 264

Cherkassky, Shura, 485

Chlumberg, Hans, 329

Chopin, Frédéric, 32, 35, 37, 61

Christensen, Lew, 315–16, 323

Churchill, Mary S., 90, 166

Citkowitz, Israel, 136, 162, 179–80, 183, 185–88, 195, 238, 248, 258, 273, 277, 278, 477

Clarke, Henry Leland, 274, 278, 327

Claudel, Paul, 48, 53, 461

Cleobury, Stephen, 423

Cliburn, Van, 513–14

Clurman, Harold, 30, 95, 174, 268; on Copland the man, 5, 8, 62, 234; on Copland's music, 262, 272, 448, 450, 551; Copland on, 263; and Copland, 29, 50–56, 81–83, 94, 237, 238, 247–48, 267, 277, 280, 336–37, 547; Chávez, 217; Rosenfeld, 99–100; Stieglitz, 101; Sykes, 152, 153; leftist politics, 105, 259–61, 622 n. 31, 656 n. 10; theater, 54–55, 131–32, 144, 257–62, 296

Cochran, Alfred, 347

Cocteau, Jean, 85, 171, 309

Cohn, Roy, 455–57, 459

Cole, Chris, 542–43

Cole, Hugo, 119, 303

Coleman, Ornette, 118

Collins, Judy, 504, 589 n. 36

Composers' Collective, 161, 273–74, 275–76, 278–79

Cone, Edward, 286, 448

Confrey, Zez, 43, 115

Conte, David, 196, 448, 506, 542, 544

Contreras, Salvador, 227

Coolidge, Elizabeth Sprague, 391, 392, 445

Coombs, Lillian, 17, 22, 25

Copeau, Jacques, 55

Copeland, Abe, 15

Copland, Aaron: as conductor, 19, 92, 127–28, 136, 327, 383, 405, 434, 532–41, 660 n. 11, 660 n. 16; as critic, 75, 159, 215, 254; dementia, 198, 252, 546–47; end of compositional career, 516–17, 553–54; family, 15–22; financial matters, 8–9, 21–22, 88–93, 193, 226, 265, 287, 291, 303, 310, 329, 333, 334, 366, 379, 387, 391, 419, 424, 428, 437, 470, 493, 510; Jewish background, 23–29, 554; homosexuality, 24, 39–40, 202–03, 234–38, 554, 609 n. 73; last will and testament, 547–48; as lecturer, 92, 95, 176, 182, 283–84, 292, 455, 462, 464, 523; leftist politics, 39, 186–87, 270–87, 296; McCarthyism, 4, 125, 191, 276, 285, 451–59, 479, 533, 550; Pan-Americanism, 104, 221, 222, 232–33, 307, 426; pets, 12–13; as pianist, 12, 32, 34, 36, 46, 89, 134, 136, 137, 140, 145, 150, 226, 356; reception in England, 332, 520; residences, 16, 51, 93–97, 264; romantic friendships, 40, 152–53, 180–85, 195, 238–52, 305; as teacher, 90, 182, 186, 189, 191–92, 194, 207–09, 214, 232, 248, 280; travels, 57, 96–97, 141, 183–84, 225, 228, 230, 240, 460, 462–65, 535, 584 n. 27; university positions, 90, 91, 178, 192; women composers, 212–13, 252, 534, 611 n. 106; Zionism, 27, 38, 328

AWARDS AND FELLOWSHIPS: American Academy's Gold Medal, 459; Congressional Gold Medal, 460; Fulbright, 461; Emmy, 509; Grammy, 476; Guggenheim, 89; honorary doctorates, 459; Kennedy Center, 460; MacDowell Medal, 460; Medal of the Arts, 460; Medal of Freedom, 460; Motion Picture Academy, 343, 346, 383, 432, 437, 496; Music Critics' Circle, 404, 417; Prix de Paris, 76; Pulitzer Prize, 404; RCA Victor, 86

INTEREST IN: literature, 13–14, 42–43; motion pictures, 13, 73; opera, 34, 478; religions, 27–29, 143, 437; tennis, 12, 73; theater, 13, 31, 54, 130, 131; the visual arts, 13, 102

MUSICAL STYLE, TECHNIQUE, INTERESTS: "additive" technique, 325, 352;

American folk music, 161, 174, 191, 279–80, 292–93, 308, 320, 334, 358–59, 367–68, 398, 399, 409, 420, 432, 436, 475–6, 503–04, 553; Americanism, 32, 65, 107, 132, 165, 175, 417, 521, 522, 523–24, 526–31, 552–53, 659n. 39; chaconne, 491, 500, 504; collage, 10–11, 135, 300, 421, 432, 496, 529, 555; compositional process, 9–12; contrapuntal techniques, 78, 138, 384; Eastern verse, 41, 78; Hammond organ, 330; harmony, 41, 137, 146, 331, 397, 495, 555; heckelphone, 289; homosexuality, 525–31; jazz and popular music, 33, 43–44, 48, 57, 83, 113–20, 127–38, 145–46, 148, 262, 289, 353, 426–27, 484, 503, 527, 551–52, 553; Jewish contexts, 33, 38, 77, 127, 135, 137, 144–46, 148, 289, 331, 518–24, 525, 553; Latin-American folk music, 230–31, 289, 299–300, 353, 368, 415, 425–26, 508, 553; medieval music, 480, 483, 504, 553; microtones, 83, 85, 129, 137, 145; misc. folk musics, 116, 224, 330, 375, 381–82, 409; modality, 77, 129, 138, 345, 352, 468; neoclassicism, 132, 138, 289, 384, 526; octatonic scale, 42, 80, 85, 137, 138, 150; orchestration, films, 341, 382, 430, 435–36; orchestration, general, 10, 126, 148, 176, 186, 311, 368, 416, 529; palindrome, 416; pandiatonicism, 297, 333, 397, 515; percussion, 335, 494, 508, 603n. 53; rhythm, 80, 138, 147–48, 489, 505, 555, 590n. 40, 594n. 14; saxophone, 134, 311, 331, 387; self-borrowing, 11, 566n. 25; twelve-tone method, 68, 80, 120, 138, 145–47, 229, 231, 445–48, 482, 495, 499, 506–07, 513, 553, 650n. 33

THOUGHTS ON: aleatoric music, 465; electronic music, 466; film music, 342, 348–50; government support of the arts, 286–87; radio, 313; rock, 118–119; university composers, 286

WORKS (BALLET): *Appalachian Spring,* 7, 27, 41, 83, 99, 105, 122, 124, 154, 155, 163, 170, 188, 205, 232, 246, 262, 300, 308, 332, 355, 388–406, 422, 445, 448, 476, 497, 498, 520,

533, 537, 541, 544, 555; *Billy the Kid,* 67, 85, 99, 109, 155, 174, 189, 191, 200, 212, 300, 302, 307, 314–25, 326, 343, 364, 366, 367, 369, 373, 374, 399, 478, 497, 526, 552, 555; *Dance Panels,* 214, 437, 486–90, 497, 522, 533; *Grohg,* 76, 78, 80, 81–87, 125, 129, 292, 293–94, 525; *Hear Ye! Hear Ye!,* 86, 90, 116, 136–37, 155, 291–95, 319, 320, 339, 427, 533; *Rodeo,* 67, 99, 174, 191, 196, 197, 213, 300, 334, 363–74, 388, 397, 419, 497, 498, 526, 535, 555

WORKS (CHAMBER): *Capriccio,* 33; *Duo,* 497, 511–13, 516, 552, 555; *Elegies,* 297; *Hommage à Fauré,* 79; *Lament,* 27, 36, 38; *Movement,* 80; *Nonet,* 172, 490–92, 499–500, 504, 552, 555; Piano Quartet, 197, 232, 248, 440, 445–50, 482, 512, 553; *Poème,* 39, 42; *Schumanniana,* 36; *Sextet,* 211, 289, 290, 291, 512; *Sonata Movement,* 76; *Two Pieces* for string quartet, 79–80, 140–141; *Two Pieces* for violin and piano, 136–37, 148, 179, 275, 293, 294, 330; *Two Preludes,* 42; *Threnody I and II,* 513; Violin Sonata, 67, 69, 327, 352, 383–86, 511, 555; "Ukelele Serenade," *see Two Pieces* for violin; *Vitebsk,* 27, 36, 38, 141, 142–46, 152, 157, 272, 275, 300, 523, 555

WORKS (CHORAL): "Las Agachadas," 374–75; *Canticle of Freedom,* 198, 478, 479–80; *Four Motets,* 27, 77, 328; "The House on the Hill," 137–38; "An Immorality," 137–38, 293, 330; *In the Beginning,* 27, 95, 176, 421–23, 533, 555; "Into the Streets," 275–76, 304; "Lark," 327–28; "Song of the Guerrillas," 383; "What Do We Plant?" 303–04; "The Younger Generation," 383

WORKS (FILM SCORES): *The City,* 66, 99, 102, 188, 337–40, 347, 380, 409, 494; *The Cummington Story,* 407, 408–10, 425, 515; *The Heiress,* 11, 91, 247, 433–38, 440–41, 475, 492, 488, 526; *The North Star,* 378–83, 410, 434, 533; *Of Mice and Men,* 91, 340–48, 351, 367, 382, 391, 415, 526, 550; *Our Town,* 7, 91, 188, 332, 342,

Index

Index

Index

Index

Odets, Clifford, 27, 257, 258, 259–62, 263–67, 273, 281, 283, 296, 330, 336–37, 340, 351, 470
O'Donnell, May, 404
O'Hara, Frank, 237, 305
Ohlsson, Garrick, 136
Oja, Carol, 166, 253, 255, 526
O'Keefe, Georgia, 100, 101
Olivier, Laurence, 439
Olmstead, Andrea, 165, 166, 168
Onnou, Alphonse, 142
Orbón, Julián, 206, 231, 232
Orff, Carl, 489
Ormandy, Eugene, 295, 312, 404–05, 509
Ornstein, Leo, 36, 44, 97–98
Orozco, José Clemente, 218, 613 n. 13
Orrego-Salas, Juan, 4, 230, 231, 232, 233, 254, 442
O'Shea, Patrick, 544
Ostrowska, Djina, 46
Ottaway, Hugh, 419
Ouspensky, 28
Overton, Hall, 119
Ozawa, Seiji, 539

Packer, Herbert, 458
Paderewski, Ignacy, 18, 32, 33
Page, Ruth, 181, 291–95, 367, 393
Page, Tim, 501
Paine, John Knowles, 108
Palestrina, Giovanni P., 59, 60, 72
Palmer, Robert, ix, 198, 206, 358, 383, 637 n. 9
Paradise, Timothy, 386
Parker, Dorothy, 330
Parker, H. T., 155, 156
Parker, Horatio, 98, 108
Parker, Robert, 216
Parsi, Hector Campos, 231
Pärt, Arvo, 464
Payne, John Howard, 346
Paz, Juan Carlos, 229
Peale, Norman Vincent, 21
Pears, Peter, 73–74, 467, 469
Peck, Donald, 539
Penderecki, Krysztof, 465, 492
Pentland, Barbara, 206, 213, 611 n. 106
Perlis, Vivian, ix, 9, 24, 76, 80, 111, 244–45, 246, 252, 285, 458, 459, 515, 537, 542, 545, 546, 547, 548
Persichetti, Vincent, 254, 384, 546

Petrassi, Goffredo, 206, 463
Pettersson, Gustaf Allan, 463
Pettiford, Oscar, 117
Pettis, Ashley, 276
Peyser, Joan, 600 n. 15, 646 n. 34
Picasso, Pablo, 13, 51, 153, 323, 377
Pidgeon, Walter, 452
Pipkov, Lyubomir, 71
Pisani, Michael V., 587 n. 7
Piston, Walter, 49, 51, 66, 149–50, 159, 163, 164, 169, 174–77, 216, 310, 360, 384, 407, 408, 421, 498, 527, 530, 554
Pitoéff, Georges, 55
Plaistow, Stephen, 491
Plotts, Donald, 251–52
Poe, Edgar Allen, 393
Pokrass, Daniel and Dmitry, 381
Pope, Stuart, 92, 93
Porter, Andrew, 546
Porter, Quincy, 164
Posselt, Ruth, 385
Poulenc, Francis, 48, 57, 66–67, 254, 527
Pound, Ezra, 51, 55, 135, 137–38, 593 n. 37
Powell, Bud, 117
Powell, John, 109
Preston, Simon, 127
Previn, André, 347, 436, 445, 528
Prokofiev, Sergei, 34, 48, 57, 64, 70–72, 75, 121, 122, 265, 282–83, 350, 430, 554
Proust, Marcel, 55
Purcell, Henry, 72, 107, 491, 534

Rabaud, Henri, 537
Rachmaninov, Sergei, 48, 61, 98
Radakiewicz, Henwar, 338
Raksin, David, 347, 437
Rameau, Jean-Philippe, 64
Ramey, Phillip, 5, 6, 13, 27, 61, 77, 111, 160, 169, 171, 177, 185, 192, 204, 209–10, 212, 215, 244, 285, 362, 514–16, 517, 525, 543, 547
Ramey, Samuel, 469
Rampal, Jean-Pierre, 512
Ravel, Maurice, 35, 36, 41, 46, 48, 54, 58, 64, 85, 92, 186, 208, 210, 214, 298, 464
Read, Gardner, 206
Reagan, Ronald, 460
Reck, David, 118
Rector, Jennifer, 328
Reger, Max, 58, 61

Music in American Life

Behind the Burnt Cork Mask: Early Blackface Minstrelsy and Antebellum American Popular Culture   *William J. Mahar*

Going to Cincinnati: A History of the Blues in the Queen City
   Steven C. Tracy

Pistol Packin' Mama: Aunt Molly Jackson and the Politics of Folksong
   Shelly Romalis

Sixties Rock: Garage, Psychedelic, and Other Satisfactions   *Michael Hicks*

The Late Great Johnny Ace and the Transition from R&B to Rock 'n' Roll
   James M. Salem

Tito Puente and the Making of Latin Music   *Steven Loza*

Juilliard: A History   *Andrea Olmstead*

Understanding Charles Seeger, Pioneer in American Musicology
   Edited by Bell Yung and Helen Rees

Mountains of Music: West Virginia Traditional Music from *Goldenseal*
   Edited by John Lilly

Alice Tully: An Intimate Portrait   *Albert Fuller*

Long Steel Rail: The Railroad in American Folksong (2d ed.)
   Norm Cohen

The Golden Age of Gospel   *Text by Horace Clarence Boyer; photography by Lloyd Yearwood*

Aaron Copland: The Life and Work of an Uncommon Man
   Howard Pollack